THE NEW GROUNDWORK OF BRITISH HISTORY

BOOK TWO

THE NEW GROUNDWORK OF BRITISH HISTORY
is issued in the following forms:

COMPLETE—55 B.C.–A.D. 1939.
BOOK ONE—55 B.C.–A.D. 1603.
BOOK TWO—1603–1939.
SECTION TWO—1485–1714.
SECTION THREE—1603–1783.
SECTION FOUR—1688–1939.
SECTION FIVE—1783–1939.

Bk. II (F 938)

THE NEW GROUNDWORK OF BRITISH HISTORY

(THE NEW "WARNER AND MARTEN")

BY

GEORGE TOWNSEND WARNER, M.A.

Sometime Fellow of Jesus College, Cambridge
late Master of the Modern Side in Harrow School

SIR C. HENRY K. MARTEN, K.C.V.O., M.A.

Late of Balliol College, Oxford, and late Provost of Eton College

D. ERSKINE MUIR

Final Honours, School of Modern History, Oxford:
Sometime Scholar of Somerville College, Oxford

BOOK TWO

1603 – 1939

BLACKIE & SON LIMITED
LONDON AND GLASGOW

BLACKIE & SON LIMITED
16/18 William IV Street,
Charing Cross, London, W.C.2
17 Stanhope Street, Glasgow

BLACKIE & SON (INDIA) LIMITED
103/5 Fort Street, Bombay

BLACKIE & SON (CANADA) LIMITED
Toronto

First published 1943
Reprinted 1944, 1945 (twice), 1946, 1947
Reprinted, with minor adjustments, 1949
Reprinted 1950, 1952, 1953, 1954, 1955
1956, 1957, 1958

Printed in Great Britain by Blackie & Son, Ltd., Glasgow

Bk. II (F 938)

PUBLISHERS' PREFACE

The first edition of Warner and Marten's *Groundwork of British History* was published in 1911, and the book has been a standard text-book in schools ever since. It has been revised several times, through its many editions and impressions, and now advantage has been taken of the years of the war to carry out a *complete overhaul* of the work, so as to bring it into line with the current requirements of *School Certificate Examinations* and with the most recent historical research.

The revision has been carried out by Mrs. D. Erskine Muir, with the approval of Mr. Warner's Trustees and of Sir Henry Marten, who has made many valuable suggestions and read the proofs. Mrs. Muir possesses high qualifications for her task and wide experience as a teacher and examiner in History.

The period from 1830 to 1939 is entirely new. The text up to 1830 has been rearranged so as to assist those working for School Certificate Examinations and certain chapters have been revised in the light of modern historical views. The text of Book One, however, is still substantially as written by Mr. Warner and of Book Two up to 1830 as Sir Henry Marten wrote it.

Notes, Time-Charts, and other teaching equipment have been provided by Mrs. Muir, who has also provided a selection of questions from actual School Certificate papers.

The book is arranged in twelve sections each corresponding to a recognized " period " in British History.

NOTE

For permission to include questions from past School Certificate examination papers, grateful acknowledgment is made to the following Examination Boards: the University of Bristol [B], the University of Cambridge (Local Examinations Syndicate) [CL], the Central Welsh Board [CWB], the University of Durham [D], the University of London — General School Examination [LGS], and Matriculation Examination [LM], Northern Universities Joint Matriculation Board [NUJB], the Oxford and Cambridge Schools Examination Board [O & C], the Oxford Local Examinations Board [OL], and the University of Wales [UW]. The letters in square brackets are the abbreviations that have been used in the Examination Questions throughout the book.

CONTENTS

BOOK TWO — 1603–1939

FROM THE UNION OF THE CROWNS TO THE PRESENT DAY

PERIOD SIX — 1603–1688

THE STRUGGLE BETWEEN CROWN AND PARLIAMENT

PERIOD SEVEN — 1688–1714

THE STRUGGLE WITH FRANCE AND THE GROWTH OF CONSTITUTIONAL MONARCHY

PERIOD EIGHT — 1714–1783

THE EXPANSION OF BRITAIN AND THE FINAL CONTEST WITH THE CROWN

PERIOD NINE — 1783-1815

THE GREAT STRUGGLE WITH FRANCE; REVOLUTION AND NAPOLEON

PERIOD TEN — 1815-1867

INDUSTRIAL DEVELOPMENT: ABUSES AND REFORMS

COLOURED MAPS

TEXT MAPS AND DIAGRAMS

BOOK TWO

FROM THE UNION OF THE CROWNS TO THE PRESENT DAY

1603–1939

PERIOD SIX

THE STRUGGLE BETWEEN CROWN AND PARLIAMENT

1603–1688

CHAPTER 34

JAMES I (1603–1625) AND HIS FOREIGN POLICY

The development of England at every stage has been largely influenced by the character of its monarchs. But it may be doubted whether at any other period more depended upon the character of the sovereign than during the first half of the Seventeenth Century, when, as we shall see, most difficult questions arose both at home and abroad. It will be as well, therefore, to say something at once about the first two kings of the house of Stuart who sat upon the English throne — about James I, who succeeded Queen Elizabeth in 1603, and reigned till 1625, and his son, Charles I, who reigned from 1625 till 1649.

Character of James I

James I has been described as the most learned man who ever occupied a British throne. He was highly educated. In his youth he was something of a prodigy,[1] and in later life he wrote tolerable verses, whilst his speeches and prose writings were vigorous and clever.[2] He was exceptionally well informed, especially in theology, and well versed in

[1] At the age of ten "he was able, *extempore*," wrote a contemporary, "to read a chapter out of the Bible out of Latin into French, and out of French after into English."

[2] His writings include *A Counterblast to Tobacco*, a violent attack upon the practice of smoking.

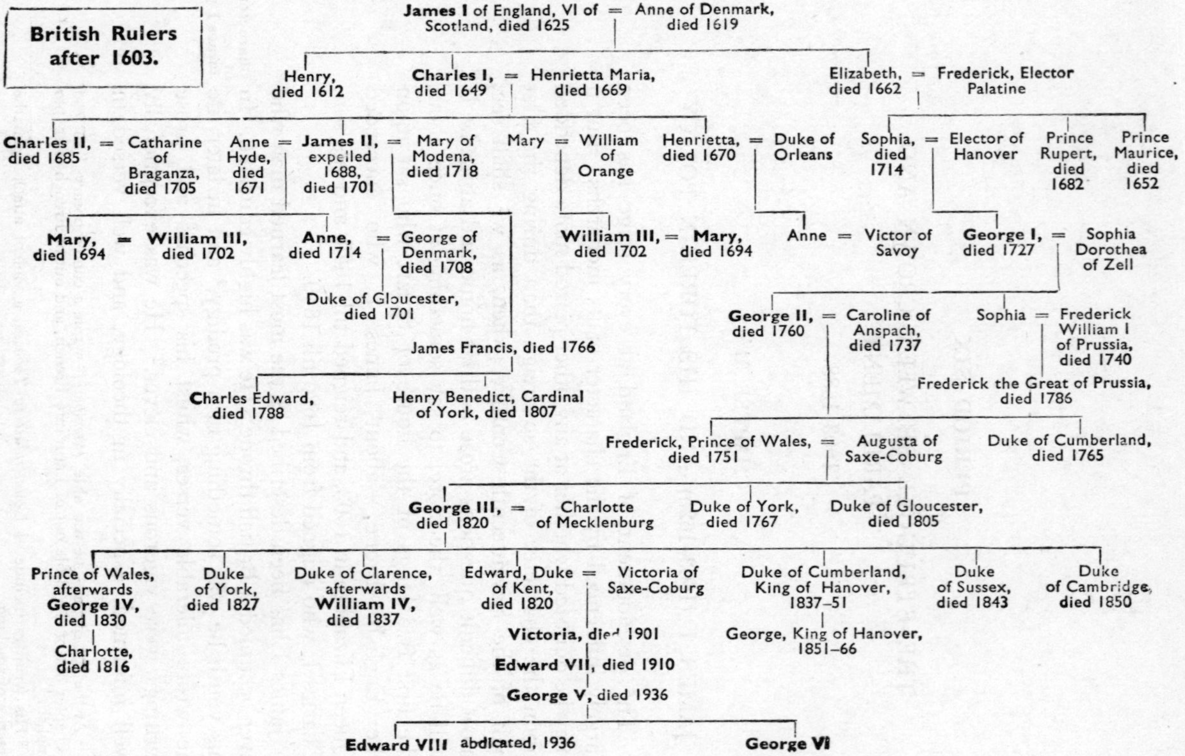
British Rulers after 1603.
James I of England, VI of Scotland, died 1625 = Anne of Denmark, died 1619
Henry, died 1612
Charles I, died 1649 = Henrietta Maria, died 1669
Elizabeth, died 1662 = Frederick, Elector Palatine
Charles II, died 1685 = Catharine of Braganza, died 1705
Anne Hyde, died 1671 = James II, expelled 1688, died 1701 = Mary of Modena, died 1718
Mary = William of Orange
Henrietta, died 1670 = Duke of Orleans
Sophia, died 1714 = Elector of Hanover
Prince Rupert, died 1682
Prince Maurice, died 1652
Mary, died 1694 = William III, died 1702
Anne, died 1714 = George of Denmark, died 1708
William III, died 1702 = Mary, died 1694
Anne = Victor of Savoy
George I, died 1727 = Sophia Dorothea of Zell
Duke of Gloucester, died 1701
James Francis, died 1766
Charles Edward, died 1788
Henry Benedict, Cardinal of York, died 1807
George II, died 1760 = Caroline of Anspach, died 1737
Sophia = Frederick William I of Prussia, died 1740
Frederick the Great of Prussia, died 1786
Frederick, Prince of Wales, died 1751 = Augusta of Saxe-Coburg
Duke of Cumberland, died 1765
George III, died 1820 = Charlotte of Mecklenburg
Duke of York, died 1767
Duke of Gloucester, died 1805
Prince of Wales, afterwards George IV, died 1830
Charlotte, died 1816
Duke of York, died 1827
Duke of Clarence, afterwards William IV, died 1837
Edward, Duke of Kent, died 1820 = Victoria of Saxe-Coburg
Duke of Cumberland, King of Hanover, 1837–51
George, King of Hanover, 1851–66
Duke of Sussex, died 1843
Duke of Cambridge, died 1850
Victoria, died 1901
Edward VII, died 1910
George V, died 1936
Edward VIII abdicated, 1936
George VI

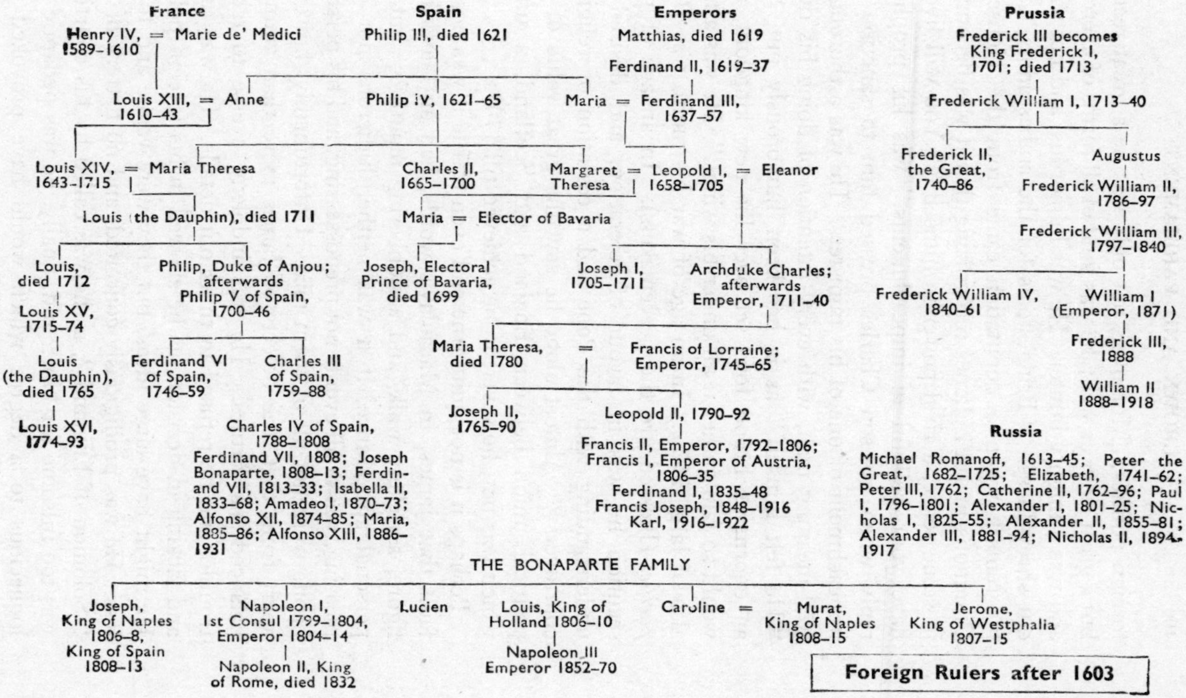

Foreign Rulers after 1603

foreign politics. Moreover, not only was he a great reader, but a great rider as well; he was fond of all forms of exercise, and was a mighty hunter. He was humorous, and not without shrewdness. " Bring stools for the ambassadors," was his remark when a deputation came from the House of Commons in 1621, James recognizing that it was becoming, in some sense, a rival power to himself. " You will live to have your bellyful of impeachments," was his prophetic reply when his son Charles pressed him to sanction the impeachment of one of his ministers. He was a thoroughly well-meaning man, with every intention of doing his duty. " He felt himself," as it has been humorously put, " as an enormous brood fowl set over his new kingdom, and would so fain gather it all under his wings." He was a man also of large ideas. In an age of war his motto was *Beati pacifici* (Blessed are the peacemakers). In an age of persecution he was in favour of toleration, and desired an understanding with the Pope and a cessation of religious controversy. Almost alone he saw the great value of the political union between England and Scotland, a union which was not, however, to be achieved till 1707.

Perhaps it is not quite true and even if true it was not his fault that James, in Macaulay's words, had an " awkward figure, a rickety walk, and a slobbering mouth "; but his personal appearance, if it was neither ludicrous nor displeasing, was at all events not prepossessing, and his personal habits were not all of them nice. Unfortunately, however, apart from that, the defects of James more than counterbalanced his virtues. He was indolent, averse to taking trouble, and he refused to think out details. He was timid and lacking in decision, as he showed in his foreign policy. He might have large ideas, but they were vague and formless. He was prodigiously conceited, and no flattery of this " Solomon of England ", as he was called by his courtiers, was too fulsome for him; and, finally, he was pedantic and loquacious to a degree which would have provoked any

English House of Commons at any period. James was, in truth, unsympathetic and tactless, and, as was natural in a Scot brought up in Scotland, entirely ignorant of the ordinary opinions of the ordinary Englishman. The French King once called James "the wisest fool in Christendom" — perhaps that is the best description of him.

His son and successor was very different. The portraits of Vandyck and the fate of the "martyred" King have combined to prejudice most people in favour of Charles I. And, indeed, he was not without many attractive characteristics. He was gentle in character, devoted to his wife and children, artistic (before the Civil War he had acquired the best picture gallery in Europe [1]), and fond of good literature, and more especially of Shakespeare. Moreover, he was a hard worker at the business of his kingdom. But as a ruler he showed his weak side. He was a silent, obstinate, self-absorbed, unimaginative man, who never knew what anyone else was thinking about. He was untrustworthy — he would make promises, but with all sorts of mental and private reservations, and consequently he often failed to keep them. No one who has not followed his intrigues in detail, either at home or with foreign powers, can understand how difficult he was to deal with. He would pursue at the same time three or four contradictory plans, and it is not surprising, therefore, that his policy should have been futile. It might be said of him, as was said of another ruler, "that his head was as full of schemes as a warren was full of rabbits, and, like rabbits, his schemes went to ground to avoid notice or antagonism".[2]

Character of Charles I

Such was the character of the two Kings. We must now

[1] Unfortunately the Commonwealth sold most of the pictures after the King's execution; and they are now to be found in various foreign collections, and especially in Paris, Madrid, and Leningrad.

[2] Yet the summing up of his character by one of his advisers, Edward Hyde, Lord Clarendon, deserves to be remembered: "To conclude, he was the worthiest gentleman, the best master, the best friend, the best husband, the best father, and the best Christian, that the Age in which he lived had produced, and if he was not the best King, if he was without some parts and qualities which have made some kings great and happy, no other Prince was ever unhappy, who was possessed of half his virtues and endowments, and so much without any kind of vice."

Position of England in 1603

see in what manner James I dealt with the problems which faced him. We may take, first, those that arose in foreign affairs, since the desire to get money to take part in foreign politics profoundly affected the relations between the Stuart kings and their parliaments (*Note 59*). In some respects England's position in 1603 was far more secure than it had been before. When James VI of Scotland became James I of England these two countries, after hundreds of years of rivalry, were at last united under one king. Hitherto, for England's Continental foes, Scotland had been the most convenient of allies; when English energies were absorbed in foreign wars Scotland always had the opportunity of making an invasion, an opportunity of which she not infrequently took advantage. But henceforth, Scotland is, generally speaking, the ally and not the foe of England in her foreign undertakings. Moreover, there were no rivals to the throne whom foreign powers could support, and the succession seemed secure. Again, there was no danger to be apprehended from Spain. Englishmen during the first half of the seventeenth century, and even later, continued to hate the Spaniards, but they no longer had reason to fear them. Consequently England was not vitally concerned in affairs on the Continent, as she had been under Elizabeth through fear of Spain's ambitions, and as she was to be later owing to the ambitions of France.

James's policy of peace

We need not concern ourselves with James I's policy in the years previous to 1618. Until his death, in 1612, *Lord Salisbury*, James I's minister, had the controlling influence, and a cautious policy of peace was pursued. After Lord Salisbury's death, James designed marriages for two of his children. One, *Elizabeth*, later known from her great beauty as the " Queen of Hearts ", married, in 1613, the Elector Palatine of the Rhine, the grandson of William of Orange and the leader of the Calvinistic party in Germany. On the other hand, for his son *Charles*, James designed a marriage with the daughter of the King of Spain, the great champion of the Papacy. With this object he opened negotiations in 1617, which, though they ended in failure, were regarded with great suspicion and disfavour by James's subjects.

Condition of Germany in 1618

In 1618 there broke out in Germany the war known as "*the Thirty Years' War*". The war developed into a gigantic European struggle, which gradually drew in all the chief states in Europe, and it was destined to have vast consequences. To understand the war, and the part Great Britain played in it, something must first be said as to the condition of Germany at this period. Germany, in the seventeenth century, consisted of some three hundred states bound together in a confederation called the Holy Roman Empire, at its head being an Elected Emperor who held office for life. There was a good deal of friction between the rulers of the various states as to the constitution of Germany, some wanting to tighten the bonds of the Confederation and to exalt the powers of the emperor, and others holding contrary opinions. But, of course, the great line of division in Germany at that time was between the Protestants and Roman Catholics, the former being on the whole predominant in the north and the latter in the south of Germany.

The Bohemian election (1619)

In 1619 an event occurred which brought on a crisis. The most important person in Germany was the head of the *House of Habsburg*, and he was always elected Emperor.[1] Not only did he govern large Austrian dominions, but he ruled Hungary as well. In addition to this, he was King of Bohemia. But the crown of *Bohemia* was, like that of Hungary, in theory elective, and the House of Habsburg was staunchly Catholic, whilst the nobles in Bohemia were mainly Protestant. Consequently the nobles of Bohemia took advantage, in 1619, of the death of the Emperor to make a change of dynasty, and offered the crown to a Protestant, Frederick, the Elector Palatine, who was, as stated

[1] A Habsburg was always elected emperor from 1438 until the close of the Holy Roman Empire in 1806, except for a brief period in the eighteenth century, when the Austrian dominions were ruled by a woman.

above, James's son-in-law. Frederick asked James's advice as to whether he should accept it, but James was slow in making up his mind,[1] and Frederick accepted the throne before James had come to any decision.

Beginning of Thirty Years' War (1619-22)

"That prince," said the Pope, referring to Frederick, "has cast himself into a fine labyrinth." The Pope was right. The Catholic powers in Germany at once combined to support the claims to Bohemia of Ferdinand, the new Emperor and head of the Austrian dominions. Frederick, on the other hand, was not cordially supported by the Protestant princes in Germany. His forces were consequently defeated, in little more than an hour, at the battle of the *White Hill*, just outside *Prague*; and he was expelled from Bohemia (1620). But that was not all. The Duke of Bavaria invaded and occupied that part of Frederick's dominions known as the Upper Palatinate, which bordered his own territory (1621). The King of Spain, both as an ardent Catholic and a cousin of Ferdinand's, also intervened, and proceeded to send an army from the Netherlands to occupy the Lower Palatinate, which lay on the Rhine (1622). The result of the opening stage of the war was, therefore, that the Elector Palatine lost not only his new kingdom, but his hereditary possessions as well.

England's policy

We must now see what part Great Britain played in these proceedings. Public opinion in England had been enthusiastic in support of Frederick, the Protestant husband of an English princess.[2] It wanted to force a Protestant policy upon the Government, and clamoured for an immediate war with Spain. In this public opinion was right. The Spanish King would probably not have occupied the Palatinate at all if he had felt convinced that it would have led

[1] The matter, of course, was urgent, but all the answer Frederick's agent could extract from James was, "I will consider of it".

[2] The enthusiasm even extended to the lawyers, and thirty gentlemen of the Middle Temple swore on their drawn swords, after the fatal battle outside Prague, to live or die in the service of Queen Elizabeth; and Charles, who was devoted to his sister, was so much upset by the news of this battle, that for two days he shut himself up in his room and would speak to no one.

to hostilities with England. But he was well served by Gondomar, his ambassador in London, who was much more aware of James's timidity and indecision than James was himself, and knew exactly how, by a mixture of firmness and flattery, to manage him. And therefore, though English volunteers went out to fight on the Continent, and the House of Commons enthusiastically passed motions in Frederick's favour,[1] nothing else happened. James, indeed, wished to be the peacemaker of Europe, and sent numberless embassies to the Continent; but he never realized that diplomacy, unbacked by armed force, was useless, and that the differences between Protestants and Catholics in Germany were, at that time, too deep to be settled merely by a little judicious management.

The Spanish marriage and the journey to Madrid (1623)

Having failed to prevent the Spanish occupation of the Palatinate, James thought he could get the Spaniards to surrender it if he arranged a marriage between Charles and the Spanish Infanta, and he accordingly reopened the negotiations which he had begun in 1617. Finally Charles — fancying himself in love with the Infanta, whom, by the way, he had never seen — and Buckingham, James's favourite, persuaded James to let them go to Madrid and woo the Infanta (1623). Travelling under false names as " Tom and John Smith ", they crossed the Continent, and arrived at Madrid at eight o'clock one night. But the Spanish statesmen in return for the marriage, instead of being prepared to give up the Palatinate, tried to extract from Charles concessions for the Roman Catholics in England.[2] Charles made all sorts of promises — which no one knew better than himself that he could not have kept; and finally came back in disgust, to be received with acclamations and bonfires,[3]

[1] The members waved their hats " as high as they could hold them " when one motion was put to the vote.

[2] Charles was allowed only one interview of a purely formal nature with the Infanta; he tried to effect another of a more informal character by leaping into a garden where she was walking, but the Infanta, who did not care for Charles, rushed away shrieking.

[3] There were a hundred and eight alone between St. Paul's and London Bridge.

not so much because he had returned as because he had returned without the Infanta. Buckingham and Charles were now all for war to recover the Palatinate. James yielded and Parliament voted the money, and an army was collected (1624). But the army was, to quote a contemporary, " a rabble of raw and poor rascals ", and never reached its destination, being diverted to another siege in 1625. In the same year James died, with the Palatinate still unrecovered.

The expedition to the Palatinate (1624)

CHAPTER 35

JAMES I AND DOMESTIC AFFAIRS

1. PLOTS AGAINST THE KING

James I; the Bye and Main Plots (1603)

We must turn now to the internal history of England under the first Stuart king. Despite the fact that before Elizabeth's death there were other possible successors, James was fortunate in that his accession to the throne met with almost universal approval. There were, however, three unsuccessful plots against him. The first was rather an absurd plot, known as the *Bye Plot*, the object of which was to kidnap the King at Greenwich and to capture the Tower of London; it was designed by one Roman Catholic and betrayed to the Government by another. The evidence given by one of the conspirators led the Government to suspect the existence of the second plot, known as the *Main Plot*, the alleged object of which was to put, with Spanish aid, the Lady Arabella Stuart on the throne.[1] The details, are, however, obscure and uncertain, and it is very doubtful whether there was ever such a plot at all (1603).

The chief interest of the Main Plot lies in the fact that

[1] The Lady Arabella was, like James, descended from Margaret, the elder daughter of Henry VII; but, unlike James, she had been born in England, a fact which, in the eyes of some lawyers, gave her a better title to the throne.

Sir Walter Ralegh,[1] the soldier and seaman, the prose writer and poet, the explorer and courtier of Elizabeth's day, was accused of being implicated in it. Ralegh, after a most unfair trial, was condemned to death for treason. But he was reprieved, and imprisoned in the Tower. He employed his time in writing a *History of the World* and in making chemical experiments.[2] Thirteen years later, in 1616, he obtained his freedom in order to find a gold mine on the Orinoco River, of which he had heard on one of his journeys. But his expedition was disastrous. He had a bad crew, he lost his best officers by disease, and he was unable, owing to sickness, to go up the river himself. Worst luck of all, since his last journey a Spanish town on the river had been moved from a position above the mine to one below it. Consequently Ralegh's men had to pass the town on their way to the mine. The Spaniards attacked them, or they attacked the Spaniards — one or other was inevitable — and Spanish blood was shed. On Ralegh's return the Spanish ambassador clamoured for his punishment. James I was at that time engaged in the marriage negotiations of Charles and the Infanta. He yielded, therefore, and executed Ralegh on the old charge of treason, and in so doing was guilty of an act for which posterity has never forgiven him (1618).[3]

Sir Walter Ralegh

The third plot was the famous *Gunpowder Plot.* The Roman Catholics had hoped much from a son of Mary Queen of Scots; and James, on his accession, was inclined to be tolerant, and excused the Roman Catholics from the fines which they paid for not going to their parish churches,[4]

The Gunpowder Plot (1605)

[1] Ralegh's name has been spelt in seventy different ways. He himself signed his name variously in the course of his life, but he never signed it in the way it is often spelt now, i.e. Raleigh.

[2] Amongst other things he compounded drugs, and his " great cordial or elixir " had a wonderful reputation.

[3] Ralegh was warned, it is only fair to James to say, that any hostilities against the Spaniards would cost him his life; and in his over-eagerness to get free from the Tower, Ralegh asserted that the mine was neither in nor near the King of Spain's territories, a statement which he must have known to be untrue.

[4] They were extremely heavy — £20 a month, or else the confiscation of two-thirds of their property.

The immediate result of this concession was an invasion of Roman Catholic priests from abroad — no less than a hundred and forty in six months — and such signs of activity that James felt obliged to reimpose the fines and to banish the priests. It was this which prompted the Gunpowder Plot (1605). Its leader, Robert Catesby, was something of a hero — of great strength and fascinating manners, and a real leader of men, with magnetic influence over others — but very wrongheaded, and driven to desperation, almost to madness, by the persecution which the Roman Catholics had endured. Amongst the other conspirators was Guy Fawkes, who came of an old Yorkshire family, and had seen much warfare in the Netherlands. The plan of the plot was to blow up the House of Lords when the King and the members of both Houses of Parliament were assembled in it at the opening of the session; to capture James's son, Charles, and proclaim him king; and then to inform other Roman Catholics of the success of the plot at a hunting match which was to be arranged in the Midlands, and with their aid to organize a Roman Catholic Government.

The plotters first tried to dig a mine from an adjacent house through the foundations of the House of Lords; then they hired a cellar, or rather a room on the ground floor, underneath the House of Lords, and put in it two tons of gunpowder in barrels. Finally, however, one of the conspirators, appalled at the enormity of the crime, sent a letter of warning to a cousin of his who was a member of the House of Lords (Lord Monteagle), and who gave the letter to the Government. Consequently, the night before Parliament met, the barrels were discovered, and Guy Fawkes with them; and subsequently he and the other conspirators were either killed in fighting or executed. The result of the plot was that laws of extreme severity were passed against the Roman Catholics — laws, for instance, which excluded them from all professions, which forbade them to appear at Court or within ten miles of London unless employed in business there, and which made the fines against them even more severe. Parliament was always clamouring for these laws to be put into execution, though James occasionally, and Charles very often, failed to enforce them.[1]

2. THE KING'S MINISTERS

We must now say a word as to James's advisers during his reign. The King, on his accession, retained in office, as chief minister, Robert Cecil, the son of Elizabeth's great minister, Lord Burleigh, and created him *Earl of Salisbury*.[2] "He was fit to prevent things going worse, not fit to make them better," was the judgment upon him of Bacon, his cousin. The remark was uncousinly and somewhat unjust. A man of vast industry and sound sense, a capable financier, a clever manager of the King's business in Parliament, Salisbury, up till his death in 1612, did good work at home and had a large share in directing England's foreign policy.

Lord Salisbury's ministry (1603-12)

After 1612 James employed favourites to carry on his Government. This was not only because he enjoyed the society of a lively companion during his leisure, but because he desired to have a person who was wholly dependent upon himself, and who could be imbued with his ideas and could then carry them out; in fact, he thought that, through favourites, he might be an absolute ruler with little trouble to himself. His first choice was singularly unfortunate — a Scotsman named *Carr*, whom he created Lord Rochester, and afterwards Earl of Somerset. Lady Essex divorced her first husband in order to marry Carr, and she and her new husband were subsequently found responsible for the murder of a distinguished man, who happened to be her

James and his favourites — Carr and Buckingham (1612-25)

[1] An attempt has been made to show that there was really no Gunpowder Plot, and that the whole affair was contrived by Lord Salisbury, James I's minister, in order to discredit the Roman Catholics; but this is very unlikely.

[2] James used to call him familiarly his "pigmy", or his "little beagle", owing to his shortness of stature.

personal enemy.[1] James consequently dismissed Carr from all his offices (1616), and kept him a prisoner in the Tower for the next six years.

The King's next choice was better. *George Villiers*, who eventually became *Duke of Buckingham*, had an attractive personality, with agreeable manners and a merry laugh.[2] He was the friend of some good people, such as Abbot and Laud, both Archbishops of Canterbury; of Bacon, who hoped through Villiers to carry out his political ideals; and even of the man who was eventually to impeach him, Sir John Eliot. Moreover, he proved himself a very fair soldier and an energetic Lord High Admiral. But his character was spoilt by his rapid rise. He was too impulsive and volatile to be a statesman; and " if it is only just ", as has been said, " to class him among ministers rather than among favourites, he must rank amongst the most incapable ministers of this or any other century ". At first, however, Villiers was only concerned with matters of patronage; not till towards the end of James's reign did he have much influence upon the King's policy.

Francis Bacon (1561-1626)

Of all the people living at that time, *Francis Bacon*, the historian, essayist, and philosopher, possessed the greatest ability and the widest views. He was a strong supporter of the monarchy; but he loved it, it was said, because he expected great things from it. He saw the necessity for harmony between King and Parliament; the function of the Parliament was to keep the King informed of the wishes of his people, and of the King, through Parliament, to keep the nation informed of his policy. In the early part of James I's reign, Bacon's cousin, Lord Salisbury, prevented him having much influence, perhaps from personal jealousy or dislike. But, after Salisbury's death, Bacon became in

[1] His name was Overbury. He was something of a poet, and a great friend of Carr's. He had tried to prevent Carr marrying Lady Essex, and Lady Essex, in revenge, contrived to season with white arsenic the confectionery Overbury ate.

[2] James used to call him " Steenie ", from a fancied resemblance to a picture of St. Stephen.

1613 Attorney-General, and from 1618–21 was Lord Chancellor. In those capacities he exercised much influence in the legal side of the struggle by upholding the theory that the Judges should support the King: " they shall be lions," he said, " but yet lions under the throne."

3. THE KING AND PROTESTANT PARTIES

Religion: The Anglican party

We turn from the King's ministers to trace the King's policy. It was on questions of religion that people in those days felt most acutely, and these were amongst the first to occupy James's attention on his accession (*Note 60*). We have already noticed the upshot of his attempt to tolerate the Roman Catholics, and we must now see how he dealt with the Protestants. It may be convenient at this stage to say something of Protestant parties in seventeenth-century England. *Firstly*, there was the *Anglican*, or, as it came to be called at the time, the *Arminian* [1] party, the strong party in the Church of England, of which Archbishop Laud was later to be the leader. In politics the members of this party were believers in the " divine right " of kings. In matters of Church government they were strong upholders of the power of the bishops; and they believed that the bishops, by succession from the Apostles, and the priests, through ordination by the bishops, had been given special powers. With them the Communion service was in a special sense a means of grace. Laud, by his extreme intolerance brought, in later years, much odium upon the Anglican party; and its members, partly because of their liking for vestments and a rather elaborate ritual, and partly because of the doctrines held by some of the more extreme amongst them, were suspected by their enemies of being in sympathy, if not in alliance, with the Church of Rome. But the Anglican party included among its members in the seventeenth century some singularly attractive characters, such as George

[1] After the name of Dr. Arminius, a Dutch divine, who died in 1609.

Herbert, the poet, and Lancelot Andrewes, the Bishop of Winchester, and one of those chiefly responsible for the Authorized Version of the Bible; it had interests in the historic side of the English Church and in preserving its continuity from the Early Church; and it did much to improve the order and beauty of the church services throughout England.

The Puritans

And then, *secondly*, there were the various bodies of people we may group together under the name of *Puritan* (*Note 63*).[1] In dealing with the Puritans three things must be borne in mind. In the first place, many of the popular views held with regard to the Puritans are erroneous, being due to the caricatures drawn of them after the Restoration of 1660. The Puritans, for instance, were not all drawn from the inferior social class; on the contrary, many of the best type of English gentlemen of that day held Puritan opinions. They were not averse to all pleasure and amusement. They did not wear their hair short, and did not speak through their noses. Secondly, we must remember that the great majority of Puritans still belonged to the Church of England; the great and final division between Churchman and Nonconformist did not come till the reign of Charles II. Thirdly, the term includes a large variety of opinions—just after the Civil War it was estimated that there were a hundred and seventy different sects, nearly all belonging to what we now call the Puritan party. Some Puritans were disposed to acquiesce, for instance, in the rule of bishops, if moderately exercised, whilst others detested and made the most violent attacks upon them. Then, especially during and after the Civil War, the *Presbyterians* (see p. 443) became a great force, and wished to impose their system of church government and their doctrines on everyone else. The *Independents*, however, believed in the right of every man to think for himself, and in what they called " liberty

Presbyterians and Independents

[1] These people would, however, have repudiated the name in the earlier part of the seventeenth century; indeed it was regarded as a nickname and term of reproach.

for tender consciences", so long as those consciences were not those of Roman Catholics. And, finally, there were — as there are in every movement — various groups of extremists, who, we shall find, were a dangerous element at the time of the Commonwealth.

Attitude towards Roman Catholicism

All classes of Puritans, however, were united on certain matters. They were all agreed, for instance, in their detestation of Roman Catholicism. It is difficult for us now to realize the intensity of the feeling of large numbers of Englishmen against the Roman Catholics, or to justify the severity of the laws against them. But we must remember that the persecutions of Queen Mary's reign were still fresh in men's minds,[1] that the Roman Catholics had been concerned in various plots against Elizabeth, and that the Armada was looked upon as a Popish Armada. Moreover, the Gunpowder Plot of 1605 was regarded — quite wrongly — as a plot in which the Pope and the English Roman Catholics as a body were implicated. Then, again, the Roman Catholics were not aiming merely at toleration for themselves; they were a large and increasing body, and they wanted England to become a Roman Catholic country. Lastly, it must be borne in mind that the Puritans looked upon the Pope as Antichrist, upon the ceremonies of the church which he ruled as idolatrous, upon the doctrines — to quote the House of Commons — of Popery as "devilish", and upon its priests as "the corrupters of the people in religion and loyalty". They would, indeed, have regarded a return to Roman Catholicism as a moral and religious catastrophe for the nation.

Apart from their hatred of the Papacy, the various sections among the Puritans had other views in common. They all opposed the claims of bishops and priests to special powers, and they disliked ornaments and vestments and an elaborate

[1] Foxe's *Book of Martyrs* (first published in 1563) was regarded as a sort of second Bible at this time, and was chained to the desk in a great many Parish churches; its vivid accounts helped to keep alive the memory of the Marian persecutions.

ritual in church. They were all more or less followers of Calvin; that is to say, they believed in predestination, the doctrine that some are foreordained to salvation and others are not; and they looked upon the Communion as a commemorative feast in memory of our Lord's death, and not as a special means of grace. Above all, they made the Bible their rule of faith and of conduct; they had an intense feeling of responsibility towards God for all that they did, and all the power which came from the conviction that He was on their side in their struggle against what they thought was wrong.

Dislike of toleration

There is, perhaps, one more point to bear in mind in dealing with religious parties in England, and for that matter in Scotland as well. No religious party, whether Roman Catholic, or Arminian, or Presbyterian, desired merely toleration for itself; they all, except perhaps the Independents, desired to persecute those who disagreed with them. Toleration, "that hellish toleration", as a Scottish divine once called it, would satisfy few; each party wanted every other religious party exactly to conform to its own views and practices, or else to be suppressed.

Elizabeth and the Puritans

It was inevitable that some of the religious opinions held by the Puritans should clash with those held by the Monarchy. Even in Elizabeth's day there was, at times, no little friction. In the early years of her reign had occurred what is known as the *Vestiarian Controversy* — clergymen with Puritan leanings objecting to wearing the surplice and to certain of the ceremonies enjoined in the Prayer Book. Then, later on, the more advanced Puritans, chiefly at Oxford and Cambridge, had advocated a Presbyterian form of government and had attacked the bishops, with the result that a dozen of them had been sent to jail. Others, again, had organized meetings, called *Prophesyings*, at which various religious subjects were discussed, and clergymen learnt how to preach sermons. But Elizabeth thought that theological discussion would provoke too much independence of thought; and she much preferred a clergyman to read to his congregation an extract from "the Book of Homilies" (which had been issued at the same time as the Prayer Book) rather than to preach to his congregation a sermon of his own composition — indeed, she thought one or two preachers quite a sufficient allowance for each county. She, therefore, disliked these clerical gatherings and sternly repressed them. And when the House of Commons, in which there was a strong Puritan element, ventured to discuss problems of ecclesiastical government or doctrine, the Queen mercilessly snubbed them.

The Puritans, however, on James's accession were inclined to be well-disposed to him, for they expected much from him. James had been brought up in Presbyterian Scotland, and the Puritans believed that his attitude towards them would be sympathetic. They consequently lost no time in presenting him with a *Millenary Petition* — so called because it was supposed to be signed by a thousand ministers [1] — asking for certain reforms. A conference, which included the two archbishops and six bishops on the one side and four Puritans on the other, was held at *Hampton Court* to consider the situation (1604).

The Hampton Court Conference (1604)

The King himself presided and behaved at first with admirable impartiality. Then, at the end of the second day, a Puritan mentioned the word "Presbytery". Now James, though the Puritans did not know it, hated the Presbyterian form of religion, with its outspokenness and its democratic government, as he had experienced it in Scotland. "A Scottish Presbytery," he said, "agreeth as well with a monarchy as God with the devil. Then Jack and Tom and Will and Dick shall meet, and at their pleasure censure me and my council." [2] The Conference soon broke up, and its only

[1] As a matter of fact it was not signed at all, though it had received the support of eight hundred ministers.

[2] "Stay, I pray you," James went on, "for one seven years, and if then you find me pursy and fat, and my windpipes stuffed, I will perhaps hearken unto you; for let that government be once up, I am sure I shall be kept in breath."

The Authorized Version of the Bible (1611)

result — though it was a very important result — was the preparation of the *Authorized Version of the Bible* (which appeared in 1611); the Puritans otherwise went away disappointed and empty-handed. James himself became a strong supporter of the extreme Anglican position, and a strong believer in the maxim "No bishop, no king"; if once the authority of the bishops was overthrown (*Note 61*), that of the Monarchy itself, he felt, would be threatened.

4. THE KING AND PARLIAMENT

Puritanism and Parliament

The Puritans, if they found no favour with the Monarchy, found plenty of support in the House of Commons. In every Parliament of James I and Charles I, and to an increasing extent as the years went on, there was a strong Puritan element in the Lower House, and eventually that element became supreme. It is this fact that largely accounts for the differences between the first two Stuart kings and their Parliaments. The Lower House was fanatically anti-Catholic; the two kings were inclined to be tolerant to the Catholics, James because he was naturally of a tolerant disposition and Charles because he had married a Roman Catholic wife. The Crown supported the Anglican or Arminian position in the English Church; the majority in the House of Commons was strongly opposed to the Arminian doctrines and regarded with considerable suspicion all the King's High Church appointments.

Causes of struggle between King and Parliament

There were, however, many other causes besides religious differences for the struggle round which centres the chief interest of the seventeenth century, the struggle between King and Parliament (*Note 62*). Of these we must say something before tracing the history of the struggle in detail. One cause of the struggle undoubtedly was the absence of external danger, already referred to in the last chapter (p. 408). It is often said that an Englishman can think of only one thing at a time. For a great part of Elizabeth's reign his mind was taken up with dangers from abroad. When Elizabeth's life alone stood between her subjects and anarchy or a foreign domination, it was no time to discuss rights and privileges. But by 1603 these dangers were over. The defeat of the Armada in 1588 meant the destruction not only of Philip's ambitions, but also of the Tudor dictatorship — for it was no longer required. Englishmen might, therefore, safely devote themselves to criticizing and reforming their own government.

Character of the House of Commons

Another cause of the struggle was the development, during the sixteenth century, of the national character. That century, it has been said, saw the birth of the modern Englishman. He had realized his possibilities in enterprise, in seamanship, in literature; the Reformation and the Renaissance had taught him to think and to reason for himself; he had become more self-reliant, more self-confident, perhaps more self-willed. He was, in a word, ready for a greater share in the government of his country. And more especially had come the development of the middle classes. The battle of English liberty in the seventeenth century was fought, not so much by the nobles or by the people, as by the squire, the merchant, and the lawyer; these were the classes which had developed in Tudor times, and it was from these classes that the members of the House of Commons were drawn. Very often they were ignorant, especially about foreign affairs; sometimes they did not realize the difficulties of the Government and brought absurd charges against the ministers. But they were men, for the most part, uncorrupted and incorruptible; independent and yet moderate; patient though very persistent. In the earlier stages of the struggle the lawyers chiefly fought the war of words in the House of Commons; they were, as Bacon said, the "vowels" of the House, the remaining members merely the "consonants". But when it came to the war of swords, it was the country gentlemen who made the best use of them.

England, then, was not distracted by foreign dangers; and she had developed a class of citizens who could think and act for themselves. Even during Elizabeth's reign the relations between the Queen and her Parliaments were not always perfectly harmonious. It is true that only eleven Parliaments were called, and that hardly any outlived a single session of some six weeks' duration; and that Elizabeth, as she frankly stated on one occasion, called them "not to make new laws [1] or lose good hours in idle speeches", but to provide supplies for the expenses of her government. Nevertheless, on occasions the House of Commons had exhibited an independent and almost pugnacious temper, which indicated that the nation would not continue to look on quietly while the Crown and its ministers governed, and that it was time for a reconsideration of their respective rights and duties. With James I that reconsideration came, and it was significant that at the opening of his first Parliament there was a record attendance. The time had come, as the House of Commons declared in the very first year of James's reign, to "redress, restore, and rectify" those actions which in the reign of Elizabeth they had "passed over". Questions of government, plain and broad questions, pressed for an answer.

Questions at issue:

There were questions of theory which went to the foundation of all authority. By what title did the King hold his throne? By hereditary divine right, as the King and the bishops and many others believed, or by virtue of an Act of Parliament? If the King ruled by divine right, criticism either of his words or of his actions was obviously wrong; a subject must yield passive obedience to a divinely appointed ruler. Or again, what was meant by the King's *Prerogative*? The King's party held that it was a sort of reserve power residing in the King to do ultimately what he liked; to override, if he thought reasons of State demanded it, all the

(a) Divine Right

(b) Prerogative

[1] The Queen was no believer in new laws, and in one year she vetoed no less than forty-eight out of the ninety-one bills which had been passed by both Houses of Parliament.

ordinary laws of the land. The Parliament party held, on the other hand, that law was the ground of all authority, and that the King possessed his powers by law, and must at all times be regulated by law. Where, again, did sovereignty reside? Did it rest with the King alone, or with the King and Parliament combined?

It is obvious that all the practical questions that arose, such as those concerning the power of the King to raise money without the consent of Parliament, and to imprison people without trial, or the power of the Parliament to call ministers to account for their actions, depended upon an answer to these questions. Nor were the answers at all clear. The powers of the monarchy were ill-defined, and the English Constitution was neither then nor at any other time of a rigid type. The King's party had just as decided opinions as the Parliamentary party; and both could bring strong arguments in support of their respective views. And as time went on, the differences between these views became irreconcilable; till at last the sword — and the sword alone — could settle them.

(c) Practical Questions

"I found Parliaments when I came here," said James once, "so I had to put up with them." One can sympathize with the King, for it is obvious that the Stuarts succeeded to an exceedingly difficult situation in regard to their Parliaments. But James, instead of relieving the situation, merely aggravated it. A wise man once said that the rights of kings and peoples never agree so well together as in silence. James, however, was both loquacious and pedantic. He was always wanting to define matters of government which had much better be left undefined, and to theorize concerning powers which he might have exercised, in practice, without notice, but which, uncompromisingly enunciated, were bound to provoke opposition.

We have no space to enter into the details of James's relations with his Parliaments, but we may take, as an example of his tactlessness, an incident which occurred at

James and Godwin's case (1604) the opening of his *first Parliament* (1604). The King's court had disallowed the election to the House of Commons of a man called *Godwin*, on the ground that he was an outlaw, and that James in a proclamation had said that no outlaws were to be elected. The House of Commons declared that it was their privilege to settle disputed elections. James answered that their privileges were his grant and ought not to be quoted against him, and a controversy at once ensued as to the origin of parliamentary privileges and the king's power to abrogate them. In the end James allowed the House of Commons to settle the matter of the election; but it was not an auspicious beginning.[1]

In the first Parliament of James I, also, an extremely Bate's case (1606) important question of taxation was brought up. The ordinary revenue of the king was derived partly from independent sources, such as crown lands and feudal dues, bringing in about £250,000 a year; and partly from a duty on all imports called tunnage and poundage,[2] a duty which was granted to the king on his accession for the term of his life, and which brought in about £150,000 a year. Two or three years after his accession, James began to impose, on certain articles, extra duties over and above what he was allowed to impose by tunnage and poundage. A merchant called *Bate* refused to pay the extra duty on currants, which was one of these articles. But the judges decided that he must pay not only because the ports — the gateways to the kingdom — belonged to the king, but also because it was the king's right and duty to regulate trade in what ways he thought desirable for the good of the State (1606). The result of this decision was that the Government imposed

[1] "The state of monarchy", James said to his Parliament in 1611, "is the supremest thing upon earth; for kings are not only God's lieutenants upon earth and sit upon God's throne, but even by God Himself they are called Gods; as to dispute what God may do is blasphemy, so it is sedition in subjects to dispute what a king may do in the height of his power." This is another example of the King's loquacious tactlessness.

[2] So called because a certain sum was paid on every tun of wine and pound of merchandise imported.

extra duties upon a whole mass of other articles as well, and the King's revenue was increased. These extra duties, known as *Impositions*, were, of course, a constant source of contention, and were strenuously opposed by this and other Parliaments.

The Parliament of 1621; revival of impeachment

The King dissolved his first Parliament in 1611, and for the next ten years there was no Parliament except in 1614, when one sat for two months; it is known in history as the "*Addled Parliament*" because no laws resulted from it. But in *1621* the loss of the Palatinate by Frederick, and the possibility that England might be engaged in a war for its recovery, led James to call his *third Parliament*. This Parliament was very important. In the first place the House of Commons revived its right of impeachment, its right to prosecute the king's ministers or office holders before the House of Lords. This was a weapon of tremendous power which had not been used since 1459; and it was a weapon which later on was to be used with great frequency. The House of Commons began by impeaching some holders of monopolies. It went on to accuse the Lord Chancellor, Francis Bacon, Lord Verulam, of receiving bribes. Suitors in those days often used to give presents to judges. But there is no doubt also that Bacon had in some cases, probably through carelessness, received presents before he had given his decision, and that these presents were given with a corrupt intention; there is no proof, however, that Bacon received them as bribes or that they in any way influenced his decision.[1] We may agree with Bacon's own judgment: "I was the justest judge that was in England these fifty years. But it was the justest censure in Parliament that was these two hundred years." Bacon was

[1] In one case, a lady, who had a series of suits being heard before Bacon, drove down to York House, Bacon's residence, with £100 in her purse. "What is that," said Bacon on her entrance, "that you have in your hand?" "A purse of my own making," was the lady's reply, "which I hope your lordship will accept." "What Lord," replied Bacon, "could refuse a purse of so fair a lady's working?" But, as a matter of fact, though Bacon took the purse and the £100, his final decision was not at all in favour of this lady litigant.

deprived of his chancellorship and died shortly afterwards.

In the second place, this House of Commons upheld its liberty of speech. The House of Commons was strongly, almost fanatically, anti-Catholic and anti-Spaniard, and it met at the time that James was proposing a marriage between Charles and a Spanish princess with a view to the restoration of the Palatinate. It accordingly drew up a petition to be presented to the King, in which it begged that Charles might marry one of " our own religion ", and expressed with some bluntness its opinion of the Pope and his " dearest son " the King of Spain. Such a petition coming in the crisis of his negotiations with Spain was, from the King's point of view, exceedingly embarrassing; and James wrote an angry letter against the " fiery and popular spirits " in the House of Commons who had dared " to argue or debate publicly matters far above their reach and capacity ", and forbade the House " henceforth to meddle with anything concerning our Government or deep matters of State ". Fortunately for English liberty, the House of Commons maintained its courage; and in the candle-light on a dark December day, it drew up a Protestation declaring its freedom of speech. The King thereupon dissolved the Parliament, imprisoned some of its members, and sending for the journal book of the House of Commons tore the Protestation out of it with his own hands (1622). But, nevertheless, the House of Commons had shown there was one place in the kingdom where an Englishman might say what he liked.

Liberty of speech

In the *fourth Parliament* (1624) we pass into smooth waters, for Parliament had got the war with Spain which it desired. Moreover, Buckingham and Prince Charles supported the House of Commons in their impeachment of Middlesex, the Lord Treasurer. Shortly afterwards James died (1625).

This brief summary will have shown that the rift had begun between the Crown and Parliament in the reign of

King James. The House of Commons had made a decided advance; it had revived impeachment, upheld its privileges, and protested against impositions. James's character, it must be admitted, had been peculiarly fitted to open dangerous questions; in the reign of his successor they would have to be answered.

CHAPTER 36

CHARLES I (1625–1649)

1. CHARLES I'S FOREIGN POLICY (1625–1649)

Charles I and the war (1625-6)

When Charles I came to the throne, the Protestants were fighting for their existence in Germany, but a new champion had arisen on behalf of the Protestant cause in the person of the *King of Denmark*. Charles agreed to pay him £360,000 a year for the conduct of a war in Germany. He paid one instalment of £46,000 — and that was all. For one thing, Charles had obtained, largely through his own fault, insufficient supplies of money from Parliament. For another, soon after Charles made the engagement to the Danish king, he and Buckingham, who largely controlled the King's policy, came to the conclusion that the Protestantism of Germany might best be succoured and the Palatinate recovered by an attack upon the Spanish ports. It was, doubtless, a roundabout plan to attack the King of Spain in order to put pressure on the Emperor to restore Frederick, but a naval war with Spain was sure to be popular, and it was easier than campaigning in Germany. Accordingly an expedition was organized to *Cadiz*, which was to repeat Drake's exploit, sack the town, and capture the treasure fleet coming from America. But the expedition came to hopeless grief and took neither Cadiz nor the treasure fleet

(1625).[1] The next year the King of Denmark, with soldiers clamouring for pay in consequence of the failure of the English subsidies, was obliged to take the offensive, was decisively defeated, and accordingly returned to his own country (1626). Charles's initial interference in the Thirty Years' War had, therefore, been disastrous.

Difficulties with France (1625-6)

Meantime Charles had got into difficulties with France. At the end of his father's reign he was engaged to marry a French princess, *Henrietta Maria*, and on his accession he married her. By the terms of the marriage treaty concessions were promised to the Roman Catholics in England, and James also, just before his death, had undertaken to lend ships to the French King. The French King and his famous minister, Richelieu, wanted to use the ships to aid them in a war against the Protestants in France, the Huguenots as they are called. Charles, after futile endeavours and discreditable subterfuges to evade his father's promises,[2] was obliged to lend them — to the great wrath of his subjects in England.

The Rhé expedition (1627) and Buckingham's assassination (1628)

Later on, the King of France demanded that the promised concessions to the Catholics in England should be granted, and in 1627 the two countries gradually drifted into war. Buckingham was himself sent with an expedition to capture a fort in the *Isle of Rhé*, in order to assist *La Rochelle*, the Huguenot stronghold on the west coast of France which the French King was still besieging. At that time there was no standing army, and a force largely composed of the riff-raff of the country was not likely to be successful.[3]

[1] The expedition had started in the stormy month of October, with pressed crews and soldiers, with ships whose hulls were rotten and whose sails — at all events in the case of one ship — dated from the Armada; and the food was exceedingly bad, " such as no dog in Paris garden would eat ", said a contemporary. On reaching Cadiz, the men got drunk, and the ships finally returned home with scarcely enough men to work them.

[2] Amongst other things, a mutiny was arranged so that the ships might not be given up.

[3] When an army had to be raised, each county had to contribute a certain number of men. The lord-lieutenants, as in this case, took advantage of the occasion to get rid of those who, it was desirable, " should leave their county for their county's good ". Buckingham's troops were ignorant alike of marksmanship and discipline, and after being drilled for a fortnight at the seaside, were dispatched on the expedition.

Buckingham, however, did well, and inspired his men with courage, if not with enthusiasm; and, but for the fact that, through no fault of his own, the French managed to revictual the fort, and that, through contrary winds, reinforcements failed to leave England, he might have succeeded. As it was, Buckingham came back discredited in the eyes of the country. Before he could fit out another expedition, the tenpenny knife of a disappointed officer called Felton, who thought, as many others thought, that the assassination of Buckingham was a meritorious act, closed his career (1628).

Charles's inaction (1629-49)

With Buckingham's death, " there was an abrupt transition ", it has been said, " from a policy of adventurous activity to one of utter inaction ". Charles would make proposals, at one and the same time, to France for an alliance against Spain, and to Spain for an alliance against France. He would offer to help *Gustavus Adolphus*, the King of Sweden, the new champion of Protestantism in Germany, and not the King of Denmark, and then to help the King of Denmark and not Gustavus. One ambassador said to Charles, " The truth is you pull down with one hand as fast as you build up with the other ": and the criticism was a just one. Moreover, circumstances were against the prosecution of an active policy. At first, Charles had no money to back his schemes; and later he had his hands full with his quarrel with his own subjects. As a result, the influence of Great Britain in foreign affairs became a negligible quantity for the remainder of Charles's reign.

Later stages of the Thirty Years' War

The Thirty Years' War, therefore, ceased to be influenced by or to influence Great Britain; and we can only briefly allude to its later developments. *Gustavus Adolphus* had a brief spell of brilliant success and was then killed at the famous battle of *Lützen* [1] (1632). The Protestant cause appeared hopeless. But Richelieu, though he suppressed Protestants in France, was willing to support them in

[1] At the crisis of the battle, a thick November mist obscured the sun, and Gustavus, losing his way, was killed by the enemy.

Germany by force of arms so as to weaken the house of Habsburg. During the later stages of the war, the French armies exerted a decisive influence and were brilliantly successful. The war came finally to an end in 1648, France and Sweden acquiring large parts of what had been German territory, whilst the German states were left more disunited and independent than before the war broke out. Upon Germany and the German nation the effects of the war, material and moral, were appalling — indeed, in the opinion of Bismarck, the great Prussian statesman, Germany was still suffering from these effects in 1880.

Failure of English policy — its causes

It must be confessed that England's foreign policy during the first half of the seventeenth century was both inglorious and ineffective. Many explanations may be offered. There was no standing army, and consequently no force behind English diplomacy; and if England went to war, her hastily trained levies had little chance against more experienced soldiers. Parliament again, though keen for war, did not, as a matter of fact, provide either James or Charles with sufficient money to wage it effectively — though in the case of Charles it was, as we shall see, largely his own fault for not explaining what he intended to do. Moreover, ill fortune attended the English efforts. But the chief cause of the futility of English policy lay in the characters of James and Charles; the indecisive and timid policy of the one and the tortuous and contradictory policy of the other could only result in failure. Nor must we forget that England's failure enabled France, by becoming the ally of the German Protestants, to establish a predominance which was before the end of the century to threaten the independence of nearly every other country in Europe.

2. CHARLES I AND DOMESTIC AFFAIRS (1625–1642)

Turning now to domestic affairs it will be apparent from what has been already said that Charles succeeded to no

Charles I and Henrietta Maria

easy inheritance. He had been left an incompetent and impetuous minister in Buckingham, and unfortunately that minister had more influence in Charles's reign than he had enjoyed even in the later years of King James. At home there was an empty treasury and a Parliament which was beginning to feel its power; and abroad, things were going badly for the Protestants in the Thirty Years' War. Moreover, Charles's wife was to be of no assistance to him. *Henrietta Maria* was a vivacious and attractive person, but, unfortunately, as time went on, she interfered more and more in affairs of State, and had more and more influence over her husband. The Queen was quite ignorant of English customs and the English character. She was a Roman Catholic in a strongly Protestant country, and was always striving to obtain concessions for those of her own religion. She actively intrigued, in times of difficulty at home, for assistance from abroad; and she held the most extreme political opinions with regard to the King's authority and the wickedness of those who opposed it.[1]

Causes of dispute between Charles and his Parliaments

Charles called three Parliaments during the first four years of his reign, and quarrelled with each one of them. Then for eleven years he governed without a Parliament. Finally, a war with Scotland and the consequent need of money forced him in 1640 to call two Parliaments, the second of which reduced his powers, and eventually civil war broke out in 1642. Such is briefly the history of Charles's relations with his Parliaments. The subjects of dispute were many. There was, as in James's reign, the religious difficulty. Charles was an Anglican High Churchman, and because of his wife was inclined to tolerate the Roman Catholics; Parliament was Puritan and anti-Catholic. Parliament distrusted the King's ministers, Buckingham in the first four years, and Strafford and Laud in 1640; the King, on

[1] "Of the many women, good and bad," it has been said, "who have tried to take part in affairs of State, from Cleopatra, or the Queen of Sheba downward, nobody by character or training was ever worse fitted than the wife of Charles I for such a case as that in which she found herself."

6

the contrary, thought these ministers able and efficient, and any parliamentary criticisms of them factious and impertinent. Parliament, in the early years of Charles's reign, was angry at the failure of the English foreign policy; and in later years, because of the Court intrigues with foreign powers.

But underlying all these disputes lay the questions indicated in the last chapter: Where did sovereignty reside? Who had the responsibility for the government of the country? The Parliament wanted, rightly or wrongly, a greater control of the government; Charles, rightly or wrongly, was unwilling to concede it — there lay the whole difficulty. We regard it now as an easy task to bring the powers of Crown and Parliament into harmony. But this dual control was not easy to arrange, and perhaps was impossible to obtain without friction. As a matter of fact, a Civil War occurred in 1642 and a Revolution in 1688 before an arrangement could be made — and even then it proved not to be permanent (*Note 64*).

Charles's first Parliament (1625)

Charles's *first Parliament* met in *1625*,[1] just after the King had arranged to pay very large subsidies to the King of Denmark and to send a fleet to attack Spain. Obviously large sums would be required. But Charles's reticence and want of frankness proved a fatal impediment. There were no Blue Books or White Books and no daily newspapers in those days, and it was difficult for members of Parliament to know what was going on. Though members knew, of course, that a great religious war was in progress in Germany, and were anxious that England should help the Protestants, they were yet unfamiliar with recent developments. But Charles would neither explain his policy, nor depute anyone else to do so. Consequently, as one member said, "They knew not their enemy", and the statement was literally true. Nor did Charles explain his needs; he made a definite

[1] Even an outbreak of the plague in London did not prevent an attendance at the opening of Charles's first Parliament which beat the record established when James I came to the throne.

demand for the navy, but only hinted at the largeness of the sums he really required. Consequently Charles only got one-seventh of the amount of money which he needed.

Tunnage and Poundage granted for one year

At the same time Parliament granted tunnage and poundage to the King only for one year, though for the last two centuries it had been granted the king for life. Here Parliament was wrong. The Monarchy could not get on without the money. It had to meet the ordinary expenses of government; moreover, the Court spent more money than in Elizabeth's day whilst the great rise in prices, owing to the influx of silver from the New World had made the king's revenue worth less than before. The decision, however, in Bate's case (p. 426) made it legal for Charles to go on levying the customs without Parliamentary sanction, and he accordingly did so. In this, as in the succeeding Parliaments, the Puritan majority had apprehensions about religion, for the King favoured Anglican High Churchmen such as Laud,[1] and also allowed the administration of the laws against the Roman Catholics to become somewhat lax.

The second Parliament (1626); Buckingham's impeachment

Charles's *second Parliament* met in *1626*, after the loan of ships to the French King and the disaster to the Cadiz fleet had occurred (p. 429). The House of Commons first demanded that an inquiry into the Cadiz disaster should precede any grant of supply, and wanted especially to investigate Buckingham's conduct. Charles held that he and not Parliament must be the judge of the capacity of his ministers: "I would not have the House to question my servants," he said, "much less one who is so near me." The House of Commons then went a step further, and under Eliot's leadership impeached Buckingham. *Sir John Eliot* was a Cornishman, a man of lofty nature, and a great orator, but apt — as those possessing the qualities of an orator often are — to exaggerate, and take either a better or a worse view of a man than he deserved. In 1625 he had expressed

[1] Laud supplied the King with a list of clergy marked either O for Orthodox or P for Puritan, so that only those might receive promotion whom Laud considered Orthodox.

a hope to Buckingham that he might be "wholly devoted to the contemplation of his excellencies". But in the next year, when he saw, as he said, "our honour ruined, our ships sunk, our men perished, not by the sword, not by the enemy, not by chance, but by those we trust", his indignation knew no bounds. In a speech of wonderful power he applied to Buckingham the words in which Tacitus characterized Sejanus [1]: *Sui obtegens, in alios criminator; juxta adulatio et superbia.* "If he is Sejanus, I must be Tiberius," was Charles's comment on this comparison, and he never forgave Eliot as a consequence. Buckingham's impeachment led Charles to dissolve the second Parliament.

The *third Parliament* met two years later, in *1628.* Charles was needlessly rude in his first speech. If the Parliament did not supply his wants, he must, he said, use all means which God had put into his hands. "Take not this as a threat," he added, "for I scorn to threaten any but my equals." This was an unpromising beginning; but Parliament had more important causes of dissatisfaction than the King's speech. The Rhé expedition had failed (p. 430). Parliament was still nervous about religion. Moreover, the King had recently levied a forced loan. But this was not all. Five

The Five Knights

knights had refused to pay the forced loan, and had been imprisoned. When brought up in a court of law, the justification for their imprisonment had been given as "the special command of the King". The Crown lawyers argued before the judges that the King must have, for the safety of the State, the power to commit people to, and to keep them in, prison without trial. That is true enough; but the danger was, as it has been well said, that the King was making the medicine of the constitution its daily food. Moreover, the knights' lawyers held that such a power as the King claimed was plainly contrary to an Englishman's liberty and to Magna Carta. The judges before whom the

[1] Sejanus was governor of the praetorian troops, and for many years controlled the policy of the Emperor Tiberius.

case was tried had given no definite ruling in such a difficult matter, though they had refused to release the knights from prison.

The third Parliament lost no time in trying to check what was held to be an abuse of the King's power, and drew up the *Petition of Right*. The first article declared that loans and taxes without consent of Parliament were illegal, and the second that all arbitrary imprisonment without cause shown was illegal. The third article of this petition forbade the billeting of soldiers in private houses;[1] and the fourth, the exercise, in time of peace, of martial law, which too often had meant no law at all. The King, after trying every means of evasion, finally gave his consent to this petition; and, though he violated every one of its articles, the Petition stands as a great landmark in the struggle.

The Petition of Right (1628)

It was after the Petition was passed that Wentworth, who had been one of the chief leaders of the House of Commons, joined the King. The second session of the third Parliament met in 1629. Parliament maintained that the King had not kept his promises with regard to the Petition of Right, and dissensions between King and Parliament grew more bitter. Charles determined to dissolve Parliament, but before he could do so occurred the celebrated scene when, with the Speaker held down in the chair and the doors locked, three resolutions were passed, proposed by Eliot and hence often called *Eliot's Three Resolutions*. They declared that whoever proposed innovations in religion, and whoever either proposed or paid taxes without the consent of Parliament, was an enemy to the kingdom and a betrayer of its liberties. These three resolutions — combining the grievances which the House of Commons felt in religion and in politics — were the last that the third Parliament (1629) was to pass, for it was at once dissolved;

The dissolution of Parliament (1629)

Eliot's Three Resolutions.

[1] Soldiers, raised for an expedition abroad, were sometimes billeted in private houses, and were not infrequently an intolerable nuisance. Some people in Essex complained, for instance, that the Irish quartered there broke the furniture, and threw the meat into the fire if it did not win their approval.

and Eliot, the most noble-minded of all in that struggle, was put into the Tower and died there.[1]

We have now come to the end of the first period of the conflict. On the whole, though Parliament was sometimes unduly suspicious, sometimes rather niggardly in its supplies, and always intolerant in matters of religion, it had shown itself more patient, more practical, more clear-headed than either the kings or their advisers, and it is difficult to resist the conclusion that it was in the right. But this must not blind us to the fact that Parliament was seeking to establish a control over the king and his advisers which had not been exercised in Tudor times, and it was not unnatural that the Crown should resist such attempts.

3. ARBITRARY GOVERNMENT, 1629–1640, AND GROWING DISCONTENT IN ENGLAND AND SCOTLAND

Arbitrary government (1629-40)

The next eleven years saw no Parliament — the longest interval England has known in her history since Parliament began (*Note 65*). They are usually called *The Eleven Years' Tyranny*. We must, however, beware of regarding a year without a Parliament as anything exceptional; in Elizabeth's reign, for instance, Parliament on the average met only every third year. Nor must we regard Charles as a wicked despot, destroying the rights, the goods, and the lives of his people. The period, on the contrary, was one of prosperity for the nation at large; with the exception of Eliot, no political martyr lost his life; and the King, on the whole, kept within the letter of the law as it was interpreted for him by judges, who might, however, with reason be deemed somewhat accommodating.[2] Yet none the less they were

[1] Eliot's son petitioned that the body might be buried at Port Eliot, the Cornish home of the family. But Charles was implacable. "Let Sir John Eliot," wrote the King on the petition, "be buried in the church of that parish where he died"; and accordingly he was buried in the Tower.

[2] The judges also would be likely to be on the side of the Crown, for lawyers go by the latest precedent, and would maintain that the Stuarts might well do as the Tudors had done.

dangerous and critical years for England; and when they were over, the people of England showed that they were determined that a repetition of such absolute rule should not occur.

We must say something about the advisers of Charles during this period. No one succeeded to Buckingham's commanding position in Charles's councils. Yet amongst the King's advisers two figures stand out pre-eminent — *Thomas Wentworth (Note 66)*, eventually created *Earl of Strafford*, and *William Laud* (*Note 66*). Wentworth, a member of an old family with large estates in Yorkshire, had supported the Crown when he first entered the House of Commons; but in the early Parliaments of Charles I he was one of the leading critics of the King's policy, and the Petition of Right in particular was largely due to his initiative. Then between the two sessions of the third Parliament he joined the King's side, and was made a peer (1628). For this change Wentworth has been unsparingly attacked, called a political apostate, the First of the Rats, and compared to Lucifer.[1] And, indeed, it is impossible to deny that Wentworth was inconsistent, that he did things when in authority which he would have been the first to condemn when in opposition, or that self-interest was probably one of the motives which influenced him.

Thomas Went-worth, Earl of Strafford

Wentworth, however, was one of those strong, masterful, able people who have an unlimited confidence in their own capacity, and very little in that of anyone else. He had been with the Opposition because he distrusted Buckingham and specially disliked his foreign enterprises, and because of the arbitrary acts which the Government had committed. But he was never really of the Opposition; he had no sympathy with the Puritan leanings of the majority, and felt contempt for many of his fellow-members. Moreover, he was no believer in Parliamentary government — govern-

[1] See Lord Macaulay's *Essay on Hallam's History*.

ment, in his view, was to be for the people, but not by them. To him princes were, to use his own expression, the " indulgent nursing-fathers to their people ", and the authority of a king " the keystone which closeth up the arch of order and government ". And only by allying himself with the King could he show, it must be remembered, his capacity for administration. Wentworth therefore joined the King, and was made President of the North in 1628, which gave him the control of the northern counties. In 1632 he became Lord Deputy of Ireland, and it was in Ireland that he was to exhibit the strength and weakness of his statesmanship (see p. 506). Then in the summer of 1639 he became Charles I's principal adviser, and quickly made himself the most hated man in England.

Laud

Wentworth's great friend was *Laud*. He and Laud were alike in that energy and whole-hearted devotion to the King's service, and in that determination to get things done which was expressed in their letters to one another by their watchword " Thorough ". Laud was the son of a clothier at Reading. He had been educated at Reading school and St. John's College, Oxford. He became President of St. John's, and was noted for his opposition to the Puritans. He was next made Bishop of St. David's; in 1628 he became Bishop of London, and five years later Archbishop of Canterbury. It was Laud who directed the ecclesiastical policy of the Government. In that policy there is much that can be praised. Large sums of money were spent in the erection and restoration of churches. Order and decency were enforced in the Church services. Laud made, through deputies, a visitation of all the dioceses in his archbishopric, and found much to amend: the chapter of a cathedral neglecting to preach and often absent; the aisle of one church being used by the bailiff of a local lord to melt the lead which had been stripped from the roof; the aisle of another being used for cock-fighting, the vicar himself being present.[1] Moreover, Laud was no respecter of persons, and attacked wrongdoing in however high quarters it might be discovered.

But, with all his energy and goodness, Laud was unsympathetic and narrow-minded, a man who thought that everyone must believe in the High Church doctrines which he believed in, whether he be English, Irish, Scot, or even French or Spaniard. Through his control of the Press he tried to stop the publication of all views antagonistic to his own. But it was especially in the Courts of Star Chamber and High Commission that Laud made his evil reputation.[2] Laud, with his sharp tongue and irritable temper, always voted for the biggest punishment upon theological offenders, and it was chiefly due to him that such barbarous punishments were inflicted as flogging and branding and the cutting off of ears. If Laud saved the Church of England, as in Mr. Gladstone's judgment he did, from being bound in the fetters of an iron system of compulsory and Calvinistic belief, he was also responsible for driving the moderate Protestants into the arms of the Puritans.

The difficulties of Charles were mainly financial, for his income from Crown lands and feudal dues, from tunnage and poundage and Impositions was insufficient. He had therefore to find other sources. Thus he caused all those who held lands by feudal tenure or of a certain value — over £40 a year — to become knights and to pay fees for the honour, or else to be fined for refusing it. He fined nobles and others whose ancestors had encroached — perhaps hundreds of years before — on the limits of the Crown forests. Various companies, on paying certain annual payments, were granted monopolies of the commonest articles of use,

Finance

Knighthood

[1] Laud also stopped St. Paul's Cathedral being used as a club for gossip by the men of fashion, or as a playground by those of more tender years, and he insisted that men should not come into church with their hats on.

[2] These courts had been established, the one in the reign of Henry VII and the other in that of Elizabeth; they tried a man in secret, without a jury, and made prisoners give evidence against themselves.

such as bricks, salt, and soap.[1] Then the Navy was very weak; Barbary corsairs had actually landed and wintered in Dorset in the winter of 1624–25. So, in 1634, Charles levied a tax called *ship-money* from the maritime towns and counties, the proceeds of which were to be used for providing new ships for the Navy and repairing those already in existence. For this tax there were many precedents in time of war, but now Charles imposed it in time of peace. A year later, he issued a "second writ of ship-money", as it was called, and levied it from the whole country — a very unpopular move.

Ship-money (1634)

Up till *1637*, though there had been great dissatisfaction, there was little resistance to the King. With that year, however, the struggle began — it has been well called the first year of the Revolutionary Epoch. Popular feeling had the opportunity of showing itself in *June*. Prynne, a lawyer, Burton, a clergyman, and Bastwick, a doctor, were sentenced for attacks on the bishops,[2] to lose their ears, to be fined £5000, and to be imprisoned for life. They suffered the first part of this sentence in Palace Yard. Prynne[3] had already lost part of his ears for an attack upon the stage four years previously, but his case had then aroused little interest. Now, however, all London came to show its sympathy. His path and that of his fellow sufferers was strewn with flowers, many people wept, and there was an angry yell when Prynne's ears — or what remained of them — were sawn off. Then in *November*, 1637, came the famous trial of *John Hampden*. The King had issued a third writ of ship-money, and it looked as if he was going,

The beginning of the Crisis (1637)

John Hampden

[1] In Tudor times it was the business of the State to regulate trade; and Charles I in much that he did merely carried out the Tudor system. Thus the Star Chamber was used to proceed against Corn Engrossers, and real attempts were made to find sensible work for the unemployed. So also the monopoly system was part of the scheme of Paternal economic government. The real difficulties were, first, that Charles from want of money abused the system; and, second, that the English people were becoming more and more Individualistic in outlook.

[2] The bishops, Bastwick had written, were the enemies of God and the King, and the Church which they governed was as full of ceremonies as a dog is full of fleas.

[3] During the course of his life he wrote two hundred books and pamphlets. He wrote all day, his servant bringing him every three hours a roll and a pot of ale "to refocillate his wasted spirits".

without Parliamentary sanction (this was the root of the trouble), to make it a permanent tax. Hampden, a Buckinghamshire squire of importance, refused to pay. The case was heard, and the judges decided by seven to five that ship-money was legal. The case aroused intense interest, and the arguments of Hampden's lawyers were circulated over the entire kingdom. In the same year the opinions of the greatest literary figure of the period on Laud's rule were shown in the writing by Milton of *Lycidas*.

In Scotland, however, even more than in England, the year 1637 is one of importance.

The Church of Scotland

During the lifetime of *John Knox* (died 1572) it seemed as if the Scottish Church might ultimately accept a modified form of Episcopacy, but under *Andrew Melville*, who succeeded John Knox in the leadership of the Scottish Church, the view prevailed that all ministers were of equal status, and *Presbyteries* were erected to perform the administrative duties formerly associated with bishops. The Scottish Church thus became definitely Presbyterian in its government. Under this system there are four Church Courts. Each congregation has its *Kirk Session* consisting of the minister and elders, both elected by the congregation.

The Presbyterian Courts

The congregations are grouped into sixty *Presbyteries*, each congregation being represented on the Presbyterial court by its minister and one elder. Three or more Presbyteries compose a *Provincial Synod*, twelve in number, meeting twice a year. The supreme court of the Church, the *General Assembly*, meets once a year. Its members are ministers and elders elected by the Presbyteries.

On to this Presbyterian system James the Sixth of Scotland (First of England) sought to graft bishops.[1] He, and,

[1] Bishops were popular neither in Scotland nor in England. Thus one English writer calls the bishops "not the pillars but the caterpillars of the Church"; another in a parody of the Litany says: "From plague, pestilence, and famine, from bishops, priests, and deacons, good Lord, deliver us." The Scots are not behindhand — one calls the bishops "beastlie bellie-gods" regardless of the fact that some bishops, at all events, lived ascetic lives and were decidedly spare of frame; and another characterizes them as "bunchy knobs of papist flesh".

Policy of James VI

after him, Charles I, believed in the Divine Right of Kings, while the people of Scotland believed no less ardently in the Divine Right of the General Assembly, and denied the right of the civil authority to interfere in any way in the affairs of the Church. The General Assembly had influence that extended beyond ecclesiastical affairs, and was, in fact, a representative body which was the centre of opposition to royal despotism. On the other hand the Scottish Parliament, or Council of Estates, was a feudal assembly whose business was controlled by the "*Lords of the Articles*", in the nomination of whom the king had a large say. Therefore conflict between Crown and Church was almost inevitable. King James showed much tenacity of purpose, and by 1612 he had fully established Episcopacy in Scotland, without, however, abolishing the Presbyterian Courts. He then sought to modify the forms of worship, and by diplomacy and intimidation the General Assembly was induced to pass, in 1618, what were called, from the place of meeting, the *Five Articles of Perth.* Of these Articles, perhaps the most unpopular was the enforcement of kneeling at Communion, which savoured to the Scottish mind of idolatry.

Church and State

Five Articles of Perth (1618)

Charles came to the throne in 1625, and in twelve years had united the whole Scottish nation against him. To begin with, his marriage with a Roman Catholic met with much unfavourable comment. Then he frightened the nobles by an attempt to recover some of the lands which they had obtained from the Church at the Reformation. Finally he aroused the anger of the whole people by his determination to establish complete uniformity with the Church of England by doing away with the Presbyterian Courts and by imposing a new Prayer Book similar to the English Prayer Book. The particulars in which it differed from the English Prayer Book were universally held to be due to the influence of Archbishop Laud, and to be in a Popish direction. "It was," said a contemporary, "a Popish-English-Scottish-Mass-Service-Book."

Charles I and the new Service Book (1637)

Riot in St. Giles' (1637)

Laud's Liturgy was used for the first time in St. Giles' Cathedral, Edinburgh, on Sunday, 23rd July, 1637, and provoked a riot — traditionally stated to have been started by a woman called Jenny Geddes — which was really the beginning of a revolution. Charles might have retrieved the situation by withdrawing the Service Book, but this he refused to do. Then opposition to the Prayer Book grew into a demand for the abolition of Episcopacy, and a zealous Presbyterian organization known as "The Tables" was practically ruling Scotland in defiance of King and Council. Still Charles persisted, and in 1638 opposition to him culminated in the *National Covenant*.

The National Covenant (1638)

The National Covenant was first signed in Greyfriars Churchyard, Edinburgh, on 1st March, 1638, and copies were sent all over Scotland. Everywhere it was signed with the utmost enthusiasm, the signatories pledging themselves "to adhere to and defend the true religion", by which they meant Protestantism in general, and the Presbyterian Church in particular.

The Glasgow Assembly (1638)

This at last awakened Charles to the seriousness of the situation. He offered to withdraw the Service Book and to permit a free General Assembly and a free Parliament to meet. But it was too late. When the General Assembly met in Glasgow in November, only Covenanters were admitted to membership, and Hamilton, the Royal Commissioner, seeing that the Assembly would demand his assent to Acts abolishing Episcopacy, dissolved it in the name of the King. But the Assembly continued to sit, though an unconstitutional body, and with great gusto annulled the Five Articles of Perth, cancelled the Service Book, deposed the bishops, abolished Episcopacy, and reintroduced strict Presbyterianism.

First Bishops' War (1639)

Naturally the King refused to sanction the Acts of this Assembly, and it was clear that war was inevitable. It broke out in 1639 and was known as the *First Bishops' War*. The Covenanters under Alexander Leslie, "that old, little, crooked soldier", a veteran of many Continental campaigns, took up position on Duns Law, near Berwick. The King came north with a force, miserable in numbers and equipment, and could do nothing but agree, by the *Pacification of Berwick*, to the Scottish demands, the chief of which was that another General Assembly should meet. This did meet in August, and all the measures of the Glasgow Assembly were again passed. In addition, the Assembly passed a new Act making the signing of the Covenant compulsory on the whole nation. All these Acts of Assembly received the royal assent, but Charles, who was as determined as ever to have his own way, refused to sanction the parliamentary measures necessary to make them legally enforceable. The situation was, therefore, unchanged, and in 1640 the *Second Bishops' War* broke out. The meeting of the Short Parliament in England showed the Scots that they had no reason to fear that the English nation would support Charles, and they accordingly invaded England and marched to Newcastle-on-Tyne. Charles met Scottish representatives at Ripon, and had no alternative but to agree to the continued occupation of Newcastle till a settlement could be reached. In August, 1641, he granted all the Scottish demands, and paid the expenses of the army at Newcastle, which amounted to £850 a day, and the Scots went home. In September, Charles visited Edinburgh in the hope of obtaining Scottish help against the rapidly growing opposition of the English Parliament. He was most gracious, yielding to all Scottish demands, and lavishing honours and other signs of favour on the leading Covenanters, but he failed in his main purpose. His actions at this time, however, had this effect, that, when the Civil War did break out, Scotland had no quarrel with him, and had no call to support either side. Nevertheless, by this time the Covenanters were dreaming a new dream. They dreamed of uniformity of Church government in England and Scotland, not on the Episcopal model as Charles had hoped, but on the Presbyterian model; and they now worked to make the dream a reality.

Second Bishops' War (1640)

Charles in Scotland (1641)

4. THE SHORT AND THE LONG PARLIAMENTS (1640–1642)

We must now trace the influence of Scottish affairs upon English politics. The Scottish rebellion, it has been said, gave back to England her Parliamentary system. For eleven years Charles had done without Parliament. But the money he had was only just enough for current expenses; any extra strain would break down Charles's system and make a Parliament inevitable. After the First Bishops' War was over, Strafford arrived in England, and, by his advice, in order to obtain funds to renew the war with Scotland, a Parliament was summoned. That Parliament — called the *Short Parliament* — met in *April, 1640*, and it lasted but three weeks. The King tried to bargain for subsidies in return for giving up ship-money, but he failed; and Parliament, when it proceeded to petition for a peaceful settlement with Scotland, was dissolved. This Parliament brought to the front a Somersetshire squire named *Pym*, who was to show himself a great Parliamentarian. He was a clear and cogent speaker, a clever tactician, and the possessor of unbounded energy. In a speech of two hours — an exceptionally long speech for that period — he attacked the misgovernment of the King, and summed up his political creed by declaring that " the powers of Parliament are to the body politic as the rational faculties of the soul to a man ". And he quickly achieved for himself a position which led his enemies to call him, in the next Parliament, " King Pym ".

English affairs; The Short Parliament (1640)

The Second Bishops' War followed the dissolution of the Short Parliament. In the peace which ended it Charles, as we have seen, promised to pay £850 a day to the Scottish Army. But with this large sum of money required, he was compelled to summon another Parliament and, what is more, to listen to its demands.[1] The House of Commons

[1] As it was, Charles had to seize £130,000 of bullion from the Mint, and merchants could not meet the Bills of Exchange. This caused immense dislocation, and was one of the things which turned the merchant class against Charles.

was, at that time, an aristocratic and not what we should now consider a democratic assembly; and the Parliament which met in *November, 1640* — to be known in history as the *Long Parliament* — was composed, it has been said, of the very flower of the English gentry and educated laity.

The Long Parliament meets (Nov., 1640)

Work of the Long Parliament

The work of this Parliament for the first nine months of its existence was the abolition of the arbitrary power of the Crown (*Note 67*). Now at last, after nearly forty years, some of the questions at issue between King and Parliament were to be definitely settled. The House of Commons during these nine months worked with practical unanimity — a fact which shows how universal the dissatisfaction with the King's government had been. Under Pym's leadership laws were passed declaring that this particular Parliament was not to be adjourned or dissolved without its own consent, and that, in future, Parliaments must be summoned every three years (the *Triennial Act*). Arbitrary courts — such as the Star Chamber and the Court of High Commission — were abolished; and taxes, such as ship-money, were declared illegal, and tunnage and poundage also without consent of Parliament. Only on a Bill for the abolition of Episcopacy — the Root and Branch Bill — was there great divergence of opinion.

Arbitrary Power Abolished

Prerogative courts

Illegal taxation

Along with these laws came the punishment of the King's former advisers. Some, however, had fled overseas, but others were imprisoned and impeached,[1] and amongst these were the two greatest, Laud and Strafford. Laud was not beheaded till 1645, but to the popular imagination "Black Tom Tyrant", as Strafford was called, was the embodiment of the arbitrary power of the King. In the words of a contemporary, "the whole kingdom was his accuser", and when he was impeached for treason it was felt that his trial would decide the question whether government was to be in future by the King's prerogative alone or by King and

Impeachment of ministers

The Trial of Strafford (1641)

[1] In the whole course of English history there have been only seventy impeachments, and of this number a quarter took place between 1340 and 1642.

Parliament combined. But it was impossible to prove that Strafford had been guilty of treason: he might have been guilty of acts against the nation, but not of acts against the King. Of his government in Ireland, which was one point of attack, he made a very able defence. It was universally believed — possibly rightly — that Strafford had advised the King to utilize the Irish army to overawe English resistance. But the only evidence of this was found in a copy of the notes taken at a Privy Council meeting by one of its members, in which Strafford was reported to have said: "You have an army here you may employ to reduce this kingdom", and from the context it was impossible to judge whether "this kingdom" referred to England or Scotland.

Eventually the House of Commons gave up the impeachment and passed instead a Bill of Attainder, condemning him as guilty of treason.[1] The bill was sent up to the House of Lords, which, after some hesitation, passed it. The only hope of life left to Strafford lay in the King. After two days of agonizing doubt Charles, with his palace surrounded by an angry crowd, afraid that if he held out his beloved Queen herself would be impeached,[2] and advised to surrender by his Council, by the judges, and by some of the bishops, and even by Strafford himself, eventually gave his consent to the bill. Strafford, brave and noble to the end, was executed on Tower Hill (May, 1641).[3] To the 200,000 who were present, as well as to the great majority of Englishmen, his execution was necessary for the safety of the nation.

Execution of Strafford (May, 1641)

At the end of the summer of 1641 Englishmen had come to the parting of the ways, and the work of the Long Parlia-

[1] Consequently they had not got to prove his guilt; they merely asserted that he was guilty and ought to be executed, and voted upon the measure.

[2] The House of Commons intended to impeach the Queen for her intrigues with foreign powers if the King had refused to pass the bill.

[3] "I thank God," he said, when he took off his doublet at the scaffold, "I am not afraid of death, nor daunted with any discouragement rising from my fears, but do as cheerfully put off my doublet at this time as ever I did when I went to bed."

Split in Parliament

ment was to be no longer unanimous. The final split between the two parties came in the debates on the *Grand Remonstrance* (*November*). Previously to this Charles had made a journey to Scotland (*September*) with the hope, no doubt, of organizing a party favourable to his cause — a hope in which he was disappointed. It was whilst he was playing a game of golf in that country in *October* that he heard news of the Irish Catholic rebellion [1] (p. 508). That rebellion had important results in England. Even its horrors were exaggerated in the accounts received in England. Consequently Protestant feeling was inflamed and affected the King, because he was suspected of some complicity with the rebels. Moreover, to suppress the rebellion an army would be necessary. This aroused a fresh question of the very greatest consequence — Who was to control the army, the King or the Parliament? Upon the answer hung the liberties of England.

The Grand Remonstrance

It was now that Pym brought forward the document known as the *Grand Remonstrance*. This was, partly, a recapitulation of all the evil deeds of which Pym and the Puritan party held Charles to be guilty. But it also contained a scheme of reform for the future which was much too advanced for many at that period. It proposed, for instance, that only ministers should be appointed of whom the House of Commons should approve, and that a Synod of Divines should be summoned to make religious changes. Such proposals would, in the opinion of many, have shattered the power of king and bishop alike. The debates upon them were keen and protracted. Churchman was ranged against Puritan, and constitutional Royalists like Falkland and Hyde, who still wished the King to direct the Government, against those like Pym, who were grasping at sovereignty, and wished Parliament to exercise direct control over the ministers. The Remonstrance was finally carried, long after midnight, in the early morning of *23rd November*, but

[1] According to tradition, Charles finished his game.

only by eleven votes. In the excitement members clutched their swords. "I thought," said one, "we had all sat in the Valley of the Shadow of Death." The Civil War was not far off.

To attempt a *coup d'état* and to fail is fatal. Yet this was the fortune of Charles. On *4th January, 1642*, hearing that the House of Commons intended to impeach the Queen, he decided to forestall such an action by accusing the five leading members of the House of high treason for intrigues with the Scots. Included in this number were Pym and Hampden. Charles determined to arrest the five members himself, and went down to the House of Commons accompanied by a guard of some 400 men.[1] But, through an indiscreet friend of the Queen's, the five members had learnt the King's intention, and when Charles entered the House he found, to use his own words, that "the birds had flown". For the King to enter the House of Commons in this fashion was, of course, a scandalous breach of its privileges, and when he left it there were loud and angry cries of "Privilege! Privilege!" There is no need to detail the history of the next seven months. Both sides tried to obtain control of the militia, and Parliament passed a bill with this object, which Charles vetoed. Both sides made preparations for war. In April Hotham, the Governor of Hull, went so far as to refuse the King admittance to that town. And on *22nd August*, at Nottingham, the King's standard was set up.[2] The great Civil War had begun.

The attempt on the five members (Jan., 1642)

Civil War (Aug., 1642)

[1] It is said that Charles hesitated on the morning of the 4th to carry out his design, but the Queen urged him on. "Go, you coward," she cried, "and pull out these rogues by the ears, or never see my face more!"

[2] According to Clarendon, it was blown down the same night by a very strong and unruly wind — an inauspicious beginning.

CHAPTER 37

THE CIVIL WAR (1642–1645)

Supporters of two parties

In the great Civil War the bulk of the nobility and the gentry and their tenants were on the side of the King, whilst the majority of the townsmen and yeomen fought for Parliament (*Note 68*). Yet it would be a mistake to regard the war as one of class against class. Eighty peers fought for the King, thirty fought against him, and 175 members of the House of Commons belonged to the Royalist party. Geographically, a line drawn from the Humber to Southampton roughly divides the two parties: east of that line is, on the whole, Parliamentary; west of that line, with the important exceptions of Bristol, Gloucester, and Plymouth, is on the whole, Royalist. The real line of division is, however, political — as to whether King or Parliament shall be supreme — and perhaps, above all, religious, the Anglican against the Puritan.

Resources of both parties

Summing up the advantages possessed by either side, it should be noted that the Parliamentary party had possession of the city of London, and that its cause was probably supported by two-thirds of the population and three-quarters of the wealth of the country. Fewer troops also were employed by Parliament in the garrisoning of small detached forts and fortified country houses. Moreover, the navy was on the side of Parliament, and could be employed not only to ward off foreign aid, but also to carry troops and protect the coast towns. The Parliamentary forces undoubtedly contained the better infantry, but at that time the bayonet had not been invented. Consequently half the infantry were pikemen, and useless beyond the reach of their fifteen-feet pike, and half were musketeers, and therefore useless for hand-to-hand fighting. Moreover, the musketeer's task in those days was a harassing and laborious one, and he took a long time to fire his musket.[1] Therefore the infantry were greatly handicapped, and we find in the Civil War that the battles were won by the cavalry.

But it was in the cavalry in the opening stages of the war that the Royalists had such a great advantage, for they possessed better riders and better horses (*Note 69*). Moreover, the Royalists had the King and the unity of aim and command which his presence should have given; they had at first more experienced and better leaders; and during the first two years of the war strategical ability was confined to the King's party. Above all, in *Prince Rupert*,[2] not yet twenty-three, the nephew of Charles, the Royalists had not only a born cavalry leader — brave, inspiring, energetic — but a general capable of planning a decisive campaign. Prince Rupert also was a leader who had profited by the new Swedish tactics to make his men charge hard and reserve their pistol fire till the charge had gone home.[3] Rupert and the other Royalist leaders should have proved more than a match for a general with so little initiative as the Parliament's first commander, Lord Essex, possessed, or for "sweet meeke" Lord Manchester, as he was called, both of whom, moreover, were "half-measures" men, "not wanting to beat the King too much". Rupert, however, was to exhibit a certain sharpness of temper in counsel which made him a difficult man to work with, and, above all, an impetuousness in battle which was to ruin the King's cause.

[1] A musketeer had to extract powder from a flask and pour it into the muzzle of his musket, to put a bullet which he had previously deposited in his mouth into the muzzle, to ram the bullet home, to fit the musket into a rest (it was too heavy and too long to be without one), and finally to ignite the powder with a match (a twisted strand of tow), which had probably in the preceding operations been scorching the back of his hands.

[2] His mother was the Princess Elizabeth, who married the Elector Palatine. She had the reputation of being a very devoted mother; but according to one of her daughters, she much preferred the society of dogs and monkeys to that of her own children when they were young.

[3] The old tactics for cavalry were to advance slowly, to "caracole", as the expression went, up to the infantry, to discharge pistols, and then to retire.

The campaign of 1642

The aim of the King in the *first* year of the war (*1642*) was to *march upon London with one army*. Starting from Shrewsbury, he outmarched Essex, who was also coming from the Midlands, but then turned to meet him at *Edgehill* (October).[1] Both wings of the Royalist cavalry were successful, but Rupert pursued too far, and in the excitement the reserve cavalry of Charles — called the " show-troop ", for it consisted largely of well-dressed landed proprietors — joined the pursuit. Consequently the Royalist infantry was hard pressed, and Rupert after a lengthy absence only returned in time to make the battle a drawn one. The King was, however, able to continue his march, but when he got as close to London as *Turnham Green* he found his progress barred by 24,000 Londoners, and accordingly retired to Oxford. Military critics disagree as to whether Charles should have tried to force his way to London; but his army was never to get so near the capital again.

Edgehill (1642)

The campaign of 1643; the triple advance upon London

In the *second* year of the war (1643) the King designed a *triple advance upon London.* Lord Newcastle,[2] after subduing the north, was to march south; Hopton, after subduing the south-west, was to advance east; Charles was to keep Essex employed, and advance upon London when the others were ready. In the spring and summer the outlook was black for Parliament. Newcastle won *Adwalton Moor* (1st June), and in consequence secured a large part of Yorkshire. In the west Bristol was taken by Rupert, and Hopton utterly defeated Waller, the rising general on the side of Parliament, at *Roundaway Down* in July. It was this battle which led Pym to begin serious negotiations with the Scots for the

[1] It was usual, in the Civil War, for the armies to wear " field signs " to distinguish them. Thus, at Edgehill, the Parliamentarians had orange scarves; at Newbury they wore green boughs; and at Marston Moor, white handkerchiefs or white pieces of paper in their hats. Later, in the New Model Army, the uniform was red — hence red became the colour of the British army.

[2] Newcastle once spent £20,000 in entertaining James I at Welbeck, Ben Jonson writing the masques on that occasion. Subsequently he became tutor to the Prince of Wales (afterwards Charles II).

loan of an army, and which caused the few members of the House of Lords left in London to propose to the House of Commons that most abject terms of peace should be made with the King — terms only rejected in the House of Commons by seven votes. In the centre, meanwhile, the King had lost Reading, but the Parliamentarians had been beaten in a skirmish at *Chalgrove*, near Oxford, a skirmish in which Hampden was killed.

Importance of London

In *September*, *1643*, however, the tide turned. "*Hull* and *Plymouth*", it has been said, "saved the Parliamentary cause." Newcastle's Northerners with Hull untaken refused to advance south, as they feared to leave their homes and property at the mercy of their foes in that town. Hopton, though he continued to advance east, found his army dwindling away because his Westerners had similar fears with regard to Plymouth. Meanwhile Charles, unable to advance on London unsupported, had advanced to besiege Gloucester early in August, and in September Essex successfully relieved it. Charles, however, intercepted the army of Essex on its return journey at *Newbury*, but he failed, after an indecisive battle, to prevent the return of Essex to London. In the battle Lord Falkland, one of the noblest figures in the war, was killed. In October, Hull, which Newcastle had besieged, was relieved as the result of a battle at *Winceby*, in which Cromwell, the future leader of the Puritans, was conspicuous. Only in the south did Hopton continue his victorious advance.

Battle of Newbury (1643)

Parliament and the Scottish alliance

In the last month of the year the Parliament suffered a great loss in the death of Pym. Before his death, however, he had succeeded in negotiating an alliance with the Scots. Both sides had appealed to the Scots, but the Presbyterians, feeling that if the King triumphed over Parliament he would inevitably try to subdue them, determined to throw in their lot with Parliament. The Scottish terms were uncompromising — Presbyterianism must be the future religion of England. Parliament, in the *Solemn League and Covenant*,

The Solemn League

and Covenant (1643) accepted the condition with qualifications,[1] and in return obtained from Scotland an army of 20,000 men — a force which enabled it to win the war.

With *1644* the war took a somewhat different shape. Each side had secured an ally; the Scots had joined Parliament, and to balance them Charles brought a force over from Ireland. But the tide ran strongly for Parliament. The Scottish army was of immense assistance, whilst the Irish soldiers, who were worthless troops and hated as Catholics, merely alienated a large number of the King's supporters.[2] Moreover, the army of the Eastern Association — an association of Eastern Counties formed originally for defensive purposes only — left its own district, and under Lord Manchester prepared to take an active part in the war; and in March the defeat of Hopton meant the loss of all hope of a successful invasion of Sussex and Kent by the Royalists.

The campaign of 1644

In July, 1644, came the great Royalist defeat at *Marston Moor*. Newcastle, who had been besieged in York by the Scots and by Fairfax and Manchester, was relieved by Rupert, and shortly afterwards a great battle was fought between the combined Royalists and the Parliamentary forces. The battle of Marston Moor was notable because of the large number of the men employed: the Royalists were seventeen thousand, and the supporters of Parliament were twenty-six thousand in number. But, above all, the battle was important in that Prince Rupert was to find his match. Oliver Cromwell, a Huntingdonshire squire, had trained for the Eastern Association a body of cavalry composed, as he said, of " men of religion ", who could stand up to the " men of honour" serving in the Royalist cavalry. More-

Marston Moor (July, 1644)

[1] The Church of England was to be reformed " according to the Word of God and the example of the best reformed Churches ". The second half of the sentence refers to the Scottish Church in particular, but the first half might be and was variously interpreted by Scots and English.

[2] The Irish rebels were regarded with horror by the English, and the use of them by Charles had the same effect in England then, it has been well pointed out, as the employment of Sepoys would have had if a similar crisis had arisen in England just after the Indian Mutiny of 1857.

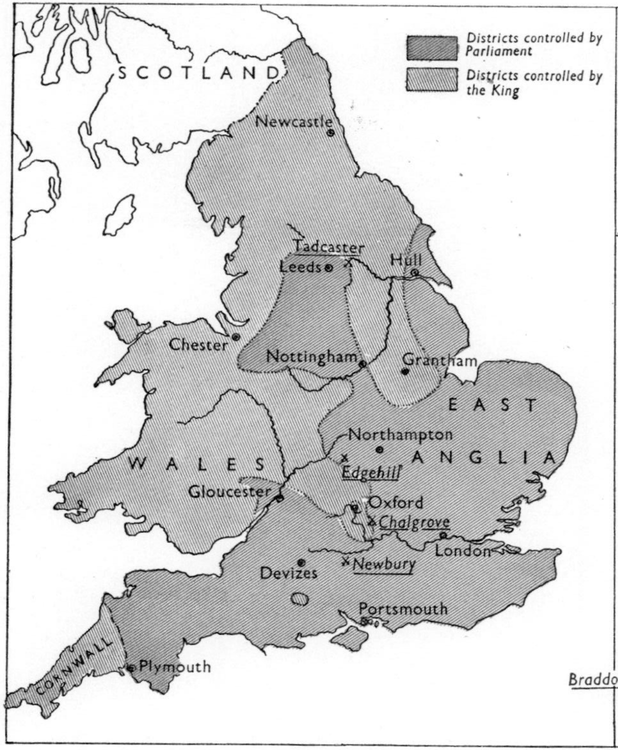
Districts controlled by Parliament
Districts controlled by the King
SCOTLAND
Newcastle
Tadcaster
Leeds
Hull
Chester
Nottingham
Grantham
EAST ANGLIA
WALES
Northampton
Edgehill
Gloucester
Oxford
Chalgrove
London
Devizes
Newbury
Portsmouth
CORNWALL
Plymouth

1643

Districts controlled by Parliament at the beginning of 1645
Districts controlled by the King at the end of 1645
Districts lost by the King during 1645
Dunbar (1650)
Philiphaugh (1645)
Newcastle
Carlisle
Scarborough
Marston Moor
York
Preston (1648)
Bolton
Pontefract
Newark
Lichfield
Naseby (1645)
Worcester (1651)
Cropredy Br.
Gloucester
Oxford
London
Newbury
Maidstone (1648)
Langport
Taunton
Lyme
Exeter
Lostwithiel
Plymouth
Braddock Down
0 40 80 120 Miles

1645

THE CIVIL WAR

F 938

over, Cromwell was a leader who could make his cavalry charge as hard as Prince Rupert, but who, unlike Rupert, could keep his men in hand for a further movement. At seven o'clock in the evening Cromwell charged.[1] He defeated, with the aid of the Scottish horse, Rupert's cavalry, then wheeled round and dispersed the Royalist cavalry who had been successful on the other wing. Meantime, the Scottish infantry in the centre were hard pressed. Cromwell, however, quite untiring, came to their assistance and then helped to annihilate the " Whitecoats ", as Newcastle's own infantry regiments were called. It was Cromwell who won the battle — indeed, the three chief generals on his side were at one period fugitives from the field — and the result of the battle was not only that Newcastle retired abroad, but that the six northern counties were lost to the King.[2]

Failures of Parliamentarians

Yet, in spite of this victory, Parliament did not make progress. At the end of August Charles managed to surround *Essex's* army at *Lostwithiel*, in Cornwall, and though Essex himself escaped by sea, and his horse broke through the Royalist lines, his infantry had to capitulate. Charles, however, on his return in October, found his way barred at *Newbury* by another army under Manchester and Essex. The battle which followed, like the first battle fought there, was indecisive, though, but for Manchester's want of enterprise, Charles would not have got through, as he succeeded in doing, to Oxford.

Second Battle of Newbury (1644)

The second battle of Newbury brought to a head the dissatisfaction which Cromwell and others felt with the " half-measures " men and their lack of energy. This dissatisfaction led to the *Self-denying Ordinance* being carried in Parliament, under which members of Parliament resigned

[1] The Royalist leaders thought there would be no fight that day. Newcastle had gone to his great coach, called for a pipe of tobacco, and settled down for the evening.

[2] Here is Cromwell's own description of the battle: " We never charged but we routed the enemy. The left wing, which I commanded, being our own force, saving a few Scots in our rear, beat all the prince's horse, and God made them stubble to our swords. We charged their regiments of foot and routed all we charged."

The Self-denying Ordinance and the New Model Army

their commissions in the army. Accordingly Manchester and Essex retired, though Cromwell, who resigned because he was a member of the House of Commons, was reappointed to a command. Parliament also resolved to reorganize the army. As a consequence, the Parliament obtained just what it wanted. The *New Model* army, as it was called, was a force well-officered,[1] with regular pay, and especially strong in its cavalry and artillery. It was not bound by local ties, and it could "go anywhere and do anything". Above all, Fairfax [2] was made the commander and was given absolute control, without interference by Parliamentary commissions, whilst Cromwell was put in charge of the cavalry.

The Battle of Naseby (June, 1645)

The result of the New Model was seen in *1645* at the battle of *Naseby* (June). Rupert beat the wing opposed to him, it is true, but pursued too far. Cromwell was successful on the other flank, then re-formed his cavalry, and, as at Marston Moor, charged the Royalist infantry who were pressing the Parliamentarians. Cromwell made one more charge at Rupert's returning cavalry, and the day was won. The battle was decisive. It cost Charles half his cavalry, all his infantry and artillery, and most of his best officers. Moreover, it revealed to the nation his intrigues with foreign powers, for the cabinet containing much of his correspondence was captured. "The King and the kingdom", says Clarendon, the Royalist historian, "were lost at Naseby"; and after Naseby the war soon ended. To the south-west Fairfax was successful at *Langport*, and in September Bristol was retaken by Fairfax.

But, meantime, in Scotland a brilliant attempt had been made to retrieve the King's fortunes. Some two months after the battle of Marston Moor in 1644, a Scottish nobleman, the Marquis of *Montrose*, the "Great Marquis".

[1] It is a mistake to suppose that the officers were not gentlemen — thirty out of thirty-seven colonels were of gentle birth.

[2] Fairfax was a very brave man, a vigorous commander, and an excellent disciplinarian, besides being conspicuous for generosity to his opponents. He was also a lover of learning, and when he captured Oxford in 1646 his first care was to send a strong guard to preserve the famous Bodleian Library.

opened a campaign on behalf of Charles. He had signed the National Covenant in 1638, and had fought for the Covenanters, but he had always affirmed his devoted loyalty to the Crown. The alliance of the Covenanters with the English Parliament was to his mind an act of disloyalty to the Sovereign, and he took the only course open to him as a royalist and a man of honour — he offered his sword to the King. With forces which never exceeded four thousand foot and two hundred horse he won, within the space of twelve months, no less than six battles. His only permanent force was a contingent from Ireland of some sixteen hundred, consisting mainly of Scotsmen who had served in the Irish war; but he also got various clans to assist him.

Montrose's successes in Scotland (Sept. 1644-Aug., 1645)

The first victory was won on 1st September, 1644, at *Tippermuir*, near Perth — won by a rush upon a newly levied army.[1] Then after a victory at *Aberdeen* — marred by the excesses of his troops in the town after the battle — Montrose turned upon Argyll. Joined by the Macdonalds, the mortal foes of the Campbells, he penetrated into the Campbell country and won a decisive battle at *Inverlochy*[2] over double his numbers. Finally, after two other successes, he won the battle of *Kilsyth*, near Glasgow (15th August, 1645), though here, it has been said, the mistakes of his enemy were so enormous that it would have been difficult not to beat him.

Failure of Montrose (Sept., 1645)

After the battle of Kilsyth, Glasgow submitted, and it seemed as if all Scotland might be recovered for the King; Montrose even hoped to cross the border with twenty thousand men. But his victories were at an end. The Macdonalds deserted him to go and renew their fighting with the Campbells. The Gordons went away for some reasons of personal pique. In the Lowlands, where Montrose now

[1] In their flight after the battle ten of the good citizens of Perth, it is said, "bursted with running".

[2] Argyll himself was on a barge in the loch during the fight, perhaps because he had dislocated his shoulder three weeks previously; but his enemies had another explanation of his conduct.

was, he obtained no support; the General Assembly had excommunicated him, and his Irish soldiers were regarded as " instruments of Satan ". Moreover, two months before the last victory at Kilsyth, had come the fatal day at Naseby. Part of the Scottish forces in England were, therefore, free to operate against Montrose, and marched north. Consequently Montrose's forces were overwhelmed at *Philiphaugh* (near Selkirk, September, 1645), and, after the battle, he himself, at the King's command, went to the Continent. The Civil War both in England and Scotland was now practically over, and was finally completed when Charles in May, 1646,[1] surrendered himself to the Scottish army, and when the city of Oxford capitulated in the following June.

CHAPTER 38

THE COMMONWEALTH (1649–1653) AND THE PROTECTORATE (1653–1659)

1. DOMESTIC AFFAIRS

Parties after the war; the King

The great Civil War was over, but the termination of the war still left great questions undecided. How was England in future to be governed? What form of Christian religion was to be the State religion, and how far was toleration to be extended to those who could not agree with it? These questions, difficult enough in themselves, were complicated by the number of parties who wished to share in their settlement. There was, *first* of all, *Charles I*; the King had been vanquished, but no one at first wished to abolish the monarchy. He played the part that might have been expected of him. Too high-minded and too high-spirited to give up either the Church of England and her bishops, or

[1] He left Oxford with his long locks cut and his beard altered; he journeyed to Harrow, surveyed London from that spot, and then by a circuitous route reached the Scottish army in Nottinghamshire.

the control of the ministers and the army, he was not high-minded enough to avoid pretending that he would do so. Designing, as he said himself, to " set his opponents by the ears ", he intrigued not only with each party in turn or even simultaneously, but also with the Catholics in Ireland and the great minister, Mazarin, in France.

The Scottish army and the Parliament

There was, *secondly*, the *Scottish army*, determined, as a matter of conscience, to see that Presbyterianism was permanently established in England as the Parliament had promised in the " Solemn League and Covenant ". Then there was, *thirdly*, the *Long Parliament* — shorn, of course, of the hundred and seventy-five Royalists who had joined the King in the Civil War. The majority in this Parliament wished Charles to reign indeed, but not in any real sense to govern; on the other hand, it was afraid of the New Model Army. In matters of religion it was anxious to impose Presbyterianism upon the whole people of England, and had already — with the aid of Scottish Commissioners and a body of people called the Westminster Assembly of Divines — taken steps to make it the established religion in England.

The Extremists and the New Model Army

Fourthly, there gradually emerge — as in all big movements — various groups of *Extremists*: Democrats, who wanted annual parliaments and universal suffrage; Levellers, who wanted all men to be equal; and idealists, who thought the Fifth Monarchy[1] was about to be achieved under their own beneficent rule. *Lastly*, and above all, there was the *New Model Army*. In this army the Independents predominated; they were indifferent as to what form of established religion was set up, but were determined to secure toleration for " tender consciences ", and to be free from the absolute control either of Anglican bishops or of Presbyterians. An army of forty to fifty thousand men, well trained, well officered, and well disciplined, was bound to be irre-

[1] The last of the great monarchies referred to in the prophecy of Daniel (*Daniel* ii. 44).

sistible in politics if it chose to interfere.[1] Moreover, in Oliver Cromwell it possessed unquestionably the greatest man of this epoch.

Oliver Cromwell

Born at Huntingdon in 1599, of a good family, *Cromwell* became a member of Parliament at the age of twenty-nine. In 1642, at the age of forty-three, his military career began, and it was not to close till he was fifty-two. He had made his reputation in the cavalry during the Civil War, and to him was due the chief credit for organizing and training horsemen that could rival Prince Rupert's. In his cavalry tactics he, like Rupert, did not make the mistake of firing before charging, but, unlike Rupert, he did not rely, it has been said, so much upon the pace as upon the weight and solidarity of his charge.[2] In his campaigns, both during the Civil War and later, he showed that, though not perhaps a great strategist, he possessed real genius in seeing the critical points of a battle, and untiring energy in following up a victory.

In politics, so far, he had not made much mark. As a member of the Long Parliament, however, he had shown himself greatly interested in religious questions, and a keen partisan; " if the Grand Remonstrance had not passed," he said, " I would have sold all I had the next morning, and never seen England more." In the years after the Civil War was over, his most striking characteristic, especially in his negotiations with King or Parliament, is the long hesitation and indecision he shows in making up his mind; and then, when a decision has at last been arrived at, the " swift, daring hammer-stroke ", as it has been called, that follows.

The time has long gone by when Cromwell was regarded as a hypocrite, half knave, half fanatic. A man of intense religious feeling, who looked upon all he did as due to

[1] Enemies as well as friends bear witness to its discipline. Punishments, when inflicted, were apt to be severe; for blasphemy or cursing, soldiers were sometimes bored through the tongue with a red-hot iron.

[2] His cavalry did not gallop, but charged in close order, to use Cromwell's own words, at " a pretty round trot ".

God's providence, he possessed at the same time strong practical common sense. "Trust in God and keep your powder dry" is said to have been the advice he gave to his soldiers — and the saying illustrates this double aspect of his character. His speeches are somewhat intricate and sometimes unintelligible, but they reveal a man of masterful energy who never lost sight of his ideals. Though a hater of the Roman Catholic religion and not very lenient to supporters of the Anglican bishops, he was large-hearted; and his ideas of toleration, inadequate as they seem to us to-day, were far more liberal than those generally prevalent during his own lifetime. If, when he came to supreme power, he showed himself anxious to put down undesirable amusements and to make life in England more serious, it must not be supposed that he was averse to all pleasure. On the contrary, he was fond of music and of writing verses; he loved good horses, and was a bold jumper and a skilful driver.[1]

Though Parliament ordered the sale of the King's collection of pictures, in order to fill up some of the deficit left by war, Cromwell intervened to save what he could. It is owing to his personal action that the famous Mantegnas at Hampton Court were kept for the nation.

The history of the fourteen years that follow the Civil War can be briefly put. The New Model Army began to interfere in politics, and finally became supreme, with Cromwell as its leader. It then tried to base its authority upon the consent of the English people as expressed in Parliament — and in this it failed, and England was in reality governed by a military dictator. But we must follow the stages in a little more detail.

The years 1646-60

[1] A team of six horses did run away with him, however, in Hyde Park, while he was Protector, to the great joy of his enemies, who wrote numberless lampoons on the subject.

2. THE EXECUTION OF THE KING (1646–1649)

Period I: June, 1646–Jan., 1649. (a) Charles and the Scots

In these fourteen years we may take, as a *First Period*, the two and a half years that elapse from the fall of the city of Oxford until the execution of the King (June, 1646–January, 1649). They are years of negotiations and intrigue, of which the merest outline must suffice. First of all, the King was with the Scottish army, which retired to Newcastle. He refused to accept the Solemn League and Covenant, as the Scots pressed him to do, and he refused to accept the terms which Parliament proposed — terms, indeed, that would have taken all power away from him. As he refused their terms, the Scottish army could not take him back to their own country; and they finally — having been promised by Parliament £400,000 for their expenses — handed the King over to Parliament, and then recrossed the Tweed [1] (February, 1647).

(b) Parliament and the army

The next step was that Parliament proceeded to quarrel with the army. The differences were partly religious. Parliament was a supporter of Presbyterianism. The army consisted largely of Independents, who objected just as much to the rule of the presbyter as to the rule of the priest, and who wanted liberty for "tender consciences". The Parliament — reasonably enough, now that the war was over — wished to reduce the army by one-third, and proposed to transfer the bulk of what was left to Ireland, to finish the war in that country. But it revealed its jealousy of the army by proposing to break up its old organization. Moreover, it was foolish enough to think that the army would be satisfied with six weeks' pay, when in the case of the infantry eighteen weeks' and in the case of the cavalry forty-three weeks' pay was owing. The army naturally objected, and elected men called "agitators" (i.e. agents)

[1] "The Scotch army", it was said, "sold their king as Judas sold his Master", and accepted the money as "blood money", to "their own eternal infamy"; but it is difficult to see what other policy they could have pursued.

to make known their grievances. Finally *Cornet Joyce* and a body of soldiers seized the King at Holmby House,[1] in Northamptonshire, where he was residing, and carried him off to the army headquarters at Newmarket (*June, 1647*); [2] whilst the army itself approached London, and insisted upon the retirement from the House of Commons of the eleven members most hostile to it. This was the first — but by no means the last — direct interference of the army with the Parliament. Cromwell had tried to mediate between them, but finally joined the army.

The army seizes the King

Like a later monarch, Louis XVI of France, Charles now had the chance offered him of keeping his throne by accepting a settlement. He first was approached by the army, which asked him to negotiate with them. Drawn up by Ireton, Cromwell's son-in-law, the *Heads of the Proposals*, as the army terms were called, recognized Episcopacy as the State religion, but allowed toleration for others. They set up a Council of State to manage foreign affairs and the army, and left for ten years the appointment of ministers with Parliament.[3] The King was perhaps unwise to refuse these terms.

Charles and negotiations for a Settlement

(c) The army and the King

But Charles preferred to turn to the Scots, and this opens another stage in the tangled history of these negotiations. There had been in Scotland, especially amongst the nobles, a reaction in favour of the King, and the Scots were angry at the success of the Independents, and still hoped that Presbyterianism might be enforced upon England. At the suggestion of the Scottish Commissioners, the King, in *November*, *1647*, effected his escape, and fled to *Carisbrooke Castle*, in the Isle of Wight, the governor of which

(d) The King and the Scots again

[1] At Holmby Charles was allowed to ride about the country with an escort, and to play bowls in the gardens of the neighbouring country houses.

[2] " Where is your commission?" said Charles to Joyce on his arrival. " Here," answered Joyce, pointing to his soldiers. " It is as fair a commission," was Charles's answer, " and as well-written a commission as any I have seen written in my life."

[3] They also arranged for a redistribution of seats and a revised system of election closely resembling that finally adopted in the Reform Bill of 1832.

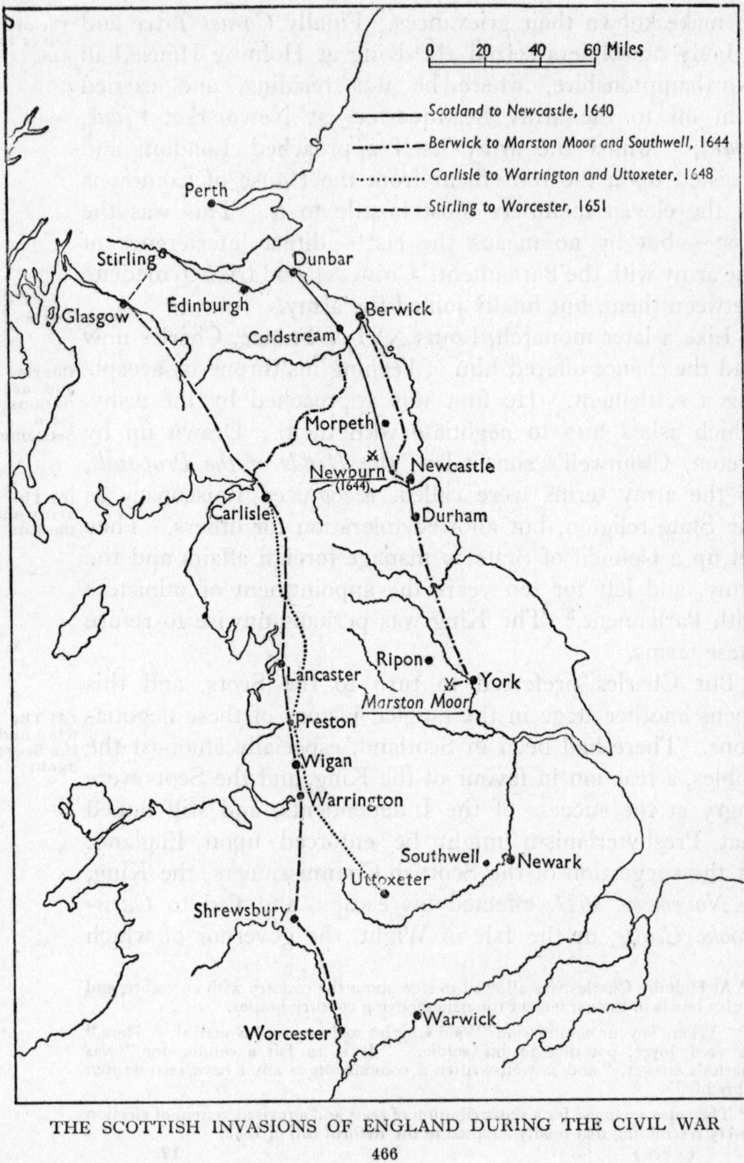

THE SCOTTISH INVASIONS OF ENGLAND DURING THE CIVIL WAR

place, however, remained, contrary to the King's expectation, faithful to the army. Consequently he was kept a prisoner, but he managed, nevertheless, to complete his negotiations with the Scots. Two days after Christmas Day, 1647, Charles signed a treaty called *The Engagement*,[1] by which, in return for his restoration to the throne of England, Charles promised to establish Presbyterianism in England for three years, and to suppress other sects.

The Second Civil War (1648)

As a result of "the Engagement" the Duke of Hamilton and a Scottish army invaded England in 1648; the Royalist risings also took place in Wales and in the south-east of England. But the Second Civil War, as it is called, was a half-hearted affair. Scotland was divided, the majority of the Presbyterian ministers, so potent in influence, being against the expedition to England. The Scottish army lacked enthusiasm, and was moreover ill equipped — only one man in five knew how to handle musket or pike, and there was not a single piece of artillery. Consequently, whilst Fairfax subdued the south-east and took Colchester, Cromwell, in a campaign of great energy, interposed his army between Hamilton and Scotland. He destroyed at *Preston* an English Royalist force attached to the Scottish army, and, in a relentless pursuit of thirty miles, caused the Scottish army to capitulate, ten thousand prisoners falling into his hands (*August*, *1648*). Finally, Cromwell entered Scotland, and restored the influence of Argyll, the head of the Presbyterian party.

Scots invade England

Meantime, during the war, the King was again negotiating with Parliament, and was making concessions which he had no intention of keeping. But the end was near. Cromwell and his army had gone to the war with the intention of bringing that "man of blood", as they called the King, to account on their return. When they did return, to find Parliament carrying on negotiations with the King, they

[1] The treaty was signed, wrapped in lead, and buried in the castle garden until it could be safely taken away.

resorted to force. On *6th December, 1648*, Colonel *Pride* and a body of red-coated musketeers, standing at the door of the House of Commons, excluded a hundred and forty-three of its members from entering. "Pride's Purge" completed, the remaining members — now only about ninety in number — decided to set up a tribunal to try the King.[1]

The execution of the King (Jan., 1649)

The result of the trial was a foregone conclusion; and at four minutes past two in the afternoon of *30th January, 1649*, on a scaffold erected outside the Banqueting Hall of Whitehall, the King was beheaded.[2] Never had Charles shown himself to possess such nobility and kingliness of character as in his last days. There is a story that Cromwell, in the middle of the following night, visited the King's body, looked at it mournfully, and murmured the words, "Cruel necessity!"[3] The cruelty of the execution no one will deny; its necessity has been matter of controversy from that day to this. The deed, at all events, shocked public opinion at the time.[4]

3. ENGLAND AS A REPUBLIC

Period II (Jan., 1649-April, 1653).

So began the Commonwealth (*Note 70*). We may take as a *Second Period* the *four* years between *January, 1649*, and *April, 1653*. The Government during these years was in the hands of the House of Commons which had been returned to the Long Parliament in 1640; but by successive purgings

[1] The trial took place in Westminster Hall, and the place where Charles stood is marked by a brass tablet. As the galleries were crowded with spectators, including ladies, the President of the Court took the precaution to wear a shot-proof hat, which can still be seen at Oxford.

[2] The King, it is said, wore two shirts in consequence of the cold, so that he might not shiver and appear to be afraid, and he walked so fast from St. James's to the Banqueting Hall at Whitehall, outside which he was executed, that his guards could scarcely keep up with him.

[3] The story is told by Lord Southampton, who had leave to watch by the body that night. The figure of the visitor was muffled; but from his voice and gait Lord Southampton took him to be Cromwell.

[4] When the executioner showed the King's head to the thousands gathered at Whitehall, "such a groan arose", writes an eyewitness, "as I never heard before and desire I may never hear again".

The "Rump" Parliament

it had been, out of an original total of four hundred and ninety members, "winnowed, sifted, and brought to a handful "[1] of some ninety members. This *Rump* Parliament, as it was called, governed England with an authority which no assembly in England, before or since, has possessed.[2] It was government by a "single-chamber", the most extreme form of Republicanism. With no monarchy and no House of Lords to control it — they were both abolished after the King's execution — it could pass what laws it pleased, pursue whatever policy suited it, and it could not be legally dissolved except of its own free will. It entrusted the administration of the country to a *Council of State* of forty-one, the great majority of which were members of the "Rump", and to various committees, on each of which sat persons with special knowledge of the particular branch of administration committed to it.

Cromwell, the Levellers, and Ireland

The authority of the "Rump" Parliament really rested, of course, on the authority of Fairfax, Cromwell, and the New Model Army; and it was chiefly for that reason that it suppressed its enemies with such success. The Extremists first of all seemed formidable after the King's execution. But Cromwell was no Leveller or Fifth-Monarchy man, and he saw the danger of such opinions. "We must break them," he said, "or they will break us," and he suppressed with great energy a mutiny in the New Model Army. Ireland was the next scene of Cromwell's activity. Nearly all parties in that country had combined, after the execution of Charles I, to support his son; how Cromwell conquered Ireland, however, is described elsewhere (p. 509) (*Note 74*).

As to the position of Charles I's family, they were now exiles in France, where Henrietta Maria had been sent, with her four children, by her husband when his position grew

[1] The words are Cromwell's.

[2] Of course the "Rump" had no claim whatsoever to be considered representative of the nation. Neither the towns nor country districts of four counties, of which Lancashire was one, had any representative at all; Wales had only three, and London one.

desperate. The elder son was now recognized by all Royalists as Charles II, but clearly in England his supporters were in a hopeless minority. His chief hopes lay in Scotland, and here, therefore, the first efforts to place him on the throne began. There were two parties in Scotland. On the one hand Montrose wanted a rising of pure Royalists to be organized in the Highlands. On the other hand, Argyll wanted Charles II to adopt the Covenant, and to impose Presbyterianism upon all his three kingdoms. Montrose, publicly disowned but secretly encouraged by Charles, did attempt to raise the Highlands. But he was defeated, captured, and hanged in his "red scarlet coat" in the Grassmarket at Edinburgh (May, 1650).[1] Meantime, in the same month that Montrose was executed, Charles agreed to the terms of Argyll; Presbyterianism was to be imposed in the King's dominions, and in all Scottish affairs Charles was to refer to the General Assembly and the Scottish Parliament. Shortly afterwards Charles landed in Scotland.

Scotland and Charles II

Execution of Montrose (1650)

There ensued a war between England and Scotland (*Note 74*). Cromwell, on his return from Ireland, invaded Scotland,[2] but he was outmanœuvred by Leslie, the Scottish commander, and was cornered in the peninsula of *Dunbar*, with no base but his ships. With his army, in his own words, "poor, shattered, hungry, discouraged", and with Leslie secure on the hills and ready to attack if he tried to escape, the outlook for Cromwell was black. But then Leslie, instead of waiting, "shogged"[3] his right wing still farther to the right on to the low ground, so that he might hold the road by which Cromwell could escape. In so doing, Leslie's left wing became isolated, whilst his centre, being still up in the hills, was unable to manœuvre easily. Cromwell saw this, and next morning attacked and rolled up the right

Battle of Dunbar (3rd Sept., 1650)

[1] "The leader of warlike men," it has been said, "swift and secret in his onslaught, the poet, the cavalier, the soul of air and fire, the foremost to head a forlorn hope, at last the forsaken victim of a forsaken cause, Montrose is for ever dear to the imagination."

[2] Fairfax refused to command an army against the Scots.

[3] i.e. moved on; the word is Cromwell's.

wing, whilst the rest of the Scottish army, entangled between a hill and a ravine, was helpless. Cromwell lost only twenty men, but the Scots lost three thousand in the battle besides ten thousand prisoners [1] (*3rd September, 1650*).

Cromwell then marched on to Edinburgh, and in 1651 took Perth. His departure, however, towards the north of Scotland, had left the way open to England, and Charles, with a Scottish army, entered England by Carlisle and reached *Worcester*. Here, however, Cromwell, who had returned south, caught him up, and blocked his way to London. On the anniversary of Dunbar, Cromwell attacked Charles from both sides of the river, and after "as stiff a contest", in Cromwell's words, "for four or five hours, as ever I have seen," absolutely defeated him (3rd September, 1651). Though Charles himself escaped and got eventually to the Continent,[2] yet not one troop of his cavalry or one company of his infantry succeeded in following his example. Worcester decided the Royalist cause up till the Restoration of 1660; though there were numberless Royalist plots, they were never really serious. The battle also destroyed the independence of Scotland. An English army invaded that country, took its strong places, and Monck, who was a general in the army, governed it for the rest of the Commonwealth.[3] Commissioners were sent who obtained the consent of the Scots to union with England, and though the bulk of the nation was hostile, they had perforce to agree.

Battle of Worcester (3rd Sept., 1651)

Cromwell and his victorious army were now free to take part in politics. The "Rump" Parliament made reforms too slowly to please them, and they wished it to dissolve,

Cromwell and the "Rump" Parliament

[1] When the Scots were defeated "the Lord General", said one of Cromwell's captains, "made a halt and sang the hundred and seventeenth Psalm" till his horse could gather for the chase — another instance of his practical piety.

[2] Charles had six weeks' wandering in England, full of adventures, before he finally got across the Channel from Brighton. He had to hide in an oak at one place, and in a "priest's hole", up a chimney, in another. He witnessed in a village the rejoicings at the news which had been received of his own death. In another village the blacksmith said he had not heard that "that rogue Charles Stuart, had been taken". "If that rogue were taken," answered Charles, "he deserves to be hanged more than the rest for bringing in the Scots."

[3] For the later history of Scotland, see p. 511.

though for some months they allowed it to continue. But when Cromwell found that its members were arranging for a new Parliament, to which they should not only all belong, but also from which they should have the power of excluding other members, his patience was exhausted. He came down to the House, "clad in plain black clothes and grey worsted stockings", and lectured its members. Then, with the aid of his soldiers, he fetched the Speaker down from the chair, took away "the bauble", as he called the mace, evicted the members, and locked the doors. According to Cromwell, "there was not so much as the barking of a dog" at this forcible ejection; indeed, all were tired of the "Rump's" rule.

4. CROMWELL'S SUPREMACY

Period III (April, 1653- Sept., 1658)

We now come to our *Third Period*, the five and a half years that elapse between the dissolution of the "Rump", in *April*, *1653*, and the death of Cromwell, in *September*, *1658*. The monarchy, the Extremists, the Irish, the Scottish army, and the remnants of the Long Parliament had been in turn suppressed. Cromwell and the army were at last supreme. The problem before Cromwell was, however, a difficult one — so difficult indeed that he never solved it (*Note 70*). On the one hand, he desired a State based on free elections with an efficient system of Law, not indeed democratic in the modern sense, but managed by the Middle Class. On the other hand, he desired a Godly State, which was to force men to be moral — in his sense of the word. How was he to combine those desires, if the English people did not agree with his ideas of what a Godly State should be? He and his army wished, as it has been humorously put, to fix a legal wig upon the point of the soldier's sword. Unfortunately for them, however, their rule was not based upon great popular support. Consequently the wig fell off, and the naked sword only was visible. Parliaments were frequently called, but they were bound, unless nominated by the army leaders or purged of hostile elements, to be unmanageable.

At first it was impossible to allow ordinary elections to Parliament, so the army, through the Council of Army Officers, selected an assembly of persons of whom they approved. This included representatives of Scotland and of Ireland. Scotland had been promised a share in legislative power, in return for accepting union with England, and she now sent thirty members to the British Parliament which was thus the first United Parliament. Sometimes it is called " Barebone's Parliament " after one of its members.[1] The Speaker was the Provost of Eton and many notable men sat in it. Unfortunately, it was too visionary and unpractical. It wished to reduce the law into the " bigness of a pocket book ", and therefore angered the lawyers; it proposed to find money for the army in a way which the army thought made the chances of being paid exceedingly remote. Finally, its projects with regard to the religious system raised such a hornet's nest that Cromwell was only too thankful when the moderate element in the Assembly, by getting up early one morning, before their opponents were ready, carried a motion that the Assembly should surrender its power to Cromwell, and dissolve (December, 1653).

First United Parliament of Great Britain

The next experiment was a new Constitution, drawn up by the Army led by a band of officers with Lambert at their head. It was known as the *Instrument of Government*. Cromwell was to be called Protector, and to have the executive power and a fixed sum for the purposes of government. Parliament, consisting of one House, was to possess the legislative power. But Parliament was controlled by the Protector, because he alone could summon it, he could veto any of its acts which were contrary to the principles of the new Constitution, and he could dissolve it after it had sat

The Instrument of Government: the Protectorate

[1] " Praise-God Barebones ", a leather-seller of Fleet Street.

Dictatorship five months. If not dissolved, it was to sit for three years and then a new Parliament must be elected. Cromwell himself was to be controlled, to a certain extent, by a Council of State which was created under the Instrument, and by the fact that, if he wanted additional money over and above the fixed sum allowed him, Parliament alone could grant it.[1]

There now begins what in modern times we would call a dictatorship. Cromwell was head of the State, and his rule rested on the army. He was thus a true military dictator. He was to rule England for the next six years, and this experiment is of interest because it shows the typical successes and failures of such a system. Thus Cromwell was extremely successful abroad, he raised England's prestige to great heights, his army and navy won great victories. At home, his repressions made him unpopular, and yet he was bound to refuse liberty to his opponents. He crushed Ireland and forced her into submission, but he meant to give her representation in the English Parliament.

He himself believed in Parliamentary rule, and indeed the whole case against the Monarchy was bound up with it, yet he " could neither rule with Parliament nor without ". He personally believed in religious toleration, and his quarrels with Parliament first arose because he wished to allow it, and the Puritans did not.

First Protectorate Parliament (1654)

The *First Protectorate Parliament* met in *1654*, and began by discussing the new Constitution. One hundred of its members refused to sign an undertaking to be faithful to the Commonwealth and the Protector and had therefore to be excluded. The members who were left, however, evinced a desire to reduce the army and cut down its expenses. Moreover, they proposed to abolish toleration by drawing up a list of " damnable heresies ", to which no one was to adhere, and of twenty " articles of faith ", which no one was to

[1] In some respects Cromwell's powers were very similar to those possessed by the President of the United States of America to-day. It may be noted, too, that the " Instrument " gave Great Britain a written constitution, another point of resemblance with the U.S.A.

dispute. Cromwell wished Parliament to proceed to practical reforms, such as that of the Chancery and Criminal law, but he could not induce members to devote their energies to anything but endless debates on the Constitution. He had to wait for five months under the Constitution, but he interpreted the month to be "lunar" and not "calendar" and dissolved this intolerant Parliament as soon as he could.

After the dissolution Cromwell tried for a time a new experiment in local government. England was divided into eleven districts, each under an official called a "*Major-general*", whose business it was to supervise the militia, to prevent Royalist plots, and to stimulate the local authorities in enforcing the various laws relating to conduct and morality which had recently been passed. Nothing made the Puritan rule so unpopular as this "poor little invention", as Cromwell called it, for people resented it as the act of a military despotism.

The Major-generals

Cromwell was still anxious to rule with Parliament, rather than without, so, in the summer of *1656*, he summoned another Parliament — the *Second Protectorate Parliament*. The "Major-generals" had proved so unpopular, that the elections resulted in a large number of persons being returned to Parliament who were known to be hostile to the Government. As a precautionary measure, one hundred of these members were excluded from taking their seats. The remainder showed their belief in Cromwell by presenting to him a new Constitution known as the *Humble Petition and Advice*, under which the Council of State was to be abolished, Cromwell was to be made King and given larger powers, and a second House was to be created. Cromwell hesitated long over his new title. It was, he said, to him personally "but a feather in his cap", but there were great practical advantages in it, if only because, as one member said, the kingship was bounded "like an acre of land", and people would understand its powers. The

Second attempt to rule with Parliament

Second Protectorate Parliament (1656-8)

army was, however, opposed to the title, and Cromwell therefore refused it, whilst accepting the other changes.

The Second Protectorate Parliament then met again in its reformed condition; but many of Cromwell's supporters in the Lower House had been transferred to the new upper one, whilst the hundred members who had been excluded returned to the Lower House. Hence difficulties at once recurred; the Lower House discussed the functions and composition of the Upper House, and even the powers of the Protector himself; and in February, *1658*, Parliament was dissolved. Seven months later, on 3rd September,[1] Cromwell died, with the problem of how to combine popular control with his own rule still unsolved.

Death of Cromwell (3rd Sept., 1658)

5. FOREIGN POLICY OF THE COMMONWEALTH

England, it has been said, was more warlike during the period of the Commonwealth than she had been at any other time since the Hundred Years' War with France. But, as we have seen, till the end of 1651 the military energies of the Commonwealth Government were occupied in fighting its Royalist foes. Cromwell, on land, was winning Dunbar and Worcester; Blake, on sea, was sweeping Royalist privateers from the Channel and the Mediterranean, and forcing the colonies to recognize the rule of the Republic. In 1652, however, the Commonwealth was free to interfere with its Continental neighbours; and with the best army in Europe, composed of some forty thousand men, and a fleet to which it added two hundred and seven ships, its interference proved to be of a decisive character (*Note 71*).

Holland was England's first foe. It might have been expected that these two States, being both Republics and both Protestant, would have combined.[2] But England and

[1] The anniversary of Dunbar and Worcester.

[2] A suggestion, indeed, for a political union was actually put forward by England, but it came to nothing.

Holland were keen commercial rivals. "We are fighting," said a member of the Long Parliament, "for the fairest mistress in the world — trade." Holland had, so far, been the conqueror. The Dutch had shut the English out from trade in the East Indies. They had almost acquired a monopoly of the carrying trade; they were, it was said, "the wagoners of all seas". In the autumn of 1651, however, the "Rump" Parliament passed a *Navigation Act*, by which goods coming to England were to be carried in English ships, or in ships belonging to the country from which the goods came.[1] If ever an Act, it has been said, did make a nation great, it was this one; and the enormous development of English shipping in the years that follow must be largely attributed to its influence. But in fostering English shipping this Act struck a heavy blow at the Dutch. Then other questions arose between the two nations. An informal "sort of a war" was going on between the English and French on sea, and England claimed to seize French goods on Dutch ships, a claim which the Dutch resisted. Finally, there was a question of honour; the English held that Dutch ships should lower their flag to English men-of-war in the Channel, and the Dutch were naturally averse to recognizing such a right. Over this point came a collision between the Dutch and English fleets near Dover, and then the war began (May, 1652).

The causes of Dutch War (1652)

The Navigation Act (1651)

In the war that ensued the English had the advantage of more solidly built and more heavily armed ships, and, though they were without such a great tactician as the Dutch possessed in Tromp, they had in *Blake* a commander who combined great care in the organization of his fleet with brilliant daring in action. The war, which lasted from 1652–54, was crowded with sea battles. Tromp defeated Blake off *Dungeness* in November, 1652, and obtained

Incidents of war (1652-54)

[1] This policy was not, however, a new one, for Navigation Acts of one sort or another had been passed ever since the reign of Richard II, but they had not been effectively carried out.

command of the Channel.[1] But in the following February, 1653, Blake regained the command after a three days' battle off *Portland*. The English ships were able to inflict great damage upon Holland's extensive commerce. In the course of the war no less than one thousand four hundred Dutch ships were captured, including one hundred and twenty men-of-war, and towards its close no Dutch merchantman could show itself in the Channel (*Note 72*). (See map, p. 495.)

Cromwell's triumphs

Cromwell's chief triumphs were won abroad, where he made England feared and courted. One great aim, of course, of Cromwell's foreign policy was to prevent the restoration of the Stuarts by foreign aid. His other two aims were to maintain and to extend, first, the Protestant religion, and then English commerce. Here Cromwell showed that intense religious feeling, combined with practical common sense, which has been noticed already. Cromwell at first pursued a policy of peace and sought alliance with the Protestant powers. In April, 1654, the Dutch war came to an end. The Dutch agreed to salute our flag in British seas and to expel Royalists from their country, whilst they tacitly acquiesced in the Navigation Act. Treaties of alliance followed with Denmark, Sweden, and Portugal, which gave England important commercial concessions.

Cromwell's alliances (1654)

Cromwell's energy soon found a fresh opportunity for action. The Thirty Years' War had ended in Germany in 1648, but war still lingered on between Spain and France. Each of these powers was anxious to secure his support. But Cromwell's terms were high. He proposed to *Spain* that Englishmen should have liberty for the exercise of their religion in the Spanish dominions, and freedom of trade with the Spanish West Indies. "This is to ask for my master's two eyes," was the reply of the astonished Spanish ambassador. Then Cromwell determined upon a colonial

[1] It was after this battle that Tromp was said to have put a broom at his masthead to show that he had swept the English off the sea; but such a story of so modest a man as Tromp is probably untrue.

war with Spain. An expedition was sent to capture Hispaniola in the Spanish West Indies (1655).[1] But the attack upon that island was a disastrous failure. Jamaica, however, was captured, and Cromwell proceeded to colonize it with characteristic vigour.

The expedition to the West Indies (1655)

The expedition to the West Indies by no means exhausted Cromwell's activity in 1655. Blake was sent to the Mediterranean on a cruise; he made a fine attack on Tunis, whose Bey had refused to give up some English prisoners, but the voyage is chiefly interesting as marking the beginning of England's activity in the Mediterranean Sea. In the same year some horrible atrocities committed by the Duke of Savoy, with the connivance of the French, on the Protestants who lived in the Vaudois valleys in Savoy, aroused angry protests from Cromwell.[2] The French King, therefore, anxious to secure Cromwell's alliance, put pressure upon the Duke to stop the massacres, and Cromwell was regarded throughout Europe as the saviour of the Protestants.

Attack on Tunis (1655)

Shortly after this successful intervention Cromwell made a treaty with France, and war was formally declared between England and Spain in the beginning of 1656. The year 1657 saw a great naval success. The English fleet, under Blake, found the Spanish treasure fleet at Santa Cruz, protected by the forts. Entering the harbour with the flowing tide, Blake succeeded, before he retired with the ebb tide, in sinking, blowing up, or burning every Spanish ship.[3] The following year (1658) it was the turn of the soldiers. The French and English determined to besiege Dunkirk, the possession of which would give the English " a bridle for the Dutch and a door into the Continent ". Six thousand of the New Model Army combined with the French. They took the chief part in a battle waged near the

The attack at Santa Cruz (1657), and capture of Dunkirk (1658)

[1] Such an expedition would not necessarily in those days involve a formal war between England and Spain in Europe.

[2] See Milton's celebrated Sonnet on " The Late Massacre in Piedmont ".

[3] Blake died on his homeward journey on board his ship at the very entrance of Plymouth Sound, 7th August, 1657.

fort, and earned for themselves the nickname of "the Immortals". Shortly after this Dunkirk fell. But then Cromwell died, and in the confusion which followed nothing more could be done. "Cromwell's greatness at home," said Clarendon, "was a mere shadow of his greatness abroad"; and with this admission from the great Royalist historian we may be content to leave the study of the Commonwealth's foreign policy. The Commonwealth had done something, at all events, to restore the prestige which England had lost in Europe under the first two Stuarts.

6. EVENTS LEADING TO THE RESTORATION (1658–1660)

Period IV: (Sept., 1658-May, 1660). The Army and Parliament.

We now come to the *Fourth Period* — a year and a half of great complexity, between *1658* and *1660*. "There is not a dog that wags his tongue, so great a calm are we in," wrote one man, when Richard, Cromwell's son, was made Protector. The calm was not to continue for long. A new Parliament met; the officers of the army quarrelled with it; and Richard, after trying to mediate, threw in his lot with the officers, and dissolved it. A fortnight later Richard resigned.[1] The army decided to recall the "Rump". The "Rump" — consisting now of some sixty or seventy members — wanted to limit the powers of the new commander-in-chief, and to provide that in future all commissions in the army should be signed by the Speaker, and therefore to a certain extent be controlled by him. Moreover, they threatened the freedom of conscience so dear to the army. Eventually "Honest John" *Lambert*, the darling of the soldiers, a brave and generous if unstable man, surrounded the House and stopped the entrance of members, and once again the army was triumphant.

[1] At the Restoration Richard Cromwell had to fly to the Continent. He came back to England twenty years later, and died in 1712. "Gentle and virtuous, but became not greatness" is the verdict passed upon him by a contemporary. His nickname "Tumbledown Dick" is a more disrespectful version of the same characterization.

But then another general appeared, determined, with the aid of a large army and £70,000 in his treasury, to put an end to what he called the "intolerable slavery of sword government", and to call a free Parliament. This was the commander-in-chief in Scotland, *George Monck.* On 8th December, 1659, he reached Coldstream; Lambert, who had gone north to meet him, found his army dwindling away, and was unable to do anything. Marching to London, Monck restored the members of the Long Parliament, including those originally evicted by Pride's Purge, but only so that they might make arrangements for a new and free Parliament being called. When these arrangements were completed, the elections took place amid great excitement; and a vast majority came back in favour of the restoration of the Stuarts. Monck had already suggested to Charles what proposals it was advisable for him to make. Charles adopted them in a *Declaration* which he issued to the English people from *Breda.* The Declaration was received with enthusiasm, and on 29th May, 1660, Charles re-entered London, "the ways strewed with flowers, the bells ringing, the streets hung with tapestry, and the fountains running with wine". The Commonwealth was at an end (*Note 70*).

Monck and the Restoration

Declaration of Breda (1660)

The rule of Cromwell and the Commonwealth had certainly not been above criticism. It is quite arguable to say that individual liberty and the right of free speech were threatened to a greater degree under the Commonwealth than during the reign of Charles I. Moreover, though taxation was three times heavier than it was during Charles I's reign, the Commonwealth had a deficit of half a million yearly. Again, if the Commonwealth showed toleration to Jews and Quakers, its treatment, if not of Anglicans, at all events of Roman Catholics, might be considered severe. And of course it is easy enough to scoff at the "rule of the saints by the sword", and ridicule their attempts to make men more virtuous by passing Acts against swearing and duelling, horse-racing, cock-fighting, and bear-baiting,

The rule of the Commonwealth

and by trying to enforce more strictly the keeping of the Sabbath. Yet, for all that, there was much to admire. The Commonwealth government was, it has been said, a more tolerant one than any which had existed since the time of the Reformation. It maintained good order, and did, as a matter of fact, succeed in suppressing some amusements of a highly undesirable character. Its constitutional experiments were ingenious and interesting; and its attempts to reform the Court of Chancery and to reduce legal expenses wholly praiseworthy. Much of the work it attempted to do was, indeed, very modern in outlook — and that is, perhaps, why it failed at that time. Above all, its Foreign Policy raised England from the low position it had reached in the time of the Stuarts, whilst it has been said that no previous Government had such imperial instincts as Cromwell's.

CHAPTER 39

THE BEGINNINGS OF THE BRITISH EMPIRE

Beginnings of Empire (1603-88)

When James I ascended the throne in 1603, the British Empire was non-existent. Attempts had been made to colonize Virginia, but they had failed; the East India Company had been formed in 1600 for the promotion of trade with the East, but its first expedition had not returned from the East Indies when Elizabeth died.[1] With the Stuarts, however, the beginnings of Empire came, and the seventeenth century is, therefore, from an imperial as well as from a domestic point of view, a very important one. And it is worth pointing out that the successful development of this Empire in the seventeenth century was largely due to private enterprise (*Note 83*).

[1] It returned six months after James's accession with one million pounds of pepper.

We may turn to affairs in the East first. It was under Portuguese auspices that the route to India and the Far East by the Cape of Good Hope had been discovered in 1502, and during the sixteenth century Portugal had been successful in preserving a monopoly of the Eastern trade for her own merchants.[1] But in the seventeenth century both the Dutch and English nations determined to secure some share in that trade. In the Far East the Dutch proved themselves persistent and intrepid traders. The Dutch East India Company conquered the Spice Islands from the Portuguese, and established their own supremacy. The English East India Company also endeavoured to trade in the Far East, but the Dutch Company was wealthier and stronger. Disputes between Dutch and English occurred, and culminated in the massacre at *Amboyna* (1623), when ten Englishmen were executed on a trumped-up charge of conspiring with some Japanese soldiers against the Dutch governor of that place.[2] Soon after this the English practically gave up their attempts to compete with the Dutch for trade in the Far East, and they did not re-enter the contest till the close of the eighteenth century. **Dutch supremacy in Far East**

On the mainland of India the English East India Company met with greater success. It had to encounter the hostility of the Portuguese, but, despite that, it managed to prosper. In 1612, it established its first depot for goods, or " factory ", as it was called, at *Surat*, on the west coast of India.[3] Others followed at *Madras* (1639), *Bombay* (1661), and *Calcutta* (1690). At the close of the seventeenth century a rival company to the East India Company was **English " factories " in India**

[1] A few Englishmen did, however, succeed in reaching India in the reign of Elizabeth. The first Englishman known to have visited India was a Jesuit, Stephens by name, in 1579.

[2] No reparation was extracted from the Dutch for this flagrant injustice for thirty-one years; then Cromwell insisted on a large money indemnity being paid to the English company and to the relatives of the executed men.

[3] Leave would not have been obtained from the native ruler for this factory to be established but for the fact that Captain Thomas Best had won a great reputation for the English in that same year by defeating, on four successive occasions, an overwhelming force of Portuguese ships.

started in England; but the two companies amalgamated in 1709, and the united company quickly developed trade. So far the object of the English in India had been merely the extension of trade; how the East India Company in later years obtained an empire in India which stretched from Cape Comorin to the Himalayas must be explained in a later chapter. (See p. 638.)

Foundation of Virginia (1607)

Meantime, whilst the English merchants were developing a substantial trade in the East, English colonists had built up many settlements in the West. The first successful attempt was made in *Virginia*. In May, 1607, some hundred emigrants landed in Chesapeake Bay and founded the settlement of Jamestown. But the colony had great difficulties at first, though, when the adventurous Captain John Smith[1] was for a short time President in 1608, things progressed more favourably. The colony did not, however, really prosper until the arrival of Lord De la Warr in 1610. His short governorship was the turning-point in the early history of Virginia, and the colonists soon received large reinforcements in numbers from the mother country.

The Pilgrim Fathers (1620)

Then, in 1620, came the foundation of the Puritan colonies farther north. Many Puritans had fled, during Elizabeth's reign, from England in consequence of persecution, and settled in Holland. One hundred of these men got leave from James to found an English colony in America. Returning to England, the "*Pilgrim Fathers*", as they came to be called, started from Plymouth on board the *Mayflower*, landed in Cape Cod Harbour, and founded the little settlement of New Plymouth. The misgovernment and intolerance of Charles led to their numbers being largely aug-

[1] If his autobiography may be believed, John Smith had fought against the Spaniards in the Low Countries and the Turks in Hungary. He had been thrown overboard by the crew of a French ship in a storm because he was considered a Huguenot. Saved by another ship, he had again fought against the Turks, and defeated three Turkish champions in single combat. Subsequently he was taken prisoner and sold as a slave; but he killed his master, a Turkish pasha, made his escape, and returned to England. His career in America is made famous by his marriage with the Indian princess Pocohontas (*La Belle Sauvage*).

mented before long; indeed, it is said that nearly twenty thousand colonists sailed from Old to New England, as the group of the more northern colonies was called, between the accession of Charles I and the meeting of the Long Parliament in 1640.[1] And so the northern colonies, of which *Massachusetts* became far the most important, were gradually formed.

Development of Colonies under Charles II

The reign of Charles II proved an extremely important one in the history of our American colonies. For one thing, *North* and *South Carolina* were founded and named after the King. Above all, the territories of the English in America became continuous. The Dutch had colonized the territory which lay between the northern and southern settlements of the English. In the Dutch war of 1665, however, an expedition was sent, and these colonies were captured; and in the subsequent peace the Dutch formally relinquished them. New Amsterdam became *New York*, named after James, Duke of York, and the colonies of *New Jersey*, *Delaware*, founded by Lord De la Warr, and *Pennsylvania*, founded by the Quaker, William Penn, were established.

Condition of American Colonies

Of the relations between England and her American colonies we shall have something to say later on; it is sufficient to say here that to most of them an English governor was sent out, and that the degree of independence enjoyed by each colony varied. But, like all mother countries at that time, England regarded her colonies as a source of wealth, and the colonial trade was carefully regulated for the benefit of English merchants. As to the character of the colonies themselves, there were striking differences between them. The "New England" colonists[2] were Puritans by religion, inclined to be democratic in government, and they were hard-working, keen, if somewhat

[1] There is a story, though there is no reliable evidence to support it, that in 1636 Cromwell and John Hampden, despairing of their country, took their passage to America, but that the vessel was stopped by an order in Council.

[2] Massachusetts, Connecticut, New Hampshire, and Rhode Island, comprised New England.

austere men. The southern colonies [1] were more aristocratic, and in them the Church of England was established by law. There the climate was hot, and the chief products were tobacco and rice, the cultivation of which was worked by slaves. The colonists were owners of plantations, many of which were very large. The central colonies [2] were composed of somewhat heterogeneous elements, and every variety of race and religion might be found in one or other of them. With such differences between these various groups, it was not likely that the colonies would find combination an easy matter, and indeed there were continual disputes, chiefly about boundaries, between them. Unity was not to come till the oppression of the mother country — or what was considered by the colonists to be oppression — roused the colonies to common action in 1775; and less than a century after this the underlying differences between the North and the South were to produce the American Civil War of 1861.

Other parts of Empire

Of the other parts of our Empire developed or acquired in the seventeenth century we must say little. In the West Indies the small island of *Barbados* was successfully colonized in 1626.[3] The resources of *Jamaica*, captured by Cromwell in 1655, were quickly developed, and this island was also the home of the Buccaneers [4] who preyed upon Spanish commerce in the Caribbean Sea. Meantime, settlements were made in *Newfoundland* and the *Bahamas*, whilst various points on the West African coast were secured, and in 1651 *St. Helena* was occupied by the East India Company. *Bermuda* was first settled by Sir George Somers in 1609, and the Crown took over the Government in 1684.

[1] i.e. Virginia, Maryland, North and South Carolina, and Georgia, which was founded in 1732.

[2] i.e. New York, New Jersey, Pennsylvania, Delaware.

[3] Barbados was stoutly Royalist, and held out against the Commonwealth until 1652.

[4] The most famous of these is perhaps Captain Dampier.

CHAPTER 40

CHARLES II (1660–1685)

1. FIRST PHASE: DOMESTIC AFFAIRS

We must now trace the internal history of the twenty-eight years that elapse between the Restoration of 1660 and the Revolution of 1688.

With the Restoration we are conscious of a lowering in the ideals of the nation. Both the rival parties in the previous troubles had produced fine personalities, men actuated by lofty motives, and exhibiting nobility of character. With the Restoration we begin, it has been said, the life of modern England, and the Age of Heroics gives way to the Age of Common Sense. Charles was a king in keeping with such an epoch. Since the age of fifteen he had been, but for the brief campaign in 1651, an exile from his country, and now he entered London as King, in 1660, on his thirtieth birthday. He had the Englishman's love of exercise — he was devoted to tennis[1] and hunting, and would often walk from Whitehall to Hampton Court. But in business he was sometimes indolent, and his frivolity was incurable. "Naturally I am more lazy than I ought to be," was his own frank confession; and he was engaged in chasing a poor moth, as Pepys describes in his diary, whilst the Dutch guns were heard roaring in the Thames. He was thoroughly selfish and unprincipled, and prepared to sacrifice religion, friends, or ministers, if he found such a course the more convenient for his own interests. Moreover, his life in exile had been a very demoralizing one for him, and when he returned to England his Court was notorious for its licence and corruption, and for the evil influence exercised by women such as Lady Castlemaine and the Duchess of Ports-

Characters of Charles II and James II

[1] He used to play in the summer at 5 o'clock in the morning.

mouth. Finally, he was at heart a Catholic, but was too prudent in politics, or too lukewarm in faith, to venture to declare himself.

His brother James who was later to succeed him as James II, was in some respects a better man than Charles, though his own life was not above reproach. In his brother's reign, James earned as a soldier the praise of a French general, and as a sailor he fought well at sea and administered the navy with tolerable efficiency at Whitehall. He possessed energy and sincerity, and he proved himself a kind master and father. Yet Charles had many more interests than James in Nature, in Science [1], and in Art. He was more good-humoured, and he had a gift of wit which was denied to James. Moreover, he was a far abler man. "The King," said one observer, "could see things if he would; the Duke (i.e. James, then Duke of York) would see things if he could." James was a bigot, a man given to extremes in all things. He was an ardent Roman Catholic, and those who did not agree with him must be heretics; he was a believer in absolute monarchy, and those who opposed him were rebels. Charles, though of the same opinions, and not without a certain persistency in endeavouring to support them, was more pliable, more tactful, content to bide his time, and determined above all things "not to go on his travels again". James, perhaps, succeeded to a more difficult situation, but the differences in their respective characters largely account for the fact that whilst Charles reigned for twenty-five years and found himself in a stronger position at the end of his rule than he was at its beginning, James's reign came to an abrupt conclusion in less than four years.

Settlement of the kingdom (1660-1)

Charles had made four promises in his *Declaration* signed at *Breda* before his return to England, the performance of these promises, however, being conditional upon the consent of Parliament. *First*, *arrears of pay* were promised to the soldiers. These were paid, and the New Model Army, with

[1] The Royal Society was founded in Charles II's time.

the exception of a regiment known as the Coldstream Guards, was disbanded. *Secondly*, Charles had promised a *general amnesty*. Charles himself was not revengeful, and was quite willing to forgive and to forget. Parliament, however, in the Act of Indemnity and Oblivion which it passed made many exceptions. Thirteen regicides (i.e. those who had signed the death warrant of Charles I) were executed and twenty-five persons were imprisoned for life, whilst Cromwell's body was barbarously dug up from its grave in Westminster Abbey, hanged at Tyburn, and buried under the gallows.[1]

The land question

Thirdly, Charles had promised *security of tenure* to those who had obtained land under the Commonwealth. The land question proved a very complicated one. Eventually it was settled that all lands belonging to the Church and the Crown, and all lands which had been confiscated by the Commonwealth Government, should be returned to their previous owners, whilst the private sales of land held good, though they had been often made in order to pay the heavy fines inflicted upon recalcitrant Royalists by the Commonwealth. It was a compromise which pleased neither party and inflicted hardship on both; but perhaps this could hardly be avoided.

Religion

So far matters had been settled by the Convention Parliament, but this Parliament found itself unable to come to an agreement over the *fourth* promise of Charles — the *promise of liberty of conscience*. Charles had tried to effect a compromise through a conference between leading ecclesiastics; but the attempt was a failure, and it was left to a new Parliament to deal with the question. That Parliament is known in history as the *Cavalier Parliament*, and it lasted from 1661 to 1679. It was remarkable during the first few years of its existence for its exuberant Royalism; indeed, it was more Royalist, so the saying went, than the King himself.

The Cavalier Parliament (1661-79)

[1] The site is in Connaught Square.

The Clarendon Code (1661-5)

On the religious question the Cavalier Parliament proved itself to be more Anglican than even the ordinary High Churchman, and between 1661 and 1665 four Acts were passed against the Puritans, and a time of persecution set in (*Note 77*).

Religious persecution

By the first of these Acts, the *Corporation Act*, no one could be a member of the municipal bodies which governed the towns and controlled the election of Members of Parliament unless he took an oath denying the lawfulness, under any pretext whatever, of taking up arms against the king, and received the Communion according to the rites of the Church of England. This Act sought to deprive the Puritans of their hold upon the towns and the House of Commons. By the *Act of Uniformity* every clergyman and schoolmaster was obliged to take a similar oath of non-resistance and declare his "unfeigned consent and assent" to everything contained in the Book of Common Prayer, in which six hundred alterations had just been made, of a trivial character mostly, it is true, but in an anti-Puritan direction. No less than two thousand clergymen *refused to conform* to this Act, and were deprived of their livings. By the *Five-Mile Act* these two thousand dispossessed clergymen were not allowed to come within five miles of their former livings or of any corporate town unless they took the non-resistance oath imposed by the Corporation Act, and promised not "to endeavour at any time any alteration of government either in church or state". By the *Conventicle Act* religious meetings — other than those of the Church of England — were forbidden, under penalty of imprisonment for the first, and transportation for the third, offence. These Acts helped to complete the severance between the Church of England and the more advanced Puritans. They are sometimes known as the *Clarendon Code*. But this is unjust, because, though Clarendon was the chief minister at the time, neither he nor the King was the instigator of those laws; and the King himself was no persecutor.

Beginning of Nonconformity

The Amnesty, the Land, and the Religious Questions had all been settled, at least temporarily, but one problem still remained which no party in the State had hitherto satisfactorily solved — how were the powers of the Monarchy and the Parliament to be harmonized? It might appear, at first sight, that the Monarchy, at the Restoration, recovered all its old authority. The King, as before, chose his own ministers and conducted the home and foreign policy of the country. Though feudal dues were abolished, the King was granted by Parliament a revenue for life from customs and excise. In one respect, indeed, Charles was more powerful than his predecessors in that he had a small standing army of some five thousand men, which was increased as the reign progressed.[1]

Powers of the Crown after 1660

But, in reality, the King was not in his old position of power. The arbitrary courts, such as the Star Chamber, were no longer in existence. The Restoration, it has been said, was not only a restoration of the Monarchy but of the Parliament as well, and the wishes of that Parliament could no longer be ignored. "The King of France", said a shrewd observer, "can make his subjects march as he pleases; but the King of England must march with his people." Moreover, in 1667 the Parliament made a great advance; it secured that additional grants of money to the Crown should be appropriated for particular objects, and that a Parliamentary audit should be made to ensure that the money was so expended. This meant that Parliament not only voted money, but could control and manage the way it was expended.

During the first seven years of Charles's reign (*1660–67*),

[1] A regiment of foot (the Coldstream) and a regiment of horse (the Blues — so called from their uniforms) were made up of "New Model" soldiers; besides these there were the regiment of Grenadiers, composed chiefly of Cavaliers, and two troops of Life Guards, whilst a troop of horse and a regiment of foot, known later as the Royal Dragoons and the Queen's Regiment, were required for the defence of Tangier. The Royal Scots and the Buffs were also created in Charles II's reign, the one being recruited from Scotsmen who had fought for the King of France, and the other from those who had served under the banner of Holland. The Scots Greys were also formed in Charles II's reign.

The Ministry of Clarendon (1660-7)

Lord Clarendon, the author of the famous *History of the Rebellion*, was the chief minister; indeed he had such influence that Charles, a contemporary said, was but "half a king" whilst he was in power. As Edward Hyde, Clarendon had been a member of the Long Parliament, and had approved of its measures until the Grand Remonstrance was brought forward. Though not responsible for the Clarendon Code, he was perhaps too intolerant a High Churchman; but he was moderate in politics, upright and hard-working, and his great object was to establish a balance of power as between King and Parliament. Partly in consequence of his very moderation, he became in time unpopular with all classes. The King got tired of his lectures; the courtiers sneered at his morality; the Royalists disliked him for his supposed leniency to the Puritans over the amnesty and the land questions; whilst the Nonconformists hated him for the Code. Moreover, the marriage of his daughter, Anne Hyde, with James, Duke of York, the King's brother, made him appear self-seeking; and the sale of Dunkirk to France, for which Louis XIV, the French King, was said to have bribed him,[1] caused him to be accused of corruption.

Clarendon's unpopularity was increased by two disasters for which he was in no way responsible. The Great Plague of 1665 killed one-fifth of the population of London,[2] besides raging in the provinces. The Great Fire in the following year swept away two-thirds of London's houses, and not far short of a hundred of its churches, including St. Paul's; it was indeed fortunate for England that she had Sir Christopher Wren to rebuild so many of them.[3] Finally, in 1667, the whole nation held Clarendon responsible for

[1] According to Pepys, the Diarist, the common people called the great house which Clarendon was building for himself, in Piccadilly, Dunkirk House, "from their opinion of his having a good bribe for the selling of that towne".

[2] For four months previous to the arrival of the Plague there had been no rain, and this made the capital very insanitary.

[3] Wren built St. Paul's and fifty-two churches in London.

the appearance of the Dutch fleet up the Thames. And so Clarendon was dismissed by the King, was impeached by Parliament, and retired into exile.[1]

2. SECOND PHASE: FOREIGN POLICY OF CHARLES II

England in the period of the Commonwealth had secured a position of great influence in Europe. With the return of the Stuarts, in 1660, she was soon to lose it. Between the restoration of Charles II, in 1660, and the revolution which his brother, James II, brought upon himself after three years of rule, there elapse twenty-eight years. During those years the *King of France*, *Louis XIV*, who reigned from 1643 till 1715, is the central figure in European politics. With the aid of a large revenue, capable ministers, and wonderful generals, he had already secured for the Crown, before the Restoration, absolute power at home and a pre-eminent position in Europe. By the time of the Revolution of 1688 his ambitions and resources were, as we shall see, a menace to every state in Europe.

Position of France under Louis XIV (1643–1715)

Charles returned to England in 1660 under obligations to no foreign power. But from the first he was attracted towards France (*Note 78*). His mother was French; his first cousin, Louis XIV, was such a king in France as he would have liked to be in England. Moreover, Charles wanted to foster the commercial welfare of England, and he looked upon Holland, not France, as the rival of the country over which he ruled. And so he married his sister, Henrietta, the only person whom he ever really loved, to the French Duke of Orleans, brother of Louis XIV, and he himself married Catherine of Braganza, the daughter of the King of Portugal, with whom Louis XIV was in alliance. Catherine, as her dowry, secured two useful possessions for England — *Bombay*, which Charles leased to the East India Company

Charles II's policy towards France

[1] Hyde Park was created out of the gardens surrounding the great new house which he had built for himself and which was confiscated at his fall.

for the trivial rent of £10 a year, and *Tangier*, an important strategic port, which encouraged England to hope that "she might give the law to all the trade of the Mediterranean". Moreover, Charles sold Dunkirk to the French (1662). The sale was unpopular, but wise; for Dunkirk was expensive to keep up, useless strategically, and the King could not afford to maintain garrisons there as well as at Tangier.

Sale of Dunkirk (1662)

Meantime the commercial ambitions of Holland and England, especially in Africa and the East Indies, led to continual disputes between the ships of the rival nations and to attacks upon each other's commerce.[1] The trade rivalry between the Dutch and the British was fierce, and the Government of Charles II was bombarded with petitions against the Dutch. Finally war was declared against Holland in 1665, and this was to be a war waged by England with the object of crushing a trade rival (*Note 79*).

Second Dutch War (1665–7)

In this war France was nominally in alliance with Holland, though she took no prominent part in the military operations, which were nearly all at sea. The battles were fiercely contested, and a large part was played in them by fire ships — the torpedo boats of that time. The King's brother, James, Duke of York, won a great battle off *Lowestoft*, in which, with the loss of one ship, he inflicted on the Dutch a loss of twelve ships.[2] In the next year (1666) Monck and Rupert, no longer generals on land but "generals at sea", unfortunately separated their fleets, and Monck was defeated in a battle lasting for four days, and hence called "*The Battle of the Four Days*", which was fought between *North Foreland* and Dunkirk. Monck's ships behaved well and "fought", it was said, "like a line of cavalry handled according to rule". In 1667 an indelible disgrace was inflicted upon England. Lack of money caused

[1] Two English companies — the Turkish Company and the East India Company — estimated their losses, in consequence of Dutch depredations, at £700,000.

[2] After the battle James went to bed, and, as a consequence of misunderstood orders, the Dutch fleet was not pursued.

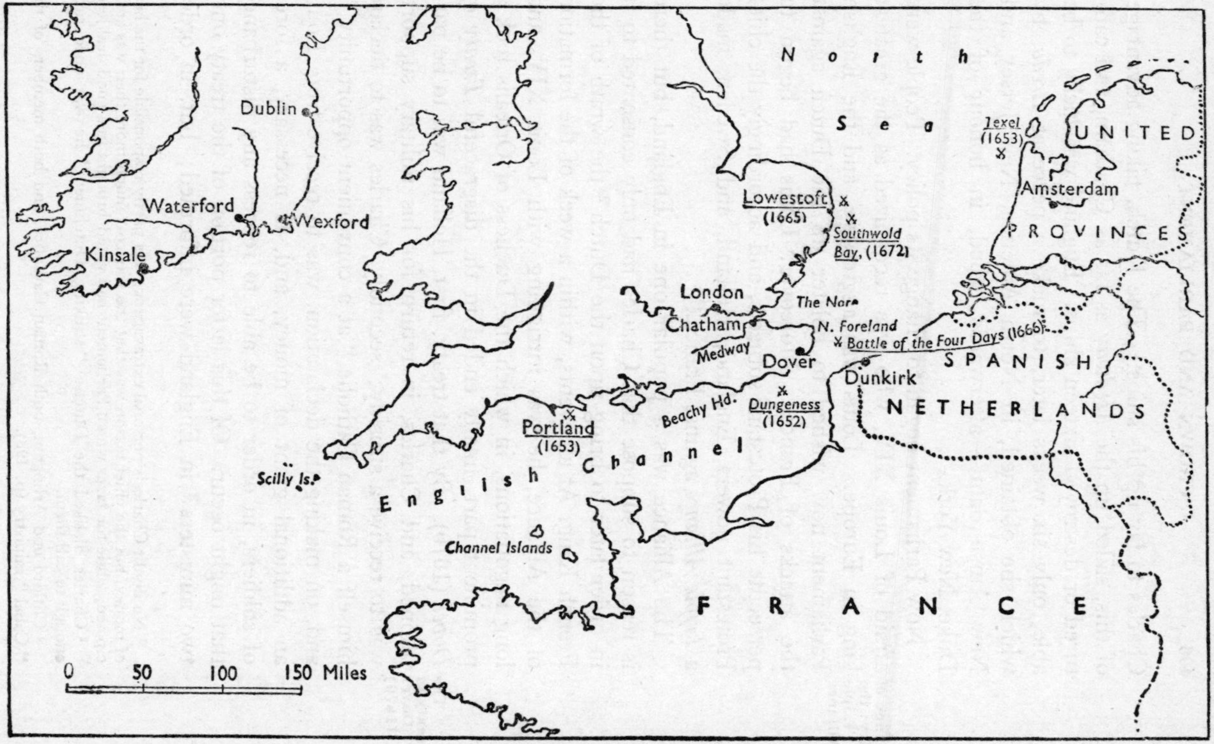

THE NAVAL WARS, 1649–1674

Charles to lay up his ships.[1] The Dutch, taking advantage of this, sailed up the *Medway* as far as Chatham, and captured or destroyed sixteen ships. England was lucky to be able, only six weeks later, to make a peace at *Breda*, by which she obtained, in North America, New Jersey and New Amsterdam — afterwards called, in honour of the Duke, New York.

Change of policy: the Triple Alliance

Now Parliament began to change its policy. People were afraid of Louis XIV, who was recognized as the greatest king in Europe. Louis was aggressive, and the English Parliament now wished to bolster up the Dutch against the attacks of France. Moreover, Louis had begun to persecute his Protestant subjects, and accordingly the chief Protestant powers, England, Holland, and Sweden, made a *Triple Alliance* against France.

The Treaty of Dover (1670)

The Alliance was a popular one in England, but there is reason to suppose that Charles had only consented to it in order later to bring upon the Dutch[2] the wrath of the French King. At all events, within a week of the formation of the Alliance, he was intriguing with Louis XIV, and long negotiations, in which the Duchess of Orleans took a prominent part, finally ended in the disgraceful *Treaty of Dover* (1670). By that treaty, first, Holland was to be partitioned, and Charles, in return for his military support, was to receive a subsidy; secondly, Charles was to declare himself a Roman Catholic " at a convenient opportunity ", and, on making the declaration, was to receive from Louis an additional grant of money, and, if necessary, a force of soldiers, in order to be able to repress any disturbance that might occur. Of this latter portion of the treaty only two ministers[3] in England were informed; but, in order

[1] No doubt Charles's personal extravagance was partly responsible for the lack of money, but the chief reason was that the war cost much more than was anticipated, while the taxes which Parliament had voted brought in a good deal less.

[2] Charles disliked the Dutch: " stinking Dutchmen " he was once rude enough to call them.

[3] Clifford and Arlington, both Roman Catholics, and both members of the " Cabal " ministry (p. 498).

to deceive the other ministers and the nation, a "sham treaty" was drawn up, which had reference only to the proposed war with the Dutch. With the treaty of Dover the creditable portion of Charles's foreign policy terminates. In the war which followed in 1672 the Dutch made an heroic resistance. They cut their dykes and surrendered part of their land to the sea, in order to preserve it from the French; and their fleet, though defeated off *Southwold Bay*, more than held its own in the latter portion of the war. In 1674 England was glad to make peace. The power of Holland, however, was broken, and gradually a large portion of her trade fell into English hands.

Third Dutch war (1672–74)

From 1674 to 1688 England ceased to be of importance in foreign affairs. Occasionally the King showed some independence of France, as, in 1677, when the Princess Mary, the daughter of the Duke of York, married William of Orange, the ruler of Holland. But for the greater part of the time the English kings were the pensioners of Louis XIV. That monarch paid Charles II large sums of money for the prorogation of Parliament, and when he seemed to be too independent he bribed the Opposition in Parliament instead. Finally, Charles, a year before he died, gave up Tangier in order to please Louis XIV. When James II came to the throne in 1685, the French ambassador was the chief supporter of his disastrous policy. Meantime Louis XIV's powers and ambitions were extending, and when the Revolution of 1688 came, his ascendancy was threatening all Europe.

Foreign policy (1674–88)

Decline of English prestige

3. CHARLES II AND THE ATTEMPT AT PERSONAL RULE

After Clarendon's fall, Charles largely directed his own policy. For the next five years (*1667–73*) his chief ministers were five in number, and came to be known from the initial letters of their names as the *Cabal* Ministry. Two of them,

The Cabal Ministry (1667–73)

Clifford and *Arlington*, were Roman Catholics. *Buckingham*, the third member of the group, was "everything by starts, and nothing long"; in the fickleness of his opinions, the changeableness of his occupations, and the immorality of his life he was highly characteristic of that epoch. The fourth, *Ashley Cooper*, afterwards Lord Shaftesbury, was a person who was accused of changing sides always at the right moment for himself (*Note 80*). He was undoubtedly a very able statesman. He was, in religious matters, in favour of toleration. He was keenly interested in colonial and trade development, and thus a supporter of the war against the Dutch. And he is regarded by some historians as the first great party leader in the modern sense, and as the founder of modern Parliamentary oratory. *Lauderdale*, the last of the five, and perhaps the wickedest, governed Scotland.

The Cabal, however, was in no respect like a modern Cabinet. Its members were not of the same opinions; they had no leader; and they were not consulted together. It was during the existence of the Cabal that there came the Triple Alliance, the secret Treaty of Dover — of which only Clifford and Arlington knew — and the Third Dutch War (p. 497). Just before the Dutch War began, Charles, in accordance with his agreement with Louis XIV, tried to secure toleration for Roman Catholics, and incidentally for Dissenters as well, by issuing what was called a *Declaration of Indulgence*, suspending the penal laws against Roman Catholics and Dissenters (1672). But Parliament objected, and Charles had not only to withdraw the Declaration, but to agree to a *Test Act* by which no one was to hold any office of State who refused to take the sacrament according to the Church of England (1673). This Act caused the Duke of York to retire from the Admiralty, and Clifford and Arlington to retire from the Ministry. Charles then dismissed Shaftesbury, and the Cabal Ministry came to an end (1673) (*Note 82*).

The Declaration of Indulgence (1672) and the Test Act (1673)

For the next few years (*1673–78*) Charles's chief minister was *Danby*, who was an Anglican in religion, and the King gave up, for the time, his attempts to restore Roman Catholicism in England. These years are a maze of intrigues. The Cavalier Parliament was getting restive. Shaftesbury, on being dismissed by the King, had at once begun to organize an opposition in both Houses, which soon became formidable. Meantime the French King was at one time subsidizing Charles in order to get Parliament prorogued, and at another trying to bribe the Opposition to oppose the King. The nation was nervous and uneasy. Then an event happened which made it panic-stricken.

Ministry of Danby (1673–78)

In the autumn of 1678 a man called Titus Oates made a statement to a London magistrate declaring the existence of a *Popish plot*, the objects of which were to murder the King, to put the Duke of York in his place and to bring a French army into England. Shortly afterwards the magistrate[1] was found dead, having been obviously murdered. At once the nation, always in dread of Popish plots, took alarm, and a panic began. Every word of Titus Oates was believed, though he was really a thorough scoundrel.[2] Other informers sprang up in every direction; and Roman Catholics were tried and executed on the flimsiest evidence. Protestants carried flails to protect themselves from imaginary Roman Catholic assaults, whilst the Houses of Parliament without one dissentient declared a " damnable and hellish plot " to be in existence. Of course, there was in a sense a plot — in which Charles himself was implicated by the Treaty of Dover — to restore Catholicism in England, but the details of this particular plot were a pure fabrication. Shaftesbury and the Opposition, however, made unscrupulous use of the plot. For they were anxious to divert the succession from Charles II's brother James to an illegitimate

The Popish Plot (1678)

[1] Sir Edmund Berry Godfrey.

[2] He had been expelled successively from his school, the Navy, and two Jesuit Colleges, besides having had writs issued against him on two occasions for perjury.

son of the King's, known as the Duke of Monmouth; and they hoped that this proposal would, in consequence of the alleged plot, meet with much popular support.

Three short Parliaments (1679–81)

In the same autumn (1678) some negotiations which Danby had, by Charles's command, undertaken for the supply of money from the French King were discovered, and Danby was impeached. Charles, to save him, dissolved the Cavalier Parliament, which had sat since 1661 (January, 1679). There followed in a space of two years three short Parliaments (1679–81). The first of these insisted upon committing Danby to the Tower despite the King's pardon, thereby developing the principle of the responsibility of ministers. It also passed, through Shaftesbury's influence, the very important *Habeas Corpus Act*, the object of which was to ensure that a man who was imprisoned should be brought up for trial as soon as possible.

Habeas Corpus Act

In all three of these short Parliaments, however, the chief topic was the Bill for excluding James from the succession, the Opposition being resolved to make an effort to prevent the accession of a Roman Catholic. Hence Shaftesbury and the Opposition pressed for the succession of the Protestant Duke of Monmouth, who, they held, was a legitimate son of Charles, the marriage certificate of his mother with Charles being secreted (so it was alleged) in a certain " black box ". Charles, however, said he would rather see his son hanged than legitimize him. It was during this time that Political Parties were first organized. At first they were known under the names of *Petitioners* and *Abhorrers*, from the fact that one party petitioned for the calling of Parliament, whilst the other expressed their abhorrence of any encroachment on the King's Prerogative; later they came to be called by their respective opponents, *Whigs* (Scots *whig*, to jog along) after the name of certain fanatical Scots Covenanters, and *Tories* (see p. 510) after some wild Irish Roman Catholic rebels; and the names are still in use to our own day. The last of the three Parliaments was sum-

The Exclusion Bill: the Protestant Succession

moned by the King to meet not in London, where the mob was fiercely hostile to the Court, but at Oxford in the Convocation House; and men came armed — so great was the excitement. But it had only lasted a week when Charles dissolved it, and the Exclusion Bill was still unpassed (1681).

Now Charles appeared to have matters his own way. The alarms caused by the Popish Plot died down, and people were ashamed of what had been done. The execution of Lord Stafford, a blameless Roman Catholic peer of over seventy years of age, for alleged complicity in the Popish plot, made people realize the wildness of the exaggerations which they had hitherto believed. The opposition therefore lost popularity. Shaftesbury had to take refuge abroad, where he died, a refugee, and Monmouth was banished. Then came a plot to kill the King, on his way back from racing at Newmarket. This plot, called after the place where the ambush was to be laid, *the Rye House Plot*, was discovered, and Charles took advantage of it to execute, quite unjustly, two important Whigs, Russell and Sidney (1683).

Supremacy of Charles (1681–85)

The Rye House Plot (1683)

Having thus crushed his opponents Charles meant to go further. He defied the Test Act and restored his brother James to office. In the years from 1681 to 1684, thanks to the annual pension he secretly received from Louis XIV, he had governed without Parliament. Now he set to work to control elections to Parliament. He did this by changing the Charters of London and of sixty-five of the large towns, which formerly returned " Whig " members.[1] Charles in these selected boroughs now nominated the governing corporations, and thereby made sure that the corporations would send up to Parliament only members whom he approved.

How far he would have succeeded, and how far Parliament would have been manipulated by him, cannot be known, for in February, 1685, he was suddenly taken ill. Realizing that he was dying, he sent secretly for the old

[1] He altered the Charters under a writ " Quo Warranto ".

priest who years before had helped him to escape from Worcester, and after receiving the Sacrament as a member of the Roman Catholic Church, he died.

CHAPTER 41

JAMES II (1685–1688)

Accession of James II (1685)

James II succeeded without difficulty (*February, 1685*) on his brother's death. It was felt that he had been treated hardly over the Exclusion Bill, and he had the support of all moderate people. Parliament, enthusiastically loyal, voted him a large income; and even when the fabricators of the Popish Plot were most barbarously treated — Oates received three thousand four hundred lashes in three days [1] — it was felt that they had only got what they deserved.

Monmouth's Rebellion (1685)

Moreover, the successful crushing of two rebellions strengthened the King's position. *Argyll* in Scotland rose in support of Monmouth; but he could only get some of his own clan, the Campbells, to help him, and he was captured and beheaded. *Monmouth* himself landed in Dorset, and persuaded the country people of that county and of Somerset to join him in large numbers. He tried a night attack upon the King's forces at *Sedgemoor*, which might have been successful but for the fact that an unsuspected and impassable ditch stopped his advance. As it was, the attack failed, and Monmouth was subsequently captured and then executed (July, 1685). The Chief Justice, Jeffreys by name, accompanied by four other judges, was sent down to the West to try the rebels, and, in what is called "*the Bloody Assizes*", hanged over three hundred and transported some eight hundred,[2] thus bringing upon himself

[1] Oates subsequently joined the sect of Baptists, and used often to preach from the pulpit of Wapping Chapel; but he was finally expelled by the sect "as a disorderly person and a hypocrite".

[2] These eight hundred were presented to various courtiers, who sold them to slavery in the West Indian plantations.

a reputation for cruelty which will last as long as history is read.

For the first nine months of his reign, till towards the close of 1685, James himself behaved with some moderation. The ease with which the two risings were quelled, however, encouraged him to a more extreme policy. He increased the numbers of the standing army, which was a very unpopular institution, to thirty thousand men. He began a systematic policy of officering it with Roman Catholics, by making use of the *dispensing power*, a power by which the judges held he was able to dispense, in the case of particular individuals, with the laws passed against the Roman Catholics. He changed his ministers, moderate men like Halifax or High Churchmen like Rochester giving way to Roman Catholics and recent converts to that religion like Sunderland; and in Ireland he made Tyrconnel, a bigoted Roman Catholic, viceroy. He showed his intention of converting the University of Oxford by appointing a Roman Catholic to the Deanery of Christ Church and by substituting Roman Catholic for Protestant Fellows at Magdalen College; and therefore incurred the hostility of that University, which had always been the most loyal supporter of the House of Stuart. He re-established the High Commission Court and issued a *Declaration of Indulgence*, suspending the penal laws against the Roman Catholics and Dissenters. He prorogued and finally dissolved his first Parliament (July, 1687), and he then made preparations for "packing" another one by calling on the Lords-Lieutenant to provide him with a list of Roman Catholics and Nonconformists suitable as Members — a demand which led most of them to resign.

James's tyranny (1686-88)

Such conduct on the part of James alienated not only those classes who had fought against his father but also the classes — the country gentlemen and the clergy — who had fought for him. In the early summer of 1688 the crisis came. In *May*, the King issued a *second Declaration of In-*

The crisis (May-June 30, 1688)

The Seven Bishops *dulgence*, and ordered it to be read in churches. The Archbishop of Canterbury and six other bishops drew up a protest, and James decided to try them for libel. On *10th June* a son was born to James by his second wife, Mary of Modena. People had so far been content to await the advent of a new reign, in the hope that James's Protestant daughter Mary and her husband William of Orange, the ruler of Holland and a strong Protestant, would succeed. But now James had a successor who would be educated as a Roman Catholic. Moreover, it was widely believed that the child was not really the child of James and his wife, but had been brought into the palace in a warming-pan. On *30th June* the Seven Bishops were acquitted, and on that night there was a scene of indescribable enthusiasm and rejoicing in London. On the same evening seven men of importance, representing different shades of opinion, met and drew up a letter inviting William to bring an army over to England and to restore to its people their liberties.[1]

Birth of a son

At this moment Louis XIV offered James his assistance. James, not appreciating his danger, refused it. Fortunately for William, Louis then moved his troops from the Netherlands frontier to wage a campaign in Germany. With Holland no longer threatened by a French army, William felt himself justified in coming to England, especially as he had received assurances of help from leaders of the English army and navy. He landed at Torbay on *5th November, 1688*, and received support at once. Later he was joined by John Churchill (afterwards the famous Duke of Marlborough), the chief man in the army, whilst an insurrection, supported by Anne, James's second daughter, took place in Yorkshire. James tried conciliation, but it was already too late. He then tried flight, and was ignominiously brought back to London. Finally, William, having arrived in London, sent James to Rochester. There only lax guard

The Revolution of 1688

[1] The letter was signed in cipher and conveyed by Admiral Herbert (afterwards Lord Torrington), who, disguised as a common sailor, managed to reach the Dutch coast in safety.

was kept over him, and James again escaped — to William's great satisfaction — and at 3 a.m. on Christmas Day, 1688, landed in France. James's reign was over,[1] and so at last was the long struggle of King and Parliament (*Note 84*). The Revolution of 1688 was, as we shall see, to produce wide-reaching changes in our system of government.

CHAPTER 42

IRELAND AND SCOTLAND UNDER THE STUARTS

1. IRELAND

The Plantation of Ulster 1608

We must now turn to consider what had been the history of Ireland under the Stuarts. Soon after James I came to the throne, an opportunity arose of developing the system of "plantation" begun in the reign of Elizabeth. In 1607 the *Earls of Tyrone and Tyrconnel*, the heads of the two great Irish tribes in *Ulster*, fearing that they were about to be attainted for treason, fled from the country. The Government then proceeded to confiscate the lands of these two clans. It held that the lands belonged to the two earls, the heads of the tribes; but, by Irish theory and custom, these lands belonged to the tribe, and it is difficult to justify the course pursued by the English Government. Some of the lands — the worst part of them — were restored to the Irish; but over half a million acres were given to settlers from England and Scotland and to the City of London and its twelve City Companies. Nor was Ulster the only province affected. Adventurers flocked over to Ireland, inquired into the titles of land in various districts, and, where they were non-existent or

[1] During his first flight, on 11th December, James had thrown the "Great Seal" into the Thames at Vauxhall, the seal being the symbol of authority without which no deed of Government was valid. This date was subsequently taken as the legal date of James's "Abdication".

defective, obtained the grant of them from the Government.

Strafford in Ireland (1633-40)

The next important stage in the history of Ireland is marked by the *rule of Strafford* who was Lord Deputy from 1633 to 40. In many ways his government was admirable. He made the officials attend to their business, and endeavoured, with some success, to put a stop to jobbery. He found an army half-clothed and half-armed, undrilled and unpaid; he transformed it into an efficient fighting force well disciplined, well officered, and well paid. The Irish Sea, before his rule, was full of pirates; but under Strafford piracy was sternly and successfully repressed.[1] To his initiative was due the development of the flax industry in Ireland with money which he himself subscribed. He improved the Protestant Church; restored order to the Services; and encouraged clergymen of ability in England to come over and take benefices in Ireland.[2] Finally, he summoned the Irish Parliament, and made it pass some excellent laws.

Plantation of Connaught proposed

Strafford's rule was then, for many things, worthy of great commendation. But his conduct was, in other ways, of an exceedingly arbitrary character, and his treatment of individuals was often very high-handed. It is, however, in his proceedings with regard to *Connaught* that he showed himself at his worst. He wished to "plant" that province, as Ulster had been "planted" a few years earlier. With this object he caused an inquiry to be made into the titles of the landholders, and intimidated and browbeat the juries into giving verdicts which would justify him in confiscating the lands. Before, however, he could bring over settlers the condition of affairs in England led him, as we have seen, to leave Ireland in 1640.

[1] Strafford himself experienced the inconveniences of piracy, for a pirate ship, the *Pickpocket*, of Dover, captured linen belonging to him worth £500.

[2] The condition of the Protestant Church in Ireland had been deplorable. A few years before Strafford came to Ireland the Archbishop of Cashel had held, besides his archbishopric, three bishoprics and seventy-seven livings. Strafford found on his arrival that the Earl of Cork had appropriated the revenues of a bishopric worth £1000 a year for a rent of £20. The earl, however, did not keep them for long when Strafford heard of it, and had to disgorge.

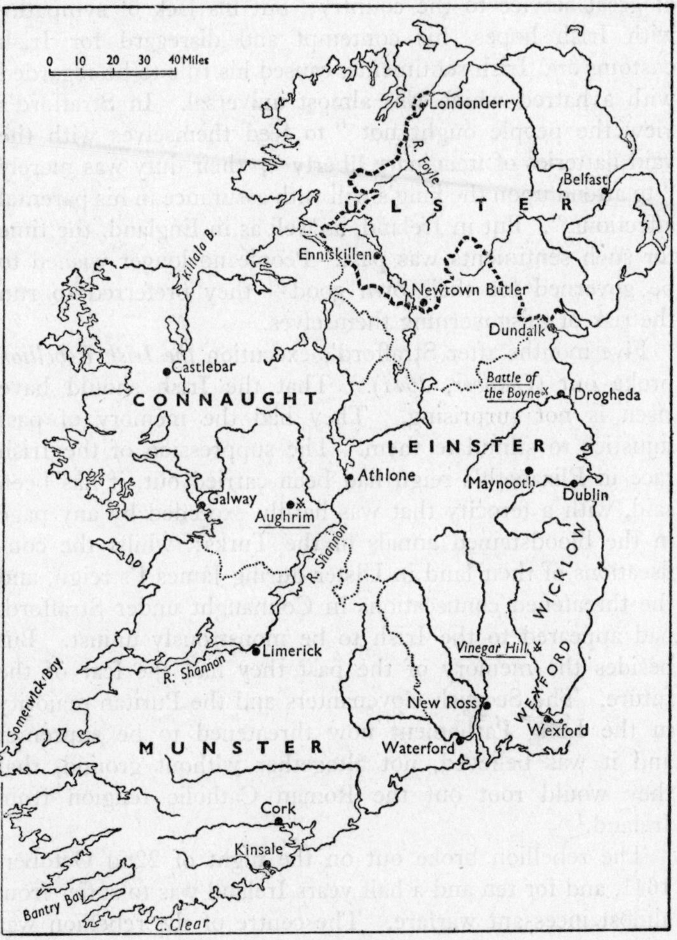

IRELAND SINCE 1603

The dotted line is the boundary between Northern Ireland and Eire

Few will deny that Strafford's masterful energy had been of great service to the country; but his lack of sympathy with Irish hopes, his contempt and disregard for Irish customs and Irish sentiments, caused his rule to be regarded with a hatred which was almost universal. In Strafford's view the people ought not " to feed themselves with the vain flatteries of imaginary liberty "; their duty was merely " to attend upon the king's will with assurance in his parental affections ". But in Ireland, as well as in England, the time for such sentiments was past. People no longer wished to be governed for their own good — they preferred to run the risk of misgoverning themselves.

The Irish Rebellion (1641)

Five months after Strafford's execution *the Irish Rebellion* broke out (*October, 1641*). That the Irish should have risen is not surprising. They had the memory of past injustice to stimulate them. The suppression of the Irish race in Elizabeth's reign had been carried out, it has been said, with a ferocity that was hardly exceeded by any page in the bloodstained annals of the Turks; whilst the confiscations of their land in Ulster during James I's reign, and the threatened confiscations in Connaught under Strafford, had appeared to the Irish to be monstrously unjust. But besides the memory of the past they had the fear of the future. The Scottish Covenanters and the Puritan majority in the Long Parliament now threatened to be supreme; and it was believed, not altogether without ground, that they would root out the Roman Catholic religion from Ireland.[1]

The rebellion broke out on the night of 22nd October, 1641, and for ten and a half years Ireland was to suffer from almost incessant warfare. The centre of the rebellion was at first Ulster, where the English and Scots were driven from their homes and endured the most fearful hardships,

[1] It was reported in Ireland that a member of the Long Parliament had said that the conversion of the Irish Papists could only be effected with the Bible in one hand and the sword in the other, whilst Pym had prophesied that Parliament would not leave one priest in Ireland.

and from Ulster it spread to Wicklow. In a rebellion at such a period some massacres were perhaps inevitable; and modern historians estimate that about four thousand Protestants were killed and that double this number died of famine or exposure. These figures are horrible enough, but to the Puritan imagination in England the number of victims was far greater, and by some people was put at one hundred thousand, and by others even as high as three hundred thousand.[1] It was natural, therefore, that the Long Parliament should pass, in angry vengeance, two laws against the Irish Catholics, the one declaring that no toleration should be granted to the Catholic religion in Ireland, and the other confiscating two and a half million acres of land in that country for the benefit of those who subscribed towards the suppression of the rebellion. The chief result of such laws, again, was to embitter feeling in Ireland, and led to many Catholic gentlemen joining in the rising.

Persecution of Irish Catholics

In 1642 the situation was complicated by the outbreak of the Civil War in England, and affairs in Ireland became so entangled, owing to the variety of parties, that a brief summary is hardly possible. It is sufficient to say that Charles, in the course of the Civil War, made attempts to secure aid from the Irish, and that a few did come over; but otherwise nothing definite was done. Then, in 1649, when Charles was executed, all parties in Ireland combined, for a brief period, in order to secure the recognition of his son as king, as the prospect of rule by the "Rump" Parliament was detested by all alike.

Irish affairs (1642-49)

Consequently Cromwell was sent over to subdue Ireland. But before he arrived a Colonel Jones had defeated the combined army at *Rathmines*, and the Irish, till they could gather fresh forces, had to rely on their ability to hold out in their fortresses. Cromwell, however, quickly stormed

Cromwell in Ireland (1649-50)

[1] This number is a third more than the total estimated Protestant population in Ireland.

Drogheda and *Wexford*,[1] and before he left Ireland had obtained possession of the whole coast except Waterford. The conquest which Cromwell had begun his son-in-law, Ireton, completed, and by April, 1652, the whole of Ireland was subdued.

The condition of Ireland at the end of this long period of warfare was pitiable. Over one-third of the population, it is estimated, died during these ten years of bloodshed and misery. Much of the land was out of cultivation, and a great deal of country depopulated. The inhabitants were further reduced, as thousands of Irishmen went to serve in foreign armies, and some hundreds of boys and girls were shipped to Barbados and sold to the planters.

Rule of Commonwealth

The war was followed by fresh plantations. Enormous quantities of land were distributed to Cromwell's soldiers and other Protestant settlers, whilst some of the previous landholders were given compensation in Connaught. At the same time the exercise of the Catholic religion was rigidly suppressed. But, in Ireland as in Scotland, Cromwell's rule had some merits, and on the whole fair order was maintained.[2] Ireland was given representation in the British Parliament, and above all she enjoyed the benefits of free trade with England.

The Restoration in 1660 brought to Ireland the same

[1] Cromwell put the whole garrison to death at Drogheda; "I do not think thirty of the whole number escaped with their lives," he wrote. By the rules of war at that time the garrison of a place which had refused to surrender and was then stormed was liable to this fate. Cromwell, however, defended his conduct on the ground that the garrison had been concerned in the massacres of 1641 and that severity on this occasion would lead other garrisons to surrender at once. It may be doubted whether this severity had this result, and, as a matter of fact, no member of the garrison had been concerned in the previous massacres. Both at Drogheda and Wexford Cromwell put to death all the priests he could find, by knocking them on the head, as he himself put it.

[2] Measures had to be undertaken for the extermination of two pests — wolves and Tories. The former had increased enormously during the war, and one man was allowed to lease an estate, only 9 miles from Dublin, at a very cheap rate, on condition that he kept a pack of wolfhounds and "a knowing huntsman". Tories (Gaelic *toruidhe*, to rob) were discontented Irish soldiers who had lost their holdings in the Cromwellian settlement, and had retaliated by murdering the new colonists and stealing their cattle. Five pounds was offered for the head of a wolf, and as much as twenty pounds for the head of a really bad Tory.

difficulty over the land question as had occurred in England — what was to happen to the Cromwellian settlers? Eventually it was settled in this way: those landholders who could prove that they had no share in the rebellion of 1641 recovered their lands, whilst the Cromwellian holders of them received compensation elsewhere. But the arrangements were not satisfactory; a good many innocent Roman Catholics did not, as a matter of fact, recover all their lands, and some recovered none. The general result was this. In 1640 two-thirds of the landholders had been Roman Catholic. After 1665 one-third belonged to the *native* interest, including families of Anglo-Norman descent and mainly Catholic; one-third belonged to the *Irish* interest, i.e. the settlers of Elizabeth's and James I's days or their descendants, mainly Protestant; one-third to the *English* interest, i.e. the Cromwellian settlers.

Ireland under Charles II

The land-owners

The reign of Charles II was a period of peace for Ireland. For a great part of the time Ormonde was the ruler, and under him a discreet toleration was exercised, and the country enjoyed repose. In the reign of Charles II, however, Ireland not only lost her free trade with England, but began to suffer from the laws which the influence of jealous English merchants and farmers secured in the English Parliament. But of that we shall have something to say later on (*Note 75*).

2. SCOTLAND UNDER THE COMMONWEALTH AND LATER STUARTS (1651–1688)

At the Battle of Worcester, 1651, the Scottish army was destroyed as a fighting force, and Scotland was occupied by an English army and subjugated. Till the Restoration in 1660 she was governed, on the whole successfully, by George Monck and English Commissioners. Taxation, it is true, was heavy, but justice was done in civil and criminal cases far more effectively than ever before. The tyranny of the Presbyterian Church was broken, and some efforts in

Scotland under the Common-wealth (1651-60)

the direction of toleration were made. The Highlands were pacified and good order maintained throughout Scotland.[1]

Scottish members sat in the British Parliament and Scotland secured Free Trade with England, and her prosperity was, as a consequence, greatly developed.

Then came the Restoration. One result of it was that Scotland lost her Free Trade with England, though she recovered her independence. Another was that the supreme authority of the King was restored. And along with his supremacy in political affairs Charles desired to have supremacy in ecclesiastical matters. So he restored Episcopacy in Scotland and determined to maintain it at all costs. The Presbyterians, who had had things their own way from 1638 to 1651, still pressed for the execution of the provisions of the Solemn League and Covenant (see p. 455). But the King in his zeal for Episcopacy was as extreme and intolerant as were they in their claims for Presbyterianism. All existing holders of livings had to be reinstituted by bishops and had to renounce the Covenants. Many ministers, especially in the South-west, refused, and they were, in consequence, "outed" from their charges, and their places were taken by others, often by uneducated and vicious men. People who refused to go to church were fined, and laws of ever increasing severity were passed against persons attending "Conventicles", as religious meetings held outside church were called. There was a good deal of persecution, particularly after a Covenanting rising (the Pentland Rising) in 1666. Lauderdale, who became Royal Commissioner in 1667, did attempt reconciliation, but there was little response, and the Covenanters began to hold their meetings in lonely and inaccessible moorlands. Consequently Government efforts to put them down increased in ferocity, dragoons being employed to hunt Covenanters, often with ruthless injustice, and in 1678 a horde of 8000 Highlanders was

Scotland and the Restoration

Episcopacy restored (1661-62)

The Covenanters

[1] "A man may ride over all Scotland", said a contemporary, "with a switch in his hand and a hundred pounds in his pocket, which he could not have done these five hundred years."

brought to the South-west, where it spoiled, murdered, and looted.

Murder of Sharp; Drumclog, and Bothwell Bridge (1679)

Early in 1679 James Sharp, Archbishop of St. Andrews, who had deserted the Covenanters and had become one of the main persecutors, was done to death by some fanatics,[1] and a few weeks later a body of Covenanters declared their defiance of all civil authority. At Drumclog, in Lanarkshire, they defeated Graham of Claverhouse, who had been sent to suppress conventicles. Elated by their small victory, they marched on Glasgow, but were met at Bothwell Bridge on the river Clyde and defeated by Monmouth.[2]

The "Killing Time" (1681-87)

For a time after Bothwell Bridge Scotland was treated with more moderation, but when James, Duke of York, afterwards James VII, became Royal Commissioner in Scotland in 1681, the " Killing Time " began, and there was a fierce persecution of the Presbyterian zealots, or Cameronians as they were called from their leader Richard

[1] From an account written by one of the nine men concerned in the death of Sharp, it is clear that, though the murder had been decided on, the actual meeting with the Archbishop on Magus Moor, near St. Andrews, was accidental. Sharp was a particularly despicable character, but it is not possible to regard his death as being anything but a very brutal murder. The Covenanters concerned believed that they " had a clear call to execute God's justice " — " John Balfour stroke him on the face, and Andrew Henderson stroke him on the hand and cut it, and John Balfour rode him down; whereupon he, lying upon his face as if he had been dead, and James Russell hearing his daughter say to Wallace that there was life in him yet, . . . went presently to him and cast off his hat, for it would not cut at first, and haked his head in pieces. . . . James Russell desired his servants to take up their priest now." Having carried out what they conceived to be their mission they " went to prayer, first together, and then each one alone, with great composure of spirit, and enlargement of heart more nor ordinary, blessing the Lord, who had called them out and carried them so couragiously thro' so great a work." This episode and these quotations go far to provide a key to the strength and the weaknesses of the Covenanters.

[2] In face of the enemy, the Covenanters, instead of preparing for battle, began to dispute about the object of the rising; the zealots insisted that they were striving to establish Presbyterianism as supreme over all other forms of Church government, and the moderates thought they should aim at something which might be attained — the free exercise of their own form of worship. The moderates also pointed out that these questions could be settled later, and that in the meantime their first task was to defeat Monmouth. But the argument continued and though a nominal settlement of the differences was reached, internal dissension continued, the Covenanting army dwindled away, no preparations were made for battle, and many of the Covenanting leaders failed dismally. " The Lord took both courage and wisdom from us," is the summing-up of one of the moderates.

Cameron. Persecution reached its height with the accession of James to the throne in 1685, the increased intensity being perhaps a result of the futile rebellion of the Earl of Argyll in support of Monmouth (p. 502). In 1687, however, James granted an Indulgence to Presbyterians and Roman Catholics alike. This put an end to persecution, and gave the Presbyterians liberty "to serve God after their own way and manner", but it also paved the way for the introduction of Roman Catholicism which James so eagerly desired, and it was accompanied by the dismissal of Protestants from offices of State and their replacement by Roman Catholics, and by the handing over of Holyroodhouse to the Roman Catholics. Thus, when the Revolution came in 1688, Scotland was full of discontent.

James VII and II (1685-88)

NOTES ON PERIOD SIX (1603–1688)

RULERS OF ENGLAND AND SCOTLAND

JAMES I (1603–1625)
CHARLES I (1625–1649)
THE COMMONWEALTH (1649–1653)
THE PROTECTORATE (1653–1658)
CHARLES II (1660–1685)
JAMES II (1685–1688)

IMPORTANT FOREIGN RULERS

FRANCE:	LOUIS XIII (1610–1643)
	LOUIS XIV (1643–1715)
SPAIN:	PHILIP IV (1621–1665)
THE EMPIRE:	FERDINAND II (1619–1637)
SWEDEN:	GUSTAVUS ADOLPHUS (1611–1632)
	CHRISTINA (1632–1654)
BRANDENBURG:	FREDERICK WILLIAM (1644–1688)

NOTE 59. — JAMES I: FOREIGN POLICY

Aimed at peace, and thought to attain it through *dynastic marriages.*

1. First aimed at *Protestant alliance,* so (1613) married his daughter Elizabeth to Frederick of the *Palatinate.*

   Outbreak of the Thirty Years' War in Germany. Frederick as a Protestant was chosen King of *Bohemia* by the Protestants there (1619), and the Emperor attacked him, not wishing for a Protestant King. James led Frederick to believe he would support him, but he did not. Frederick was defeated and lost all his dominions.

2. Also aimed at *Catholic alliance,* so planned to marry his son Charles to the daughter of the King of *Spain* (1617). England disliked the "Spanish" match, which roused great opposition. (James also executed Ralegh in 1618 to please the Spaniards.) When that failed, he planned to marry Charles to daughter of the King of *France.* (This gave England a Roman Catholic Queen, whose sons, Charles II and James II, later became Catholic.)

Note 60.—JAMES I: RELIGIOUS POLICY

1. Strongly opposed to the *Puritans* due to his dislike of Presbyterian government in Scotland. Many sects of Puritans, and none of them believed in toleration.

   At *Hampton Court Conference* (1604) James decided against Presbyterians and in favour of Bishops.

2. James was tolerant, and gave relief to *Roman Catholics*. This, and his policy of alliances with Catholic Spain, greatly enraged his subjects.

   But in 1605 the *Gunpowder Plot*, by Roman Catholics, caused James to carry out anti-Catholic laws with great severity.

3. Caused " authorized " version of the Bible to be issued — his greatest deed.

Note 61.—JAMES I: PERSONAL POLICY

1. Believed in " Divine Right of Kings " which declared all power " flowed from the king ". This led to the struggle with Parliament.
2. Had as his advisers, first Elizabeth's statesmen, then replaced them by worthless favourites, *Earl of Somerset* and *Villiers, Duke of Buckingham.*
3. Tried to secure support of *Judges*, and, if they did not decide in his favour, dismissed them. Hence corrupt justice.
4. Favoured peace, and believed Alliance between Protestant England and Catholic Spain would make for peace.
5. Drove Puritans into opposition. By tolerance towards Roman Catholics roused anti-Papal feeling in England.

Importance of James I's Reign.

Though himself learned, tolerant, and peaceable, his policy sowed the seeds of later civil war, for he *antagonized the Puritans, exaggerated the power of the Crown,* and *made the monarchy unpopular* by his favourites.

Called " wisest fool in Christendom " because though very learned, so far as book-learning went, he had no common sense. He was ruled by bad men, and all his actions alienated different people and succeeded with none.

Note 62.—JAMES I AND PARLIAMENT

Quarrelled over;

(*a*) **King's theory of Divine Right.** Parliament stood for theory that " sovereignty " lay with King and Parliament; James stood for theory that royal " prerogative " could over-ride Parliament.

(*b*) **Right of Election to Parliament.** James declared he could set aside an election (Godwin's case) (1604).

(*c*) **Taxation.** James levied "*impositions*" which were not sanctioned by Parliament (Bate's case) (1606).

(*d*) **King's Ministers.** Parliament "impeached" the King's ministers, i.e. prosecuted them in the House (1621).

(*e*) **Freedom of Speech.** Parliament declared its right to freedom of speech (1622).

Note 63. — PURITANISM

Appears under Queen Elizabeth, is thwarted by James I, leads opposition to Charles I, and splits away from Church definitely under Charles II.

Puritans all *originally members of Church of England.* Drawn largely from well-to-do middle classes, and later some of nobility.

Many *variations between Puritans,* some of whom did not object to Bishops. All objected to Roman Catholics and to ritual. Hence roused to opposition by Laud's efforts to restore ritual. All based their own religion on the Bible. *Few believed in toleration* (only the Independents to whom Cromwell belonged) and all wished to impose their views on others.

Puritans have suffered greatly from the false ideas about them spread after the Restoration. They did oppose brutal sports such as bull- and bear-baiting; also vulgar and coarse shows, such as often disgraced the theatres, or even village sports. But they did not oppose art and beauty. Milton wrote *Comus* as a masque to be acted with music, Cromwell encouraged music and saved Mantegna's pictures for the nation.

They were *driven to oppose the Crown* partly because Charles I persecuted non-conformers to Laud's High Church ideas, partly because they came to stand for champions of liberty against the King's overriding of Parliament.

Note 64. — CAUSES OF CHARLES I'S QUARRELS WITH HIS PARLIAMENT

1. **Religion.**

Charles was High Church Anglican, and Parliament was strongly Protestant. Charles's wife was Roman Catholic and Charles was inclined to tolerate Catholicism. Parliament was strongly anti-Catholic. Laud and Charles tried to impose their High Church ideas on the Puritans.

2. **King's Ministers.**

Parliament now began to try to dictate to the King whom he should have for his *ministers,* and went on to try to control the policy of the ministers. Parliament distrusted the ministers, and refused to grant money, as they believed Buckingham would mis-spend it (as over Cadiz expedition). Later Parliament attacked Strafford and Laud.

3. **Foreign Policy.**
Parliament disagreed with Charles's foreign policy and later distrusted the King and Queen's intrigues with foreign powers.

4. **Taxation.**
Parliament was determined to prevent the King from raising money except with Parliament's consent. Charles tried to get money in various ways;

(*a*) *Tunnage and poundage*, which he expected Parliament to grant without demur for his life, but which Parliament would only grant for one year.

(*b*) Raised forced loan, and imprisoned the Five Knights who refused to pay (1628).

(*c*) *Ship-money*, which he levied from all counties, whether sea-coast counties or inland (1634).

NOTE 65.—CHARLES'S EFFORTS TO RULE WITHOUT PARLIAMENT

1. Tried to get on without Parliament and therefore had to do without appeals for money.
   (*a*) Kept out of wars.
   (*b*) Tried to economise.
2. Tried to raise money in other ways. *Distraint of knighthood, ship-money, sale of monopolies.*
3. Used "prerogative" powers and "prerogative courts" to try persons objectionable to the King. *Star-Chamber* and *High Commission.*

In defence of Charles we must note:

(*a*) That country was very prosperous.

(*b*) That no one was put to death.

(*c*) That the King had the law behind him, for the judges upheld his actions.

(*d*) That the aims of Parliament to control of policy were new and were not supported by all.

NOTE 66.—STRAFFORD AND LAUD

Both urged the King to strong government ("Thorough").

1. **Strafford** (1593–1641) first opposed misgovernment of Buckingham. After his death, Strafford thought the King would now rule better. Disliked Parliament's efforts to control ministers.

   (*a*) Joined Charles's party. Governed the *North* very well (1628).

(*b*) Sent to *Ireland*, as Deputy, and governed well, though severely; started industries such as flax-growing; began to train an army for the King (1633).

(*c*) Sent for by Charles to help him over the crisis of the Bishops' War (1639). Advised Charles he must call Parliament, and Parliament at once brought in an *Act of Attainder*. This meant he was condemned by a vote of the House, and he was executed (1641).

2 **Laud** (1573–1645), worked with Strafford.

(*a*) He urged the King to force his ritualistic views on the nation.

(*b*) He used *Court of High Commission* to try ecclesiastical cases. Prevented England from becoming Calvinistic.

(*c*) He drove the Puritans into violent opposition. Those who attacked the Bishops were most severely punished (*Prynne*).

(*d*) Finally, he imposed the English Prayer Book and Service on *Scotland*. This led to the " Bishops' War ", which in turn meant summoning of Parliament and the trial and execution of Laud.

Note: Real issue was *who was to be supreme*, King or Parliament, and Charles gradually forced this upon everyone. *Therefore, his efforts failed* because he united many people against him, some on religious grounds, and others on political. His religious policy ended in provoking the Scots to make war, and once he embarked on war, Charles was bound to call Parliament, for he could not get enough money for his various expeditions.

Note 67. — THE LONG PARLIAMENT (1640–1660)

1. **Abolished Arbitrary Power of the Crown.**

(*a*) Taxation of all sorts (ship-money, etc.) only to be imposed with consent of Parliament (1641).

(*b*) Parliament to be summoned every Three Years (*Triennial Act*) (1641).

(*c*) Prerogative Courts (Star Chamber, High Commission) to be abolished. People must be tried by jury (1641).

2. **Attacked the King's Advisers.**

(*a*) Strafford tried and executed (1641)

(*b*) Laud imprisoned 1640 (later executed — 1645).

3. **Attacked the Intrigues of the Queen** (and the King) with France. Irish Rebellion gave rise to belief that the Crown was plotting with the Catholics, and meant to use Irish troops (1641).

4. Finally, believing war was at hand, Parliament brought in a **Bill to gain control of the militia**, i.e. of armed forces. Charles vetoed this. Signal for war (1642).

NOTE 68.—OPPOSING PARTIES IN THE CIVIL WAR

1. (*a*) Advantages of the Parliamentary Party.

(i) Held London and chief ports, such as Hull and Plymouth, and was supported by at least two-thirds of the population and controlled three-quarters of wealth of country.

(ii) Parliament did not waste its troops in garrisoning county castles.

(iii) Navy was on side of Parliament.

(*b*) Advantages of Royalists.

(i) Military advantage at first for cavalry was then the decisive force, and Royalists had better horsemen. Had better commanders at first.

(ii) Had unity of command, through the King.

(iii) Had prestige of Crown.

(iv) Could collect taxes and import duties.

2. Opposing Theories of Parties.

(*a*) (i) Parliament believed in *control of taxation, liberty of the subject, trial by jury,* and "ancient liberties" as set out in Magna Carta.

(ii) Parliament opposed the King's *religious policy* and believed he was betraying Protestantism.

(iii) Parliament believed the *nation was sovereign,* and the King must act in accordance with wishes of the people.

(*b*) (i) King believed that he, not Parliament, was upholding the Constitution; that he "had right" to Tunnage and Poundage for life.

(ii) He believed he was head of the Church and must stand firm for its organization under Bishops.

(iii) He believed his power came from "Divine Right" and not from the people.

Thus, the war was partly fought for religious, partly for constitutional reasons.

NOTE 69.—STAGES OF THE CIVIL WAR (1642–1651)

1. Aim of the King to take London.

(*a*) Failed in first year (1642) at Turnham Green.

(*b*) In second year (1643) made triple advance on London:

(i) From north, where King was victorious.

(ii) From west, where Rupert was victorious.

(iii) From east, where King did not succeed.

London saved because *Hull* in north and *Plymouth* in west held out, and royalist armies could not leave them in their rear.

2. Both sides appealed to **the Scots,** who decided to support Parliament, which accepted the *Solemn League and Covenant* (1643).

   Charles brought over Irish, but they were ineffective, compared with the Scots.

3. **The " Eastern Association "** with Cromwell was now fully trained, and left its own district to fight in the north. Great victory at *Marston Moor* (1644).

4. This led **New Model Army,** with good cavalry and good officers, to " go everywhere ". Won *Naseby* (1645). " The King and the Kingdom lost ".

The New Model Army:

(*a*) Was well paid, as Parliament had plenty of money.
(*b*) Numbered 50,000 men.
(*c*) Won the second Civil War in four weeks.
(*d*) Defeated Charles II at Worcester (1651).

NOTE 70.—THE COMMONWEALTH: EXPERIMENTS IN REPUBLICANISM (1649-1659)

1. **Commonwealth.**

(*a*) *Different parties.* Royalists, still in large numbers; Presbyterians, backed by Scots; Extremists such as Levellers (very strong republicans) and Independents who were more tolerant; the Army who controlled situation.

(*b*) *Cromwell* had supreme influence and used it for moderate republicanism. Therefore:

(i) Negotiated with King, to disgust of extremists. Scots and Presbyterians now support King. Leads to 2nd Civil War and execution of the King (1649).

(ii) Quarrelled with Scots who objected to Army's support of Independents, and wished to enforce Presbyterianism on England. Cromwell opposed this. Hence 3rd war (1648) and defeat of Scots at *Dunbar* (1650) and of Charles II at *Worcester* (1651).

(*c*) *Single chamber government. The Rump* created by:

(i) *Pride's Purge* (Dec., 1648) and 90 M.P.s left. Set up single chamber government. Council of State; Army Council; and the Rump Parliament.

Cromwell can rule " neither with Parliament nor without ". He and Army quarrel with Rump and dissolve it (1653).

(ii) *Barebone's Parliament* (1653) contained representatives from Ireland and Scotland, thus representative of United Britain. Very unpractical. Dissolved 1653.

2. **First Protectorate** (1653–56).

New Constitution. *The Instrument of Government creates Protectorate* (1653). Parliament of *one House*; Protector to have *veto* on such acts as were contrary to constitution, and *power to dissolve* it after five months. *Council of State* to assist Parliament to control taxation. This Parliament wished to reduce army, and to persecute non-Presbyterians. *Cromwell wished for toleration* so dissolved Parliament (1655). Turned to the Army for advice and help.

3. **Second (Revised) Protectorate** (1656–59).

Cromwell tried to settle the country by rule of *Major-Generals* in eleven districts. This army-rule so unpopular he called another Parliament, which drew up *Humble Petition and Advice* (1656); an effort to go back to the old government of England with *Lords and Commons*, and Cromwell was asked to become King. Refused the Crown but set up *Revised Protectorate* with a nominated Upper House, larger Lower House. The two Houses at once quarrelled over their powers, and Cromwell dissolved them. Death of Cromwell (1658).

Note: These experiments *failed* for three reasons:

(*a*) Parliament was *not representative* of the country for elections not free, and large body of Royalists not represented.

(*b*) Parliament consisted of *intolerant* persons who wished to persecute other forms of religion, and this Cromwell and the army would not allow.

(*c*) The *army hence could not agree* with either of the other parties of the State. The "Instrument of Government" and "Humble Petition" are *written constitutions* and show the difficulties of settling powers of the two Houses.

NOTE 71. — CROMWELL'S FOREIGN POLICY

His policy based on determination:

(*a*) *To prevent restoration of the Stuarts.* Achieved because France and Spain at war, and both wanted England's help, so neither would help Stuarts.

(*b*) *To maintain Protestant religion.*

(i) Offered terms to Spain: — Cost of war to be borne by Spain; Calais to be restored to Britain; trade to be allowed with Spanish colonies; English to be unmolested by Inquisition. Spain refused terms (1654).

(ii) Offered terms to France: — Cost of war to be borne by France; Dunkirk to be British; persecution of Vaudois to cease. France accepted terms (1655). Hence military alliance with France (1657) obtained concession for Protestants, and fought Spain, which was bigotedly intolerant.

(*c*) To *advance English commerce,* hence war with Dutch, our commercial rivals.

1. **1652–53. First Dutch War, fought over Commerce.** *Navigation Act* (1651), passed by Rump, said goods coming to England must come in English ships.
2. **Peace** made by Cromwell as Protector (1654), followed by *Protestant alliance* of Holland, Denmark, Sweden, and England.
3. **Spanish War.** War abroad between Spain and France. *Cromwell supported France* (1654–57):
   (*a*) Fought colonial war against Spain in *West Indies*, and took many islands from Spain (1655–58).
   (*b*) Expedition to *Mediterranean* very successful (1655). English supreme in Mediterranean.
   (*c*) French to gain English support, forced *Savoy* to cease persecution of Protestants (Milton's sonnet "Avenge, oh Lord! thy slaughtered saints") (1655).
   (*d*) Attack on *Dunkirk*, Spanish possession, which was captured after *Battle of the Dunes* (1658).
   Note: Cromwell's alliance with France criticized as Spain was declining power and France was becoming aggressive. Cromwell's decision made on religious grounds.

Note 72. — ENGLISH SEA-POWER UNDER CROMWELL

Period of great glory for the navy. In *Blake*, Cromwell had one of our greatest sailors. Sea-power now became England's great source of strength. Blake (1599–1657) had been a country gentleman, and fought in Civil War, but when sent to sea proved a nautical genius, just as Cromwell proved a natural military genius. English also had better ships — more stoutly built and better armed.

1. In **Civil War,** Blake defeated *Rupert,* and blockaded him in Lisbon, defeated Portuguese fleet, and then destroyed Rupert's fleet in the Mediterranean (1651).
2. In **First Dutch War** Blake faced powerful navy under *Van Tromp.*
   (*a*) **1652**. Van Tromp defeated Blake in Straits of Dover in *May.* Dutch had command of Channel. Blake defeated Dutch in the Downs in *September.* Van Tromp defeated Blake at Dungeness in *November.* English took refuge in the Thames.
   1653. Three days' battle off *Portland* won by Blake in *February.* English gained command of Channel. Drawn battle in *June.* Victory of English in *November.* Van Tromp killed.
   (*b*) Dutch commerce injured, and 1400 Dutch ships captured. Dutch merchant ships driven off sea.
   Peace (1654) gave England great commercial successes.
3. **War with Spain.**
   (*a*) Fleet under Admiral Penn attacked West Indies, army under Venables failed to take Hispaniola (1655) but took *Jamaica* (1655).

(*b*) Expedition to Mediterranean. Blake attacked Bey of *Tunis* (first appearance of English fleet in Mediterranean) (1655).

(*c*) Attacked Spanish treasure fleet off *Santa Cruz* (Teneriffe) and destroyed whole fleet, under fire from forts. Death of Blake on return voyage (1657).

Note 73. — CROMWELL'S CAREER (1599–1658)

1. Came from **yeoman stock**, lived life of small land-owner in the Midlands till over forty. Was intensely religious, but tolerant. Believed Charles I responsible for arbitrary government which must be checked, and guilty of bloodshed of civil war. Also held Charles worthy of death because he believed Charles wished to call in French against the people. Sat in Parliament as member for Huntingdon (1628). Member of Long Parliament. Helped to draw up Root and Branch Petition and Grand Remonstrance (1641).

2. A Great Army Leader.

(*a*) Organized the Eastern Association (1643), and then the New Model (1644). Insisted on strict discipline. Trained the Parliamentary army as cavalry men, in which at first the Parliamentary forces were lacking.

(*b*) Never lost a battle. But note at several he was saved by the mistakes of his enemies: Rupert at *Naseby* (1645) and Scots at *Dunbar* (1650).

3. As Statesman:

(*a*) Always stood for religious toleration, hence continued quarrels with his various Parliaments.

(*b*) In foreign policy stood for England playing a great part abroad, and was so successful that the two Catholic autocratic monarchies, Spain and France, competed for his help.

(*c*) Saw importance of sea-power.

But note, he failed to establish settled government at home, and all his constitutional experiments failed, for his rule was based on the army, and not on popular support. Hence he could never have either a freely elected Parliament or could he ever rule with any selected Parliament he summoned.

After the Restoration his body taken from its grave in Westminster Abbey and hanged at Tyburn.

Note 74. — CROMWELL'S RELATIONS WITH SCOTLAND AND IRELAND

1. Scotland.

(*a*) After 1st Civil War, Scotland wished to force England to become Presbyterian. Cromwell and his supporters opposed this, and offered to Charles I (*Heads of Proposals*, 1647) to maintain Episcopacy in England. Charles chose Scots alliance, so in 1648

Scots invaded England on Charles's behalf. Cromwell defeated them at *Wigan*, at *Warrington*, and at *Preston* (1648). Entered Scotland and put Argyll in power.

(*b*) After death of Charles I, Scotland supported Charles II, who promised to set up Presbyterianism in England (1650).

Cromwell invaded Scotland, and won battle of *Dunbar* (1650). Took Edinburgh and Perth. Scots forced to make peace and accept General Monck as Governor.

2. **Ireland.**

(*a*) In 1649 Irish supported Charles I. ***Cromwell*** went over and took *Drogheda* and *Wexford*. Showed great cruelty and put Drogheda garrison to death, and " all the priests he could find ".

(*b*) *Ireton* then conquered rest of Ireland.

(*c*) Land confiscated and *settlement* made by English. (Irish peasants left on the land but English landlords placed over them in three quarters of the whole island.) Catholic religion suppressed as far as open worship concerned.

(*d*) Called *representatives from Ireland* to the " Barebones " Parliament, and granted free trade.

Cromwell's policy in Ireland is in opposition to his usual toleration. He believed Ireland would supply armed forces for the Stuarts and that " severity " would check this. He failed, and his policy inflicted great suffering and ruin in Ireland. Population fell by over one-third in this period.

Note 75. — SUMMARY OF IRELAND UNDER THE STUARTS

1. **James I** suppressed the *rebellion of Tyrone in Ulster* (1607). Confiscated lands of Tyrone and Tyrconnel and ***planted Ulster***, largely with Presbyterian Scots (1610).

2. **Charles I** sent *Strafford* (1633–40). He restored order, revived trade, developed flax industry, raised an army, improved Protestant church. Called *Irish Parliament*, and transacted useful business through its means.

But he " planted " ***Connaught***, turning out landlords and bringing in others.

When *Long Parliament* met, ***Irish rebelled***, fearing worse treatment at hands of Puritans (1641). First took form of attack on Scottish Presbyterians in Ulster (3000 killed). Long Parliament declared for no toleration for Catholic religion in Ireland, and for confiscation of land of rebels.

3. Ireland recognized **Charles II** as it detested rule of Puritans. Rose on behalf of Charles. **Cromwell** defeated and crushed Irish, massacre of garrison of Drogheda (1649). Irish Presbyterians called to Barebone's Parliament (1653). Ireland given free trade with England.

4. Restoration of Charles II.

(*a*) Difficulty over land settled by landowners who had not rebelled in 1641, being restored to lands, and Cromwellian settlers given land elsewhere. *Result*: after 1665, one-third of landowners were native Irish Catholics, one-third were Protestant settlers of Elizabeth's and James I's plantations, one-third were Cromwellian settlers.

(*b*) Ormonde governed Ireland and granted religious toleration to Catholics (1661–1665).

(c) But free trade was abolished, and Ireland suffered from restrictions on her trade.

5. James II.

(*a*) Roman Catholic Lord-Lieutenant, Lord Tyrconnel. Ireland to be ruled on separate lines.

(*b*) After 1688 revolution, James supported by Ireland. Protestants resist. Siege of Londonderry. Battle of Enniskillen (1689). James defeated at Battle of the Boyne (1690).

(*c*) Ireland conquered for William III by Churchill and Ginkel. Irish signed the Capitulation of Limerick (1691), which promised that Roman Catholics should have the same privileges as in the reign of Charles II. These terms not kept. Penal code against Roman Catholics passed.

NOTE 76. — THE RESTORATION

Restoration Settlement. Made by the army under Monck. to end "slavery of sword government". Charles II accepted Monck's suggestion and issued the Declaration of Breda (1660).

1. **Declaration of Breda** made the following provisions:
   (*a*) A "free" Parliament to be elected and King to rule with it.
   (*b*) Lands bought by persons under the Commonwealth not to be confiscated, i.e. Royalists whose lands had been taken, did not have them restored.
   (*c*) Religious toleration was promised (but this was not kept).
2. **Monarchy Restored,** and it was treason to take arms against the Crown, but actually everyone knew that if the King governed arbitrarily, Parliament and the nation would not stand it.
3. **Parliament Returned,** with King, Lords, and Commons, and Parliament kept control of all taxation, and hence control of the King.
4. **Church of England Restored,** and though "no man to be called in question" for his religion, the Parliament which met was strongly Anglican, and proceeded to persecute Puritans.

5. **General Amnesty** except for the "regicides" who had signed Charles I's death warrant, 13 of whom were executed, and 25 imprisoned for life. (James II, 25 years later, was revengeful enough to order Judge Jeffreys to condemn Alice Lisle, the widow of one of the regicides. Charles II was himself merciful and would have preferred no executions at all.)

NOTE 77.— THE CHURCH AND THE BEGINNINGS OF NON-CONFORMITY

The Puritans had not wished for toleration under the Commonwealth and the Anglicans would not have it under Charles II. So we have (*a*) persecution; (*b*) rise of non-conformity; (*c*) attempts of Charles to get toleration for Roman Catholics, which failed.

1. **Persecution by the Anglicans.**
Parliament passed the *Clarendon Code* (called after Lord Clarendon, the Chancellor) to persecute non-conformists. The Code consisted of:
(*a*) *Corporation Act* (1661). All members of Corporations had to take Holy Communion according to rites of Church of England. Corporations controlled elections in many of the boroughs of members of Parliament. Hence this largely *disfranchised non-conformists.*
(*b*) *Act of Uniformity* (1662). All clergy to be ordained by Bishops, and to use Book of Common Prayer; all schoolmasters to be licensed by Bishops. This meant that 2000 Ministers now resigned their livings and became "dissenters".
(*c*) *Conventicle Act* (1664). No one might attend any religious service other than those of Church of England.
(*d*) *Five-Mile Act* (1665), No non-conformist minister or schoolmaster might come within 5 miles of any town.
This was meant to strike at non-conformists in the towns, where they chiefly were to be found, for it meant they could not educate their children, and their ministers could not in any way keep in touch with them.
Note: The "Code" did not make everyone into members of the Church of England; it drove numbers into "dissent", and it set these people apart. From now on the "dissenters" found it hard to get educated.

NOTE 78.— CHARLES II AND FRANCE

Foreign policy turns on Charles's relations with France.

1. First act of his minister Clarendon was to *sell Dunkirk to the French* (1662). Louis XIV aimed chiefly at conquest of the Dutch, needed help of English navy. Also wished to see England become Catholic.

Hence he and Charles combined to outwit Parliament and force England into line with French schemes. In Charles's defence is urged that he believed English interests were helped by destruction of Dutch power.

2. Charles negotiated *alliance with France*, and his sister Henrietta married Louis XIV's brother; Charles married Catherine of Braganza, Portugal being ally of France (1665).

3. Followed this by making *war on the Dutch* (1665–7). Policy was highly unpopular, and in 1667 peace of Breda signed. England joined Holland and Sweden in alliance against France.

4. *Triple Alliance* of England, Holland, and Sweden against France (1668).

   Louis determined to detach England, so in 1670 he and Charles made *secret Treaty of Dover*. Under this Holland to be partitioned; Charles to receive money from Louis; Charles to declare himself a Roman Catholic, and at suitable moment to accept French army to force England to become Roman Catholic.

   Following the treaty Charles *made war on the Dutch again*, but he and Louis both failed to conquer that country, and in 1674 England made peace.

5. Charles now on the surface abandoned French alliance in response to Parliament's clamour, and made *marriage treaty with Holland* (1677) — his niece and heiress Mary married William of Orange.

6. Parliament now very suspicious of Louis and Charles. The *Popish Plot* (1678) was thought to mean replacement of Charles by the Catholic James, with support of France. Charles, horrified by Parliament's repression of the plot, *accepted pension from France*, and ruled without Parliament till his death in 1685.

Note 79. — THE DUTCH WARS OF CHARLES II

Cromwell had fought the First Dutch War (1652–53) to secure commercial advantages. Charles II fought the Second and Third Dutch Wars chiefly in alliance with France, which gained advantages as France had no fleet equal to the war.

1. **Second Dutch War.** 1665–67. England and France against the Dutch. De Ruyter the Dutch admiral; Prince Rupert and Monck (now Albemarle) the English admirals.

   (*a*) English won *Battle of Lowestoft* (1665), but three-day *Battle of the Downs* (1666) quite inconclusive.

   (*b*) Charles neglected the navy, spent no money on it, and laid up ships as " economy ". Hence, in 1667. Dutch sailed up the *Medway*, and burnt the English fleet at anchor. *Peace of Breda* followed, and England gave up trading stations in East Indies. Received part of " New England " (New York, Delaware, and New Jersey), but at that time these considered valueless.

2. Parliament, with the country, now bitterly opposed to Charles's policy, and did not wish to help Catholic France to crush Protestant Holland. Insisted on the *Triple Alliance* of England, Holland, and Sweden (1668).

3. Charles broke this, as soon as he could, and declared **Third Dutch War** (1672–74). (Result of Secret Treaty of Dover.)

English fought indecisive actions off *Solebay* (second Southwold battle), and in their attacks on the *Texel* were defeated and driven off. Charles compelled to call a Parliament for money. Parliament insisted on *peace* (1674) and *marriage alliance with Holland* negotiated later (1677).

NOTE 80. — IMPORTANCE OF SHAFTESBURY (ANTHONY ASHLEY COOPER) (1621–1683)

1. Began as an opponent of the Crown in the Long Parliament (1641). Sat in Barebones Parliament (1653). Supported restoration. Made minister by Charles II (1660).

2. A member of the famous " Cabal " or Ministry (Clifford, Arlington, Buckingham, Ashley Cooper, Lauderdale), so called from initials of members (1669).

Ashley believed in toleration.

3. Hence soon led to suspect Charles II's double dealing and after *Treaty of Dover* (1670) led opposition. Regarded as first " party " leader.

Called his party the " Country " party, opposed to the " Court " party. Nicknames became " Whigs " and " Tories ".

4. When Charles attempted to pass *Declaration of Indulgence* (1672), Shaftesbury led attack and secured *Test Act* (1673). Charles then dismissed him (1673).

5. Shaftesbury whipped up feeling over *Popish Plot* (1678) because he believed that Charles and Louis XIV were plotting to make England Roman Catholic. (The secret clauses of Treaty of Dover were not known till recent times, but Shaftesbury suspected their existence and they prove he was right as to intentions of the two Kings).

6. *Danby's* negotiations with France were discovered, 1679, and Shaftesbury got *Habeas Corpus Act* passed (1679). This is of the greatest importance, for it prevents any person being imprisoned without trial.

7. Shaftesbury now began to work for the *Exclusion Bill* to exclude James II from succeeding to the throne, as a Catholic.

(*a*) First Bill (1679) provided heir to the throne should be James's Protestant daughter Mary, married to William of Orange. Charles dissolved Parliament to stop Bill.

(*b*) Brought in Second Bill (1681), not saying who should succeed. Shaftesbury meant it to be *Monmouth,* Charles's eldest illegitimate son, and hoped to produce some sort of proof that Charles had married Monmouth's mother. Charles dissolved Parliament.

(*c*) Third Bill (1681) introduced at Parliament held at Oxford. Monmouth now named as heir in the Bill. Charles dissolved Parliament and never called another, getting money from Louis XIV to make him independent.

Note: *Habeas Corpus Act* is regarded as a great safeguard of liberty. Any person arrested can demand trial at next session, and if not tried, judge must grant a writ of " habeas corpus ", ordering the person in charge to release the prisoner. Thus no one can be imprisoned for unknown cause, or for " political reasons " when no crime has been committed. The Act has been " suspended " in times of great emergency, e.g. by Pitt in the Revolutionary wars, and again in the 1914–18 war it was suspended on the grounds that persons were highly dangerous against whom no crime could be proved. The outcry was so great that the Act was restored after one year.

Note 81. — CHARLES II'S ATTEMPT AT PERSONAL RULE

1. Charles tried first to secure French help to make him independent of Parliament. *Secret Treaty of Dover*, 1670.

2. Tried to get toleration for Roman Catholics — by the *Declaration of Indulgence* (1672) suspending the laws against Catholics and Dissenters. Parliament would not agree, and passed *Test Act* (1673) instead, obliging all holders of office to be communicants of Church of England.

3. Charles negotiated for more money from France, through Danby (1678). Discovered, and Danby impeached and *Exclusion Bill* brought forward to exclude James II from throne. Charles, to prevent its passing, dissolved Parliament at Oxford (1681).

4. Charles now ruled without Parliament with help of subsidies from France.

(*a*) Shaftesbury, who had led opposition, fled abroad.

(*b*) Charles dropped Test Act and restored James to his offices (1681).

(*c*) Set to work to gain control of Parliament by changing the Charters of the Corporations, which returned the members to Parliament (1683).

NOTE 82. — EFFORTS OF CHARLES II AND JAMES II TO GAIN "TOLERATION"

Aimed really at getting toleration for Roman Catholics. Included Dissenters in effort to win them over. Dissenters refused to accept the "declaration" as dreaded Roman Catholicism so much.

1st Declaration, which remitted all penal laws for Catholics and Dissenters issued by *Charles II* (1672), when Parliament was not sitting. Parliament when summoned repudiated whole idea and counter-attacked by Test Act.

2nd Declaration (1687) by *James II* again offering "toleration" to both. Again refused by Dissenters.

3rd Declaration (1688) issued by James, and bishops and clergy ordered to read it in Churches. *Seven Bishops* refused. Tried, on James's orders, for sedition, but acquitted by jury amid popular rejoicings. Signal for fall of James.

Toleration finally granted by William III (1689). Allowing freedom of worship to all *Dissenters* who would take oath of allegiance.
(Complete toleration not granted till 1828, when *Test and Corporation Acts* finally abolished, i.e. *Catholic Emancipation.*)

NOTE 83. — THE BEGINNINGS OF THE BRITISH EMPIRE

1. (*a*) Early attempts to colonize Virginia under Elizabeth had failed.
(*b*) First progress came from the East.
(i) *East India Co.* formed under Elizabeth (1600), but trade in the East hampered by the Dutch. In 1623 Dutch executed some Englishmen at *Amboyna* and English abandoned trade with islands.
(ii) On mainland of India English had to meet competition of *Portuguese* (1612). First factory at *Surat*, then others at *Madras* (1639), Bombay (1661), and Calcutta (1690).
(iii) Cromwell took *Jamaica* (1655).
(iv) *Bahamas* settled in 1666. *St. Helena* taken in 1651.

2. **Development of America.**
(*a*) *Virginia* colonized in 1607–10. Successful under Lord De la Warr.
(*b*) Farther north, *Pilgrim Fathers* left England (1620) under James I and sailed to *New England*. Under Charles I many more followed. Massachusetts chief colony. Consisted of Puritans flying from Anglican persecutions.
(*c*) *Maryland* founded (1634) by the Roman Catholic Lord Baltimore, as refuge for Roman Catholics.

(*d*) Under Charles II, first advance again in the south.

(i) Where the *Carolinas*, called after Charles, were founded (1663).

(ii) Then, in the north, settlements acquired from Dutch, by Treaty of Breda (1667), *New York, New Jersey*, and *Delaware*.

(iii) Then *Pennsylvania* founded by William Penn, the Quaker (1680), who fled from the persecutions under Charles II.

Thus the colonies stretched in a strip all along the seaboard, and consisted of persons of different religions, but all of English nationality.

Note 84 — THE REVOLUTION OF 1688

The revolution aimed at (1) maintaining the Protestant religion and State; (2) at ending the efforts of the Stuarts to rule arbitrarily. (What Charles II worked for secretly, James worked for openly.)

1. James II's Religious Policy.

(*a*) Had suppressed Monmouth's rebellion (1685), which aimed at a Protestant succession, with the greatest cruelty.

(*b*) Used his *dispensing* power to dispense with the Test Act, and appointed Roman Catholics as *judges*, and as *officers of the army*.

(*c*) Made Tyrconnel, a Roman Catholic, viceroy in Ireland.

(*d*) Appointed Roman Catholic to Deanery of Christ Church, Oxford, and put in Roman Catholic Fellows at Magdalen College, Oxford.

(*e*) Re-established the Court of High Commission to try ecclesiastical cases.

(*f*) Issued a Declaration of Indulgence and advised all Bishops and clergy to read it.

(*g*) Dismissed his moderate ministers and replaced them by Roman Catholics.

2. James and the Army.

Appointed Roman Catholic officers, raised the numbers of the army to 30,000, and brought troops to Hounslow Heath to overawe London.

3. James and Parliament.

He "dispensed" with the laws, thus completely setting aside all Parliamentary government. He began to prepare to "pack" Parliament by ordering Lords-Lieutenant to send him lists of suitable Roman Catholics and non-conformists to be elected members.

Finally, revolution made inevitable by the birth of a son (June, 1688), who would be a Roman Catholic. Hitherto heir had been the Protestant Princess Mary.

TIME CHART FOR PERIOD SIX (1603–1688)

	England, Scotland, Ireland.	Dates.		Other Powers.	Dates.
James I (1603–1625)	James I succeeded to throne; Millenary Petition.	1603			
	Hampton Court Conference.	1604			
	Gunpowder Plot.	1605			
	Colonization of Virginia.	1607			
	Plantation of Ulster.	1608			
				Murder of Henry IV of France; Accession of Louis XIII.	1610
	Dissolution of James I's First Parliament; Authorized Version of Bible.	1611			
				Marriage of Frederick, Elector Palatine, and Elizabeth, daughter of James I.	1613
	Death of Shakespeare.	1616			
	The Five Articles of Perth; Execution of Ralegh.	1618	Thirty Years' War.		
	Sailing of the *Mayflower*.	1620			
	James's Third Parliament meets; fall of Bacon.	1621			
	Visit of Charles and Buckingham to Madrid.	1623			
				Richelieu, Chief Minister of France (1624–42).	1624
	Marriage of Charles and Henrietta Maria.	1625			
Charles I (1625–1649)	War with France; Expedition to La Rochelle.	1627		War between England and France.	1627
	Petition of Right; Buckingham assassinated.	1628			
	Charles's 3rd Parliament dissolved; no Parliament for 11 yrs.	1629			
				Death of Gustavus Adolphus of Sweden at battle of Lützen.	1632
	Wentworth goes to Ireland; Laud Archbp. of Canterbury.	1633			
	Hampden's Case; New Prayer Book in Scotland.	1637			
	The National Covenant.	1638			
	First Bishops' War; English factory started at Madras.	1639			
	Short Parliament; 2nd Bishops' War; Long Parliament.	1640			
	Strafford executed; Irish Rebellion; Grand Remonstrance.	1641			
	Beginning of Civil War; Battle of Edgehill.	1642			
	Solemn League and Covenant.	1643		Accession of Louis XIV; Mazarin, Chief Minister (1643–61).	1643
	Battle of Marston Moor.	1644			
	Battles of Naseby and Philiphaugh; Laud executed.	1645			
	King surrendered to Scots.	1646			
	Second Civil War.	1648		Treaty of Westphalia.	1648

TIME CHART FOR PERIOD SIX (1603–1688) — *Continued*

Reign	England, Scotland, Ireland.	Dates.	Other Powers.	Dates.
Commonwealth and **Protectorate** (1649–59)	Execution of Charles; Cromwell in Ireland.	1649		
	Battle of Dunbar.	1650		
	Battle of Worcester; Navigation Act.	1651		
	First Dutch War.	1652		
	Expulsion of the Rump; Barebone's Parliament; Cromwell, Protector.	1653		
	First Protectorate Parliament; Peace with Dutch.	1654	Alliance between England and France; War with Spain.	1654
	Capture of Jamaica.	1655		
	Second Protectorate Parliament; Humble Petition and Advice.	1656		
	Blake at Santa Cruz.	1657		
	Capture of Dunkirk; Death of Cromwell.	1658		
	Richard Cromwell Protector.	1659	Peace between France and Spain.	1659
Charles II (1660–1685)	Declaration of Breda; Restoration of Monarchy.	1660		
	Corporation Act; Irish Act of Settlement.	1661		
	Act of Uniformity; Acquisition of Bombay; Dunkirk sold.	1662		
	Conventicle Act; Capture of New Amsterdam.	1664		
	Second Dutch War; The Plague; Five Mile Act.	1665		
	The Great Fire of London.	1666		
	Dutch in Medway; Treaty of Breda; The Cabal Ministry	1667		
	Triple Alliance.	1668		
	Treaty of Dover (Charles II and Louis XIV).	1670		
	Third Dutch War; Battle of Southwold Bay; Declaration of Indulgence.	1672	William of Orange becomes Stadtholder in Holland.	1672
	Test Act; Fall of Cabal.	1673	Murder of John and Cornelius de Witt.	1673
	Death of Milton; Peace with Dutch.	1674		
	Marriage of Princess Mary and William of Orange	1677		
	The Popish Plot.	1678	Treaty of Nimwegen between France and Holland.	1678
	Habeas Corpus Act.	1679		
	Dissolution of Oxford Parliament; Pennsylvania founded.	1681		
	Rye House Plot.	1683	Death of Colbert.	1683
James II (1685-8)	Monmouth's and Argyll's Risings; The Bloody Assizes.	1685	Revocation of Edict of Nantes.	1685
	Declaration of Indulgence.	1687		
	James Edward born; Trial of Bishops; William III arrives.	1688	Louis XIV invades Germany.	1688

EXAMINATION QUESTIONS ON PERIOD SIX
(1603–1688)

1. To what extent was the great Civil War the result of religious causes? (LGS 1935)

2. What were the aims of James I in his foreign policy? How far did he succeed in carrying them out? (LGS 1937)

3. Say what you can in favour of the foreign policy of James I. (LGS 1932)

4. Summarize the chief complaints of James I's Parliaments. How far were they justified? (OC 1938)

5. What can be said in defence of *either* the foreign policy *or* the domestic policy of James I. (OC 1936)

6. Give an account of the colonization of North America by the British in the reigns of James I and Charles I. (NUJB 1935)

7. What were the chief causes of the civil war? (NUJB 1939)

8. Give an account of the relations between King and Parliament between the accession of James I (1603) and the dissolution of Charles I's third Parliament (1629). (NUJB 1938)

9. Account for the defeat of the Royalists in the Civil War. (OC 1931; D 1932)

10. Account for the failure of the Commonwealth to survive. (OC 1938)

11. What were the chief difficulties which faced Cromwell as Protector, and how did he try to overcome them? (LGS 1932)

12. Show the influence of *either* Scotland *or* Ireland on English history between 1629 and 1660. (LGS 1936)

13. How much of the work of the Long Parliament was permanent? (OC 1939)

14. Describe the work of Oliver Cromwell after the death of Charles I. (LGS 1937)

15. What exactly were Cromwell's powers from 1654–58? Why did he fail to establish a permanent republican government? (B 1932)

16. State the main facts of Oliver Cromwell's dealings with (*a*) the Irish, and (*b*) the Scots. (NUJB 1936)

17. " The Restoration was a triumph less of the Monarchy than of the Church of England ". Explain this statement with reference to the period 1660–88. (CL 1932)

18. Describe the main events of the three Anglo-Dutch wars of the seventeenth century. (NUJB 1937)

19. Both Charles I and Cromwell found it impossible to govern with Parliaments. Why? (OC '32)

20. Was Charles II's foreign policy advantageous to England? (OC 1935)

21. What were the causes and results of the English naval wars with the Dutch? (OC 1936)

22. Give a brief history of religious affairs during the reign of Charles II. (LGS 1920)

23. What were Charles II's principal aims and how far was he successful in achieving them? (OC 1939)

24. Describe social life in town and country in the latter part of the seventeenth century. (B 1931)

25. The Revolution of 1688 was as important an event in European as in English history. Discuss. (LGS 1924)

26. Explain why Charles II succeeded in retaining his throne, and why James II lost it. (LM 1925)

27. Why and how did James II unite the most important sections of the English Nation against himself? (LGS 1937)

28. Charles II and James II both wished to rule as absolute monarchs. Explain (*a*) the means adopted by each for this purpose, and (*b*) why Charles II succeeded and James II failed. (NUJB 1937)

29. Describe the growth of the party system under Charles II. (LGS 1935)

PERIOD SEVEN

THE STRUGGLE WITH FRANCE AND THE GROWTH OF CONSTITUTIONAL MONARCHY

1688–1714

CHAPTER 43

WILLIAM AND MARY; AND ANNE

1. WILLIAM III (1689–1702) AND MARY (1689–1694)

The accession of William III and Mary marks what is known as the "peaceful" Revolution, for really it settled the question which had occupied the country throughout the period when Stuarts sat on the throne of England. Parliament had finally won in its contest with the Crown.

The details of the Revolution Settlement have now to be considered (*Note 85*). The great result of the Revolution upon our system of government was that henceforth the bulk of the king's revenue was obtained by *annual* grants from Parliament, and that Parliament had therefore to meet every year. As a consequence, Parliament acquired the complete control of finance, and, with that, an increasing control of the administration. Gradually, also, the relation between the two Houses of Parliament underwent alteration. The House of Commons has had, since 1407, the sole power to initiate Bills involving the grant of public money or the imposition of taxation, and in the reign of Charles II it denied the right of the House of Lords to amend such Bills. Consequently, with the increasing control of Parliament in financial affairs, the Lower House became the

Parliament and the control of finance

more important; though, as we shall see, individual members of the Upper House could, up till 1832, largely influence the composition of the House of Commons.

Moreover, as the result of the Revolution, two Acts were passed, the one at the beginning of William and Mary's and the other at the end of William's reign, which limited the power of the Crown. The *Declaration* or *Bill of Rights*, which was drawn up and passed through Parliament in 1689, completed the work which Magna Carta had begun. Its clauses may be briefly summarized. First, William and Mary were declared to be King and Queen, and the succession to the throne was settled upon their children, and, failing them, upon James's other daughter, Anne; and a clause was added that no person who was a Roman Catholic or who married a Roman Catholic could succeed to the throne.[1] Secondly, it declared to be illegal: (*a*) the " pretended power " of the Crown to suspend laws; (*b*) the power of dispensing with laws " as it hath been exercised of late " by the Crown; (*c*) the existence of the Court of High Commission and similar courts. Thirdly, Parliament was to be freely elected, to have freedom of speech and to meet frequently, and there was to be no taxation without its consent. Fourthly, a standing army was declared illegal. This clause is still in force, and the army is only made legal by an Act passed every year, called the Army (Annual) Act — and this is another reason why Parliament has to be called annually.

The Bill of Rights (1689)

The Protestant Settlement

Dispensing power abolished

Taxation

The Army (Annual) Act (1689)

The second measure was the *Act of Settlement*, passed in 1701. The first question to be arranged was that of the succession, for William and Mary were childless and all the children of the Princess Anne had died.[2] The Protestant representative of the House of Stuart who had the best claim

Act of Settlement (1701)

[1] It has been calculated that this clause has taken away the eventual claims to the succession of nearly sixty persons.

[2] The Duke of Gloucester, the only one to survive infancy, died in 1700 when nearly eleven years of age; eight months before his death he celebrated Queen Elizabeth's birthday in high spirits, " firing all his guns and making great rejoicing ". It may be noted that the birthday of the great Queen, 7th September, was kept as a national day of rejoicing throughout this period.

was Sophia, the granddaughter of James I (her mother was Elizabeth who married the Elector Palatine) and the wife of the Elector of Hanover. The crown was accordingly settled upon "the most excellent Princess Sophia, and the heirs of her body, being Protestants". With regard to the other clauses in the Act of Settlement, some were inserted because of William's personal unpopularity and because of the jealousy felt with regard to his foreign policy at that time. Thus the monarch was not to leave the kingdom without the consent of Parliament, and England was not to be obliged to engage in wars for the foreign possessions of the Crown. But these articles were soon modified or repealed. Two clauses are, however, of permanent importance. Henceforth judges could only be dismissed after being convicted in the Law Courts, or after an address by both Houses of Parliament — and the king, therefore, lost his power of dismissal which had been so useful in previous reigns. No pardon by the Crown could be pleaded to an impeachment by the House of Commons — a clause which finally established the responsibility of the king's ministers for all acts of state.

Hanoverian Succession

The judges

The ministers

Though the Crown still continued to select the ministers, and, in William's reign at all events, to control the home and foreign policies of the country, the Revolution had secured, therefore, for the individual Englishman his political liberty and for the Parliament which represented him complete control of taxation and, subject to the king's veto, of legislation. In two other respects the Revolution had important effects. Hitherto all publications had, under an annual *Licensing Act*, been subject to a rigorous censorship.[1] In 1695 the House of Commons decided not to renew the Act, and thus was secured the Liberty of the Press for which half a century previously Milton had ardently pleaded — though that liberty was still somewhat curtailed by the

Liberty of the Press (1695)

[1] In Charles II's reign printing was confined to London, York, and the two Universities, and the number of "master-printers" was only twenty. All new works had to be examined and licensed before they were published.

severity of the laws of Libel[1] and by heavy stamp duties upon newspapers. Secondly, something was done to make religious restrictions less severe (*Note 86*). By the *Toleration Act* (1689) liberty of worship was allowed to those who could subscribe to thirty-six of the thirty-nine Articles in the Book of Common Prayer, i.e. practically all except Roman Catholics and Unitarians. But the Nonconformists were still excluded from office under the Test and Corporation Acts passed in the reign of Charles II. The Toleration Act marked, nevertheless, a great advance, and from that time the feeling of tolerance steadily increased. After the accession of the House of Hanover in the eighteenth century an Act was annually passed excusing the Nonconformists from the penalties which they had incurred for holding any office. Complete toleration to all sects, including Roman Catholics, was not, however, to come till the nineteenth century.[2]

The Toleration Act (1689)

We must now say something about the details of the domestic history. William and Mary established their position with greater ease than might have been expected. The death of Dundee at the Battle of Killiecrankie (p. 546) and the flight of James to France after the Battle of the Boyne (p. 546) led to the submission of Scotland and Ireland. In England itself there was surprisingly little opposition. One of the Archbishops, four bishops, and four hundred other clergymen, known as the *Non-jurors*, refused to take the oath of allegiance to William and Mary, and consequently were deprived of their benefices — and that was all. Yet, though there was little opposition, there was also little loyalty to the new sovereigns. Statesmen and warriors were alike

Lack of loyalty to William and Mary

[1] These libel laws were mitigated by an Act passed in 1792.

[2] Though the Nonconformists obtained toleration, severe laws continued to be passed against the Roman Catholics. Thus in 1699 a law was passed rendering any priest liable to perpetual imprisonment for celebrating Mass; and a friar named Atkinson, who was convicted through the evidence of his serving-maid — she was rewarded with a gift of £100 — was imprisoned for thirty years at Hurst Castle, finally dying there in 1729 at the age of seventy-three. But these vindictive laws were not as a rule enforced by the Government, and the Roman Catholics, as a whole, were allowed to have their worship undisturbed.

faithless. Danby, who was the chief minister for five years, Marlborough, the general, and Russell, the victor of the Battle of La Hogue, all intrigued with James whilst holding office under William and Anne. Parliaments were often unfriendly, and there was one plot against William's life.[1]

Characters of William and Mary

No doubt Englishmen ought to have been grateful for the benefits of the Revolution, but perhaps their want of loyalty to William and Mary is not altogether surprising. The King himself was interested in foreign politics alone. England was to him merely a factor in his war with France; "he had", as a contemporary said, "to take England on his way to France". His individual opinions, moreover, were not likely to make him popular. In religion he was a Calvinist, and he was therefore distrusted by the very powerful High Church party in the Church of England. In politics, though the Tory opposition to the war compelled him in 1695 to depend for a time upon a Whig ministry — the Whig Junto, as it was called — yet for the greater part of his reign he tried to ignore parties, and to rule with ministers drawn impartially from Whigs and Tories; as a consequence, he obtained the hearty support of neither party. Nor was William's personality an attractive one. Diminutive in stature, thin and fragile-looking, his appearance was only redeemed by the brightness and keenness of his eyes. His manner was cold and repellent, and his habits unsociable;[2] and the few friends that he possessed were all Dutchmen. Moreover, his health was wretched, and inclined to make him irascible and peevish. William had none of the outwardly attractive qualities which would have secured the affection of his English subjects; and they failed to do justice to the magnanimity which he showed in dealing with his enemies, his patience and calmness in times

[1] The idea was to kill the King in a narrow lane near Turnham Green, as he was returning from his usual Saturday hunt; but the plot was discovered.

[2] "He spoke little and very shortly," said a contemporary, "and most commonly with a disgusting dryness." Long and solitary hunting expeditions in the New Forest were his only recreation, and he disliked conversation and all indoor games.

of crisis, or the unwearying industry which he displayed in public affairs. Mary, on the other hand, was an affable, kind-hearted, genial queen; it was a saying at the time that "she talked as much as William thought, or her sister, the Princess Anne, ate". Mary's death, in 1694, was consequently a great blow to William's position, and after that his unpopularity steadily increased.

The Opposition to William after 1697

After the conclusion of the war with France, in 1697, opposition to William's policy came to a head. A *Tory Parliament* attacked — with some reason — the enormous tracts of land which the King had granted to his Dutch favourites in Ireland. Moreover, a standing army was still very unpopular, and Parliament insisted — with great stupidity — upon reducing the armed forces in England to seven thousand men. Then, again, Parliament was jealous of his foreign policy, and consequently passed those clauses in the Act of Settlement to which reference has already been made. William, indeed, was so worried by the Opposition that he seriously thought of resigning his crown, and had even drafted a proclamation for that purpose. Englishmen, in truth, were somewhat ignorant of foreign politics; and the greatness of the work accomplished by William, not only for England, but for Europe, was never realized. The King, however, had the satisfaction before his death of feeling that the nation was strongly supporting him in the War of the Spanish Succession, the opening of which he just lived to see (1702).

Financial Features of Reign: (1) The National Debt (1693)

Two features in our National Finance make their appearance during the reigns of William and Mary. The first was the *National Debt*, which dates from 1693. By 1697 it had reached £20,000,000; by 1713, £78,000,000; and by 1815 it was to rise to the stupendous total of £840,000,000.[1] The

[1] The National Debt helped to rivet the Commercial Classes to the Revolution Settlement, because it was thought that if the Stuarts returned they would repudiate the Debt. It therefore helped to cause the alliance between the Whig aristocracy and the merchants, as both depended for their power or prosperity in the eighteenth century on the Hanoverian dynasty.

Government borrowed money to finance the wars, and citizens lent that money in return for interest. This gave the people of the country a very sound investment for their savings, while it also enabled the terrible burden of the wars to be spread out, and prevented that burden from crushing out all trade and industry. The other was the *Bank of England*, which was founded in 1694, and which gave a solid foundation to England's commercial and imperial development in the next century. In 1695 occurred the *restoration of the currency*; the old money, which was much worn, and was often "clipped" round the edges, was called in, and a new coinage was issued, whose milled edges made clipping impossible in the future.

(2) Foundation of Bank of England (1694)

2. A PERIOD OF FOREIGN WARS (1689–1714)

The Revolution of 1688 ushered in a period of prolonged conflict for Great Britain. Between 1688 and 1815 she was engaged in a series of seven great wars, which occupied no less than fifty-six years. Of these wars five begin and the other two end as wars in which Great Britain's chief opponent is France, and we must try to understand the general causes of the hostility between these two countries before examining the particular causes of each war (*Note 88*).

The conflict with France (1689–1815)

First of all, there were the ambitions of France in Europe. France wanted to extend and to strengthen her eastern frontier with the ultimate object of making the River Rhine her boundary.[1] This could only be accomplished at the expense, in the south-east, of the German States and, in the north-east, of the Netherlands. The Netherlands were divided. Part of them, called Holland or the United Provinces, was independent: part of them, corresponding to the modern country of Belgium, belonged to the King of Spain up till 1713, when it came under the rule of Austria,

[1] The Rhine, the frontier of old Gaul, was the great object of French ambition. An old proverb ran —

Quand Paris boira le Rhin
Toute la Gaule aura sa fin.

and was thenceforward called the Austrian Netherlands. The frontier between France and what is now Belgium was no natural boundary, such as a river or a range of mountains, but on each side of it had been built a great chain of forts known as the "Barrier Fortresses". Those on the Belgian side were slowly and steadily passing into the hands of France as she pushed her frontier forward. Once they were all, or nearly all, in her hands, France might be able to seize not only Belgium, but Holland as well. But with the independence of Holland, England's own fortunes were linked. The French, if they obtained outlets in the North Sea, would threaten our maritime position and thus our national security. For that reason England insisted that the "Barrier Fortresses" should be garrisoned wholly or in part by soldiers from Holland.

The Barrier Fortresses

The ambitions of France were not only concerned with the acquisition of the Rhine frontier. At various times between 1689 and 1815 her rulers attempted, if not to annex the country, at all events to control the policy of Spain by means of a close family alliance or a treaty. Moreover, Louis XIV (1643–1715) at the beginning, and the French revolutionaries and Napoleon (1793–1815) at the end, of the period had achieved a position in Europe which threatened the independence of all other States.

France and Spain

The causes of this constant warfare between England and France were not, however, solely European. The ambitions of France and of England clashed, as will be shown later, throughout the world. In India and in the West Indies, in North America and in North Africa, a great struggle had to be contested to decide between their competing ideals of expansion. And if contemporary statesmen, with rare exceptions, attached more importance to the European than to the Imperial aspect of the struggle, to us to-day it is the struggle for Empire that must always possess the greater interest.

World ambitions

We must now deal with the wars in detail. And first we

will take the two wars that were fought between 1688 and 1713. The position of Louis XIV in 1688 was unique. His army, although it had been engaged in continual wars, had suffered no serious reverse in battle for over forty years, and his navy was equal to those of Holland and England combined. In Louvois the King possessed the best war minister, in Vauban the best engineer, and in Tourville the best admiral of the age; and though Condé and Turenne, his greatest generals, were dead by 1689, he still had Luxembourg and Villars. With such resources at his command, Louis, during his reign, had added to his dominions many of the frontier fortresses in the Netherlands already referred to, and, farther south, Alsace, Franche Comté, and the great fortress of Strasbourg. He was threatening further annexations at the expense of the Netherlands and of Germany. The English kings, Charles II and James II, had been his pensioners, and he had hopes of securing for his family the succession to the throne of Spain. The Revolution in England, however, ruined the plans of Louis XIV. To a king of England who was dependent upon Louis for money and upon his ambassador for advice succeeded William III, the ruler of Holland, one whose whole life had been devoted to resisting France. William had already in 1688 formed a League against France, and the support of England in 1689 was the coping stone to that alliance. "Without the concurrence of the realm and power of England," said William later, "it was impossible to put a stop to the ambitions and greatness of France."

The position of Louis XIV

The war which followed is known in Continental history as the *War of the League of Augsburg* (*1689–97*). To us it is better known as the *War of the English Succession*, for Louis XIV was supporting James II, and therefore its issue decided whether William or James was to be king of England. For the first two years of the war (*1689–90*) English military operations were confined mainly to the British Isles and to the sea (*Note 88*). In Scotland, John

The War of the English Succession (1689-97)

The war from 1689-90

Graham of Claverhouse, Viscount Dundee, raised the Highlanders on behalf of James, and routed, in the space of two minutes, just beyond the Pass of *Killiecrankie*, William's forces under the leadership of Mackay (June, 1689). In the battle, however, Dundee was mortally wounded, and with his death all the energy was taken out of the movement, which quickly subsided.

(a) In Scotland: Battle of Killiecrankie (1689)

Meantime, in Ireland, James II arrived with French money and troops. In Ireland the situation was far more serious than in Scotland, for, in addition to the bitter religious feeling, there was the racial hatred between the Irish inhabitants and the English and Scottish settlers. A war between Catholics and Protestants at once broke out. The Protestants in the North were attacked and the two Protestant strongholds, *Londonderry* and *Enniskillen*, besieged. But the Protestants in Londonderry held out heroically for one hundred and five days till they were relieved, whilst those in Enniskillen attacked their besiegers and won the Battle of *Newtown Butler*.

(b) In Ireland: the Siege of Londonderry (1689)

Subsequently William himself came to Ireland, and won a victory at the *River Boyne* (1st July, 1690). The battle was notable for the variety of nations engaged in it. Of James's forces, over a third were French, and the commander-in-chief was a Frenchman. On William's side, about half were natives of England, and, of course, he had many Irish Protestants from the north of Ireland and some two thousand Dutchmen fighting for him; the rest of his force included Huguenots, Prussians, Danes, and Finlanders. James shortly afterwards fled back to France, and in 1691 the war in Ireland came to an end. John Churchill, the future Duke of Marlborough, had a brilliant campaign, and took Cork and Kinsale, whilst Ginkel, a Dutch general, won a desperate battle for William at *Aughrim*. A few months later, in the autumn of 1691, *Limerick*, the last great Catholic fortress, surrendered, and with its capitulation William's position in Ireland was secure.

Battle of the Boyne (1690)

(c) On the Sea

On the sea, in these two years, Louis XIV missed his chances. With a superior fleet, and with the best admiral of the day in Tourville,[1] he should, according to military historians, have isolated Ireland from England so as to give every assistance to James; instead of which William was allowed to pass over to Ireland unmolested, and his communications were never threatened even for an hour.

Battle of Beachy Head (1690)

Tourville, however, on 30th June, 1690, the day before the Battle of the Boyne, met at *Beachy Head* a combined Dutch and English fleet under Lord Torrington. The latter, who was inferior in force, wished to refuse battle with his van and centre and to fight only a rearguard action.[2] But the impetuous Dutch van insisted on fighting, and were very severely handled; and had Tourville followed up his victory, the result might have been disastrous.

The war from 1691-97: (a) On the Sea

Battle of La Hogue (1692)

During the rest of the war (*1691–97*) England obtained the supremacy at sea. In 1692 came the victory off *La Hogue*. Tourville, on this occasion vastly inferior in force, had fought with credit a rearguard action against the English admiral, Russell. But, after the battle, the French fleet had to retire in some disorder, and many ships retreated through the dangerous "Race of Alderney", which is between that island and the mainland. Thirteen of the French ships, however, were unable to get through, took refuge at La Hogue, and were burnt by Russell's fleet. That victory, received in England with tremendous and perhaps exaggerated enthusiasm, saved England from fear of invasion, and gave to her the command of the Channel.[3]

[1] Tourville had served in the French fleet for thirty years, and had seen service in the Anglo-Dutch wars and against the Barbary pirates. He was a practical seaman as well as a good tactician; indeed it was a saying at the time that he could act in any capacity from a ship's carpenter to an admiral.

[2] The Government had information that the enemy's ships-of-the-line numbered only sixty, and ordered Torrington with his fifty ships to engage them. Torrington counted with his own eyes — or rather with his one eye, as he had lost the other in an explosion — eighty ships of the enemy, and was unwilling to fight, but he had to obey orders.

[3] "During several days," says Macaulay, "the bells of London pealed without ceasing. Flags were flying on all the steeples. Rows of candles were in all the windows. Bonfires were at all the corners of the streets. And three Lords took down with them £37,000 in coin to distribute among the sailors."

The French, however, then took to commerce-destroying and did considerable damage, especially when they captured one hundred out of four hundred ships of a convoy bound for Smyrna. In 1694 an interesting event occurred. William sent a fleet to the Mediterranean, where it saved Barcelona from capture and consequently Spain from French control, and by wintering at Cadiz and returning to the Mediterranean in the next year exerted considerable influence upon the course of the war.

(b) In the Netherlands

On land during these years (1691–97) the English operations are confined to the Spanish Netherlands. The war was chiefly a war of sieges. William as a soldier was painstaking but mediocre; his opponent, Luxembourg, was brilliant but indolent. Consequently William generally lost the battles; but Luxembourg took no advantage of his victories. William's designs were excellent. Thus he tried to surprise Luxembourg at *Steinkirk* in 1692; but he wasted time by a preliminary cannonade of artillery which lasted one hour and a half, and by an elaborate deployment of infantry which was already late in arriving. Luxembourg, though genuinely surprised, marshalled his troops with great rapidity and won a victory. In the next year (1693) William was beaten at *Neerwinden*. But by sheer tenacity and strength of purpose he clung on, and two years later he won his first great success by recapturing the strong fortress of Namur.

The Treaty of Ryswick (1697)

Finally, by 1697, France was exhausted. She had been fighting a coalition of Great Britain, Holland, Spain, the Empire, and some of the German States. Now she could not continue the struggle, and at the *Treaty of Ryswick* she recognized William as King of England, and gave up all her conquests since 1678 except Strasbourg. The war had been an uninteresting one. The English had, however, done well. They had secured the supremacy at sea. They had learnt some valuable lessons under William's leadership, lessons whose effect was to be shown in the subsequent wars under

Marlborough. They had secured an honourable treaty, and, above all, had helped to inflict the first decided check on the ambitions of Louis XIV.

The Spanish Succession and the Partition Treaties (1698-1702)

We turn now to the causes of the next war — *the War of the Spanish Succession.* That two monarchs should arrange for the distribution of the territories belonging to a third monarch in anticipation of his death and without consulting either him or his ministers seems an indefensible proceeding. Yet this is what happened in 1698. The circumstances were, it is true, peculiar. The Spanish dominions included not only Spain, but the Spanish Netherlands, Milan and Naples, Sicily and Sardinia, besides vast possessions in the West Indies and South America. Charles II, the King of Spain, had no children or brothers, but he had two sisters and two aunts. Of the two aunts, the elder had married the French king, and the younger the emperor. They were all dead, but their respective sons, Louis XIV and the Emperor Leopold I, had married, the one the elder and the other the younger of the two sisters of the Spanish King.[1] Thus the children of Louis and of Leopold combined both sets of claims. Here was a difficult situation. It was quite obvious that neither Louis XIV nor Leopold nor their eldest sons could be allowed to add the enormous territories of Spain to those either of France or Austria. It was hopeless to deal with Charles II, who was sickly and half-witted. Consequently Louis XIV and William III proceeded to draw up Partition Treaties by which a baby, the grandson of Leopold (child of his daughter Maria) and the heir to the Electorate of Bavaria (but, of course, not heir to the Empire), was to succeed to the greater part of the Spanish dominions (1698).

First Partition Treaty (1698)

Second Partition Treaty (1700)

Unfortunately the Bavarian baby died of smallpox. Another treaty was accordingly drawn up (1700), under which the Archduke Charles, the *second son* of the emperor, was to obtain the bulk of the Spanish inheritance, but the Dauphin of France was to have Naples and Milan.[2] It is

[1] See table on p. 405. [2] Milan was to be exchanged for Lorraine.

hardly a matter for surprise that the King of Spain, when he heard of these Partition Treaties, flew into a violent passion, and that his queen smashed some of the furniture in her room. Charles II of Spain subsequently sickened, and on his deathbed was persuaded to leave all his possessions to Philip of France, the *second* son of the Dauphin (1700). Louis XIV, after some hesitation, accepted the will and threw over the treaty. Philip was therefore declared King of Spain. A Bourbon had displaced a Habsburg, and Louis XIV might well have said — as he is wrongly reported to have said — "Henceforth there are no Pyrenees."

The will of Charles II (1700)

Louis XIV's acceptance of the will would not, in itself, however, have produced the war, for, after all, it was his second and not his eldest grandson that succeeded. Other actions of the French King made war inevitable (*Note 88*). In the first place, he expelled the Dutch from the Barrier Fortresses, which they garrisoned, and substituted French troops, and thus showed his intention of making a further advance in the Netherlands. Secondly, he expressly reserved the rights of Philip to the French throne. Philip's elder brother was delicate and not expected to live long, and Philip might therefore succeed not only to Spain but to France as well. Thirdly, he showed by his policy that he was attempting to secure for France the commercial concessions which England had obtained for trade with Spanish America. Finally, on James II's death, in 1701, he recognized James's son — the "Old Pretender" as he is called — as James III, King of England. For Louis XIV, after recognizing William's title at the Peace of Ryswick, to support the Pretender four years later, was the one thing needed to make England as enthusiastic as William for renewed war. The war, therefore, broke out in 1702, but William died before he could take any part in the fighting.

Causes of renewal of war

3. REIGN OF QUEEN ANNE (1702–1714): THE GREAT WAR

The Princess Anne succeeded to the throne, under the terms of the Bill of Rights, on William's death in 1702. The chief part of her reign was to be occupied by the great War of the Spanish Succession which now broke out.

The reign of Queen Anne (1702–14)

To summarize a war which lasted for over ten years, and which was fought in Italy and Germany, in the Netherlands, and in Spain, is no easy task. At the opening of the war, England, Holland, Austria, and most of the German States were on one side, and they were joined later by Portugal and Savoy; on the other side were France, Spain, and Bavaria. The great figure in the war, so far as the Allies were concerned, was *John Churchill*, created *Duke of Marlborough*. Born in 1650, he had seen service in Holland as a colonel in the French service during Charles II's reign,[1] had subsequently by his coolness saved the situation at Sedgemoor in that of James II, and had undertaken some very successful operations in the south of Ireland under William III. No one can deny either his avarice or his faithlessness. He deserted James II twice. He betrayed, it is said, the secret of two expeditions to Louis XIV in William III's reign, and in one year was concerned in two plots against him. He was consequently dismissed from his appointments, and he did not recover favour till towards the close of William's career. Yet, though faithless in his political principles, his military friendship with Prince Eugene, the most famous of the other allied generals, and his political friendship with Godolphin, the English minister at home, showed that in his relations with individuals no one could be a more loyal or more admirable colleague. Moreover, he was not only a great general, but a great diplomatist as well — the best of his age, according to Voltaire. Strikingly handsome, with a manner described by a contemporary as irresistible, he

The War of the Spanish Succession (1702-13)

Marlborough (1650-1722)

[1] Turenne, the French general, is said to have called him "the handsome Englishman", and to have won a bet that Churchill would recover a post with half the number of men who had failed to defend it.

needed all his powers of negotiation during each winter, so that he might induce the allies to furnish him with adequate forces during the following summer.

His tactics

As regards Marlborough's tactics, military critics agree in praising the effective use which he made of all arms. He insisted upon accuracy in infantry shooting, and taught all ranks to fire simultaneously and not, as the French did, consecutively. He made the cavalry, after the example set by Rupert and Cromwell, rely on the momentum of their charge rather than on their firing, and he showed great capacity in utilizing them at the critical moment with decisive effect. He handled the artillery with remarkable skill, more especially at Blenheim, where every gun was laid under his own eye. No less praiseworthy was the quickness with which he saw the weakness of an enemy's position; of this quickness the best example was perhaps at Ramillies. As a strategist, Marlborough was superb. Many of his schemes were upset because of the opposition of the Allies, and more especially of the Dutch; but those that he carried into execution show that Marlborough deserves the distinction of being called the greatest general that this country, or, if we may believe Bolingbroke, any other country, has produced. At all events, of hardly any other general can it be said, as it can be said of Marlborough, that he never fought a battle which he did not win, or besieged a place which he did not take.

Marlborough's objects

In order to understand Marlborough's operations, it must be remembered that, at the opening of the war, the French were in possession of the Spanish Netherlands. Marlborough's earlier campaigns, therefore — with the exception of the greatest of them all, that of Blenheim (1704) — had for their objective the expulsion of the French from the Spanish Netherlands. The later campaigns aimed at the conquest of the French barrier fortresses with a view, finally, to an advance into the interior of France.

In the first two years of the war (1702–3) no big engage-

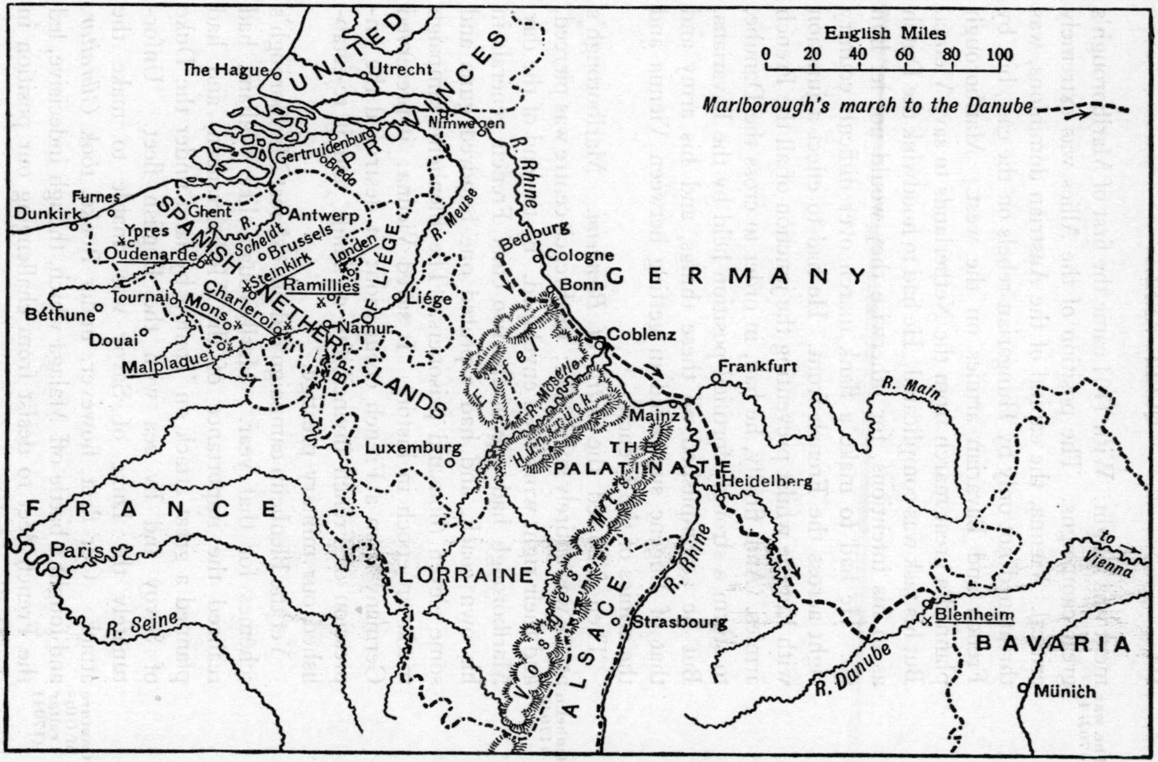

MARLBOROUGH'S CAMPAIGNS

The war (1702-4)

ment was fought. With 1704 came the first of Marlborough's great campaigns. The position of the Allies was extremely critical. Vienna, the capital of the Austrian dominions, was threatened not only by Hungarian rebels on the east, but by French and Bavarian armies on the west. Marlborough planned a great march from the Netherlands to save Vienna. But his task was complicated. He had to hoodwink the Dutch as to his intentions, for otherwise they would not let him go. He had to make a flank march over difficult country right across the French front. He had to effect a junction with Eugene whilst preventing the junction of all the French armies. And, finally, he had, in order to cross the Danube, to storm a strongly fortified position held by the Bavarians. But he accomplished all these things, and his army and that of Eugene succeeded in getting between Vienna and the armies of the French.

Blenheim (1704)

Then followed the *battle of Blenheim.* Marlborough's attack was entirely successful; the French centre was pierced, and their right wing then enveloped. By the end of the day Marlborough had one of the two chief French generals in his own coach, and had captured one hundred guns and some eleven thousand prisoners. The Blenheim campaign marks an epoch in history. It saved Vienna; it preserved Germany from a French occupation; it destroyed the impression of French invincibility on land; and it re-established our military prestige.

Yet the Blenheim campaign did not exhaust Marlborough's schemes for that year. Marlborough, like William, had realized the importance of the Mediterranean, and had planned a great attack on Toulon by land under the Duke of Savoy and by sea with the English fleet. Unfortunately the Duke of Savoy was unable to make the attack. Our fleet, however, under Rooke, took *Gibraltar*, and fought a battle off Malaga which, though indecisive, led the French fleet to desist from challenging our position in the Mediterranean.

Capture of Gibraltar (1704)

The next important year is *1706*. First, the French were evicted from Italy in consequence of a great battle won by Eugene near Turin. Then, in the Netherlands, Marlborough won the battle of *Ramillies*. He was threatening the strong fortress of Namur, and the French general had concentrated his forces to protect it. In the battle which ensued Marlborough won a victory which he followed up with such rapidity, that by the end of the year the French had lost not only Antwerp and Brussels, but nearly the whole of the Spanish Netherlands.

Battle of Ramillies (1706)

The third success of the Allies in 1706 was won in Spain. Two years previously the Allies had determined to attempt to put the Archduke Charles on the Spanish throne. At first not much was done, but in 1705 Peterborough captured *Barcelona*[1] by a brilliant feat of arms, and occupied Catalonia and Valencia. In 1706 the Allies under Galway marched from Portugal and occupied Madrid, whilst Peterborough and his army marched from the east and effected a junction. Later in the year, however, Madrid had to be evacuated, and the joint army retreated to Valencia. But the year had been so disastrous to Louis XIV, that he offered terms of peace that the Allies would have done well to accept.

The war in Spain (1705-6

The year *1707* was a set back to the Allies, as Eugene failed in an attempt to invade France, Marlborough could do nothing in the Netherlands, and in Spain Galway was severely defeated at *Almanza* owing to the flight of the Portuguese contingent, which left the English to contend against a force three times their number. In the following year (*1708*), however, Marlborough won another great victory at *Oudenarde*, which led to the practical completion of the capture of the Spanish Netherlands and also to the

Oudenarde (1708)

[1] The evidence for this and other achievements of Peterborough depends upon the *Memoirs* of Captain Carleton, which were for long accepted as genuine by historians, and which were edited in 1809 by Sir Walter Scott. It was later proved, however, that these memoirs are fictitious, and that they were written probably either by Defoe or Swift, and there is good reason for thinking that the credit for the capture of Barcelona really belongs to Peterborough's subordinate officers.

capture of Lille, one of the most important of the French barrier fortresses. Moreover, the English captured *Minorca*, and by so doing secured what was most important — a harbour in the Mediterranean in which a fleet could winter; whilst stormy weather led to the failure of a French expedition which was sent up the Firth of Forth to capture Edinburgh. Louis again offered peace, and was prepared to preserve for Philip only Naples and Sicily. The terms he offered now were actually far better than those the Allies were in the end to obtain. The Allies insisted that he should also, if necessary, assist them in expelling Philip from Spain by force. Such a proposal naturally not only infuriated the French King, but the French nation as well, and gave them both fresh energy for the war. And then, in *1709*, came the last and the most costly of Marlborough's victories, *Malplaquet*, and the capture of Mons.

Capture of Minorca (1708)

Malplaquet (1709)

Our great series of successes ended with Malplaquet. French enthusiasm revived. The Allies became slack, and a Tory Ministry in favour of peace succeeded to power in Great Britain. This Ministry dismissed Marlborough in 1711, and Ormonde, his successor, was given instructions — which he was to keep secret from the Allies — not to undertake offensive operations.[1] In Spain the Allies, though they managed temporarily to occupy Madrid, were defeated in two battles in *1710*; and the accession in the following year of the Archduke Charles to the Austrian dominions, and his election as Emperor, altered the whole situation.

Recovery of France (1710-13)

Now that, in 1711, the Archduke Charles had succeeded to all the Austrian dominions, it was absurd for Great Britain to go on fighting in order that he might succeed to the Spanish dominions as well. But the difficulty was that our allies, the Dutch and the Austrians, would not agree to a peace. What then was Bolingbroke, the joint

[1] This was perhaps the most dishonourable action ever done by a British Government. Ormonde, in obedience to instructions from home, finally withdrew his forces altogether, though there was a brilliant opportunity of defeating the French.

head of the Government, to do? He had already begun to open up negotiations with France behind the back of the Allies, and these were now continued. Eventually in 1713 a series of treaties was signed at *Utrecht*.[1] By these treaties Philip kept Spain and the New World, but was excluded from the succession to the French throne (*Note 89*). The Emperor Charles was given the Spanish dominions in Italy and the Netherlands. The Dutch were allowed to garrison the Barrier Fortresses. With regard to Great Britain, the Protestant succession was recognized. She obtained from France Newfoundland (leaving to the French certain fishing rights which were the cause, later, of many difficulties) and Nova Scotia, and from Spain Gibraltar and Minorca, thereby establishing her position in that sea which has been called the "keyboard" of Europe. Spain also gave to Great Britain the monopoly of the slave trade with Spanish America — not then regarded as either inhuman or wicked — and the right to send one ship a year to Porto Bello in the Spanish Main.

The Treaty of Utrecht (1713)

Great Britain had therefore gained her original objects in going to war. She had made, moreover, very important additions to her Empire; and there is some truth, if also some exaggeration, in the verdict of an historian that if at the Armada England entered the race for colonial expansion, she won it at the Treaty of Utrecht. Further, the peace, though it checked French ambitions, was not a vindictive one against France, and therefore that country did not, after it, harbour the desire for a future "war of revenge". Englishmen must remember, however, to their shame that the people of Catalonia, who had fought bravely for the Allies throughout the war, were left to the vengeance of Philip — and a terrible vengeance it proved to be.

[1] Treaties were signed between France, Spain, Holland, and England at Utrecht in 1713, but the treaty between France and Austria was made in the following year at Rastadt.

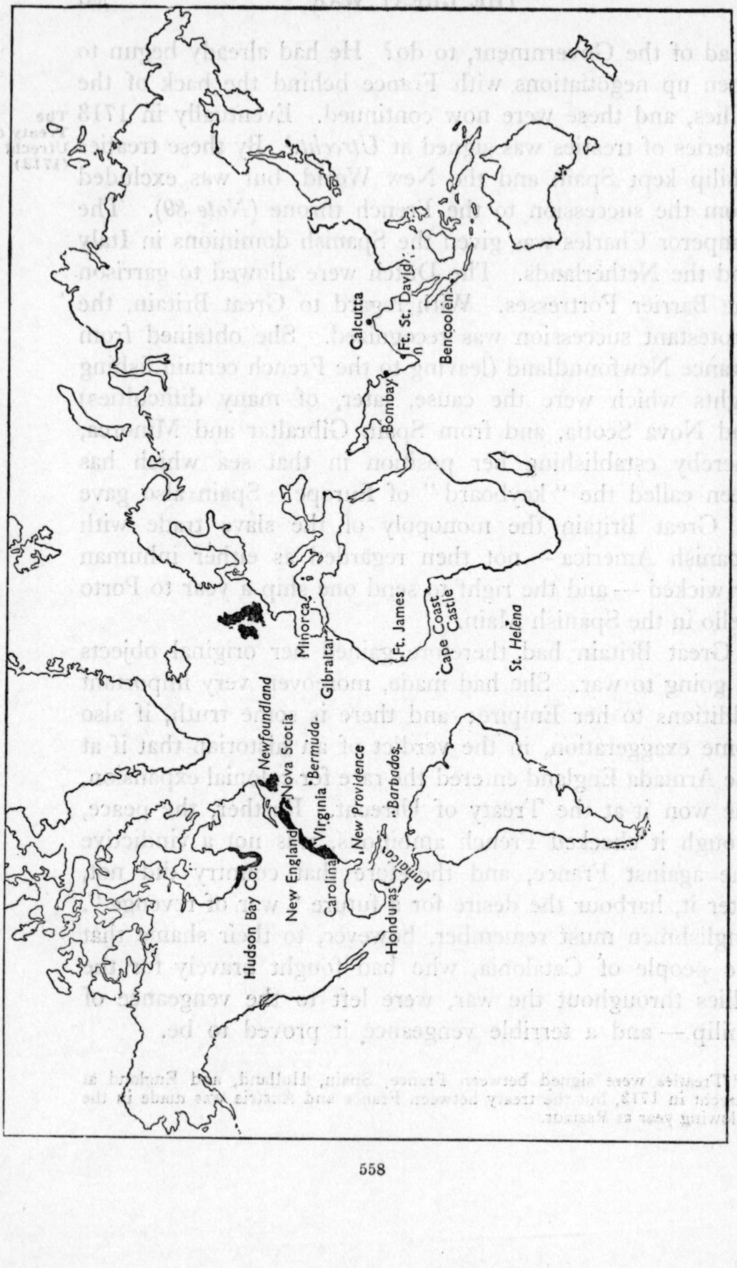

THE BRITISH EMPIRE IN 1714

4. DOMESTIC AFFAIRS UNDER ANNE

The Union with Scotland (1707) — perhaps the most important event in Anne's reign—will be discussed later (*Note 91*). The history of the domestic politics whilst Anne was Queen remains to be narrated. Two features deserve special notice. One is the fierceness of the party strife, especially towards the close of the reign, when it extended even to the ladies of the two parties, who, it is said, patched upon different sides of their faces, and had different designs upon their fans. It is to the struggle over the Exclusion Bill in Charles II's reign that these two great parties, known as Whigs and Tories — nicknames given to those parties by their respective opponents — owe their origin, and in Anne's reign the differences between them were sharply defined (*Note 92*). The Whigs were in favour of Toleration, whilst the Tories were strong upholders of the Church of England, and were jealous even of the liberties which the Dissenters had recently acquired under the Toleration Act. The Whigs upheld the constitutional government that had developed as a result of the Revolution, but the Tories still had ideas of divine right and passive obedience. The Whigs supported the War of the Spanish Succession, the Tories, on the other hand, in the earlier stages of the war, wished it to be chiefly maritime, and in the later stages were opposed to it altogether. Finally, whilst all the Whigs were in favour of the succession, on Anne's death, of the Electress Sophia of Hanover and her son George, many of the Tories favoured James II's son.

Whigs and Tories

The other feature to be noticed in Anne's reign is the close connection between politics and literature. In those days the reporting of speeches in Parliament was forbidden, whilst the age of public meetings had not begun. But the increased interest that was being taken in public questions and the increased importance of Parliament made it neces-

Politics and literature

sary for the rival parties to influence the country; and this was done through the papers and pamphlets of the great literary men of the period. Thus *Addison*, a Whig and the editor of the *Spectator*, eventually became a Secretary of State, though he never opened his mouth in the House of Commons; whilst *Swift*, a Tory and a clergyman, composed pamphlets which had enormous political influence, and, when towards the end of Anne's reign the Tory party was in power, used to dine every week with the two leaders of the Government, in order to assist in formulating their policy.

Godolphin's ministry (1702-10)

There were two ministries during Anne's reign. The first was under the leadership of *Godolphin*, who was in close alliance with Marlborough. Of the latter something has been said already. Of the former Charles II once remarked that "little Sidney Godolphin was never in the way and never out of the way". He seems to have been a shrewd statesman, though his personality has left curiously little impression. At first the members of the Government were drawn from both parties, but the growing hostility of the Tories to the war led to the ministry becoming increasingly, and in 1708 completely, of a Whig complexion. Two of the Tories who were dismissed in 1708 were *Robert Harley* and *Henry St. John*, both of whom immediately began to scheme the overthrow of the ministry.

Godolphin's ministry has justly been called "one of the most glorious in English history", for under its rule occurred the great achievements of Marlborough and of Peterborough, the captures of Gibraltar and Minorca, and the Union with Scotland.

Causes of its fate

Godolphin's Ministry came to an abrupt termination in 1710. The causes were many. The war was becoming unpopular, and it was urged with some force that Great Britain should have accepted the terms of peace offered by Louis XIV in 1706, and the still more favourable offers of 1709. Moreover, Marlborough was ambitious to be made

Captain-General of the British forces for life — an ambition which frightened Englishmen into thinking that he wished to be a second Cromwell and which therefore brought unpopularity on the Whig ministers though they had not supported the proposal.

Then, again, the Queen became hostile to the ministry. Though she was a person of no intellectual attainments, and appears to have had little influence in the actual administration of her Government, she was extremely popular with all classes for her kindness of heart, and because, as she said of herself, she was "perfectly English".[1] She disliked a purely Whig ministry, and she could not forgive the Whigs for their attacks upon her husband, Prince George of Denmark, whilst he was alive, or for their suggestion, soon after his death, that she should take thoughts of a second husband. Moreover, the Queen was very subject to the influence of those of her own sex. For some time the influence of the Duchess of Marlborough had been supreme. The Duchess was a very self-willed, masterful, and somewhat quarrelsome lady; about 1708 she quarrelled with the Queen, as she did subsequently with her son-in-law, her granddaughter, and even her doctors.[2] Mrs. Masham (Abigail Hill) who had strong Tory connections,[3] succeeded to the first place in the Queen's affections, and the change was ominous for Godolphin's ministry.

Queen Anne

Sarah Churchill, the Duchess of Marlborough

Above all, Anne was a strong supporter of the Church of England; and it was the cry of "the Church in danger"

[1] The Queen had no taste for literature and music, and for some years never heard even her own band play. But she was fond of hunting, and in her later years used to follow the stag-hunt in Windsor Forest in an open chaise drawn by one horse, "which she drives herself", wrote Swift, "and drives furiously, like Jehu".

[2] The duchess got a portrait of her granddaughter, blackened its face, and hung it up with the inscription: "She is much blacker within". In 1740 she had lain a great while ill, without speaking. Her physicians said: "She must be blistered, or she will die." She then called out: "I won't be blistered, and I won't die." And, as a matter of fact, she was not blistered, and she did not die — till four years later.

[3] She was a cousin of Harley's and to him she owed her introduction into the royal circle.

that finally brought about the downfall of the Whigs. A certain Doctor Sacheverell, whose chief recommendations to favour were a fine presence and a good voice, preached a sermon before the Lord Mayor, in which he advocated Passive Obedience, said that the Church was in danger of schism, and attacked the ministers, calling them amongst other things "wiley Volpones", in allusion to a nickname of Godolphin. The Government was foolish enough to take notice of the sermon and impeached the doctor. There was great popular excitement. The Queen, on her journey to the trial at Westminster Hall, was greeted with shouts of "We hope Your Majesty is for the Church and Doctor Sacheverell". Sacheverell became a popular hero and was acclaimed by cheering mobs, and after the trial was over — as a result of which he was sentenced to a light punishment [1] — he had a triumphal progress through the provinces on his way to Shropshire.[2] The Queen then took action. The Whigs were dismissed and the Tories were called to office. Parliament was dissolved and in the new House of Commons there was a large Tory majority (*Note 92*).

The Sacheverell trial

Whig ministry falls (1710)

This rise to power of the Tories was important, for it was to affect the history of the next reign (George I). The two leaders of the party were Harley (created *Earl of Oxford*) and St. John (created *Viscount Bolingbroke*). These two were really opposed to each other, and their intrigues in the end were to ruin their party and drive the Hanoverian heirs to depend upon the Whigs. Harley possessed personal courage and was a great patron of literature — his famous collection of manuscripts, now in the possession of the British Museum, is priceless. In politics he was

Tory ministry (1710-4); Harley and St. John

[1] He was forbidden to preach for three years — a possibly agreeable punishment.

[2] The Sacheverell case is interesting as being one of the earliest political movements in which ladies took an active share, and the ladies were enthusiastic admirers of the doctor. "Matters of government and affairs of State", wrote a contemporary, "are become the province of the ladies. They have hardly leisure to live, little time to eat and sleep, and none at all to say their prayers." The Duchess of Marlborough, however, did not agree with her own sex in the matter — she described Sacheverell as an "ignorant and impudent incendiary"

a moderate. Hence he was liable to be accused of being irresolute in his decisions and dilatory in their execution. This moderation led him also sometimes to be shifty in his dealings with his Tory colleagues, and not averse to negotiations with his political opponents. Hence he has been called the " mole " in the politics of that day, because he was always burrowing. Bolingbroke has been described as a " brilliant knave ". No one will deny his brilliancy. Swift said that he was the greatest young man he knew. Pope went further and declared him to be the greatest man in the world, whilst Pitt said that he would rather recover one of his speeches than " all the gaps in Greek and Roman lore ". His style provided a model for Gibbon the historian, and his political ideas were not without their influence upon statesmen who lived so recently as Disraeli. His knavery is more open to doubt, but it is certain that his actions and policy were not quite so disinterested and straightforward as he makes them out to be.[1] Bolingbroke was impetuous, and a strong party man; and he soon supplanted Harley in the affections of the Tories. " Members ", said Bolingbroke of the House of Commons, " grow fond like hounds of the man who shows them sport, and by whose halloa they are wont to be encouraged." And Harley was too fond of running with the hare to be able to cheer on his followers.

Measures of ministry: Occasional Conformity and Schism Acts

The Tory ministers proceeded to secure the objects which their supporters had most at heart. They tried to strengthen the Church and to weaken the Nonconformists by passing the *Occasional Conformity* (1711) and the *Schism Acts* (1714). The first Act was directed against the habit of the Nonconformists of qualifying for office by taking the Communion every now and again in an Anglican Church, and thus evading the Test and Corporation Acts; the second Act tried to deprive the Nonconformists of their hold upon education by forbidding anyone to teach without a licence

[1] " Ah, Harry," his father is reported to have said to him after he went to the House of Lords, " I always said you would be hanged, but now you are made a peer, I suppose you'll be beheaded."

from a bishop. To make the war unpopular Swift's genius was employed in the composition of pamphlets such as "The Conduct of the Allies", and Marlborough himself was dismissed from his employments, accused of peculation, and attacked with such violence that he left the country. The war, conducted half-heartedly for a year or two, was, as we have seen, terminated in 1713 by the Treaty of Utrecht (*Note 89*).

Then came the question of the *Succession to the throne*. The peaceful succession of the House of Hanover has been called the "greatest miracle in our history"; if it was not that, it was undoubtedly at one time unlikely. The majority of the people were probably Tory in sentiment, and would have preferred a Stuart, especially as the Electress Sophia of Hanover and her son George, if not unpopular, were completely unknown in England.[1] Men known to be supporters of the Stuart succession were put into positions of trust by the ministry, the Earl of Mar, for instance, being given control of Scotland, and the Duke of Ormonde being made Warden of the Cinque Ports. Two things, however, prevented the continuance of the House of Stuart on the throne of England. In the first place, James the Second's son, James Edward, the Old Pretender as he was called, refused — and it was greatly to his credit — either to change or to dissemble his Roman Catholic religion. Consequently in England the Tories found themselves torn between their affection for the Anglican Church and their allegiance to the Stuart dynasty, while the Scottish nation was divided into those who had a passionate romantic loyalty to the Stuarts and those whose devotion to Protestantism made support of a Roman Catholic an impossibility.

The succession question

The Religion of the Stuarts

In the second place, Anne died too soon. There were dissensions between the Tory leaders, but Bolingbroke

[1] Of course, by the Act of Settlement the Princess Sophia was the successor to the throne, but Queen Anne, beyond inserting her name in the Liturgy, did nothing to recognize her claim, and never invited the princess to England or gave her a title.

The death of Queen Anne

managed to get rid of Harley, who was dismissed from the ministry. It is uncertain what Bolingbroke really intended, but it is probable that he was working for the succession of the Old Pretender. Events, however, moved too quickly for him. Two days after Harley's dismissal Anne fell very seriously ill. A council meeting was summoned to discuss the situation. Two Whig dukes who were Privy Councillors suddenly entered the meeting and, as they were legally entitled to do, took part in the discussion. As a result, it was resolved that the Treasurer's staff — the symbol of authority — should be given to Shrewsbury, a moderate Whig, and Anne, on her deathbed, gave it to him. On Anne's death, whilst the plans of Bolingbroke were still undeveloped, George I, through Shrewsbury's influence, was proclaimed King (the Electress Sophia being dead). Had the Queen lived six months, or even six weeks, longer, our history might have been very different.

5. SCOTLAND UNDER THE LATER STUARTS

Condition of Scotland in 1689

The condition of Scotland on William III's accession was deplorable. It was rent by religious feuds. There was little wealth and few industries, and every bad harvest produced a famine. The Lowlands suffered from the depredations of the Highlanders — and even as late as 1747 it was reckoned that £5000 worth of cattle were annually "lifted", whilst another £5000 were paid by various owners to save their cattle from that fate. The Highlands were in a barbarous condition; the chief had almost supreme authority over the members of his clan;[1] and plunder, it has been said, was at once "the passion, the trade, and the romance of the Highlander".

The reigns of William and Mary and of Anne mark the beginning of a happier and more prosperous period for

[1] Some chiefs had a private executioner of their own; and the town of Perth, in 1707, sent a request to Lord Drummond for the occasional use of his executioner — a request which was very courteously granted.

Scotland. One fearful atrocity, it is true, was committed. The Battle of Killiecrankie (p. 546) and the death of Dundee (1689) did not at once terminate hostilities, and some of the clans still refused to recognize the new sovereigns. At last a proclamation was issued, promising pardon to all who took an oath of allegiance to the new Government before the last day of 1691. Only two chiefs had not taken the oath by the appointed day, and of these, one, Macdonald of Glencoe, failed merely because he had made it a point of honour to delay till the last possible moment, and had then gone to the wrong place to take the oath. Sir John Dalrymple, the joint Secretary of State, was completely out of sympathy with the Highlanders, and determined to make a signal example of the people of Glencoe. Troops were sent there commanded by their hereditary enemy, Campbell of Glenlyon, who, after being entertained by the Macdonalds for a fortnight, suddenly made an attack upon them and brutally murdered the chief and thirty-seven of his clan (1692).

The Glencoe massacre (1692)

The condition of Scotland, however, rapidly improved after the Revolution of 1688. The Bank of Scotland, founded in 1695, was an incentive to trade; the Habeas Corpus Act, passed in 1701, and similar to that passed in England thirty years before, protected the liberty of the individual. But to three things, above all, did Scotland owe her prosperity. In the first place, Presbyterianism, the religion of the great majority, was made, in 1689, the established religion, whilst the Episcopalians obtained toleration. Hence Scotland obtained what she most needed — the cessation of religious strife — though a small sect of Presbyterian extremists refused to enter the Establishment, and persisted in demanding the enforcing of the Solemn League and Covenant. Secondly, a law was passed in 1696 establishing schools in every parish, and Scotland, long before England, enjoyed a widespread measure of education.

Causes of improvement

Thirdly, the Union between England and Scotland was

achieved in 1707 (*Note 91*). There had been great difficulties in the way. English merchants did not wish to give commercial concessions or English Churchmen to recognize Presbyterianism. Scotland was legitimately proud of her nationality and had no wish to have her individuality absorbed in that of England. And, moreover, Scotland attributed to English jealousy and deliberate obstruction the failure of an attempt made by her merchants in 1698 to develop a trading centre at the Isthmus of Darien (now Panama). It gradually became clear, however, that the slender monarchic union would have to be either broken, or very considerably strengthened. Endless complications might arise when Anne died. After long negotiations the Union was at last completed. By its terms Scotland was allowed forty-five members in the House of Commons and sixteen peers in the House of Lords; she contributed one-fortieth to the Land Tax and was paid nearly £400,000 for sharing in the English National Debt. Scotland was to preserve her own Law Courts, whilst a separate Act secured her Presbyterian church. Above all, free trade was established between England and Scotland, and Scotland was allowed to trade with the colonies. Scotland was at last given her industrial opportunity, and soon her shipping and manufactures proved formidable rivals to the shippers and manufacturers of England. Moreover, no one can fail to realize the immense share Scotsmen have had in developing the British Empire.

The Union between England and Scotland (1707)

The Darien Scheme (1698)

The Terms of the Union

Effects of the Union

Yet the Union was not popular for some time. In Scotland, during the Rebellions of 1715 and 1745, one of the cries was for the abolition of the Union. In England the Scots were long unpopular, and at the beginning of George III's reign Bute's Scottish ancestry was one of the causes of his great unpopularity when Prime Minister. But gradually the national prejudices faded away, and the natives of both countries learnt to appreciate the immense advantages each derived from the Union. Henceforth the histories of England and Scotland are linked together.

NOTES ON PERIOD SEVEN (1688–1714)

RULERS OF ENGLAND AND SCOTLAND

WILLIAM AND MARY (1689–1694)
WILLIAM III (1694–1702)
ANNE (1702–1714)

IMPORTANT FOREIGN RULERS

FRANCE:	LOUIS XIV (1643–1715)
SPAIN:	CHARLES II (1665–1700)
	PHILIP V (1708–1746) — first of the Bourbon Kings of Spain.
EMPIRE:	LEOPOLD I (1657–1705)
	JOSEPH I (1705–1711)
	CHARLES VI (1711–1740)
BRANDENBURG:	FREDERICK I (1688–1713)
SWEDEN:	CHARLES XII (1697–1720)

NOTE 85. — EFFECTS OF THE REVOLUTION OF 1688

1. Parliament really gained the upper hand, for

(*a*) *King's revenue now granted annually*, hence Parliament had to meet every year.

(*b*) House of Commons denied right of Lords to amend money Bills. *Appropriation of Supplies* meant that money must be spent on purpose for which it was voted.

2. Power of the Crown limited by two very important Acts.

(*a*) **Bill of Rights** (1689).

(i) Crown could only be held by a Protestant.

(ii) Declared illegal the "suspending" or "dispensing power" lately claimed by the Crown.

(iii) All prerogative courts illegal.

(iv) *Parliament* to be freely elected, have freedom of speech, and no taxation without its consent.

(v) Standing army illegal — this provision was contained in the corollary *Mutiny Act*, which said that troops could not be kept under arms for longer than twelve months. (To this day an annual Army Act has to be passed.)

(*b*) **Act of Settlement** (1701).

(i) Settled the Crown on Protestant line (i.e. the *Protestant* grand-daughter of James I, Princess Sophia, wife of the Elector of Hanover. Other claimants who were Roman Catholics were thus disqualified.

(ii) Judges only to be dismissed after address by both Houses of Parliament.

(iii) No pardon by Crown could be pleaded for impeachment — this made ministers responsible.

(iv) Persons holding office of profit under the Crown might not sit in Parliament (repealed in 1706). Kings must not involve Britain in war to defend other possessions.

Neither of these last two provisions was kept. *Ministers* (who hold offices of profit) are in the House of Commons and owing to this can defend measures there and are responsible for presenting measures. William III and George II both involved England in foreign wars which were largely fought over foreign possessions.

(*c*) *Triennial Act* (1694) ordered General Election every **3** years (now is 5 years). Thus, the Crown was no longer independent of Parliament, for had to ask annually for money; the army was under Parliament's control through need for annual Act; the King's ministers were responsible to Parliament; and the judges were independent of the Crown.

NOTE 86. — EFFECTS OF THE REIGN OF WILLIAM III

1. (*a*) **Religious Toleration** began. William resolved on toleration and passed the Act of Toleration (1689) — allowing freedom of worship.

(*b*) **Freedom of Press** helped, as "Licensing Bill" no longer renewed, so censorship abolished.

2. Finally **put an end to "Divine right"**, for William and all subsequent kings owed their throne to the decision of Parliament, embodied in the Act of Settlement.

3. "Whigs" had called William to power, so **a period of Whig rule followed,** which encouraged commerce as the Whigs tended to be supported by commercial classes, Tories by landlords.

4. **England drawn into continental struggle against France,** as William being ruler of Holland was resolved to save Holland from France. (Some historians say that for the first time foreign policy was the only interest of the reign.)

NOTE 87. — WILLIAM III AND SCOTLAND AND IRELAND

1. The Scots accepted the Revolution.

(*a*) They recognized William as King, and he recognized Presbyterianism as religion of Scotland (1688).

(*b*) Some of the Scots, under Graham of Claverhouse, rose for James II, and won battle of *Killiecrankie* (1689). Later, rebellion collapsed.

(*c*) Amnesty offered to all by a certain date. *Macdonald of Glencoe* late in accepting amnesty; *Massacre* of Glencoe (1692) brought about by their neighbouring foes, the Campbells. William was blamed, but probably never understood what was being done.

2. The Irish stood by James II, who landed with French troops (1689).

(*a*) Ireland rose for him. *Londonderry* and *Enniskillen*, loyal to William, and besieged (1689).

(*b*) 1690. William went to Ireland and won *Battle of the Boyne* James returned to France — and died there in 1701.

(*c*) *Treaty of Limerick* (1691), promised Irish Catholics the same privileges they had under Charles II. Not kept. Roman Catholics excluded from Irish Parliament, and

(*d*) Protestants passed the Penal Code which forbade Roman Catholics to own land, or belong to professions, and all priests "banished" from land (latter never enforced).

NOTE 88. — ENGLAND AND THE WAR OF THE SPANISH SUCCESSION (1702–1713)

1. Why England entered the War.

(*a*) To check absolute preponderance of France, which would have followed had Louis gained control of Spain.

(*b*) To safeguard English trade, which was threatened by Louis who sent French troops to take the Netherlands and Italy, and who granted France privileges in trading with these countries.

(*c*) To prevent restoration of the Stuarts, which was favoured by France as Louis recognized the son of James II (the "Old Pretender") as King of England.

2. England's Part in the War.

(*a*) **Drove the French out of Holland.** This was achieved as follows:

(i) 1702. Marlborough defended the Dutch frontier against the French.

(ii) *Austria saved* by *Battle of Blenheim* (1704) when Marlborough drove French army from Vienna and drove them back over the Rhine. He was supported by Austrians, under Prince Eugene. Bavaria, France's ally, forced to make peace.

(iii) *Marlborough* won *Battle of Ramillies* (1706), took 8 great fortresses from France, and conquered part of the Spanish Netherlands (Belgium).

(iv) Won *Battle of Oudenarde* (1708) and took Lille. Won *Battle of Malplaquet* (1709) and took Mons, the last great fortress in French hands. Way open to France itself.

(*b*) **For a time won Spain** for the Imperial candidate, Charles III. Gibraltar captured (1704). Barcelona and Madrid taken (1706). Finally English defeated at *Almanza* (1707). Minorca captured (1708). English lost Madrid (1710).

(*c*) **Gained Supremacy at Sea.**

(i) Admiral Rooke destroyed the Spanish treasure fleet at Cape Finisterre (1703).

(ii) Britain by capture of *Gibraltar* (1704) and *Minorca* (1708) gained control of Mediterranean.

The wars checked Louis's ambitions, saved Holland, and indirectly helped Great Britain, but the nation had been unwilling to go to war, and grew tired of it.

Note 89. — CLOSE OF THE WAR OF SPANISH SUCCESSION

Attempts of Louis to obtain Peace.

(*a*) 1706 *after Ramillies* Louis offered terms of partition. Charles to have Spain; Philip of France to have Italian possessions. Rejected.

(*b*) 1708 *after Oudenarde* Louis offered to withdraw his support of Philip. Rejected by Whigs, who demanded that he should make war on Philip.

(*c*) 1709 *after Malplaquet* Louis offered to help allies with money against Philip, but would not declare war on him. Rejected by Whigs.

Treaty of Utrecht (1713) ended the war. It was brought about because nation was tired of war, and the Whigs falling from power, the Tories, who were a " peace party ", made peace at once.

(Tories dismissed Marlborough and negotiated peace with France without consulting their allies).

The results of the war were:

1. *France* kept her early conquests, including *Alsace*, and Louis's grand-son became King of Spain, as Philip V.
2. *Holland* recovered her territory and her safety was guaranteed by the line of great barrier fortresses. Saved from French conquest.
3. *Spain* accepted Philip of France as King; gave up Italian possessions and the Spanish Netherlands. *Thrones of France and Spain never to be united.* (This had been one of chief causes of war.)

4. *Austria* gave up claim to Spanish throne, but got instead Milan, Naples, and the Spanish Netherlands.

5. *Great Britain* gained:

(*a*) Gibraltar and Minorca in Europe.

(*b*) Nova Scotia, Hudson Bay Territory, and Newfoundland in America.

(*c*) Commercial treaties with Spain and Holland. By Spanish *Treaty of Assiento* England could supply Spanish colonies with slaves.

(*d*) Recognition by France of the Protestant succession and Pretender expelled from France.

Thus, comparing the gains with the causes, Britain really achieved her objects, for aggression of France was defeated, and both France and Holland were so exhausted by the struggle that Britain which had suffered far less, went ahead commercially and politically, owing to her immense gain in prestige due to Marlborough's victories.

NOTE 90. — FINANCE AND COMMERCE UNDER THE LATER STUARTS

As the *Whigs* had brought about the Revolution of 1688, they gained long ascendancy. Being supported largely by the commercial classes, great attention was paid to commerce.

1. **Bank of England** founded (1694) by Paterson, encouraged by Montagu, the Chancellor of Exchequer. Government borrowed $1\frac{1}{4}$ millions, and subscribers of this formed a company. Government paid interest on the loan, guaranteed the Bank, and gave it a Charter.
   This helped British finance and commerce, as it enabled money to be loaned for great undertakings, with security.

2. **National Debt** funded (1693). Montagu arranged that the money for the enormously expensive wars should be borrowed from business men, but *capital not to be repaid*, only annual interest paid, and guaranteed by Government.

   (*a*) This meant that expenditure on wars was spread out: if it had been raised and paid for out of taxes, taxation would have been so heavy that all trade and industry would have been ruined.

   (*b*) The loans provided a perfectly safe investment, and encouraged people to save.

   (*c*) So many people lent money to the Government in this stock that great stability was gained for the Protestant rulers, as any restoration of the Stuarts might have meant repudiation of the money loaned to William's Government.

3. Great attention paid to Britain's commercial interests in the policy of the Government. Thus, at Utrecht (1713) Britain gained by commercial clauses. She also gained by the subordination of the Dutch to the English in the war.

4. **Darien scheme** (1695–1700) by Scots to form an overseas trading company. Object to buy trade concession at " Darien ", i.e. Isthmus of Panama. Failed. This made Scots readier for Act of Union, to enable them to share in English trading concession.
5. Restoration of the **currency;** old money called in, and new money was " milled " round the edge, which prevented clipping.

NOTE 91. — ACT OF UNION WITH SCOTLAND, 1707

One of the most important events of Anne's reign. Hitherto countries only united by the Crown. Hence the Scots could not share, e.g. in trading companies.

Under the Commonwealth Scotland was united to England and shared in benefits of English trade. On the Restoration of Charles II, this Union was ended.

Scotland had passed its Habeas Corpus Act and founded its own Bank of Scotland. Had established toleration in 1689. In 1696 set up " public " schools.

Events leading up to Union.

1. After Revolution of 1688, Scots did not accept English settlement of succession.
2. In 1703 Scots passed *Act of Security*. English succession of Anne only to be accepted by Scots if England granted free trade with Scotland and allowed Scots to control own affairs. Bill vetoed by Anne.
3. In 1704 Scots again passed Act of Security — now accepted by Anne.

Act uniting England and Scotland passed in 1707.

One *Kingdom of Great Britain* formed, with one sovereign and one Parliament.

Formerly opposed because England did not want to recognize Presbyterianism as State religion of Scotland, nor grant commercial privileges.

Terms of Act:

1. Scotland given 45 members in Commons, 16 peers in Lords (her peers elected by the other Scottish peers).
2. Scotland to contribute one-fortieth of land tax.
3. Scotland kept her own law courts, and her own laws (Scottish Law differs from English Law, and is based on Roman Law).
4. Presbyterianism recognized as State religion of Scotland.
5. Free trade established between the two countries.
6. Scotland to be allowed to trade with the English colonies.

NOTE 92. — GROWTH OF PARTIES UNDER LATER STUARTS

1. **Origin of Parties.** Grew up under *Charles II*. Shaftesbury reckoned the first party leader.

(*a*) *Whigs* opposed Charles II, for they objected to French alliance and dreaded Catholicism. Worked up feeling over Popish Plot (1678), in order to secure exclusion of James.

(*b*) *Tories* believed in " divine right " and passive obedience. Supported Crown and Church of England.

(Names came from Whigs, a term used in Scotland for strong Presbyterians; Tories used to denote Irish Roman Catholics.)

2. Parties under William and Mary (1688–1702).

Both parties invited William to England, as Tories driven to oppose James II's Roman Catholic policy (1688).

(*a*) *Tories* opposed the (Dutch) war with France, and wished for neutrality. Hence Tory ministers dismissed by William (1696); opposed toleration and wished to maintain privileges of Church of England. Stood for power of Crown.

(*b*) *Whigs* supported the war and wished for Dutch alliance. Supported toleration for Dissenters. Stood for power of Parliament.

(*c*) *Both parties* united to pass Act of Settlement (1701) which settled the Crown on Protestants.

3. Parties under Queen Anne (1702–1714).

Note: Anne's Ministries at first contained members of both parties. Marlborough and Godolphin at first reckoned as Tories, gradually became Whigs.

(*a*) *Tory Ministry* (1702–8).

1702–4. Tory Ministry, with a few Whigs. War of Spanish Succession. Tories gradually ceased to support war.

1704–6. Moderate Tories in office, extreme Tories dismissed. Marlborough's influence supreme through his wife's friendship with the Queen. War successfully waged.

1706–8. Whigs given posts in Ministry. Union with Scotland strengthened Whigs (1707).

(*b*) *Whig Ministry* (1708–10).

(i) All Tories resigned. Marlborough supreme. War continued.

(ii) Gradual unpopularity of war. Sarah Churchill displaced in Queen's favour by Abigail Hill (Mrs. Masham), a Tory.

(iii) Quarrel over the Church. *Sacheverell* incident lost the Whigs the Queen's support (1709).

(*c*) *Tory Triumph* (1710–14).

Harley (Earl of Oxford) and St. John (Bolingbroke) in office.

(i) Peace made at Utrecht (1713). Marlborough dismissed.

(ii) Non-conformists attacked, Schism Act passed.

(iii) Tories began to work for *succession of Stuarts* to the throne, with safeguards against arbitrary rule. " Old Pretender " came over in secret to see Anne.

TIME CHART FOR PERIOD SEVEN (1688–1714)

Sovereign.	Great Britain.		Dates.		Other Powers.	Dates.
William III (1689–1702) and Mary II (1689–1694)	Bill of Rights; Toleration Act.	War of English Succession,	1689	or War of League of Augsburg.		.
	Battle of the Boyne; Battle of Beachy Head		1690			.
			.			.
	Massacre of Glencoe; Battle of La Hogue.		1692			.
	National Debt funded.		1693			.
	Death of Mary; Bank of England started.		1694			.
	Darien Scheme.		1695			.
			.			.
			1697		Peace of Ryswick.	1697
			.		First Partition Treaty.	1698
			.			.
	Death of Duke of Gloucester (heir to throne).		1700		Charles II of Spain dies; 2nd Partition Treaty.	1700
	Act of Settlement; Death of James II.		1701		Prussia becomes a Kingdom, Frederick I.	1701
Anne (1702–1714)	Godolphin's Ministry.	War of Spanish	1702	Succession.		.
	Scottish Act of security vetoed.		1703			.
	Scottish Act of Security passed; Blenheim.		1704			.
			.			.
	Battle of Ramillies.		1706			.
	Act of Union between England and Scotland.		1707		Death of Aurangzeb, Great Mogul.	1707
	Battle of Oudenarde; Minorca captured.		1708			.
	Battle of Malplaquet.		1709			.
	Tory Ministry under Harley and St. John.		1710			.
			.		Charles VI becomes Emperor.	1711
			.			.
	Treaty of Utrecht.		1713			.
	Death of Anne.		1714			.

EXAMINATION QUESTIONS ON PERIOD SEVEN

(1688–1714)

1. Did William III's foreign policy prove of benefit to England? (OC 1936)

2. State the terms of the Treaty of Utrecht. Why was it important? (LGS 1936)

3. How did the Revolution of 1688 affect (*a*) Scotland, and (*b*) Ireland? (LGS 1937)

4. Give an account of the work of the Duke of Marlborough. (NUJB 1937)

5. What were the chief changes in the constitution affected by (*a*) the Bill of Rights; (*b*) the Act of Settlement? (OC 1935)

6. Write a short account of *two* of the following: (*a*) the economic development in the eighteenth century of the British colonies in North America; (*b*) the English woollen industry in this period; (*c*) the establishment of the Bank of England; (*d*) enclosures in England in this period. (NUJB 1938)

7. Why did England take part in the War of the Spanish Succession? (OC 1938)

8. Describe the rivalry between Whig and Tory parties in the reign of Anne and George I. (NUJB 1938)

9. Describe the series of Acts passed on the accession of William III for securing the liberty of the subject. (LGS 1920)

10. Account for and describe William III's long struggle to weaken the power of France. How far was his object attained? (OL 1927, '28)

11. Trace the growth of the principle of religious toleration during the seventeenth century. (LM 1921)

12. What justification can be urged for the participation of England in the War of the Spanish Succession? (LM 1923)

13. What were the conditions leading up to the Union of the English and Scottish Parliaments? (LGS 1937)

14. Why did Britain enter the War of the Spanish Succession? What did she gain by doing so? (LGS 1937)

PERIOD EIGHT

THE EXPANSION OF BRITAIN AND THE FINAL CONTEST WITH THE CROWN

(1714–1783)

CHAPTER 44

THE HANOVERIAN DYNASTY

1. DOMESTIC POLITICS AND THE FIRST TWO GEORGES

On the death of Anne, the Elector of Hanover became King, and ascended the throne as George I.

George I (1714-27), and George II (1727-60)

The new dynasty cannot have been said to have presented the nation with a very attractive monarchy in its first two Kings. A contemporary said of George I that "he had no notion of what was princely"; whilst George II was somewhat coarse, occasionally irritable, and not over-generous — he only made one present to Walpole, who was his minister for fifteen years, and that was a diamond with a flaw in it. Neither of the two Kings was much interested in science, art, or literature.[1] Both of them quarrelled with their eldest sons.[2] But whilst George I quarrelled also with

[1] There is a story that George I, when congratulated by some courtier on becoming King of England, said: "Rather congratulate me in having Newton for a subject in one country and Leibnitz in the other." But the story lacks confirmation, and there is no reason to suppose that George I realized the greatness either of the discoverer of the law of gravitation or of the inventor of the differential calculus.

[2] George I was so much displeased with his son, the future George II, that he appears to have entertained a suggestion that the son should be seized and sent to America, "where he should never be heard of more"; for Queen Caroline, George II's wife, found in George I's cabinet after his death a letter from the First Lord of the Admiralty containing this proposal.

his wife and kept her in prison for over thirty years, George II was very much attached to Queen Caroline (she died in 1737), who was indeed a remarkable woman, keenly interested in the philosophy and literature of her time, and exercising considerable influence upon politics.

Both George I and George II, however, possessed characteristics which should have appealed to their new subjects. They were keen soldiers. George I began his fighting career at the age of fifteen, and commanded the forces of the Empire for a short period during the War of the Spanish Succession, whilst George II led a great cavalry charge at Oudenarde, and, donning the same old uniform thirty-five years later, fought like a lion at Dettingen. Both Kings were truthful and trustworthy, loyal to their friends and not vindictive to their opponents. Moreover, it is very greatly to their credit that, though they were absolute rulers in Hanover, they never overstepped the constitutional limits imposed upon them in Great Britain, and they had the good sense to rely for counsel in British affairs upon their British advisers and not upon any German ministers or favourites. It was hardly to be expected that George I, who came to the throne at the age of fifty-four and did not know a word of English, should understand or care for British politics; he spent half his time in Hanover, and his influence in Great Britain was small. George II, though also devoted to Hanover, knew more of Great Britain, and, as he possessed shrewdness and common sense, was a factor of considerable importance in domestic affairs.

The Whig Government (1714-20)

The accession of George I in 1714 made the Whigs supreme. The Tories were tainted with Jacobite sympathies, and for forty-five years (till after the accession of George III) the Whigs remained in secure possession of the Government. The Whigs had an immense majority in the first Parliament of George I, and they carried through some notable measures. First, they introduced greater *toleration*, by repealing the persecuting Acts of Anne's

Tory ministers (the Occasional Conformity and Schism Acts). Then, hoping to gain security, they passed the *Septennial Act* (1716) which allowed Parliament to sit for seven years. This was clearly better than the limit of three years imposed in the reign of William.[1] Parliament, as a result of the Revolution of 1688, had obtained control of legislation and taxation. William III, however, as has been pointed out, chose his own ministers and directed both the home and foreign policy of the nation; and even Anne often presided at meetings of the cabinet [2] — as the meetings of heads of departments came to be called — and directly appointed the ministers. But with the accession of the House of Hanover came a great change, and it may be convenient here to summarize the chief features of the constitution during the hundred years after 1714 (*Note 93*).

The Prime Minister

"The Act of Settlement had given us," it has been said, "a foreign sovereign; the presence of a foreign sovereign gave us a Prime Minister." George I could not speak English — Walpole, after 1721 the King's chief minister, had to brush up his Latin in order to converse with the King in that language — and George II only spoke it with a strong German accent; while neither of the two Kings was sufficiently interested in or intimate with British politics to comprehend its details. Consequently neither of them attended cabinet meetings; and George III, when he came to the throne in 1760, was unable, despite his desire, to do so owing to the precedent set by his predecessors. Hence it was natural that one minister should preside over the cabinet and direct its proceedings; and gradually it came about that he and not the King appointed his colleagues to

The cabinet system

[1] This arrangement held good till 1911, when the life of a Parliament was changed to five years.

[2] The privy council had grown too large for consultative purposes; consequently an inner royal council had developed, which was first called a "cabinet" in the reign of Charles I. After the Revolution the cabinet became an established institution. A statesman of Anne's reign illustrated the difference between the privy council and the cabinet thus: "The privy council were such as were thought to know everything and knew nothing, while those of the cabinet thought that nobody knew anything but themselves."

the ministry, and that he obtained the title of Prime Minister. Moreover, the King, as he was not present at the cabinet meetings where the details were discussed, gradually lost the power of deciding on what was to be done. He would be told that such and such had happened, and that the advice of his minister was to do this. If he did not understand, or were careless, or not interested, he agreed without further comment. Gradually, the other characteristics of our present system of cabinet government were evolved: ministers were chosen from the same party; they became jointly responsible for the policy pursued; and they became dependent for the continuance of their power, not upon the king, but upon the House of Commons. Hitherto the Crown had decided, though the ministers might be consulted; but as time goes on the position is reversed — the ministers decided, though the Crown might be consulted. Moreover, the Crown ceased to refuse its assent to bills passed by Parliament, Anne being the last sovereign who exercised this right.

The King's ministers

We must beware, however, of two mistakes in tracing the history of cabinet government. In the first place, we must not antedate its full development. In the eighteenth century, for instance, the leader of the ministry would have repudiated the title of Prime Minister owing to its unpopularity. Members of a cabinet not infrequently gave individual and contradictory advice to the king and seldom retired from office at the same time. Moreover, the Crown was still a very great force and still a real factor in the administration of the country; indeed, it might be said that the ministers of the eighteenth century had to serve two masters — the Crown and a majority of the House of Commons. And when there was no disciplined or organized party, as happened especially in George III's reign, the monarchy counted for a great deal in politics.

Slowness of its development

In the second place, it must not be imagined that the power which the Crown lost was gained by the people, that monarchy gave way to democracy. Britain in the eighteenth century, it has been said, was ruled by a "Venetian oligarchy". It was an oligarchy not, indeed, as exclusive, but almost as omnipotent, as in that famous republic, although its power was based, not, as in Venice, on the wealth derived from commerce, but mainly on the power derived from the possession of large landed estates. Educated at one of the large public schools, intermarrying with one another, meeting each other constantly in the small and exclusive society of the London of that day, a few family clans composed in the main the governing classes of the period. The leaders of such families as the Pelhams, the Russells, and the Cavendishes were found constantly in the higher, and their relatives in the lower posts of each Government. In one cabinet half the members were dukes, and in another there was only one commoner. This landowning oligarchy not only at times "encircled and enchained the throne", but to a large extent dominated the House of Lords, and possessed enormous influence in the House of Commons. **Power of the aristocracy**

The House of Commons was, up till the passing of the Reform Bill in 1832, a very undemocratic body. The representation was most unequal; Cornwall, for instance, because it was a royal duchy and therefore subject to the Crown influence, returned as many members as the whole of Scotland. In the English and Welsh counties the franchise was limited to freeholders, namely, those who owned their own land — not, of course, a large number. In the English and Welsh boroughs the franchise was confined to members of the corporation; in the city of Bath, for instance, the number of voters was only thirty-five. Moreover, whilst towns becoming so important as Manchester or Birmingham had no representatives at all, there were a great many small and insignificant boroughs, with a very few voters, which returned one and sometimes two members. Many of these boroughs were either "rotten" or "pocket" boroughs. A "rotten" borough was generally sold to the highest bidder, very often **Composition of the House of Commons** **"Rotten" and "Pocket" boroughs** some rich merchant.[1] A "pocket" borough belonged to an individual, generally a neighbouring landowner, who nominated a member to represent it. In the middle of the eighteenth century it was said that no less than fifty members of the House of Commons owed, in some measure, their seats to the influence of the Duke of Newcastle, whilst, a little later, Sir James Lowther (Lord Lonsdale) practically nominated nine members, known as "Sir James's Nine-pins", who had to vote as he directed.[2]

In Scotland the electoral system was just as unrepresentative. The county of Bute possessed but twelve voters, whilst in the burghs the elections were controlled by a few individuals. Just before the Reform Bill of 1832 it was reckoned that with a population of over two and a quarter millions Scotland had only three thousand electors, and it was said that more votes were cast at a single by-election in Westminster than in a Scottish general election. Moreover, the ministers responsible for Scottish affairs had an enormous influence, which they exercised to secure members favourable to the Government in power.[3]

Corruption in politics

Politics was regarded as a lucrative profession, and a minister in the eighteenth century might expect to be able to endow his relatives and supporters with desirable offices, which combined a small amount of work with a large amount of remuneration.[4] Loyalty to a party or a minister was

[1] In 1730 the price for the lifetime of a single parliament was £1500; in 1830, £7000.

[2] About the time of the accession of George III, the number of members representing English constituencies was 489. Of these 80 represented the counties and were almost entirely the landed gentry. Of members representing boroughs, the election of 32 was controlled by the Government, and of just on 200 by some 100 patrons. Of the other 180 members, many had bought their seats or had the seats bought for them.

[3] Thus the Duke of Argyll and his brother were supreme during part of Walpole's ministry, and Henry Dundas during Pitt's rule (1783–1801) had such authority that he was known as Harry the Ninth, and practically all the Scottish members were his supporters.

[4] Thus Horace Walpole, the letter writer, was the third son of Robert Walpole, the Prime Minister. Whilst still a boy at Eton his father gave him the offices of Clerk of the Estreats and Comptroller of the Pipe, which produced about £300 per annum. At the age of twenty he became Usher of the Exchequer, which was worth from £1000 to £1500 a year. His duties were not exacting; they

generously rewarded; in George III's reign, for instance, no less than three hundred and eighty-eight peerages were created, most of them for political services. There were many places and pensions, and a large number of members had either one or the other.[1] But this was all part of the political system of that day. The direct bribery of members of Parliament, however, to obtain their votes on a particular occasion was rare; and owing largely to the influence of such statesmen as the elder, and to a lesser extent the younger Pitt, and to a bill passed at the end of the century which reduced the number of places and pensions, the standard of political morality was steadily improved. And by no means all politicians found politics remunerative: the Duke of Newcastle was in public life for nearly fifty years, and found himself at the end of it some £300,000 the poorer as a consequence.

Placemen

The political system in existence between 1714 and 1832 did, as a matter of fact, produce many statesmen of distinguished ability, who guided Great Britain on the whole very successfully through very difficult times. Many of our greatest statesmen, including Walpole, Canning, Fox, the two Pitts, Gladstone, and Palmerston, began their political career as representatives of "pocket" boroughs. Of course it is quite true that the House of Commons was not acutely sensitive to public opinion and did not readily reflect every change in the nation's ideas. But if the nation really felt strongly about anything, its feelings would in the end prevail in the House. And in some ways the system was good, for it gave the House a stability and the member an

were "to furnish papers, pens, ink, wax, sand, tape, penknives, scissors, and parchment to the Exchequer and Treasury, and to pay the bills of the workmen and tradesmen who serve these offices". On his father's death, Walpole received in addition £1000 a year from the collector's place in the custom house. All these offices Walpole held for the rest of his life. Of his two brothers, one held the lucrative office of Auditor of the Exchequer, and the other was Clerk of the Pells.

[1] In the Parliament elected in 1761, it is estimated, there were 50 ministers and civil servants, 50 court officials, 50 holders of sinecures, 37 Government contractors, and 10 holders of secret service pensions.

independence which were valuable. And though the landed classes had the chief, it must not be supposed that they had the sole power, or that the professions and trade and industry were not represented; on the contrary, lawyers and merchants, naval and army officers, civil servants and diplomats were present in the House of Commons and helped to make it a real microcosm of the nation.[1]

2. THE JACOBITE RISINGS OF 1715 AND 1719

Character of period (1714–60)

It must be admitted that the period known as the early Hanoverian had some unattractive characteristics. " Soul extinct; stomach well alive " is the verdict of one distinguished historian on this epoch. Indeed, it cannot, except towards its close, be called an inspiring one. In politics there was a good deal of corruption, and no great principle to ennoble the strife between the party factions. In religion, the Church of England, it has been said, slept and rotted in peace, and its leaders — the bishops — were in some cases hardly Christians. A period of peace was followed by a period of war, in which for a time many of our soldiers and seamen showed conspicuous incapacity. In literature, the poetry of the period has been criticised as being too artificial and epigrammatic. But the merits of its greatest poet, Pope, somewhat underrated in the nineteenth century, are now more fully recognized, whilst in the period was written one of the most widely-read poems in the world — Gray's *Elegy*. Moreover, it was a period of growing toleration in matters of religion, and of growing common sense in the affairs of the world; the country grew prosperous, and trade and industry increased; and the nation obtained, for the first half of this epoch, what perhaps it most needed at that time — an interval of repose. Nor must we forget that this epoch

[1] In the Parliament elected in 1761, 169 members were Irish peers or the sons of peers, and 101 were baronets or the sons of baronets. There were 50 merchants, 40 practising lawyers, 21 naval officers, 59 army officers, 7 civil servants, and 5 diplomats.

produced in John Wesley one of the greatest religious leaders in England's history.

Such a period, however, was not one in which men would be ready to lead forlorn hopes in support of lost causes. Tory squires and Oxford undergraduates might still continue to toast the Stuarts,[1] but the mass of the nation quietly acquiesced in the Hanoverian succession (*Note 93*). Only in Scotland, and especially in the Highlands, was active devotion shown to the House of Stuart, and Scotland was the centre of the two rebellions which took place. The first rising was in 1715, and is known, from the name of its leader, as *Mar's Rebellion.* There were to be risings in the Highlands under the Earl of Mar himself, and in the Lowlands of Scotland; in Cumberland, under a Mr. Forster; and in the west of England, where the Duke of Ormonde was to land. But the rising in the west came to nothing. The two Scottish forces should have combined for a joint attack upon Stirling, which commanded the communications of Highlands and Lowlands; but the Lowlanders went south instead of north, and along with the men of Cumberland were taken prisoners at Preston. On the same day Mar met the Hanoverian army at *Sheriffmuir*, and though the battle was indecisive, the right wing of each army soundly defeating the wing opposed to it, Government troops blocked the road to Edinburgh, and the rebellion fizzled out.

The 'Fifteen

The causes of the failure of the rising were many. To begin with, its leaders were incompetent, and no one had much faith in Mar, "bobbing John" as he was called. The Old Pretender did indeed land in Scotland, but not till after Sheriffmuir had been fought, and not only did he bring neither men nor money with him, but he also proved a very dispiriting and frigid leader. Moreover, Louis XIV had just died, and the Regent Orleans, who governed during

Causes of failure

[1] Under such disguises as Job, standing for James III (the Old Pretender), Ormonde, and Bolingbroke; or £3. 14*s*. 5*d*., which denoted James III and the two foreign kings who were expected to assist him, Louis XIV of France and Philip V of Spain.

the childhood of Louis XV, wished to keep on good terms with Great Britain. Consequently no help came from

THE JACOBITE RISING OF 1715

France. Finally, the Whig Government dealt energetically with the situation.[1]

In 1719 a small Spanish force under the Earl Marischal

[1] The Old Pretender, or the Chevalier de St. George as he is called, left Scotland in less than six weeks. Subsequently he married a granddaughter of the King of Poland, his two sons being Charles Edward (d. 1788) and the Cardinal of York (d. 1807). He himself died in 1766, and in 1819 George III erected a monument to his memory in St. Peter's at Rome.

landed in Scotland and was joined by about a thousand clansmen led by the Marquis of Tullibardine. Government troops, however, defeated and scattered them at Glenshiel.

3. WALPOLE

The danger of a Stuart restoration had thus been safely overcome. Now, however, came difficulties in another direction, namely finance.

The South Sea Bubble (1719)

A company had been formed in 1711 to secure the trade of the South Seas. It had prospered, and in 1719 it offered to take over the National Debt, that is to say, to become the sole creditor of the Government, and to buy out, either by cash or by shares in the Company, all other creditors. The Company proposed to pay £7,000,000 for this privilege — for as such it was regarded — and to reduce the interest which the nation was paying. The Government accepted the offer, and the more willingly as the Company had paid considerable bribes to the less honest of its members. The directors of the Company thought that the close connection with the Government which would result from the Company being its sole creditor would be a gigantic advertisement and inspire confidence. And so it proved. Everyone, including philosophers and clergymen, and even in its corporate capacity the Canton of Berne, began to buy shares in the Company. The £100 shares went up by bounds and reached £1000. There followed a craze of speculation. Numerous companies were formed, none too foolish to lack subscribers.[1] And then came the reaction, and the bubble burst. People began to realize that the South Sea Company's shares could not possibly be worth what had been paid for them, and tried to get rid of them. Consequently the shares fell even quicker than they had risen,

[1] One financier brought out a company to promote "a certain design which will hereafter be promulgated"; and even this company did not lack subscribers.

and hundreds of people who had bought when the stock was high lost their fortunes.

Fall of the ministry (1720)

At once there was a cry for vengeance. It was seriously proposed to tie the directors up in sacks and throw them into the Thames. Revelations regarding the bribes to the ministers came out, and the Government was ruined. Of the two leaders, Sunderland resigned, and Stanhope, who was honest, had a fit when an unjust charge of corruption was brought against him, and died. Of the other ministers, one committed suicide, another was sent to the Tower, whilst the smallpox accounted for a third. The way was thus left open for Walpole, who had not been officially connected with the South Sea Company's transactions, though he had made a profit of 1000 per cent by judicious buying and selling of its shares on his own private account.

Character of Walpole

Robert Walpole was a typical product of his time (*Note 94*). By birth a Norfolk squire, and educated at Eton, he was a cheerful, good-natured, tolerant person, and a keen sportsman, who, it was said, always opened the letters from his gamekeeper first, however important his other correspondence might be.[1] He was a man of considerable common sense, and a prodigiously hard worker. He never appeared to be in a hurry, and he had the invaluable faculty of forgetting his worries. " I throw off my cares," he said, " when I throw off my clothes." As he said, however, of himself, he was no saint, no reformer, no Spartan. A cynical, coarse person, he lacked all enthusiasms. With him there was no ideal for his country to seek to attain in external affairs, no passion to lessen the sum of human misery at home. Such a statesman may make a nation prosperous, but he can never make a nation great. It was fortunate for Great

[1] Parliament owes its Saturday holiday to the fact that Walpole on that day used always to hunt with his beagles at Richmond. Pope, the great friend of Walpole's chief opponents, has borne witness to his social qualities:

" Seen him I have; but in his happier hour
Of social pleasure ill exchanged for power:
Seen him uncumbered with the venal tribe,
Smile without art and win without a bribe."

Britain that, after she had waxed fat under a Walpole, she had a Pitt to inspire her to action.

The twenty-one years of Walpole's administration, from 1721–42, contain, it has been said, " no history ". In foreign affairs Walpole maintained till near the close of his ministry a policy of peace, which was very beneficial to England. In domestic affairs little happened. In our financial history, however, Walpole's rule was very important. Walpole undoubtedly was a great financier. He restored credit after the South Sea panic. He found, it is said, our tariff to be the worst in Europe; and by abolishing duties on a great number of articles he made it the best. In all the details of financial administration he was excellent; if he could not, as George I said he could, make gold out of nothing, he could make it go a long way.

Walpole's rule (1721–42)

Finance

Walpole's administration, again, marks a stage in the evolution of cabinet government. Walpole has been called our first prime minister, because he practically appointed all his colleagues and insisted that they should have the same opinions as himself. He, however, was no believer in cabinet councils, and preferred to discuss public affairs with two or three of his colleagues at the more convivial and less controversial dinner table. But if a minister differed from him he had to go — either to govern Ireland like Carteret (1724); or to be the first leader of an organized Opposition like Pulteney (1725), whose tongue Walpole feared, it was said, more than another man's sword; or to grow turnips like Townshend (1730), the brother-in-law and Norfolk neighbour of Walpole.

Development of Cabinet Government

Though Walpole was supreme in his ministry, he had to encounter considerable opposition from other quarters. Bolingbroke, who had fled to the Continent on George I's accession, had been allowed to come back to England, and, though excluded, as one of the conditions of his return, from using his great powers of speech in the House of Lords, wielded his pen with great effect in a weekly paper

Walpole and the Opposition

called *The Craftsman*.[1] He and the Tories, though not very numerous themselves, had as their allies in opposing Walpole an increasing number of the older Whigs under Pulteney, who were discontented with Walpole's monopoly of power, and of the younger Whigs called " the Boys ", including a rising statesman in William Pitt, who unsparingly attacked Walpole's system of bribery and corruption. Walpole, however, held his own. He had the support of both George I and George II, and especially of Queen Caroline until she died in 1737.[2] Moreover, his mixture of shrewdness, good sense, and good humour made him an excellent leader in the House of Commons; and these qualities, besides the power which he could exercise through the gift of places and pensions, and the possession by some of his chief supporters of " pocket boroughs ", served to secure him a fairly docile majority.

Walpole was careful, moreover, to avoid raising great antagonisms. Whilst allowing the Dissenters in practice to hold office in towns and elsewhere, he would not, for fear of angering the Church, formally repeal the laws which forbade them to do so. In another matter he gave way to popular feeling. In 1733 he introduced an *Excise Bill*.

The Excise Bill (1733)

Under this Bill duties on wine and tobacco were to be paid, not on their arrival in port, but only if and when they were taken for *internal* consumption in Great Britain out of the warehouses where they were to be placed on arrival. The object of the Bill was to check smuggling and to make London and other places free ports by allowing goods to be re-exported without paying any duty. The Bill, however, met with tremendous opposition. An army of excise

[1] The first number of *The Craftsman* appeared at the end of 1726, and the last number in 1736. It was published at first twice and then once a week, and amongst its contributors, besides Bolingbroke himself, were Swift, Pulteney, Pope, and Arbuthnot.

[2] Queen Caroline on one occasion succeeded in convincing the King with arguments Walpole had used to her, though unconvinced by them herself. She had great influence over the King, cf. the old couplet:

> " You may strut, dapper George, but 't will all be in vain;
> We know 't is Queen Caroline, not you, that reign ".

men, it was alleged, would be created, who would swamp the elections with their votes, and who would invade Englishmen's homes to see that the duty had been paid, reducing British subjects to a condition of slavery. The citizens of London prayed to be heard against the Bill, and sent a petition escorted by coaches that stretched from Westminster to Temple Bar. The soldiers were on the point of mutiny because they thought that the price of their tobacco would be raised. The whole country took up the cry of "No slavery, no excise", and numbers of people marched about with badges on their hats bearing this and similar inscriptions. In the House of Commons the Opposition attacked the Bill with great fury, and Walpole's majority sank to seventeen. When this occurred, Walpole felt he must yield. "This dance", he said, "will no further go"; and, to the great popular delight, the Bill was abandoned.[1]

Three years after the withdrawal of the Excise Bill, Walpole's Government became very unpopular in Scotland. As a result of the Union of 1707, the customs duties in that country had been increased so as to tally with those in England, and consequently many Scots thought themselves justified in eluding them. Smuggling was therefore regarded with an indulgent eye in Scotland, and was so general as to be almost one of its minor industries. In 1736 two notorious smugglers, who had robbed a custom-house officer, were convicted and ordered to be executed in Edinburgh. One of them made himself a popular hero by chivalrously aiding the escape of the other,[2] and there was consequently a huge and sympathetic crowd at his execution. The execution

[1] Even Samuel Johnson, some twenty years after, so far forgot the impartiality of a lexicographer as thus to define the word "excise" in his Dictionary: "a hateful tax levied upon commodities, and adjudged not by common judges of property, but by wretches hired by those to whom excise is paid".

[2] The two prisoners had planned to escape from prison by enlarging the window in their cell. One of them, however, stuck in the aperture, and not only was unable to get out himself, but prevented the egress of the other. But, on the following Sunday, he attacked the guard at the close of divine service, and endeavoured to escape. He failed, but prolonged his struggles to distract the attention of the guards, thus enabling his fellow-prisoner to get away.

over, there was some disorder, and stones were thrown at the town guard. Its commander, *Captain Porteous*, gave orders for the guard to fire, and some people were killed. Popular fury was aroused. Captain Porteous was tried and condemned to death. But he was reprieved by the Government, and the mob then took matters into their own hands and hanged him on a dyer's pole.[1] Walpole's Government accordingly tried to pass a Bill punishing the city of Edinburgh, but its terms were so stringent that they were opposed by all the Scottish members and had to be considerably modified. Walpole's position in Scotland was further weakened by the defection of the Duke of Argyll, who had enormous influence; consequently in the new Parliament of 1741 only six Scottish members supported Walpole.

The Porteous Riots (1736)

Meanwhile Queen Caroline's death in 1737 had deprived Walpole of his chief ally, whilst in the same year the Prince of Wales joined the Opposition. Finally, the Opposition forced on the war with Spain in 1739 (p. 599), and Walpole's mismanagement of it helped to secure his defeat and resignation in 1742. Walpole's rule had not been an inspiring one. But his policy of peace abroad and inactivity at home had two results: it made the Hanoverian dynasty secure, and it gave the country a breathing space which enabled her to endure the exertions demanded during the later wars of the century. Moreover, Walpole's strong, clear common sense had been of great value in matters of practical administration, whilst his financial ability had done much, and would, but for a factious opposition, have done more to develop the prosperity and trade of the country.

Fall of Walpole (1742)

Walpole had been a great minister, but the same cannot be said of the men who followed him. The Whigs still continued their long hold of office, and *Carteret*, *Pelham*, and the *Duke of Newcastle* were the new leaders.

The new Government had now to meet what threatened to be a very formidable danger, and here they really reaped

[1] See Scott's *Heart of Midlothian* for a full account of the Porteous Riots.

the advantages which Walpole's rule had sowed. The peace and prosperity which he had secured for Britain made the country willing to support the Hanoverians whom he had served, and when another attempt was made tc bring back the Stuarts, England did not support it (*Note 93*).

4. THE JACOBITE RISING OF 1745

The 1745 Rebellion: the Young Pretender

The Jacobite rising in 1745 was a more formidable affair than either of the preceding attempts, though in the interval between 1719 and 1745 Jacobitism had become almost entirely a Scottish movement. This rising took place during the War of the Austrian Succession soon after the battle of Fontenoy (p. 601), where Great Britain had lost great numbers of her bravest troops. The hero of the '45 was Charles Edward, the son of the Old Pretender, whose daring and attractive personality well fitted him to lead the Highlanders to victory. Though France had refused to give him any help, he was determined to win back the throne of his fathers, and in July he landed at Moidart in the north-west cf Scotland with only seven men. Some of the Highland chieftains knew well the folly of his attempt, and Lochiel and Macdonald of Boisdale tried to dissuade him. But he would not listen to them, and, seeing his determination, they decided to give him their support. Some other clans joined in, and Charles marched south. Cope, the opposing general, came north from Edinburgh to meet him, but made a tactical error, and Charles, who had been joined by a very capable officer, Lord George Murray,[1] entered Edinburgh unopposed and advanced to meet Cope, who had returned by sea, at *Prestonpans*. Crossing by night a marsh which was supposed to be impassable, Prince Charles at daylight found himself within two hundred yards of the enemy; and his Highlanders, charging successively the artillery, the cavalry, and the infantry, won a decisive

The Battle of Prestonpans

[1] He had a son at Eton who was very anxious to fight for King George.

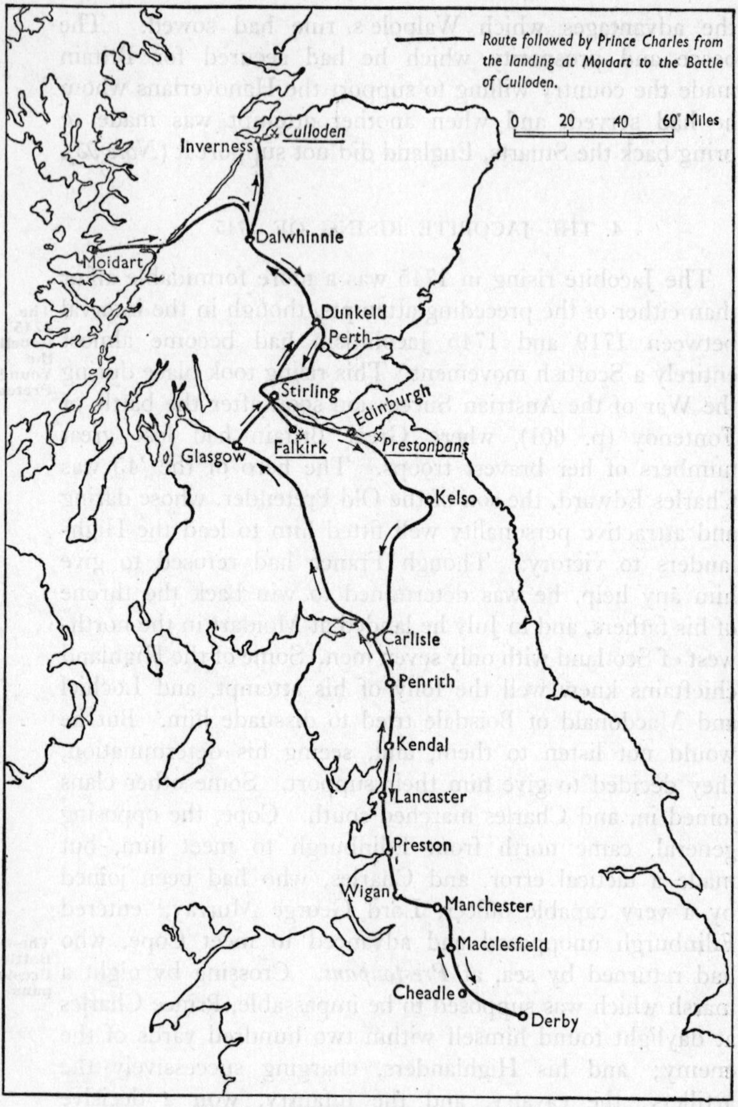
Route followed by Prince Charles from the landing at Moidart to the Battle of Culloden.
0 20 40 60 Miles
Culloden
Inverness
Dalwhinnie
Moidart
Dunkeld
Perth
Stirling
Edinburgh
Falkirk
Prestonpans
Glasgow
Kelso
Carlisle
Penrith
Kendal
Lancaster
Preston
Wigan
Manchester
Macclesfield
Cheadle
Derby

THE JACOBITE RISING OF 1745–1746

victory in under ten minutes (September). "They ran like rabets", wrote the Prince of the enemy (the spelling is his own); "not a single bayonet was blood-stained."[1] Scotland seemed to be at his feet.

The invasion of England

General Wade, meanwhile, had been sent north to Newcastle with ten battalions (seven of which were composed of foreigners) to prevent an invasion of England. Prince Charles, against the advice of his ablest advisers, advanced south, then suddenly — to avoid Wade — swerved west, entered England by Carlisle, took Manchester, and reached Derby — within one hundred and twenty-five miles of London. Whether he ought to have advanced farther will always be a matter for dispute. Had he but known that Newcastle, one of the chief ministers of the day, was restlessly pacing his room in an agony of doubt as to whether to join the Pretender or not, that George II himself had made all preparations to retire to Hanover, and that people were rushing in wild panic to get their money from the bank, he might have proceeded. As it was, Prudence in the person of Lord George Murray said "No"; for Wade was with one army in the north, Cumberland with another in the Midlands, and yet another lay near London, whilst the Prince's own army was dwindling and recruits were not coming in. The Scottish Lowlands, which had gained much from the Union, were apathetic where he had expected enthusiasm, and the north of England had "given him not the least encouragement". Consequently Prince Charles, against his own wishes and in very bad grace, retreated; and when he had once begun, he could not stop.

March to Derby

Reasons for retreat

Suppression of rising

The rebellion henceforward became, as a contemporary said, "a rebellion on the defensive", and was bound to fail. Prince Charles, however, reached Scotland safely, and won a victory at *Falkirk* (January, 1746). The Duke of Cumberland was then appointed to the chief command in

[1] The Highlanders were delighted; they had, they said, a prince "who could eat a dry crust, sleep on pease-straw, eat his dinner in four minutes, and win a battle in five".

Scotland, and showed a great energy in drilling his troops and in teaching them to meet a Highland charge. Whilst the men in the rear rank were to fire volleys, those in the front rank were to kneel with bayonets fixed, and each man was to thrust at the Highlander on his right front, the right being the Highlander's unprotected side. After a clever winter campaign in a mountainous country, Cumberland met Prince Charles at *Culloden*, near Inverness, and won a complete victory (April, 1746), though he obtained the horrible appellation of " Butcher ", from the cruelty which he showed after the battle, his troops being ordered to show no mercy and to kill all they captured.[1]

The Battle of Culloden (1746)

After the rebellion was over, many Scotsmen were executed. Prince Charles himself, with £30,000 on his head, after wandering for five months amongst the moorlands and mountains and islands of the west, was, through the heroism of Flora Macdonald, able to effect his escape, and eventually died in 1788.[2] The British Parliament passed a stringent Disarming Act. Parliament also abolished the hereditary jurisdiction of the Highland chiefs — many of whom had taken part in the insurrection — and tried, though without success, to abolish the national dress. With the failure of the rising, the hopes of the Jacobites were for ever crushed. Before long the Highlanders were to show on many a battlefield the same splendid loyalty to the House of Hanover as they had shown to the House of Stuart, for Pitt during the Seven Years' War formed two Scottish regiments, which did magnificent service, especially on the " Heights of Abraham ".

The reform of the calendar

Peace having thus been re-established, the country once more settled down. Only one matter of interest need be mentioned, and that was the reform of the calendar. Hitherto

[1] Cumberland celebrated his 24th birthday on the night before Culloden Charles Edward was one year his senior.

[2] Through Flora Macdonald's help he escaped to Skye disguised as an Irish spinning-maid, and subsequently got safely to France. In 1750 he revisited England, of course disguised, and " in the new church in the Strand " made a Declaration of his Protestantism, hoping thereby to gain additional support.

in Great Britain the old Roman calendar had been used, and not the corrected calendar adopted first by Gregory XIII in 1582, and subsequently by nearly all European nations. The old calendar was several days wrong, and the ministry, in order to rectify it, omitted some days in September, 1752, calling the 3rd of September the 14th. Great irritation was aroused by this change, many people thinking that they had been defrauded by the Government of these days; hence came the popular cry, " Give us back our eleven days ". Another change was made at the same time, and the legal year in future was to begin on 1st January, and not, as heretofore, on 25th March.

CHAPTER 45

FOREIGN POLICY AFTER 1714

British relations with France

To the conduct of foreign affairs, and the events which led to the great wars of George II's reign, we must now turn. For twenty-six years after the signing of the Treaty of Utrecht — from 1713 to 1739 — Great Britain enjoyed a period of repose. Both France and Great Britain wished to uphold the Treaty of Utrecht, and for a great part of this period each country was ruled by a peace-loving minister, *Walpole* being chief minister in Great Britain from 1721–42 and *Fleury* being responsible for French policy from 1720–29. Hence not only were there no hostilities, but even at times an alliance or informal co-operation between these two powers — a very unusual state of affairs in the eighteenth century.

Great Britain and Spain

England and France were thus transformed from age-long enemies to allies. But the hostility which Great Britain had felt towards France was now transferred to *Spain*. In 1718 Spain wished to seize Sicily, and Britain prevented

Battle of Cape Passaro (1718)

this by sinking her fleet off *Cape Passaro*.[1] Later Spain tried to recover Gibraltar and Minorca, but again Britain prevented her.

A few years later trade controversies with Spain became acute. The Spaniards jealously tried to exclude all other nations from trading with their enormous possessions in South America, though they failed to develop the trade on their own account. But British ships did a great deal of illicit trade with Spanish America, especially through the solitary British ship which under the terms of the Assiento clause of the Treaty of Utrecht was allowed to be sent there annually. This ship, whilst in the Spanish port, was emptied of its cargo each day, and refilled under cover of night by small boats from other ships outside the harbour.

Jenkins's ear (1739)

The Spaniards, not unnaturally incensed at these proceedings, had retaliated by searching on the high seas British ships whose destination might be Spanish America, and treating British sailors with great brutality. Consequently, British feeling was roused, and the politicians opposed to Walpole, then the chief minister, thinking they had got a good party cry, took care to fan the indignation. Finally, anger reached boiling-point when a certain Captain Jenkins produced his ear in a bottle before the House of Commons, and asserted that it had been cut off by the Spaniards. He was asked " what his feelings were when he found himself in the hands of such barbarians ", and he answered in words which were probably suggested to him beforehand, but which had the effect desired by the opposition of stimulating patriotic fervour: " I commended my soul to my God, and my cause to my country." [2] Walpole,

[1] The Spanish fleet of eighteen sail was utterly destroyed by an English fleet of twenty-one sail under *Admiral Byng*. Part of the Spanish fleet fled, and took refuge inshore. A Captain Walton was sent in pursuit, and his dispatch announcing his success is said to be the shortest on record and to have run as follows: " Sir, we have taken and destroyed all the Spanish ships which were upon the coast: the number as per margin. Respectfully, &c., G. Walton." But, as a matter of fact, this was only the ending of the letter.

[2] It has been doubted whether Jenkins ever really lost an ear at all, or, if he did, it has been asserted that he lost it in an English pillory. According to

unable to withstand popular opinion, after futile negotiations with Spain, declared war in 1739.

The year 1739 ushered in a new and prolonged period of conflict (*Note 95*). The war with Spain, somewhat discreditable to our honour in its origin, was discreditable to our arms in its conduct. An attempt on *Cartagena*, in Spanish America, was a miserable failure, and our only success was a voyage round the world undertaken by *Anson*, who captured an enormous amount of treasure on the west coast of South America.[1]

The war with Spain (1739)

But meanwhile, in 1740, another Succession War broke out. This had to do with Austria. Charles VI, the emperor and ruler of the vast Austrian dominions — known to us already, in the Spanish Succession War, as the Archduke Charles — had one child, a daughter, *Maria Theresa*. He persuaded nearly all the European powers to recognize an arrangement known as the *Pragmatic Sanction*, by which it was laid down that all his kingdoms and territories should pass undivided to this daughter. But on Charles's death, in 1740, the Elector of Bavaria, the husband of Charles's elder brother's daughter, claimed the Austrian dominions. The King of France supported him and sent two armies across the Rhine. Meanwhile Frederick II, known in history as Frederick the Great, who had just succeeded to the Prussian throne, disregarded his promise to Charles to recognize his daughter, and seized Silesia, which belonged to Austria.

The Austrian Succession War (1740–48)

Feelings of chivalry and also fears of what might happen to the Austrian Netherlands impelled Great Britain to assist Maria Theresa, and, moreover, the Electors of Hanover

Great Britain enters the war

Jenkins's story, the ear had been cut off in 1731 by a ferocious Spanish captain, by name Fandino, who was himself captured by a British frigate eleven years later after a desperate resistance.

[1] Anson succeeded in capturing the great treasure-ship that sailed every year from Manila to Acapulco. The treasure he secured, worth some £500,000, was paraded through the city, on its way to the Bank of England, in a procession of thirty-two wagons, the ship's company marching alongside with colours flying and band playing.

were traditional allies of the House of Habsburg. Hence, once again, England and France, though they did not declare formal war till 1744, found themselves engaged in hostilities. The military operations in which we took part were at the outset somewhat complicated, and it is sufficient to say that the position of Maria Theresa was at first very precarious, but that the loyalty of her subjects, and especially of the Hungarians, saved her.

Carteret's policy (1742–44)

Carteret became, on Walpole's resignation in 1742, responsible for our foreign policy. A gifted man, with great knowledge of European politics, and with the advantage, rare at that time, of being able to talk fluently in German, he belongs to the small number — perhaps fortunately small — of foreign secretaries who wished Great Britain to play a large part in Continental politics. He succeeded, first, in negotiating a peace between Frederick and Maria Theresa, by which Prussia withdrew from the struggle, and then in combining nearly all the German powers, with the exception of Prussia, against France. An army composed of English and Hanoverians, under the command of Lord Stair and accompanied by George II himself, was directed to evict the French from Germany. But the army soon found itself

Dettingen (1743)

in an apparently hopeless position at *Dettingen*, with no food, with the River Main on one flank and impenetrable mountains and forests on the other, whilst its advance and retreat were covered by French forces. Fortunately the French left their strong position, and the British were able to make a decisive charge and snatch a victory from the jaws of defeat.[1] As a consequence, the French troops retired from Germany, and the situation was relieved.

The coalition of German powers, however, soon broke up. Prussia again took up arms against Austria, and

[1] George II's horse, frightened by the crackle of musketry, ran away with him at the beginning of the battle; the King, therefore, fought during the remainder of the time on foot, saying that he could trust his legs not to run away with him. He behaved with the utmost bravery, encouraging his soldiers: "Steady, my boys; fire, my brave boys, give them fire; they will soon run." In honour of the victory, Handel composed a Te Deum.

Carteret, owing to his unpopularity at home, retired from office. Meanwhile, a French force of 80,000 men, under the famous Marshal Saxe, invaded the Austrian Netherlands, and, despite the efforts of the British, it was everywhere victorious. In 1745 the British were defeated at *Fontenoy*, though the infantry won great glory by a magnificent charge, which was finally checked by the Irish Brigade serving in the French army.[1] In the same year the rising of the Young Pretender (see p. 593) led to the withdrawal of the British troops from the Continent. The French proceeded to occupy nearly the whole of the Austrian Netherlands, and when the British returned two years later they met with no success.

Fontenoy (1745)

The war was ended in 1748 by the Treaty of *Aix-la-Chapelle*. Maria Theresa was left in possession of the Austrian dominions, including the Austrian Netherlands, though Prussia kept Silesia; otherwise no change of importance took place. The war, however, so far as Great Britain and France were concerned, was not merely European. The French took Madras in India. We took Louisburg, the great port of Cape Breton Island, the Gibraltar, as it has been called, of the New World. These two places were exchanged at the peace. Concerning the right of search, the original cause of the war with Spain, nothing was said at all.

Treaty of Aix-la-Chapelle (1748)

CHAPTER 46

THE SEVEN YEARS' WAR: AMERICA, INDIA, AND PITT

1. AMERICA

The Treaty of Aix-la-Chapelle settled nothing permanently. It was only a truce, and a few years later, in 1756, a mightier war broke out — the *Seven Years' War* (*Note 96*).

[1] It was at Fontenoy that the young Duke of Cumberland so distinguished himself by his bravery that he was given command of the troops sent to Scotland to fight the Young Pretender.

The British and French in North America

The rival ambitions of Great Britain and France in America and in India had to be adjusted — and the sword alone could do that. Something has already been said about our colonies in North America. The British colonies — thirteen in number — stretched along the shores of the Atlantic. To the north of them lay the French possession of Canada, to the south and west of them French Louisiana. The French ambitions were brilliant in conception. Just as in later times the French desired a sphere of influence that would stretch from the east to the west of Africa, so in the eighteenth century they wished to join Louisiana and Canada by occupying the land behind and to the west of the British settlements. At first sight the French ambitions might seem absurd; for the French colonists in Canada numbered only some 60,000, and the English colonists were nearly a million and a half. The French colony was united, and autocratically governed by capable French officials. The thirteen English colonies, on the other hand, were entirely separate in government, and often ill-disposed to one another; and all attempts to combine them for joint action had hitherto been complete failures. Moreover river valleys favoured the French designs. Throw a cork into the River Alleghany at its source near Lake Erie, and it will eventually find its way — if it meets with no obstacles — by the River Ohio and the Mississippi, to the Gulf of Mexico. Mountains — the Alleghany Mountains — on the other hand, interposed a natural barrier to the British expansion westward.

After the Treaty of Aix-la-Chapelle events moved fast in America. The French seemed likely to achieve their ambitions. If they could cut off the English on the north and south, and close in on them from the west, the English would be surrounded and shut up in a limited space, and could then be gradually squeezed out and either conquered or evicted from North America. Hence the French began to build a great chain of fortresses to serve the twofold purpose of forming a link between their northern and southern

The French forts

possessions and of hemming in the British. South of Montreal they had already built, on the shores of Lake Champlain, two forts at *Crown Point* and at *Ticonderoga*. They now developed the building of a line of forts from north to south to secure the river valleys. Meantime the British, owing partly to the disunion of the colonies themselves and partly to the procrastination of the home government, had done nothing except the building of *Oswego* on the south side of Lake Ontario. Then in 1754 came the building by the French, near the western boundary of Pennsylvania and at the junction of three rivers, of *Fort Duquesne*; and the last link, it has been said, in the French chain of forts was forged. Its building at once led to war in America. Two attempts to capture it were made, the first under Washington in 1754, and the second under Braddock in 1755; and both were disastrous.[1] The outlook for the French in America was bright, when in 1756 formal war was declared between Great Britain and France.

Fort Duquesne (1754)

2. INDIA

But in the east as well as in the west, in India as well as in America, French and British ambitions clashed. Though on the west coast *Bombay* belonging to the English East India Company and *Mahé* belonging to the French East India Company lay far apart, their factories on the east coast were in the same districts. In the north the English *Calcutta* lay close to the French *Chandernagore*, whilst in the south the French *Pondicherry* lay between, though at some distance from, *Madras* and *Fort St. David*. Both companies had reached a point when for their future commercial development some interference with the politics of the interior was probable. It was, however, the condition of India itself which made that interference inevitable.

English and French East India Companies.

[1] Braddock, who had pushed forward with twelve hundred men, was caught in an ambush some seven miles from the fort, and lost nearly two-thirds of his force. He himself fought most bravely, and, after having five horses shot under him, was mortally wounded, and died next day.

The races of India India, it must be remembered, is not a country like France or Germany, but a large Continent. Its area is almost equal to, and its population is greater than, that of all Europe if Russia is excluded. The inhabitants of this vast continent speak some fifty languages, and from the Northern Pathan to the Southern Tamil there is a great diversity of customs and manners; and they are divided into races which, in the words of a recent viceroy, differ from one another "as much as the Esquimaux from the Spaniard or the Irishman from the Turk". It may be urged that the Hindu religion gives a certain unifying influence; but it must be borne in mind that the Mohammedans — to say nothing of other religious sects such as the Parsees and Sikhs — constitute a very strong minority.[1] Moreover, the Hindus are themselves divided into some 3000 castes, the members of which have little social intercourse with one another; and their religion, it has been said, exhibits the worship of innumerable gods and an endless diversity of ritual. The religion of the well-educated Brahmin — the highest caste — may be called a form of Deism; the religion of the ordinary Hindu peasant embraces the worship of many local deities, and almost every village has its own particular objects of veneration.

The great Mohammedan dynasty, generally known as the Mogul dynasty, had, for a time, brought nearly the whole of India under its control. Established in the sixteenth century, it had gradually extended its power, especially under *Akbar* — the contemporary of Elizabeth — and *Aurangzeb*. But with the death of the last-named in 1707 the empire had begun to break asunder and India fell into a condition of anarchy. From the north the King of Persia came in 1739 and sacked Delhi, the Mogul capital. The Afghans after six successive invasions established themselves in the Punjab, until finally they gave way, towards the end of the century, to the Sikhs. In the north-east the rulers

Its anarchical condition after 1707

[1] According to the last census, the Hindus number at the present time about 70 per cent of the total population.

of Bengal and Oudh were practically independent. In Central India, the Marathas — Hindu tribes — made expeditions north and east from their two great centres at Poona and at Nagpur. In the south the Nizam of Hyderabad was the greatest potentate, and the Nabob of the Carnatic in the south-east was his vassal. In the south-west the ruler of Mysore was shortly to possess formidable power.

Dupleix in India (1741–54)

In the constant rivalries between these various States lay the opportunity for European interference. And in 1741 a Frenchman, by name *Dupleix*, of exceptional ability and ambition, was appointed Governor of Pondicherry. He determined to take advantage, in the south, of this state of affairs. During the War of the Austrian Succession he devoted his energies to the capture of Madras, only to be obliged to give it back at the peace. But there followed disputed successions in Hyderabad and in the Carnatic. Dupleix and the British each supported a rival pair of candidates. One of the French candidates triumphed at Hyderabad; the other secured the whole Carnatic save Trichinopoly, and even that place was besieged and seemed likely to fall.

Clive and the Siege of Arcot (1751)

It was at this critical moment in 1751 that the position was saved by *Robert Clive*. The son of a small Shropshire squire, he had — after a somewhat turbulent boyhood — gone to India to act as a clerk in the East India Company.[1] When Dupleix attacked Madras, he had volunteered for service, and both then and subsequently made his mark as a soldier. He now proposed, as a diversion, an attack upon *Arcot*, the capital. His proposal was accepted, and with a small force he succeeded in capturing it. This bold action had the effect he desired, and the siege of Trichinopoly

[1] He was, even in early life, of a somewhat pugnacious disposition, and, at the age of six, was described as "out of measure addicted to fighting", whilst, later on, the shopkeepers of Market Drayton, so tradition says, used to pay "a small tribute of apples and halfpence" to Clive and a band of his schoolfellows in order to preserve their windows from molestation. Clive, when he reached India, was for some time profoundly unhappy, and tried to commit suicide, but the pistol did not fire.

was raised. But this was by no means all. He had now to defend Arcot until relief came. With two hundred and thirty men he held on for fifty days, though he had to defend two breaches, the one of fifty and the other of ninety feet, against an army of ten thousand men. From the successful defence of Arcot, as Macaulay says, dates the renown of the British arms in the East. We had shown that we were not mere pedlars but fighters as well. Further successes led to the triumph of the British candidate in the Carnatic, and in 1754 Dupleix was recalled. Yet, as in Canada, the struggle was not over; and the Seven Years' War was to prove as important for its effects in India as for those in Canada.

3. THE SEVEN YEARS' WAR

The Seven Years' War did not begin formally till 1756.

Outbreak of Seven Years' War (1756)

But, as we have seen, hostilities between Great Britain and France had occurred in America and in India long before the war broke out in Europe. The capture and defence of Arcot by Clive occurred in 1751, the English attacks on Fort Duquesne began in 1754, whilst in 1755 hostilities spread to the sea, on which the British captured two French men-of-war carrying soldiers to Canada. Finally, in the early months of 1756 the French attacked Minorca; and with this last event war was regularly declared between the two countries.

Rivalry of Prussia and Austria

It was not only, however, the rivalry between France and Great Britain that brought about the war, but also that between Austria and Prussia. Maria Theresa had no intention of allowing Frederick to retain Silesia; she felt its loss so keenly that she could not see a native of that country, it was said, without weeping. The only question was as to the partners which the rival powers would take. In the War of the Austrian Succession the allies on each side had been dissatisfied with one another. For this and for other reasons the old alliances were reversed in the Seven Years' War. Austria and France — hitherto the great European rivals — for once made alliance together, and subsequently persuaded Russia to join them; and Great Britain bound itself to Austria's rival, Prussia.

The Seven Years' War, so far as Great Britain is concerned, may be divided into two periods. The first two years (1756–57) were years of almost unrelieved failure. The *Duke of Newcastle* (see p. 608) for the greater part of the time was chief minister. Procrastinating and ignorant, timid and undecided, he was "unfit", said George II, "to be Chamberlain to the smallest Court in Germany"; and it would certainly be difficult to find anyone less fitted to carry on a great war. He was a man of vast incompetence, always in a hurry and bustle and never doing anything. He has been described as a "hubble-bubble" man, his manner and speech resembling the bubbling of a Turkish pipe.[1] But his personal influence over various "pocket" boroughs returning members to the House of Commons, and his vast fortune spent in securing others, gave him a position which enabled him to be in high office almost continuously for over forty years. He and his ministry were so incapable that they could not survive the beginning of the Seven Years' War (1756).

The Duke of Newcastle (1754–56)

Commanders, both on land and sea, uninspired by the Government at home, planned their strategy without thought, and fought their battles by obsolete and formal methods. Consequently, at the beginning of the war, Great Britain was in terror of invasion, and to her disgrace

British failures in the war (1756–57)

[1] Newcastle was for a long time responsible for the administration of the American colonies, and two stories are told of his ignorance in that capacity. After being minister for many years someone told him that Cape Breton was an island and was not on the mainland, and he exclaimed delightedly: "Cape Breton an island! Wonderful! — show it me in the map. So it is, sure enough. My dear sir, you always bring us good news. I must go and tell the King that Cape Breton is an island." On another occasion a general suggested that some defence was necessary for Annapolis; on which Newcastle, with his "evasive lisping hurry", replied: "Annapolis, Annapolis! Oh! yes, Annapolis must be defended; to be sure, Annapolis should be defended — pray, where is Annapolis?"

Hessians and Hanoverians were brought over to defend her own shores.

Byng and Minorca

Meantime, *Byng* was dispatched with a fleet badly provisioned and poorly equipped to relieve *Minorca*, which had been attacked by the French. Off that island he fought an indecisive action with the French fleet when he ought to have avoided a battle and confined his attention to harassing the French communications. He then, supported by the advice of a council of war, returned home, leaving Minorca to be taken by the French. The nation was furious. Byng was tried for neglect of duty, found guilty, and shot on the quarterdeck of his own ship in Portsmouth Harbour — a scapegoat for the incompetence of the British Government and the want of seamanship on the part of the British navy.[1]

America

In America, the British lost *Oswego* and *Fort William Henry*, and an intended attack on Louisburg came to nothing. In

Germany

Germany, the Duke of Cumberland, George II's son, who had been sent to protect Hanover and to cover the western frontier of Prussia from a French invasion, was defeated at *Hastenbeck*, and forced to sign the *Convention of Klosterseven*, by which he agreed to evacuate the country (1757).[2] Only two wonderful victories won by our ally, King Frederick of Prussia, over the French at *Rossbach* and over the Austrians at *Leuthen* saved the situation.

The last five years of the war (1758–63) are, on the other hand, years of almost untarnished glory. Midway in the

Pitt and Newcastle (1757–61)

year 1757 *William Pitt* formed a coalition ministry with the *Duke of Newcastle*, Newcastle managing the patronage and

[1] Byng, who was the son of the admiral who had won the battle off Cape Passaro in 1720, was unfortunate in being the first victim of a new rule. Officers could previously be shot for "cowardice" or "disaffection"; but "negligence" had recently been added as a capital offence, and Byng came under this charge because he was found guilty of not having done his utmost to save Minorca. Voltaire's *mot* on this execution is well known; it was done, he said, "pour encourager les autres".

[2] George II was very angry as a consequence, and on Cumberland's return to London only gave him an interview of four minutes, telling him that "he had ruined his country and spoiled everything". At cards that evening, when the Duke entered the room, the King said openly: "Here is my son who has ruined me and disgraced himself!"

business details whilst Pitt was left to conduct the great war with which his name will be for ever connected (*Note 97*).

Pitt, after an education at Eton, went into the cavalry. He entered Parliament in 1735. He became an opponent, first as leader of "the Boys", of Walpole's corruption, and second, of Carteret's continental foreign policy; and the violent expression of his views was so congenial to the old Duchess of Marlborough that she left him a legacy of £10,000. Subsequently he had become paymaster of the forces in Pelham's administration, but had refused to take the enormous perquisites which had hitherto been connected with that office. From 1757 to 1761 Pitt was the real ruler of Great Britain. No doubt he was inconsistent, and in youth when in opposition attacked measures which he subsequently supported when in power. He has been described, and not without truth, as something of a charlatan. He loved ostentation and lacked simplicity. He was always something of an actor, and even for the most unimportant interviews his crutch and his sling (for he was a martyr to gout) were most carefully arranged.[1] And it must be admitted that his conduct to other ministers was overbearing and at times almost intolerable.

Pitt

But Pitt was a great man. As an orator he was superb. "His words", wrote one contemporary, "have sometimes frozen my young blood into stagnation and sometimes made it pace in such a hurry through my veins that I could scarce support it." Another said that you might as soon expect a "No" from an old maid as from the House of Commons when Pitt was in the height of his power.[2] Absolutely

[1] Pitt was very fond of reading aloud the tragedies of Shakespeare to his family, but, whenever he came to any light or comic parts, he used to give the book to someone else to read. "This anecdote", says a distinguished historian, "is characteristic of his whole life. He never unbent. He was always acting a part, always self-conscious, always aiming at a false and unreal dignity."

[2] Many stories illustrate the extraordinary power Pitt possessed over the House of Commons. On one occasion a member who was attempting to answer Pitt was overcome either by Pitt's glance or a few words which he spoke, and sat down in fear and confusion. Someone afterwards asked a person who was present "whether the House did not laugh at the ridiculous figure of the poor

incorruptible himself, he and his son, the younger Pitt, did more than any other two men to raise the standard of English public life. Quite fearless, he had the courage to stand up for unpopular causes — as in the case of Byng — when he saw an injustice was being done. It was of course as a war minister that he was greatest. But Pitt was one of those rare statesmen who had great views on all things. Unfortunately for Great Britain he held high office only from 1757 to 1761, and again for a brief period from 1766 to 1767. If he could have stayed in office longer, Ireland might have been pacified, America might not have been lost, our Indian Empire might have been at an earlier date organized, and parliamentary reform sooner accomplished. For not only had he great views himself, but like a prophet of old he could inspire a nation to noble deeds and high thoughts.

Pitt had all the qualities necessary for a great war minister. He combined supreme self-confidence with the power of inspiring others. "I believe," he said of himself, "I can save this country and that no one else can." "No one," said an officer, "can enter his closet without coming out of it a braver man." He had the capacity for selecting good men; no doubt he appointed some bad officers, but Hawke and Wolfe and Ferdinand of Brunswick are great names which attest his judgment. Above all, he had not only the genius of conceiving great and sound strategical designs, but also the capacity, with infinite patience and thoroughness, to plan their execution. No doubt he was arrogant and overbearing. He threatened to impeach one colleague who opposed him, and another complained that his language was of a kind seldom heard west of Constantinople. But

Success of Great Britain, and Pitt's influence

member". "No, sir," he replied, "we were all too much awed to laugh." On another occasion Pitt began a speech with the words "Sugar, Mr. Speaker". The combination of Pitt's somewhat theatrical gestures and appearance with such simple words as these caused some members to laugh. Pitt turned round on these members, repeated the word "sugar" three times, and then said, "Who will now dare to laugh at sugar?" And the members sank, we are told, into abashed silence.

these very qualities enabled him to become the only genuine war minister Great Britain has had since the development of cabinet government, a minister possessing the almost undisputed control of the army and the navy as well as of the diplomacy of the country. For his ally Pitt had Frederick, King of Prussia, and it was through the combination of these great men that the foundations of the modern Empire of Great Britain and of the modern Kingdom of Prussia were securely laid.

Strategy of Pitt

Pitt's strategy was briefly as follows. Assistance must be given to the King of Prussia. Even the generalship of Frederick the Great would not have enabled Prussia to withstand alone the combined forces of Austria, France, and Russia. Moreover, it was part of Pitt's policy to absorb French energies as far as possible in Europe. "We shall win Canada," Pitt said, "on the banks of the Elbe." Consequently he not only paid subsidies to Frederick of Prussia, but also maintained in Germany an army partly British and partly Hanoverian under *Ferdinand of Brunswick* to protect Hanover and the western flank of Prussia from the French. In addition he attacked various places on the French coast. These attacks, though not very successful,[1] kept the French nation in a continual state of alarm, and led, according to Pitt's information, to some thirty thousand French troops being employed in defensive work at home instead of in aggressive operations elsewhere. In the West Indies and in the East Pitt's object was, at first, to protect British commerce, and later, to extend British possessions. His chief energies, however, were concentrated on the conquest of Canada; it was there we were to make the first bid for victory whilst the French wasted their efforts on the Continent.

The campaign of 1758

In 1758 the initial successes began. In America, three separate armies advanced; the first, it is true, failed to take Ticonderoga, but of the others, one, with the aid of the

[1] An opponent of Pitt's spoke of them sneeringly as "breaking windows with guineas", and they were undoubtedly expensive.

fleet, captured Louisburg, and the other Fort Duquesne. Two raids were made on the French coast. The first went to St. Malo and destroyed a great deal of French shipping; but the second, after doing much damage at Cherbourg, revisited St. Malo, and on this occasion had to make a disastrously precipitate retreat. In Germany, Ferdinand of Brunswick was able to reach the Rhine, though he had to retreat later on. And just before the end of the year an expedition which had been dispatched to West Africa captured the French settlement of Goree.

The year of victories (1759)

With 1759 came a year more fruitful of successes than any other in our history. Upon Canada Pitt planned a twofold advance. Amherst was to take Ticonderoga, which he did, and to reach Quebec — which he was unable to accomplish. Wolfe, one of Pitt's favourite officers, was selected to command the soldiers and Saunders to command the sailors of another expedition which should go up the river St. Lawrence to attack Quebec. Saunders, in spite of fog and contrary winds, took the fleet and the transports up the St. Lawrence without mishap.

The attack on Quebec

Quebec stands upon a rocky promontory at the junction of the river St. Charles and the river St. Lawrence. Montcalm, the French commander, had fortified the bank of the river St. Lawrence from the point where the river St. Charles joins it to a point some eight miles down stream where another river, the Montmorency, flows into it. Wolfe had, with inferior forces, to fight an enemy who was strictly on the defensive. He at once seized the Isle of Orleans, which lay below Quebec. But he could not succeed in tempting Montcalm from his entrenchments, and an attack made upon the French from across the river Montmorency was a failure. The summer wore on and matters looked hopeless.

Meantime, however, some of the British ships had succeeded in passing the Quebec batteries, and in getting above the city. It was this achievement which enabled

Wolfe to make his master-stroke. The cliffs on the north bank of the St. Lawrence above Quebec are steep and precipitous, but about a mile and a half beyond that fortress Wolfe had discovered a zigzag path which led to their summit. He determined to attempt a night attack at this place, and accordingly made arrangements, with great skill, to divert the enemy's attention from that quarter. Below Quebec, Montcalm's attention was occupied by a bombardment from the main body of the fleet under Saunders, whilst the garrison in the city itself had an energetic attack directed upon it from the opposite bank. Meanwhile Wolfe himself and a large part of his troops had embarked in the ships which were above Quebec. On the night of the attack the ships were some six miles above the intended landing-place so as to distract the attention of Bougainville, who with a large force was watching these ships, from Wolfe's real objective.

Brilliantly conceived, the plan was no less brilliantly executed. About 2 a.m. on the morning of 13th September, the ships' boats, laden with soldiers, started on their journey. They deceived two sentinels on the bank by pretending to be some expected French provision boats, and then a small landing-party got on shore, climbed up the path, surprised the small guard at the top of the cliff, and covered the landing of the rest of Wolfe's forces.

The news of this exploit was, of course, conveyed to Montcalm and Bougainville. The latter waited for the news to be confirmed, and was any way too far off to be of service; but Montcalm, after some hesitation, through being uncertain of Saunders's intentions, hurried up and marshalled his men on the *Heights of Abraham*. Towards ten o'clock the French advanced. The British waited till they came within thirty-five yards, gave two murderous volleys, and then charged, the newly-enlisted Highlanders especially distinguishing themselves. In twenty minutes the battle was over, and was followed by the capture of Quebec. The

The Heights of Abraham (13th Sept.)

heroes of each side, Montcalm and Wolfe, were mortally wounded.[1]

Elsewhere almost as great successes occurred. An expedition sent to the West Indies failed, indeed, to take Martinique, but took *Guadeloupe* instead. In Germany, Ferdinand, with an army composed of various nationalities, had to retire before two other armies and leave Hanover unprotected. By a brilliant counterstroke he suddenly attacked one French army at *Minden*. Nine battalions of British infantry, though exposed to a cross fire of artillery, charged through three successive lines of hostile cavalry and tumbled them to ruin; and but for the failure of Lord George Sackville to follow up so magnificent a charge with the cavalry, the victory might have been an overwhelming one.

Battle of Minden (1st Aug.)

Meanwhile the French had been planning the invasion of England. The fleets at Toulon and at Brest were to unite and to convoy the troops across. The Toulon fleet left harbour; but it was discovered going through the Straits of Gibraltar, and Boscawen, the British admiral, started in pursuit in under three hours — a wonderful performance. By the end of the next day the greater number of the French ships had been dispersed or destroyed off *Lagos*, on the south coast of Portugal, and the remnant had retired to Cadiz (18th August). The Brest fleet took advantage of the absence of Hawke's blockading fleet, which had been driven away by a fierce storm, to escape, and sailed south.[2]

Battles of Lagos (18th Aug.) and Quiberon Bay (20th Nov.)

[1] Wolfe, at the age of sixteen, fought in the battle of Dettingen, and had to act as adjutant of his battalion. At the age of twenty-two he was given command of a regiment, and proved himself an admirable commander. He was a person of literary tastes. As his boat was going down the St. Lawrence on the night of the attack, he is said to have quoted some lines of Gray's Elegy, exclaiming: "Now, gentlemen, I would rather have written that poem than take Quebec!" George II had a high opinion of Wolfe's capacity. On one occasion someone said to him that Wolfe was mad. "Mad, is he?" was the King's answer; "then I wish he would bite some of my other generals."

[2] Hawke had entered the navy in 1720 at the age of fourteen. To Hawke is due what has been called a veritable revolution in naval strategy, for he instituted in 1759 the system of a blockade over the French port of Brest. He did this effectually for a period of six months from May to November, 1759. The French fleet finally escaped only because a very bad storm forced Hawke to take refuge at Tor Bay.

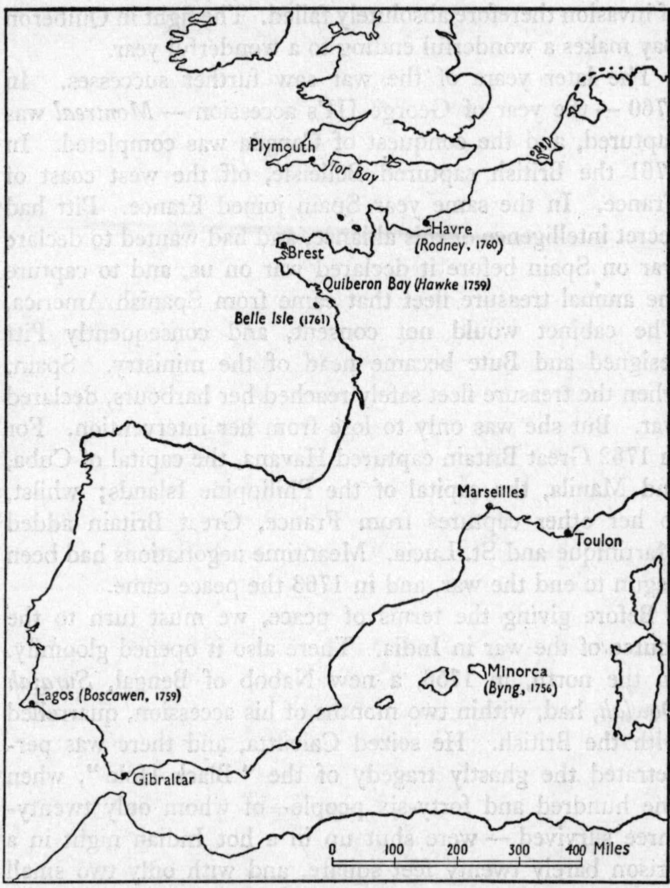

THE NAVAL WAR IN EUROPEAN WATERS, 1756–1763

But Hawke pursued it to *Quiberon Bay*, and on a lee shore during a November gale, in a bay full of reefs and shoals, fought it, captured two of its number, and destroyed two others. The remainder of the French fleet was dispersed, seven ships taking refuge up a river, from which they only escaped some fifteen months later. The French plan of invasion therefore absolutely failed. The fight in Quiberon Bay makes a wonderful ending to a wonderful year.

British successes (1761–62)

The later years of the war saw further successes. In 1760 — the year of George III's accession — *Montreal* was captured, and the conquest of Canada was completed. In 1761 the British captured Belleisle, off the west coast of France. In the same year Spain joined France. Pitt had secret intelligence of this alliance, and had wanted to declare war on Spain before it declared war on us, and to capture the annual treasure fleet that came from Spanish America. The cabinet would not consent, and consequently Pitt resigned and Bute became head of the ministry. Spain, when the treasure fleet safely reached her harbours, declared war. But she was only to lose from her intervention. For in 1762 Great Britain captured Havana, the capital of Cuba, and Manila, the capital of the Philippine Islands; whilst, to her other captures from France, Great Britain added Martinique and St. Lucia. Meantime negotiations had been begun to end the war, and in 1763 the peace came.

The war in Bengal

Before giving the terms of peace, we must turn to the course of the war in India. There also it opened gloomily. In the north, in 1756, a new Nabob of Bengal, *Surajah Dowlah*, had, within two months of his accession, quarrelled with the British. He seized Calcutta, and there was perpetrated the ghastly tragedy of the "Black Hole", when one hundred and forty-six people—of whom only twenty-three survived — were shut up in a hot Indian night in a prison barely twenty feet square, and with only two small barred windows. Clive came up from Madras and retook Calcutta. In 1757 — in the very same month that Pitt took office — he won on the field of *Plassey* with three thousand men, and with only eight guns, a victory over an army of fifty thousand men with forty guns. Clive was materially helped by the treachery of Meer Jaffier, one of the nabob's generals, and by the fact that a thunderstorm wetted the enemy's gunpowder, whilst tarpaulins protected

Battle of Plassey (1757)

his own; but even so, it was superb audacity on the part of Clive to risk a battle. That victory marks the beginning of the political ascendancy of the East India Company in Bengal; the Company put Meer Jaffier on the throne, and was given in return a substantial amount of land round Calcutta.

The war in Southern India

In the south matters had begun badly, as in the north, and the French took Fort St. David and besieged Madras; but they were quickly driven away. Brilliant success was to follow. In the year of victories — in 1759 — the capture of *Masulipatam* gave the English East India Company not only some eighty miles of coast line in the Circars, but substituted English for French influence at the Court of the Nizam of Hyderabad; whilst in the following year, at *Wandewash*, Eyre Coote won a victory over the French which led to the capture of Pondicherry and the other French settlements.

Battle of Wandewash (1760)

The Treaty of Paris (1763)

The Treaty of Paris in 1763 (*Note 96*) ended the war which had been so glorious to our arms. In America, Great Britain received Canada, the French territory on the east of the Mississippi, Cape Breton Island, and all other islands in the River and Gulf of St. Lawrence, besides Florida, which she received from Spain in exchange for Havana (Cuba). In the West Indies, she received Dominica, Tobago, and Grenada; in the Mediterranean, Minorca; and in Africa, the settlements on the river Senegal. But Great Britain gave back a good deal. To Spain she returned rich Havana and Manila — the news of the capture of the latter was not received till negotiations were practically completed. France recovered Belleisle and Goree, strong Martinique and wealthy St. Lucia; and her settlements in India were restored to her on condition that she should not fortify them. To France also was ceded the right to fish off the Newfoundland coast, and two small islands were given to her for the use of her fishermen. No doubt if Pitt had been in office the terms would have been better; but, even as it is, the peace marks a great stage forward in the advance of our empire. With regard to Germany, France agreed to give up all the territories which she had occupied in that country. Frederick the Great held, however, that the British by negotiating a peace separately with the French had basely deserted him; and though the charge was not true, it affected Prussian sentiment towards Great Britain for a considerable period.

CHAPTER 47

JOHN WESLEY AND THE RISE OF METHODISM

In the early Hanoverian period, the nation, it has been said, had sunk into a condition of moral apathy rarely paralleled in our history. It was due, above all others, to John Wesley, that Great Britain, towards the middle of the century, was roused from her spiritual torpor, and of this man and his influence something must now be said (*Note 98*).

John Wesley and the Methodist movement

John Wesley's influence on the religious life of the nation was similar to that exercised by Pitt on the political life. Wesley had been educated at Charterhouse and Oxford. After taking orders, he returned to Oxford as a Fellow in 1729, and for the next six years was the leader of a small society for mutual improvement, the members of which, including his brother Charles, the famous hymn writer, and George Whitefield, were known in the University by the nickname of *Methodists*. Subsequently Wesley was a minister for two years in Georgia, the newly founded colony in America. On his return to England he began the work which has made him so famous. In 1739 he built the first of his chapels at Bristol, and formed the first of his regular Methodist societies in London. Above all, the year 1739 saw the system of open-air preaching adopted which was to carry the message of the gospel to hundreds of thousands of people.

The activity shown by John Wesley and his colleagues, Charles Wesley and Whitefield, was astonishing. Of the three, Whitefield was probably the greatest preacher, and he, during the thirty-four years of his ministry, is said to have preached on the average ten sermons a week to audiences numbering sometimes as many as thirty thousand.[1] His record, however, is surpassed by that of John Wesley, who, in the half century preceding his death in 1791, is estimated to have delivered forty thousand sermons, and to have travelled a quarter of a million miles, the greater part of it on horseback. Their preaching affected all classes — the miners of Cornwall, the soldiers in the army, the negroes in Georgia, as well as a section of fashionable society in London. Nor was the activity of the three confined to England and Wales, for the whole world was their parish. Whitefield made over twelve journeys across the Atlantic, and Wesley had a missionary tour in Scotland when over eighty years of age.

George Whitefield

Activity of the Methodists

Throughout his life Wesley remained a member of the Church of England. But gradually the movement which he initiated became independent of that Church. His doctrines concerning sin and conversion were disliked by many in the Anglican Church. The chapels which he built were designed to be supplemental to the parish churches; before long they became rivals. Quite early in his career, in 1737, Wesley had instituted "lay" preachers, and in 1784 he even began to ordain ministers; and after his

Methodism and the Church of England

[1] No popular preacher has probably ever had such influence as Whitefield. He had a voice which could be heard by thirty thousand people in the open air, but which was managed with such skill that he could pronounce, a contemporary said, an unpromising word like Mesopotamia in a way to produce tears from his audience. Of his powers of vivid description many stories are related. Even such a pattern of propriety and aristocratic conduct as Lord Chesterfield, when Whitefield was relating the story of a blind man deserted by his dog and losing his way on a dangerous moor, lost all self-control, and bounded out of his seat as the blind man neared a precipice, exclaiming, "Good God! he's gone!" One of Whitefield's admirers held that a sermon of his would only reach its highest perfection at the fortieth repetition.

death the Wesleyans formed themselves into definite and separate organizations.[1]

Influence of Wesley on the English nation

Yet John Wesley is not to be remembered only as the founder of a new religious organization. He was a great social reformer as well as a great religious leader, and to him, perhaps in a greater degree than to any other man, is due the increased kindliness and humaneness which was exhibited in the later part of the eighteenth century, and the development of practical efforts to deal with the problems of poverty, inadequate though those efforts still were But above all else we may put his influence on the religious life of the whole British people. A great French thinker, who visited the country soon after the accession of George I, was of opinion that there was no such thing as religion in England; and there is no doubt that the early period of the Hanoverian rule was singularly lacking in religious activities and enthusiasms. It is the imperishable glory of John Wesley that he restored Christianity, as has been said, to its place as a living force in the personal creed of men and in the life of the nation.

CHAPTER 48

GEORGE III (1760–1820)

The very long reign of George III saw many important developments. We have to study first the King's attempt to revive the power of the Crown; then the loss of the American colonies; developments in India; the outbreak of the Revolutionary and Napoleonic wars; and lastly the troubled history of Ireland.

[1] How much the various Methodist societies have grown may be realized by statistics. On Wesley's death, in 1791, the members of his societies numbered seventy-six thousand, and the preachers three hundred; at the present time, throughout the world, there are over fifty thousand ministers, nearly ninety thousand lay preachers, and between twenty and thirty million adherents belonging to the Wesleyan communities.

1. DOMESTIC AFFAIRS TO 1782 AND THE ATTEMPTS OF GEORGE III TO REVIVE THE POWER OF THE CROWN

George III, the grandson of George II, was throughout his reign a popular monarch. And in many ways he deserved his popularity. He was a devoted husband, and except when his sons were at fault — and they often were — an affectionate father. He was simple in all his tastes, sincere in his religion, and imperturbably brave.[1] He was not without interests in art and literature; his library was a magnificent one, and most of the drawings at Windsor were purchased by him, whilst he had a fine collection of miniatures and gems. Moreover, having been born and educated in Great Britain, he could glory, as he said, in the name of " Briton ", whilst his fondness for the public schools, his devotion to hunting,[2] and his keenness as a farmer showed that he shared the interests of the Englishmen of his day. But his education had been inadequate, and he could hardly be considered a learned monarch; his English was ungrammatical, his spelling inaccurate, and his stock of general knowledge somewhat slender, whilst he is said to have expressed an opinion that Shakespeare wrote " much sad stuff ".[3] Moreover, he had been brought up in great seclusion by his German mother, and suffered from an inability to see anybody's point of view but his own. Consequently he was sometimes ignorant and bigoted in his opinions, and self-confident and obstinate in upholding them; and it is melancholy to think that a monarch in many ways so estimable should have spent so much of his life, as has been said, in

Character of George III

[1] Not even a shot fired at him as he was entering his box at a theatre prevented him from enjoying his usual nap during the interval between the play and the afterpiece.

[2] He was so fond of riding that even when he was blind he used to take long rides in Windsor Park, accompanied by a groom with a leading-rein.

[3] It is worth remembering, however, that George III, when recovering from his first attack of insanity, asked for *King Lear*. That same evening, on seeing his three eldest daughters, he said of the play: " It is very beautiful, very affecting, very awful. I am like poor Lear, but, thank God, I have no Regan, no Goneril, only three Cordelias."

obstinately resisting measures which are now almost universally admitted to be good, and in supporting measures which are as universally admitted to be bad. To him, perhaps more than to anyone else, does Great Britain owe the loss of her American colonies, the failure to pacify Ireland, the delay of parliamentary reform, and the long continuance of the slave trade. Yet it must be remembered in his defence that the views which he held were those of the average Englishman of that day, and that the blame, where there is blame, must be shared by the King and his subjects alike.

His desire for power

George came to the throne determined to govern as well as to reign. " George, be a king ", were the words which his German mother, so it is said, constantly repeated to him. And a real king George was determined to be. For such an attempt the time was opportune. Some distinguished men, such as Bolingbroke, had advocated during the reign of his predecessor that the monarchy should recover its lost power. The King could rely on the devoted support of the Tories, who were by this time completely reconciled to the Hanoverian dynasty. And through places and pensions and secret service money — though the amount of this has been exaggerated — he could influence many votes, whilst a body of men known as the " King's Friends " were prepared in the House of Commons to act according to his wishes. George meant to choose his ministers from any party or group that he liked — and also to dismiss them; and this, of course, he could do so long as these ministers could command a majority in the House of Commons.

His policy was quite clear — he aimed not at taking away from Parliament its control over taxation, but at choosing his own policy, and, above all, at choosing his own ministers. He aimed at gaining control of Parliament through a " King's Party ". It was the Crown's policy in this second direction which brought it into open conflict with those who wished to uphold liberty (*Note 102*).

The first use George made of his position was to exercise

his choice of ministers. The great Whig party were divided by quarrels, and the King could play off one section against the other.

The King and his Ministers

Thus within a year of his accession Pitt quarrelled with his colleagues and resigned. He wished to continue the French war, but the country wished for peace, and the majority of the Cabinet shared that view. So in 1761 Pitt left office, and much to the misfortune of the nation went into opposition.

Pitt

His place was first taken by the *Earl of Bute*, formerly the King's tutor. Bute was extremely unpopular in England, partly because he was a Scot, partly because he was considered a favourite of the queen-mother. So violent was the feeling against him that he had to employ a bodyguard of boxers while he was in London. There were better reasons for the universal distrust felt of him. He used bribery most extensively to secure power, and here we have the appearance, on a large scale, of the weapon George was to use so disastrously both for himself and the nation.[1]

Bute's ministry (1762–63)

Bute fell from office in 1763, and he was succeeded by *George Grenville*, who was a lawyer, and who used his special qualifications in a most unfortunate way. In the first place he took a "legal" view of the quarrel with the American colonies (see p. 627). In the second, he tried to stifle the criticisms which were being aroused by the King's government. Thus he began an attack on the liberty of the press. No. 45 of a paper called the *North Briton* contained a somewhat stringent criticism on the King's Speech at the opening of the Parliamentary session, a speech which as usual was only read and not composed by the King. The writer of the criticism was *John Wilkes*, the editor of the paper and a Member of Parliament. The Government decided that the article constituted a criminal libel and

Grenville's ministry (1763–65)

John Wilkes and the "North Briton", No. 45

[1] Bute's ministry was notorious for its bribery; on one morning, it is said, no less than £25,000 was expended in purchasing votes.

issued a "general warrant" (i.e. one in which no names are mentioned) for the arrest of the "authors, printers, and publishers" of the *North Briton.* The arrests (forty-nine in all) were carried out, but Wilkes claimed that, as a member of Parliament, he could not be arrested for libel. This claim was upheld by the Lord Chief Justice and Wilkes was accordingly released.

The House of Commons (or rather the Government) was not satisfied, however, declared that Parliamentary privilege did not extend to libel, and expelled Wilkes from membership of the House. Before the libel action came up for trial, Wilkes fled to France. We shall hear of him again.

The King and Grenville

The Wilkes case added to the unpopularity of the Government; public opinion supported Wilkes and considered general warrants illegal. Grenville, too, by his pertinacious and tiresome loquacity,[1] had made himself disliked by the King; and consequently he had to resign in 1765. "I would sooner meet Mr. Grenville," the King is reported to have said a little later, "at the point of my sword than let him into my cabinet." And Grenville never held office again.

Rockingham's ministry (1765–66)

Grenville was succeeded by *Lord Rockingham,* who tried to conciliate the colonies and repealed the Stamp Act. He also declared general warrants illegal, thus trying to undo the harm Grenville had done. Unluckily Pitt would not serve under him, and in 1766 George III dismissed Rockingham and called on Pitt to form a ministry and Pitt agreed.

Chatham's ministry (1766–68)

George III hoped much from this, for Pitt was not only honoured by the whole nation, but had declared that he would govern in accordance with the King's wishes, and this was more likely since he had quarrelled with all other parties. But actually Chatham's day was done. He had long suffered terribly from gout, and he had become so eccentric that he would withdraw for weeks and shut him-

[1] "When he has wearied me for two hours," the King complained, "he looks at his watch to see if he may not tire me for one hour more."

self up, refusing to see anyone or to answer letters or messages. Thus the actual conduct of affairs fell into the hands of his incapable subordinates. Finally in 1768 Chatham gave up office altogether. His successor was the somewhat idle *Duke of Grafton*, who resumed the attack on the press.

Grafton's ministry (1768–70)

In 1768 Wilkes returned to England and was elected Member of Parliament for Middlesex. Parliament declared, however, that because of his expulsion he could not sit. He refused to acquiesce in this, and when fresh elections were ordered in the county of Middlesex, he stood again, and was triumphantly re-elected, to the cry of "Wilkes and liberty". An extraordinary struggle followed. Three times he was "expelled" from the Commons, and then Middlesex proceeded to re-elect him. After another election in which Wilkes was successful the House simply declared his opponent elected, though Wilkes had received 1143 votes and his opponent only 296. Such unconstitutional action was bitterly resented, and now there appeared the famous *Letters of Junius*, attacking the Government with a violence which was extraordinarily effective.[1] Grafton resigned in 1770.

Wilkes and liberty

The Letters of Junius

At last George obtained the minister he wanted, and for the next twelve years, from 1770 to 1782, he was largely his own prime minister. The nominal head of the Government was *Lord North*, a good-humoured, easy-going, tactful person, who was quite content to leave the initiative in policy and even the details of administration to the King.[2] The chief interest of this Government lies in its policy towards the American colonies and to this we must now turn.

The King and Lord North (1770–82)

[1] No writer, it has been said, ever surpassed "Junius" in condensed and virulent invective. Amongst others, Lord George Sackville, Grattan, Burke, Gibbon, Lord Chatham, Lord Temple, the brother of George Grenville, and Sir Philip Francis have been credited with the authorship of the letters; the two last-named seem to be the least unlikely.

[2] On two occasions the King actually summoned and presided over a cabinet meeting, delivering on the first occasion a "discourse" which "took up near an hour in delivering".

2. GREAT BRITAIN AND NORTH AMERICA (1763–1783)

We have to deal in this section with the causes and course of one of the most important crises in our history — the War of American Independence. Our very success in the Seven Years' War made our position in North America one of peculiar difficulty. "With the triumph of Wolfe on the Heights of Abraham", it is said, "began the history of the United States". The conquest of Canada freed the American colonies from danger of absorption by the French; and by so doing enabled them to stand by themselves and to become independent of the mother country. Moreover, the great expenses that fell, as a consequence of the war, upon the mother country led to an attempt to tax the colonies, which caused the Puritan democrats of the North and the Anglican, aristocratic, and slave-owning planters of the South to unite for the first time in a common opposition.

Influence of Seven Years' War on American colonies

Up till the end of the Seven Years' War, no other colonies in the world had been so well treated as those in British America. In matters of government, indeed, many of the colonies had in the course of the eighteenth century attained a large measure of self-government. The governor of each colony was generally appointed by the Crown; but the Colonial Assemblies had acquired the right to initiate legislation, and by their control of the finances — and in some colonies of the governor's salary as well — could bend the governors to their will. Great Britain, however, regulated the trade of the colonies — sometimes to her own advantage. Thus the manufacture in America of steel or woollen goods, or even of hats, was limited or forbidden, so as not to compete with British imports. All goods from Europe had first to be landed in Great Britain, and the colonies were also subject to the Navigation Act. Some of the chief colonial products, such as tobacco and cotton, could be exported only to Great Britain. But the colonies had compensations. Many of their products, such as grain and

Trade restrictions

fish and rum, they could export where they liked. They got the protection of the British Fleet and Army. The colonies in the North were able, owing to the Navigation Acts, to develop their shipping. The inhabitants of Great Britain were allowed to smoke only American tobacco. And the restrictions on American trade were largely evaded by systematic smuggling.

In 1763 *George Grenville* became the chief minister in Great Britain. Four things then occurred which began the trouble. First, he found that the revenue from the American customs was only about £2000 a year, and not unnaturally he tried to put some check on the vast amount of smuggling which these small figures indicated — a step strongly resented by the colonists. Secondly, in order to protect the British West Indies, a law had been passed in 1733 putting very heavy duties on molasses or liquid sugar coming to the British North American colonies from the French West Indies, molasses being required, especially in Boston, for the making of rum, and being cheaper in the French than in the British West Indies. Smuggling had made this law ineffective. But now Grenville, though halving the duty on foreign molasses, saw that it was levied, and this increased the colonial irritation. Thirdly, the British Government, anxious to prevent the frauds and abuses which had been formerly committed in obtaining lands from the Indians, issued a Proclamation forming large parts of the land of the colonies into a reserve for the Indians, and forbidding all fresh grants of land by the Red Indians except through the colonial superintendents appointed by the Crown. This seemed to the colonists to be doing away with their rights of independent and indefinite expansion, and caused great suspicion and resentment. Then, fourthly, Grenville decided that it was necessary for the defence of the American colonies, not only against the French but against the Indian tribes, to keep a small standing army in America.[1] Grenville

Grenville's policy (1763–65)

(a) Customs revenue

(b) Duty on molasses

(c) Indian reserves

(d) Standing army in America

[1] A Red Indian, called Pontiac, had invaded the colonies in 1763, and only with great difficulty, and mainly by British troops, was the invasion repelled. This showed the necessity of keeping a standing army in America.

was not unreasonable in thinking that the colonies themselves should contribute something towards the cost of the army. For the resources of Great Britain were being subjected to a severe test. The Seven Years' War had nearly doubled the National Debt. Taxation was heavy and included even taxes on wheels and window panes. Moreover, Britain was threatened by a coalition of France and Spain, countries which were preparing for an attack in the near future.

Nor was Grenville's particular proposal unreasonable. He suggested that the colonies should pay only one-third of the expense of this army by means of an Act under which all legal documents should bear stamps. But he allowed a year's delay for its discussion, and told the agents of the colonies that, if the colonies would raise the money in any other way, he would be quite content; and only when they failed to suggest any alternative scheme was the *Stamp Act* passed through the British Parliament (1765). Moreover, legally the British Parliament had undoubtedly the right to pass the Stamp Act imposing this taxation on the colonies. But it was natural that a liberty-loving people should object to being taxed by a Parliament in which they were unrepresented, and which belonged to a country three thousand miles away that would lessen its own burdens by the amount of money it could raise from them. "No taxation without representation" has been the watchword of English liberty; and it proved a cry which it was difficult for Englishmen to resist. Moreover, the thin-end-of-the-wedge argument was a strong one; if the colonies acquiesced in this tax, would others not be imposed? Consequently the colonies, already irritated by Grenville's other measures, used the year which he had allowed them not for discussion but for agitation. When the Act was finally passed and came into operation, there were riots, a governor's house was sacked, and collectors were burnt in effigy. No one used the stamps; and — most ominous of all — delegates from nine

The Stamp Act (1765)

out of the thirteen colonies met together to protest, thus showing an unprecedented unity of purpose.

Repeal of Stamp Act (1766)

The opinions of British statesmen differed when news of these proceedings reached England. Grenville stood out for Great Britain's legal rights, and others, like Burke, thought the Act inexpedient, and were not concerned with its legality. Chatham thought that the British Parliament had no right to impose an internal tax on the colonies, and proclaimed that the Americans would be slaves if they had not resisted. Meanwhile, on Grenville's retirement from office, *Rockingham* succeeded as Prime Minister. Adopting a conciliatory policy, he repealed the Stamp Act, though an Act was passed at the same time declaring that Great Britain had a right to tax the colonies. The Americans were delighted; and all danger of serious trouble seemed to be at an end (*Note 99*).

Townshend's new duties (1767), and their partial abolition (1770)

But then came another dispute, due to a brilliant and unreliable man, *Charles Townshend*, who was Chancellor of the Exchequer in *Lord Chatham's* ministry. In 1767, at a time when Chatham was totally incapacitated by illness, Townshend *imposed duties on tea, glass, and paper* imported into the American colonies. He contended that as these were external taxes levied at the ports, and not internal taxes, the colonists could not object. The money derived from these taxes — estimated to bring in some £40,000 a year — was to go to pay the governors and officials whose salaries had hitherto been paid by the Assemblies. This was to cut at the root of colonial self-government and aroused the strongest opposition. Accordingly, in 1770, *Lord North's* ministry — which had come into office in that year, and was to remain in power for the next twelve years — abolished the duties on glass and paper. But, with incredible folly, the duty on tea was retained, in order to assert the right of taxing.

Small incidents are exaggerated when two peoples are irritated with one another, and at this time various occurrences exasperated feeling on both sides. We can only

Unfortunate incidents (1770–73)

refer to two of them. British regiments had been subjected to various kinds of insult from the townspeople in Boston. Finally a mob surrounded some soldiers, and after calling them "Rascals, lobsters, and bloody backs" (because they were liable to be flogged), proceeded to snowball them. In the confusion a volley was fired, and four people were killed. The affair was magnified into a massacre, even into "the massacre", by the colonists, and great indignation was aroused (1770). The other incident inflamed feeling in Great Britain. One of the King's ships, the *Gaspee*, engaged in repressing smuggling, was boarded one night by some American colonists and burnt (1772), and the perpetrators of this outrage were never punished.

The Boston "massacre"

Other events soon afterwards finally brought about war. The East India Company — at that time in great financial difficulties — was allowed to export its tea direct to America without going to Great Britain first; consequently the Company would only have to pay the threepenny duty per pound levied on tea imported into America. The more extreme of the colonists, however, thought this was only a trick of the Government to reconcile the colonists to the tax by cheapening the cost of tea, and consequently when the ships of the Company arrived in *Boston* a number of men disguised as Mohawks boarded them, and threw their three hundred and forty chests of tea into the sea (1773).

The Boston Tea-party (1773)

The British Parliament now acted with severity. An Act was passed modifying the Constitution of Massachusetts, transferring to the Crown the appointment of many of the officials, and prohibiting public meetings except by leave of the Governor; the port of Boston was closed, and thousands were thrown out of work. *Gage*, a soldier, was made Governor of Massachusetts, and additional troops were sent out. The other colonies, however, supported Massachusetts, and a Congress representing all the colonies except Georgia was held at Philadelphia. This Congress drew up a Declaration of Rights, demanded the

Outbreak of war (1775)

The American Congress

repeal of thirteen Acts of Parliament, and initiated a boycott — to use a modern word — of British goods. Lord North then tried conciliation, but it was too late, for the war had already begun with a skirmish at *Lexington* (1775).

Declaration of Independence (1776)

In the next year, on 4th July, 1776, came the famous *Declaration of Independence* in which the thirteen colonies finally broke their allegiance to Great Britain, though many people in the colonies did not approve of this step (*Note 100*). With that Declaration began the independent history of the United States. Whether that independence could have been prevented is doubtful. No doubt the British Government was partly to blame; it was, it might be urged, ignorant and unsympathetic, and its policy was vacillating. No doubt, also, the character of the colonists in the North was, in Pitt's phrase, "umbrageous" (i.e. they took umbrage easily) and quarrelsome, whilst there were extremists amongst the colonists who wished to reduce British control to a vanishing point, and who, to use Burke's phrase, "were ready to snuff the approach of tyranny in every tainted breeze". But the circumstances were extraordinarily difficult and perhaps no statesmanship at that time could have overcome them. Two points may be noted in conclusion. First, it was only because the colonists were Englishmen with an Englishman's idea of liberty and self-government that they rebelled — no other colonists would have done so. "No one but Englishmen," says an American historian, "established American independence, and this they did on the basis of English history." Secondly, the colonies, by the time of the accession of George III, had grown up, but the mother country had failed to realize it, and that was perhaps the chief cause of the difficulties.[1]

[1] "Is there not something extremely fallacious", said an American contemporary, "in the commonplace image of the mother country and children colonies? Are we children of Great Britain any more than the cities of London, Exeter, or Bath? Are we not brethren and fellow-subjects with those in Britain?"

"The British Empire was doomed to be broken asunder," says an American historian, "but it was brought to that disaster by the insistent demand of Englishmen in America for the full enjoyment of those liberties which England had fostered beyond any other country of the world."

The War of American Independence (1775–83)

To conduct a campaign[1] three thousand miles away, in a country a thousand miles long and covered with forest, was, for Great Britain, a difficult task. We may compare the British failure in the War of Independence with the successes won in the Seven Years' War, and may wonder at the very different outcome of that war. Yet the answer is that in the Seven Years' War we were really fighting France in North America, and both combatants were then equally far from their bases. In the War of Independence we were fighting the Americans themselves, who, of course, were fighting in their own territory, while we were fighting from our distant base. Moreover, when France joined in the American war, she for a time deprived us of that essential factor, command of the sea. Yet, at the outset the task should not have been insuperable, considering the circumstances of her opponents. The American colonist did not like moving far from his home. Moreover, he only enlisted for short periods, and therefore might leave, and not infrequently did leave, his fellow-colonists in the crisis of a campaign. He was, besides, inclined to be insubordinate, "regarding", said one general, "his officer as no more than a broom-

[1] The following summary of the war will make it more intelligible: —

	Political History	Military Operations (v) British victory; (d) British defeat	
1775.	Congress assumes sovereign authority.	Lexington; Boston blockaded; Bunker's Hill. American expedition to Canada.	
1776.	July 4. Declaration of Independence.	Evacuation of Boston; Brooklyn (v); capture of New York; occupation of New Jersey; Trenton (d).	
1777.		Brandywine (v); Saratoga (d).	
		(*a*) *America*	(*b*) *Maritime and India*
1778.	France declares war; death of Chatham.	Evacuation of Philadelphia.	
1779.	Spain declares war.	Savannah captured (v).	Siege of Gibraltar begins.
1780.	Holland declares war. Armed Neutrality.	Charlestown captured (v); Camden (v).	Hyder Ali invades Carnatic.
1781.		Guildford (v); Yorktown (d).	Porto Novo (v).
1782.	Lord North resigns; negotiations for peace.		Loss of Minorca (d); battle of Saints off St. Lucia (v); Siege of Gibraltar raised (v).
1783.	Peace of Versailles.		

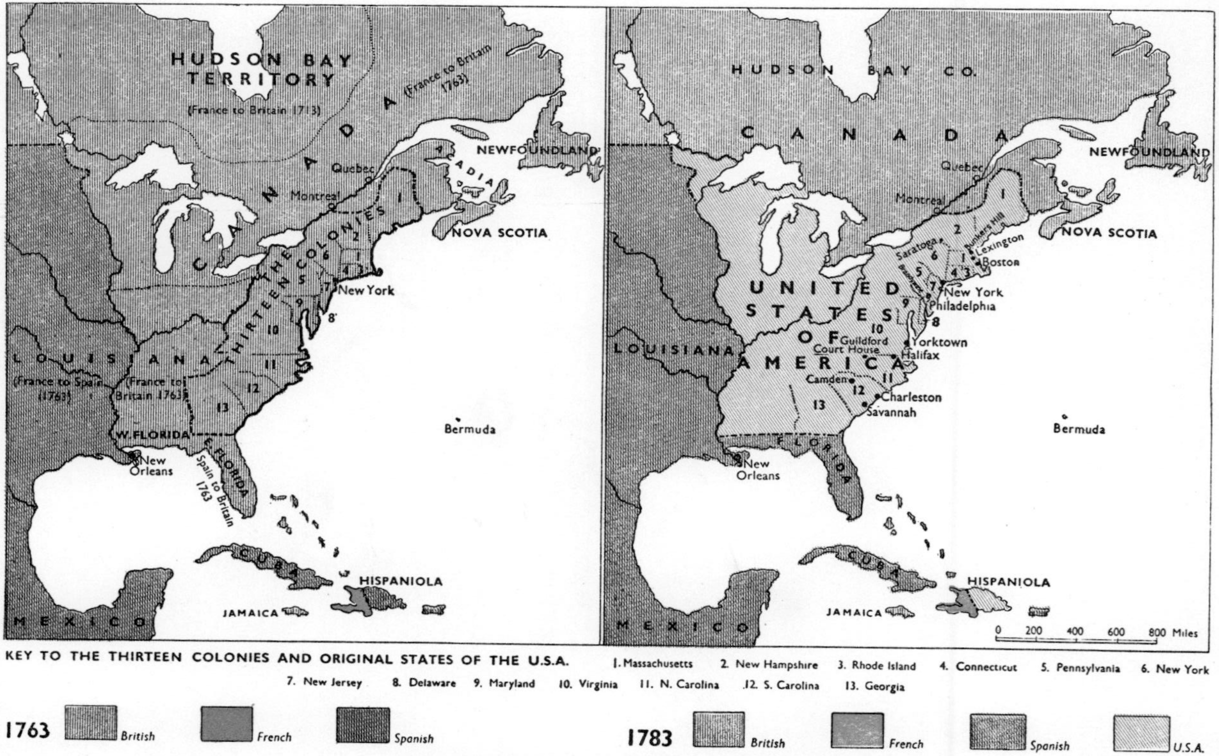

NORTH AMERICA IN 1763 AND IN 1783

stick", especially if serving under the command of officers from any other colony but his own. The Congress, which supervised the generals, was loquacious and incompetent, whilst "peculation and speculation", in the words of the commander-in-chief, were rife amongst the contractors. And finally, a large number of the colonists were either loyal to the mother country or indifferent to the cause of both combatants.

But the British made the mistake of underestimating their enemy; one expert, for instance, declared that four regiments would be sufficient to conquer America. They made inadequate preparations for the dispatch of reinforcements to the army in America when they saw that war was probable; and they began the war in a half-hearted way, with ideas of conciliation and compromise, forgetting "that it is impossible to wage war on the principles of peace". The British, also, not only failed to produce a great general, and fought largely with hired German troops, but possessed in *Lord George Germaine* — the Lord George Sackville who refused to charge at Minden — a minister of war who was to exhibit conspicuous incapacity. The colonists, on the other hand, had in a Virginian planter, *George Washington*, a man as commander-in-chief who, without being perhaps a great general, was untiring in organization and persistently courageous and steadfast even in the darkest periods of the war.[1]

The war lasted for eight years, and is the story of missed opportunities (*Note 101*). During the earlier period the British might have won victory on land but bungled too much. During the latter part of the war, they had lost command of the sea, and that enabled their enemies, France and Spain, to intervene decisively on the side of the colonies.

[1] Washington, a country gentleman of wealth and position, fought against the French and Indians before and during the Seven Years' War, having been made adjutant of the Virginian forces at the age of nineteen and commander-in-chief at the age of twenty-three; in Braddock's expedition of 1754 he showed great bravery, and had four shot-holes in his coat.

Lexington and Bunker's Hill (1775)

In the first campaign, in 1775, the war centred round Boston. The British and Colonists came into conflict at *Lexington*, and though the British seized the stores at which they aimed, yet the attacks on them showed how well the colonists could fight. The British Commander was Gage, and he entirely under-estimated his opponents, with the result that he was involved in the costly fight of *Bunker's Hill.* Here Gage sent his tired troops up a hill on a very hot day, to make a frontal attack on an entrenched position. Though the British took the hill after three attempts, they lost two fifths of their numbers. Gage then did nothing more, and allowed Washington, who had hardly any ammunition, to attack Boston.

American attack on Canada (1775)

The colonists then carried the war into Canada. They sent an expedition to capture Quebec, which, however, held out successfully against them. The British Government had already foreseen danger in this direction and had given concessions (in the Quebec Act, 1774) to the Roman Catholics who now rallied to Britain (see p. 637) and the American expedition met with no support.

British successes (1776)

The failure of this plan seemed, indeed, to be a prelude to American defeat. Gage was replaced by *Lord Howe*, who defeated Washington at *Brooklyn* (1776), took New York, drove Washington away, and over-ran New Jersey. Despite a successful attack by Washington on a German detachment at *Trenton* on Christmas Day, the year closed with prospects looking bad for the colonists, who had hardly any troops left, and bright for Great Britain.

British disaster (1777)

All was altered by the disaster which was now to overtake Great Britain. A plan was made for a final joint attack on Washington.[1] *Burgoyne*, one of the commanders of the British army in Canada, was to cross the frontier and move down southwards. Howe, commanding the British troops

[1] So great was the muddle that to this day it is not clear from the official papers what exactly was contemplated, or which of two plans was decided upon. Lord George Germaine is said never to have opened his official letters, and Howe is said never to have received his orders.

in New York, was to move northwards and join him. Howe wished first to attack Philadelphia, and he did so, and also defeated Washington at the battle of *Brandywine*. But then all went wrong. Burgoyne, who had never expected Howe to delay, had taken *Ticonderoga*, and then struggled on through thickly wooded country, where his supplies began to run out. He was surrounded, and with his whole army of 4000 men surrendered at *Saratoga* (October, 1777). This disaster was later seen to have been the turning-point of the war, and emboldened by the British reverse first France, and then Spain, now declared war upon us.

Brandywine (1777)

Ticonderoga (1777)

Saratoga (1777)

France and Spain declare war

Moreover, disputes arose over the rights of neutrals at sea. Great Britain declared that enemy goods on board neutral ships could be captured (i.e. she denied the doctrine put forward by the neutrals of " free ships, free goods "), and this led to disputes with other powers. As a result, Holland joined the ranks of Britain's enemies and war was declared between the two powers, while Russia, Denmark, and Sweden formed an *Armed Neutrality* which was hostile to Great Britain.

Sea power

Holland declares war

Armed Neutrality (1780)

Thus, not only was the number of Britain's enemies most formidably increased, but the importance of sea-power became overwhelming. Spain attacked Gibraltar, the route to India was menaced, and attacks were made on the West Indies.

The British fleet had been allowed to deteriorate since the Seven Years' War, while the French fleet had grown stronger. The French navy was now almost equal in numbers to the British fleet, and it had adopted new tactics, which were to become extremely successful, of firing at masts, sails, and rigging.[1] This inferiority of the British at sea was to become decisive, for it reacted on the position of the troops in America.

Weakness of the British navy

In 1780 the British (now under *Clinton*) were in New

[1] Modern critics think that the British should therefore have confined themselves to blockading the enemy ports.

The Surrender of York-town (1781) York, and decided to co-operate with the many "loyalists" in the southern States. *General Cornwallis* was therefore dispatched to Carolina where he captured Charlestown, and won an engagement at *Camden*, and another at *Guildford Court House*. He then moved to the coast to wait at *York-town*, in Virginia, for the British fleet to bring him reinforcements. But instead of the British, the French fleet arrived, and blockaded him while Washington appeared with a large army and cut him off on land. His position seemed quite hopeless, for the French fleet could bombard him from the sea, and Washington from the land. He was obliged to surrender.

Meanwhile French troops had been landed in the north, and soon Britain was left with nothing in her hands but New York itself.

Attacks by France and Spain Elated by this series of events, France and Spain now attacked Great Britain with vigour. In the West Indies all her islands were captured except Barbados and Jamaica. **Loss of Minorca (1782)** In the Mediterranean Minorca was taken, and the siege of Gibraltar (which had already lasted for three years) was pressed on.

So threatening was the outlook that public feeling in England forced the King to dismiss Lord North. It became clear that peace must be made. Two successes came most opportunely to give Great Britain better bargaining power. *Admiral Rodney* had been sent to deal with the French fleet which had worked such havoc in the West Indies. **Battle of the Saints (1782)** He met them off Dominica, and in the *Battle of the Saints* (a group of tiny islands) won a decisive victory [1] (1782).

In the same year *Gibraltar* was saved. The French and Spaniards made a great combined attack by sea with 49

[1] When war broke out between France and Great Britain, Rodney was at Paris in an impecunious condition, and his creditors refused to let him go home. A French nobleman, however, chivalrously came to his rescue with a loan, and Rodney returned. During his two and a half years of command in the American War, Rodney captured a French, a Spanish, and a Dutch admiral, and added twelve line-of-battle ships, all taken from the enemy, to the British navy, including the *Ville de Paris*, the great ship which the city of Paris had given to the French King

ships, and by land with 40,000 men. The attack was beaten off by Eliott, the governor, and his garrison of 7000 men. A British fleet appeared, drove off the enemy, and raised the siege, which had lasted for three years and seven months.

Gibraltar saved (1782)

The two events made Britain's enemies ready to negotiate, and preliminaries of peace were begun. In 1783 treaties were concluded at *Versailles*. The independence of the United States was recognized, and, in spite of their efforts to save them, the British had to leave such of the loyalists who did not emigrate to Canada to the mercy or rather to the vengeance of their fellow-colonists. Great Britain gave up to Spain, Minorca and Florida; and to France, Tobago, Senegal, and Goree, besides restoring to her St. Lucia and the Indian settlements which had been taken from France during the war.

The Treaties of Versailles (1783)

The American War of Independence deprived Great Britain of one empire; but it strengthened the foundations of another.

In 1774, as has been already noted, the British Parliament had passed the Quebec Act for Canada. This Act had extended the boundaries of Canada, had set up a form of government by a Governor and a nominated Council, made French law the law of the land, and had in effect recognized and supported the Roman Catholic Church as the national church of Canada. This Act was very unpopular with the English colonists in the thirteen American colonies, and was one of the contributory causes of the war; they especially disliked the clause extending the boundaries of Quebec at the expense, as they thought, of their further expansion, and the clause recognizing the Roman Catholic Church. But by the French colonists of Canada it came to be regarded as the *Magna Carta* of their history, and it did much to reconcile them to their conquerors.

The Quebec Act (1774)

CHAPTER 49

GREAT BRITAIN AND INDIA (1763–1823)

Condition of India (1763)

We must now turn back from the West to the East, from America to India, where these years from 1763 to 1783 are hardly less important. Two things must be borne in mind. First, India was still in a state of anarchy. The boundaries of States were constantly shifting; there was no such thing, it was said at the time, as a frontier in India. Adventurers sprang up who carved out new States for themselves, or usurped the thrones of old ones; and the Great Mogul Emperor was under the tutelage now of one potentate and then of another. In the second place, the East India Company was in a very undefined and uncertain position after the Seven Years' War was over. The Nabob of the Carnatic and the Nizam of Hyderabad were its allies. It possessed some territory, but not much, on the east coast, and round Bombay and Madras. In Bengal, however, its position was peculiar. Except for Calcutta and some districts near it, the Nabob still governed that province. But he was the Company's nominee, and — put briefly — it may be said that his object was to extract as much money as possible from the country, whilst the Company's officials collected from the Nabob what money and privileges they could obtain, collectively for the Company and individually for themselves.

Such a position in Bengal was bound to lead to difficulties, and it very quickly did. The Nabob who had succeeded Meer Jaffier quarrelled with the Company, massacred some Europeans at Patna, and fled to his neighbour, the Nabob of Oudh. Both Nabobs, however, were defeated at the decisive battle of *Buxar*. It was necessary then to regulate our position. Fortunately *Clive* became Governor of Bengal six months after the battle, and in the

Battle of Buxar (1764)

short space of twenty-two months made great changes (1765–67). In the first place, he obtained from the Mogul Emperor the financial administration of Bengal and Bihar; and thus the East India Company became practically the governors of a country three-quarters the size of France. Secondly, he made an alliance with the Nabob of Oudh, his idea being that the Nabob's territory might be a useful buffer against aggressions from the west, either on the part of the Marathas or the Afghans. Thirdly, and above all, he supplemented the inadequate salaries of the officials, and forbade them to take part in private trading — thus initiating the series of reforms which was eventually to make the British rule in India, so far as British officials at all events were concerned, perhaps the purest in the world. It is sad to think that Clive should have come home to be attacked in Parliament for corruption,[1] and soon afterwards, under stress of disease and anxiety, to commit suicide (1774).

Clive's reforms (1765–67)

Trade and not conquest had in the past been the object of the East India Company, good dividends rather than warlike distinctions. Consequently the British Government had not interfered with the Company, beyond renewing its charter from time to time. But now that the Company had become the owner of a vast territory, the British Government was bound to assume some portion of the responsibility, more especially as after Clive's departure matters fell into great confusion (*Note 103*). Consequently, in *1773*, a *Regulating Act* was passed by *Lord North.* A governor-general and council of four members were appointed, with control over all the Company's possessions in India. Hence some unity of control was secured. But the Act was in other respects unsatisfactory. The governor-general was liable to be much hampered by the council, all of whose members had equal votes, and both were exposed to some interference

The Regulating Act (1773)

[1] It was in the course of his examination before a parliamentary committee that Clive, describing the temptations to which he was subjected, exclaimed, " By God, Mr. Chairman, at this moment I stand astonished at my own moderation!"

from the judges who were appointed under the same Act.

The first governor-general was *Warren Hastings*.[1] He found himself from the first terribly hampered by the Council, since one of the members sent from England was Sir Philip Francis, who came out with the preconceived idea that Hastings was both oppressive and corrupt. Francis won over two of the Council to his side, and thus Hastings was outvoted and could not carry any of his measures. This lasted for two years until one of his opponents died. Thwarted now by the Council, now by the incompetent governments of Bombay or Madras, with a temper, as he said, " almost fermented into vinegar by the weight of affairs and by everlasting teasing ", he yet managed to do a vast amount. He divided Bengal into districts for purposes of government, arranged its land revenue, and organized its civil service.

Warren Hastings Governor-general (1774–85)

Above all, Warren Hastings by his resourcefulness and courage saved our position in India at a critical time. The disaster at Saratoga and the consequent alliance of the French with the American colonists had its effect upon affairs in the East no less than in the West. French agents intrigued with the Marathas, and Warren Hastings found himself involved in a war with fighting tribes who were almost a match for our arms. Moreover, in Southern India the French secured in Suffren an admiral, and in *Hyder Ali* an ally who brought our Indian Empire to the verge of ruin. Hyder Ali, who had usurped the throne of Mysore, was, though ignorant of the alphabet, a very remarkable man. In alliance with the French, he suddenly invaded the plains of the Carnatic, and in three weeks had wellnigh extinguished our power (1780).[2] But Hastings was equal to the occasion. Within twenty-four hours of hearing the news at Calcutta

India during the War of American Independence (1778–82)

Hyder Ali

[1] He was a Westminster boy, and had been sent to India at an early age, to the great grief of his head master, who thought his classical attainments would be wasted in that arid and commercial atmosphere.

[2] There is a celebrated description of this invasion, and of the havoc it wrought, in Burke's speech on the Debts of the Nabob of Arcot.

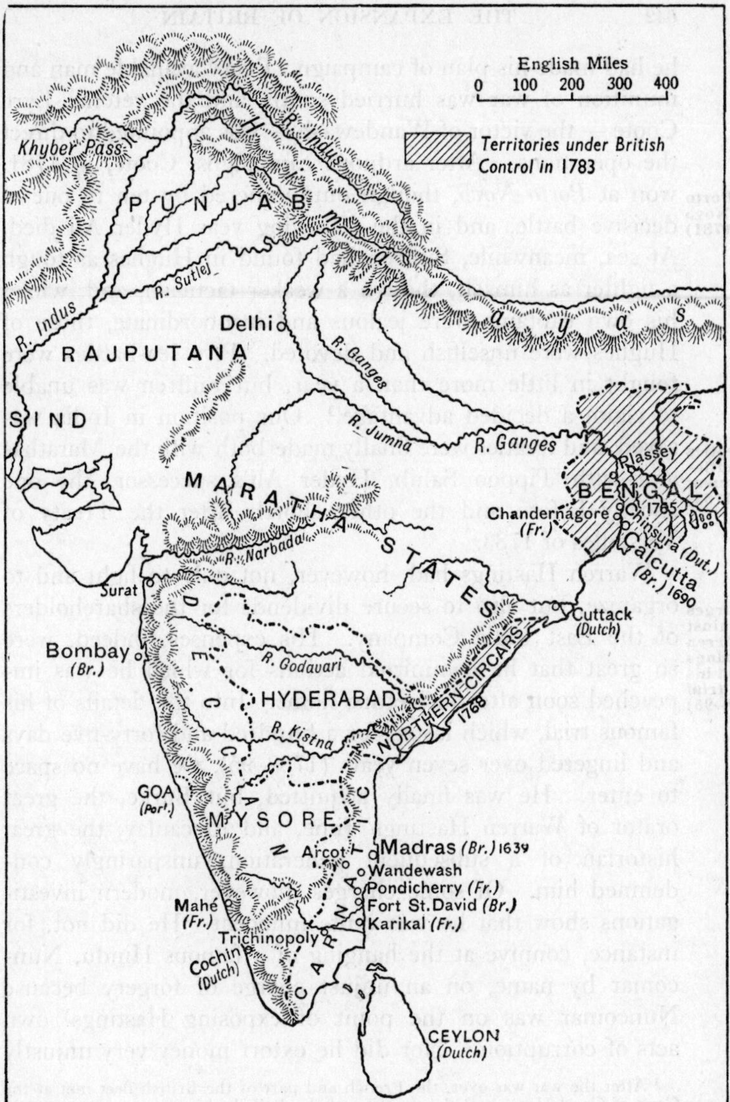
English Miles
0 100 200 300 400
Territories under British Control in 1783
Khyber Pass
PUNJAB
HIMALAYAS
R. Indus
R. Sutlej
R. Indus
Delhi
RAJPUTANA
R. Ganges
R. Jumna
R. Ganges
SIND
MARATHA STATES
Plassey
BENGAL
1765
Chandernagore (Fr.)
Chinsura (Dut.)
Calcutta (Br.) 1690
R. Narbada
Surat
Cuttack (Dutch)
DECCAN
Bombay (Br.)
R. Godavari
HYDERABAD
NORTHERN CIRCARS
1768
R. Kistna
GOA (Port.)
MYSORE
CARNATIC
Arcot
Madras (Br.) 1639
Wandewash
Pondicherry (Fr.)
Fort St. David (Br.)
Karikal (Fr.)
Mahé (Fr.)
Trichinopoly
Cochin (Dutch)
CEYLON (Dutch)

INDIA, 1707–1783

he had made his plan of campaign. Every available man and munition of war was hurried south, and the veteran Eyre Coote — the victor of Wandewash — was appointed to direct the operations. After arduous campaigns, Coote, in 1781, won at *Porto Novo*, though outnumbered by ten to one, a decisive battle, and in the following year Hyder Ali died. At sea, meanwhile, Suffren had found in Hughes as tough a fighter as himself, though a weaker tactician, and, whilst his own captains were jealous and insubordinate, those of Hughes were unselfish and devoted. Five sea-battles were fought in little more than a year, but Suffren was unable to claim a decided advantage.[1] Our position in India was saved, and treaties were finally made both with the Marathas and with Tippoo Sahib, Hyder Ali's successor, the one shortly before and the other shortly after the Treaty of Versailles of 1783.

Porto Novo (1781)

Treaties of Settlement (1783)

Warren Hastings had, however, not only to fight and to organize, but also to secure dividends for the shareholders of the East India Company. His expenses, indeed, were so great that he committed actions for which he was impeached soon after his return home. Into the details of his famous trial, which lasted for a hundred and forty-five days and lingered over seven years (1788–95), we have no space to enter. He was finally acquitted, but Burke, the great orator of Warren Hastings' time, and Macaulay, the great historian of a subsequent generation, unsparingly condemned him. Of some charges, however, modern investigations show that he was quite innocent. He did not, for instance, connive at the hanging of a famous Hindu, Nuncomar by name, on an unjust charge of forgery because Nuncomar was on the point of exposing Hastings' own acts of corruption.[2] Nor did he extort money very unjustly

Charges against Warren Hastings and his trial (1788–95)

[1] After the war was over, the French and part of the British fleet met at the Cape of Good Hope, and the captains of the British ships at once hastened in a body to pay their respects to the great French commander.

[2] Nuncomar was hanged for forgery, but there is no reason for believing that the decision was an unjust one, or that Warren Hastings had anything to do with it.

from the blameless mother and grandmother of the Nabob of Oudh, cruelly torturing their blameless ministers; the truth being that the Begums — as the mother and grandmother were called — had departed from Oudh with a large sum of money which really belonged to the State, and that probably only slight coercion was needed to induce the ministers to return it.

In other matters Warren Hastings may have acted unwisely, as, for instance, when he let troops out on hire to the Nabob of Oudh for the suppression of the *Rohillas*, a turbulent tribe of Afghans; or inflicted upon the Rajah of Benares an enormous fine because he refused to pay a sum of money for the expenses of the war. But though it is impossible to justify everything that Clive or Hastings did, we must remember that to the former is due the beginning of our Empire in India, and that the latter not only succeeded in retaining, in the darkest days of our Imperial existence, every acre of land that we then possessed in India, but in leaving our dominions strengthened and organized. Warren Hastings is a not unworthy beginner of that long line of governors-general and viceroys of whom it has been said that they represent a higher level of ruling qualities than has been attained by any line of hereditary sovereigns, or by any line of elected presidents.

India. Pitt's India Act (1784)

It may be convenient at this stage to proceed with the history of India during the forty years after Warren Hastings' retirement from India. Lord North's Regulating Act of 1773 had proved a failure. Consequently, just previously to the retirement of Warren Hastings, the younger *Pitt* passed, in 1784, an Act reorganizing the government of our possessions in India. The governor-general was given greater powers, and henceforth, subject to a *Board of Control* sitting in London, directed the politics and the diplomacy of our Indian Empire. In future the governor-general was, as a rule, a person of high birth and connections sent out from Great Britain; and as both the governor-general

The Board of Control

and the Board of Control were appointed by the King acting on the advice of his ministers, the British Government became directly responsible for our Indian policy. In the appointment of other officials, however, and in matters of trade the East India Company was left supreme, though the Government had to confirm the higher appointments.

Marquis Cornwallis Governor-general (1786–93)

The first governor-general under the new system was the *Marquis Cornwallis* (1786–93), the defender of Yorktown. In his administration three points deserve notice. In the first place, by his own personal example and by his measures he still further purified the administration. Secondly, he made in Bengal a permanent settlement of the land revenue, by which the tax-collectors in that province — *zemindars* as they were called — were practically converted into landlords paying a fixed rent to the government, a policy the expediency of which has been much debated. Thirdly, though he left Great Britain with the intention of pursuing a peaceful policy, he found himself obliged to make war on Tippoo Sahib of Mysore. After a skilful campaign he was successful, and forced his adversary to make peace and to lose half his territories.[1]

Marquis Wellesley Governor-general (1798–1805)

After an interval, Richard Wellesley, better known as the *Marquis Wellesley*, the elder brother of the great soldier who eventually became Duke of Wellington, was made governor-general. A brilliant scholar at Eton, he obtained this office at the age of thirty-five. He found on his arrival in India, in 1798, a situation which required the exercise of all his abilities. French ambitions were reviving. French officers, by drilling and organizing the troops of native rulers, had not only improved those troops immensely but had obtained very great influence for themselves — one of them was deified after his death and is still worshipped in Southern India. Tippoo Sahib, who proved himself a hard-

[1] Cornwallis found, like subsequent viceroys, that his work was very laborious and harassing. "I have a great deal more business every day", he wrote to his son, "than you have in a whole school-day, and I never get a whole holiday."

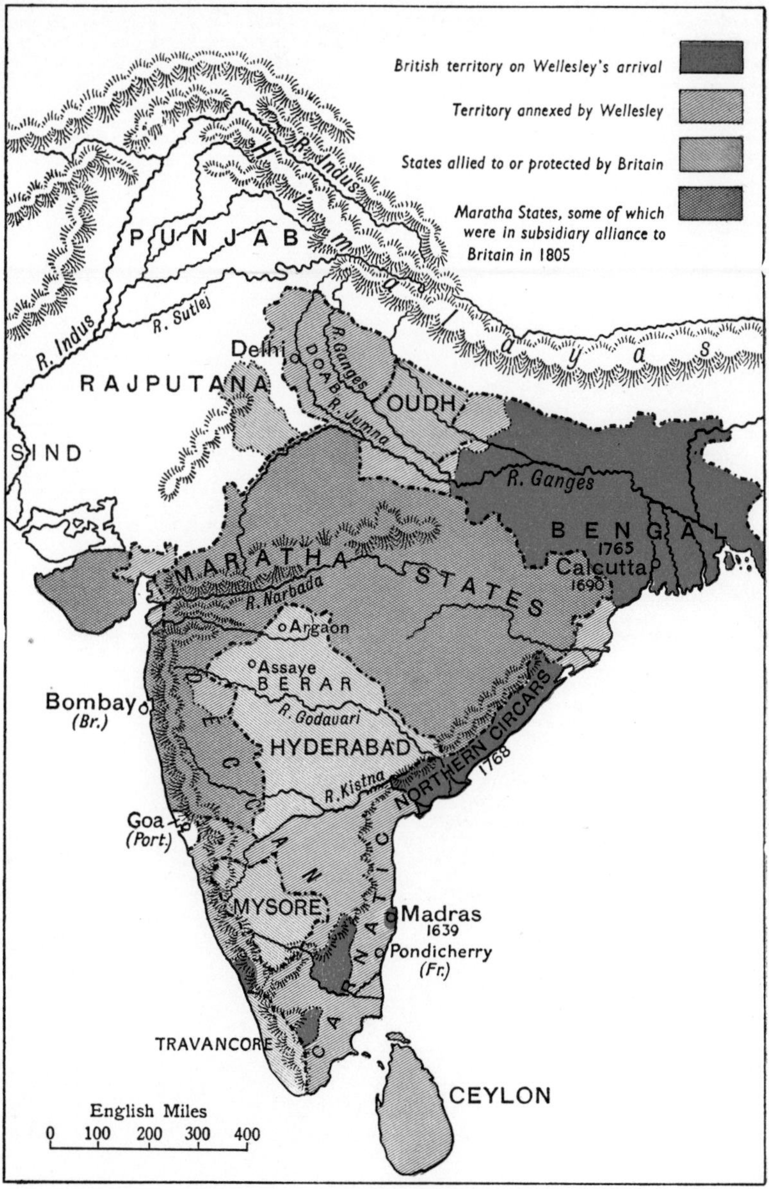
British territory on Wellesley's arrival
Territory annexed by Wellesley
States allied to or protected by Britain
Maratha States, some of which were in subsidiary alliance to Britain in 1805
R. Indus
Himalayas
PUNJAB
R. Sutlej
R. Indus
Delhi
DOAB
R. Ganges
R. Jumna
OUDH
RAJPUTANA
SIND
R. Ganges
BENGAL
1765
Calcutta
1690
MARATHA STATES
R. Narbada
Argaon
Assaye
BERAR
R. Godavari
Bombay
(Br.)
DECCAN
HYDERABAD
NORTHERN CIRCARS
1768
R. Kistna
Goa
(Port.)
MYSORE
CARNATIC
Madras
1639
Pondicherry
(Fr.)
TRAVANCORE
CEYLON
English Miles
0 100 200 300 400

INDIA, 1784–1805

F 938

working ruler as well as a brave and resourceful soldier, had made an alliance with the French in order to realize his supreme object — the downfall of the British. Above all, three weeks after Wellesley reached Madras, Napoleon himself started on the Egyptian expedition, and, if successful, might have proceeded to India (p. 679).

Into the details of Wellesley's great proconsulship limits of space forbid us to enter, and we must only allude to its chief results. First, Wellesley persuaded the Nizam of Hyderabad to expel the French officers in his service, and arranged that, in return for the Nizam giving up part of his territory, the East India Company should maintain an army for his defence. Then he turned against Tippoo Sahib, and the brilliant capture of *Seringapatam* by *Baird* resulted in Tippoo's death.[1] A large part of Mysore was annexed by the Company, a small part was given to the Nizam, and the remainder was handed over to the representative of the old Hindu dynasty which had ruled there before its expulsion by Hyder Ali. Other annexations in Southern India followed, the result of which was that most of the Carnatic came under direct British control. Hence our territories in the south were enormously extended.

Wellesley's policy in the south

Capture of Seringapatam (1799)

In the north, Wellesley's operations were no less important. He made a treaty with the Nabob of Oudh similar to that made with the Nizam, the Company in exchange for territory, including Rohilcund, maintaining an army for the Nabob's defence. War subsequently followed with some of the Maratha leaders, of whom the most formidable was Sindhia, whose troops had been trained by French officers. Arthur Wellesley — the future Duke of Wellington — won the battles of *Assaye* and *Argaum* in 1803,[2] the

Wellesley's policy in the north

Battle of Assaye and Argaum (1803)

[1] He was buried with military honours under an escort of British grenadiers, and his family was taken under British protection. The last of his sons, whom Queen Victoria was much interested in seeing in 1854, died in Calcutta in 1877.

[2] See Tennyson's "Ode on the Death of the Duke of Wellington":

"This is he who far away
Against the myriads at Assaye
Fought with his fiery few and won."

Battle of Laswarri and capture of Delhi (1803)

former by an attack of superb audacity against an army twice his strength. Lake won the battle of *Laswarri* and captured Delhi, and with its capture the Mogul emperor came under British control. Later on came a war with Holkar, another Maratha leader, whose irregular horse were famous throughout India. Against him our army met with a disaster, and the East India Company and the British Government, already frightened by the immensity of the recent annexations, and the cost of the military operations, recalled Wellesley in 1805. Under Wellesley important reforms had been made in administration. But it is chiefly for his extension of our empire that he is remembered; for in the space of seven years he had made our territories continuous from Delhi to Calcutta and from Calcutta to Cape Comorin; he had destroyed or weakened our most dangerous foes; he had closed India to the French, and had exalted Great Britain to be the suzerain power in India.

Extension of Empire under Wellesley

Lord Hastings Governor-general (1814–23)

For nearly ten years after Wellesley's departure little occurred in India. It was a period of inaction and of non-intervention. But the anarchy in various parts of India soon necessitated British action. Enormous bands of brigands, "human jackals", roamed over Central India, burning and killing and robbing wherever they went. Sometimes these *Pindaris*, as they were called, crossed into British territory and did immense damage. Such a state of things could not continue, and on *Lord Hastings*' arrival as governor-general (1814–23) our policy was changed into one of action. Lord Hastings first had a war with *Nepal*— the home of the brave Gurkhas — which led to some annexation of territory and to a satisfactory settlement of our relations with that country. In 1817 came the struggle with the Pindaris, which led also to a war with the Marathas. The result was that both Pindaris and Marathas submitted; a good deal of territory was annexed, including the territories of the Peshwa of Poona, whilst the boundaries of the

War with Nepal

various native states in the centre of India were delimitated. There for the present we may leave Indian affairs. Thanks chiefly to Wellesley and Hastings, the British power had been substituted in India for that of the Great Mogul. That eastern empire which had been the dream of Napoleon's ambition had become an accomplished fact with his greatest enemies.

Nor is India the only part of our empire which was developed in the later part of the eighteenth and the beginning of the nineteenth century. The discoveries of *Captain Cook* between 1768 and 1779 had given to Great Britain the opportunity of developing a third great continent in Australia. How the opportunity was utilized will be told later.

CHAPTER 50

DOMESTIC AFFAIRS—FOX AND BURKE

Party Struggles: Fox and Burke

We must now go back to see how matters had developed at home while such great deeds were on foot abroad. While the war with America had dragged along its disastrous course, the dissatisfaction aroused in Great Britain at the mismanagement and blunders was very great. People blamed the ministers, and they blamed the King for choosing them. In addition the growing power of George III was regarded with alarm, and in 1780 a motion was carried in the House of Commons that the "influence of the Crown has increased, is increasing, and ought to be diminished". In the same year came a formidable ultra-Protestant riot, owing to an Act of Parliament repealing some of the laws against the Roman Catholics: its leader was *Lord George Gordon*, and all London east of Charing Cross was at the mercy of a mob, till George III himself ordered the troops to disperse

The Gordon Riot (1780)

the people without waiting to read the Riot Act.[1] The proposal of a similar Bill for Scotland, granting concessions to the Roman Catholics, aroused such an uproar in that country that it had to be abandoned. Finally, in 1782, after the capitulation of Yorktown and the loss of Minorca, Lord North insisted upon resigning — to the great disgust of the King, who never forgave him for his " desertion ", as he called it; " remember, my Lord," said the King, on parting from him, " that it is you who desert me, not I you."

The Rockingham Whigs (1782)

The King had now to recall the Whigs, and Rockingham once more became Prime Minister. This ministry was made celebrated by the outstanding individuals who now gave the party unequalled brilliance. The chief of these were Charles James Fox and Edmund Burke.

Fox

Charles James Fox (*Note 105*) was a strange mixture of virtues and vices. He has been described as the most genial of all associates and the most beloved of all friends. He was a great lover of literature, and read through his Homer, it was said, every year. He was energetic in all that he did, whether in taking writing lessons when secretary of state to improve his handwriting, or in swimming and cricket, and he became, through constant practice, an incomparable debater.[2] Yet, before he was twenty-four he ran through a fortune by gambling, and was the leader of every sort of extravagant fashion — including red-heeled shoes and blue hair-powder. His political life was varied. Beginning as a Tory and a member of Lord North's ministry, he became a Whig during the American War, and developed into a Radical as a supporter of the French Revolution. He might be called the founder of the Liberal Party, as he bridged the

[1] For four days London was in the hands of the mob; Newgate prison was destroyed and its 300 prisoners released; Roman Catholic chapels were burnt: and a distillery was attacked, with the result that immense casks of spirits were broken, and many of the mob died as a result of drinking too much. The leader, Lord George Gordon, eventually became a Jew and died a madman (see Dickens' *Barnaby Rudge*).

[2] In one session he spoke at every sitting except one, and he always regretted that he had abstained from speaking on that occasion.

gap between the old Whig Party and the new Whigs who pressed for Parliamentary Reform. Whatever views he held he supported passionately. As a statesman, however, he failed to gain the confidence of the King or of the nation, and from the time he left the Tory ministry in 1774 till the time of his death in 1806, he was only in office for twenty months.

Of *Edmund Burke* (*Note 106*) it has been said that, " Bacon alone excepted, he was the greatest political thinker that has ever devoted himself to the practice of English politics ". An Irishman by birth, and educated at Dublin University, he became, when thirty-six years of age, secretary to Lord Rockingham, and a Whig member of Parliament (1765). He was a keen Whig and a great writer and talker. His speeches had enormous influence; for all politicians read them, though members of Parliament did not always listen to them, as they were long and awkwardly delivered.[1] Possessed of wonderful knowledge, he formed opinions which posterity has agreed were generally right. Thus he was in favour of a policy of conciliation with the American colonies; he supported the claims of the Roman Catholics for emancipation, and of the Dissenters for complete toleration; he wished to reform the penal code and the debtors laws; and he attacked the slave trade. But though he wished to diminish the corruption of Parliament, he was a great admirer of the British constitution as it then existed, and he was opposed to any extension of the franchise or redistribution of the constituencies. Moreover, he had a great horror of any violent reforms, and hence became an impassioned opponent of the French Revolution, as was shown in his " Reflections " upon it.

Burke

Samuel Johnson once said that Burke and Chatham were the only two men he knew who had risen considerably above

[1] Burke spoke with a strong Irish accent, his gestures were clumsy, and his delivery was described as execrable. Yet of one of his speeches in the Warren Hastings impeachment a contemporary wrote: " Burke did not, I believe, leave a dry eye in the whole assembly ".

the common standard, and it is an extraordinary thing that Burke should never have had a seat in any cabinet. He did not, however, belong to one of the governing families, and his Irish extraction made Englishmen inclined to distrust him. Moreover, his judgment was occasionally warped to such an extent by his imagination, as in the charges which he brought against Warren Hastings, that it became entirely unreliable. But of his writings one of the greatest English historians has said, "The time may come when they may no longer be read; the time will never come in which men will not grow the wiser by reading them."

Whig Reformers

The Whigs hoped to check the corrupt power which the Crown had acquired, and for this purpose they now brought in (through Burke's influence) an *Economical Reform Bill.*

The "Economical Reform" Bill

This reduced the number of offices and pensions and disfranchized all "revenue officers". Up to this time these "officers", who were appointed by the Crown, were so numerous that they actually formed one-tenth of the voters of the country. Other measures included the grant of an independent Parliament to Ireland (see p. 711).

Shelburne's ministry (1782–83)

When Rockingham died, the King chose as Prime Minister *Lord Shelburne*, a very able but unpopular man who was so much distrusted and disliked by Fox and Burke that both resigned office rather than serve under him.

To Shelburne fell the unenviable task of making the peace, and when the terms of the Treaty of Versailles became known (see p. 637) his enemies made capital out of it. Fox and Burke united with Lord North and Shelburne was out-voted in the House and driven from office.

The Fox-North ministry: The "Infamous Coalition" (1783)

For a brief while these incongruous allies held power. The *Duke of Portland* acted as head of the new ministry, but Fox was its chief figure. He could count on North's stolid placidity [1] and he hoped he himself could accomplish

[1] There is a story that, during the War of American Independence, after Fox had denounced a member of Lord North's ministry in most scathing terms, Lord North came up to Fox and said laughingly, "I am glad you did not fall on me, Charles, for you were in high feather to-day."

much. Yet brilliant as were Fox's talents, he could not get either the nation or the King to accept this ministry. Many people were disgusted at an alliance between such opponents, Fox the advanced Whig, and North the extreme Tory. Clearly such an alliance had no solid base. When Fox brought in his *India Bill*, his enemies saw their chance. This Bill proposed to take over the powers of the East India Company and to govern the Indian provinces through Commissioners and officials, all of whom would naturally be appointed by Fox's government. The King acted. He could no longer control the Commons, but he had absolute control of the Lords. He sent messages stating that " whoever voted for the bill would be considered his enemy ", and as a result the measure was thrown out, and the Coalition ministry resigned.[1]

Their place was taken (December, 1783) by a young man of twenty-four, William Pitt the second son of the great Earl of Chatham, and with his appearance a new period began.

[1] Fox had " sol i his birthright for a mess of pottage ", for after these few weeks in power, he was out of office for twenty years.

NOTES ON PERIOD EIGHT (1714–1783)

BRITISH SOVEREIGNS

George I (1714–1727)
George II (1727–1760)
George III (1760–1820)

IMPORTANT FOREIGN RULERS

France:	Louis XV (1715–1774)
	Louis XVI (1774–1793)
Empire:	Charles VI (1711–1740)
Austria:	Maria Theresa (1740–1780)
Prussia:	Frederick William I (1713–1740)
	Frederick II — " The Great " (1740–1786)
Russia:	Peter I — " The Great " (1689–1725)
	Elizabeth (1741–1762)
	Catherine II — " The Great " (1762–1796)

MINISTRIES IN GREAT BRITAIN (1714—1783)

Stanhope–Townshend:	(1714–1717)
Stanhope:	(1717–1721)
Walpole:	(1721–1742)
Carteret:	(1742–1744)
Pelham:	(1744–1754)
Newcastle:	(1754–1756)
Devonshire–Pitt:	(1756-1757)
Newcastle–Pitt:	(1757–1761)
Bute:	(1761–1763)
Grenville:	(1763–1765)
Rockingham:	(1765–1766)
Chatham:	(1766–1768)
Grafton:	(1768–1770)
North:	(1770–1782)
Rockingham:	(1782)
Shelburne:	(1782–1783)
Fox–North:	(1783)
Pitt:	(1783–1801)

Note 93. — THE HANOVERIAN PERIOD

1. Effects of the Hanoverian Succession.

(*a*) George I was a foreigner, and could not speak English. Hence his *Prime Minister* acquired great power and influence. Cabinet system developed, with *Cabinet of one party* and head acting as link with the Crown.

(*b*) *The Whigs* were supreme, and carried measures for toleration and Septennial Act (Parliament to sit for 7 years) to keep themselves longer in office (1716).

(*c*) *Oligarchy* in power; a band of great Whig noble families, but the bulk of the people had very little power or influence.

(i) This led to corruption, for the party in power could give away places and pensions and so secured votes in the house.

(ii) In the elections to Parliament, the bad representative system enabled wealthy men to buy up seats (rotten and pocket boroughs).

2. Revolts against the Hanoverians

(*a*) *The First Jacobite Rebellion*, 1715.

(i) Led by Earl of Mar in the Highlands; by Forster in Cumberland; and Irish were to land in the west. Mar fought at *Sheriffmuir*, but battle indecisive one, and a Spanish force later defeated when it landed in Scotland.

(ii) No French help came; Louis XIV died, and Regency did not want war with England.

(iii) The " Old Pretender ", James Francis Edward, did not land in Scotland till after Sheriffmuir, Jan., 1716; came without troops and was so uninspiring he thoroughly damped down his supporters. Left after one month.

(iv) English government acted promptly and with success.

(*b*) *Second Jacobite Rebellion*, 1745–46. Charles Edward the " Young Pretender " landed.

(i) Took Edinburgh. Won Battle of *Prestonpans*.

(ii) Invaded England, via Carlisle (English army was guarding the other, eastern route), and marched by Manchester to *Derby*. Turned back, because English had one army guarding London, another in the north ready to cut him off and a third in the Midlands.

(iii) Retreated to Scotland and won Battle of *Falkirk*. Retreated to Highlands and defeated at *Culloden* (1746).

Initial successes won because Great Britain was occupied in war abroad. Failed because English did not join Prince Charles Edward. Hanoverians firmly established, partly owing to Walpole's prosperous ministry and Great Britain would not accept a Roman Catholic sovereign.

NOTE 94. — WALPOLE (1676—1745)

1. **Financial Measures.**

(*a*) Very successful financier. Rose to power through his skill over the *South Sea Bubble*. Restored credit after the panic (1720).

(*b*) Reformed the tariff, reducing duties on articles.

(*c*) Set up the " Sinking Fund " to pay off the capital of the National Debt by setting aside one million a year from taxation and using the interest on that to repay loans to Government (1729).

(*d*) *Excise Bill* (1733). To make wines and spirits pay duty only when taken out of bonded warehouses for consumption. Would have stopped smuggling into England. Fiercely opposed, on ground that inspectors would " pry " into men's private affairs so *dropped by Walpole.*

2. **Cabinet Rule.**

Walpole acted as Prime Minister, and head of his *Cabinet.* If a minister disagreed, he dismissed him from office.

3. **Reasons for his Fall.**

(*a*) Unpopular over Excise Bill.

(*b*) Unpopular over *Porteous Riots* (1736). A Scottish smuggler was to be executed, the crowd rescued him and Captain Porteous fired on the crowd. Tried for deaths of persons in mob, reprieved, was lynched by mob. Walpole highly unpopular for Government's part.

(*c*) Death of *Queen Caroline,* his ardent supporter (1737).

(*d*) Opposition stampeded country into war with Spain over "*Jenkins's Ear*". Walpole utterly against the war; conducted it so tepidly, forced to resign (1742).

4. **Results of Walpole's Ministry.**

Britain had 20 years of peace and prosperity, Hanoverians settled down, and country grew rich.

NOTE 95. — WARS WITH SPAIN AND AUSTRIA

1. Britain anxious to trade with Spanish America, but Spaniards dreaded this. War of " *Jenkins's Ear* " over this trade (1739).

2. **War of Austrian Succession** (1740–48).

Maria Theresa of Austria, was to succeed her father the Emperor by the set of treaties called " Pragmatic Sanctions ". Frederick the Great of Prussia attacked her, and France joined him. *Great Britain supported Maria Theresa,* because she did not want France to get the Austrian Netherlands (Belgium), and King George as " Elector of Hanover " was ally of Maria Theresa.

British won battle of *Dettingen* (1743) and drove French out of Germany (1743).

British defeated at *Fontenoy,* in the Netherlands (1745).

As "Young Pretender" landed this year in Scotland, Britain was ready for peace by *Treaty of Aix-la-Chapelle.*

(*a*) Britain got Madras, which French had captured in the war.

(*b*) French regained Louisburg, which we had captured in war.

(*c*) Maria Theresa kept Austria but Frederick the Great got Silesia.

NOTE 96.—THE SEVEN YEARS' WAR (1756–1763)

Was fought in Europe, in India, and in America.

1. In India.

(*a*) The East India Company traded under Charter in India, and had French company to contend with (Clive was originally simply a clerk employed by the Company). The Mogul empire had broken up and the *French* under Dupleix had tried to secure *Madras*. Before the war broke out in 1756, *Robert Clive* had already been extending the Company's territory. Clive attacked the capital *Arcot*, took it and held it against the French (1751). *Madras* given to Britain at Treaty of Aix-la-Chapelle.

(*b*) In 1756 Surajah Dowlah of Bengal put British into the *Black Hole of Calcutta*. Clive marched from Madras, and won the battle of *Plassey* — led to annexation of *Bengal*.

(*c*) In the south, English took *Masulipatam* and Eyre Coote won battle of *Wandewash*, which led to capture of *Pondicherry* (1761).

(*d*) By *Treaty of Paris* (1763) Britain kept all her territory except Pondicherry. After 1765 Clive returned as Governor of Bengal, and a system set up whereby East India Company ruled, together with the Nawab. Clive checked corruption and organized the State.

2. In America.

The French settlements lay inland, along the rivers, while the *British held the sea-board.* The French received a good deal of help from the French government; the English colonists, having been largely people who broke away from England, had much less encouragement.

(*a*) French held Canada, and down in the south held Louisiana. Wished to join these possessions by a line of forts, and so hem the British into an enclosed space. Built these forts by 1754 (Crown Point, Ticonderoga, Oswego, and Duquesne).

British tried to take *Duquesne* and failed. When war broke out, attacks on *Oswego* and *Louisiana* failed (1757).

(*b*) *Pitt* planned double attack. Amherst to advance from Ticonderoga and Wolfe to go up River St. Lawrence, and both to meet and attack Quebec. *Wolfe took Quebec* (1759).

3. **Europe.**

(*a*) Early *disasters*. Byng failed to save *Minorca* in 1757; British defeated in Germany at *Klosterseven*.

(*b*) *Pitt revolutionized the war*. Subsidies sent to Frederick the Great, and army sent to Germany, won battle of *Minden*, 1759.

(*c*) French had planned invasion of Britain, but our naval victories at *Lagos* and *Quiberon Bay* (1759) destroyed the French fleet entirely.

(1759, the *Year of Victories*, saw British victorious at *Quebec, Minden, Lagos, Quiberon Bay, Masulipatam*).

4. **Treaty of Paris** (1763), ended Seven Years' War.

Great gains for Britain:

(*a*) In America got Canada; all French territory east of Mississippi; Cape Breton Island (which commanded river St. Lawrence); Florida.

(*b*) In West Indies got Dominica, Tobago, Grenada.

(*c*) In India kept control of Madras and Bengal.

(*d*) In Africa got Senegal.

(*e*) In Mediterranean got Minorca.

France recovered Pondicherry; right to fish off Newfoundland; Bellisle, Martinique, and St. Lucia.

Spain recovered Havana and Manila.

Note 97. — PITT THE ELDER; LATER LORD CHATHAM (1708–1778)

A great war-minister, just as Walpole had been great peace minister.

1. Chose good commanders and backed them up. Supported Clive, though he was not actually his employer (1759).

2. Understood sea-power. Saw it was vital to war in America and India, but that French fleets must be blockaded in French harbours and destroyed if they came out.

3. Understood importance of keeping France occupied in Europe, so poured out lavish subsidies to Frederick the Great of Prussia. Thus France could not keep up war in India and America, and Pitt said he " won Canada on the banks of the Elbe ".

4. Could not work with George III (1760), who wished to revive power of Crown.

5. Did not approve war with the American colonies, and declared we should not tax them without their consent (1775).

6. Was extremely honest, fought against corruption, raised the level of public life, was a great orator, and was universally respected by all parties. Greatest achievement the extension of British Empire in India and America.

NOTE 98. — WESLEY AND RISE OF METHODISM

1. John Wesley (1703–91), originally member of Church of England. With his brother Charles and friends, tried to start movement of reform, at Oxford (1729).

2. After a visit to America, returned to England and began his " mission " (1738). Aimed at reaching the poor, who did not attend church, and would not have been specially welcomed by the Tory clergy.

Preached to such various peoples as negroes of Georgia, miners of Cornwall, soldiers in army, and rich in London; often preached in open-air.

3. Chapels meant to be additional to Churches, but clergy distrusted his methods and his views on " conversion " from sinful ways.

Gradually began to set up " lay preachers " and later " ministers ". This led to split off from Church of England.

4. Very wishful to improve conditions of the poor, amongst whom his missions were held. Wesley is largely responsible for start of movement to improve conditions of life amongst the working-classes.

NOTE 99. — THE LOSS OF THE AMERICAN COLONIES (1775–1783)

1. Causes of the Quarrel.

(*a*) *Economic.* The colonies could not trade direct with other countries, and could not manufacture in competition with British goods. The Navigation Acts forced them to send goods to Great Britain for re-export.

But colonies had protection of British fleet, could develop shipping in which to send their goods to Britain, and had steady market for their products.

(*b*) *Political.* British government objected to colonists obtaining land from Indians, often by fraud, and forbade acquisition of Indian lands. Britain had to keep a large army to defend colonists from Indians and French, and now thought colonists should contribute one-third of cost.

(*c*) *Financial.*

(i) British proposed to tax colonists (Stamp Act) (1765) to pay for contribution to army, *but* said colonists could raise the money in any other way they liked. Many in Great Britain, including Chatham, agreed with the views of the colonists, that they could not be taxed internally by a Parliament in which they were not represented.

(ii) Townshend then imposed *duties* to pay for colonial officials (1767). This held to hinder self-government, and led directly to revolt.

(Tea duty was protest, for East India Company now allowed to export tea direct to America, instead of via Britain, so duty was actually reduced to 3*d*. per lb. Boston Tea-party, 1773).

NOTE 100. — THE DECLARATION OF INDEPENDENCE. 4TH JULY, 1776

This is one of the most important documents in the study of history, for it puts into words the doctrines which underlie all democratic rule.

"When in the course of human events it becomes necessary for one people to dissolve the political bonds which have connected them with one another, and to assume among the powers of the earth the separate and equal station to which the laws of nature and of nature's God entitle them, a decent respect to the opinions of mankind requires that they should declare the causes which impel them to the separation.

"We hold these truths to be self-evident, that all *men are created equal*; that they are endowed by their Creator with *certain unalienable rights*; that among these are life, liberty, and the pursuit of happiness; that to secure these rights, governments are instituted among men, *deriving their just powers from the consent of the governed*; that whenever any form of government becomes destructive of these ends it is the right of the people to alter or abolish it, and to institute a new government, laying its foundation on such principles and organizing its powers in such form, as to them shall seem most likely to effect their safety and happiness.

"Such has been the patient sufferance of these colonies; and such is now the necessity which constrains them to alter their former system of government. The history of the present King of Great Britain is a history of repeated injuries and usurpations, all having, in direct object, the establishment of an absolute tyranny over these States. To prove this, let facts be submitted to a candid world."

Then follows a list of alleged acts of tyranny committed by the Government against the colonists.

"We, therefore, the representatives of the United States of America, in general Congress assembled, appealing to the supreme Judge of the world for the rectitude of our intentions, do solemnly publish and declare that these united colonies are and ought to be, Free and Independent States; that they are absolved from all allegiance to the British Crown, and that all political connection between them and the State of Great Britain is, and ought to be, totally dissolved. . . ."

NOTE 101. — STAGES IN THE WAR OF AMERICAN INDEPENDENCE

1. (*a*) Just before Declaration of Independence (1776) war centred round Boston. British lost *Bunker's Hill* (1775), and Americans invaded Canada, but were repulsed.

(*b*) Howe defeated George Washington at *Brooklyn*, and took New Jersey (1776).

(*c*) Joint British attack on Washington failed, and Burgoyne surrendered at *Saratoga* (1777).

2. **Holland, France, and Spain now declared war on Great Britain,** while **Russia, Denmark, and Sweden** formed the hostile **Armed Neutrality** against her (1778–79).

Importance of sea-power now shown. Great Britain fighting 3000 miles from her base.

(*a*) For Spain attacked Gibraltar, and the West Indies and Minorca.

(*b*) Britain lost command of the sea to the French and could not send reinforcements (1778).

(*c*) Cornwallis reached *Yorktown*, and expected to be helped by British fleet, but French fleet arrived instead, and he had to surrender (1781).

(*d*) French troops landed.

3. **Desperate Position of Great Britain.**

Peace, with loss of colonies inevitable.

Slightly better terms obtained by the naval victory off Dominique called "Battle of the Saints" (1782), and the relief of Gibraltar (1782), though these partly offset by loss of Minorca (1782)

4. **Treaty of Versailles** (1783).

(*a*) Thirteen colonies obtained their independence.

(*b*) Great Britain gave up to Spain Florida and Minorca. To France, gave up Tobago and Senegal and St. Lucia.

But, note effect on Canada where, by *Quebec Act* (1774), the Canadians were granted a Governor and nominated council, and thousands of "loyal" Americans crossed into Canada.

Note 102. — GEORGE III: ATTEMPT TO REVIVE PERSONAL POWER OF THE CROWN

Interest of George III (1760–1820) lies in the fact that he meant to rule as King. He was British born and bred, and understood British politics. He never meant to work without Parliament, but aimed (*a*) at control of Parliament; (*b*) at destroying all opposition in the country.

1. Formed *King's party* by offering pensions and places to those who would vote in accordance with his wishes. Collected large body pledged to vote for him.

2. Desired *Prime Minister* who would be subservient to him. Bute (1761), Grenville (1763), and North (1770).

3. Objected to opposition, hence the attacks on *Wilkes*. Grenville issued the "general warrants" (1765) (these did not name the per-

sons to be arrested). Parliament led by the King's friends also refused to recognize the *Middlesex elections*, when Wilkes was repeatedly elected (1768–69).

4. During American war, power of the King's party so great that motion carried condemning its increase (1780).

   When peace necessary, and North resigned, Whigs returned to power and passed the *Economical Reform Bill*, reducing greatly the number of offices to be filled by the Crown, and thus checking corruption (1783).

   Rise of Pitt, King's helplessness after the disaster of the American war, ended George's attempts (1783).

Note 103. — INDIA UNDER GEORGE III

After Clive's conquests, the East India Company became a great ruling power. Thus *North's Regulating Act* (1773) to set up a Governor and Council of 4 to administer it; English judges to administer English laws.

1. **Warren Hastings** (1732–1818) the first Governor-General (1773).

   War. (*a*) Had to hold India while the war raged in America, and France attacked Britain in India.

   French allied with *Hyder Ali* of Mysore (1780). Defeated through Hastings and Eyre Coote at *Porto Novo* (1781). Hastings sent troops to Madras and Bombay. French admiral Suffren defeated at sea.

   (*b*) Deposed the Begums of Oudh (1781), who were governing the country disgracefully. Then hired out troops to the new Nabob of Oudh to enable him to crush the *Rohillas*.

   Peace. (*c*) He tried to reorganize the land system, with new assessments for taxation.

   (*d*) Codified the laws, and set up new commercial dues.

   On his return to England (1785), Hastings was accused of corruption, and after a trial lasting seven years (which ruined him) was acquitted (1795). He saved India from the French, he introduced many reforms and gave efficient and honest administration. But he was thwarted by having always to act with his Council of four, some of whom opposed him (notably Francis, said to be the author of Letters of Junius). Hence Pitt saw need for reform.

2. **Pitt.** In 1784 passed the *India Act*. This gave the Governor-General greater power, made him responsible to a Board in London; Governor and Board appointed by the Government, no longer by East India Company, and thus Government became responsible for India, though Company still carried on administration.

TIME CHART FOR PERIOD EIGHT (1714–1783)

Sovereign.	Prime Minister.	Great Britain.	Dates.	Other Powers	Dates.
George I (1714–1727)		Whig Ministry.	1714		
		Mar's Rising.	1715	Accession of Louis XV.	1715
		Septennial Act.	1716		
		Alliance of Britain, France, Holland.	1717		
		Battle of Cape Passaro.	1718	Death of Charles XII of Sweden.	1718
		South Sea Bubble.	1720		
	1721–42 Sir Robert Walpole (Whig)				
				Death of Peter the Great.	1725
George II (1727–1760)		Indemnity Act for Dissenters.	1727	Spain attacks Gibraltar.	1727
		Excise Scheme.	1733	War of Polish Succession.	
		Porteous Riots.	1736		
		Death of Queen Caroline.	1737		
		War against "Jenkins's Ear".	1739	Spain.	
		Anson's Voyage	1740	Accession of Maria Theresa to Austria and of Frederick the Great to Prussia.	1740
		Dupleix, Governor of Pondicherry	1741	War of Austrian Succession.	
	1742–44 Wilmington.	Battle of Dettingen.	1743		
		Fontenoy. Charles Edward's Rising.	1745		
	1744–54 Henry Pelham (Whig).	Battle of Culloden. French take Madras	1746		
				Peace of Aix-la-Chapelle.	1748
		Defence of Arcot by Clive.	1751		

TIME CHART FOR PERIOD EIGHT (1714–1783) — *Continued*

Sovereign	Prime Minister	Great Britain		Dates.		Other Powers.	Dates.
George II (1727–1760)	Newcastle.	Braddock's Expedition.		1755			.
	Devonshire.	Black Hole of Calcutta; Loss of Minorca.	Seven Years' War.	1756	Seven Years' War.		.
		Battle of Plassey.		1757			.
				.			.
	Newcastle. (with Pitt).	Year of Victories.		1759			.
		Battle of Wandewash; Capture of Montreal.		1760			.
George III (1760–1820)		Bridgewater Canal; Pitt resigns.		1761		Family Compact (France and Spain).	1761
	Bute.			.		Catherine II reigns in Russia.	1762
	Grenville.	Treaty of Paris.		1763			.
		Battle of Buxar; Hargreaves' Spinning Jenny.		1764			.
		Stamp Act; Watt's Steam Engine.		1765			.
		Stamp Act repealed; Declaratory Act.		1766			.
	Rockingham.	Townshend's duties.		1767			.
	Chatham.	Cook's First Voyage to Australia; Chatham resigns.		1768			.
	Grafton.			.			.
		Boston Massacre.		1770		Dauphin Louis marries Marie Antoinette.	1770
				.			.
	Lord North. 1770–82	Burning of the *Gaspee*.		1772		First Partition of Poland.	1772
		Boston tea-party; North's India Act; Warren Hastings Governor-General of India (till 1785).		1773			.
		Quebec Act.		1774		Accession of Louis XVI.	1774
		Battles of Lexington and Bunker's Hill	American War of Independence.	1775			.
		American Colonies declare Independence.		1776			.
		Surrender of Saratoga.		1777			.
		Death of Chatham.		1778	American War of Independence.	France joins America	1778
		Crompton's "Mule".		1779		Spain joins France.	1779
		Siege of Gibraltar by Spaniards and French (1779-1783)				Holland joins France. Death of Maria Theresa.	1780
				.			.
		Minorca, which had been regained by Britain in Treaty of Paris, now lost.		1781			.
		Surrender of Yorktown					
	Rockingham	North resigns; Independence of Irish Parliament.		1782			.
	Shelburne Portland.	Treaty of Versailles.		1783			.

EXAMINATION QUESTIONS ON PERIOD EIGHT

(1714–1783)

1. Describe the rising of the Young Pretender in 1745 and account for his failure. (LGS 1937)

2. Trace the events which led up to the Act of Union with Ireland in 1800. (LGS 1937)

3. State (*a*) the merits, and (*b*) the defects of Walpole's work. (NUJB 1935)

4. Show how Walpole (*a*) obtained and (*b*) lost power. (LGS 1936)

5. What circumstances led to the rise and what to the fall of Walpole? (LM 1923; OC 1930)

6. Show how Cabinet government developed under George I and George II. (NUJB 1930)

7. How was the British Empire affected by control of the sea during the period 1756–83? (NUJB 1935)

8. " Peace and retrenchment." How far were these the inspiration of Walpole's administration? (OC 1937)

9. Describe the work of Clive and Warren Hastings in India. (LGS 1937)

10. Compare the services of Clive and Warren Hastings to the expansion of British rule in India. (OC 1937)

11. Sketch the career of Warren Hastings in India. Why and with what justice was he impeached? (LGS 1936)

12. Describe *either* the development of communications in the Industrial Revolution *or* the rise of the Lancashire cotton industry in this period. (LGS 1936)

13. Account for the failure of the rebellions of 1715 and 1745. (LM 1931; OC 1931; D 1931)

14. Give an account of the Methodist movement and indicate its results. (CL 1930)

15. " The task of John Wesley and the elder Pitt was to counteract the bad effects of Walpole's ministry ". Comment. (CL 1932)

16. How did William Pitt influence the conduct of the Seven Years' War? (OC 1933)

17. Give an account of the work of the elder Pitt (Chatham). (NUJB 1938)

18. Give an account of the part played by Britain in *either* the War of the Austrian Succession (1740–8) *or* the Seven Years' War (1756–63). (NUJB 1937)

19. Were the American Colonists justified in rebelling against the English Government? Give reasons for your answer. (NUJB 1937)

20. Why did we lose the American colonies? (OC 1935)

21. " Be a King ". Did George III succeed in breaking down the limits of constitutional Kingship? (OC 1937)

22. How do you explain (*a*) the English success in the Seven Years' War, and (*b*) the English failure in the American War of Independence? (LGS 1936)

23. Describe the career of Charles James Fox. What were his chief aims and how far was he successful in fulfilling them? (LGS 1935)

24. Describe and account for the attitude towards the French Revolution of (*a*) Pitt, (*b*) Burke, and (*c*) Fox. (OL 1927; NUJB 1932)

PERIOD NINE

THE GREAT STRUGGLE WITH FRANCE; REVOLUTION AND NAPOLEON

1783–1815

CHAPTER 51

PITT, THE YOUNGER: HIS FIRST MINISTRY

William Pitt the younger had been born in 1759, the great "year of victories". He had shown great promise as a child [1] and young man, and when he entered Parliament in 1780 he at once made his mark. Shelburne had surprised everyone by making him Chancellor of the Exchequer, and now, when only twenty-four years of age, he was Prime Minister (*Note 107*).

Pitt's first ministry (1783–1801)

His government was looked on at first almost as a joke, and having been formed on 19th December, 1783, was called the "mince-pie administration" as likely to end when Christmas festivities were over. Fox and North, however, had completely misjudged both the nation and the man with whom they had to deal. Pitt, despite various defeats in the House, held on. His courage and resourcefulness, coupled with the extreme violence of the opposition,

[1] William Pitt as a child was very precocious. At the age of seven, when told that his father had been raised to the peerage, he said "that he was glad he was not the eldest son, but that he could serve his country in the House of Commons like his papa". At the age of twelve he wrote his first poem, and when a year older his first play — with a political plot. At the age of fourteen and a half, when he did not weigh much more than six stone, he went to Cambridge — the story, however, that his nurse brought him there in a carriage and stayed to look after him lacks confirmation.

won him increased support; and when in April he dissolved Parliament he came back amidst great popular excitement with a decisive majority, no less than one hundred and sixty of Fox's supporters — Fox's martyrs they were called — losing their seats.[1] For the next seventeen years Pitt, trusted alike by the King and the nation, reigned supreme.

Pitt and the King

With the accession of Pitt, though the King was still able to exercise at times very great influence, his system of personal government came to an end. For one thing, the King had a minister whom he trusted; and for another, he could not afford to quarrel with Pitt, for if so he would have been thrown back on the Whig opposition. Moreover, the King's health began to decline. Brain troubles incapacitated him for a time in 1788. Increasing blindness, which became serious in 1805, made him retire more and more from public business. After 1811 the madness which had so long threatened led to his complete withdrawal, the Prince of Wales for the remainder of the reign acting as regent, under conditions, however, which left the chief power with the ministers.

Pitt's home policy: finance

As a financier Pitt began well. The country was prosperous, but the national finances were not in a satisfactory condition. Pitt was a personal friend of *Adam Smith*, whose famous book *The Wealth of Nations* had been published in 1776, and he was convinced by this book that trade should be freer from restraints; for as international trade consists in one nation exchanging its goods for those produced by other countries, duties which prevented foreign goods from coming into Britain, checked our goods from going out in exchange. Pitt therefore lowered many duties on imports, and abolished others. His new "Book of Rates"

Customs duties revised

[1] The most exciting election was at Westminster where Fox was a successful candidate. The poll was open for forty days, and there were continual conflicts between a body of seamen whom Fox's naval opponent, Lord Hood, had brought up to London, and the hackney chairmen, who supported Fox. The King, of course, favoured Hood, whilst the Prince of Wales was an active ally of Fox. But Fox's most successful canvasser was the beautiful Georgiana, Duchess of Devonshire, who really won the election.

made duties in many instances so light that it ceased to be worth while to smuggle.

He went on to make a commercial treaty with France, under which each country lowered the duties on goods produced by the other; the effect was that more British goods, such as cotton and cutlery, were exchanged for French wine and silk. As the Industrial Revolution progressed (see p. 739) production became cheaper and Great Britain had more goods to exchange for those of other countries.

Commercial Treaty with France

Pitt would have liked to extend "free trade" to Ireland, but unfortunately he failed to carry this measure (see p. 715) (*Note 110*).

In India the "Regulating Act" of Lord North had proved a failure, and *Pitt's India Act* was now passed in 1784. This Act left administration to the East India Company, but gave all control over political matters to the Board of Control appointed by the British Government (p. 643).

Pitt's India Act (1784)

In other parts of the world Pitt undertook reforms. In Canada Lord North's *Quebec Act* (1774) had been made to conciliate the Canadians, especially the French Roman Catholics, and keep them loyal during the American War of Independence. Thus it set up a government-nominated Council, extended the boundaries of Quebec, and recognized the Roman Catholic Church as the national Church of Canada. Since then streams of "loyalists" had left the independent United States of America, and poured across the frontiers into the parts of Canada which lay to the east and to the west of the French frontiers. There they multiplied and prospered. But differences of race and religion caused friction with the older French settlers, and the two sections quarrelled bitterly.

Pitt and Canada

In an attempt to remedy this, Pitt, in 1791, passed his *Canada Act*, which divided Canada into two, an eastern province called *Lower Canada* or Quebec and a western

Canada Act (1791)

province called *Upper Canada* or Ontario. Each had its own governor and a certain amount of self-government. In this way Pitt hoped to satisfy both parties, and he trusted that in time the French province would acquire the taste and aptitude for self-government which the English settlers possessed so strongly.

Australia

Under Pitt's rule too, began the first settlement in Australia. Captain Cook had discovered the continent, and in 1786 it was decided to use it for the transportation of convicts who, owing to the loss of the American colonies, could no longer be sent out, as formerly, to the plantations of Virginia or Carolina. The Home Secretary of that year was *Lord Sydney*, and since he was responsible for all prisoners, the spot chosen for the first convict settlement in the new land was called after him.

Pitt and Parliamentary reform

Though Pitt owed his position in the first place to the King's support, he was aware of the faults of the Parliamentary system, and he was prepared to do something for reform. Accordingly he brought in a Bill to disfranchise thirty-six "rotten boroughs", each of which returned two members to Parliament. These boroughs were entirely in the hands of "patrons" who owned them, and Pitt proposed to buy these men out and give them compensation (one million pounds was the sum proposed). The seats were to be redistributed and given to the large new towns which were now springing up all over the country. His measure did not pass the Commons and Pitt was soon diverted from all reforms by the crisis which arose in foreign affairs.

Europe was now on the verge of one of the greatest upheavals in history, the French Revolution. While all Europe was affected, England suffered through the effects which the revolution produced upon Pitt; it meant his abandonment of all reform, and the eventual adoption of a policy of repression which was sometimes harsh and even cruel.

CHAPTER 52

THE FRENCH REVOLUTION AND THE GREAT WAR (1789–1802)

1. THE FRENCH REVOLUTION

The French Revolution, 1789; its causes

Throughout the eighteenth century France had suffered from a government which was often incompetent and arbitrary, a court which was extravagant and at times frivolous, and an aristocracy which clung to its privileges — above all that of not contributing to the chief taxes — whilst it was apt to neglect its duties. She endured a system of taxation which had every possible fault, and which left to the poor peasant only one-fifth of his earnings for himself. Moreover, the people had no share in the government, and the States-General — which had in the Middle Ages corresponded in some measure to the English Parliament — had not met since 1614.

The close of the eighteenth century, however, found people's minds prepared for change. A brilliant writer, *Voltaire*, had attacked various abuses, particularly those connected with the Roman Catholic Church, and had created, it is not too much to say, the critical atmosphere of his generation. A seductive philosopher, *Rousseau*, had taught people to look back to an imaginary golden age when there was no oppression and no poverty because there were no kings, no nobles, and no priests. In the same year that these two writers died, in 1778, the French monarchy had appealed to its subjects, as we have seen, to support liberty in America; it is not surprising that the French people should seek liberty for themselves when financial difficulties at last forced the King to summon the States-General in May, 1789.

France was at heart loyal, and a great king might have

Course of Revolution (1789)

made reforms which would have staved off a revolution. But *Louis XVI*, the King, though well-meaning and amiable, was vacillating and undecided, whilst his Queen, Marie Antoinette, though beautiful, was unpopular and indiscreet. The King had no scheme of reforms and no scheme of coercion — he merely let things drift. Consequently events moved quickly after the meeting of the *States-General* at *Versailles*. On previous occasions, the States-General had sat and voted in three estates, representing the nobles, clergy, and people respectively. But on this occasion the representatives of the people insisted on all the orders sitting and voting in one house, and by their pertinacity achieved their object. Then, on *14th July*, the men of Paris took the *Bastille*, the great fortress dominating eastern Paris — and its fall was regarded throughout Europe as the sign of the downfall of absolute monarchy in France.[1] In October, the women of Paris, impelled by fear of famine, marched to Versailles, and brought the King, the royal family, and the States-General to Paris, thinking that they would thus be sure of supplies of bread; and, as a consequence, the government and the assembly became, as time went on, increasingly subject to the influence of the Parisian populace.

The year 1790 was taken up with the task of reorganizing
1790 France — with removing abuses in Church and State, in taxation and in the law, in the army and navy. The King's attitude was uncertain, and sometimes he sided with the reformers and at other times he opposed them. Finally,
1791 however, in June, 1791, he escaped from Paris and fled towards the eastern frontier of France. But he was captured at Varennes and was henceforth regarded by many as a traitor because he had fled towards the foreigner.

[1] To the popular imagination the Bastille was impregnable, and its dungeons were full of untried prisoners. As a matter of fact, the Bastille was only defended by a hundred and twenty soldiers, most of them old, and by fifteen cannon, only one of which was fired; and there were only seven prisoners, of whom four were forgers, two were madmen, and the other had been put there by the request of his family.

In 1792 Austria and Prussia declared war and invaded France. In August of that year the Paris mob stormed the Tuileries palace, where Louis XVI lived. Then the Prussians attacked Verdun, " the gateway of France ", and during the panic caused by the news of its imminent fall occurred the awful September massacres in Paris, when hundreds of people who had been imprisoned because of their suspected hostility to the Revolution were barbarously murdered. A new assembly, called the Convention, met towards the close of September. This assembly declared France to be a Republic, and a few months later the King was put to death (January, 1793).[1]

The Convention (1792)

The King beheaded (1793)

The French Revolution affected profoundly every state in Europe. Its ideas of " Liberty, Equality, and Fraternity " were popular with European peoples, whilst they aroused the apprehensions of European monarchs. In Great Britain, at first, the Revolution was regarded with sympathy. Pitt watched it with no unkindly eye " as a spectator ", to use his own words, and saw no reason why it should affect British policy. Poets such as Wordsworth and Coleridge saw in it the dawn of a new era of happiness and freedom; whilst Radical clergymen preached in its favour, and Radical politicians corresponded with its leaders and formed revolutionary societies. The Whigs thought it bore a resemblance to their own " glorious " Revolution of 1688; and Fox, the chief Whig leader, in particular gave the Revolu-

British opinion and the Revolution

[1] Marie Antoinette was guillotined in October. Louis XVI's son, the Dauphin, died in 1795, at the age of fifteen. For six months in the year previous to his death he was in a ground-floor room, without light, and often in winter without a fire, and in solitary confinement, his meals being passed to him through a grating.

After the execution of the King the extreme section in the Convention, the Jacobin or Mountain party, overthrew the more moderate section, and the " Reign of Terror " ensued (June, 1793–July, 1794), in the last seven weeks of which nearly fourteen hundred people were sent to the guillotine in Paris alone. The extremists then lost their power, and a more moderate government followed. At the end of 1795 the Convention Assembly was dissolved, and the government was put under the control of two Assemblies and of a committee called the *Directory* (1795–99). Finally, in October, 1799, Napoleon, after his return from Egypt, overthrew the Directory, and became supreme as *First Consul* (The Consulate, 1799–1804), and in 1804 he was elected *Emperor*.

tion his enthusiastic approval, exclaiming of the capture of the Bastille, "How much the greatest event that has happened in the world, and how much the best!"

Many individuals warmly sympathized with it, because they believed it would redress wrongs, and help the poor.[1] But, as the Revolution became more violent, opinion altered. **Causes of change in opinion** Burke, the greatest of all Whigs, who from the first, unlike others of his party, had regarded it with suspicion, published in November, 1790, his "Reflections on the French Revolution", in which he expressed his detestation of it "in its act, consequences, and most of all in its example", and prophesied that its ultimate result would be anarchy; the book made a profound impression not only in Great Britain but in all European courts. Moreover, atrocities such as the September massacres horrified public feeling. Above all, the French revolutionaries were not content to leave other countries alone. They intrigued with revolutionaries in this country, and riots in Dundee, Sheffield, and elsewhere showed the dangers of their exhortations. In the autumn of 1792 other events occurred which hastened on war. The French proclaimed that they would give **Aggression of France** assistance to any nation that rose for its liberty — which was equivalent to a declaration of war against the monarchies of Europe. They occupied the Austrian Netherlands (they had begun war with Austria in the previous spring), and declared the river Scheldt open to commerce; this river, in order to develop the trade of Holland and Great Britain, had been for a long time, under European treaty, closed to all vessels by the Dutch government, and in declaring it thus open the French government showed a flagrant disregard of all treaty rights.[2] Moreover, France threatened to invade Holland. Once again, as on other

[1] Diaries of such different persons as the poet Cowper, and the governess, Miss Weedon, express these views.

[2] The estuary of the Scheldt was in Dutch territory; ever since 1648 the Dutch had been recognized as having control of it and had excluded all foreigners from it, thereby ruining Antwerp and developing the prosperity of their own port of Amsterdam.

occasions, Great Britain felt that her own independence was bound up with that of Holland. Then followed the execution of Louis XVI in the beginning of 1793; and war was declared in February. Pitt had striven to maintain peace as long as he could; but the extremists in France had made peace impossible (*Note 108*).

2. THE WAR WITH REVOLUTIONARY FRANCE

The First Coalition (1793–96)

The war which began in 1793 was waged at first against revolutionary France. Britain joined with those powers which were already at war — Austria and Prussia — and at the same time Holland, Spain, and Sardinia joined in. This great group of allies formed what is called the *First Coalition*. Great Britain sent vast sums of money, as subsidies, to the allies whose armies were already on the French frontiers. Indeed, from their great camps in Belgium, Paris could have been reached in twelve marches.

Pitt was to be the guiding force in Great Britain during the great struggle, and it is generally admitted that, unlike his father Lord Chatham, he was not successful as a war minister. This was in part caused by the mistaken policy he adopted, which wasted British resources, and in part by Pitt's own character.

Character of the younger Pitt

Pitt, in his relations with his colleagues and the members of his party, seems to have been cold and reserved; a good deal of marble, they complained, entered into his composition, and it required much effort on the part of an interviewer to produce even a momentary thaw.

It has been urged against Pitt that he was jealous of able men, and preferred to be the one man of genius in a cabinet of commonplace men; indeed, his second ministry was composed of such feeble elements that the wits said it consisted merely of " William and Pitt ". He showed no signs whatever of his father's gift for choosing good men to carry out his ideas, and this weakened all his operations.

Pitt, however, if not perfect, must be reckoned a great prime minister. Honest and incorruptible himself, he, like his father, did much to raise the standard of morality in public life. Above all, it was his indomitable courage and self-confidence that enabled Great Britain to weather the storm that was caused by the French Revolution and by Napoleon. To the French, Pitt was always the arch-enemy who had to be subdued, the real centre of opposition to their designs. That the French Assembly should in 1793 have solemnly declared Pitt to be "the enemy of the human race" is the greatest compliment they could have paid him. "England has saved herself", he said in his last speech, "by her exertions, and will, as I trust, save Europe by her example." That she had done the one and was to accomplish the other was perhaps as much because of William Pitt with all his shortcomings in the conduct of the war, as it was of Nelson or of Wellington.[1]

Pitt's mistakes

Apart from the difficulties raised by his character, Pitt's policy shows serious mistakes. The chief faults urged against him are that he misused sea-power and that he frittered away Britain's strength in futile expeditions, and so wasted his resources. Certainly the early years of the war proved very inglorious.

The Coalition against France and its failure

The first attack on Revolutionary France was made by the Coalition in the summer of 1793. Surrounded on all sides, and attacked by the trained armies of Europe, Revolutionary France could only oppose them by her untrained mobs. Moreover, she had to deal with Royalist risings within her borders and with the struggle between different parties even amongst the Revolutionaries. All the world shared Pitt's belief that she could not hold out against such a combination. It was owing to this mistaken belief that the war would be a short one, that Pitt based all his financial measures on wrong conceptions. He was so confident that

[1] Canning's comment on Pitt is worth quoting: "Whether Pitt *will* save us, I do not know, but surely he is the only man that *can*."

the struggle would be very short, that he decided to pay for the war by loans, and made no sufficient effort to raise money by taxation. This error had the gravest results when the struggle dragged out far beyond Pitt's expectations.

Causes of its failure

Coalitions of European powers have seldom worked harmoniously. The allies, as a contemporary said, wanted to hunt the sheep before killing the dog; instead of a joint advance upon the capital, each was intent upon securing the frontier fortresses which it could claim at the peace. Moreover, they were jealous of each other and had no commander to direct the whole operations. Meantime, the armies of France, with their country threatened, exhibited a patriotism and an enthusiasm which carried all before them. The generals represented literally the survival of the fittest, for those that failed were nearly always dismissed and sometimes guillotined. Above all, the new Government that France had evolved left the control of the war to one man, and that a man of genius, Carnot.

Military operations (1793–96)

Consequently, though in the summer of 1793 there were eight foreign armies on French soil, and Lyons, Toulon, and Brittany had risen against the Revolution, before the end of the year these risings had been put down and all the foreign armies but one had been expelled. In the following year, 1794, the French drove the allies not only from Belgium but from Holland as well, and secured the Rhine frontier that they had been striving for so many centuries to obtain.[1] Holland therefore dropped out of the Coalition, and in 1795 both Prussia and Spain withdrew from it. With 1796 came Napoleon's famous campaign in Italy, in which, after invading Piedmont and forcing its ruler, the King of Sardinia, to withdraw from the war, he defeated the Austrians in a succession of battles, then marched to within ninety

[1] In 1794 the French won sixteen pitched battles, took one hundred and sixteen towns and two hundred and thirty forts, and captured ninety thousand prisoners and three thousand eight hundred cannon; and they opened the next year with capturing the Dutch fleet, which was embedded in the ice, by a cavalry raid.

miles of Vienna and obliged the Austrians at the beginning of 1797 to make peace.

The British army and the Government

It must be confessed that Great Britain played a somewhat inglorious part in the military operations from 1793 to 1796. No doubt her allies were largely to blame — Great Britain was heading a crusade, it has been said, with an army of camp followers. But her statesmen had done nothing in the years after the American war to profit by its lessons. As a consequence, at the beginning of the French war, both officers and men, whether cavalry or infantry, were untrained, whilst the artillery was worse than at any other previous period of its history. In the course of the war, the Government, at its wits' end to get recruits, adopted the pernicious system of promoting those officers who succeeded in enlisting a certain number of recruits, and sent out regiments of boys instead of men to tropical climates — which, in the case of most of them, meant certain death. In equipment, the Government was scandalously negligent. It failed to send out greatcoats to soldiers campaigning in the Netherlands during the winter, or boots for those fighting in tropical districts infested with dangerous insects. Troops were sometimes sent out who had never fired a shot, or with wholly insufficient supplies of ammunition; and the arrangements for transport and hospitals were inconceivably bad.

British failures: (a) Against France

Next among the causes of failure was the fact that our small army was frittered away on a variety of objects. In the first year of the war (1793) the royalists of *Toulon*, the great naval port of France, called in the English, but the expedition sent out under Hood proved a total failure and had to withdraw. Another little force was sent to help the Royalists who had risen in *Brittany*, but that too failed. A third expedition sent to *Dunkirk* was also obliged to withdraw partly owing to the incompetence of its commander, the King's second son, the Duke of York. Farther afield a very large force was sent to the *West Indies*, but the greater part died of disease. The net results of a five years' campaign were the capture of Martinique and St. Lucia, and a treaty with the " Black Emperor ", the negro Toussaint l'Ouverture, who had made himself master of the greater part of San Domingo.

(b) In the West Indies

At sea Pitt entirely failed to realize the importance of preventing the French from using their sea power. At first their navy was greatly affected by the Revolution and the royalist rising at Toulon was very threatening. But Pitt made no effort to blockade the French ports, and thus their fleet was reorganized and put to sea. It was able to carry troops to the West Indies, it was able to send an army to Ireland, and it was able to convoy grain across the Atlantic. *Lord Howe* was sent, in 1794, to cut off the grain fleet, and he defeated the French in the Battle of the *Glorious First of June*, fought off Ushant, but though technically he was victorious, the corn ships slipped through during the engagement and reached Brest safely. Finally, by failing to command the coast road to Genoa, as it possibly might have done, the fleet did not check the French campaign in Italy which in 1796 gave Napoleon his wonderful successes and forced us to evacuate the Mediterranean.

(c) At sea

The Glorious First of June (1794)

In this same year of 1796, too, the French were able to send a fleet to attack us in Ireland. Their ships put out of Brest, with fifteen thousand troops on board, and set sail for Bantry Bay. Their commanders, however, were in a ship which lost touch with the fleet [1] and the winds proved persistently contrary, so that the French had finally to retire without landing in Ireland at all.

French attempt on Ireland (1796)

[1] The French fleet left Brest just as night was coming on, and Pellew, the commander of a British frigate which was watching the port, attached himself to the French fleet, just out of gunshot, and by making false signals, burning blue lights, and sending up rockets, played havoc with the commander-in-chief's orders, and got the fleet into hopeless confusion.

3. ISOLATION OF GREAT BRITAIN

Desperate position of Britain in 1797

The chance of crushing France had been lost in 1793, and in 1797 Great Britain found herself in a desperate position. France had conquered the Netherlands, and controlled the Dutch fleet. She had made an alliance with Spain, and practically controlled the Spanish fleet too. Great Britain had been deserted by her allies, Prussia and Austria and Russia, who had been engaged on the eastern side of Europe in carving up Poland. She was left alone to deal with her enemy [1] (*Note 111*).

Battle of St. Vincent (1797)

In 1797 the French and Spanish fleets wished to join together. Had they done so, they would have formed a most dangerous combination. Admiral *Jervis* was sent to prevent this, and met the Spanish fleet off *Cape St. Vincent*. Nelson distinguished himself at this battle, which was a complete victory for Great Britain.

Mutiny in the navy (1797)

At this point occurred the great mutiny of the fleet. The ships at Spithead protested against their grievances, which were many and great; very poor pay and part of that embezzled by paymasters, wretched food, very severe discipline, and very little leave. Lord Howe whom they loved and trusted was sent to investigate, and he promised them redress. But what "Black Dick", as the sailors lovingly called Howe, could promise did not satisfy the more extreme element at the other station, the North Sea station of the *Nore*. Here the leader, Parker, was definitely republican. He wanted officers to be elected by seamen, and he flew the red flag of the "floating Republic". The Government did not attempt compromise here, and the mutiny was suppressed and the leaders hanged. Yet, in spite of their action, the men never wished to refuse to fight the enemy.[2]

[1] In 1797, a week after the Battle of Camperdown (see p. 679), Napoleon forced the emperor to sign the Treaty of Campo Formio.

[2] During the mutiny the British had kept up their blockade of the Dutch fleet with only two ships, as all the others mutinied. Duncan, the admiral, kept making signals as though the mutinous ships were still under his command, and the Dutch fleet consequently did not stir.

No sooner was the mutiny ended than the ships put to sea to meet the Dutch. The hostility of that country to Great Britain made her willing to side with Napoleon, and again had the French and Dutch been able to join forces they would have made a most powerful combination. Admiral Duncan, with the fleet of the Nore to reinforce him, dealt with the Dutch, and in a terrific battle off *Camperdown*, in the mouth of the Texel, he defeated them entirely.

Victory over the Dutch at Camperdown (1797)

Danger then shifted to the Mediterranean. Napoleon in 1798 began to plan his invasion of Egypt. He took Malta from the Knights of St. John, and set sail for Alexandria. Nelson who was in command in the Mediterranean did not know what Napoleon's plan was, and a storm prevented the frigates bringing him information. But he guessed that Napoleon's destination was Egypt. Nelson's fleet reached Alexandria first, but found no one there, and turned back to Sicily. Napoleon who had gone round by Crete reached Alexandria, disembarked, and won the *Battle of the Pyramids*, against the Mamelukes, who then governed the country, and took Cairo.

The Mediterranean

Nelson heard of Napoleon's arrival in Egypt, sailed back to Alexandria, and upon 1st August sighted Napoleon's fleet at anchor in *Aboukir Bay* close to the mouths of the Nile. The French fleet had made the two great omissions of not anchoring their fleet as close to the shore as possible and of not joining their vessels by chains. Nelson could trust his captains, as he said, "to find a hole somewhere", and they quickly realized that they were able to pass on both sides of the French ships as well as between them, and to concentrate their forces first on the van and then on the centre and rear of the French fleet. Beginning at six o'clock in the evening, the battle lasted far into the night and continued the next morning. The French flagship, *L'Orient*, blew up at 10 p.m., and before the battle was over eleven out of the thirteen French ships had been captured or sunk. It was a brilliant victory, in which all the captains,

The Battle of the Nile (1st Aug., 1798)

fighting, as Nelson said, "like a band of brothers", had distinguished themselves.

4. THE SECOND COALITION AND ITS FAILURE (1798–1800)

The Second Coalition (1798)

The Battle of the Nile had great consequences. Not only were the French unable to help their Indian ally, Tippoo Sahib (*Note 117*), but the British obtained control of the Mediterranean, and their former allies now prepared to join them once more. Russia first took the lead, Austria and Turkey followed, and what is known as the *Second Coalition* was formed (*Note 111*).

Siege of Acre (1799)

At first things went well for the allies. The British took Minorca and blockaded Malta and Brest.[1] Napoleon, who was marooned in Egypt by the destruction of his fleet, tried to move north through Syria and attacked *Acre*. But *Sir Sydney Smith* held out bravely, and was helped in the defence by the great guns which Napoleon had tried to send by sea and which had been captured by the British. Napoleon had to retreat back to Egypt, and in his continued absence the troops of the Coalition won successes in Germany and in Italy. Sydney Smith sent newspapers giving an account of these to Napoleon, doubtless meaning to annoy him. Napoleon, however, was thereby stirred on to a desperate act. He abandoned his army, and in a small sailing ship managed to dodge the British fleet and reached France, safely. There he overthrew the revolutionary government of the Directory, and gave himself the post of First Consul. He was in fact now the dictator of France (Christmas Day, 1799).

Napoleon returns to France: the coup d'état of 1799

[1] St. Vincent's maxim was to be "close in with Ushant (the island outside Brest) in an easterly wind", which was the favourable wind for the escape of the French fleet; and only once during St. Vincent's command (which lasted 121 days) did the main fleet off Ushant fail, owing to fog, to communicate with the in-shore squadron stationed between Brest and Ushant. St. Vincent made himself very unpopular by ordering that when vessels went home to refit or take in stores, their officers were not to sleep on shore or go farther inland than three miles.

The Russians and Austrians had quarrelled, and Russia now left the coalition. Napoleon, after restoring order in France, determined to attack the Austrians, who were fighting in Italy. He crossed the Alps, took the Austrians in the rear, and won the great victory of *Marengo* (1800). This gave him north Italy, and the victory of another French army over the Austrian force at *Hohenlinden* (1800), compelled the Austrians to make peace (1801).

Marengo (1800) and the collapse of the Coalition (1801)

Great Britain had thus lost all her allies, and the second coalition had failed. France was stronger than ever. At this juncture Britain was involved in serious difficulties with Ireland (see p. 716), as a result of which Pitt resigned, and his place was taken by the incompetent Addington.

5. RENEWED ISOLATION OF GREAT BRITAIN: PEACE OF AMIENS

Worse misfortunes were now to come, for Britain's former allies turned against her. They were alienated by the difficulties created by their position as neutrals which conflicted with Britain's theories of *contraband*. No country denied that a neutral ship carrying contraband, or attempting to enter a blockaded port, was liable to seizure. The quarrel arose over what constituted contraband. The British included food and stores, such as hemp which Russia exported. They seized goods belonging to the enemy, even when carried on neutral ships under control of their own country's warships. They also held that a vessel could be seized even if the port to which it was bound was only blockaded " on paper ", not effectively — that is to say, there might be no adequate force present.

Contraband and blockade

Napoleon stirred up the discontented neutrals and at the end of 1800 Russia, Denmark, Sweden, and Prussia formed the *Second Armed Neutrality* which threatened Britain with war. This closed the whole Baltic to us, and deprived our fleet of materials it badly needed, such as

The Second Armed Neutrality (1800)

timber and hemp. Against this Britain was resolved to act.

The battle of Copenhagen (1801) The British fleet under the command of *Sir Hyde Parker* was dispatched to attack the Danes. He sailed for *Copenhagen*, and there sent Nelson in to force his way up the straits in front of the capital. Nelson succeeded brilliantly, silenced the Danish batteries on shore, and sank the Danish fleet.[1] The Danes abandoned the Armed Neutrality, and so opened the Baltic once more to the British.

Almost at the same time (1801) the British won successes at sea in the West Indies, and at Alexandria *Abercromby* entirely defeated the French army which had been left behind by Napoleon in Egypt. The assassination of the Czar Paul placed on the throne of Russia Alexander I who favoured Great Britain. He at once left the Armed Neutrality and made a treaty with Britain.

The Treaty of Amiens (1802) Both sides were now exhausted, and at this juncture efforts were made towards peace. Great Britain was ready for it, burdened as she was by a gigantic debt and governed by a pacific minister; and so was Napoleon. Before the end of the year the preliminaries were signed, and developed into the *Treaty of Amiens* in 1802. "It was a peace," said a contemporary, " of which everyone was glad and nobody proud." Great Britain gave up all her conquests save Ceylon and Trinidad, whilst France retained the country which is now called Belgium, and the Rhine frontier.

Reflections on the conduct of the war For nearly the whole of its course, the war had been conducted by Pitt and his lieutenant Dundas. In Macaulay's opinion, Pitt's war policy was that of a driveller; and it has been said of Dundas that he was so profoundly ignorant of war as to be unconscious even of his ignorance. The judgments are somewhat harsh. But it is impossible to read

[1] Parker, the British commander-in-chief, allowed Nelson to make this attack with part of the fleet whilst he remained outside with the remainder of the ships. When, after three hours' fighting, the Danes seemed to be holding their own, Parker hoisted the signal to " discontinue the action ". But Nelson exclaimed to an officer, "You know, I have only one eye — I have a right to be blind sometimes," and then putting the telescope to his blind eye exclaimed, " I really do not see the signal!"

the details of the war without realizing that our statesmen not infrequently failed to take sufficient advantage of the opportunities offered them, had no clear or consistent idea of their objectives, and made the task of the generals always difficult and sometimes impossible by providing them with inadequate or ill-equipped forces. Hence much of the war is disappointing; but in the West Indies, in the Netherlands, and above all in Egypt our soldiers fought bravely, and some of our generals — and more especially Abercromby — exhibited considerable capacity, whilst the navy won for itself immortal glory.

CHAPTER 53

THE NAPOLEONIC WAR (1803–1815)

1. ATTACK ON ENGLAND: TRAFALGAR

Causes of the renewal of war in 1803

The Peace of Amiens was merely a truce, for the reorganization of France failed to satisfy Napoleon's ambitions, and his aggressive policy made the renewal of war inevitable (*Note 112*). The First Consul annexed Piedmont and Elba. As a mediator he intervened in Germany and reconstructed the boundaries of its States so as to suit French interests; he sent thirty thousand soldiers to Switzerland and gave that country a new constitution. Above all, he virtually annexed Holland, and thus once again British supremacy was threatened in the North Sea. But Napoleon's ambitions were not limited to Europe. The official report of a French colonel who had been sent to Egypt aroused great indignation in Great Britain, for the colonel expressed the opinion that six thousand French troops would be sufficient to recapture that country; and the fact that this report was published in the official French newspaper showed that Napoleon had not renounced French ambitions in that quarter. We now know also — though Great Britain did not realize it at the time — that Napoleon had designs upon the Cape of Good Hope, upon India, and upon Australia. Napoleon on his side made bitter complaints because Great Britain, contrary to the terms of peace, still retained Malta in her hands, and because the British newspapers made attacks upon him. War eventually broke out in 1803. It was fortunate, perhaps, that it came as quickly as it did. Napoleon was building a very large fleet, which might have successfully challenged our maritime supremacy if time had been given for its completion.

When we wonder why the peace did not last, we can see, looking to what Napoleon was to become, that his ambitions would not let him be content with what he had achieved. But at the time people hoped for a lasting peace, and many English took advantage of it to visit the Continent, especially France, which had been closed to them since the Revolution of 1789.[1]

The war which now broke out into fresh fury, is called the Napoleonic War, for it was waged against the Empire of Napoleon and no longer against the France of the First Republic. In its first phase, which lasted from May, 1803, until October, 1805, the main interest centres in Napoleon's plans for the invasion of England. To carry out his great scheme, Napoleon stationed at and near Boulogne nearly a hundred thousand soldiers [2] — the soldiers who were afterwards to win such a wonderful series of victories on the Continent; and for the transport of this army he built over 2000 flat-bottomed boats, specially suited for transport and beaching. But the British held command of the Channel, and here Napoleon's plans broke down.

The attempted invasion of England (1803–5)

His battle fleet was concentrated in four places, the great

[1] Haydon the painter was one, and he gave a very interesting account of his experience in his autobiography, describing amongst other things the pleasure many of the French felt when Sunday was restored as a day of rest.

[2] Napoleon hoped to have 150,000 men; as a matter of fact, during the critical months of 1805, he had only 93,000 men.

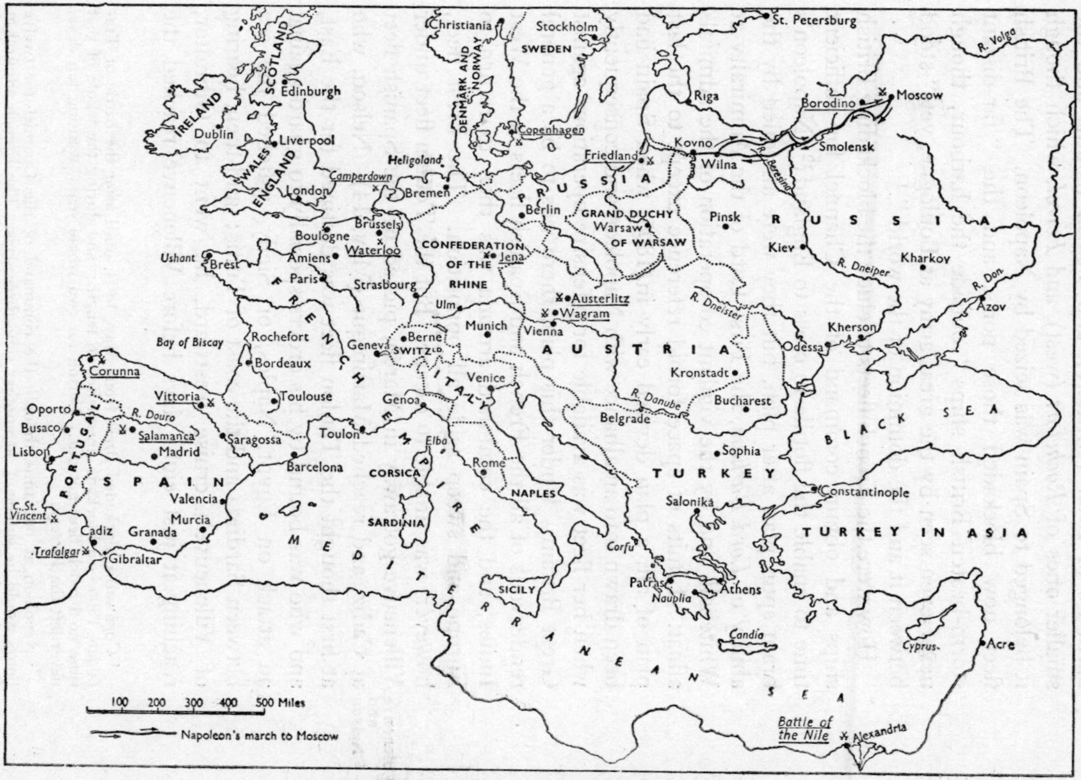

EUROPE IN THE TIME OF NAPOLEON

harbours of *Brest* (Brittany), and *Toulon* (south) and the smaller ones of *Rochefort* (west), and *Ferrol*, which though it belonged to Spain was seized by Napoleon. The British fleet now blockaded those ports, and the "far-distant storm-beaten British ships" outside the harbour, though never even seen by the great army at Boulogne, yet "stood between it and the dominion of the world".[1]

How were the French fleets to elude the blockading British ships and obtain command of the Channel for sufficient time to enable the flotilla to cross to England?[2] Napoleon's brain spun plan after plan, but they were all foiled by the ability of *Lord Barham*, the First Lord of the Admiralty at Whitehall, and by the vigilant co-operation of the admirals afloat. Limits of space forbid reference except to the last plan of all, a plan devised early in 1805, when Spain had been drawn into an alliance with Napoleon and consequently when her fleet was available for offensive operations against Great Britain. Under this plan, there was to be a general rendezvous of all the French and Spanish fleets in the West Indies, and the combined armada was then to return to Europe and sweep aside all opposition. The Brest fleet, however, was unable to escape. But the Toulon fleet under Villeneuve got away in March, picked up the Spanish fleet at Cadiz, and reached Martinique (May, 14). Nelson, who at first thought the Toulon fleet was destined for the East, and who was bound by his orders specially to guard against an attack on Egypt, Naples, or Sicily, watched the sea between Sardinia and the coast of Tunis; and then, hearing of Villeneuve's cruise westward, he went to Gibraltar, reaching it just eight days before Villeneuve reached the

Villeneuve and Nelson

[1] Cornwallis blockaded Brest from May, 1803, until after the battle of Trafalgar, 1805 — a blockade unequalled in length; and during the whole of that time no French fleet got out. Nelson for two whole years, wanting ten days, never left the *Victory*.

[2] Napoleon at one time thought the command of the Channel for twelve hours would be sufficient, at another time three days. The French admiral at Brest thought "at least a fortnight was necessary", as the Channel was too stormy to be always practicable for the transport-boats.

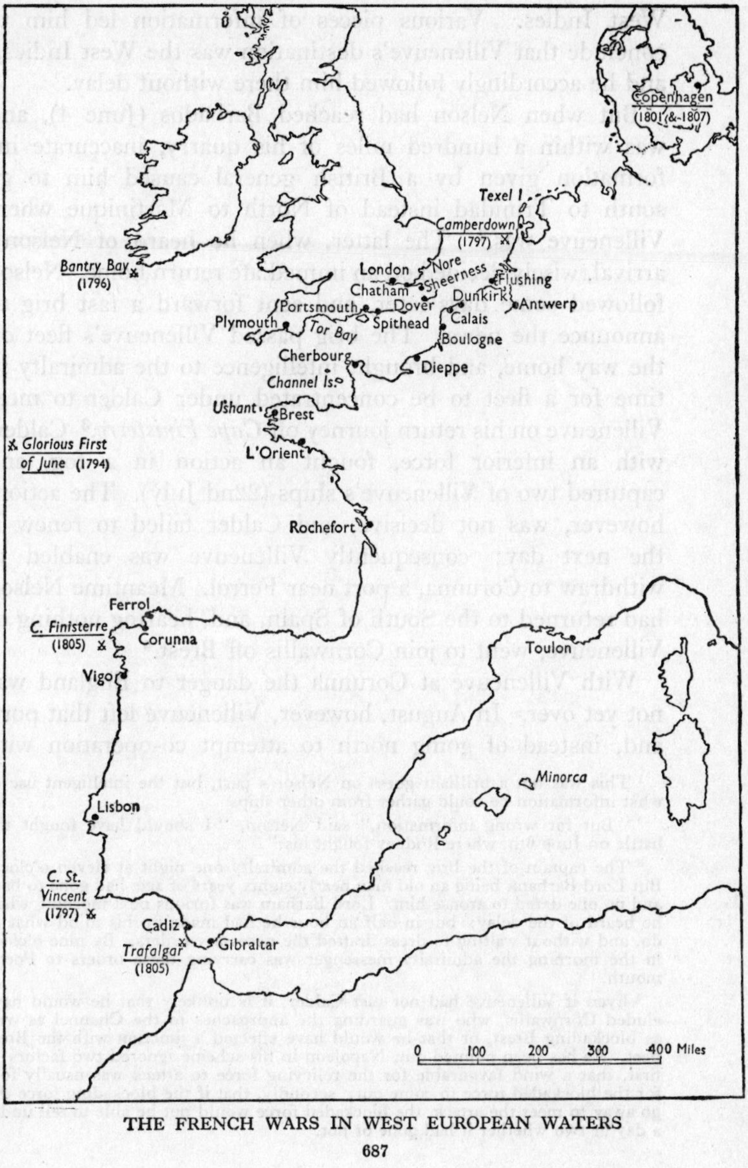

THE FRENCH WARS IN WEST EUROPEAN WATERS

West Indies. Various pieces of information led him to conclude that Villeneuve's destination was the West Indies,[1] and he accordingly followed him there without delay.

But when Nelson had reached Barbados (June 4), and was within a hundred miles of his quarry, inaccurate information given by a British general caused him to go south to Trinidad instead of North to Martinique where Villeneuve was.[2] The latter, when he heard of Nelson's arrival, wisely decided on an immediate return home. Nelson followed some days later, and sent forward a fast brig to announce the news. The brig passed Villeneuve's fleet on the way home, and brought intelligence to the admiralty in time for a fleet to be concentrated under Calder to meet Villeneuve on his return journey off *Cape Finisterre*.[3] Calder, with an inferior force, fought an action in a fog, and captured two of Villeneuve's ships (22nd July). The action, however, was not decisive, and Calder failed to renew it the next day; consequently Villeneuve was enabled to withdraw to Corunna, a port near Ferrol. Meantime Nelson had returned to the South of Spain, and, hearing nothing of Villeneuve, went to join Cornwallis off Brest.[4]

With Villeneuve at Corunna the danger to England was not yet over. In August, however, Villeneuve left that port, and, instead of going north to attempt co-operation with

[1] This was not a brilliant guess on Nelson's part, but the intelligent use of what information he could gather from other ships.

[2] "But for wrong information," said Nelson, "I should have fought the battle on June 6th, where Rodney fought his."

[3] The captain of the brig reached the admiralty one night at eleven o'clock. But Lord Barham, being an old man nearly eighty years of age, had gone to bed, and no one dared to arouse him. Lord Barham was furious next morning when he heard of the delay; but in half an hour he had made up his mind what to do, and without waiting to dress drafted the necessary orders. By nine o'clock in the morning the admiralty messenger was carrying these orders to Portsmouth.

[4] Even if Villeneuve had not met Calder, it is unlikely that he would have eluded Cornwallis, who was guarding the approaches to the Channel as well as blockading Brest, or that he would have effected a junction with the Brest fleet. As has been pointed out, Napoleon in his scheme ignored two factors — first, that a wind favourable for the relieving force to attack was usually foul for the blockaded force to come out; secondly, that if the blockading force did go away to meet the attack, the blockaded force would not be able to tell under a day or two whether it had gone or not.

the Brest fleet, he went south and entered Cadiz. There he was shortly afterwards blockaded by the British fleet, and Napoleon had to give up all ideas of invasion. By now Great Britain was fully roused to her danger, the country would no longer be content with Addington as its leader, a general demand arose for the recall of Pitt, and accordingly in 1804 he replaced Addington as prime minister. He succeeded in forming another coalition against France — the third that he formed — consisting of Russia, Austria, Great Britain, and Sweden (1805). Accordingly Napoleon marched his army away from Boulogne to attack Austria. Meantime Villeneuve was watched by Nelson, who had, after a short rest in England, returned to his command. Villeneuve, however, could not lie idle while the British assumed the offensive, as they began to do, in the Mediterranean; urged on by Napoleon, and on the point of being superseded, he ventured to leave Cadiz, intending to check the British operations against Naples. But Nelson attacked him and the battle off *Cape Trafalgar* resulted (21st October).

The Third Coalition (1805)

The allied fleet of thirty-three ships of the line, after it left Cadiz, was discovered by Nelson in a slightly curved line some five miles long. Nelson had previously determined to make an attack upon the centre and rear of the allied fleet, with his own twenty-seven ships arranged in two columns. Of one of these columns Collingwood was in command with orders to attack the rear ships, whilst Nelson himself led the other with the object of fighting the centre and keeping off the van ships of the enemy. The action began about noon. Collingwood in the *Royal Sovereign* outdistanced the ships of his own column,[1] and for a quarter of an hour fought the enemy single-handed. Somewhat later Nelson's column got into action. Nelson's ship, the *Victory*, led, and

Battle of Trafalgar (21st Oct., 1805)

[1] "See how that noble fellow Collingwood carries his ship into action!" was Nelson's comment, and almost at the same time Collingwood exclaimed, "What would Nelson give to be here!" It was just before Collingwood began his attack that Nelson issued his famous signal, "England expects every man to do his duty."

her first broadside dismounted twenty guns and killed or wounded some four hundred men of the enemy. The fighting was carried on with fierce determination by both sides; but the British gunnery proved its superiority, and eventually, out of thirty-three ships of the enemy, the British captured nineteen. In the course of the battle, however, Nelson was wounded in the spine by a musket ball and died in the hour of victory.[1] "It does not become me to make comparisons," Lord St. Vincent had written previously, "there is but one Nelson." And later generations have endorsed this verdict (*Note 114*).

Death of Nelson

2. THE ATTACK ON BRITAIN'S TRADE: THE CONTINENTAL SYSTEM

Trafalgar destroyed the naval power of France, but the mere fact that the war was to last for another ten years shows how overwhelmingly great was Napoleon's power on land. Indeed he was on the verge of some of his greatest victories. Just six weeks after Trafalgar, he won the great victory of *Austerlitz* (2nd December, 1805) which crushed Austria, forced her to make peace, and ended the Third Coalition. The news came to Pitt just when his health had finally broken down. His words "Roll up the map of Europe, it will not be wanted these ten years," were extraordinarily prophetic. The shock really killed him, his friends said he had "an Austerlitz look", and in six weeks he was dead.

Austerlitz (1805)

Death of Pitt (1806)

The British Government now had to face a terrible situation. Napoleon went from triumph to triumph. He overwhelmed the Prussians at *Jena* in 1806, he defeated the Russians at *Friedland* in 1807, and the Czar Alexander decided to come to terms. He met Napoleon at Tilsit, and there the two made an alliance, dismembering Prussia and

Jena (1806)

Treaty of Tilsit (1807)

[1] Just before his death Nelson was told that 14 or 15 of the enemy ships had surrendered. "That is well," he answered, "but I bargained for 20."

reorganizing the rest of Germany, and making common cause against Great Britain.

The Continental System

This was to prove the climax of Napoleon's power. Only Britain still held out against him, and if he could not defeat her at sea, or invade her on land, he yet hoped to defeat her by the use of another method. He determined to starve

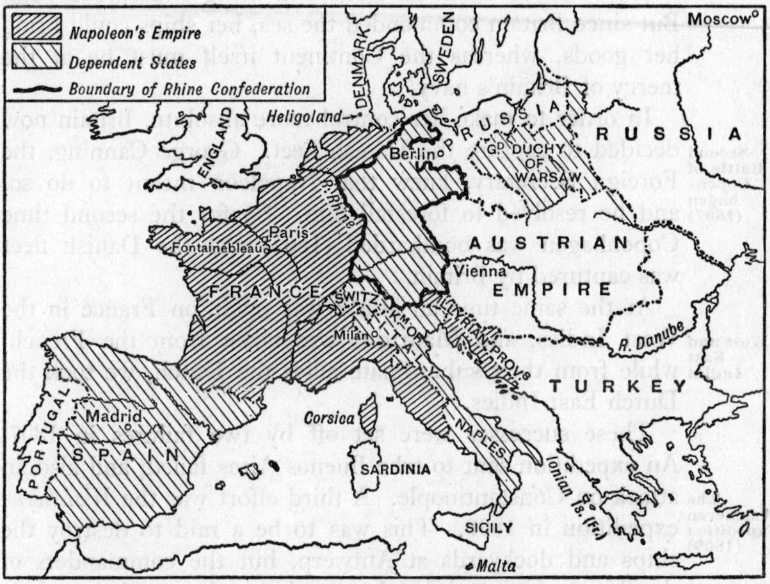

THE CONTINENTAL SYSTEM

her out and to strangle her trade. With this object he had issued, at the end of 1806, the famous *Berlin Decrees* which set up what is called the *Continental System* (*Note 116*). The British Isles were declared to be in a state of blockade, though there was not one French ship within miles of any British port. No ships coming from Great Britain and Ireland or her colonies might enter any port of France or any of her allies; all goods of British origin could be seized. The "system" was to be adopted by Prussia, Austria,

Russia, and all the countries under Napoleon's control, such as Holland, the rest of Germany, and most of Italy.

Britain retaliated by *Orders in Council* which declared all the ports from which Britain was excluded to be themselves blockaded, and forbade any neutral ships to enter them save by licence from Britain. The general result of this economic warfare was to check all trade and bring widespread ruin. But since Britain commanded the sea, her ships could bring her goods, whereas the Continent itself must be at the mercy of Britain's navy.

Second Battle of Copenhagen (1807)

In order to make her control more absolute, Britain now decided to capture the Danish fleet. George Canning, the Foreign Secretary, knew that Napoleon meant to do so, and he resolved to forestall him. So for the second time Copenhagen was bombarded (1807) and the Danish fleet was captured by Britain.

West and East Indies

At the same time an attack was made on France in the West Indies, and Mauritius was taken from the French, while from their subordinate allies the Dutch, we took the Dutch East Indies.

The Walcheren Expedition (1809)

These successes were set off by two failures in 1807. An expedition sent to take Buenos Aires failed, and also an attack on Constantinople. A third effort was the *Walcheren* expedition in 1809. This was to be a raid to destroy the ships and dockyards at Antwerp, but the commanders of the fleet and army refused to work together, and the whole affair was a failure.[1]

[1] The Walcheren Expedition gave rise to an epigram, better known perhaps than the expedition itself. The naval leader was Sir Richard Strachan and the army commander, Chatham, Pitt's elder brother:

Great Chatham, with his sabre drawn,
Stood waiting for Sir Richard Strachan;
Sir Richard, longing to be at 'em,
Stood waiting for the Earl of Chatham!

3. ATTACK ON SPAIN

From Napoleon's point of view, the success of his blockading plan depended on prohibiting the Continent from trading with Britain. He was therefore led on by this necessity to further aggression. He annexed *Holland* and joined her to France. Then he began the Spanish enterprise which was to prove so fatal (*Note 113*). In 1807 he first attacked and annexed *Portugal*, and in 1808 he forced the King of Spain and his heir to abandon the throne of Spain, which Napoleon at once bestowed on his brother Joseph. His position now seemed supreme. The French empire included *France*, *Belgium*, the land up to the *Rhine*, and *Piedmont* and *Tuscany*. As King of Italy, Napoleon had the direct rule, in addition, of *Lombardy* and *Venetia*. As Protector of the *Confederation of the Rhine*, he controlled the policies and the armies of nearly all the German powers except Austria and Prussia, both of which were, however, quiescent. Russia was his ally. Of his brothers, Louis was King of *Holland*, Jerome King of *Westphalia*, and Joseph King of *Spain*, whilst his brother-in-law, Murat, was King of *Naples*. Yet with all his power, and all these vast resources, he had really already sown the seeds of his own defeat, for his attack on Spain and Portugal gave Britain her opportunity. Portugal was Britain's "oldest ally" and to her an army was dispatched under *Arthur Wellesley*. He defeated the French at *Vimiero*, and by the *Convention of Cintra* (1808) they undertook to evacuate Portugal. The mistake was made, however, of granting the French army leave to return to France and of sending them back in British ships instead of sending them as prisoners to England. This roused the greatest indignation in England[1] and Wellesley was recalled. Meanwhile the Spaniards succeeded in forcing eighteen thousand Frenchmen to surrender at *Baylen*, a notable achievement.

Napoleon's position (1808); further aggression

Vimiero (1808)

[1] Contemporary cartoons show John Bull politely escorting the French army back to France where Napoleon greets them with astonished pleasure.

Napoleon at once decided to go to Spain himself, and at the head of a vast army he marched to Madrid. From there he intended to go to Lisbon, but now *Sir John Moore*, who had been sent to command the small British forces, made a threatening move down from the north. This would have meant that he could get between Napoleon and his base and cut him off from France. Napoleon determined to free himself from any such danger, and with his large force he set off to attack Moore. He intended to thrust westward and get between Moore and the coast, where the British fleet lay, ready to take off the British troops who were much outnumbered. Eventually Napoleon left the pursuit to Soult. It was a race between French and English who should reach *Corunna* first. Moore's army marched over mountainous country, covered with snow, at an average of seventeen miles a day. He reached Corunna, and while the rearguard fought off the French, the main army was taken off safely by the British fleet, though Moore himself was killed in the action (January, 1809).

Napoleon in Spain

The retreat to Corunna (1809)

4. THE PENINSULAR WAR AND THE FALL OF NAPOLEON (1809–1814)

After the embarkation of the British troops, Napoleon thought that the Spanish rising was " nearly at an end ". But he was quickly to be undeceived, for in April, 1809, Wellesley arrived in the Peninsula for the second time. With Wellesley's operations the campaigns known in our history as the *Peninsular War* really begin. The difficulties which Wellesley had to overcome were very great. Opinion at home was much divided as to the expediency of the war and the abilities of Wellesley himself; consequently he had to be cautious — " if I lost five hundred men without the clearest necessity ", he said, " I should be brought to my knees ". The British officers with him were for the most part at first inexperienced; the men were sometimes six

The Peninsular War (1809–14)

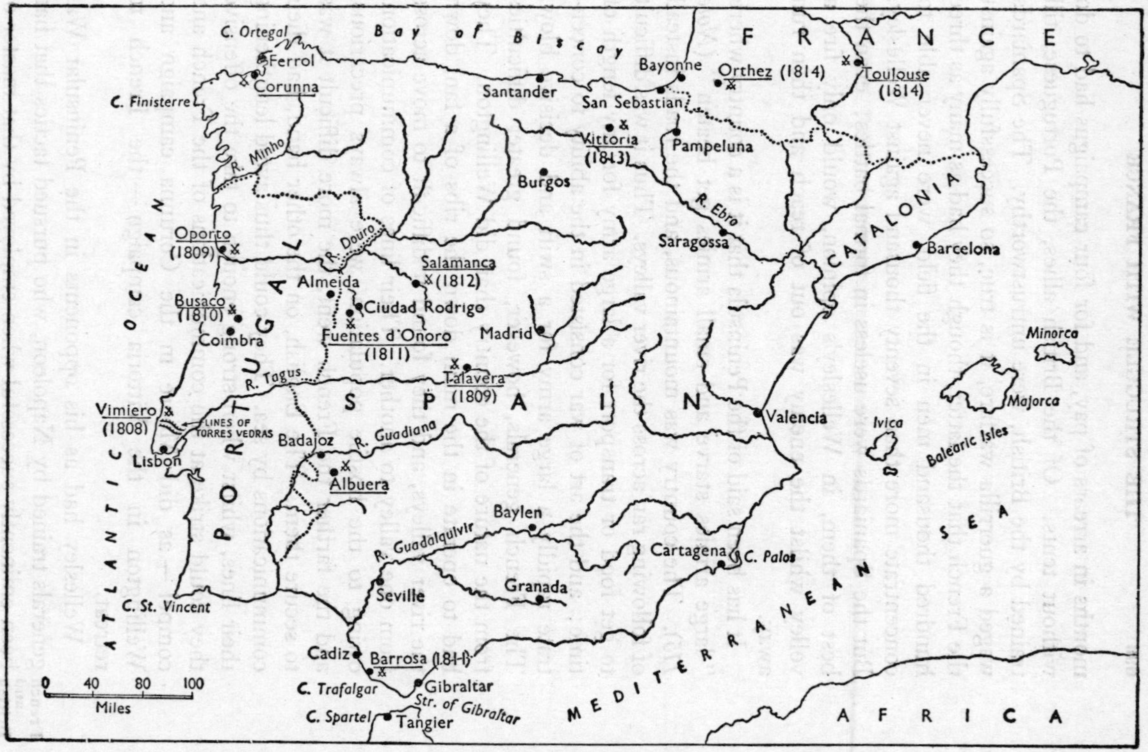

THE PENINSULAR WAR

months in arrears of pay, and for four campaigns had to do without tents. Of the British allies, the Portuguese, till trained by the British, were untrustworthy. The Spaniards waged a guerrilla warfare, it is true, so successfully against the French that the latter, though they had as many as three hundred thousand men in the field, were never able to concentrate more than seventy thousand against Wellesley. But the Spaniards were useless in formal battles; even the best of them, in Wellesley's opinion, would only fire a volley whilst the enemy was out of reach and then run away.

It has been said of the Peninsula that it is a country where "large armies starve and small armies get beaten" (*Note 115*). The country was mountainous, and the roads instead of following ran across the river valleys. Thus it was difficult to get food or transport for a large army for any length of time; and the art of war consisted in the ability to concentrate rapidly a large army for a swift and decisive blow. The French generals, however, found greater difficulties from the nature of the country than did Wellington. They had to operate in the main down the ribs of a fan, down the river valleys, and they found it difficult to move across from one valley to another. Their lines of communication, owing to the hostile population, were always precarious, and the farther the French went, the more difficult it was to secure them. The English, on the other hand, had their communications by sea. They could thus avoid lengthening their lines, whilst when strong enough to take the offensive they could strike at the communications of the French and compel — as did Moore in the Corunna campaign and Wellington in the Vittoria campaign — the French to retreat.

French and British tactics

Wellesley had as his opponents in the Peninsular War generals trained by Napoleon, who pursued tactics that had been eminently successful when employed by that master of the art of war. Briefly, Napoleon's tactics at this time were to concentrate his artillery fire upon the point selected for attack; and then to throw at the weak spot either a great mass of cavalry or else a great mass of infantry in columns of nine, eighteen, or, as at Waterloo, twenty-four deep, the columns being preceded by a cloud of nimble skirmishers who occupied the enemy's attention. Wellesley's genius, however, was equal to these tactics. First, in order to preserve his troops from the enemy's fire, he kept his troops till the last possible moment out of sight — behind a wall, for instance, or the crest of a hill. Second, when the French cavalry charged, he relied on the solidity of a British square. But when he was fighting the French infantry column, he had his men in line, two deep. This formation, so long as it remained steady, had great advantages; through its length it could outflank the enemy, and it could pour at a closely massed column a deadly fire to which only the leading files of a column could reply.[1] The British line would fire one or two volleys at short range, so short that the soldiers often waited to see the white of their enemies' eyes before firing. They would follow up this attack with a bayonet charge before the enemy had time to recover, and then retire to await a fresh charge from the forces opposed to them.

Our intervention in the Peninsula was not altogether popular in Britain. Many politicians thought it a waste of men and materials, and as the Continental System began to make itself felt, our dwindling resources made the strain of this distant war very heavy.

In addition, at first Wellesley did not achieve any great success. In 1809 he drove the French out of Portugal and himself made a dash into Spain. He hoped to reach Madrid; but after winning an engagement at *Talavera*, not far from the capital, he could not advance since the Spaniards failed to support him, and Napoleon sent vast reinforcements

The Talavera campaign (1809)

[1] Wellesley took care to prevent his own line being outflanked, and protected it in front by a powerful line of skirmishers, so that the skirmishers of the enemy should not harass it.

under his commander, *Masséna.* In consequence Wellesley not only had to retreat, but the French pursued him into Portugal, and declared that they would drive the English " into the sea ".

The Crisis of 1810

The news of the French advance filled Britain with gloom. Had Wellesley been driven out, possibly peace would have been made and Napoleon left in possession of his conquests. But Wellesley saved himself and his army. He had retreated right back to Lisbon, which stands on a peninsula. Across the neck of land he had already prepared a great defence work. This consisted of three lines, *the lines of Torres Vedras*, immensely strong, consisting in part of water-works, of barricades, and of fortified gun emplacements. The area in front of these lines had been evacuated and cleared.

The lines of Torres Vedras (1810–11)

Thither the British troops retreated, and when the French pushed on, hoping now for swift victory, they found themselves before an impregnable position, which they could not storm. Nor could they obtain supplies, and after a " siege " of five months, Masséna had to withdraw his starving troops and return to Spain.

In the Peninsula itself, matters settled into a period of waiting. Wellesley, who had (1809) been made a peer with the title of Lord Wellington[1] for his success in saving the army, remained in Portugal, and in 1811 only two engagements were fought (one at *Fuentes d'Onoro*, one at *Albuera*). But in 1812 there came a change.

Fuentes d'Onoro and Albuera (1811)

Napoleon had quarrelled with the Czar, largely over the Continental System which hit Russia very hardly. He resolved to invade Russia. For this enterprise he collected the " Grand Army " and withdrew many of his best troops from Spain. History has few greater tragedies to record than the fate of Napoleon's expedition. Before he started, Napoleon received the homage of kings and princes at a brilliant gathering in Dresden. He then entered Russia

Napoleon in Russia (1812)

[1] He was created a Duke in 1814.

with an army of over six hundred thousand men — a larger and more motley army than any seen since the time of Xerxes. After fighting a most murderous battle at *Borodino*, he entered the capital of Russia, *Moscow* — but only to find it a deserted city, whilst on his arrival large parts of it were set on fire by incendiaries. After a brief stay he decided to retire, and on his return journey had to endure the awful rigours of a Russian winter and the pitiless and persistent attacks of the Russian cavalry. Less than sixty thousand of his troops eventually crossed the Russian frontier in fighting condition. Napoleon himself left his troops before the end and hurried home accompanied by only three companions. He finally returned to Paris in a hackney coach.

The retreat from Moscow (1812)

This preoccupation of the French with Russia gave Wellington his opportunity. While Napoleon was marching into Russia, Wellington was marching into Spain.

Wellington's opportunity (1812)

The two main roads from Portugal were guarded on the Spanish side by two great fortresses, *Ciudad Rodrigo* and *Badajoz*, between which lay the opening to Madrid, and both of which Wellington captured. The main French army lay at *Salamanca*, and a small force was dispatched by the French in an effort to cut Wellington's communications. This force he utterly wiped out " in less than ten minutes ", and went on to defeat the whole main body.

Ciudad Rodrigo and Badajoz (1812)

Salamanca (1812)

The effect of this victorious advance was to drive the French out of southern Spain. Joseph Bonaparte fled from Madrid, and Soult led the retreat of the French troops north to *Burgos*. Wellington pursued, but could not take the city, and lost thousands of lives when he was compelled to fall back. He had to evacuate Madrid and returned once more to Salamanca (*Note 115*).

In 1812 an important change occurred in Britain. *Lord Castlereagh* became Foreign Secretary (a position which he held till 1822), and he set to work at once to infuse fresh energy into the struggle against Napoleon. He believed

Castlereagh

that the Russian campaign gave Europe a fresh chance to combine more successfully than before against France. He succeeded in inducing Prussia, Sweden, and Austria to join in the attack, and these powers now allied with Great Britain and Russia to form the *Fourth Coalition*, which was at length to secure victory.

The Fourth Coalition (1812)

The allies attacked in 1813, and the great assault was made upon the French in Germany. Napoleon concentrated his troops at *Leipzig*, and there the great four days *Battle of the Nations* was fought. It ended in the total defeat of the French, and the Emperor, after having suffered enormous losses, retreated with only a few troops to France.

The War of Liberation

The Battle of the Nations (1813)

At the same time, in Spain, Wellington drove the French army, which had been further depleted by Napoleon in order to obtain reinforcements in Germany, away from Salamanca towards the Pyrenees. At *Vittoria* he defeated Joseph's army and cut off its retreat (1813). Joseph himself escaped over the mountains. Wellington pressed on, took San Sebastian and Pampeluna, crossed the Pyrenees, and invaded France.

Vittoria (1813)

Now France was attacked from two sides. Napoleon had refused the generous terms offered to him by the allies. In the north-east he fought his great defensive campaign against the allied armies which poured over the frontier. He was unable to save Paris, though this campaign is reckoned by some to have been one of the greatest efforts of his career. In the south-west Wellington moved forward, won the battle of *Orthez*, and advanced on *Toulouse*. Just before he captured the town, Napoleon had abdicated. The war was over.

The Invasion of France (1814)

Orthez and Toulouse (1814)

The campaigns in the Peninsula had been of inestimable importance. It cost Napoleon, according to Wellington's calculations, not far short of half a million men; Napoleon himself called it a "running sore"—a constant drain of money and men. It re-established the prestige of the British army, and it gave Spain the opportunity of showing that no

The importance of the Peninsular War

despot, however powerful, can trample upon the independence of a proud nation.

So after close on twenty years of war France was beaten back to her own borders. The reasons of her first successes and her eventual failure lie deeper than the genius of Napoleon and the counterbalancing dogged accuracy of Wellington — the compensation which Fate gave us[1] — they lie in what is greater than great men, namely great ideas. At the beginning France stood as the champion of *Liberty*. Hence, wherever the invading French went, they were more or less welcomed as liberators by the people. This was so in Italy, and Holland, and Germany. Thus the resistance in these countries was often half-hearted. Briefly, it was the new ideas of the Revolution fighting against kings and princes, representatives of the old despotism — and the kings were beaten. As time went on, however, it was revealed that the French did not practise what they preached. They made " war support war ": they lived at free quarters in the countries they nominally came to set free, and a taste of this soon lost the favour they had at first won. Napoleon made the change plain. A despot himself, his armies rapidly became the oppressors of Europe instead of its liberators, and this soon bred a national hostility to him. It could not work at once, because his armies were so enormously superior. But this feeling of *Patriotism*, which he roused everywhere against him — indeed almost created in Germany — triumphed in the end. So in the contest of the peoples of Europe against one despot, Napoleon was bound to go down. Rightly is the fight of Leipzig (his first great defeat in a pitched battle) called the Völkerschlacht, " The Battle of the Nations ". It was national patriotism which crushed him.

Causes of Napoleon's downfall

[1] Both generals were born in 1769. " Fate owed us this compensation " was the comment subsequently made. Curiously enough, they were both at school in France at the same time; Wellington at Angers and Napoleon at Brienne. They received their first commissions within a few months of each other in 1785–86, and also their lieutenant-colonelcies. They ended their fighting careers on the same day. But they never met, though it is believed that Wellington caught sight of Napoleon through his glass at Waterloo.

The same fact is revealed in another way. At first all the wars which France had to wage in Europe were short. Austria was the only country which kept up a fairly continuous war, and even she had made peace four times before Leipzig. Shattering defeats at Rivoli, Marengo, and Hohenlinden, Austerlitz and Wagram brought her to the ground. Of the others, Prussia and Russia joined for brief periods; Spain and the German States wavered now to one side, now to the other. Great Britain alone was constant, but at first could find no decisive point of attack. Victories at sea and the capturing of colonies could not end the war. But when she found and fostered a national spirit of resistance in Portugal and Spain, Napoleon's downfall began. The Peninsular War is the first *long* war with which he had to grapple, and he could not end it, partly because of the patriotic, though guerrilla, warfare which Spain fought, and partly because he could not strike at the heart of the sea-power which supported Spain. His troops entered almost every European capital; but they could not reach London. And so the long struggle in Spain gave Europe time to rally.

War between Great Britain and the United States 1812-14)

Meantime, whilst Wellington was fighting in the Peninsula, Great Britain found herself involved in a new war. The "Continental System" and the British retaliatory measures had placed the United States and other neutral countries in an almost intolerable position. A neutral ship, if it was sailing to or from a British port, might be seized by the French; if it was not, it might be seized by the British. Moreover, the British had searched United States merchant vessels, and even on one occasion a United States war vessel, for British seamen who had joined American ships to avoid being impressed into British men-of-war. Disputes led to war being declared in 1812. In the earlier stages of the war, though Captain Broke in the *Shannon* upheld our prestige by causing the American frigate *Chesapeake* to surrender in fifteen minutes, the American frigates — so equipped as to be almost ships of the line — won many successes over the lighter-armed British frigates; and United States privateers took some five hundred British merchantmen in seven months. The land operations of the United States across the Canadian frontier were, however, a failure. The Canadians, whether of French or of British descent, combined with the British regulars to resist the invasion, and fought with great courage and persistency. Eventually Great Britain, in 1814, after Napoleon's abdication, was able to send a large fleet and her Peninsular veterans to America. Washington was taken, but an attack upon New Orleans failed, and peace was made at the end of the year.

5. THE "HUNDRED DAYS" (1815)

The Congress of Vienna, and Napoleon's return from Elba (1815)

Napoleon, on his abdication, had been given Elba — a small island off Tuscany — to rule as an independent principality. Meanwhile the Bourbon line in the person of Louis XVIII — a brother of Louis XVI — had been restored in France, and a great *Congress* — in which Lord Castlereagh represented Great Britain — was held at *Vienna* to settle the affairs of Europe. The congress had not completed its labours when suddenly it heard of Napoleon's return to France. The temporary absence of the British frigate which watched Elba had enabled Napoleon to escape and to land in France with eight hundred men. He was received in France by his old soldiers with enthusiasm, and reached Paris on 20th March, 1815, without so much as firing a shot. Then begins the period known in history as that of "*the Hundred Days*". Louis XVIII had to fly. Napoleon reconstituted the Government, and announced that he was going to pursue a policy of peace toward other countries and to grant liberal institutions to France. But the allies put no trust in Napoleon's promises. The Congress of Vienna outlawed him, and declared him to be an enemy and disturber of the peace of the world. Each of the big powers — Great Britain, Austria, Russia, and Prussia —

undertook to supply a hundred and fifty thousand soldiers, whilst Great Britain as usual was to provide subsidies.

Napoleon's plan of campaign

The plan of the allies was to make a joint advance upon Paris. But in June only the British and Prussians were ready. In Belgium, Wellington had about eighty-five thousand men under his command; one-third were British (very few of whom had seen any service before), one-third Germans, and one-third Dutch Belgians. Blücher, the Prussian general, commanded some hundred and twenty-four thousand Germans. Wellington and Blücher were acting in concert, and their combined armies were spread over a very much extended line, not far short of a hundred miles in length, and some miles away from the French frontier. Napoleon's idea was to make a sudden and unexpected attack on the centre of the allied line; this would enable him to push his own forces like a wedge between Wellington and Blücher, and, as their bases lay in opposite directions, the one to the west and the other to the east, to defeat them in detail. Leaving Paris on 12th June, Napoleon marched to the frontier, passed through Charleroi, and by the evening of the 15th he himself was in front of part of the Prussian forces which lay at Ligny, whilst Ney, his chief commander, was some seven miles farther west at Quatre Bras, where some of Wellington's troops were posted.

Ligny and Quatre Bras (16th June 1815)

"It was the finest thing ever done," said Wellington of Napoleon's performance, "so rapid was it and so well combined." The allies were surprised and outmanœuvred; but, fortunately for them, both Napoleon and Ney wasted the morning of the 16th, and this delay enabled Blücher and Wellington — the latter of whom had attended the Duchess of Richmond's famous ball at Brussels on the previous evening — to concentrate a large part of their forces. In the afternoon of the 16th came two battles. Napoleon beat the Prussians at Ligny. Ney at first crumpled up Wellington's lines at Quatre Bras, but the stubbornness

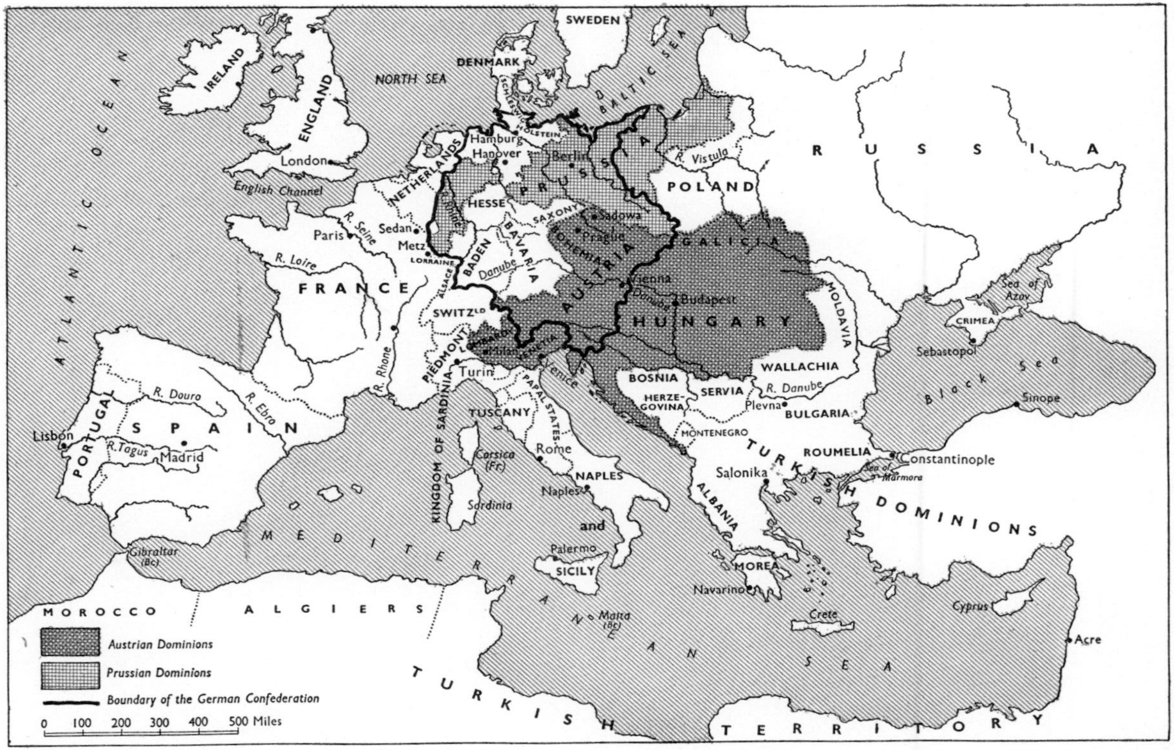

EUROPE AFTER THE PEACE SETTLEMENT IN 1815

F 938

of the British soldiers, and the fact that Napoleon had withdrawn, without Ney's knowledge, part of Ney's right wing to assist in Blücher's downfall, led to his final repulse.[1]

Movements of armies (17th June)

The day after these two battles — the 17th of June — was occupied with marches. At dawn the Prussians retreated, not east towards Namur, their base of operations, as Napoleon had expected, but north in order to keep in touch with Wellington. About ten o'clock Wellington began to retreat north. Napoleon himself, worn out with the exertions of the previous few days, again wasted the morning, and not till about 2 p.m. did Grouchy, one of Napoleon's generals, start in pursuit of the Prussians, and Napoleon himself in pursuit of Wellington. Nightfall found Wellington in position near Waterloo and Napoleon's troops beginning to arrive there, whilst the Prussian army was sixteen miles away at Wavre, and Grouchy, who had only just discovered the Prussian line of retreat, was some way to the south of it. During the night Wellington received promise of help from Blücher and determined to hold his ground.[2]

The Battle of Waterloo (18th June)

On the 18th came the battle of Waterloo. The two armies were drawn up facing each other across a shallow valley, at a distance of about a mile apart. For eight hours, from eleven in the morning till seven in the evening, Napoleon hurled his troops against the positions of the British and their allies. His attacks were all repulsed, and the arrival of the Prussians to reinforce Wellington coincided with the failure of the Old Guard sent forward by Napoleon as his last effort. The Emperor drove from the battlefield and his army disintegrated in flight. Four days later (22nd June) he

[1] The Duke of Wellington had a very long day on the 16th. He left Brussels in the morning, and rode out beyond Quatre Bras; then he visited Blücher at Ligny, and warned him of the dangerous position he had taken up. He had therefore ridden over forty miles before the battle of Quatre Bras began, and he remained in the saddle till nightfall. A general officer found him late that night, when his troops were asleep, chuckling over some English newspapers which had just arrived!

[2] It is said that the Duke of Wellington himself rode over to Wavre during the night of the 17th, and got personal assurance of support from Blücher — but the story lacks confirmation. He received a message anyway before dawn on the 18th.

abdicated. He subsequently surrendered to the commander of a British man-of-war, and was sent by the British Government as a prisoner to St. Helena, where he died six years later (1821).

The Treaty of Paris (1815)

After Waterloo, the *Congress of Vienna*, which had been sitting since before the *Hundred Days*, concluded its work, and peace was finally signed at *Paris*. France obtained better terms than might have been expected. This was partly due to the fact that her representative, Talleyrand, stressed the fact that the allies were making peace with a France ruled over by the restored monarchy of the Bourbons, and not with revolutionary or Napoleonic France. Moreover, Great Britain, represented by Castlereagh and Wellington, did not wish to see the other powers, especially Prussia, given too much, and they wanted to settle thorny problems on a fair basis of compromise.

Therefore, France was left with the boundaries she had before the Revolution. Prussia was not allowed to take Alsace-Lorraine. Only the conquests made by the Revolution and by Napoleon were taken from France. Thus Belgium and Holland were now set free from French domination and united into one independent State. In Spain the Bourbons were restored. In Italy, the Bourbons returned to Naples, while, in the north, Venetia and Lombardy were given to Austria. Prussia was given half of Saxony (for Saxony had been the firm ally of Napoleon), and she also acquired the Rhineland. Poland, which had been partitioned during the Revolution, and had been partially restored by Napoleon (in his formation of the Duchy of Warsaw) was again obliterated, Russia receiving the lion's share.

Of her conquests, Great Britain kept Malta, Mauritius, and the Cape of Good Hope. She had taken the Cape from the Dutch when they were under Napoleon, and she now paid them compensation. Her gains did not seem extensive, but their importance was only realized later.

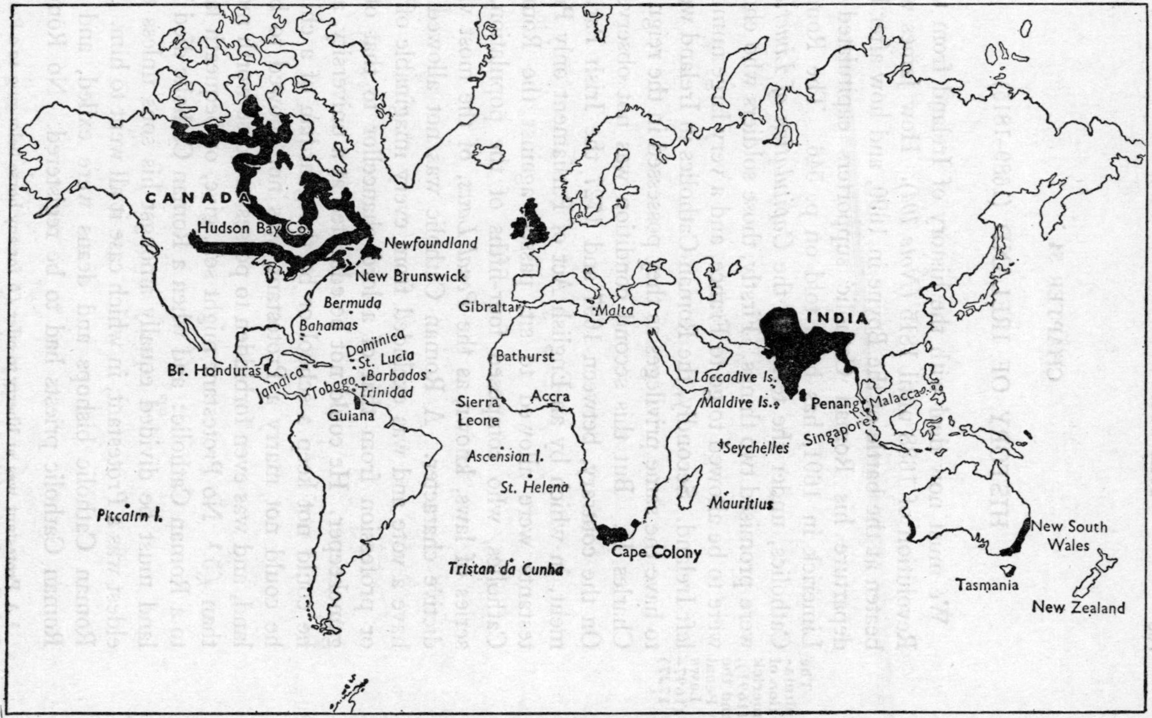

THE BRITISH EMPIRE IN 1815

CHAPTER 54

HISTORY OF IRELAND (1689–1815)

The Capitulation of Limerick (1691), and the Penal Laws (1697–1727)

We must now deal with the history of Ireland from the Revolution of 1688 until 1815 (*Note 104*). How James was beaten at the battle of the Boyne in 1690, and how after his departure his Roman Catholic supporters capitulated at Limerick in 1691, has been told on p. 546. The Roman Catholics, under the terms of the *Capitulation of Limerick*, were promised two things. Firstly, those soldiers who chose were to be allowed to go to France, and a very large number left Ireland. Secondly, the Roman Catholics in Ireland were to have the same privileges as they possessed in the reign of Charles II. But this second condition was not observed. On the contrary, between 1697 and 1727 the Irish Parliament, in which by an English Act of Parliament only Protestants were allowed to sit, passed against the Roman Catholics, who composed four-fifths of the population, a series of laws, known as the *Penal Laws*, of the most vindictive character. A Roman Catholic was not allowed to have a vote and was excluded from every imaginable office or profession from that of a lord chancellor to that of a gamekeeper. He could not be educated at a university, and he could not keep a school or be the guardian of a child; he could not marry a Protestant, was not allowed to buy land, and was even forbidden to possess a horse worth more than £5.[1] No Protestant might sell, give, or bequeath land to a Roman Catholic: and when a Roman Catholic died his land must be divided equally amongst his sons unless the eldest was a Protestant, in which case it all went to him. All Roman Catholic bishops and deans were exiled, and all Roman Catholic priests had to be registered. No Roman

[1] A Protestant was at liberty to offer £5 for any horse belonging to a Roman Catholic, who was bound to accept the offer.

Catholic chapel was allowed a bell or a steeple, and pilgrimages to holy wells were forbidden.

Quite apart from the exclusion of the Roman Catholics from any share in the government of their country, the political condition of Ireland stood in great need of reform. All laws passed in the Irish Parliament had still, under Poynings' Act of 1495, to receive the assent of the privy council in England, whilst the Parliament in England, in the reign of George I, arrogated to itself the right of passing laws binding upon Ireland. It must be remembered also that the Irish Parliament had practically no control over the officials who governed Ireland, these being appointed and supervised by the Government in England, and it was an additional grievance that the highest of these officials were almost invariably Englishmen. The viceroys were Englishmen, often spending four-fifths of their time in England; the Protestant bishops were nearly all Englishmen, and some of them never came to Ireland at all;[1] and only one Irishman in the whole course of the eighteenth century was made lord chancellor.

Political condition of Ireland

The Irish Parliament itself needed drastic reformation; half the members of its House of Lords were Protestant bishops, whilst over two-thirds of the members of its House of Commons were nominated by individuals, no less than sixty seats belonging to three families; and, as has already been pointed out, no Roman Catholic could vote at an election or sit in either House of Parliament. Moreover, till past the middle of the eighteenth century, there was no fixed term for the duration of a parliament. Consequently a parliament lasted for an indefinite period, and one existed in the eighteenth century for over thirty years.

The Irish Parliament

Even worse perhaps than the political was the economic

[1] One divine held the bishopric of Down for twenty years; he never went near it during the whole of that time, but lived at Hammersmith. Of two bishops appointed at the same time in the eighteenth century, it is said that one sent down to his diocese twenty-two cart-loads of books and one hogshead of wine; the other, however, was content with one load of books, but dispatched to his palace twenty-two hogsheads of wine.

Economic Condition of Ireland

condition of Ireland. That island is naturally a great pasturing country; its cattle and its wool were at one time the best in Europe. It might have become a great manufacturing country as well. But the selfishness of English farmers and manufacturers stifled its enterprise. The English Parliament had already, in Charles II's reign, forbidden the importation into England of cattle, sheep, and swine, alive or dead. It proceeded, in William III's reign, to prohibit altogether the exportation of Irish woollen manufactures, and to confine the export of Irish unmanufactured wool to England alone, where the wool had to pay heavy import duties.[1] Irish industries were thus ruined. But this does not exhaust the evils from which Ireland suffered. As a consequence of the Irish support to James II, a great deal of land had been confiscated, and it is reckoned that, after the Revolution, three-fourths of it belonged to owners of British descent.

Irish landlords

A large number of these owners lived in England in the eighteenth century, and let their land to people called "middlemen", who often rackrented and exploited the smaller tenants to whom they sublet. The wretched Irish peasant, paying rent to a middleman, tithes to the Protestant clergyman, and dues to his Roman Catholic priest, had in some cases, it was said, "hardly the skin of a potato to subsist upon".

Irish emigration

Such were the conditions in Ireland in the earlier part of the eighteenth century, and they all combined to degrade and to debase the great mass of the population and to make the country a most unhappy one. The more energetic and ambitious Irishmen, indeed, left their own country to pursue their fortunes elsewhere. Spain, for instance, possessed five Irish regiments, and within a hundred years a quarter of a million Irishmen, it is said, joined the Irish Brigade in France. It was that brigade which took the chief share in defeating the British at Almanza and at Fontenoy, and

[1] It is true that after 1743 the British Government encouraged the flax and linen industry at Belfast; but that was inadequate compensation.

which caused, so tradition says, George II to say at Dettingen, "Curse on the laws which deprive me of such men". To Austria Ireland supplied some of her best generals, and to Russia two field-marshals,[1] whilst Coote's opponent at the hard-fought battle of Wandewash was of Irish extraction.

Relaxation of Penal Laws (1778-82)

We must now see how the conditions in Ireland were gradually improved during the later portion of the eighteenth century. In the first place, it was found impossible in practice to carry out the laws imposing restrictions on the exercise of the Roman Catholic religion, and even before the middle of the century these laws were to all intents and purposes obsolete. The American War of Independence brought further relief to the Roman Catholics; for the British Government, anxious to conciliate opinion in Ireland, encouraged the Irish Parliament to repeal the laws prohibiting Roman Catholics from buying land (1778), and before the war was over other concessions followed.

Abolition of Commercial Code (1780), repeal of Poynings' Act (1782), and creation of Independent Parliament (1782)

But the American War of Independence had more important effects even than this. It brought up the whole question of the relations of Great Britain to her dependencies — and Ireland might almost be called a dependency, and in some ways was much worse off than the American colonies. Above all, it gave Ireland an opportunity of pressing her claims in a way that could not be resisted. During the later stages of the war, Great Britain, hard pressed by her foes in every part of the world, had to withdraw the bulk of the troops from Ireland. The country was in imminent danger of an invasion from France; and was indeed, at one period, in "daily, almost hourly expectation of it". Quite spontaneously, Irishmen, of all creeds and classes, organized themselves into a body called the Irish Volunteers to protect their country from a French

[1] One of these was the famous Peter Lacy. He began his martial career at the age of thirteen, fighting in defence of Limerick. Subsequently he entered the Russian service, fought against Danes, Swedes, and Turks, and finally became Governor of Livonia. He is credited with having converted the Russian troops from the worst troops in Europe to some of the best, and even in modern times a division of the Russian army was still called after him.

invasion. Nearly all the landed gentry became volunteers, the Duke of Leinster, for instance, commanding the Dublin contingent. Volunteer rank was given precedence in society, and great sacrifices were made to supply funds. The movement was entirely independent of the Government, who indeed regarded it, and with reason, with a considerable apprehension. For the volunteers, when they realized their power, began, like Cromwell's Ironsides, to interfere in politics, and demanded an independent Parliament and the abolition of the restrictions upon Irish industries;[1] "England", as an Irish orator said, "had sown her laws in dragons' teeth, and they had sprung up armed men." Moreover, in *Henry Grattan* Ireland had found a parliamentary leader of exceptional ability and force of character, who directed the movement in the Irish Parliament with great distinction. The British Parliament was powerless to resist. In 1780 the restrictions on Irish trade and industries were abolished. Two years later, in 1782, Ireland obtained her legislative independence, Poynings' Act being repealed and the British Parliament giving up the right to pass laws binding upon Ireland.

Grattan's Parliament (1782)

The Irish Parliament now had a brief period of lively activity. The leader of the reformers was Henry Grattan, whose wonderful gifts as an orator brought him fame. At the time it was said that there was no one but Chatham himself who had such power of inspiration. He was a Protestant, but he now devoted himself to the effort to remove all the disabilities from which the Roman Catholics suffered. He declared: "The Irish Protestant cannot be free until the Irish Catholic ceases to be a slave." He was opposed by the Government officials who ruled in "Dublin Castle" and who were entirely hostile to any reforms. Yet Grattan might in time have won his way, had it not been for the effect on both Britain and Ireland of the events

[1] The uniforms of the volunteers — scarlet, green, blue, and orange — were all manufactured in Ireland so as to encourage home industries.

abroad, which not only stopped efforts at reform, but led to a period of repression.

The effect of the French Revolution on Ireland itself was most important (*Note 118*). Men saw that in France religious disqualifications had been abolished, the equality of man proclaimed, and government on a democratic basis set up. In Ireland the Roman Catholics wanted emancipation, that is, the right to vote and to hold offices; the Protestants wanted Parliamentary reform. Moreover all sections united in wishing for redress of economic grievances.

Effect of French Revolution in Ireland

Henry Grattan had led the moderate party, advocating Catholic emancipation and Parliamentary reform. But he did not believe in universal suffrage: "I want," he said, "to combat the wild spirit of democratic liberty by the regulated spirit of organized liberty." He wished to preserve the union with Great Britain, and declared that Ireland must support England in time of war.

Grattan

Wolfe Tone now formed an extremist party, which aimed at "breaking the connection with England, asserting the independence of our country, uniting all Irishmen in place of the denominations of Protestants and Catholics." In 1792 he and *Lord Edward FitzGerald* formed an organization called "The United Irishmen" in which they sought to unite the Presbyterians of Ulster and Roman Catholics of all Ireland against the rule of England. Thousands joined it and its influence grew rapidly.

Wolfe Tone and the United Irishmen (1792)

Pitt saw that something must be done, and in 1793 the Irish Parliament (which consisted of Protestants, elected by Protestants) was induced to pass an Act giving the vote to Roman Catholics in Ireland, though they might not sit as members. Then, in 1795, Pitt sent as Viceroy, Lord Fitzwilliam, who was himself one of the Whigs who had rallied to Pitt, and who believed that Roman Catholics should be given complete political equality. He announced this as his policy, and urged it in the dispatches which he sent home. The Irish were full of hope and rejoicing. Pitt's govern-

Pitt's Policy: Franchise granted to Roman Catholics

Lord Fitzwilliam (1795)

ment, however, refused to support Fitzwilliam, repudiated his policy, and recalled him.

The effect on Ireland was disastrous. Convinced now that nothing would be done to redress their grievances, the Irish turned to treason, and the "United Irishmen" began secret negotiations with the French. In 1796 the Revolutionary government sent an armed force of 15,000 to invade the country, which attempted a landing in *Bantry Bay*, but failed.

Attempted French landing (1796)

Disorders broke out especially in Ulster, and led to atrocities on both sides. Consequently in 1797 Pitt ordered the "disarming of Ulster". This was carried out by soldiers; and some Welsh and German troops sent into the country bullied and even tortured the people on the pretext of searching for arms.

Such methods produced their natural results. The Irish rose in open rebellion. The avowed objects of the leaders were to secure Catholic emancipation and Parliamentary reform. The peasants joined because they wished for abolition of tithe. Many Irishmen too now believed that their country could prosper only if she broke away altogether from England and got rid of the commercial burden on her prosperity. They hoped that the French would send them aid.

Rebellion of 1798

The rebellion failed utterly. The British government had known of the plot, and on the eve of the outbreak arrested the leaders, the best known of whom was Lord Edward FitzGerald.[1] The French help was not forthcoming, for Napoleon, who had thought of invading Ireland, had already

[1] Lord Edward FitzGerald was one of the seventeen children of the first Duke of Leinster. He served in the American War of Independence and was severely wounded, his life only being saved by a negro, who afterwards became his devoted servant. Subsequently FitzGerald was in Paris during part of the Revolution, attended the debates of the Convention Assembly, and was imbued with revolutionary ideas. He joined the United Irishmen on his return, and was one of the organizers of the Rebellion. A price was put on his head by the Government, and through treachery he was seized in a feather-dealer's house in Dublin. He killed one of his captors, but was himself severely wounded, and died shortly afterwards in prison.

started on his Egyptian expedition when the rebellion broke out. The peasants, left to themselves, made a despairing effort, but they were easily crushed at *Vinegar Hill* in Wexford. A small body of French, led by Wolfe Tone, arrived weeks later and was surrounded and captured at Lough Swilly.[1]

After the Rebellion was over, Pitt felt that the only way to preserve the connection of Ireland with Great Britain, and to secure any harmony between Roman Catholics and Protestants in Ireland itself, was by means of a Union between Great Britain and Ireland, similar to that between England and Scotland. Irish opinion was, however, against such a union. But lavish promises of peerages and honours — forty-one persons were either created peers or raised a step in the peerage — and very generous money compensation to those individuals who held "pocket boroughs",[2] secured a majority sufficient to pass the measure through the Irish Parliament. Moreover, though no explicit promise was made, the Roman Catholics were given to understand by the Government that Catholic emancipation would form a sequel to the passing of the Union. Thus the *Act of Union*, despite Grattan's speeches against it, was finally passed through the Irish Parliament in 1800. By its terms four Irish bishops and twenty-eight peers, who were to be elected for life by the whole body of Irish peers, were to sit in the House of Lords, whilst Ireland was to contribute a hundred members to the House of Commons. Ireland was to keep her separate judicial system and her separate executive — dependent, of course, upon the British ministry. There was to be absolute free trade between Ireland and Great Britain, and Ireland was to contribute two-seventeenths to the revenue of the United Kingdom.

Act of Union (1800)

Thus ended the Irish Independent Parliament after an

[1] Tone committed suicide in prison, before he could be executed.

[2] Over £1,250,000 was expended in this fashion, and two peers received £52,000 and £45,000 respectively for their boroughs.

existence of eighteen years. It had possessed some able speakers and statesmen; it had passed some useful laws; and, on the whole, considering the difficulties which it had to meet, it was not unsuccessful. The understanding about Catholic emancipation came, most unfortunately, to nothing. George III became firmly convinced that the grant of such emancipation would be contrary to his coronation oath, and would not agree to it, and Pitt consequently resigned office in 1801.[1] Our period consequently ends with Catholic emancipation still unsecured, and the Irish Catholics consequently feeling that they had been cheated over emancipation. Moreover, the Parliament at Westminster was now saddled with the responsibility of dealing with the biggest of the Irish problems, the agrarian question; but the English at Westminster never realized their full responsibility and for a long time failed to attempt any solution.

CHAPTER 55

PITT'S HOME POLICY AFTER THE OUTBREAK OF WAR (1793–1815)

Policy of Coercion

The outbreak of war with France had a disastrous effect upon Pitt (*Note 108*). Whatever prospects there had been of improvement in the political and social condition of Britain came to an abrupt end. All reform ceased: "One cannot repair one's house in a hurricane," said a contemporary in defence of Pitt. Unfortunately, however, Pitt did not stop at cessation of reform — he began a policy of coercion. The fear of revolution in England was the cause, but actually the bulk of the country was loyal, and repression, after all, was no remedy for social ills.

[1] It is reported that the King read the Coronation Oath to his family and said, "If I violate it I am no longer legal sovereign of this country, but it falls to the House of Savoy."

In 1790 Burke had published his *Reflections on the French Revolution* which contained the warning that power in France would pass more and more into the hands of extremists. This book had a tremendous effect on Britain, and particularly on the aristocracy who had practically ruled the country for the past century. It was answered in 1791 when Tom Paine published his *Rights of Man* in which he maintained that the people of a country had the right to choose or alter the form of government as they liked. This democratic view found many followers, but in 1792 Paine issued another pamphlet in which he praised republicanism, and because of the fear roused by the march of events in France, his opinions lost their popularity.

Burke's "Reflections on the French Revolution"

Paine's "Rights of Man"

Burke and Paine may be said to represent the two extreme views, but by far the majority of the British people agreed with Burke in so far as he regarded the French Revolution as an anarchical movement. The Government was certainly of his opinion, and was especially afraid of the various bodies which they thought were spreading revolutionary ideas in Britain. Chief of these were the "Corresponding Societies", the largest of which, the "London", was under Thomas Hardy and had over three thousand members. These societies were really clubs which held meetings and published pamphlets, and their objects were no more revolutionary than an attempt to obtain universal suffrage and annual parliaments. Some members, however, openly professed sympathy with the ideas of the French Revolution, and because of this Pitt attacked the Societies and ordered the prosecution of both members and leaders. In Scotland a series of famous trials ended in the "martyrs of 1793" being sentenced to transportation, though it was impossible to prove that they had done more than ask for "more equal representation". In England, Horne Tooke and Hardy were more fortunate, for when they were tried in 1794, the juries acquitted them.

The Corresponding Societies

A serious step was taken in 1794 when the Habeas Corpus

Suspension of the Habeas Corpus Act (1794)

Act was suspended, so that a person could be kept in prison indefinitely without being brought to trial, if simply accused of "treasonable practices". A most odious system was set up of Government spies who went about the country and produced "evidence of plots". On the strength of such stories, many people were imprisoned.[1]

Repressive measures

Pitt next introduced and passed a series of Acts (1795) which made writing, speaking, or in any way "inciting against the Government" a serious offence, to be severely punished. Public meetings were made illegal unless licensed by a magistrate, and, of course, no reform meetings would be licensed. Further, by the *Combination Act* of 1799, working men were forbidden to form Trade Unions, for fear they should be "revolutionary". It was also made an act of treason to support any changes in the constitution.

Combination Act (1799)

In all these measures, considered necessary by the Government at the time, Pitt had the support of the Tories and of a large majority of the Whigs, led by Burke. Only Fox and some of his followers stuck to their principles, declared that the excesses of the French were due to the miseries they had suffered, and formed a new Whig party.

Pitt's Financial difficulties

Pitt's financial reforms all went by the board. The National Debt increased so enormously that the provision of the Sinking Fund was useless, yet he continued its operation, on the false assumption that the war would be short. Thus while on the one hand he paid money into the Sinking Fund to pay off the debt, on the other hand he borrowed far larger sums to finance the war. The commercial treaty with France naturally was not enforced. Increased taxation was needed, but Pitt took no steps to deal with the question adequately. He was so confident that the struggle would only be a short one that he preferred to borrow rather than tax. Thus he only increased the assessed taxes in 1797, and it was not till 1798 that he brought in his

[1] "Oliver the spy" became infamous for this, and even magistrates at length refused to accept such "evidence".

income-tax.[1] He also borrowed on very disadvantageous terms, paying increasingly high rates on an ill-considered system. As a result he left the nation far more heavily burdened with debt than was necessary.

Pitt and Ireland

Pitt's policy in Ireland has already been considered. Here we must note that Pitt himself, when the King refused even to consider Catholic Emancipation, resigned, in 1801. But when, in 1804, he returned to office, he took no further steps in the matter. Perhaps to do justice we must admit that he could never have induced the King to alter his resolution, for George firmly believed that to grant Catholic emancipation was contrary to his coronation oath.

Addington's ministry (1801–4)

To Pitt at his resignation in 1801 succeeded one of his followers, *Addington.* He it was who made the Treaty of Amiens in 1802, and conducted the early stages of the war when it was renewed in 1803. But he was quite unequal to the position.

> " Pitt is to Addington
> What London is to Paddington ",

sang Canning, rather unkindly. And as the administration grew more Paddingtonian, it was felt that the tried pilot must be recalled. Pitt returned to power in 1804, and lived long enough to see the crowning victory of Trafalgar in October, 1805. But six weeks later Austerlitz made Napoleon supreme in Europe, and this victory, and the impeachment of his closest ally, *Robert Dundas, Lord Melville,* for malversation of funds,[2] broke down his already enfeebled health, and in January, 1806, he died.

Pitt's second ministry (1804–6)

Pitt's opponents had intended to charge him with incapacity in the conduct of the war. His death left them

[1] This was graduated from 2*d*. in the £ on incomes of £60, up to 2*s*. in the £ on incomes over £200.

[2] A vote of censure on Melville preceded the impeachment. In the actual vote, the numbers were equal; but the speaker, after a silence of many minutes, gave his casting vote against Melville. There ensued a scene of wild exultation amongst Pitt's opponents. Pitt crushed his cocked hat over his brow to conceal the tears trickling down his cheeks; and his younger supporters, forming a screen round him, led him away from the House.

with no one to blame. It also left the King with no one to whom he could turn. He was forced to call upon Fox.

Ministry of all the Talents (1806)

A coalition ministry was formed, for all parties felt that they must unite in face of the terrible situation on the Continent. Fox, Grenville, Addington combined. Owing to the fact that the best men of all parties were included in the Ministry, it had the nickname of " *All the talents* ". Yet, because these men did not really agree on policy, nothing much could be done. Fox and his followers wished for reform of Parliament and for Catholic Emancipation, but their fellow ministers would never agree to either. Fox did succeed, in the face of bitter opposition from the King, in getting an *Army Act*, which improved army service. But the only real achievement was the passing of the Act to abolish the wicked *trade in slaves*. (Freeing the slaves was not yet possible and this Act only stopped the capture and sale of slaves as a money-making affair.) The *abolition of the Slave Trade* was the last act of Fox's life, for he died 8 months after taking office.

Abolition of slave trade

This was the only reform possible, for in the succeeding years the struggle against Napoleon absorbed all the energies of the government. Repression and growing misery characterized the first decade of the century and led on to the demand for Reform which was to follow the establishment of peace.

Portland's ministry

Fox's ministry was followed by one under the inefficient Duke of *Portland*, who took office in 1807. Though himself incapable, his cabinet included two young men, Castlereagh and Canning, both destined to lend brilliance to our foreign policy. Feeling against " revolutionary principles " ran so high that no important measures could be undertaken, for any reform was thought to lead to revolution.

The Regency (1811)

The only political event of note was the setting up of the Regency in 1811. This was necessary owing to the hopeless nature of the King's illness, and in 1812, when it was certain that he would never recover his sanity, the Prince of Wales received full powers to act as sovereign. The Prince, selfish and bad as he was, had been the friend and supporter of the Whigs. He could not, even had he wished, have struggled against the general opposition to reform, but actually he made no attempt to stick to his principles, but abandoned the Whigs at once and chose as minister the dull and reactionary *Perceval.*

Murder of Perceval (1812)

Perceval's ministry was short, for he was shot at and killed in 1812, by a lunatic, in the lobby of the House of Commons. Lord Liverpool took his place, but the whole strength of the nation, its energy and talent, seemed to be absorbed in the struggle against Napoleon, so that none was left for home affairs.

Yet we must notice that, in spite of the exhaustion caused by the long wars, the eighteenth century was remarkable in the spheres of art and literature.

Art and literature in the eighteenth century

Many of the most famous names in British art belong to this period. Hogarth, the greatest of satirical painters, lived in the first part of the century,[1] Reynolds, Romney, Raeburn, Allan Ramsay, and Gainsborough in the latter part. These men made portraiture supreme, and through them Britain could claim her greatest recognition in the world of art abroad.

In literature the first half of George III's reign was the time when Johnson, the " immortal doctor " flourished. Boswell's *Life* remains one of the great classics, and in itself has drawn many on to further study of the period. Gibbon wrote his *Decline and Fall of the Roman Empire*; Burke's speeches are still unsurpassed; while Scotland produced her greatest poet, Robert Burns. The French Revolution coincides with the appearance of the " romantic " poets, Shelley and Keats, Scott and Wordsworth, though Scott has won greater fame by his Waverley novels. Byron became celebrated in the years when the Napoleonic war

[1] Some of his best work is to be seen in the comparatively little known Soane Museum in Lincoln's Inn Fields.

raged. Jane Austen wrote her novels in the midst of that great struggle, and the whole flowering of literature which was to mark the first years of the nineteenth century, finds its seeds in the eighteenth.

NOTES ON PERIOD NINE (1783–1815)

BRITISH SOVEREIGN

GEORGE III (1760–1820)

IMPORTANT FOREIGN RULERS

FRANCE:	LOUIS XVI (1774–1792)
	FIRST REPUBLIC (1792–1799)
	NAPOLEON BONAPARTE:
	First Consul (1799–1804)
	Emperor (1804–1815)
SPAIN:	CHARLES III (1759–1788)
	CHARLES IV (1788–1808)
	JOSEPH BONAPARTE (1808–1814)
	FERDINAND VII (1814–1833)
EMPIRE:	JOSEPH II (1765–1790)
	LEOPOLD II (1790–1792)
	FRANCIS II (1792–1835)
	(Holy Roman Empire ended 1806)
RUSSIA:	CATHERINE II (1762–1796)
	PAUL I (1796–1801)
	ALEXANDER I (1801–1825)

BRITISH PRIME MINISTERS

PITT (the Younger):	(1783–1801)
ADDINGTON:	(1801–1804)
PITT:	(1804–1806)
GRENVILLE-FOX (Coalition)	(1806–1807)
PORTLAND:	(1807–1809)
PERCEVAL:	(1809–1812)
LIVERPOOL:	(1812–1827)

NOTE 104. — IRELAND IN THE LATER EIGHTEENTH CENTURY (1760–1795)

1. Political Grievances.

(*a*) By the *Penal Laws* (1727) no Roman Catholic could vote, or hold any office, or go to the University, or be a schoolmaster; or buy land. No Protestant could marry a Roman Catholic, or leave land to a Roman Catholic.

(*b*) Under the ancient Poynings' Act, all laws passed by Irish Parliament had to receive assent of the English Privy Council, but English Parliament could pass laws binding on Ireland.

(*c*) In Irish Parliament no Roman Catholic could sit, nor could any Roman Catholic have a vote, and two-thirds of members were nominated by private persons.

(*d*) All officials appointed by England, and were almost invariably Englishmen.

2. Economic Grievances.

(*a*) Irish agriculture and trade controlled, not to Irish advantage. Irish might not export to England any cattle or woollen manufactured goods. Raw wool had to pay heavy duties if sent to England.

(*b*) Land had been confiscated and three-quarters belonged to English landlords.

(*c*) Tithes had to be paid to the Episcopal Church of Ireland, though four-fifths of population were Roman Catholics.

3. Reforms during Eighteenth Century.

During American war, Britain forced to conciliate Irish, so

(*a*) *Penal Code abolished* (1778).

(*b*) *Restrictions on Irish trade abolished* (1780).

(*c*) *Irish Parliament given self-government* by repeal of Poynings' Law, and British Parliament could not pass laws binding upon Ireland (1782). This meant *legislative independence.*

4. Grattan's Parliament.

The Irish Parliament now had a brilliant period under leadership of *Henry Grattan*, who wished to remove last disability of Roman Catholics, wished for "Catholic Emancipation", i.e. that Roman Catholics should be allowed to sit in Parliament, and to hold offices (e.g. be lawyers, soldiers, etc.).

NOTE 105. — CHARLES JAMES FOX (1749–1806)

Brilliant young man, of eminent Whig family. Brilliant speaker and strong upholder of liberty everywhere.

1. *Championed American colonies*, and led the party which supported them (1775).
2. *Opposed the growth of the King's Power* and wished for Parliamentary reform.
3. Friend of the Prince of Wales, an unprincipled man, whose connection with Fox did the latter much harm, and helped to fix the King's dislike of Fox.
4. *Joined the Rockingham Ministry* (1782) on fall of Lord North; he would not serve under Shelburne. So formed alliance with former opponent North, and made the "*Infamous Coalition*" (1783). Tried to bring in a Bill to settle India (1783). Failed, and his place taken by Pitt the younger.
5. *Opposed Warren Hastings*, as believed he had oppressed Indians (1786).
6. *Great Champion of the French Revolution.* Declared people of France justified in rebelling against their government. Strongly opposed Pitt's repressive measures in Britain. Opposed the war against France (1793).
7. On death of Pitt joined the Coalition "*Ministry of all the Talents*" (1806). Wished to end war, but failed to come to terms with Napoleon. Helped to abolish trade in slaves.

Note: Fox ruined his career chiefly by accepting office in the "Infamous Coalition". of 1783, which lost him popular confidence. The King always hated him. And as the French Revolution grew more extreme, Fox, as its champion, was discredited.

NOTE 106. — EDMUND BURKE (1729–1797)

Irish by birth, entered Whig Parliament in 1765, and served under Lord Rockingham, with Fox, on fall of North.

Liberal minded in early life, and

1. Supported a policy of conciliation towards the American colonies.
2. Supported Catholic emancipation.
3. Supported complete religious toleration for all.
4. Wished for reform of penal laws, and abolition of slave trade.
5. But did not wish for extension of the franchise, nor redistribution of seats, and believed British Constitution needed no reform.

6. In later life was so bitterly opposed to the French Revolution that he supported the war, and all the repressive measures of Pitt.
7. His speeches still are some of the best English prose: most notable are *Thoughts on the Present Discontents* (a defence of the party system), *On the American Colonies* (putting the case for a self-governing colonial empire), and *French Revolution* (against violent change in government).
8. Led the attack on Warren Hastings.
9. One of the best exponents of moderate political philosophy.

NOTE 107. — WILLIAM PITT, THE YOUNGER (1759–1806)

Was Chancellor of Exchequer before he was twenty-four, and made *Prime Minister when he was twenty-four* (1783).

1. Pitt as Financier.

(*a*) Reduced duties drastically, so as to work towards freedom of trade.

(*b*) Established the Sinking Fund to reduce National Debt.

(*c*) Commercial treaty with France (1786).

(*d*) Wished for free trade with Ireland. Abolished application of Navigation Acts to Ireland (1788). Established free trade with Ireland in 1800.

(*e*) *But* after the French war broke out he abandoned the treaty with France, kept on the Sinking Fund when it was useless, and borrowed at too high rates, rather than tax. He wrongly believed war would be very short, and based his plans on this.

2. Pitt and the Empire.

(*a*) *India* — his India Act (1784) made British Government responsible for the Governor-General and his Council.

(*b*) *Canada* — his Canada Act (1791) divided Canada into two. Lower (or French) Canada, and Upper. Meant to prevent friction between the races.

(*c*) *Australia* — first settlements sent out (1788).

3. Pitt and Reform.

Desired reform of Parliament. Bill to disfranchise 36 rotten boroughs and redistribution of seats (1785). Not passed, and war ended all reform.

Wished for Catholic Emancipation, in conjunction with Act of Union (1800) but defeated by King.

NOTE 108. — PITT AND THE FRENCH WAR (1793)

1. Pitt originally did not desire war with France, and for first three years of Revolution, Britain kept aloof.

Causes of the War. In 1792 French seized the *Austrian Netherlands* (Belgium), and declared they would help any nation that rose in revolt. They declared *Scheldt open* to all commerce, and the river had been closed by European treaty to help British trade.

French threatened to invade Holland, and Britain could not let that coast be in hostile hands.

2. **Revolutionary War.**

(*a*) Pitt is not considered to have been a good war minister. He scattered the resources on small expeditions. Thus in 1793 he sent expeditions to the West Indies, to Toulon, and to Belgium.

(*b*) He had not his father's gift for choosing good men to serve under him.

He let the King give the Duke of York command of the army.

(*c*) He wasted money on subsidies to useless allies, e.g. the King of Prussia who made terms with Napoleon which suited him and would not fight when wanted.

(*d*) But, note, Pitt was hampered because all the allies were incompetent, and he suffered for their mistakes. He also never lost heart but persevered in forming one coalition after another against the Revolution. He also may be said to have been unlucky in having to contend with so great a genius as Napoleon.

NOTE 109.—CHANGE IN PITT'S HOME POLICY PRODUCED BY FRENCH WAR

1. Pitt began life as reformer, friend of Adam Smith (said " Tom Paine was right ", Paine being reformer who wrote *Rights of Man*).

2. War changed him into a reactionary, for he dreaded spread of revolutionary ideas to England.

(*a*) Considered such ideas must be stamped out, so attacked " Corresponding Societies ", i.e. reforming societies which " corresponded " with each other.

(*b*) Prosecuted all advanced reformers. A series of *political prosecutions* held. In Scotland the " martyrs of 1793 " (Muir, Palmer, etc), prosecuted or transported. In England Hardy and Horne Tooke tried (1794) but acquitted.

(*c*) " Two Acts ", 1795, made speaking or " inciting " against the Government a very serious offence. Public meetings illegal unless licensed by a magistrate.

(*d*) Any attempt to " change the British Constitution " made act of treason.

(*e*) *Combination Acts* (1800) forbade working men to combine in any body. Hence all *Trade Unions* or clubs illegal.

NOTE 110. — PITT AND IRELAND

1. Grattan's Parliament was moderate, but extremists under *Wolfe Tone* wanted complete independence of Ireland. Society of United Irishmen formed (1791).

2. Pitt saw need for reform, and in 1793 vote was given to all Roman Catholics who were £40 freeholders.

Fitzwilliam sent as Viceroy, and promised complete Emancipation. Repudiated by Pitt (1795).

3. United Irishmen plotted with revolutionary France.

(*a*) French expedition tried to land in *Bantry Bay*, but failed (1796).

(*b*) Revolt in Ulster. Pitt ordered disarming of Ulster; great severity shown (1797).

(*c*) *Irish Rebellion* of 1798 partly organized by Lord Edward Fitz-Gerald. French fleet defeated. Irish defeated at *Vinegar Hill*. French troops defeated at *Lough Swilly*.

4. Pitt Decided to Abolish Irish Parliament (1799).

Act of Union carried only by:

(*a*) Promises of pensions to induce members to vote for it.

(*b*) Promise of free trade.

(*c*) Understanding that Catholic Emancipation would be granted.

5. Act of Union (1800).

(*a*) Ireland lost her own Parliament.

(*b*) Sent 100 members to English Parliament and 28 peers.

(*c*) Ireland to contribute two-seventeenths to English revenue.

(*d*) Ireland to keep her own courts of justice and own civil service.

But, Pitt (owing to the attitude of the King) could not give Roman Catholic Emancipation, hence Irish M.P.s were all Protestants; no Roman Catholics could hold any office. Moreover, tithes were still paid to the Episcopal Church.

NOTE 111. — THE WAR WITH REVOLUTIONARY FRANCE (1793–1798)

1. Britain joined the Coalition of Austria, Prussia, Holland, Spain, and Sweden *against Republican France*. *Britain met with disaster.*

(*a*) because she sent too many small expeditions to Toulon, Brittany, Dunkirk, West Indies (*all failed*) 1793.

(*b*) at sea did not use sea-power and did not blockade French ports though Howe won *First of June*, and took Cape of Good Hope (1795).

2. After 1797 Britain made greater use of sea-power. Won Battles of *St. Vincent* and (after mutiny at the Nore) *Camperdown* (1797).

Cut off Napoleon in Egypt by *Battle of the Nile* (1798).

3. War with Napoleon — first phase, 1798–1802.

In 1799, after failure in Egypt, Napoleon returned to France and became Consul. War was now against him. Austria made peace with France.

Armed Neutrality formed against Britain by Russia, Prussia, Denmark, and Sweden (1801).

Against this Britain won *Battle of Copenhagen* (1801) and in the west captured West Indies.

4. Peace of Amiens (1802).

(*a*) Britain gave up all conquests except Ceylon and Trinidad.
(*b*) France kept Belgium and the Rhine frontier.

Note 112. — SECOND PHASE OF THE NAPOLEONIC WARS (1803–1808)

1. Causes of Second War. Europe hoped for peace after Treaty of Amiens. *Napoleon*, however, *showed he meant to renew war*. (Became Emperor in 1804).

(*a*) He was aggressive in north of Italy; annexed Piedmont and Elba.
(*b*) He sent troops to Switzerland.
(*c*) He sent expedition to Egypt.
(*d*) He began to build a huge fleet.
(*e*) Great Britain fearing war in Egypt, did not give up *Malta* as she promised in the treaty.
(*f*) Great Britain being convinced Napoleon was preparing to resume war when it suited him, decided to be first in the field.

2. Napoleon's Plans to Invade Britain.

Spain was France's subject-ally, and her fleet was to co-operate with French fleet.

(*a*) But Britain blockaded all the French and Spanish harbours.
(*b*) Special transport-fleet collected by Napoleon at *Boulogne* helpless unless battle-fleet held the Channel.
(*c*) Napoleon therefore gave up plan, and sent his army to attack Austria.
(*d*) Nelson destroyed French and Spanish fleets at *Trafalgar* (1805), and all hopes of invasion useless.

3. Napoleon Plans to Ruin Britain's Trade.

Napoleon then fell back on attempt to ruin Britain's trade.

(*a*) By *Continental System* (Berlin Decrees, 1806) no country allowed to trade with Britain. He had conquered Austria (Austerlitz, 1805), Prussia (Jena, 1806), and made alliance with *Russia* (Tilsit) (1807).

(*b*) Britain retaliated by *Orders in Council* blockading foreign ports (1807).

To ensure blockade she *captured Danish fleet* (Copenhagen, 1807), to prevent Napoleon seizing it.

(*c*) Napoleon, to make Continental System complete, seized *Holland* and *Portugal* and *Spain*.

This led to the *Peninsular War* (1808).

NOTE 113.—NAPOLEONIC WAR: THIRD PHASE (1809–1814)

1. War in the Peninsula.

(*a*) French driven from *Portugal* by battle of *Vimiero* (1808) and forced to evacuate Portugal. Moore sent to cut off Napoleon in Madrid. Retreated to Corunna where fleet met him and British army saved from capture (1808).

(*b*) *Wellington attacked in Spain.* Wellington drove French from Portugal, entered Spain, won *Talavera,* then driven out of Spain and back to coast. Entrenched himself at the lines of *Torres Vedras* (1810–11).

(*c*) *Wellington had to defend himself on the coast.* French after months retreated from Portugal and Wellington, pressing on, won Fuentes d'Onoro and Albuera (1811).

(*d*) *Wellington advanced and freed southern Spain.* While Napoleon was occupied in *Russia* (1812) Wellington entered Spain, took key fortresses of Ciudad Rodrigo, and Badajoz; won battle of *Salamanca,* drove French from Madrid, and freed southern Spain.

(*e*) *Wellington freed all Spain and invaded France.* While Napoleon was fighting the war in *Germany* which had risen against him (1813), Wellington won battle of *Vittoria,* and in 1814, while Napoleon was defending Paris, Wellington crossed the Pyrenees, entered France, and took Toulouse.

The effect of the war was to keep large numbers of Napoleon's troops engaged, and to use up his transport. French lost half a million men. It restored British prestige, and above all it encouraged other nations to resist Napoleon.

NOTE 114.—SEA-POWER IN THE FRENCH WARS

1. At first Britain did not use her sea-power, and did not blockade France. Therefore, French

(*a*) Defended West Indies and it took us five years to capture them.

(*b*) Invaded Ireland twice — Bantry Bay, 1796, and again in 1798.

(*c*) Conveyed their grain across Atlantic.

2. French conquest of Spain gave her *Spanish fleet.*
   (*a*) French and Spanish fleets to meet. Prevented at *St. Vincent* (1797).
   (*b*) French conquest of Holland gave her *Dutch* fleet. Defeated at *Camperdown* (1797). Dutch fleet destroyed.
   (*c*) French sent Napoleon to Egypt (to attack Syria and possibly stir up India), but Nelson defeated *French fleet* at *Battle of the Nile* (1798) (famous for Nelson sending in ships between French and shore, and French thus caught between two fires). As a result, Napoleon was shut up in Egypt, and French expedition failed.

3. **Armed Neutrality,** to protest against Britain preventing neutrals from trading with France.
   All the northern powers combined against Britain, namely, Russia, Prussia, Denmark, Sweden.
   Nelson destroyed the *Danish fleet* at *Copenhagen* (1801) — famous for Nelson's skill in getting through the shoals.
   (**Note:** Nelson was second in command to Hyde Parker, hence his famous " blind eye " to Parker's signal to withdraw.)
   Result: Baltic opened to Britain.

4. After Treaty of Amiens **Napoleon planned to invade Britain.**
   (*a*) Got fleet of transports ready at Boulogne.
   (*b*) Spanish and French fleets to meet in West Indies, and fleet to gain command of Channel.
   But, Nelson blockaded French and Spanish fleets in their harbours, so no junction could be made. *Brest* fleet did not get out. *Toulon* fleet did, met Spaniards and sailed to West Indies. Returning to Europe fought indecisive battle at *Cape Finisterre* (Calder, British admiral, did not renew action). French fleet took refuge in *Cadiz.* Napoleon ordered them out and Nelson met and defeated them at *Trafalgar* (1805).
   Nelson sent his fleet in two lines ahead and broke the Franco-Spanish line, and fought action with his ships parallel to allied ships.
   Result: French naval power destroyed, invasion hopeless, and Britain supreme at sea. This led Napoleon to attempt the " Continental System ", which alienated Russia and led to his downfall.

NOTE 115. — REASONS FOR FAILURE OF FRENCH IN PENINSULAR WAR

1. *French had very long lines of communication,* which could fairly easily be attacked by Spaniards.
2. *Geography of the country* was against French, for roads ran across valleys, transport very difficult, and food hard to get. French held Madrid and had to work down the valleys and could not quickly get across from one valley to another.

3. *British* did not suffer so much, for they had *command of the sea.* Thus could easily get troops and stores to Wellington, who fought the greater part of the time near the coast. At Torres Vedras, British got supplies from sea, while French starved in the devastated country.
4. Napoleon did not, after the first, go to Spain himself, but left his marshals to fight. (Soult, Masséna.)
5. He could not send adequate troops, and had to withdraw large bodies when he undertook first the Russian campaign, then had to fight " War of Liberation " in Germany, and finally defend France against invasion in north.

Note 116. — THE CONTINENTAL SYSTEM (1806)

1. **Blockade.**

   Britain blockaded French harbours, and in return Napoleon imposed the " Berlin " decrees, after his fleet was lost at Trafalgar. These set up the " Continental System " (1806).

   (*a*) Aimed at ruining British commerce by forbidding any ships from Britain or her colonies to enter any port of France or of her allies.

   (*b*) Britain retaliated by *Orders in Council*, forbidding any neutral ships to enter ports from which Britain was excluded (1807).

2. **Immediate result** was to check all trade. But, as Britain had command of the sea, and Napoleon had not, Britain could carry goods where she wished, while continent could not get anything by sea without British leave.

3. **Indirect Results.**

   (*a*) The need to close all the continent to Britain led Napoleon to extend his aggression, and made him seize Holland and Spain.

   (*b*) Also led to his quarrel with Russia, for the Czar refused to impose the system, as Russia needed British goods.

   (*c*) Great Britain, in order to prevent Napoleon acquiring the Danish fleet, attacked Copenhagen and destroyed Danish ships (1807).

   The Continental System did great damage to British trade, and impoverished the country, but France herself suffered still more, and Britain stood the strain better.

Note 117. — INDIA DURING THE FRENCH WARS (1795–1799)

1. French stirred up *Tippoo Sahib* in Mysore to rebel against Britain.

   French sent officers to drill native troops, and were very active in organizing Tippoo's army (1795).

2. French sent Napoleon to Egypt, with idea of proceeding to India. Battle of Nile cut Napoleon off from France and ruined expedition (1798).

3. Tippoo Sahib made war on British, but was defeated by Baird at *Seringapatam* (1799).

Note: In 1798 French Government hesitated whether to send Napoleon to Ireland to help rebellion of FitzGerald, or to Egypt. Napoleon himself decided this in favour of Egypt.

NOTE 118. — IRELAND IN THE FRENCH WARS

1. Ireland very strongly affected by American Revolution and French Revolution. *Wolfe Tone* wanted independence of Ireland, formed "United Irishmen" (1792), and plotted with the French (1796).

2. In 1796 *Hoche* sent French force to Ireland, and tried to land in *Bantry Bay*; winds contrary and British fleet arrived, so force never landed. Dutch fleet carrying French troops defeated at *Camperdown* (1797).

3. 1797. "Disarming of Ulster" with great cruelty.

4. 1798. Rebellion partly organized by FitzGerald. Rebellion put down by English. Irish defeated at *Vinegar Hill.* French force landed at *Lough Swilly* destroyed by British. Act of Union followed (1800).

NOTE 119. — HUMANITARIAN MOVEMENTS IN THE EIGHTEENTH CENTURY

1. Wesley and the Methodists stirred up religious feelings, and were pioneers of social reform.

2. Evangelical party supported "humanitarian" movements.

   (*a*) **Missionary work** amongst heathen. *Church Missionary Society* founded, 1799. *British and Foreign Bible Society*, 1804.

   (*a*) **Prison Reform.** *John Howard* (1726–1790) and *Elizabeth Fry* visited the prisons and urged reform of prisons and of the terribly severe Penal code.

   (*c*) **Anti-slavery Society,** founded by *William Wilberforce* (1759–1833), and supported by ***Buxton.*** Abolition of Slave Trade carried in 1806.

TIME CHART FOR PERIOD NINE (1783–1815)

Sovereign.	Prime Minister.	Great and Greater Britain		Dates.		Foreign Powers.	Dates.
George III.	1783–1801. Pitt.	Pitt (the Younger's) First Ministry.		1783			
		Pitt's India Act.		1784			
		Commercial Treaty with France.		1786		Death of Frederick the Great.	1786
		Hastings impeached; First convicts to Australia.		1788		Bread Riots in France.	1788
						French Revolution begins; Fall of Bastille.	1789
		Formation of Upper and Lower Canada.		1791			
						French Republic set up.	1792
			French Revolutionary	1793	War.	Execution of Louis XVI; 2nd Partition of Poland	1793
		Suspension of Habeas Corpus Act; Battle of 1st of June		1794			
						Rule of Directory in France (till 1799); 3rd Partition of Poland.	1795
		Death of Burke; Camperdown; St. Vincent.		1797			
		Battle of Nile; 2nd Coalition; Irish rebellion.		1798			
		Combination Laws.		1799		Napoleon becomes First Consul.	1799
		Union with Ireland.		1800			
	Addington.	Battle of Copenhagen.		1801		Alexander I reigns in Russia.	1801
		Peace of Amiens		1802			
			Napoleonic	1803	War.		
	Pitt.			1804		Napoleon proclaimed Emperor.	1804
		3rd Coalition; Trafalgar.		1805		Battle of Austerlitz.	1805
	Grenville.	Death of younger Pitt.		1806		End of Holy Roman Empire; Battle of Jena.	1806
	Portland.	Slave Trade prohibited; British seize Danish Fleet.		1807		Battle of Friedland; Treaty of Tilsit.	1807
	Perceval.	Battle of Corunna.	Peninsular War.	1809		Battle of Wagram.	1809
		The Regency.		1811			
	1812–27 Liverpool.	First Steamboat on Clyde.	War with U.S.A.	1812		March to Moscow.	1812
		Fourth Coalition (Castlereagh).		1813		Battle of the Nations.	1813
						Congress of Vienna.	1814
		Battle of Waterloo. Corn Law passed.		1815		Restoration of Louis XVIII.	1815

EXAMINATION QUESTIONS ON PERIOD NINE

(1783–1815)

1. Describe Wellington's work in the Peninsular War and account for his successes. (LGS 1937)

2. Describe the main changes in British farming and rural life between 1783 and the Agricultural Labourers revolts of 1830–1. (NUJB 1936)

3. Sketch the career of Horatio Nelson and discuss the importance of his victories. (LGS 1935)

4. How do you account for the success of the English in India during the eighteenth century? (LM 1931)

5. By what methods did George III destroy the power of the Whigs? (OL 1927)

6. What do you know of (1) town life, and (2) country life, during the eighteenth century? (OL 1930)

7. Describe the course of events which led up to the Irish rebellion of 1798. (OC 1932)

8. Describe the resistance of Great Britain to the ambitions of Napoleon between 1802 and 1815. (LGS 1936)

9. Trace the events which led up to the Act of Union with Ireland in 1800. (LGS 1937)

10. Describe the part played by Great Britain in the overthrow of Napoleon. (NUJB 1935)

11. Outline the changes in English agriculture during the eighteenth century. (NUJB 1930, '32; OC 1930)

12. Describe the domestic policy of the younger Pitt before and after the outbreak of the French Revolution, and account for any striking differences. (NUJB 1930; OL 1930; LM 1932; D 1932)

13. Describe and account for the attitude towards the French Revolution of (*a*) Pitt, (*b*) Burke, and (*c*) Fox. (OL 1927; NUJB 1932)

14. Compare the achievements of William Pitt, Earl of Chatham, with those of his son William Pitt. (OC 1925; OL 1926)

15. Give an account of Pitt's India Bill and of the circumstances which led to it. (NUJB 1931)

16. " Misguided and reactionary ". Is this a fair criticism of the domestic policy of Pitt after 1793? (OC 1929)

17. Explain why the Domestic System of manufacture was replaced by the Factory System. (NUJB 1930)

18. What is meant by the expression " Agrarian Revolution "? In what ways was it related to the industrial changes of the later eighteenth century? (CMB 1932)

19. Discuss the importance of the victories won by Nelson. (OL 1920, 1930; LM 1931)

20. Explain how England's command of the sea stood her in good stead in her struggle with Napoleon. (OL 1928; OC 1930; D 1931; NUJB 1932)

21. What was the Continental System? How far can it be said to have achieved its object? (B 1931)

22. What were the social effects in Great Britain of the Revolutionary and Napoleonic wars? (NUJB 1931)

23. Which do you consider played the greater part in the defeat of Napoleon, the success of our navy or the campaigns in the Peninsula? (OL 1925)

24. What were the main causes of the discontent and distress in England at the end of the Napoleonic wars? (LGS 1924)

PERIOD TEN

INDUSTRIAL DEVELOPMENT: ABUSES AND REFORMS

1815–1867

CHAPTER 56

GEORGE III

1. 1815 AND AFTER IN GREAT BRITAIN

The years which followed Waterloo are generally taken as beginning a new era. The century which followed saw such immense changes in every sphere of life that it forms one of the most thrilling and interesting periods in British history. To keep clear in our minds what the reigns involved, we need to consider briefly what we are going to study. **Introduction**

First, there are great social changes. The development of machinery, and the growth of our vast town population, altered the whole trend of life. The sufferings of the poor in the early part of the century were such that they led first to a great demand for political reform, and then after that to a long, gradual process of social reform. That process is still going on.

Next, there are changes abroad. The nineteenth century was the great age of Liberalism. Revolutions swept over Europe, new States were formed, great powers competed together for supremacy. England's policy was of much importance, and she produced a series of great ministers, Canning, Palmerston, Gladstone, Disraeli.

Self-governing and National movements in Europe

There were two movements of supreme importance in the nineteenth century. *First*, there was a movement for *Self-government*. The rulers of many of the States of Europe after 1815 were reactionary and despotic, and distrusted all Liberal aspirations, which they labelled as dangerous and anarchical. In many parts of Europe liberty, in the English sense, was unknown: there was no liberty of speech or of writing; public meetings were forbidden and arbitrary arrests frequent. Only one other European country besides Great Britain had a Parliament — and that was France. The growing desire felt by the people for greater individual freedom and for a greater control of the government led at times, and especially during the years 1830–32 and 1848–52, to agitations and revolutions, which were sometimes suppressed and sometimes successful. Closely allied with the movement for self-government there was, *secondly*, a movement for the realization of the idea of *Nationality*. People of the same race or speaking the same language, possessing common traditions or a common history, showed a passion to be united and to be freed from the control of alien rulers, a passion which led to the independence of Belgium in 1830, to the War of Italian Liberation in 1859, and to the final union of Germany under the leadership of Prussia in 1871.

Then, the British Empire developed, its territory was extended, and its whole policy altered. The idea of self-governing colonies was worked out.

There emained the problem of Ireland. This became so acute that her relations with Great Britain were one of the major problems which statesmen had to attempt to settle, and the effect on Britain was as important as it was on Ireland.

Trouble ahead

When peace came to Europe in 1815, all countries were so exhausted that for a while stagnation reigned. The absolute rulers were everywhere restored, and foreign policy at first had little interest for Great Britain.

It was at home that great changes took place, and here

we have to trace most important developments. Vast changes in industry; terrible distress amongst the working-classes; a total failure on the part of the Government to see or to sympathize with the state of the nation, led to upheaval. The next seven or so years show how the grievances of the " common people " became unbearable, and how they revolted against them. A harsh government tried repression and thereby drove the country to the brink of revolution.

The troubles and struggles of these years can be traced to two main causes — to the distress due to the aftermath of war, and to the further fact that Britain was now embarking on what is called the " industrial revolution ".

2. THE INDUSTRIAL REVOLUTION

The closing years of George III and the age of machinery

George III was, in 1811, recognized as unfit to rule, and the Regency was declared. The state of the country was terrifying; the " common people " were suffering and showing their discontent, yet neither Crown nor Parliament took any steps to help the nation.

Distress due to the war

In the first place the country was bound to be faced with a difficult situation created by the coming of the peace. War is destructive, and it takes time and money to repair the damage it leaves behind. Trade had shrunk away during the long war and every nation was impoverished, therefore every nation had less money to spend. Unemployment was bound to exist on a large scale, and this was made worse by the fact that all government orders stopped, and in addition thousands of soldiers and sailors were added to those wanting work.

The Industrial Revolution

This inevitable trouble was greatly increased by the fact that the beginning of the peace coincided with the development of what we call the *Industrial Revolution*, which in turn at first created more unemployment.

Machinery was now to become the great feature of industrial life, and in every direction we see men inventing new machines. If we stop to think, we can see that there is an interesting problem here. Machinery means factories, and that means that men must congregate to work in towns. Village industry and home industry must disappear. But if factories spring up, and mankind swarms together in towns and cities, then food must be brought, and also the raw materials for industry, and the resulting manufactures must be transported from the factories to the shops and to distant places, and even overseas. Thus, roads, railways, and shipping must be developed too. What is fascinating in this " revolution " is the fact that all the necessary changes appeared at the same time, and each one fitted in with the other.

First we must retrace our steps, for, though it is in some ways convenient to take 1815 as a dividing line, changes had begun in the latter half of the eighteenth century which came to fruition in the nineteenth.

Agriculture

Rotation of Crops

" Turnip " Townshend

Perhaps the first of our industries to be affected by the scientific spirit was our oldest — that of *Agriculture* (*Note 120*). Up till the eighteenth century *arable* land had, in most districts, been treated as in the Middle Ages; it was sown with corn for two years and then left fallow for a year to recuperate its fertility. The discovery was made, however, that by the cultivation of roots, the recuperative advantages of a bare fallow might be secured without the loss of a year's crop. Moreover, the roots both gave the opportunity for clearing the soil and provided food for the cattle and sheep during the winter.[1] Consequently there was more manure, and the fertility of the land was correspondingly increased. Tradition says that " *Turnip* " *Townshend*, George I's minister, was the first to realize the importance of this discovery, and to develop on his Norfolk estates a four-year rotation of crops (e.g. wheat, some form of roots,

[1] Formerly the bulk of the stock, except that required for breeding purposes, was killed about Martinmas.

barley, a mixture of clover and some form of grasses), never taking two successive corn crops off the same land; and this principle of rotation — sometimes three-year or five-year instead of four-year — was generally adopted in the latter part of the eighteenth century in England.[1]

The breeding of stock

Moreover, the scientific breeding of live stock, especially by *Robert Bakewell*,[2] the developer of the famous Leicester breed of sheep, produced such changes that by 1800 the average weight of sheep was nearly three times, and of cattle more than twice, what it was at the beginning of the eighteenth century. New forms of manure for the land, new artificial foods for stock, were also discovered. The institution, at the end of the century, of the *Smithfield Club* for the encouragement of stock breeding, and of a new Government department, the Board of Agriculture, are significant of the great interest taken in agriculture, an interest shared by George III himself, who started the model farm at Windsor and wrote articles in agricultural newspapers.

Enclosures of common land

These were not the only great changes that took place in agricultural conditions in this period. Waste lands were reclaimed and made productive by enterprising landowners. Large farms were substituted for small farms in many districts. Above all, an enormous amount of common land and open fields — no less than seven million acres in George III's reign alone — was enclosed by individuals, chiefly, of course, the neighbouring landowners, through Acts of Parliament. At the same time more capital was expended on the land, more improvements were introduced, and the enclosed land was made far more productive — it has been estimated that its produce multiplied at least fivefold. But these changes led to the decay, and even to the disappearance,

[1] There is a story that an archdeacon took a rector to task for growing turnips in a churchyard. "This must not occur again," he said. "Oh no, sir, next year it will be barley!" was the reply of the unrepentant rector.

[2] He was born in 1725 and died in 1794. People used to come from all over the world to see his bull "Twopenny" and his ram "Two-pounder"; and in his kitchen he would entertain "Russian princes, French and German royal dukes, British peers and sightseers of every description".

in many parts of England of the yeoman class and of the small farmers. In many districts they found increased difficulty in obtaining a livelihood owing to the enclosure of the common lands on which they used to feed their stock, and, moreover, they were often tempted by good offers to sell their land. Many of them sank into the position of labourers, and their condition during the earlier part of the nineteenth century was deplorable. Many of them drifted into the towns, which were now springing up, owing to the revolution in industry.

Industrial development

For the world was changed by the vast series of developments which now transformed Britain from an agricultural into an industrial country (*Note 121*). Each part of the new methods fitted into new discoveries in other branches. Thus men learnt to improve the production and use of coal, and of iron and steel, at the time when a whole series of inventors were producing various kinds of machinery, and others were developing the means of transport. Each of these advances would have been useless without the others. In combination they fitted together and entirely transformed men's lives, for they not only changed conditions of work, but they cheapened production and so made goods more plentiful. At the same time, population was increasing very rapidly, and great towns were springing up. The new population could not have lived, and the new towns could never have been created, unless roads and railways had made it possible to bring food and raw materials to them. Town life became the feature of British development. The new conditions led on the one hand to all sorts of problems in connection with housing and health. Public health had to be studied, and not only conditions in factories and workshops, but conditions in the crowded streets and houses.

In another direction, the growth of factories led the men and women who worked in them to learn to combine, and so we have the growth of Trade Unionism, leading on to Socialism and the Labour Party.

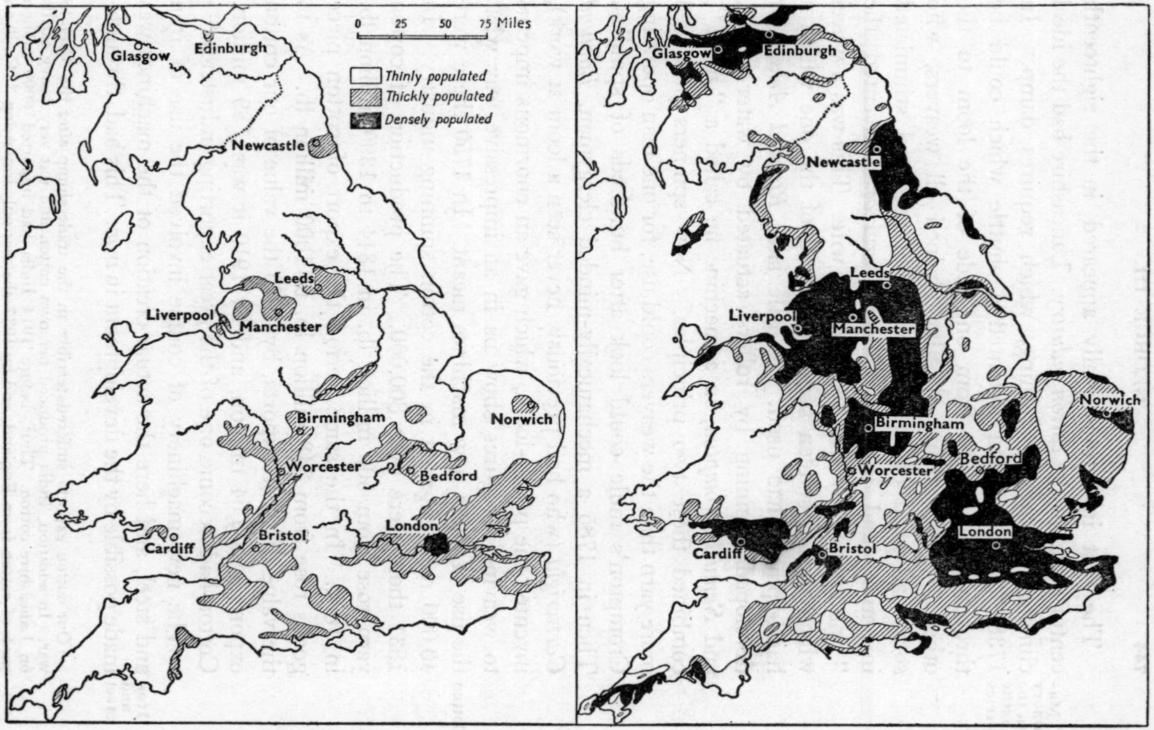

DENSITY AND DISTRIBUTION OF POPULATION BEFORE AND AFTER THE INDUSTRIAL REVOLUTION

The first inventions really appeared in the eighteenth century, and in the *cotton industry*. Lancashire had the ideal climate for cotton spinning, which requires damp. In 1738 *John Kay* had invented a shuttle which could be thrown mechanically from one side of the loom to the other. This "flying shuttle" helped all weavers, who soon had need of more yarn. This demand stimulated invention, and in 1764 *James Hargreaves* invented the "Spinning Jenny", called after his wife. This was a wheel which turned sixteen spindles instead of the one which a hand-spinner had used. A little later *Richard Arkwright* developed spinning by rollers actuated by water-power, and *Samuel Crompton*, in a machine he called a "mule", combined these two principles. Now spinners produced more yarn than the weavers could use, for one man operating Crompton's mule could look after hundreds of spindles. Then in 1785 a mechanically-minded clergyman, *Edmund Cartwright* (who had previously never seen a loom at work), invented the power-loom, which gave an enormous impetus to weaving. Figures show us in an impressive way what the use of these new machines meant. In 1750 there were 40,000 men engaged in the cotton spinning industry. In 1831 there were over 800,000. The production of cotton yarn rose from 500 million lb. in 1844 to 1300 million lb. in 1882. In the same period the export of cotton piece goods rose from 348 million lb. to 1000 million lb. As to the value of these exports, by 1870 the value of our cotton exports was £54 million, and by 1910 it was £89 million. Cotton had become one of the great exporting industries.[1]

Machinery in the textile industries

Cotton

The new machinery of course involved the use of iron and steel, and here the actual creation of the machines was made possible by the development in *iron*. This had, through-

Iron and steel

[1] Our cotton exports suffered terribly in the trade slump after the 1914-18 war. In addition, India produced her own cotton and put very heavy tariffs on Lancashire cotton. Thus, before 1914 India had imported 3000 million yards of cotton from England, and by 1937 she was only importing 334 million yards.

out previous centuries, been smelted by charcoal, and as the forests were used up, the price of this fuel rose. In 1760 coal and coke could be used, owing to an improvement in blast. *Henry Cort* discovered new ways of puddling iron, and thus by 1770 the " iron age " had begun.

Now it was only a step to the discovery of the use of steam, and *James Watt* is the man to whom we owe this. **Steam** In 1769 Watt, a maker of mathematical instruments at Greenock, made the first efficient steam engine. At first it was used only for drawing up water, but soon it was given a " rotatory " and parallel motion, and could be used for manufactures. In 1790 the first iron ships had been built, and in 1812 one of the first steamers, the *Comet*, sailed down the Clyde. In this very same year Napoleon was embarking on his great Russian campaign. He hoped to win the mastery of the world by force of arms. The " nation of shopkeepers ", whom he despised, were setting out on their campaign too, but it was one for peaceful prosperity.

Once the principle of steam-driven engines had been established, the *railway* age was at hand. In the year before **Railways** Waterloo, *George Stephenson* made his first locomotive, which was one to carry coals, and it travelled at the rate of three miles an hour. When it was suggested that lines should be laid down all over the country, great opposition was set up, for landowners objected to the idea of such traffic across their estates. Parliament rejected the first Bill for the promotion of a railway (1818). But the pressure of the new inventions was too great. Already " cotton towns " were filling the north, population was leaping up,[1] and trade called for better transport. In 1825 the first railway was opened for traffic, the *Stockton and Darlington*, and next came the *Manchester and Liverpool Railway* (1829). Once the idea was safely launched, financiers saw in railways an excellent investment. Companies were formed, hundreds of thousands of pounds were put into the ventures,

[1] In 1801 at the first census, it was 9 million; in 1821, 12 million.

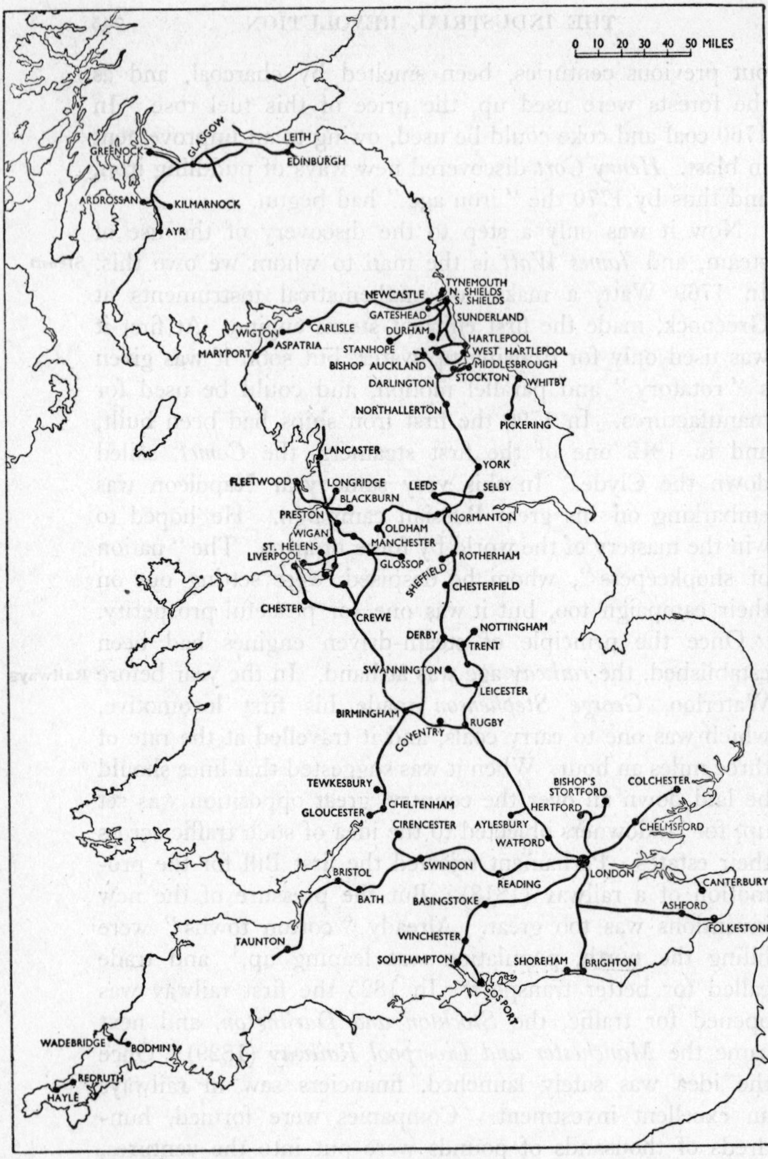

BRITISH RAILWAYS IN 1843. (Compare with the map on page 748.)

and with extraordinary speed the land was covered with a network of lines.[1]

The effect of the railways on industry was tremendous. Now the coal-fields could be opened up, especially in the north-east, and " heavy " industries could be developed wherever they were situated, since the railways could transport raw materials so easily. Thus by 1850 there were over 6000 miles of railway, linking up all the industrial districts of the north. Passengers carried in 1843 were 23 millions, in 1850 73 millions.

To look a little ahead, Queen Victoria, who was always enterprising, made her first journey by train in 1842. It was found that " third-class " traffic paid better than " first ", since there were more passengers to use it, so the *Cheap Trains Act* (1846) laid it down that one train on each line a day must carry passengers for 1*d*. a mile.

Canals and roads

But railways did not go to every place, nor were they the only means of transport. *Canals* had carried much traffic, but now the railway companies bought them up, and usually closed them in order to rid themselves of competition.

They could not deal so with the roads, and parallel with the railway development came improvement in roads. *John Macadam* in 1811 demonstrated his new surfaces, and localities which were not yet industrialized, profited from the new roads. Dickens' novels show the great part played by the coaches which carried mails and passengers.

One final invention proved again the rule that improvements in an industry call out further advance. The great use of coal meant an extension of mining, and the discovery of the steam engine caused the introduction to the mines of machinery driven by steam. At first this increase in coal-mining produced accidents in the pits, and the loss of life was terrible till *Humphry Davy's* safety-lamp was invented

[1] The labourers who worked on the railways were called " navvies ", from " navigators ", the name given to the earlier workers on the canals.

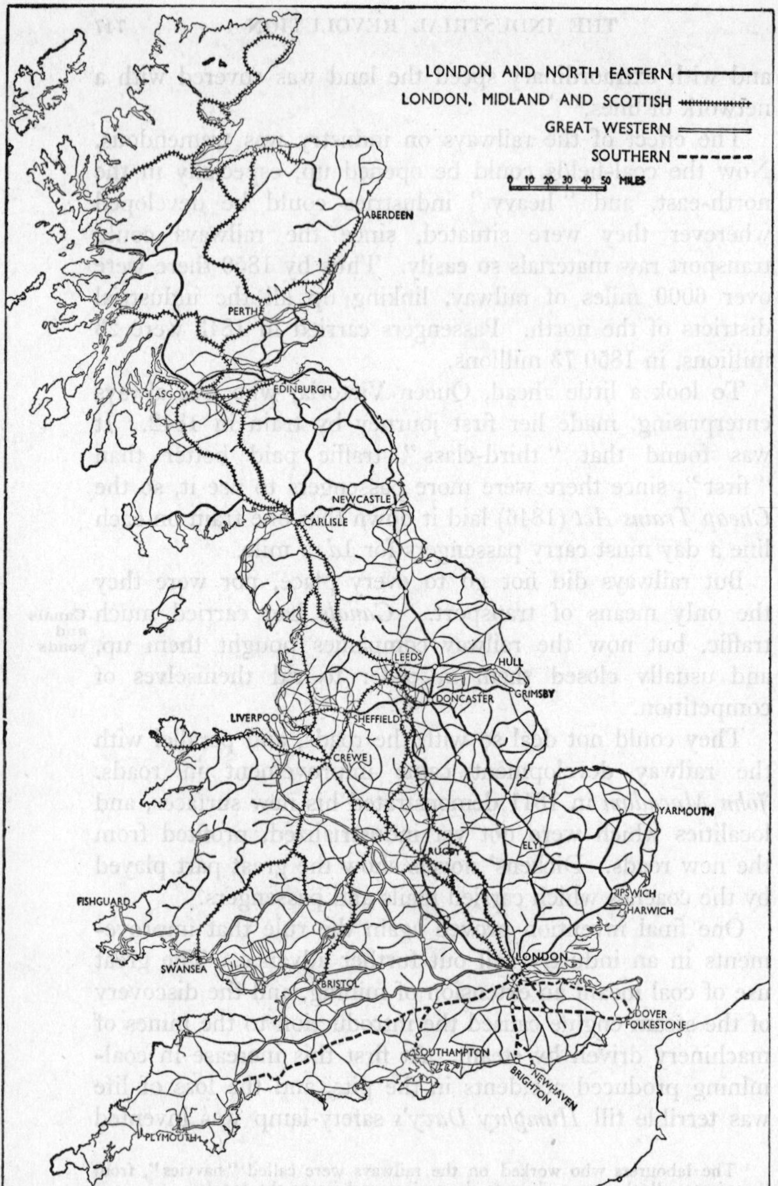

BRITISH RAILWAYS AFTER 1921. (Compare with the map on page 746.)

(1815) — it largely eliminated explosions of dangerous gases in the mines.

The safety-lamp

We know that these new inventions were in the end to improve the lot of mankind, but at first they seemed to the workers to bring only evils in their train. Machinery was destined to cheapen production, and so in time create a larger demand for goods and gradually give rise to an ever greater demand for labour. But in the first years of the new century unemployment increased and the purchasing power of wages fell.[1]

Opposition of workers

Starvation faced many, and in despair they took to violence. The "Luddite" riots, primarily due to the introduction of the new machines, occurred in the years 1811 and 1812 (called derisively after Ned Ludd, a village simpleton who was supposed to have broken some machines), and were put down with severity which too often became cruelty[2] (*Note 122*). Byron in the House of Lords pleaded for these men "meagre with famine and sullen with despair", but he was more merciful than the judges who sentenced such rioters as were caught. A terrible echo of these times comes to us in the story of a boy of fifteen who had acted as sentry to some rioters, and was sentenced to death, and who on the scaffold "called on his mother for help, thinking she had the power to save him". Yet these riots were only a beginning. For as the "post-war depression" of 1815–16 deepened, the temper of the people grew worse, in face of their helplessness. We have now to see how the Government, far from helping the working-classes, adopted a policy which increased their burdens.

"Luddite" Riots

[1] Wages during the war years rose in most industries, but not as fast as the cost of living. The case of the hand-loom workers was especially hard, because they were competing against the power-loom. Thus in 1797 a highly skilled weaver earned 26*s.* 8*d.* a week, in 1811 only 14*s.* 7*d.* These weavers could thus in 1797 buy 281 lb. of food with their wages, and only 131 lb. in 1811. Between 1790 and 1813, the cost of living, as measured in commodities, rose by 87 per cent.

[2] A very good description of home-weavers is given in *Silas Marner* by George Eliot, while excellent pictures of the machine-breaking riots are to be found in *North and South* by Mrs. Gaskell, and in *Shirley* by C. Brontë.

The Government's attitude: Castlereagh

The Prime Minister from 1812 to 1827 was *Lord Liverpool*, himself an amiable enough man, but he had no personality and was dominated by *Lord Castlereagh*. Castlereagh, though a "Liberal abroad" (see p. 756) was the opposite at home, and while his influence lasted there was misery leading to riots and disorders, which were merely suppressed, while no efforts were made to help the starving people. Yet all blame cannot be put on Castlereagh alone. Parliament supported him and urged him on. For in those days public opinion did not expect the State to cure the evils of poverty, and Parliament itself, lacking accurate information, did not know the extent of the social problem.

Financial measures

One of the first acts of Parliament (actually at the instigation of the opposition), after peace was declared, was to remove the Income Tax. This had been introduced by Pitt as a war measure, and on these grounds it was now discontinued. As the *National Debt* had naturally grown enormously owing to the heavy war expenditure, great sums of money had to be produced to pay interest on the debt. Yet now this extra taxation was not raised "directly" from the richer classes, but was met by raising the customs duties on goods.

Starvation and Poor Relief

Moreover, the people suffered specially from changes in the price of food. The artisan class did not do so badly, but the agricultural labourer could not afford to buy many commodities. Then, even more than now, bread was the mainstay of the poorer classes, and the price of bread fluctuated.[1] Parliament was in the hands of the Tories, that is to say of the owners of land. If the price of wheat were high, landlords could charge the farmers high rents. True, they declared that in this way they kept agriculture alive and employed the labourers, but the effect of the high price of corn was felt by the village labourer even more severely than

[1] It was very high after bad harvests, such as that of 1816. The price of corn, for instance, after the good harvest of 1815 went down to 55*s.* a quarter and after a bad harvest in 1817 went up in June to 111*s.* In 1822 it fell as low as 34*s.*

by the town labourer, as his wages were far lower. Indeed, the situation had been such that some years before (in 1795) at one place in Berkshire, *Speenhamland*, the magistrates of the district decided to give relief in proportion to the price of corn and the number of children in the family. This was meant to keep the large family of the very poor man from starvation, but being widely copied, it ended by meaning that farmers and employers paid very low wages, knowing that their workpeople could get this relief to supplement their wage.

Speenhamland (1795)

As the years passed, things seemed to grow worse. With the coming of peace, other nations began to compete with our shipping and develop their own manufactures. Foreign countries began to send their corn into England. The landlords would have none of this. They saw the price of corn fall by half, and many farms which had flourished in the high-price time of war, now no longer paid. Something had to be done about it, and, in 1815, the first *Corn Law* was passed, which forbade foreign corn to be imported into England until the price of English wheat was 80*s*. a quarter. This same year saw unemployment reach greater proportions than ever before. Conditions, of course, varied in different localities and different industries, but by 1816 the state of the nation was such that poor relief had risen from under two million pounds in 1790 to nearly eight million pounds in 1816.

Corn Laws passed

William Cobbett, who himself was a countryman, in his famous *Rural Rides* describes the condition of England. Thanks to his wonderful prose, the places he passed through live in our minds. He devoted all his great gifts and his unbounded energy to stir up the spirit of revolt against such conditions, using his paper the *National Register* for his propaganda.

Nor were the town-dwellers very much better off. As the textile industry had developed with the new machines, so "factory" towns appeared; builders now ran up rows of

Conditions in the towns

squalid houses, and the great mills belched out smoke overhead. In these factories, men, women, and children worked for long hours, there being no limit fixed till 1819, and even then the legal twelve hours a day was exceeded, for there was no means whatever of enforcing the Act. The workers could not combine, for that was forbidden by the *Combination Laws.*[1]

One specially difficult thing to understand is that some men, good and broad-minded in other respects, saw no need for preventing this state of things. *John Bright*, who later worked so hard to have the Corn Laws repealed, and *William Wilberforce*, who devoted his whole life to freeing the slaves, both opposed the Factory Acts. They thought that liberty was so precious that workers and employers should be free to arrange matters between them; and they believed further that the better employers would by their success force bad ones to improve their conditions. This policy of leaving *capital* and *labour* to settle their own affairs was called *laissez faire*, but it cannot be called a success, since "labour" was not strong enough to defend itself. And when such men as these disbelieved in State action, it is easily understood how the Tory Government would react. The upper and middle classes had been genuinely terrified by the excesses of the French Revolution; they were partly ignorant of the sufferings of the workers; they had no trained body of civil servants to deal with the problems, and no traditions to induce them to attempt remedies through State action.

Laissez faire

3. REPRESSION AND REVOLT

The Radicals

Such misery as the people were suffering was hard to bear. Yet no help came, and no redress, and finding Parliament obdurate, the leaders of the people began to work for reform

[1] These Acts punished "any working man who combined with another to gain an increase in wages or a decrease in hours."

of Parliament itself. The *Radical* party appeared, so called because it wished for " radical reform ". It included writers such as Cobbett, speakers such as " *Orator* " *Hunt*,[1] and the great lawyer *Jeremy Bentham*, who wrote the *Catechism of Parliamentary Reform*. The starving miserable people eagerly joined in the movement. Meetings were held in the great towns, and soon trouble broke out (*Note 124*).

In London, during November of 1816, a great crowd met at *Spa Fields*, Bermondsey, demanding universal suffrage. It formed in procession and set off to " capture the Tower ". Needless to say, it was easily dispersed and broken up, but the Government, seeing a resemblance to the French attack on the Bastille, was genuinely terrified.

Riots and repression

Riots were reported from the Midlands and from Glasgow, and the Government decided on most vigorous methods to deal with the disorders. Not content with arresting and executing the leaders of " mobs ", when they could catch and convict them, in 1817 they suspended the Habeas Corpus Act. That Act is always reckoned one of the safeguards of British liberty, for under it a man cannot be imprisoned without trial. The suspension of the Act meant that the Government could pounce on anyone and put him in prison, and that he could have no redress for he could not claim to be tried, so of course could not prove his innocence.

Still trouble increased. The first " unemployed march " came when a band of men set out (January, 1817) from Manchester, to bring a petition to the Government. They were called the *Blanketeers* as each man carried a blanket to sleep in. Their leaders were arrested at Derby, and the march brought to a stop.

The " Manchester Massacre " (1819)

Then, in 1819, the Radicals arranged for a great public meeting to be held in Manchester, at which " Orator " Hunt was to speak. Here over 50,000 people met, at St. Peter's Fields, to ask for Parliamentary reform. The magistrates were frightened, and ordered the Yeomanry

[1] So called to distinguish him from the writer, Leigh Hunt, also a Radical.

first to arrest Hunt, and then to disperse the crowd. The soldiers obeyed, and in the enclosed space hundreds were injured and eleven killed, including two women and a child. The bitterest resentment was bred by this "Manchester Massacre" and the people nicknamed it *Peterloo* in mocking comparison with Waterloo.

The Six Acts (1819)

Completely terrified by the lawlessness which they found was increasing, the Government thought only of repression. The *Six Acts*, or as the people called them the *Gag Acts* (*Note 123*) were now passed. The most important of these Acts forbade public meetings of more than fifty people, unless the Mayor or Lord Lieutenant agreed that they should be held; duties were put on newspapers and pamphlets, so that as printing became expensive, that means of airing grievances would be checked; magistrates could order private houses to be searched for arms. This panic legislation cannot be justified by fear of "French revolutionary ideas", for the war had ended four years earlier, and revolutionary France had been not only crushed but put back under the rule of the reactionary Bourbon kings. If open political agitation is made impossible, it is driven underground, and becomes plotting.[1] After the Six Acts came the *Cato Street Conspiracy* (1820). A band of men, headed by *Arthur Thistlewood*, met in a little street off Edgware Road in London and planned to assassinate the Cabinet at a dinner party, to seize the Tower, and to set up a Republic. The plot was discovered and some of the conspirators executed.

In Scotland the *Battle of Bonnymuir*, as it was called, took place. Instigated by the Government secret agents, some miners armed themselves, but were easily scattered by a troop of soldiers.[2]

For this repressive policy, Castlereagh must bear a large

[1] This is the time when the Government used spies, such as the notorious "Oliver", who went round acting not only as spies but as *agents provocateurs*.

[2] One of those executed was Andrew Hardie, ancestor of Keir Hardie, destined to be the first leader of the Labour Party and first working-man M.P.

share of responsibility. True, he was not the head of the Government, but his was the strong character which hustled the weak Prime Minister along this path. He believed in ruthless putting down of disorder, and he saw that his ideas were carried out. The people hated him, and the poets lashed at him with scorn.[1] When he committed suicide in 1822, he had become so hated that a jeering mob howled with delight at the sight of his coffin being carried through the streets of London. His death marks the end of a bad period.

Death of Castlereagh

4. FOREIGN POLICY OF CASTLEREAGH

Castlereagh had been Foreign Secretary since 1812. He had shown great energy and resolution in carrying on the opposition to Napoleon. He had largely brought about the Fourth Coalition, which finally defeated France, and he had been one of the most prominent figures at the great Congress of Vienna, which ended the war.

After 1815, England's foreign policy remained in his hands, and it has been said that he was "one of the very greatest and most constructive of British foreign statesmen". (*Note 125*).

Castlereagh's foreign policy after 1815

The long war had left Britain determined to withdraw as far as possible from continental quarrels, and the country as a whole therefore upheld Castlereagh's main policy, which may be summed up as *non-intervention.* All Europe was afraid of revolutionary ideas, and all the absolute monarchs wished to revive their powers, which had been so shattered first by the French Revolution and then by Napoleon. Castlereagh was as strongly "anti-jacobin" as any man, but at the Congress of Vienna he had stood up for two principles — the recognition of Bourbon France, and the right of States to constitutional government.

Castlereagh acquiesced in the settlement which Vienna

[1] Shelley, Byron, Coleridge, all wrote bitter satires on Castlereagh and the Government.

Castlereagh and France

imposed upon France. She had to revert to the frontiers she had held before the conquests of the Revolution and Napoleon; she was encircled by States which would check any possible aggression on her part; she was to have an army of occupation in her territory for five years. But he did not wish to see her kept out of the position to which as a great nation she was entitled, and he therefore pressed the view that, once it was definite that she had given up her "revolutionary" ideas, she should be received back into the ranks of the great powers. And there were no indemnities.

The Congress system

He was also prepared to support the retention of constitutional government wherever it had been set up. For example, he insisted that though Poland was handed over to Russia, yet she should be guaranteed her own constitutional government.

Except for the Czar Alexander First, who showed (but not for long) signs of a vague liberalism, the autocratic rulers were not liberal-minded.[1] Furthermore, they were all afraid of a revival of militant revolution in Europe, and therefore were resolved to stamp out any tendency towards popular control. This led them to oppose all forms of constitutional government in the modern sense of the term, and to restore everywhere their own arbitrary power. The position might be summed up in the words "the little kings came out into the sun again". The Czar formed the "Holy Alliance" of Christian monarchs, but Castlereagh took advantage of the fact that the ruler of Great Britain cannot undertake responsibilities in his own person to prevent the Regent from signing that treaty, calling it "a piece of sublime mysticism and nonsense". But Castlereagh did believe whole-heartedly that the Great Powers of Europe should try to take joint action to prevent the recurrence of the horrors of war. His chief claim to fame lies in this, for he both acted as a "good European", rather than in the

[1] The Emperor's Liberalism was of a kind not unknown to Liberal autocrats. "The Emperor," said one of his ministers, "would willingly have consented that everyone should be free, on condition everyone should do his will alone."

interests of his own country alone, and he endeavoured to continue, as an instrument of peace, those meetings of the Powers which had been held by the Allies during the last campaigns against Napoleon and during the re-settlement of Europe after Napoleon's fall.

The Quadruple Alliance

At first the practical aim of those meetings or Congresses, was to ensure that the Peace of Paris was duly observed, and to attain this, Castlereagh maintained the *Quadruple Alliance* between Austria, Russia, Prussia, and Great Britain. The first Congress was held at *Aix-la-Chapelle* (1818) when it was admitted that France had ceased to disturb Europe and that the Bourbons were firmly re-established on the French throne. Accordingly, the army of occupation was withdrawn from France and she was re-admitted to the rank of a Great Power, and allowed to join a new Quintuple Alliance.

Attacks on rebellious subjects

Europe might then have advanced peaceably, but unluckily reactionary views were to create discord. In 1820 a revolution broke out in Spain, and the King, in order to save his life and his throne, was obliged to grant a very democratic constitution. The Czar, horrified at this, declared it was the duty of the Congress powers to intervene in Spain and put down the constitution. Castlereagh refused, and in a memorable state paper laid down that Britain was only committed to prevent the return of Napoleon to France, and that the revolution in Spain was a purely internal affair which it was no concern of Britain's to suppress.

Further revolutions now broke out in Portugal, Naples, and Piedmont, and the Czar insisted that the powers of the Alliance must meet to deal with the situation. At *Troppau* in 1820, Castlereagh sent his brother to represent Britain. There the three Powers (Russia, Prussia, and Austria) issued a protocol, declaring that they "would never recognize the right of a people to circumscribe the power of their kings". Castlereagh not only refused to accept this protocol, he said it was "destitute of common sense", and when the Austrians entered Italy to suppress the revolutionary movements there, Castlereagh declined to take any part in such proceedings.

Great Britain withdraws

This meant that Britain was now isolated from her former allies. One more effort was made by Castlereagh to save the situation. When the Greeks rose in revolt against the Turks, Metternich would have supported the rule of the Sultan, but the Czar was ready to help the Greeks who were his co-religionists. Castlereagh agreed that one more Congress should be called, to endeavour to settle the question without war. But before that Congress met (at Verona) Castlereagh was dead. In a breakdown from overwork he committed suicide in August, 1822, and with him died the last hope of the Congress System.

CHAPTER 57

GEORGE IV (1820–1830) AND WILLIAM IV (1830–1837)

1. THE "TORY REFORMERS"

George IV and his Queen

George IV became King in 1820. His bad personal character, his selfishness and extravagance and general uselessness, made him disliked and despised. George was separated from his wife, *Caroline of Brunswick.* At his accession he tried to rid himself of her by causing the Government to bring in a Bill of Pains and Penalties, under which he could divorce her. His own immorality was so open and notorious that people's anger was aroused, and popular sympathy was on the side of the Queen. The bill had to be dropped, but at the Coronation, a fresh scandal was created. George refused to allow Caroline to be crowned, and she tried to force her way into the Abbey, but was prevented. He might have saved himself the contempt and anger his treatment of her created, for Caroline died only a few months later.

With Castlereagh's death in 1822, the discredited ministry broke up. Better days were hoped for, since the new

Government was formed of men who wished to deal with the universal discontent, not by mere savage repression, but by attempting to remove its causes. There followed a period of change and in many respects of advance. The man who now rose to power was *George Canning*, who became Leader of the House of Commons and the chief influence in the Cabinet, though the Premiership remained with *Lord Liverpool*. *William Huskisson*, an enlightened economist, became President of the Board of Trade, and a rising young man, *Robert Peel*, became Home Secretary. This new group of people broke away from the reactionary policy of the last decade and launched out on new ways (*Note 126*).

The Tory reformers

At home, a small beginning was at once made. First the *Combination Acts*, by which Pitt had forbidden workers to organize a strike, or to form Trade Unions, were repealed (1824). This was the work of *Francis Place*. He was a master-tailor of London, and a *Radical*, as the more extreme reformers were called, and he won over *Joseph Hume*, a Member of Parliament. Hume got the repeal carried through Parliament, and when employers came in deputation to point out the resulting strikes, which they said were ruining trade, Hume brought up counter-deputations of workers. It was made so clear that the workers had genuine grievances and should not be left at the mercy of their employers, that the repeal was confirmed. Working-men might now join together in association, but they must not " molest " workers who did not choose to join them.

Repeal of Combination Acts (1824)

Next Huskisson tried to remedy some of the ills of the widespread distress and starvation. He modified the *Navigation Acts* (finally abolished in 1849), and thus ships of all nations could bring goods to England, and freights and prices in consequence fell. He went further and lowered some of the duties on foreign goods coming into England. Yet how high those duties had been we can guess when we find that some of those left ranged from 15 per cent to 30 per cent. Huskisson did not wish Parliament to repeal the Corn

Reduction of customs

Laws altogether, but he did lower the duty on Colonial corn and introduced a sliding scale, and this was a little help. He gave preference to colonial products too, and subsidized emigration.

Reform of Penal Code

Desperate hunger had driven men to crime. Peel, the new Home Secretary, now tried to improve matters by reducing the severity of the punishments inflicted by the law.[1] The *penal code* was so savage, and judges and magistrates so harsh in their administration, that in one year (1819) nearly ten thousand persons had been transported to Botany Bay. More than 200 crimes were punishable by death, including stealing a sheep, and picking pockets. This gradually, as opinion became more humane, produced the effect of causing juries to refuse to convict. Men would not condemn a fellow-creature to death for stealing five shillings. Hence the terribly severe penalties began to prove ineffective. *Sir Samuel Romilly* (1757–1818) and *Sir James Mackintosh* (1765–1832) had long worked for reform. Peel adopted Mackintosh's ideas. In 1828 the death penalty was abolished except for murder,[2] and the whole code softened. Mackintosh, when he later spoke of the changes due to Peel, said, " I could almost think I had lived in two different countries."

Canning's foreign policy

Now we must turn to foreign affairs, for here the new spirit was more strongly marked, and achieved striking effects. That policy was decided by the man who was the most outstanding figure in the Government, the Foreign Secretary, Canning.

George Canning is one of the most attractive of British statesmen. His mother, whom he adored, had been an actress, and the more strict of the aristocrats of the period, such as Lord Grey, thought that this unfitted him to hold such an office as the Prime Ministership. His wit, which was sometimes cruel,

[1] The Game Laws used to be very severe. As late as 1816 an Act was passed punishing with transportation for seven years any person found by night in open ground having in his possession any net or engine for the purpose of taking any hare, rabbit, or other game.

[2] For a brief time it was also retained for forgery of a Bank of England note, for treason, and for arson in a royal dockyard.

also made him enemies. Undismayed by all the difficulties put in his way, Canning worked steadily up. He was ready to champion anyone who suffered, and perhaps for this reason he stood up for poor, vulgar, misguided Queen Caroline in her quarrels with the worthless King. For this he was naturally in disgrace with George IV, and at last in despair had accepted the office of Governor-General in India, which would end his hopes of advancement in England. His ship was on the point of sailing, when news came that his enemy and rival, Castlereagh, had committed suicide. Canning was at once asked by the Prime Minister, Lord Liverpool, to become Foreign Secretary, and he accepted.

Canning and the reactionary kings

When people accuse Great Britain of hypocrisy, they usually mean that she has acquired territories for herself while pretending to champion the rights of others. Canning's career shows that that charge was untrue in the early nineteenth century. Great Britain, under his guidance, did stand out as a champion of oppressed countries, but she gained no territory by it. Europe was passing through an odious phase. The fall of Napoleon had meant the "restoration" of the old rulers. Back they had all gone, the Bourbons "in the baggage of the allies" as the saying went. The restored sovereigns had learnt nothing; they wished to return to absolute monarchy as it had been before the French Revolution. Austria, under Metternich, had made it her business to support this reaction with all her might (believing that in such an Empire as Austria, with her many races, he could only hold the State together by combating nationalism [1]), and not only France, but Spain, Portugal, Naples, and the little States of Italy and Germany, were now pushed back under the power of rulers who were sometimes not only stupid but cruel. Thus when the *Congress of Verona*

[1] Metternich's two points were — and there was something to be said for his attitude in both of them: (1) that the Austrian monarchy, with its heterogeneous possessions, was like "an old house which would fall in pieces if you tried to repair it;" (2) that revolutions are infectious and must therefore be put down whenever they occur. "When France has a cold," he said, referring to the Revolution in France, "Europe sneezes."

met in the autumn of 1822, it was decided that France should send an army to invade Spain and destroy the newly-granted constitution. Wellington was Great Britain's envoy, and acting on Canning's instructions, he declared that Great Britain utterly refused to be a party to any interference by force. France therefore acted by herself, sent an army across the Pyrenees, abolished the Spanish constitution, and restored the hateful Ferdinand to absolute power. Canning felt most bitterly the irony of seeing the Spaniards, who had fought so long beside the British in the Peninsular War, now slaughtered by the brutal Royalist armies at the command of the King whom Great Britain had helped to restore. When, in the next year, the restored King of Spain called for a Congress to discuss Spanish America, Canning refused to send any representative of Britain, nor would he send any representative to the proposed conference to discuss Turkey and Greece. His refusal to take part was the final blow to the "Congress System" from which Castlereagh had hoped so much. On Castlereagh's side it represented an effort to substitute peaceful settlement of difficulties for the miseries and stupidities of war, but it was an effort which failed. It broke down because the reactionary Powers tried to transform the meetings into a general "police system" of interference in other States and to interpret the co-operation of the Powers in the interests of peace as a crusade against constitutional government.

South America (1826)

Canning could not save Spain, but he could and did save her South American colonies. These colonies refused to accept Ferdinand. The King asked France and Russia to supply him with troops. Great Britain commanded the sea and could stop the transport of those armies. Canning showed that he would do so when he "recognized" the independence of the South American republics of Mexico, Peru, and Chile. "I called the New World into existence, to redress the balance of the old," were his famous words.

Now the question of *Portugal* came to the fore. There

Dom Pedro was King, and his only child was a daughter. In order to win support for her, Dom Pedro offered to grant a constitution and to abdicate if the people would accept her. He was opposed by his brother, Dom Miguel, an absolutist, who was backed by the reactionary rulers of Spain. Canning declared that any ruler could grant a constitution, and the constitutionalists appealed to Britain for help. This she was bound by treaty to give, and thus Canning sent a fleet and troops to Lisbon. The Spaniards were obliged to leave the country, Miguel was defeated, and the young Queen ascended the throne and granted a constitution (1827). **Portugal**

The Greeks

Growing bolder, Canning decided to champion liberty in Europe itself. The *Greeks*, long held down by the Turks, rose to fight their War of Independence. *Lord Byron* was the most famous Englishman to volunteer to fight, and his death at Missolonghi roused passionate enthusiasm for the Greeks. But volunteers were not enough. At first Canning hesitated. Like so many statesmen, he dreaded lest the emancipation of the Balkans from the Turks would only give Russia the chance to step in. England feared Russia, and dreaded her arrival in the Mediterranean. But when it looked as if the Greeks must be overwhelmed, Canning decided to act. He joined with Russia and France, and sent the British fleet out to the Greek coast. There, at the modern *Navarino* (the scene in classical times of the more famous battle of Pylos), a chance shot started an engagement, fought just after Canning's death. The entire Egypto-Turkish fleet was destroyed and Greece soon won her freedom (1827).

The Battle of Navarino (1827)

So it may be claimed that Canning worked to secure liberty for other countries. Whether he would have gone on to carry his liberal ideas into home politics, one cannot tell. In 1827 Lord Liverpool had a stroke, and George IV offered the premiership to Canning. He accepted it, but, before four months had passed, he too was dead.

Canning's untimely death led to a strange development.

Wellington, Peel, and Catholic Emancipation

Office was taken by a Tory Ministry which was forced by stress of circumstances to go right against one of the strictest principles of Tory policy.

The *Duke of Wellington*, who still retained the great prestige he had won in the Napoleonic wars, was asked by the King to form a ministry. He did so, with Peel as Leader of the Commons. Wellington represented the stiff Toryism of the old school; Peel was, as we have seen, a reformer, yet they united in opposition to *Catholic Emancipation*, and both were now to be obliged to change their minds.

Religion still acted as a possible disability in public life, for neither Roman Catholics nor Nonconformists could hold any office under the State, or attend the universities.[1] Now a Bill was passed (1829), which freed Nonconformists from all restrictions. Roman Catholics, however, were still debarred, and at this point the state of affairs in Ireland forced the Duke and Peel to give the whole question reconsideration. For whereas in England the Roman Catholics were a very small minority, in Ireland they were the vast majority.

Ireland's grievances

Ireland had for long been filled with burning resentment at the treatment she received. The Act of Union had been carried through in 1800 on the express understanding that Catholic Emancipation should be granted, but that pledge had not been honoured (see p. 715). Therefore the Irish found themselves with no parliament of their own, and they were " represented " at Westminster only by Protestants of the landlord class. These Protestant landowners showed no sympathy for or understanding of the grievances of the Irish Catholic peasantry.

Peel had been Chief Secretary in Ireland for six years (to 1815) but he had no sympathy with Emancipation, and indeed was considered by the Irish as so anti-Catholic that they nicknamed him " Orange Peel ". He tried to keep

[1] Each year an " Indemnity Act " had hitherto been passed, to excuse Nonconformists from taking the oath.

order through *Coercion Acts*, and introduced the system of police, whom the Irish called " Bobbies " after him.[1] He was opposed by one of the greatest men Ireland has produced, *Daniel O'Connell*, called by his followers " the Liberator ".

O'Connell the Liberator (1775–1847)

O'Connell was a marvellous orator, and one of the kindest as well as one of the most popular of men. He opposed all violence, and he was determined to use only peaceful methods. He hit on the plan of inducing men to vote only for those candidates for Parliament who would promise to support Emancipation. Soon he went further. *Vesey Fitzgerald*, Member for County Clare, was in 1828 made President of the Board of Trade, and in consequence had to seek re-election. He was a Protestant landlord, but he favoured Emancipation and was personally popular. Now O'Connell decided to stand against him. He did so, and an overwhelming majority of freeholders voted for him, though, as a Catholic, he could not take his seat. This showed the absurdity of the system, and feeling began to run dangerously high. Huge meetings were held everywhere, and O'Connell's marvellous oratory aroused the wildest enthusiasm. It became clear that an explosion would come. In England itself the situation was threatening. Peel and Wellington were both opposed to Emancipation, but each of them became convinced now that unless it were granted, revolt would break out in Ireland, and might spread to England. Hours had to be spent in argument with George IV who believed Emancipation conflicted with his coronation oath to " maintain " the Protestant religion. Eventually he gave way,[2] Peel's Bill was passed, and Roman Catholics could now sit in Parliament (1829). The Army, Navy, Law, and so on were now open to them, and they were eligible for all offices

[1] The nickname followed the system to England, when Peel set up the Metropolitan Police in London in 1825.

[2] In order to win his consent, Peel had to agree to two things, the suppression of O'Connell's Catholic Association, and the disfranchisement of 405 freeholders in Ireland.

except those of Lord High Chancellor and Lord-Lieutenant of Ireland. The Tories were naturally angry with their leaders, but accepted their judgment.

Demand for "reform"

But these " reforms ", helpful as they were, were not enough. The leaders of the opposition were determined to strike at one of the roots of the trouble. The people had suffered cruelly, Parliament had not done enough to help them. Parliament, then, they said, must be changed, and power should not be left in the hands of the landowner and the rich.

Representation in Great Britain

In Great Britain the *system of representation* had not changed with changes in the population (*Note 128*). Thus each county still sent two members to Parliament, and a number of boroughs (towns) each sent two.[1] But as population had shifted, while representation remained unaltered, certain places still had the right to send members to Parliament although their inhabitants had dwindled away. (The classic example was Old Sarum, the landowner of the uninhabited " green mounds " of which could still send members up to Westminster). These were called "pocket boroughs" or " nominated " boroughs, for the owner or patron could nominate whom he chose.

Pocket boroughs

Meanwhile, the great new towns, because they were new and had recently grown up, might have no representatives at all.

Corruption

Clearly where such power lay in the hands of a few people, it was possible to control their votes. Bribery was extensively practised, and where a great local magnate could either bribe or influence the few local voters, the borough was called a " rotten borough ", and a rotten borough could even put itself up for sale.

Rotten boroughs

Only in a very few places, such as Westminster itself, was the franchise held by a considerable number of householders.

[1] In 1832 there were, for England, 84 county members and 409 borough members; and of the borough members 200 belonged to patrons and another 180 had been " bought ".

PARLIAMENTARY REPRESENTATION BEFORE 1832

BOROUGHS

Boroughs returning two members ●
Boroughs returning one member ○
Boroughs in Wales which shared a member +

Note. (i) London returned four members.
(ii) Melcombe Regis and Weymouth returned four members between them.
(iii) Oxford and Cambridge Universities each returned two members.

COUNTIES

Yorkshire returned four members. All other English Counties returned two members each. Each Welsh County returned one member.

In Ireland and in Scotland matters were, if possible, worse. When Pitt abolished the Irish Parliament he had to give a million and a half pounds in compensation to the owners of rotten boroughs; and the bulk of the Irish representatives were returned by about 50 great landowners. Scotland sent 45 members to Parliament, but they were chosen by a tiny number of voters, only 4000 for the whole country, and it was reckoned that those voters were controlled by 150 patrons.

Thus the Parliament of the early nineteenth century was not representative of the people.

There was the same injustice in the distribution of votes. The franchise (i.e. the right to vote) was held in the counties by people owning *freehold land* worth 40 shillings. In the towns there were all sorts of qualifications. In some towns the members were chosen by the Town Council.[1] In a few, they were chosen by those persons who had the hereditary position of " freemen " (burgage franchise) and in others by the owners of certain " ancient tenements ". In other cases the franchise was very wide and gave the vote to any person whose house possessed a hearth on which a pot could be boiled, these persons being nicknamed " potwallopers ".

The Whigs, led by Lord Grey, demanded parliamentary reform and the extension of the franchise. The new movement coincided with the accession of a new sovereign, for in 1830 George IV died.

Death of George IV

He has long been despised as one of the most selfish and contemptible of our kings. He deserves that contempt, for he was capable of better things. He was no fool, and his one claim to credit is that he appreciated literature [2] and art. Yet, living at a time when no one could help but know that the people were suffering, the country hard-hit, and the need for wisdom and for economy supreme, he cared for

[1] In Bath, for example, where the corporation of 35 men returned the two members.

[2] His admiration for the novels of Jane Austen led him to keep a set of her books at each of his residences.

nothing but his own vulgar dissipations, and wasted hundreds upon thousands of pounds on his senseless amusements. The court which surrounded him and the men and women who were his companions, showed nothing but the low level to which such people could sink. The middle classes and the " common folk " knew all this and resented it. They might hope that his death would coincide with a move for reform.

2. THE GREAT REFORM BILL

It is more cheerful to turn to the men who were the openers of a new chapter. *William IV*, though somewhat eccentric (his nickname was " Silly Billy ") was warm-hearted and was prepared to back parliamentary reform, now passionately desired by the country. Accordingly, *Lord Grey* in 1831 brought in his famous *Reform Bill*, which aimed at enfranchising the middle classes. It was carried by a majority of one at its second reading, amidst intense excitement.[1] When the Bill was amended in committee, Grey called for a fresh election, and the country showed its wishes by returning him with a larger majority. His Bill came triumphantly through the Commons, only to be thrown out by the Lords. Now people saw where they stood. Reform, which the nation at large demanded, was denied by the Upper House. London rioted and the mob attacked the Duke of Wellington. Bristol burst into revolt, and Birmingham threatened to send 20,000 men to march on London. Riots in Scotland were so bad that soldiers had to be sent north. Patiently Grey introduced a fresh Bill, and once more the Lords so mutilated it in Committee as to destroy its purpose. Grey resigned and the old Tory leader, Wellington, tried to form a ministry, but no one would take office. Grey once more brought in the Bill. This was one

William IV

[1] " You might have heard a pin drop," Macaulay wrote, " as Duncannon read the numbers. Then again the shouts broke out, and many of us shed tears. I could scarcely refrain." See the account in Macaulay's *Life and Letters.*

of the real crises of our history. If the Bill failed again, few doubted that open revolution would break out. Our Constitution has one curious safeguard for such an emergency. The Lords were against reform, but the King could create new lords from amongst the reformers. Grey asked that this should be done. William IV agreed.[1] Wellington, unwilling to see the Tory majority permanently swamped by the creation of more Liberal peers, advised his followers not to vote at all. Accordingly, in June 1832, the Bill passed (*Note 129*).

Terms of Reform Bill (1832)

To Liberal enthusiasts the passing of the Reform Bill was the panacea for all human ills; even children, it is said, went about their playgrounds shouting, "The Reform Bill has passed!" To the Tories, on the other hand, the passing of the Bill seemed to foreshadow the downfall of Great Britain; and the Duke of Wellington expressed the opinion that in six weeks' time Lord Grey would be out of office, and that henceforward no gentleman would be able to take part in public affairs. Yet in itself the Reform Bill appears to us a mild measure. It abolished a great number of "rotten" and "pocket" boroughs, a hundred and forty-three seats in all, and gave them to counties or large towns. The franchise in the counties was extended to copyholders[2] and *long leaseholders of lands worth £10 a year*, or to tenants-at-will of lands worth £50 a year, and in the boroughs to *holders of houses worth £10 a year*. But it is reckoned that under the Bill only one person out of every twenty-four of the whole population had a vote.

The Reform Bill of 1832, nevertheless, broke down the monopoly of power possessed by the landowning aristocracy, and by giving the vote to the middle class altered the

[1] "The King," so ran the document from the King, "grants permission to Earl Grey and to his chancellor, Lord Brougham, to create such a number of peers as will be sufficient to ensure the passing of the Reform Bill, first, calling up peers' eldest sons."

[2] A copyholder was almost as complete an owner of land as the freeholder. The land did not belong to him, but practically he could not be dispossessed of it without his consent. Copyholds were abolished in 1922.

PARLIAMENTARY REPRESENTATION AS CHANGED BY THE REFORM ACT OF 1832

Boroughs returning two members after 1832 ● *Boroughs returning one member after* 1832 ○

County members are indicated by numbers. English Counties without numbers returned 4 members each

The Reform Bills of 1867, 1884, 1918, and 1928

centre of gravity in politics. Moreover, once a Reform Bill was passed, other bills were bound to follow. In 1867 came the *second Reform Bill*, which gave the vote to the better-class artisans in the towns — and one in twelve of the population had a vote. And then, in 1884, the vote was given to the agricultural labourer in country districts and to nearly all men in towns — and one in seven had a vote. Finally, by Acts passed in 1918 and 1928, women got the vote — and so at the present time nearly two out of three of the population have votes. In fact, practically everyone has a vote who is not a minor, an alien, a criminal serving sentence, a lunatic, or a peer.

Changes in politics after 1832

The Duke of Wellington's prophecy with regard to gentlemen ceasing to be able to take part in politics proved to be signally wrong. No doubt members after 1832 were drawn from a wider circle, and more merchants and more lawyers were elected than formerly, but the old governing families, and what is sometimes called the Public School Class still had, in the nineteenth century, great influence.[1] Though, however, the character of our legislators did not greatly alter, yet the character of legislation did. The period of quiescence in legislation came finally to an end. The rival programmes of each party were full of legislative promises, and to an increasing extent, as the franchise was extended, this legislation has been passed for the benefit of the working-classes. Moreover, the methods of politics changed. Reporters were admitted to the debates. The sessions were more protracted. Members became more regular in their attendance. Again, public meetings became far more common. Canning was the first great statesman to address them, but the prejudice against ministers in high office speaking in the country lingered for some time, and even as late as 1886 Queen Victoria objected to Gladstone addressing public meetings outside his own constituency.

[1] In the House of Commons of 1865 one-quarter of the members were connected with thirty-one families; and in that of 1900 one-quarter had been educated at Eton or Harrow.

CHAPTER 58

THE FIRST WHIG REFORMERS (1832–1841)

The passing of the Reform Act seemed at first to end the long period of Tory rule. The Whigs were in, and they were pledged to deal with the state of the country. They set to work at once and a period followed which can be taken as the beginning of a real attempt to improve social conditions (*Note 130*).

The first great problem to be tackled was that of the factories. Hard times had forced parents to let their children go to work in the new factories which now covered the north and midlands. There, children of 6 or 7 years old would work for 10 or 14 hours a day. They worked in the mines, too, for long hours, under the most terrible conditions. *Lord Ashley* (better known by his later title of *Lord Shaftesbury*) took up their cause. He was a man who, in his own home, rich and aristocratic as he was, had spent a very unhappy childhood. Moved by the evangelical teaching of his old Welsh nurse, the human being who had been kindest to him, he resolved to give his whole life to those whom he recognized as poor and oppressed. He embarked on a campaign to shorten the hours of work in factories. He was fought by the owners of factories and mines on the grounds that unless these children and women were employed for these long hours, the factories could make no profits. Even enlightened men such as Cobden and Wilberforce declared that it was better for these conditions to continue, than to shorten hours, and so bring about the closing down of the works. Parliament, however, moved by terrible accounts of the state of the children presented to them by a Commission, decided on legislation. The *Factory Act* of 1833, the first really effective Act, which dealt only with textile works,

Lord Shaftesbury

Factory Act (1833)

such as cotton and woollen, forbade the employment of children under 9; limited the hours of those under 13 to 48 hours per week, and not more than 9 hours on any one day; and of those under 18 to 13½ hours. Four inspectors were appointed to see that these laws were kept. The arguments put forward by the owners proved fallacious. Factories did not close; on the contrary, trade flourished and expanded. Long hours and inefficient labour proved less profitable than the shorter times worked by adult labour, and the removal of the cheap child-labour, while raising the wages of adults, also raised the purchasing power of the working-classes.

Education (1833) The children thus set free from mine and factory, were now to be given the first step in *education.* Two private societies [1] had already set up schools in many districts. In 1833 the State gave £20,000 a year to these societies, and all children employed "part time" in cotton mills were to go to school for at least two hours a day. This was the beginning of the State education of its citizens.

Next to be dealt with came the *Poor Laws.* The terrible poverty of the early years of the century had led magistrates all over the country to follow the example of *Speenhamland* (see p. 751). "Out-relief", which meant payment of money to families in their homes, was granted so lavishly that the burden on the rates had become intolerable. Many farmers, ruined by the high rates, gave up their farms; agricultural wages, being supplemented from the rates, fell in some counties as low as 6*s.* a week, and "relief" became an expected part of the family income. It was clear that this system could not be continued. A commission of inquiry had been set up in 1832, the secretary and moving spirit

Poor Law Amendment Act (1834) being *Edward Chadwick*, and as a result a *Poor Law Amendment Act* was passed in 1834. This Act altered the system of *poor relief*, which had lasted since the days of Queen Eliza-

[1] The Church of England "National Society for Education of the Poor in the Principles of the Church of England", and the Nonconformist "British and Foreign Schools Society".

beth. The most important point was the check imposed on " out relief ". The new Act ordered the setting up of workhouses, into which the able-bodied " destitute poor " had to go, instead of receiving money and staying in their homes as formerly. Families were broken up (for the sexes were separated in the workhouses), and conditions deliberately made very unpleasant. The idea behind this measure was twofold. It was intended that the granting of help from the rates should bring with it such severe conditions that the poor would do all they could to struggle along.[1] Thus idleness and shiftlessness would be penalized. But, on the other hand, if workers could no longer get their wages made up out of the rates, employers would be obliged either to pay higher wages, or to see their workers go off to the new " workhouses ". To a certain extent these hopes were fulfilled, but at the cost of terrible suffering. Modern legislation has swept away the system of 1834, and tried to solve the problem along other lines.

Abolition of slavery: William Wilberforce (1833)

Another reform which had world-wide importance, was carried through. *Wilberforce*, though not in agreement with the Factory Acts, showed himself one of the most enlightened philanthropists of any age in his struggle for the abolition of *slavery*. If we sometimes wonder whether the world progresses, surely in the freedom given to the slaves we have a proof of real advance. Wilberforce first attacked the horrible slave trade, under which men who were free in their own country were caught, sold, and transported into slavery. This traffic had been prohibited by Great Britain in 1807, and in 1815, at the Congress of Vienna, other European powers including France and Portugal were persuaded to do the same, and Spain forbade the trade after 1820. Slavery, however, still existed in the British colonies of Jamaica and in South Africa. Here there was an economic difficulty, for if the slaves were freed, how would the plantation owners

[1] Conditions were to be " as disagreeable as consistent with health ".

run their estates on a paying basis? Slave labour is usually recognized now as inefficient and extravagant, but the ruin of the owners was a real problem. In 1833 slavery was prohibited in British Dominions and twenty million pounds were given as compensation to the owners. The slaves were to be "apprentices" for a while, but in 1838 they were completely freed. In South Africa the question led to great bitterness, for the Dutch regarded the natives as an "inferior" and therefore subject race. Quarrels over the compensation given led to the Great Trek and to much antagonism between Boers and British.

Tamworth Manifesto (1834)

At this stage William IV dismissed Melbourne's government because he objected to its policy, and decided to call in the Tories. Peel was now head of that party, and already he showed signs that he too was a reformer. He issued what is called his *Tamworth Manifesto* — in an address made at that place, in which he declared that the Tories were fully prepared for reforms, but wished to go gradually. This was important, for it foreshadowed what has come to pass, that the two great parties would unite in social reforms. In 1834, however, the country was not prepared to believe in such a change of Tory policy, and at the election, though the Tories gained 100 seats, the Whigs came back.

Lord Grey, who had piloted political reform, felt himself too old to carry out an ambitious new policy, for he was over seventy, and he insisted on retiring and making way for *Lord Melbourne*.

Lord Melbourne

Melbourne was himself an extremely attractive man. He was very handsome and rich, and had the support of an aristocratic family behind him. He loved power, and his wit and kindliness enabled him to keep his party loyal.[1]

Though himself too cynical to care deeply for reform, his ministry was now to bring in a whole series of great measures.

Two other reforms completed the work of the Whig

[1] Many sayings are recorded of him, one of the best known being his remark to his Cabinet: "It doesn't matter what we say, but we must all say the same thing."

ministry. In 1835 the *Municipal Corporations Act* gave to a large number of towns a uniform type of Town Council elected by all male ratepaying householders. The municipalities could, if they chose, undertake the work formerly performed in some places by special committees, and provide their towns with sanitation, lighting, and other improvements. More was to be done later in this direction (see p. 852). These Councils were elected by a uniform qualification which gave control to the middle classes.

Other reforms

Another step was the setting up of the *penny post*. *Rowland Hill* had for long been agitating for the improvement of the postal service. Expense and delay were still characteristic of the Post Office system at the time of Queen Victoria's accession. The charge for letters, for instance, from London to Windsor was 5*d.*; from London to Cambridge, 8*d.*; and from London to Durham, 1*s.* Letters could not be posted after seven o'clock at night, and their delivery was exceedingly slow.[1] The reforms made were due, above all, to Rowland Hill. He proved that the expense of a letter did not vary appreciably with the distance it was carried, and owing to his efforts the penny postage was at last introduced in 1840. The postmaster-general of the day opposed the change on the ground that, if it was made, the Post Office might have to convey not forty-two millions as they then did, but eight hundred and forty millions of letters annually—a number which would burst the walls of the Post Office. That particular number was exceeded threefold some forty years later, and a faint idea of the volume of business to-day may be gathered from the fact that the total weight of the stamps issued in an average year is almost 400 tons.[2]

Postage

Thus the Whig ministry of William IV made a good

[1] A letter written after 7 p.m. on a Friday night at Uxbridge, and posted at the earliest available moment, would not have reached Gravesend, distant only forty miles, before Tuesday morning.

[2] Or, put in another way, whilst every person received on the average only four letters a year at Queen Victoria's accession, each person on the average now receives 140.

Constitutional effects of reform

beginning in remedying some of the social ills of Britain. Now the King's reign closed, and a new period began. We can note here the change in our Constitution brought about by reform.

The Reform Act of 1832 shifted the balance of political power, in the sense that from then on the landowner was to lose his predominance. Gradually power was to be extended first to the middle classes, then in slow process of time to the working-classes, finally to include women. But reform shifted power in another sense too. The House of Commons became clearly the centre of authority. The House of Lords retained its theoretical rights unimpaired, for the Lords could still throw out and destroy a Bill sent by the Commons, but there was a subtle difference after 1832. In a trial of strength between the two houses, the Commons would win, and they could invoke the co-operation of the Crown, as was to be proved in the twentieth century.

The Crown

The Crown in turn became recognized as possessing influence, but not power. The sovereign must accede to the request of a Prime Minister with the country behind him. The ruler could, and in fact did, possess knowledge and experience which might be useful to a Prime Minister. Queen Victoria's long reign was to give her much more experience than that of her ministers who came and went. The Queen saw all foreign dispatches, she was consulted on all foreign affairs, and she could intervene to avoid mistakes being made. (Once in 1861 she and Prince Albert suggested modifications in a dispatch to the U.S.A.; once she changed a proclamation after the Indian Mutiny.) Thus the Queen showed herself a constitutional monarch, and her influence was accepted and respected. She acted as a link between different parts of her Empire, and, above all, she made the Crown popular.

How necessary this was, the closing years of William IV showed. The King had no children. Princess Victoria was the child of his brother next in age. But there had been no Queen since the days of Anne, and the next royal brother, the Duke of Cumberland, was suspected of being ambitious. Cumberland was hated beyond any individual in England. His arrogance, his cruelty, and his completely reactionary ideas made him detested by all. London was filled with leaflets showing on the one side his harsh repellent features, on the other giving a portrait of the innocent-looking little princess. Had Victoria not been at hand, it is clear that there would have been a major upheaval. Luckily for the nation, Victoria could rally to her all that was best. She was young and she was a girl, and when William IV died in 1837, the nation with joy accepted her as Queen. Better days were hoped for.

CHAPTER 59

QUEEN VICTORIA (1837–1901)

THE FIRST STAGE — PEEL

Queen Victoria and Melbourne

Great Britain must be reckoned very fortunate in the personalities of the people who now came to the fore. The whole country had disliked the " Royal Dukes ", the highly unattractive sons of George III.[1] People welcomed with relief the complete break brought about by the accession of a young girl, though they could not know that in actual fact she was to prove a wise and capable ruler. She was enormously helped, and through her the whole country, by the men who had the task of governing the country and starting the young Queen on her career. First, she had as

[1] But the Duke of Cambridge, grandfather of Queen Mary, made an excellent regent in Hanover until 1837, and on his return to England was, it has been said, " emphatically the connecting link between the throne and the people." The Duke of York, who was commander-in-chief for 10,000 days made the British army, according to Fortescue, its historian, " the most efficient in the world."

her Prime Minister, *Lord Melbourne*. He was very experienced, mellowed by age, and so attractive that the Queen readily made great friends with him. He encouraged her in her wish to do her best for her people, and he helped her to take up the routine of State business. But within two years of her accession, a crisis arose.

Peel and the "Bedchamber" crisis

The Whigs had gone far and fast in their reforms. The freeing of the slaves had led to a violent quarrel with Jamaica, and further trouble came over Ireland. As a result, the Whigs resigned, and *Peel* became Prime Minister as head of the reformed Tory party, now to be called *Conservative*. Peel had two avowed objects; he had to get the country's finances in order, and he meant to maintain the Corn Laws. He was to prove himself a most enlightened patriot, and to sacrifice not only his career, but even his party, to what he believed to be the interests of his country. But unluckily for himself, he had the hard, cold manner which many shy people sometimes put on to cover up their real feelings. This made him difficult to get on with, and very few people either knew him as he really was, or cared for him. The young Queen disliked him at once, and he made mistakes in dealing with her. Thus, at the very beginning (in 1839) he insisted that the Queen should dismiss two of her ladies-in-waiting, who were of the Whig party, and replace them by Tories. Victoria indignantly refused, and as a result Peel refused to form his ministry. This quarrel, known as the *Bedchamber Question*, postponed Peel's ministry for two years, but in 1841 Melbourne retired for good, and Peel's real period of office began (*Note 133*).

Peel as Prime Minister

Robert Peel was the younger son of a wealthy manufacturer. He had an excellent business head, and was a man of wide culture and very great ability.[1] Besides his

[1] When still a boy at Harrow he used to listen to the debates in the House of Commons. At Oxford he had worked very hard, studying just before his examination some eighteen hours a day, and he was the first Oxonian who obtained a double first in Classics and Mathematics; this was not possible before owing to the system of examinations.

intellectual gifts, he had one other valuable characteristic — he had the type of mind which can see that strongly held views may be mistaken. He could in fact change his mind, and therefore his policy. This trait was not only one source of his greatness, but was also the cause of his ultimate fall.

Peel's early career

He had first taken office under Lord Liverpool in 1822, as Home Secretary. Here his great task was the reform of the *Criminal Code* (see p. 760). When Wellington became Prime Minister Peel was his most eminent supporter. He had been strongly opposed to Catholic Emancipation, but the success of O'Connell in Ireland convinced him that he was wrong. He came over to Emancipation and helped Wellington to carry the measure (see p. 764).

Now he was himself head of the Government, and his great abilities had full scope. He was an excellent speaker, and his skill and tact in managing Parliament made him, in Disraeli's opinion, the greatest member of Parliament that ever lived. His immense powers of work, the clearness of his intellect, and his great experience enabled him not only to spend eight hours a day in the House of Commons attending the debates, but also to conduct a huge correspondence as well as to supervise, to an extent which no subsequent prime minister has probably ever attempted to equal, the affairs of the various departments of State. Mr. Gladstone thought Peel's ministry " a perfectly organized administration ". " Neither the Grand Turk nor a Russian despot," said Cobden, the free trader, " had more power than Peel."

Peel's administration has been called " one of the most memorable administrations of the century ", and his chief successes were won in the economic sphere.

Financial measures:

To begin with, Peel saw that more money must be raised by *direct taxation* (*Note 134*). Taxes on goods fall largely on the working-classes, simply because they outnumber the others and therefore are the largest consumers. In Peel's day taxes were levied on almost all goods, and thus the burden of taxation was unjustly distributed (since the well-to-do only paid their taxes on consumption of goods). Peel

(a) Income Tax

imposed an *income tax* of 7*d*. in the £. Pitt's early income tax had been a war-measure, and had been removed when peace came. Now Peel imposed a direct tax on incomes. He then turned to the other side of the question, and set to

(b) Tariffs

work to reduce tariffs. He reduced 1000 duties and abolished over 600, this in itself showing what the burden had been. At once trade revived — for the duties had often made goods so expensive that the market for them ceased, and the gigantic number of officials needed to collect the dues, and to check smuggling, added to the expenses of government. The reduction of duties not only relieved government expenses, but also caused a revival in trade and a general fall in the

(c) Currency

cost of living. Finally, Peel passed the *Bank Charter Act* (1844) to set the currency in order. This Act limited the number of bank notes which could be issued, and allowed the Bank of England to issue these notes only in proportion to the gold reserve it held. This measure prevented inflation, and connected the management of currency, through the Bank, with the Government.

Social reforms:

Now, too, came a series of acts carrying on the reforms of the Whigs in social conditions. *Lord Shaftesbury* (p. 773) had worked untiringly, and the Commission to investigate into the mines now presented its report. So horrifying were the conditions revealed that the conscience of Parliament,

(a) Collieries Act (1842)

and of the nation, was startled. Children under 12 worked for 16 hours a day,[1] and women and children alike acted as beasts of burden, pulling tubs laden with coal. The Act of 1842 prohibited the employment underground of women and girls, and of boys under 10. Inspectors were appointed to see that the law was observed.

The Factory Act of 1847, passed in Russell's

[1] The owners declared that they could not run the mines at a profit without child-labour. Children under 8 did not pull "tubs", but sat opening the doors or "traps" in the workings.

ministry, introduced the Ten-Hour Day. This really applied only to women and persons under 18, but as the work of the factories depended so largely on these two classes of employees, it meant that the factories could not work longer hours, and the men therefore benefited as well.

(b) Factory Act (1847)

Britain thus embarked on a period of reform, and the country seemed to be entering upon an era of prosperity after such troubled years. Less happy was the condition of Ireland, and from the West came trouble which was eventually to overwhelm Peel and his party. Peel had been Chief Secretary for Ireland, and he had been brought much into contact with O'Connell, the " Liberator ", so beloved of the Irish. Through O'Connell's efforts the Roman Catholics had won emancipation (p. 764), but they desired more. When Peel became Premier in 1841, O'Connell hoped the time had come for further concessions. He desired the repeal of the Union, and he wished Ireland to manage her own affairs. He did not want to break away from Great Britain; he was perfectly loyal to the Crown, and he was, indeed, extremely enthusiastic in his devotion to the young Queen. But he wished for an Irish Parliament and objected to the country being ruled by a Viceroy and Chief Secretary who took their orders from the Cabinet and Parliament at Westminster. O'Connell's agitation took the form of great meetings.[1] The movement grew and gathered strength. Peel was resolved to crush it. He "proclaimed" one of O'Connell's largest meetings, and forbade it to be held. O'Connell would never go against the law, and he accepted the prohibition, thus, as it turned out, losing all the support of the more extreme elements. Peel then went further and had O'Connell arrested for sedition (1843). The first trial ended in conviction, and O'Connell went to prison. On appeal, the House of Lords reversed the sentence. O'Connell,

Ireland

[1] No disorder ever occurred at any of these meetings, except that on one occasion the retiring crowd trampled down the stall of an old woman who sold ginger-bread. The meetings generally terminated with enthusiastic cheers for the Queen.

however, was completely broken. He could not win back his power over his people, and died in retirement.

Ireland was to have a strange revenge on Peel.

The Famine (1845)

She was a terribly poor country, and the peasants depended mainly on potatoes for their staple food. Now in 1845 a fearful disease appeared and attacked the crop. Men would go out to their fields and would suddenly catch a faint sickly smell borne on the wind. Then, beneath their eyes they would see their potato plants turning black and sinking away into slime. Starvation fell upon the whole wretched country. The obvious remedy was to import food, but importation was checked by the Corn Laws imposed by Great Britain.

Anti-Corn Law League

In England agitation had already been raised against these laws. *Richard Cobden* had joined with *John Bright* to form a great League, founded in 1839, to press for repeal. Cobden was a hard-headed, clear-speaking manufacturer, an excellent hand at drawing up pamphlets and leaflets, which through the penny post he could distribute up and down the land. Bright was a member of Parliament, and reckoned one of the great orators of the day.[1] These two stirred up one of the most effective political campaigns that has ever been known. Meetings and demonstrations were held all over the country. They could point to two damning facts. The poor needed food, and the price of bread was high, while the landlords profited from the high price of wheat. Plenty of foreign corn could be brought in, but that would mean a fall in the price of corn. On the other hand, Protectionists could urge that mill-owners wanted cheap corn because it meant cheap wages and that therefore they would be able to sell their cotton cheaper throughout the world and so increase their profits. There was, no doubt, exaggeration on both sides. Peel had himself gradually become convinced that the system was wrong and that the Corn Laws should

[1] His speech on the Crimean War contained a phrase which has won immortality: "The Angel of Death is abroad in the land. We can almost hear the beating of his wings."

be repealed. His party, however, was composed of landowners. The Irish famine forced his hand. In that country in 1846, each week nearly 3000 people were dying in the workhouses alone.[1] England herself could send no corn, for her crops were ruined by rain. Cobden said these rains " washed away the Corn Laws ", for Peel hesitated no longer, and decided for Repeal. His Cabinet would not agree, and Peel resigned.

Repeal of the Corn Laws (1846)

There was a brief interval when the Whigs tried to form a ministry, but here again landlords would not agree to the import of foreign corn, so *Lord John Russell* declined office. Peel came back, thinking the way clear. He was mistaken. In his party was the ambitious young Jew, *Benjamin Disraeli*, who led a revolt of the Tories against their leader, claiming that Peel was " betraying the party ". For the landowners it must be said that many honestly considered that repeal would ruin agriculture and therefore injure the country. Peel, however, remained convinced that the Corn Laws were against the interests of the people, and he was firm in his resolve not to let party considerations come before those of the nation. Deprived, through Disraeli, of the support of some of his own party, he turned to those of his opponents, the Whigs, who also favoured repeal. With their help the repeal of the Corn Laws was carried (1846).

Fall of Peel

Peel tried to convince his party that this was both inevitable and part of a comprehensive plan, for not only were the corn duties reduced to 1*s*., but taxes on live stock, meat, cheese, and butter were abolished, as well as duties on many manufactured goods. His efforts were vain. Disraeli pursued him unrelentingly, calling the Government " organized hypocrisy ", Peel himself a " sublime mediocrity ", and finally joined with the Whigs in defeating him over another measure. Peel resigned the Premiership. Lord John Russell and the Whigs came into office, and later (1852)

[1] In the four years 1845–49, the population of Ireland fell through deaths and emigration, by almost 2 million, and decreased from 8,300,000 to 6,600,000.

Lord Derby. This victory of the *Protectionists*, as they called themselves, over the " Peelites " did not last long. The Tory party split could not be healed, and in 1846 the Whigs came into power.

Peel himself continued as a member of Parliament, and his calm acceptance of the situation won him great respect.[1] But a riding accident killed him in 1850, and the fortunes of the party passed into the custody of the young man who had brought about his political eclipse.

Disraeli's triumph over Peel, however, brought disaster to himself, for the split caused in the Tory party had the effect which might have been foreseen. Peel's friends were some of the ablest men of the day. *Gladstone*, the " rising hope of those stern and unbending Tories ", was devoted to his leader, while the tough old *Duke of Wellington* was equally loyal. These men and many others could not forgive Disraeli and would not work with him. So the Tories could not keep a majority, and the Whigs triumphantly returned to power.

CHAPTER 60

WORKING-CLASS MOVEMENTS — CHARTISM: TRADE UNIONISM: CO-OPERATION

The period of Peel's ministry coincided with a time of distress, and the name of the " Hungry Forties " clings to that decade. A strange contrast was being worked out in the lives of the different classes. While exports, shipping, coal and iron production flourished and the manufacturers grew rich, the workers were hit by dear bread due to

[1] Peel himself, in the speech he made when he resigned, summed up the situation: " I leave a name severely censured by many who from no interested motives adhere to the principle of protection; I shall leave a name execrated by every monopolist — but it may be that I shall leave a name sometimes remembered with goodwill in the homes of those whose lot it is to labour and earn their bread . . . when they eat abundant untaxed food, sweeter because it is no longer leavened with a sense of injustice."

bad harvests. The years to 1840 saw an immense transference of population. England swung over from a nation with life based on an agricultural population, to one based on towns. Hence her problems altered and became those of town dwellers and workers. Thus the industrial north experienced a " hunger-revolt ", intensified by the dislike for the new Poor Law. This led to the formation of working-men's associations to " benefit politically and socially and morally the useful classes ", and this in turn gave rise to the interesting movement known as *Chartism* (*Note 131*). This strange interlude, though it ended in failure and was ridiculed at the time, later came to be treated with more respect, for it showed that the working-classes were waking up to the desire for political power and were combining together to obtain it. They realized that the reforms of 1832 had enfranchised only the middle classes, and had done nothing for the workers.

The People's Charter

In 1838, *William Lovett*, a skilled craftsman, drew up the " People's Charter ", which he hoped might be passed by Parliament. This Charter demanded six concessions — manhood suffrage, vote by secret ballot, payment of members of Parliament, abolition of property qualification for members, equal electoral districts, and annual parliaments. Most of these points have now been granted, and, indeed, we now have what the Chartists did not visualize — universal suffrage for both men and women. In those days many, especially amongst the labouring classes, rallied to the democratic ideals of the Chartists. The movement itself had two sides, one of which worked along peaceful lines and helped to win its cause by persuasion. This section was led by William Lovett himself and concentrated on drawing up petitions to Parliament, which invariably rejected them.[1] A more violent section believed that " force "

[1] The first petition (1839) contained 1¼ million signatures and was rejected by Parliament by 255 votes to 45. The second Chartist petition, in 1842, was said to contain nearly 4 million signatures, and was rejected by Parliament by 287 votes to 49.

Feargus O'Connor

alone would win the day, and this was headed by *Feargus O'Connor*.[1] For ten years from 1838, the movement grew steadily and thousands joined it. Then in 1848 revolution broke out all over Europe, and at first it seemed as if England would catch the infection. O'Connor, who had a great gift of wild oratory, raised crowds to frenzy. He became more and more extreme. The Chartists, under his influence, refused to work for the repeal of the Corn Laws, declaring that the men who worked for the League were the manufacturers who wanted the Corn Laws abolished only in order that they could lower wages. Political reform was their goal. A third monster petition was drawn up and was to be presented to Parliament by large deputations from all over the country. It was said to contain $5\frac{1}{2}$ million signatures, and this at a time when many of the working-classes could not read or write. Great expectations were aroused by the idea of this petition, and great apprehension was felt by the Government. The Duke of Wellington collected troops, and when the procession approached Westminster it was forbidden to cross Westminster Bridge. Torrents of rain fell on the disappointed crowds, which melted away without giving any trouble. The hopes of the petitioners vanished as speedily, for when the lists of names were examined, many were found to be forgeries, and the whole thing was brought to ridicule when such names as "Queen Victoria" and "Wellington" were found scrawled in. Yet, though people laughed at the Chartists then, we can perhaps better sympathize with them now. We can see how comparatively little was to be feared from "revolution" in England, for while the rest of Europe saw fighting and bloodshed, our very mild efforts scarcely troubled political life.

Actually the country was settling down to a time of peaceful development. We have learnt that trade follows what economists call a "cycle", that is to say "slumps" are

[1] He spoke, he said, "to the unshaved chins, the blistered hands, and fustian jackets of the genuine working-man."

followed by " booms ", and now the years of depression were followed by prosperity. The repeal of the Corn Laws did not ruin agriculture, for the workers of the whole country were prospering as trade revived, and had more money to spend, while the growth of population increased the demand for goods and for corn. It was the content due to prosperity which made the working-classes lose interest in the Chartists' demand for political reform.

In addition, the Chartists did not appeal to all sections of the working-classes, many of whom found an outlet for their energies in, and hoped for more from, the reforms to be obtained through two other movements, *Trade Unionism* and *Co-operation.*

Robert Owen: Trade Unions

Both these were influenced by the ideas and work of *Robert Owen*, a most remarkable man, and one who has been hailed as the founder of British Socialism. Owen was a Welshman who went to Scotland and there set up a model factory at New Lanark.[1] He came to believe that if men were to combine instead of competing, production could be so developed and distribution of wealth so equalized, that poverty would disappear. He was convinced, too, from his own experience, that decent conditions produced decent citizens. Good wages, good housing, clean conditions of work, and opportunities for education, transformed his own workpeople at Lanark. So he came to preach the idea that good environment and social justice could transform the populace.

He considered that the beginning of this programme must be made by uniting the workers in Trade Unions. This was made legal in 1824, and as the workers realized that the Reform Bill of 1832, which they had so ardently supported, brought no benefit to them, they began to join the Unions in great numbers. In 1833 Owen had the idea of amalgamating all these small bodies, and he there-

[1] He took many of his ideas from *Political Justice*, a book written by Godwin, Shelley's father-in-law.

fore founded the "Grand National Consolidated Trades Union", which was joined by every class of worker from "farm labourer to sweeps and bonnetmakers". Owen thought that the Unions could take over industry and run it co-operatively, and he would not countenance strikes. When the employers, frightened at the new movement, began to "lock out" its members, it all fell to pieces and collapsed. Trade Unionism had to develop along different lines from those of Owen's dreams. Moreover, the employing class were now growing vindictive. They saw, and dreaded, the power which combination might give. They could not now openly forbid men to organize for the improvement of their conditions, but they tried to injure the Unions in another way. In 1834 began a set of prosecutions against men who "took an oath" in support of their Unions.[1] The climax came in the case of the Dorset labourers of Tolpuddle. These men were arrested in 1834 for swearing men into a Union which intended to join the Grand Consolidated. For this they were sentenced to seven years transportation.

The Tolpuddle Martyrs

The other working-class movement which indirectly derives from Owen, had a far more prosperous future. He had begun, in London, an experiment in "co-operative selling". Members of his "society" took to a central "store" the goods which they produced. They were paid for their labour, and the goods were sold at that "cost price" with a small charge for the expenses of running the store. The experiment was a great success for a time, and then failed owing to difficulties over Owen's personality. Yet his idea lived on, and a new start was made by a little group of men in Lancashire. There, at Rochdale, in 1844, a band of weavers joined together to open a little store in Toad Lane. They combined to buy jointly first food, then general goods which they needed. By this joint buying they could get

Co-operation

[1] These actions were taken under an "Unlawful Oaths Acts" of 1797, a panic year.

The Rochdale Pioneers

things cheaper. They called themselves the *Rochdale Pioneers*. The idea spread, and, soon, from simply buying they went on to manufacture. From that handful of men, meeting in a little back lane, came a whole new idea — to produce for use and to do away with private profit. Thus, a " co-operator " paid for his goods, and then received back the " profit " which would have been made by a private trader. (This returned " profit " was called " dividend ".) The scheme worked because the " consumer " for the first time was organizing and controlling " production ". So great has the movement grown that to-day it is reckoned that one-third of the people of England belong to co-operative stores which are managed by the members themselves, and the Co-operative Wholesale Society is the largest single manufacturing concern in the land. The idea originated in England, but it has spread over the whole world.

Prosperity of middle classes

While the working-classes in this way abandoned the political agitation for the Charter and began to work up towards prosperity and to develop their organizing powers, the middle classes also grew more prosperous. From 1848 onwards was a time when everything seemed to expand. Railways were being built and steamships were being developed. Capital was needed, and so investments paid a high rate of interest.[1] So many companies were floated, that not unnaturally there was a proportion of failures, and in order to safeguard investors, the " Limited Liability " Act was passed (1837). This provided that a shareholder in a properly registered company could only lose the actual amount he had invested, and not as hitherto be liable for the entire losses incurred, even if he had only a small share.

In 1851 the general prosperity seemed to be summed up in the *Great Exhibition*, held in Hyde Park.[2] The vast glass

[1] People with money in those days could earn interest at the rate of 20 per cent, for not only was the demand for capital great, but inventions enabled that high rate to be earned through the greater production. Thus we have the Victorian business man heaping up wealth in a way which can hardly be imitated in a period when the rate is not more than 5 per cent.

[2] Amongst the visitors one of the most impressed was Charlotte Brontë.

building which enclosed even the tall trees, was to the mid-Victorian a " fairy palace " of crystal. All England rejoiced in the wealth which the Exhibition displayed, and was proud of the crowds who flocked to visit it even from the Continent.

CHAPTER 61

FOREIGN AFFAIRS — PALMERSTON

Turning now from home affairs, we find that the early Victorian era was equally remarkable abroad. In the first place, Great Britain forged ahead and became a great power, taking a prominent part in foreign affairs. In the second, the Empire expanded on clear and vitally important lines, while to make the whole subject even more interesting, a series of most remarkable men acted as her leaders — *Palmerston*, *Gladstone*, and *Disraeli*, all of whom left very definite marks on our foreign policy.

Palmerston

Palmerston is in many respects a most vivid and amusing personality. He was, in some ways, nearer to the eighteenth than to the nineteenth century in which he actually lived. He was a very cheerful, almost boisterous man, so full of confidence in himself and his country that he never troubled to consider what other men or other nations might think.[1] This gay, flamboyant attitude was characteristic. He was always bold and dashing, often reckless, in his public life. His main policy was to assert the honour and prestige of Britain on all possible occasions. Actually he started his career as a Tory, but he went over to the Whigs over the question of Parliamentary Reform, in which he believed. He supported Catholic Emancipation too, but though he thought

[1] Thus, when he went to visit Queen Victoria after the death of Prince Albert, he arrived at a court where everything literally was draped in black, dressed " in a brown overcoat, light grey trousers, green gloves and blue studs, with his whiskers freshly dyed." His rasping tone in foreign affairs won him the nickname of " Lord Pumicestone ".

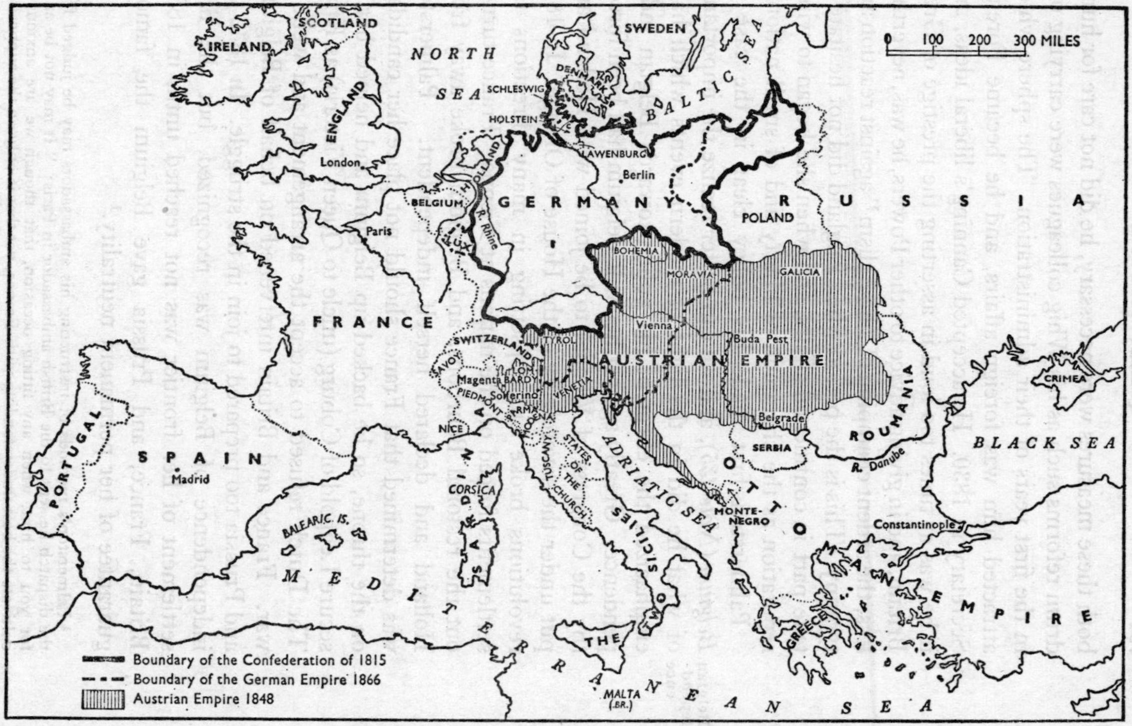

PALMERSTON'S ACTIVITIES IN EUROPE, 1833–1865

both these measures were necessary, he did not care for humdrum reforms such as his Whig colleagues were carrying out in the first years of their administration. The sphere which attracted him was foreign affairs, and he became Foreign Secretary in 1830. He accepted Canning's liberal ideas, and if he was at times too loud in asserting the prestige of Great Britain, and in giving advice to other Powers, he was, nevertheless, the ardent champion of "liberalism" against reaction and tyranny. This is the period when England did not hesitate to take part in continental affairs, and when she began to win a reputation as the champion of liberty and of small nations.

Belgian independence

Palmerston first made his policy clear in the case of *Belgium* (*Note 135*), and we can better realize the importance of what he did in the light of modern events which have emphasized the effect of his policy towards Belgian independence. Greatly against her will Belgium had been forced (by the Congress of Vienna) to be joined with Holland and put under the sovereignty of the House of Orange. In 1830 revolutions broke out, upsetting in many directions the settlements forced on the nations at Vienna. France turned out the restored Bourbons, and Belgium broke away from Holland and declared herself independent. Palmerston was determined that France should not place her candidate on the throne, so he backed up Belgium and helped her to secure Leopold of Coburg (uncle to Queen Victoria) as King. The Dutch refused to accept the arrangement and went to war. France and Britain intervened on behalf of Belgium, and Prussia too prepared to join in the struggle. In 1832 the independence of Belgium was recognized, but the final settlement of her frontier was not reached until, in 1839, Britain, France, and Prussia gave Belgium the famous guarantee of her permanent neutrality.[1]

[1] Palmerston's methods of instructing his ambassadors may be judged from the dispatch he sent to the British ambassador in Paris: "It may not be amiss for you to hint, when any fitting occasion, that though we are anxious to cultivate the best understanding with France, yet that is only on the supposition that she contents herself with the finest territory in Europe, and does not mean to open a new chapter of encroachment and conquest."

Besides Belgium, trouble broke out in *Spain* and in *Portugal.* In Spain the King died in 1833, leaving a young daughter, Isabella, but many Spaniards held that Spain could not be ruled by a woman. A large party therefore supported the late King's brother, Don Carlos, and a fierce civil war broke out. Palmerston supported the young queen, but the struggle was bitter and bloodthirsty, and was prolonged for some years. Eventually the Carlists were defeated, but their cause lingered on, and even 100 years later, in the Spanish war of 1937–39, the Carlists reappeared as a party. Palmerston backed up the young Queen of Portugal too, who was also persecuted by her uncle, Don Miguel. He seized the throne and she fled to Brazil. In 1833 her supporters drove Miguel from Lisbon. Palmerston, acting with France, secured the expulsion of Miguel from Portugal, and the firm establishment of Queen Maria on the throne (1835). In both these spheres he had English opinion behind him. **Spain**

He now embarked upon a more serious quarrel with France, over affairs in the Near East. Turkey was at this period very weak, and the Sultan was threatened by his rebellious vassal, Mehemet Ali, pasha of Egypt.[1] In 1833 Russia stole a march on the rest of Europe, and by sending her fleet to the Bosphorus forced Turkey to sign a pact of " mutual alliance " at *Unkiar Skelessi.* Palmerston was taken by surprise and could do nothing to check Russia's move. In 1840 Mehemet Ali again attacked Turkey. France at first joined with the other Powers, then secretly gave her support to Mehemet Ali, hoping thereby to win influence in Syria. When Palmerston discovered this he made an agreement with Russia, Austria, and Prussia, whereby Mehemet Ali was secured in Egypt, was promised Syria for his lifetime, but was checked in his further designs on Turkey. **Mehemet Ali**

[1] Mehemet Ali was by birth an Albanian, and began life as a trader in tobacco. He made himself master of Egypt during the Napoleonic wars. He was not without humour, and when in 1840 the four Powers deposed him, he announced that this was the fourth time he had been deposed and that he hoped to get over it as well as he had done the other times "with the help of God and the Prophet." And he did, though not so well as he had hoped.

France, which had not been consulted, was furious at being excluded from this settlement. Thiers began to threaten war, and some of Palmerston's colleagues were much alarmed. Palmerston, however, was perfectly cool. He said "One must use firm and stout language to the French government and to Frenchmen." He never believed France would go to war, and he was right. Thiers resigned, France accepted the arrangement, and it was finally agreed that during peace time Turkey should close the Dardanelles to ships of war of all nations. Palmerston's policy of co-operating with Russia and standing firm against France was completely successful, and the fear of war over the Near East countries faded away.

China

His next exploit, however, had less to commend it to his countrymen. The Chinese government was trying to forbid the importation of opium from India. Palmerston acted in the interests, as he conceived them, of British India, which derived large revenues from the trade. A quarrel arose over the question of the recognition by the Chinese of the representative of the British Crown. Palmerston in 1840 attacked China, and eventually forced her to cede us Hong-Kong and to open five other ports to British trade.

Then for a while there was an interval due to the fall of Melbourne's government and its replacement by that of Peel (1840). The new Foreign Minister, *Lord Aberdeen*, was very peaceably inclined, and did not at all wish to follow Palmerston's stormy policy or interfere with other nations. He wanted peace, and he managed to get on good terms with France. He also showed himself conciliatory towards the United States. Indeed, Canada declared that he went much too far in yielding to the Americans.

The Oregon question

There had, for example, been a dispute over the newly developed western territories, and Lord Aberdeen agreed in 1846 to what was called the " Oregon " treaty, by which the U.S.A. kept Oregon and the British received Vancouver and British Columbia.

Lord Aberdeen's conciliatory efforts carried us on quietly until 1846, but in that year Palmerston was recalled to the Foreign Office (in Lord John Russell's cabinet), and almost at once he fell out with France. The King there was now *Louis Philippe*, of the Orleanist side of the Bourbons. He was by way of being a democratic king, and walked about Paris carrying his umbrella like any ordinary French citizen. But he could not resist the temptation to add to the power of his family. Just as Louis XIV had been tempted to try to join Spain to France through marriage, so now Louis Philippe did exactly the same thing. The young Queen of Spain was old enough to marry, and Louis Philippe began to negotiate for her marriage to his younger son. Great Britain, and indeed all Europe, objected to this, for in the nineteenth century, as in the seventeenth, no one wished to see France and Spain united under one dynasty. Great Britain first suggested a Coburg prince as a husband for the Queen. This was withdrawn, but owing to a misunderstanding the French believed that we meant to persevere in this proposal. So the French King went another way to work. The young Queen was married to one of her cousins, a wretched creature who it was believed could never have children, and the Queen's sister was married to Louis Philippe's son. In this way the French thought that ultimately the Orleans family would inherit the throne of Spain. The effect of this disgraceful action was seen at once. Great Britain was furious and broke off her friendly relations with Louis Philippe. His position had always been weak, and the friendship of England had helped to keep him on the throne. Now he had lost that, and the discontented elements in France saw their chance. In 1848 a revolution broke out and he was forced to flee the country.

Palmerston and France

Disturbances began in Italy, then spread to Paris, and then to Germany. All over Europe oppressed people and races took up arms. The Italian States belonging to Austria, Hungary, Austria, all rose against the Emperor. Germany

The Revolutions of 1848

became a country where one petty ruler after another had to fly for his life. Palmerston sympathized with all these revolts, and allowed arms to be sent to insurgents whenever he could. By an irony of fate, while he did his best unofficially to forward these revolutions, he had to welcome as exiles many of the fugitive rulers. Louis Philippe came to end his days in England, and another exile was the Crown Prince of Prussia, who was, however, to return to his country and be the ruler of Bismarck's Germany.

Actually 1848, when people who believed themselves oppressed rose everywhere against tyranny, proved a year of failure. In every country, the democrats failed to unite. The autocratic rulers were able to crush one revolt after another; the Emperor Francis Joseph returned to Vienna, the Czar helped him to crush Hungary. Germany saw her rulers overthrow all the new constitutions. The hope of democratic government vanished.

Palmerston and the Queen

Palmerston had naturally infuriated the absolute rulers by his sympathy with the popular and nationalistic revolutions. His own country had on the whole approved of his policy, especially as it was realized that he made the influence of Great Britain really important abroad.

Now his high-handed ways were to bring their own punishment, and in an unexpected quarter. Queen Victoria was lively, and she had also determination. In 1840 she had married her cousin, *Prince Albert*. Modern historians have emphasized both the great influence Prince Albert had on his wife, and his own marked ability. With her marriage, the young Queen not only learnt to devote herself seriously to the task of taking her share in State business, but she was also helped by a man of great gifts. The Queen, therefore, was not likely to accept Palmerston's way of ignoring the Crown and transacting foreign affairs without due consultation or notification. His habit of withholding dispatches began to cause serious trouble, for the sovereign had a constitutional right to see such documents. The

Queen and her husband, through their vast family connections, had both knowledge of, and influence with, foreign courts. Neither would accept " Pam's " way of ignoring the sovereign. Remonstrances grew more and more vehement, and the Prime Minister, Lord John Russell, shared the royal views.

Don Pacifico (1850)

An international incident now showed the danger of Palmerston's blustering methods. A Jew, born in Gibraltar and therefore a British subject, Don Pacifico, was in business in Athens. Here he got into trouble, and a mob wrecked his house. He appealed to Palmerston on the ground that he could not obtain compensation.[1] Palmerston chose to take the matter up as an affront to Britain. He sent the fleet to seize Greek ships off the Piræus. This attack infuriated Russia (the " protector " of Greece) and France, and was taken to show British diplomacy at its worst.

Louis Napoleon

Then Palmerston went too far. In the great revolutionary year of 1848, France had abolished monarchy altogether and proclaimed the Second Republic. In 1851, *Louis Napoleon*, nephew of the Great Napoleon, by a sudden act of violence overthrew this Second Republic and made himself dictator of France. Great Britain was taken by surprise, but Palmerston, lightly abandoning his Liberal principles, quickly congratulated the ambassador of Louis Napoleon on his success, without even consulting the Cabinet or the Queen. This was too much, and he was promptly dismissed.

The incident in its far-reaching results was like a stone cast into a pond. Palmerston would not recognize his mistake. Instead, he decided on revenge. He headed a revolt against his former colleagues, and returning " tit for tat ", brought about the defeat and resignation of Lord John Russell. The Queen disliked party feuds, and she now used her influence to effect a reconciliation between the sections. She induced the former Tories who had stuck by Peel to join with the Whigs. The " Peelite " leader was *Lord Aberdeen*

[1] He actually asked for £26,000.

who became Prime Minister (1852). Far more important was the young man to whom he gave his first office — *William Ewart Gladstone* became Chancellor of the Exchequer, and one of the greatest men of the period was thus well launched on his Liberal career. Lord John Russell and Palmerston both sank their differences and took office under Aberdeen, Russell as Foreign Secretary, Palmerston as Home Secretary. This famous coalition was to fulfill all prophecies as to the ill-success which usually comes from the union of strange bedfellows, for it was to embark on one of the most futile and disastrous episodes, as far as its results went, of our history — the Crimean War.

CHAPTER 62

THE CRIMEA (1854–56)

Some people have said that the Crimean War (*Note 136*) is important only because it was instrumental in producing Florence Nightingale and her creation of modern nursing. There was more than that, however, in these campaigns. We have learnt perhaps to look at history in a broader light, and now when we think of the war of 1854 we can see certain large movements behind them. For the war was an illustration of the clash of opposing interests which perpetually disturbs south-eastern Europe. It shows the forces in opposition which have had so far-reaching an influence in modern times — the struggle between the empires of Russia, Turkey, and Austria, for the control of that debateable land, the Balkans.[1]

[1] In addition, to those who study it more closely, the Crimea is interesting for its picturesque details. Its battles and its great siege seem the last episode in "old-fashioned" warfare, before the modern armies came on the scene. Socially it was fantastic; smart young women went out to see the operations as though they were going to a picnic, and the romantic young soldiers were inspired to great deeds by *The Heir of Redclyffe*, the novel which everyone in England was reading.

The " problem of the Near East ", as it is called, centres round the *Balkans*. The countries which made up the Balkan Peninsula had for centuries been under the Turk. Serbia, Bulgaria, Rumania, Greece, had all been conquered by the Turk in the fifteenth and sixteenth centuries. In the nineteenth century they began to struggle for independence. British sympathies had been warmly on the side of Greece, and would in general have been against the Turks, had not complications arisen because of Russia. Britain dreaded the power of that vast backward country; Tsardom stood for tyranny and we feared that it stood for aggression. We believed that Russia had designs on our Indian Empire, and we were afraid of her coming down into the Mediterranean and threatening our route to the East.

The problem of the Near East

The crisis which came to a head in 1854 had been foreseen. It was due to the obvious weakness of the Turkish Empire. The Sultan's power had for long been declining, and the question which was being more or less openly discussed was as to who should divide up his territories which included, besides the Balkans, Egypt, Syria, and Palestine. Russia was then ruled by the *Czar Nicholas I*, and he said, " The bear is dying. You may give him musk, but even musk will not long keep him alive." He saw no need for a war, and suggested an amicable division of the spoils. He himself wanted access to the Mediterranean, and he suggested that Great Britain should take Egypt and Crete. France, the third power concerned, was involved through the religious question.

Turkey, the " sick man " of Europe

That question was not the cause of the war, but it was made its pretext. Russia, champion of the Greek Orthodox Church, claimed to be protector of members of that Church who were under Turkish rule, such as the Bulgars. She claimed, too, the right of guardianship over the " Holy Places "; the Church of the Holy Sepulchre in Jerusalem and the Holy Grotto in the Church of the Nativity at Bethlehem. The French, representing the Roman Church, dis-

Religious question

puted that claim. Thus men said the quarrel was over " a Key and a Star " (the Star being the silver star inlaid in the pavement to mark where Our Lord was born, the Key being that for the great door of the church at Bethlehem). Ill-will and rivalry were created, and at length Russia came out with the claim to protect all the Christian subjects of the Turks. France and Great Britain saw in this the true motive of Russian policy. They believed that Russia aimed at political control of the Balkans. Our ambassador in Constantinople was *Lord Stratford de Redcliffe*, who liked and believed in the Turks, while distrusting the Russians. He thought that the Sultan, to win our support, would agree to reform, and he believed that were those reforms granted, it was better that Turkey should retain control than that Russia should be given her chance. He pressed his views very strongly, and unluckily the Coalition cabinet, which really was formed of men whose views did not coincide, could not agree. Thus, no clear lead was given, and the Czar mistakenly thought there was no chance of war. Believing Britain would do nothing, he first occupied the two provinces bordering the Danube, Wallachia and Moldavia, and then sank a Turkish fleet at *Sinope* (1853).

War declared

Instantly Great Britain took alarm, and Napoleon III whipped up war feeling. He did not deliberately promote or desire war, but he had to conciliate public opinion in France by striking dramatic blows, and his need for earning political support made it difficult for him to avoid war if his prestige was at all threatened.

So war was declared and the French and British prepared to invade Russia. The original object of the allies, the expulsion of the Russians from the Danubian principalities, was quickly secured; but it was considered necessary for future security to cripple Russia, and for that purpose to capture *Sebastopol*, the great Russian arsenal and fort in the Crimea, the " very heart ", as it was called, " of Russian power in the East ".

"The history of the Crimean war," it has been said, "is a history of blunders." The great powers of Europe had waged no big campaign since that of 1815, and it is undeniable that the art of war had been somewhat forgotten. The allied forces landed in the Crimea, and won the battle of the *Alma* in September, 1854. But the battle, apart from the courage shown by the soldiers, reflected little credit upon the allies.[1] They besieged *Sebastopol* after a delay which enabled the Russians to improve their defences. In addition, the Russian army was heavily reinforced and was able to attack the allies at *Balaclava*. That battle was famous for one incident. Six hundred men of the "Light Brigade" made, owing to mistaken orders, a magnificent though useless charge down a valley swept by artillery from all sides, and actually managed to reach and temporarily to take possession of the enemy's guns.[2] Less than a fortnight after, the Russians made a determined attack at *Inkerman*. After a desperate battle, fought in a fog — a "soldiers' battle", if ever there was one — the Russians were eventually repulsed (5th November, 1854).

The Battle of the Alma

Balaclava and Inkerman

The allies now, however, had to fight a Crimean winter, and in the middle of November it began. For the next four months the condition of the army was terrible. The cold was intense; food and clothing were alike scanty; the transport animals all perished; the soldiers had to convert themselves into commissariat mules to bring in supplies; and the camp hospitals were miserably provided with necessities for the sick and wounded. As a consequence, the troops were attacked by cholera and scurvy, by dysentery and fever, and at one time the men in hospital were more numerous than those outside it.

The Crimean winter

[1] Lord Raglan, the British commander, was on an exposed position within the enemy's lines where he could not control the battle, whilst the bulk of the French forces went astray, and arrived too late to turn the enemy's left wing as was intended.

[2] See Tennyson's Poems. The criticism of the French commander on the charge of the Light Brigade is well known: "C'est magnifique, mais ce n'est pas la guerre."

The condition of the army was now made clear to the people at home by the dispatches of newspaper correspondents, especially of *The Times*. It became known that incompetence and corruption had left our men without stores, without clothes, without medical care. There were no bandages, no beds, not even soap to keep men and hospitals clean. There were too few doctors, and only a small number of orderlies to care for the thousands of wounded. The men had to be brought across the Black Sea to the hospital at Scutari, and when those of them who survived reached that place, it was to die in hundreds from lack of care.[1] The whole country burst into a flame of indignation. Lord Aberdeen was obliged to resign and Palmerston, whose energy was beyond doubt, became Premier (1855). More important, as it eventually proved, *Florence Nightingale* was sent out to organize the nursing and the hospitals. The career of this remarkable woman was to prove a blessing to the world at large. She was not only the " Lady of the Lamp ",[2] she was also an administrator of outstanding ability and tenacity. Her struggles with the War Office and the Army Medical authorities were to last the whole of her long life, but she emerged victorious. She bullied the officials on the spot, she bullied the officials at home; she overcame the incredible obstruction of the medical authorities; she used the press to get stores and comforts sent from England; she cleaned the hospitals and she saw that the wounded were provided with nurses, with clean beds, with clean shirts. When the war ended she returned to carry on the work, backed by her immense prestige.[3] Nursing was thrown open to women as a skilled profession, hospital hygiene was revolutionized, and not

Florence Nightingale

[1] 420 out of every 1000 died; after Miss Nightingale took charge this appalling figure fell to 22 out of every 1000.

[2] Immortalized as such in one of the most beautiful statues in London, part of the Crimea Memorial in Waterloo place.

[3] She received no official honour, though the Queen sent her a brooch. Only just before her death (in 1910) when she had become almost senile, was the honour of the Order of Merit sent to her.

only army nursing, but civilian nursing as well was transformed. Her career may be reckoned the great factor to be remembered when the battles of the Crimea themselves are forgotten.

The new year, 1855, saw great improvement in the allied position. In February Czar Nicholas died, and was succeeded by Alexander II who wished for peace. Terms could not be arranged, and the allies fought on with vigour until in September they attacked and finally stormed *Sebastopol.* This ended the war, and the *Treaty of Paris* was signed in March, 1856. The allies achieved part of their aim, the Ottoman Empire was " guaranteed " by the Powers, and the Sultan promised reforms. These reforms he never intended or attempted to carry out. As Salisbury ruefully remarked later on, we had " backed the wrong horse ". The provinces of Wallachia and Moldavia were later made self-governing and united to form the State of Rumania. The Black Sea was declared neutral; no warships were to be allowed on it, and no arsenals to be built. This clause was quietly repudiated by Russia later on (1871) when Europe was distracted by other troubles.

The Treaty of Paris (1856)

CHAPTER 63

CHANGES IN EUROPE

PALMERSTON'S LATER FOREIGN POLICY (1856–65)

The Crimean War was the only war in Europe in which Great Britain herself was involved in Queen Victoria's reign, but for the twenty years between 1845 and 1865 the world was very uneasy, and war spread over three continents. Palmerston's career epitomises English policy and brings us into touch with the great movements which were to alter the face of Europe. Two nations, Italy and Germany, were to arise and change the whole of the future.

Palmerston was considered by the nation to have retrieved the country from the disgrace which the early conduct of the Crimean War had brought upon it. He was now, by a sudden freak, to lose his popularity. *Napoleon III* was always regarded by Englishmen as a somewhat doubtful intriguer. In 1858, an Italian, Orsini, threw a bomb at him as he drove to the opera in Paris, and when the pieces of the bomb were examined, it was found that it had been made in London. It was proved, too, that the plotters had held their meetings there. The French Government were highly indignant, and Palmerston wished to placate them. Whereas both court and nation were slightly hostile to Napoleon III, Palmerston in a contradictory way, always admired him, partly because he deeply distrusted the family of Louis Philippe, and he promptly brought in a *Conspiracy to Murder Bill*, making a " conspiracy " punishable by life imprisonment. The country considered this to be giving in to French dictation in British affairs, the bill was rejected, and Palmerston resigned.

For a few months the Tories kept in office, and then a general election showed that the country had forgiven Palmerston's lapse. He came back, and with Lord John Russell and Gladstone formed what was nicknamed the *Triumvirate*. He held office for the rest of his life. During these years he gave a definitely Liberal tinge to our foreign policy, and the time is important for the great changes which took place abroad.

The Triumvirate (June, 1859)

Italy had hitherto been split up among various States and rulers, but during the early part of the nineteenth century her patriots had struggled to give her unity and independence. First the writers had stirred up her spirit,[1] and now came the turn of the soldiers and the statesmen.

Union of Italy

[1] Mazzini, her most famous republican, lived in exile in London and was a close friend of the Carlyles. Mrs Carlyle was devoted to him, but said he had not enough organizing ability to run even a Sunday School.

Cavour, Prime Minister to the King of *Piedmont*, had sent troops to fight in the Crimea in order to bring his country into prominence. Now he had his reward when Napoleon III became Piedmont's ally and sent French armies to drive the Austrians out of North Italy. Public opinion in Great Britain sympathized passionately with the cause of Italian freedom and unity, but Britain did not wish for another war. Two ships of the British fleet were sent to cruise off Sicily at the moment when *Garibaldi* wished to land with his famous *Thousand Republicans* in their red shirts, and though they were actually there to protect the British colony at Marsala, their presence was afterwards taken by the triumphant revolutionaries as a sign of British sympathy. Later Garibaldi transported his men, and conquered all Southern Italy. Palmerston, now Prime Minister, was known to hold the view that the Austrians must leave Italy, and Russell's dispatches showed that the British Government favoured the union of the Kingdom of the Two Sicilies with the new Kingdom of Italy. In this the country agreed, and finally Great Britain recognized with enthusiasm the creation of the new Kingdom of Italy (1860).[1]

The American Civil War (1861–65)

Then came a war for a different form of liberty. In the United States of America, a quarrel arose between the States of the North and those of the South, primarily over slavery, and from that over the right of certain States to break away from the Union. The Southern States had a great many negro slaves, and as settlement spread towards the great territories of the west, the Southerners wished slavery to be allowed there too. This the North opposed. The South then declared that it would break away (secede)

[1] As a matter of fact, Napoleon III had proposed to the British Government to stop Garibaldi from crossing from Sicily to the Kingdom of Naples. Russell, then Foreign Secretary, was not altogether disinclined to this. But Cavour sent Lacaita (an Italian who had become a naturalized British subject) to see Lady Russell, who was ill in bed at the time. He converted her, and she sent down for her husband, who was at that moment discussing affairs with the French ambassador. Believing her to be taken worse, he came up at once to her room. There he was also converted by Lacaita, and all idea of intervention against Garibaldi's further action was given up.

from the Union. Had this been possible, the whole principle of the "United States" would have been wrecked. Civil war broke out, waged on modern, and on horribly destructive, lines [1] (April, 1861). Great Britain suffered greatly through the war, for raw cotton, essential to Lancashire trade, could not come from the Southern States owing to the blockade. Yet though the richer classes in Britain tended to sympathize with the South, as being more akin in its way to "aristocratic" England, the working-classes supported the North, and feeling that the struggle was one for freedom, bore uncomplainingly the real hardship and starvation which resulted from the stoppage of trade.

Neutrality and the "Trent" (1861)

Neutrality always is liable to lead to troublesome incidents, and this American war brought two famous episodes. The first was called the *Trent* incident, and involved the question of the right of one nation to seize nationals or ships of another. Two Southerners were coming to Europe to seek help for their government, and they sailed in a British ship, the *Trent*. The Northerners stopped the ship and took off the two men. Great Britain was enraged and actually sent the Guards to Canada. Palmerston drew up one of his most aggressive dispatches, but the well-known action of the Prince Consort, in suggesting that the dispatch should be redrafted in a milder form, made it possible for the U.S.A. to give way and send back the two Southerners.

The "Alabama" (1862)

The other affair was even less satisfactory. A ship called the *Alabama* was built at Birkenhead to be used by the South as an armed raider, and though the British Government was informed of the fact, it delayed seizing the vessel. In consequence, it got safely to sea, and for two years did great damage to the shipping of the Northern States. The U.S.A. demanded compensation, and years later (in 1872) Gladstone, for the sake of friendly relations, paid the relatively enormous compensation of over three million pounds.

Though these episodes made tempers very hot, they did

[1] Through battle and disease over a million men were killed and crippled.

not lead even to within measurable distance of war. Much more dangerous was Palmerston's policy towards the newly arising power of *Prussia*.

Germany, like Italy, had for centuries consisted of a collection of small States. Now Prussia was forging ahead under the great statesman *Bismarck* who aimed at uniting Germany under Prussia, and meant to do this through force, or as he put it "blood and iron." He had first to check the power of *Austria*, for Austria would have liked to keep Germany under her own control. Bismarck decided to begin by winning the friendship of Russia. In 1863 the Poles under Russian domination rose in revolt. Since 1815 they had entirely lost their independence. *Poland* remained crushed and divided up between Russia and Prussia, but now she made a desperate effort for freedom. Palmerston wished to help, and sent notes protesting against the Russian treatment of the Poles. But he had no real support at home; the court wanted peace, and so did the Cabinet. Though Great Britain would not fight on behalf of Polish liberty, Bismarck showed himself fully prepared to fight against it. For one thing, he was afraid that if Russian Poland became free, Prussian Poland would also revolt. For another, he wanted to ingratiate himself with the Czar. So he sent an army to the frontier, though Russia succeeded in crushing the revolt without German aid.

Rise of Prussia: Poland

Next came a more ominous step. *Denmark* had during four centuries been connected through her monarchy with the two little duchies which formed her southern border with Germany, *Schleswig* and *Holstein*, the King of Denmark being also Duke of the two Duchies. Now there arose a dispute as to who was the real heir to the duchies. Denmark claimed them, but so did Prussia and Austria, for Holstein had belonged to the German Confederation.[1] Great Britain sympathized with Denmark, a small country trying to hold

Schleswig-Holstein (1863)

[1] Palmerston said that only three people ever understood the details of the question — the Prince Consort, who was dead; a Danish statesman who was mad; and himself.

her own against two great ones, and Palmerston led the Danes to believe that Britain would support them with arms if necessary. They accordingly refused to give in to Prussia and Austria and declared war. It then transpired that Palmerston was speaking only for himself, and that Britain had no intention of going to war on behalf of Denmark. The Austrians and Prussians accordingly proved easily victorious, and Denmark not only had to abandon her claims to the duchies, but had also to pay a very heavy indemnity. Bismarck had fought the war partly because the acquisition of Schleswig would enable Prussia to build the Kiel Canal, partly as one further step in his scheme for the union of Germany. He now saw clearly that Britain would not interfere on the Continent. The days, indeed, when Palmerston could interfere here and there, were done. His policy over Schleswig-Holstein was reckoned " Pam's greatest diplomatic defeat ", and " the fall of his prestige was almost total ". In 1865 he died, well over eighty years of age. His policy was called by his opponents one of " meddle and muddle " and of " senseless menaces ", yet his countrymen loved him, and felt a regret that under him Great Britain had not taken a more leading part in European politics.

At this point we must turn to India and see what events had passed there, for India was the scene of great upheavals.

CHAPTER 64

INDIA (1823–1858)

After 1823, India was under the control of Great Britain, and part of the country, notably *Madras* and *Bengal*, was directly governed through the great *East India Company* (*Note 137*). Other territories remained as native States, but recognized British authority in certain respects; the chief of these were *Hyderabad*, *Mysore*, and the group of States comprised in the territory called *Rajputana*, such as *Udaipur* and *Jaipur*. To the east lay *Burma*, and with this country a war was fought in 1824 which ended in Britain acquiring some territory, notably *Assam*. **Assam (1824)**

It was from the west, however, that trouble really threatened. There, across the north-western frontier lay *Afghanistan*, a wild mountainous district with a very warlike, independent people. Moreover, Great Britain believed that Russia, whose Asiatic Empire gave her an interest in India, was determined to stir up the Afghans and use them to disturb British rule. Great Britain aimed therefore at keeping the Afghans friendly, so as to checkmate Russian plans. In the year of Queen Victoria's accession, the Shah of Persia attacked Afghanistan, and it was known that he had been encouraged to do so by Russia, while in the next year (1838) Russian agents appeared at Kabul in friendly negotiations with the ruler, *Dost Mohammed* — a usurper, who had successfully overcome opposition and seized power. **Afghan wars (1838)**

A new Governor-General of India, *Lord Auckland*, was appointed in 1835. He was afraid of Russian aggression and he thought that matters had gone too far, so he decided on armed interference. His policy, which was approved by Palmerston and the Home Government, proved most disastrous, for it was both reckless and based on faulty strategy. He dispatched a British army, which took Kandahar and Kabul (1839), captured Dost Mohammed, and put on the throne *Shah Shuja*, the prince whose place had been usurped. The British forces remained for two years, during which the Afghans, though sullenly hostile, seemed crushed, but suddenly they rose (1841), murdered the British agent, and captured all the military stores. Deprived of their munitions, the British troops were really helpless, and after negotiating with Dost Mohammed's son, they decided to accept his offer of a safe-conduct and leave the country. The army of 4000 men, with 12,000 " camp-followers ", accordingly set off, in the depth of winter, to make its way down to the *Khyber Pass* **Lord Auckland**

and so to India. Such a journey in those days was a fearful undertaking, and thousands died of cold and hunger, while others were set upon by the Afghans hiding in the hills Only one man, *Dr. Brydon*, came safely through, and eventually reached Jalalabad, where there was a British garrison, with the news that every other soul had perished. The Afghans, following up their success, advanced and besieged Jalalabad itself.

Such a disaster was a severe blow to British prestige, and it was decided that it must be avenged. Two armies were sent from India (1842) one of which marched through the Khyber, relieved the garrison at Jalalabad, and went on to take Kabul, while the other went to Kandahar. After restoring Shah Shuja, these armies left, but the futility of trying to force on the Afghans a ruler who depended on the absent British, was promptly shown. No sooner had the British forces departed than the Afghans murdered Shah Shuja and restored Dost Mohammed. Nothing had really been accomplished.

The Afghan wars led to another and smaller campaign which did not reflect credit on British leaders. *Sir Charles Napier*, one of the people concerned, said: "We have no right to seize *Sind*, yet we shall do so, and a very advantageous, useful, and humane piece of rascality it will be." Sind lay at the mouth of the Indus, and was on friendly terms with Afghanistan. Its rulers, the Amirs, supported and encouraged Dost Mohammed. A treaty existed between the Amirs and Great Britain, but the British declared that this had been violated. Napier with a British force attacked and won two victories, and as a result, Sind was annexed.

Sind (1843)

Next to Sind lay the larger State of the *Punjab*, inhabited by the *Sikhs*, a fierce and warlike religious sect.[1] The

[1] The Sikh religious movement was founded about 1780, and was a reforming movement of some Punjab Hindus against what they thought were the polytheistic and idolatrous beliefs of their ancient religion. It spread rapidly, and now numbers about 3 million. "Sikh" means "learner" and these people may be thought of as "non-conformist" Hindus.

turbulence which reigned in the Punjab finally burst out into an attack on the British; a Sikh army crossed the river Sutlej and invested Ferozapore. In the war which followed (1845), the British had to fight hard, for the Sikhs were the best fighters in India, and their religious zeal caused them to be compared with Cromwell's " Ironsides ". The Sikhs were fought to a standstill, and in three weeks were defeated in a series of bloody battles, including *Firozshah* and *Sobraon*. Peace was made, but this did not last, and two years later came the second war. In this the British were commanded by *Sir Hugh Gough*. Many people thought that his tactics were faulty, for he insisted on frontal attacks and bayonet charges and apparently did not believe in the use of artillery or in out-flanking the enemy. He did not realize that the Sikhs could stand up to such fighting, and at *Chilianwala* the Sikh position was taken by the British only after the loss of over two thousand men, several guns, and the colours of their regiments — a serious matter in those days. Gough was later superseded, but before this happened he showed that he had learnt something, for at *Gujerat* he did use his artillery, and the Sikhs, after " standing two hours in hell " under the heavy fire of 84 guns, had to meet a general advance which gave victory to the British. The Punjab was then annexed (1849).

Punjab: 1st Sikh war (1845)

2nd Sikh war (1848)

Some may deplore the military conquest of these areas, but at least we can see that good ultimately came to them through British rule. Sind had not been a happy or prosperous country, and the Punjab had been the scene of perpetual strife. The two *Lawrences*, Henry and John, were sent to govern the Punjab and did everything possible to pacify the country, by reforming the laws, lowering taxation, and restoring prosperity. The full justification of British rule in these provinces was seen when the Punjab stood by the British in the great storm which soon burst upon India.

Lord Dalhousie, who had followed Hardinge in 1848, is one of the great men of the nineteenth century, and he is made

Dalhousie (1848–56) more interesting by the fact that his policy, though in some respects so well-intentioned, is yet considered to have brought such evils in its train (*Note 137*). He sums up in a sense the good side of British policy in India, in so far as he aimed at increasing the material prosperity and adding to the welfare of the people. Yet he wrought them up to a state which ended in revolt.

Dalhousie was clear in his own mind. He lived in a period when Englishmen did not doubt that British rule was a blessing, and that it was in the interests of mankind that other races should come under it. He had, therefore, no scruples when in 1852 troubles in *Burma* led to a second war and the annexation of Lower Burma. Even more important was the case of *Oudh*. There the government of the native rulers had led to great disorder and great misery, and the Nabob had been repeatedly warned that he must reform. The East India Company was still the governing body of British India, and the British Home Government and the Company decided that Oudh ought to be annexed (1856). This was accordingly done and all the valley of the Ganges was placed under the Company.

His annexations

Dalhousie then took a step which in the eyes of Indians was particularly unjust. The Indians had a well-defined rule whereby Hindu princes with no direct heirs might adopt boys to succeed them. Such adoption, though not recognized in Europe, was perfectly usual and legal in the East. Dalhousie refused to admit such a system. He laid down the rule that where a ruler had no children, his domains must at his death " lapse " to the " paramount power ". This in olden days had been the Mogul Empire, and Dalhousie insisted that the East India Company had all the rights of the former Moguls. Accordingly, he took possession of seven little States in Central India, and in view of this no native ruler felt himself secure. It should be noted that it was in these very districts—in Oudh, the Ganges Valley, and Central India — that discontent was later to swell into revolt.

The Doctrine of " Lapse "

The justification Dalhousie gave for this whole policy of bringing nations under British rule, was that thereby the native actually gained. He tried to make that claim a reality by his reforms. Already something had been done by the man who was Governor some time before Dalhousie — *Lord William Bentinck*, who had tried to bring about certain social improvements (1828–35). He had put down the horrible sect of *Thugs*, who went about secretly murdering people by strangulation, believing that in so doing they were serving their particular religion.[1] He had forbidden *suttee*, or the suicide forced on Hindu widows, whom custom compelled to burn themselves on their husband's funeral pyre.[2] The position of widows was a dreadful one in India, and this reform was accepted with comparative calm. Bentinck was a great believer in education, and to him should be given the credit for encouraging the education of the Indians. He considered, too, that they should share in the administration, and he did his best to give them posts in the service of the Government.

Bentinck's earlier reforms

Thugs put down

Suppression of suttee

Education

Dalhousie warmly approved of this policy, and he determined to carry it still further. He did his best to encourage education, and he reformed the administration. He saw, moreover, that the curse of India was her poverty, and he genuinely wished to hurry forward the development of the country. Clearly the means of communication must be improved, and so roads were built, notably one great highway running from Calcutta right up to Peshawar on the frontier, and railways. The telegraph was introduced, and a good postal system organized, run so efficiently that it was cheaper than the penny post of England. Next came the building of canals, and of great water-works to irrigate the country. All these were measures which were meant to bring prosperity, and Dalhousie believed that he was doing

Improvement of Communications

[1] These wandering bands were said to have caused the deaths of thousands in every district.

[2] During one year in Bengal alone no less than eight hundred widows were burnt to death.

nothing but good. He left the country in 1856, confident that he had served India well.

But the very reforms which he had pressed forward were soon held responsible for the disaster which was to follow. Dalhousie, men said, had gone too fast. The Indians were too backward to understand what these innovations meant — they believed that the British only wanted to consolidate their hold, and above all that they were aiming at the overthrow of the Hindu religion. Thus the new railways upset the system of caste, for different castes had to travel in the same carriage. Superstition reinforced religious beliefs, for an old prophecy said that the British rule would last for 100 years after Plassey, and that date had now come. Some even thought the wind whistling through the telegraph wires was "Bad Magic".

Dis-content aroused

Again, the richer classes were antagonized, for in Oudh the British had upset the system of land tenure, and all rulers naturally opposed the doctrine of "lapse".

Finally, the discontented were given courage by the decline in British military prestige. The disaster of the Afghan massacre had made a great impression; the tough resistance of the Sikhs had taught Indians that British troops could be faced in fair fight; and the stories of British sufferings and incompetence in the Crimean War had now filtered through to India.

The way was thus prepared for trouble, and in 1857 the Mutiny broke out. It must be clearly understood that it was in the strictest sense a "mutiny"; that is to say, it was a military revolt. The native soldiers, the Sepoys, mutinied; the people as a whole took no part.[1] The actual pretext was the introduction of a new weapon, the Enfield rifle. The cartridges had to be bitten before use, and they were smeared with grease. Like wildfire a report spread that the grease was the fat of the cow (sacred to the Hindus) and

The Mutiny (1857)

[1] Thus some authorities deliberately prefer to call the whole movement the "Sepoy Mutiny".

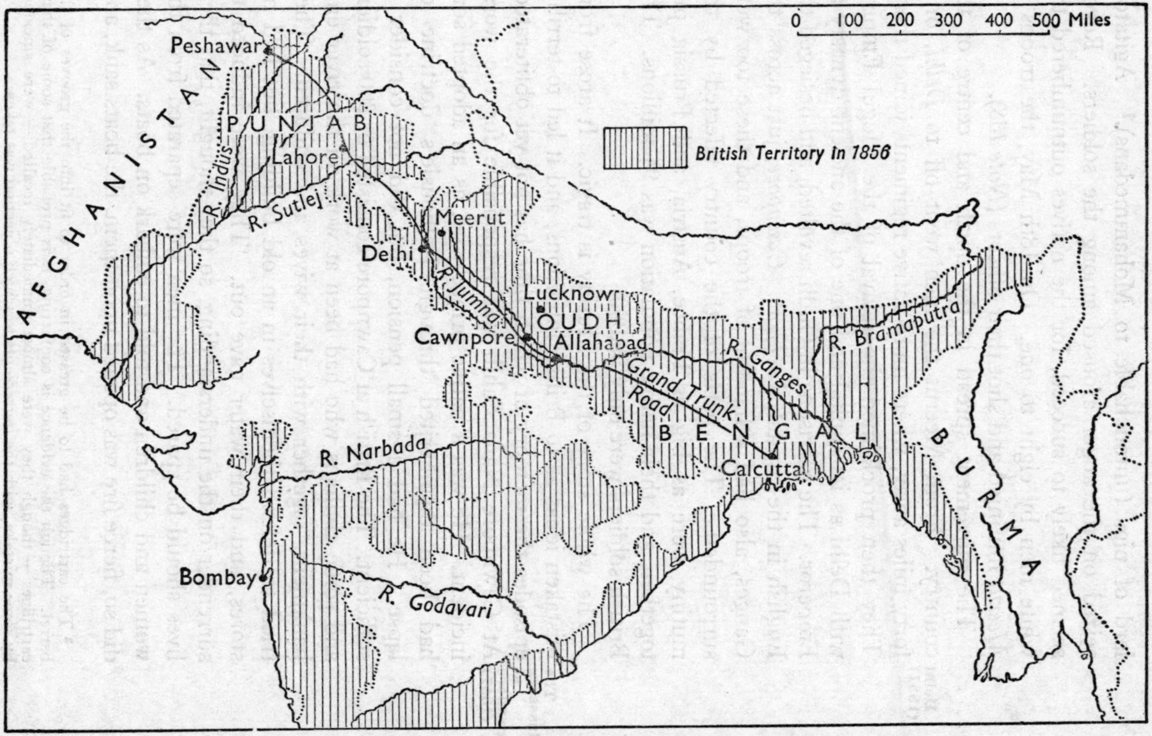

THE INDIAN MUTINY

lard of pigs (untouchable to Mohammedans).[1] Agitators seized on the anger aroused among the soldiers. Revolt seemed likely to succeed, for the natives outnumbered the white men by eight to one. On 18th May, the troops at *Meerut* mutinied and shot their officers (*Note 138*).

Delhi (1857)

The movement spread in the north and centre of the country. From Meerut the men went off to *Delhi*, only forty miles away, where more native regiments joined them. They then proclaimed the revival of the Mogul Empire, with Delhi as its capital and one of the ancient dynasty as Emperor. The garrisons in Oudh revolted, and besieged the English in the capital, *Lucknow*. *Cawnpore*, just across the Ganges, also had a handful of troops, and these too were surrounded. The parts of the country affected by the mutiny were as big as France, Austria, and Prussia put together, and their native population was 94 millions. The British soldiers were only 39,000.

The Massacre at Cawnpore (1857)

The whole story of the Mutiny is tragic. It arose from mistaken ideas as to British intentions, and it led to terrible episodes the memory of which time has not yet obliterated. At Cawnpore Nana Sahib was responsible for the worst incident. He was a native prince who, as an adopted son, had been disinherited through Dalhousie's doctrine of lapse. He had a small pension, but did not consider it sufficient. The British at Cawnpore consisted of 200 soldiers and some civilians who had been at work on the river embankment, together with their wives and children. They tried to defend themselves in an old building, but had no stores, and their water gave out. They were induced to surrender on the understanding, so they thought, that their lives should be spared. The men were separated from the women and children and told to embark on boats. As they did so, fierce fire was opened upon them, the boats sank, and

[1] The cartridges had to be greased in order to fit into the grooves of the barrel. Though the evidence is conflicting, it is probable that some of these cartridges — though they were almost immediately recalled — were smeared, by some mistake, with the ingredients to which objection was taken.

practically all were killed. The women and children were taken to an empty building, and a few days later all were killed and their bodies thrown down a well. The relieving force reached Cawnpore the very day after this massacre. Nana Sahib fled to the jungle and was never heard of again.

Other famous stories are perhaps preferable to remember, for they show the heroism which accompanied the mutiny. *Lieutenant Willoughby* at Delhi knew that his little force of eight men could never hold the great arsenal. So he blew it up and the defenders with it, rather than let the mutineers capture the great stores. *Havelock* marched, in a desperate effort to save Cawnpore, 126 miles in 9 days, in the height of the Indian summer, fighting four actions on the way. *Sir Henry Lawrence*, with 1000 British troops and 700 loyal Sepoys, held the residency at *Lucknow* against huge forces of rebels armed with artillery, who could come up to within 15 yards of the crumbling walls and makeshift defences. The garrison held out for 87 days, though Lawrence was killed at the outset of the siege. In September Havelock and *Outram* fought their way through with reinforcements, and the struggle went on for another two months, until fresh help came and the British could finally withdraw. At Delhi the " Ridge " was occupied by 4000 British who then attacked over 30,000 Sepoys holding the city itself.

Relief of Lucknow

Moreover, the Mutiny was marked by deeds which showed that in many cases the Indians stood by the British. Besides the loyal Sepoys at Lucknow, others fought side by side with their European officers at Delhi. The " Guides " and the Gurkhas there fought against the rebels and lost half their men. The Sikhs came in force from the Punjab, under Nicholson, to aid the British in the storming of Delhi. The Indian troops in Bombay and Madras refused to join in the revolt. The Indian princes either remained neutral or gave active support to the British.

Loyal Indians

Within three months the worst was over, and fresh troops (under *Sir Colin Campbell*) arrived from Britain. By

November, Delhi had been recaptured from the mutineers and the Residency of Lucknow relieved. The Mutiny was finally stamped out in Central India, and though small groups of mutineers had to be tracked down, danger was at an end (1858).

" Clemency " Canning (1856–62)

Now came the question as to what should be done. Actually the Governor-General, *Lord Canning*, was resolved that there should be no severity. He insisted on mercy, and though men called him at first mockingly " Clemency " Canning, his policy was clearly right. He was backed up too by Queen Victoria, who insisted herself on modifying in a gentler sense the words of a proclamation.[1] The Queen had been as deeply moved as anyone by the horrors of the Mutiny, but she felt herself to be indeed the sovereign of " more than a mixture of Eastern peoples ". She showed her attitude clearly when in 1877 she accepted the title of Empress of India.

Results: End of East India Company

The first and most striking result of the Mutiny was the ending of the rule of the East India Company. It was only too clear that no corporation was able to rule such territory, and the control of India passed direct to the British Government. The Secretary of State for India, with Cabinet rank, became responsible, with a council of advisers. A Viceroy represented the sovereign in India, with councils to advise him there.

The Sepoy army had hitherto been the army of the Company, and it now became part of the British forces, in which the proportion of white troops to coloured was to be one in five. Finally, it was clearly realized that more attention must be paid to the ideas and feelings of the Indians. The doctrine of " lapse " was given up and greater efforts were made to give India peace.

No more wars were to take place with India itself, but

[1] This eventually ran: " We desire no extension of the present territorial possessions . . . and our subjects of whatever race or creed shall be freely and impartially admitted to office in our service."

further trouble came in the countries beyond the borders, both east and west.

In the east, Upper Burma was annexed in 1885. In the west the trouble with the *Afghans* recurred in 1879, when another British resident was murdered at the court of the Amir. *Lord Roberts* marched to Kandahar from Kabul, and finally the British Government decided to pay the ruler of the State an annual subsidy to ensure his friendliness. As before, their true object was to check the Russians, but with the passing of time, the political situation in Europe had changed, and the distrust of Russia was replaced by fear of a common enemy. So with the opening of the 20th century Britain and Russia found themselves drawing together, and the North-west Frontier ceased to be a source of contention.

Burma (1885)

Afghanistan (1879)

As a result of the Mutiny, and of a general change in public feeling, it was realized that more must be done to improve social conditions in India. Plague and famine were the scourges which the British tried to eliminate. The Indian medical service was developed to deal with plague, and when once medical science discovered how it was carried (by rats), it became easier to prevent the fearful epidemics. As to famine, here Dalhousie's reforms at length justified themselves. When the crops failed in India, corn and rice could be imported and brought to stricken areas by the railways. As irrigation improved the cultivation of the fields, so the yield improved, and the government could and did undertake vast works to help India to feed her millions. Education, the crying need of India, where there are many millions of illiterates, was and must be a difficulty, for the cost is enormous, and so poverty-stricken a country can scarcely bear any addition to its taxation. After 1828 the British Government had tried to encourage education and set up State-aided schools. In these schools English was the common language used (for different races use different languages in various parts) and acted as a unifying force.

Social measures in India

NOTES ON PERIOD TEN (1815-1867)

BRITISH SOVEREIGNS

George III (1760–1820)

George IV (1820–1830)

William IV (1830–1837)

Victoria (1837–1901)

IMPORTANT FOREIGN RULERS

France:	Louis XVIII (1814–1824)
	Charles X (1824–1830)
	(*Revolution of* 1830)
	Louis Philippe (1830–1848)
	(*Constitutional King*)
	Second Republic (1848–1852)
	Napoleon III (1852–1870)
	(*Second Empire*)
Russia:	Nicholas I (1825–1855)
	Alexander II (1855–1881)
Emperor of Austria:	Francis II (1792–1835)
	Ferdinand (1835–1848)
	Francis Joseph (1848–1916)
Spain:	Ferdinand VII (1814–1833)
	Isabella II (1833–1868)

BRITISH PRIME MINISTERS

Liverpool:	(1812–1827)
Canning:	(1827)
Goderich:	(1827–1828)
Wellington:	(1828–1830)
Grey:	(1830–1834)
Melbourne:	(1834)

PEEL:	(1834–1835)
MELBOURNE:	(1835–1841)
PEEL:	(1841–1846)
RUSSELL:	(1846–1852)
DERBY:	(1852)
ABERDEEN:	(1852–1855)
PALMERSTON:	(1855–1858)
DERBY-DISRAELI:	(1858–1859)
PALMERSTON:	(1859–1865)
RUSSELL:	(1865–1866)
DERBY:	(1866–1868)

NOTE 120. — CHANGES IN AGRICULTURE

The eighteenth century saw *enclosure movement* — under which the great landlords enclosed common lands. (7 million acres enclosed.) Done with great harshness and unfairness, as commoners had no power and were unable to oppose Bills.

Results.

1. Small peasant owners were wiped out, Britain lost her small landowning class. Land held by great landowners and leased to large farmers with capital.
2. Agricultural labourer suffered very much. His supplementary earnings gone, and he could no longer use commons for cows, sheep, goats, or pigs, nor get fuel and bedding for his animals. Whole standard of life sank.
3. Agricultural labourers forbidden to combine and "revolts" treated with terrible severity. (Tolpuddle martyrs 1834.)

But *Agricultural methods improved.* Enclosures enabled the big farmer to improve his land. Complete change in agricultural methods.

Jethro Tull (1674–1741) invented method of sowing in rows. (Tull's Hoe.)

Lord Townshend (1674–1738) developed rotation of crops, instead of leaving a field fallow, and introduced turnips, which enabled cattle to be fed during winter, not slaughtered.

Robert Bakewell (1725–1795) improved breeding of sheep, helped by Townshend's winter feeding.

Thus meat supplies were greatly increased and this made possible the feeding of the town populations which were now springing up. Had it not been for the improvement in agriculture there would not have been food for the new towns.

NOTE 121.—THE INDUSTRIAL REVOLUTION

Began in eighteenth century, but full effects developed in early nineteenth century.

1. Machinery in the Textile Trades.

(*a*) 1733. *Kay* invented the flying-shuttle: revolutionized weaving.

(*b*) 1764. *Hargreaves* invented the spinning Jenny: revolutionized spinning of yarns.

(*c*) 1769. *Arkwright* invented spinning through rollers worked by water-power.

(*d*) 1776. *Crompton's* mule produced fine yarn by water-power.

(*e*) 1785. *Cartwright* invented power-loom for weaving.

Thus, both spinning and weaving were now on a mechanical basis.

2. Iron and Steel. New " machines " needed iron and steel.

1783. *Cort* discovered new method of puddling iron. Coal and coke used for smelting. This made production of iron easier.

3. Steam.

(*a*) 1782. *Watt* made a *steam-engine* which was developed and could be used to drive machinery.

(*b*) Ships driven by steam invented. *Comet* (1812) launched on the Clyde.

(*c*) *Stephenson*, in 1814, invented the first locomotive, and railways then followed. 1825: First railway opened—*Stockton and Darlington*.

4. Canals and Roads.

(*a*) Canals built first in 1759. *Brindley* the great engineer. Built the Manchester and Bridgewater Canal (1759–1761).

(*b*) Roads improved, by *Macadam* (1811), *Telford*, and *Rennie*.

5. Mines.

Great demand for coal, but use of machinery in mines (first steam-engine used in mines) and *Davy's safety lamp* enabled miners to work under new conditions with more safety (1815).

NOTE 122.—SOCIAL DISCONTENT IN ENGLAND (1815–1820)

1. Distress due to the long Wars.

(*a*) Return of soldiers and sailors, needing work.

(*b*) Continent now could get raw materials more easily, and began to manufacture for itself.

(*c*) War expenditure, being unproductive, means the destruction of capital, and hence war is followed by trade " slumps ".

(*d*) Heavy taxation inevitable, but Parliament acted on wrong principle, for income-tax removed and burden fell on trade and consumers through heavy duties on goods.

2. **Distress due to Industrial Revolution.**

(*a*) Innovation of machinery destroyed " domestic " industry, and *at first* many thrown out of work, e.g. hand-weavers.

(*b*) Workers forbidden to combine and so could not get higher wages. (Combination Acts, 1799 and 1800. Repealed, 1824.)

NOTE 123. — POLITICAL CAUSES OF DISCONTENT (1815–1820)

Repressive Policy of the Government.

(*a*) Habeas Corpus suspended (1817).

(*b*) *Six Acts* (*Gag Acts*), two of which forbade freedom of speech and public meetings; passed by Castlereagh in 1819–20:

(i) Act to suppress unauthorized military drilling.

(ii) Act prescribing heavier penalties for " seditious libels ".

(iii) Act putting Government Stamp on newspapers and other periodicals. (These two Acts checked freedom of the press.)

(iv) Act to prevent " seditious meetings ", i.e. stopped freedom of speech.

(v) Act authorizing magistrates to " seize arms ", i.e. check on personal liberty.

(vi) Act to prevent delay in the administration of justice in crimes of violence.

NOTE 124. — AGITATION IN ENGLAND FOR REFORMS

1811. Luddite Riots against new machines.

1. **Action of Reformers.**

Radicals, such as *Hunt* and *Bentham,* demanded political reform.

1816. *Spa Fields,* demand for universal suffrage. Riots also in Glasgow and in Midlands.

1817. March of *Blanketeers* from Manchester to London. Stopped by Government; the Blanketeers came bringing only a petition.

1819. *Peterloo,* or " Manchester massacre ". Crowd went to hear " *Orator Hunt* ", attacked by soldiers on order of magistrates.

2. **Policy of Government towards Agitation.**

(*a*) Purely repressive till 1822.

(i) Political agitation repressed (see note 123) under Gag Acts.

(ii) Social agitation for better conditions repressed under Pitt's earlier Combination Laws.

(*b*) After 1822 the Government went in for a policy of *social reforms.*

(*c*) After 1830 the Whigs demanded *political reform.*

NOTE 125. — CASTLEREAGH'S FOREIGN POLICY

1. **During the latter part of the Napoleonic Wars.**

Castlereagh (1769–1822) was responsible for the struggle against Napoleon.

He strongly supported the *Peninsular War*. Sent Walcheren expedition, the failure of which was not due to him (1809).

He urged on formation of 4th Coalition, which finally crushed Napoleon (1812).

Main idea, to be "non-interventionist" on the Continent; to let nations manage their own internal affairs; to refuse to join in the repressive policy of the Holy Alliance (1815).

2. **At Congress of Vienna** (1814).

Castlereagh and *Wellington* represented Great Britain.

(*a*) Stood for liberal policy towards France. Refused to let Prussia take *Alsace-Lorraine*.

(*b*) Insisted France must be recognized as Great Power. Objected to interference in affairs of other countries. Wished to support constitutional government (as opposed to either republican or autocratic) wherever it had been set up. Insisted Czar should guarantee a constitution for Poland.

3. **Refused to join** *Holy Alliance* of Russia, Prussia, and Austria to suppress revolutionary ideas wherever they might appear (1815).

4. **The Congress System,** i.e. periodical congresses of the nations, to be held, with idea of maintaining peace in Europe.

Castlereagh agreed to idea, but when he found the "Congress" only supported tyrannical government, he objected, and in the end withdrew.

Thus at *Troppau* (1820) the Great Powers now wished to put down revolts in Spain, Naples, and Portugal; Castlereagh objected and said they were "domestic" affairs.

1821. At *Laibach* he only sent an observer to the Congress, and ultimately after his death Great Britain withdrew from the Congress system.

NOTE 126. — THE TORY REFORMERS (1822–1832)

Reign of George IV

Canning, Huskisson, and *Peel* all reformers. (The old die-hards and reactionaries, *Sidmouth* and *Castlereagh,* were gone.)

1. **Repeal of Combination Acts** (1824). Workmen could now form Trade Unions. Carried through influence of *Place* and *Hume.*

2. **Reduction of Duties** led to fall in cost of living and revival of trade. Carried through by *Huskisson. Navigation Acts* modified (1824-26).

3. **Reform of Penal Code** carried through by *Peel* (1823–27).
4. **Religious Reforms.** *Test and Corporation Acts* repealed (1828) (this meant Dissenters could hold any office). *Catholic Relief Act* passed (all offices opened to Roman Catholics) (1829).

NOTE 127. — CANNING'S FOREIGN POLICY

Canning (1770–1827) wished to intervene to help liberal movements abroad, and opposed policy of Holy Alliance and European congresses.

1. At Congress of Verona (1822) refused to agree to French intervention in Spain.
2. Sent army to *Portugal* to prevent Spanish intervention from overthrowing the constitution (1826).
3. Revolt in *Spain* against King's tyranny was unsuccessful. But Canning supported *Spanish colonies in America* and recognized them as independent when they rebelled against Spain (1824).
4. Supported *Greeks* in their war of independence against Turkey. Battle of *Navarino* (1827).

Note: *Castlereagh and Canning are often compared* as regards their foreign policy. Both aimed at Britain's interests being supported. Castlereagh had to deal with the reaction after Napoleon and he had strongly Tory country behind him. He thought Great Britain should not " interfere " abroad. Canning, who was his bitter personal rival (they fought a duel), was bolder and more dashing. He dealt with a period when reactionary Kings had gone too far. Hence he " intervened " because he thought the Kings threatened Britain's trade interests. The country also had become less reactionary, and " reforms " had begun.

At home the Government of which Castlereagh was a member was reactionary (see note 124).

Canning was liberal and reforming. He advocated Catholic Emancipation, abolition of slavery, and freedom of trade.

NOTE 128. — REPRESENTATION BEFORE THE REFORM ACT OF 1832

1. (*a*) Each county sent 2 members, elected by freeholders, owning freehold land with an annual rental value of forty shillings.

   (*b*) Each borough sent 2 members. Elected according to the borough's charter, which varied from place to place.

   In some places only the members of the town council could vote.
2. Many boroughs were " decayed ", i.e. the people with votes had died out; e.g. *Gatton* had only 1 voter, *Pevensey* had 6, *Old Sarum* none, yet these places returned 2 members.

Other boroughs were " pocket " boroughs, where so few electors existed that they could be controlled by local magnates, e.g. Cornish boroughs had been created on purpose to give the King's party a large number of members, Cornwall being a Royal Duchy (and very sparsely inhabited).

3. Large new towns had no representation.
4. Only 80 county members for England, but 409 borough members, so boroughs controlled Parliament.

NOTE 129.—PROVISIONS OF THE REFORM ACT OF 1832

1. **Franchise Extended:**

   (*a*) In counties to copyholders and long lease-holders of lands worth £10 a year, and tenants-at-will (short leases) of £50 a year.

   (*b*) In boroughs to householders of a house with a rental worth £10 a year. (Thus property qualifications kept, but based not on ownership of land but on basis of householding. Restriction to " corporations " etc., all abolished.)

2. **Redistribution of Seats.** Rotten and pocket boroughs abolished, towns with less than 2000 inhabitants lost their representation, and seats given to large towns and counties with large population.

Result: The dependence of the franchise on land-*owners* was broken by giving votes to house*holders*, and it was certain that persons who did not rent a house, but only part of it (i.e. lodgers) would in the end get the vote.

It was a beginning, which though small did double the number of voters (had been half a million, and another half-million now added).

But only enfranchised the middle classes, and working classes had to wait nearly forty years for enfranchisement.

Note: Reform Bill *advocated* by:

(i) The Whigs, who wished to break Tory monopoly of power.

(ii) The middle classes and manufacturers, who objected to franchise depending so largely on land *owning*.

(iii) Genuine reformers who wished for enfranchisement of the workers.

Opposed by:

(i) Those Tories who wanted land-owning interest to be supreme, believing it the most important in the country, and did not realize growth of manufacturing importance of Great Britain.

(ii) All who feared " revolution " and dreaded ideas of " middle-class " agitators.

(iii) All who made money out of corrupt elections and sale of boroughs.

NOTE 130.—THE WHIG REFORMERS (1830–1834)

William IV's Reign

Government led by *Grey*, then by *Melbourne*. Policy of social reform.

1. **Poor Law Reform** (1834). Speenhamland system (1795) had given relief:

   (*a*) To supplement low wages.

   (*b*) To large families in proportion to size. Led to general " pauperization " or families living on rates.

   Act of 1834 set up workhouses, checked out-relief, and though very harsh did oblige employers to pay living wage (*Chadwick* head of Poor Law Commission.)

2. **Factory Acts.** 1833. First Factory Act, applied to *textile* workers. Limited hours of work to 8 hours for persons under 13 years, to $13\frac{1}{2}$ hours for those under 18 years. Inspectors appointed.

3. **Education.** Grants given by Government to societies which provided schools for working-class children (1833). Inspectors to see money properly spent (1839).

4. **Abolition of Slavery** (1833). Slave Trade abolished earlier (1807), but now slaves were freed.

5. **Municipal Reform** (1835). Towns given elected Town Councils and given powers to undertake public services, e.g. sanitation.

6. **Postage.** 1840. Penny post started (by *Rowland Hill*).

NOTE 131.—THE CHARTISTS (1838–1848)

1. The *Hungry Forties* led to great misery and discontent. Working classes wanted reform, in order to get redress of grievances.

   The Chartists led by *Lovett*, a moderate, and by *Feargus O'Connor*, who was violent and wished to use force.

   1st Petition, 1839.
   2nd Petition, 1842.
   3rd Petition, 1848.

2. The Charter had six points:

   (*a*) Universal manhood suffrage (in 1918 all men over 21 given franchise.)

   (*b*) Vote by Ballot, that is, votes to be secret to prevent intimidation or bribery (granted in 1872).

   (*c*) Equal electoral districts, so that numbers in each constituency should be approximately equal (granted in 1885).

(*d*) No property qualification necessary for a member of Parliament (granted in 1858).

(*e*) Members of Parliament to be paid (granted in 1911).

(*f*) General elections to be annual.

(Object was to give all men votes and to enable working-class men to sit in Parliament. All these demands have now been fulfilled except the one for Annual General Elections, which would be too expensive and distracting. In addition, as women now have votes, suffrage is *universal*).

3. *Collapse of the Chartists.*

(*a*) Extremists split the party. The Charter presented (1848), but found to have many forged names — " killed by ridicule ".

(*b*) Moderates were satisfied by gradual reforms.

(*c*) Energies of the workers diverted into other movements, e.g. Trade Unionism and Co-operation.

(*d*) Prosperity revived, Corn Laws abolished, duties on food reduced (Peel), workers became more contented.

NOTE 132. — ROBERT OWEN (1771-1858)

Owen set up model factory at *New Lanark* (1801). Believed in *co-operation* rather than competition, and in *equalization* of wealth. Believed good wages and good conditions meant good work and high rate of production.

1. Combination in **Trade Unions.**

Trade Unions legalized in 1824. Spread rapidly.

1833. Owen wished to amalgamate small unions in *Grand National Consolidated Union.*

Collapsed because:

(*a*) Owen would not countenance strikes, and

(*b*) Employers attacked the Unions.

2. **Co-operation.**

Owen started in London a scheme for *co-operative selling* (1824).

Workers produced goods and sold at central store.

Failed after a while, but idea revived by the *Rochdale Pioneers* (1844), who bought jointly, and did away with middle-man.

Movement spread, and from distributing goods, went on to produce goods. The modern *Co-operative movement* has one-third of population as members.

3. **Socialism.**

Owen believed that capital should not be held in private hands, and his friends called his views " socialism ". Term was first used in *Co-operative Magazine* in 1827.

NOTE 133. — ROBERT PEEL (1788–1850)

Chief-Secretary in Ireland (1812–18). Opposed Catholic Emancipation, as did all his party. Helped Wellington to pass *Catholic Emancipation* (1828). Regarded by his party as a "treacherous" act, but Peel believed it must be done to avoid civil war in Ireland.

1. **Penal Reform** (1822–27). Home Secretary, reformed the penal code, making it much less severe.
   Founded *Metropolitan Police* (helped to prevent crime) (1829).

2. **Financial Reform.**
   (*a*) 1819. Chairman of currency committee. Restored cash payments by Bank of England, and thus restored currency and trade.
   (*b*) Abolished many customs duties, thus helping trade.
   (*c*) *Bank Charter Act*, 1844, regularized issue of notes by Bank of England.

3. He **reformed the Tory Party** by his new programme.
   Tamworth Manifesto (1834), in which he said "Conservatives" would accept Parliamentary Reform, and any other moderate reforms. This meant transforming the old die-hard land-owning Tory party. He was *Prime Minister* in 1834–35 and in 1841–46.

4. **Social Reform;** passed Mines Act (1842) prohibiting women and girls and boys under 10 from working underground, and Factory Act (1844) limiting hours of children under 13 to 6½ hours and of women to 12 hours.

5. **Political Reform.**
   (*a*) With Wellington he passed *Catholic Emancipation* (1828), for he believed if not granted there would be civil war in Ireland.
   (*b*) Accepted Reform Bill of 1832, though his party had opposed it, for he believed revolution would come if not passed.

6. **Economic Reform.**
   (*a*) His budgets consistently reduced duties on goods (over 250 duties abolished and others reduced).
   (*b*) He repealed the Corn Laws (1846) because he saw Ireland starving and also thought workers of England would rebel if laws not repealed.

   Note: Peel was accused of ruining and betraying his party by the repeal of Corn Laws. His party was pledged to maintain them, but he carried repeal with help of the Whigs. His own party was split, and he was turned out of office. Peel claimed that he was justified, both over Catholic Emancipation and the Corn Laws, because country's interest must come before party pledges. His party felt that he had broken pledges and split the party.

Note 134.—FREE TRADE AND TARIFFS

1. 1776. **Adam Smith,** in *Wealth of Nations*, laid down doctrine that countries gained by free exchange of goods.
   Pitt convinced by book, and began to reduce duties.

2. **Huskisson** (1823) reduced duties, modified Navigation Laws, and lowered duties on colonial produce.

3. **Peel** further abolished duties and reduced others (1842). **Disraeli** did not agree with Peel's policy.

4. **Gladstone** completed abolition of more duties, and *Free Trade* made policy of Great Britain (1860).

5. **Joseph Chamberlain** returned to earlier ideas and started campaign for what he called " Tariff Reform ", i.e. duties to be put on foreign goods, but a preference (lower rates, or free entry) for *colonial products* (1903). This was part of Chamberlain's Imperialist policy. Converted Conservative party, but policy rejected repeatedly by country.

6. War of 1914–18 caused **McKenna duties** to be put on certain goods to check imports (motor cars, clocks, etc.).

7. Policy extended by Conservative government. **Accepted** by Liberals in the **National Government** of 1932, because of competition from foreign goods which were heavily subsidised by their governments.

Note 135.—PALMERSTON'S FOREIGN POLICY

Foreign Secretary, 1830–34, 1835–41, 1846–51; *Prime Minister*, 1855–58, 1859–65. Championed " Liberalism " in Europe.

1. **Belgian Independence.** Palmerston supported Belgium in her separation from Holland; secured choice of Leopold (Queen Victoria's uncle) as King (1831). *Gave guarantee of permanent neutrality for Belgium* (1839).
2. **Spain.** Supported Queen Isabella against her uncle Don Carlos (1830). Also backed Queen of Portugal (policy of asserting Britain's influence) (1834).
3. **China.** 1840. Fought the " opium war ", **compelling China to cede** us Hong-Kong and to open its ports to British trade (policy of maintaining British trading interests).
   As India sold opium to China, the war brought much blame, as fostered opium trade.

4. **France.**

(*a*) In 1840 settled Eastern Question by agreement with Russia over *Mehemet Ali* without consulting France. Distrusted Louis Philippe.

(*b*) In 1846 Palmerston quarrelled with France over King Louis Philippe's marriage treaty with Spain.

(*c*) In 1848 he strongly supported the French Revolution against Louis Philippe, who lost his throne largely as a result of losing support of Britain.

(*d*) *Resignation of Palmerston* (1851) over his congratulations to *Louis Napoleon* on seizing power in France. Done without consulting Cabinet or Queen. Palmerston forced to resign.

(**Note:** Palmerston always admired Louis Napoleon, and his later efforts to punish Orsini conspirators discredited him.)

5. **Greece.** "Don Pacifico" incident caused Palmerston to send British fleet and seize Greek ships. Russia and France both infuriated. Britain's policy regarded as too aggressive (1850).

6. **Russia.**

(*a*) Russia first alienated by Don Pacifico incident, as Russia regarded Greece as her sphere of influence (1850).

(*b*) When *Crimean War* went badly, Lord Aberdeen resigned, and Palmerston became Prime Minister, so as to prosecute the war with vigour (1855).

7. **Italy.** In 1859 Palmerston again Prime Minister. Sympathized with movement in Italy headed by *Garibaldi* and *Cavour* to unite Italy.

8. **United States.** Peel had compromised over Oregon dispute (1846). *Trent* incident led to aggressive action by Palmerston. War averted by Prince Consort (1861).

9. **Germany.** Palmerston wished to support *Danes* in struggle over Schleswig-Holstein. Misled Danes, as British would not go to war (1863).

Contrasting Views of Palmerston's Policy. Always aggressive, and made Great Britain to be looked on as interfering, but made Great Britain feared, and her prestige high on the continent. Usually wished to support all movements for liberty.

Note 136. — CRIMEAN WAR (1854–1856)

1. **Causes:**

(*a*) Turkish misrule of Balkans.

(*b*) Russia championed Christians in Balkans.

(*c*) British afraid of Russian influence, as threatening route to India. Hence Britain supported Turkey.

(*d*) Napoleon III wished to raise prestige of his Government, so asserted French influence in Holy Land.

Immediate pretext — quarrel of Russia and France over guardianship of Holy Places.

2. Events of War.

(*a*) 1854. Attack on *Sebastopol* — not pressed forward quickly enough after *Alma*.

Battle of *Balaclava* — no result as Russians got command of road to British base.

Battle of *Inkerman* — indecisive.

(*b*) 1855. Allied troops suffered terribly during winter, Nov., 1854–March, 1855.

Florence Nightingale sent out (Palmerston, Prime Minister).

(*c*) February, Czar Nicholas died. Alexander II ready to negotiate. Sebastopol taken (Sept.).

1856. Peace made in March by Treaty of Paris.

3. Results of War.

(*a*) Turkey's "integrity" guaranteed. Sultan promised reform, but did not keep promise. Czar gave up claim to protect Christians in Balkans.

(*b*) Danubian provinces given self-government, and in 1861 declared independent as Kingdom of Rumania (hence integrity of Turkey not observed).

(*c*) Black Sea neutral and no war ships allowed in it. (But Russia set this aside in 1870.)

Real result of war was to bolster up the failing power of Turkey for a while. Allies thus meant to check Russia. Later the Balkans freed themselves finally from Turkey (1912–13), but remained friendly to Russia.

Great Britain gained nothing, except development of nursing reforms due to Florence Nightingale.

NOTE 137. — INDIA. EXPANSION OF BRITISH TERRITORIES (1823–1856)

1 Part of India directly governed by East India Company (e.g. *Madras, Bengal*).

Other parts under British influence (*Hyderabad, Mysore, Rajputana*).

(*a*) In 1824 part of *Burma* annexed after *First Burmese War*.

(*b*) *Lord Auckland* (1836–41) attacked *Afghanistan* and dethroned *Dost Mohammed*. In 1841 Afghanistan attacked the British, and whole army destroyed. Second Afghan expedition to avenge this. Dost Mohammed again put on throne.

(*c*) *Lord Hardinge* fought First Sikh War. *Punjab* a Protectorate (1845).

2. **Dalhousie, Governor-General** (1848–56).
Believed (*a*) in territorial expansion of British in India; (*b*) in social reform.

(*a*) **Territorial Expansion.**

(i) Second Sikh War. *Punjab annexed* (1849). Lawrence sent to govern.

(ii) Second Burmese War. *Lower Burma annexed* (1852).

(iii) Doctrine of *lapse*. *Central Indian States* of Jhansi and Nagpur annexed (1856).

(iv) Annexation of *Oudh*, as result of Vizier's misrule (1856).

(*b*) **Social Reforms.**

Dalhousie continued the policy of *Lord William Bentinck* (1828–35), who (*a*) abolished suttee; (*b*) suppressed Thugs; (*c*) reformed finance; (*d*) gave Indians a share in government; (*e*) gave more liberty to Press.

Dalhousie (*a*) reorganized internal administration; (*b*) built canals and roads; (*c*) introduced railways and telegraph, and postal services; (*d*) encouraged education.

Dalhousie's measures all aimed at developing material resources in order to make India prosperous. His annexations aimed at bringing order to badly misgoverned provinces. Dalhousie believed British rule meant peace and prosperity.

NOTE 138. — INDIAN MUTINY (1857–1858)

1. **Causes:**

(*a*) Mutiny a *military revolt* of Sepoys. Sepoys upset by famous cartridge issue, and by order to go oversea to Burma — both against *caste* regulations.

(*b*) Supported by *native princes* because of dislike of doctrine of lapse. Confined to districts where lapse had worked harshly, and to Sepoy troops.

(*c*) General dislike of Dalhousie's reforms; customs and beliefs of the Indians upset.

(*d*) Loss of British prestige in Crimea and Afghanistan.

2. **Events of Mutiny.** First outbreak at *Meerut* (May, 1857).

(*a*) *Delhi* besieged; *Lucknow* besieged; *Cawnpore* cantonments besieged (May, 1857).

(*b*) *Cawnpore* garrison surrendered; massacre of English by Nana Sahib.

(c) *Lucknow* and *Delhi* held out and relieved (Sept. and Nov., 1857).

Note: Sikhs and Gurkhas fought for British.

3. Results of Mutiny.

(a) *East India Company abolished,* and Secretary of State, with Council in England, took over charge of Indian affairs (1858). Viceroy sent to India, with Council to advise him.

(b) Sepoy army made part of British army. Proportion of white troops to Indian increased.

(c) More attention paid to Indian ideas. Doctrine of lapse abandoned.

(d) "Clemency" *Canning* adopted policy of "no reprisals", and later Queen proclaimed *Empress of India* to emphasize British good-feeling (1877).

TIME CHART FOR PERIOD TEN (1815–1867)

Sovereign.	Prime Minister.	Great and Greater Britain.	Dates.	Other Powers.	Dates.
George III (1760–1820)	1812–27 LIVERPOOL.	Battle of Waterloo; Lord Hastings in India, 1814–23.	1815	Treaty of Paris; Louis XVIII King of France.	1815
				Congress of Aix-la-Chapelle.	1818
		Occupation of Singapore; "Six Acts"; "Peterloo"; first steamship crosses Atlantic.	1819		
				Revolutions in Spain and Naples; Congress of Troppau.	1820
George IV, (1820–1830)				WAR OF GREEK INDEPENDENCE. Death of Napoleon I; Congress of Laibach.	1821
		Liverpool's Ministry re-constructed; Death of Castlereagh.	1822	Congress of Verona.	1822
				Charles X becomes King of France.	1824
		Stockton-Darlington Railway opened.	1825	Nicholas becomes Czar.	1825
	CANNING.	Battle of Navarino; Death of Canning.	1827		
	GODERICH.	Test and Corporation Acts repealed.	1828		
	WELLINGTON.	Catholic Emancipation Act; Metropolitan Police Force founded.	1829	Treaty of Adrianople.	1829
		Manchester and Liverpool Railway opened.	1830	Revolutions in France and Belgium; Louis Philippe King of the French.	1830
William IV, (1830–1837)	GREY.	First Reform Bill.	1832		
		Abolition of Slavery in British dominions; Factory Act.	1833		
	MELBOURNE.	Reform of Poor Law.	1834		
	PEEL.	Municipal Reform Act.	1835		
		South Australia Colonized; the "Great Trek".	1836		
		Rebellion in Canada.	1837		
	MELBOURNE.	Lord Durham sent to Canada; *Great Western* crosses Atlantic.	1838		
		First Afghan War; "Bedchamber" question.	1839	Belgian Neutrality guaranteed.	1839
		New Zealand annexed; Penny Postage introduced.	1840	Alliance against Mehemet Ali.	1840

Sovereign.	Prime Minister.	Great and Greater Britain.	Dates.	Other Powers.	Dates.
Queen Victoria, (1837–1901)	1841–46 PEEL.	Chinese cede Hong-Kong.	1841		.
		Mines Act; Ashburton Treaty.	1842		.
		The Disruption in Scottish Church.	1843		.
		Factory Act.	1844		.
		Irish Famine.	1845		.
	1846–52 LORD JOHN RUSSELL.	Repeal of Corn Laws; Oregon Treaty.	1846	Spanish Marriage Question.	1846
		Factory Act.	1847		.
		Chartist Riots; Dalhousie Gov.-Gen. of India (till 1856); Second Sikh War; Anæsthetics introduced.	1848	The Year of Revolutions.	1848
		The Great Exhibition.	1851	Louis Napoleon's *coup d'état*.	1851
	DERBY	Sand River Convention.	1852	Louis Napoleon becomes Emperor Napoleon III.	1852
	ABERDEEN.	Battles of Alma, Balaclava, Inkerman. (CRIMEAN	1854	WAR.)	.
		Fall of Sebastopol.	1855	Alexander II becomes Czar.	1855
	PALMERSTON.	Peace of Paris.	1856		.
		Second Chinese War. (INDIAN MUTINY.)	1857		.
	DERBY.	East India Company abolished.	1858		.
	PALMERSTON.	Darwin's *Origin of Species*.	1859	War of Italian Unity (1859–61); Battles of Magenta and Solferino.	1859
		Maori War.	1860		.
		Death of Prince Consort; the *Alabama* incident.	1861	(AMERICAN CIVIL WAR.)	.
			.	Bismarck becomes Chief Minister in Prussia.	1862
			.	War between Prussia and Denmark.	1864
	RUSSELL. DERBY. DISRAELI.		1865		.
			.	Austro-Prussian War.	1866
		Dominion of Canada formed; Second Reform Bill.	1867		.

EXAMINATION QUESTIONS ON PERIOD TEN

(1815–1867)

1. Give an account of (*a*) parliamentary representation in England before 1832; (*b*) the changes made by the Reform Act of 1832. (NUJB 1935)

2. What were the Corn Laws and why were they repealed? (OC 1937)

3. What were the main achievements of Sir Robert Peel? (NUJB 1937)

4. Give an account of Castlereagh's work from, and including, his settlement of Europe in 1815 to his death in 1822. (LGS 1937)

5. On what grounds was the system of parliamentary representation before 1832 (*a*) attacked, and (*b*) defended? State the main changes made by the Reform Act of 1832. (LGS 1937)

6. Describe the struggle for the reform of Parliament that ended with the passing of the Reform Act of 1832. (LGS 1936)

7. What were the chief services of Sir Robert Peel to England? (LGS 1936)

8. Explain (*a*) the success of the Anti-Corn Law League; (*b*) the failure of the Chartists. (LGS 1936)

9. What were the grievances of the Chartists? (OC 1933)

10. Give an account of the establishment of Free Trade in England. (NUJB 1936)

11. How far was the distress and discontent in England between 1815 and 1832 due to the results of the Napoleonic Wars? (LGS 1935)

12. What were the causes of social discontent in England (1815–20)? (OC 1927, '29; OL 1932; LM 1932; CWB 1932)

13. Describe and compare the foreign policy of Castlereagh and Canning. (LM 1924, '25; LGS 1925; OC '29, '31)

14. Why was a reform of the Poor Law so urgently needed in the early days of the nineteenth century? (D 1931)

15. Write an account of (*a*) the co-operative movement; (*b*) the Reform of the Poor Law in 1834. (NUJB 1932)

16. Why were the Factory Acts so necessary, and what reforms did they introduce? (D 1932)

17. Outline the history and the aims of the Chartist movement. (LM 1925; OC 1929; OL 1929; NUJB 1930)

18. Discuss the aims and methods of Lord Palmerston. (LGS 1924; OC 1929; OC 1930; NUJB '32; UW '32)

19. On what occasions and with what effect did Lord Palmerston interfere abroad to check tyranny? (OL 1930)

20. Describe the chief reforms of the Whigs between 1833 and 1841. (NUJB 1938)

21. Write a short biography of Lord Palmerston. What were the chief results of his career? (LGS 1935)

22. Give an account of the development of Canada from the rebellion of 1837 to the setting up of the Dominion in 1867. (NUJB 1936)

23. Give an outline of the history of *either* Canada up to the Canadian Act of Union (1840) *or* of Australia since the colonization of S. Australia (1836). (OC 1933)

24. Trace the development of Canada in the nineteenth century. (LGS 1937)

25. What mechanical inventions promoted English prosperity in the first half of the nineteenth century? (OC 1935)

26. State the services to the British Empire of *either* Bentinck and Dalhousie *or* Disraeli and Joseph Chamberlain. (NUJB 1935)

27. Estimate Peel's services to (*a*) his party, (*b*) his country. (NUJB 1932)

28. Write an account of the Durham Report. (NUJB 1932)

29. Describe and estimate the importance of the work of Bentinck and Dalhousie on India. (NUJB 1930, 1932)

30. Examine the causes and chief events of the Indian Mutiny. (OL 1929; LGS 1922; OC 1927)

31. Give a brief description of the foreign policy of Lord Palmerston, and illustrate your account by reference to some leading events in his career. (LGS 1932)

32. State the main facts concerning (*a*) the causes of the Crimean War, (*b*) the part played by Britain in this war. (NUJB 1937)

33. Why did Britain engage in the Crimean War? (OC 1933)

34. Give an account of the growth of British rule in India from 1750–1850. (OC 1935)

35. What were the chief causes and what were the chief results of the Indian Mutiny? (LGS 1935)

36. Why did England enter the Crimean War? What were the chief results of her doing so? (LGS 1935)

PERIOD ELEVEN

POLITICAL DEVELOPMENT: IMPERIALISM AND DEMOCRACY

1867–1914

CHAPTER 65

GLADSTONE AND DISRAELI (1865–1868)

Palmerston's death, in 1865, marked the end of an epoch. Many of his associates had grown old along with him, and now they too disappeared from the political scene. Peel had died in 1850, Wellington in 1852, Lord Aberdeen in 1860. Besides his fellow-statesmen, another prominent person now pre-deceased Palmerston. The *Prince Consort* died in 1861, worn out before his time. He had led a most unselfish life, devoting himself to his wife and to her country. Though the Queen was passionately devoted to him, the English never cared for him. His stiff insistence on etiquette and his disapproval both of English sport and English laziness, annoyed them. He could not understand the nation, and in return he was distrusted. Many thought his influence too great [1] and feared that he was making the Crown too powerful. Yet he did all he could to advance science and help trade. Perhaps his most serious mistake was in the unduly severe and narrow way in which he brought up the heir to the throne.

The Prince Consort

On the Queen the effects of his death were disastrous.

[1] During the Crimea there was a popular demand that he should be interned in the Tower as a foreigner.

She shut herself up and declined to appear in public. For years she lived completely apart, refusing to visit London, to perform any state ceremonies, or to receive foreign statesmen. The people bitterly resented this and the popularity of her early years disappeared until in 1871 the illness of the Prince of Wales won her much sympathy and restored her popularity.

Meanwhile, on the empty political stage, there appeared two men who now had the way to greatness open before them — *William Ewart Gladstone* and *Benjamin Disraeli.*

Gladstone

Gladstone began life as a warm admirer of Peel. He had, like his leader, been convinced of the need to repeal the Corn Laws. He had, with his leader, suffered from Disraeli's attack on that policy. The difference thus begun at the outset of their careers, was to widen and to last throughout the lives of these two men (*Note 140*).

Gladstone was in many ways an epitome of the Victorian age. He was deeply religious and a follower of the High Church Party. He was very widely read, and a great student of the classics. He was rich, the son of a very wealthy Liverpool family. He was extremely handsome, and besides a natural dignity and severity, had a most wonderful gift of eloquence.[1] He was in many ways a strange mixture, for besides his genuine religious feeling which led him always to lay stress on the moral side of actions, he had a very subtle mind which enabled him to take a line not always clear to others. Thus his enemies, and often foreigners, accused him of hypocrisy, when to himself his actions never deviated from what he thought right. *Parnell*, one of the most formidable politicians of the day, said that Gladstone was the only opponent he really feared.

In dealing with Gladstone's career, we have to notice three separate threads: *finance*, of which he was an acknowledged master; *social reform*; and *foreign policy.*

[1] A gift wasted on Queen Victoria who complained that he " always addressed her as if she were a public meeting."

We shall deal first of all with *finance*. Gladstone for a long period acted as Chancellor of the Exchequer[1] (1859–65). His Budget Statements have always been considered as models of clearness, and he preached incessantly the doctrine of "peace, retrenchment, and reform". He aimed first at removing all barriers in trade, and his first task was the effort to lower the duties on tea and sugar and to abolish many more of those duties on goods which had remained after Peel's reforms. England now became largely a *Free Trade* country, that is to say many imports came in without paying duties. Next, he wanted to avoid spending money on armaments, for he believed such expenditure to be unproductive. He thought it best to aim at low taxation, and to leave the money in the pockets of the people. He had thought that it might have been possible to do without Peel's income-tax, but the Crimean War upset that plan. In 1860 times were more prosperous, but now Britain suffered from a fit of "nerves". She believed that Napoleon III meant to invade her, and a scare resulted in the formation of volunteer corps to defend our shores, and in the fortification of our naval ports. The expense which these measures involved, combined with the cost of restoring order after the Indian Mutiny, meant that the income-tax had to be retained, and thenceforward it became a regular feature of our taxation, though at 3*d*. in the £ it could not be thought burdensome. Great Britain was now extraordinarily prosperous, trade was increasing enormously, and revenue going up by leaps and bounds. Gladstone was easily able, therefore, to abolish a tax on paper, which he called a "tax on knowledge", since it raised the price of books and newspapers.

Finance

Free Trade

Income Tax

He also set to work to clear men's minds of the fear of France, regarding it as a harmful bogey. With the help of Cobden, the leader of the Free Traders, he negotiated a commercial treaty with France. By this treaty, each nation lowered its duties, and so French silks came into this country

Trade Treaty with France (1860)

[1] He was also Chancellor from 1852 to 1855.

more cheaply, while France lowered her tariff on British hardware. Free Trade was championed by men who came mainly from the great exporting centres of northern England, and its leaders were called the *Manchester School.* They preached that trade flourished through the exchange of goods, and that by keeping out the goods of other countries we checked the export of our own.

Free Trade: The Manchester School

Next to finance, came *reform*, and here the *Liberals*, as they began to be called, saw that the time had come for an extension of the franchise. Increased wealth had spread to all parts of the community, and now the working-classes wanted more political power. So in 1866 Gladstone drew up the second *Reform Bill.* This was intended to give votes to working-class householders. It was a moderate scheme, and would have meant that half a million of the well-to-do artisan class would have been enfranchised. What followed is a commentary on the tricks that " party " schemes can play.

Electoral Reform

Many of the former Whig party were not in favour of reform. Palmerston had always opposed it, and Lord John Russell, the Prime Minister, was very lukewarm. Indeed, his belief that the franchise was now completely satisfactory and needed no further change earned him the nickname of " Finality Jack ". Quite a large section of the Government party went even further, and were resolved to oppose all extension of the franchise. They were led by Robert Lowe, who frankly admitted that he feared to give political power to the working classes. This group was nicknamed the " Adullamites " (after the men who withdrew with David from following Saul and hid in the Cave of Adullam—1 Samuel xxii) and since that time members who have split off from their party have been said to form a " cave ". They refused to accept Gladstone's proposals, and would not vote with him. Gladstone stuck to his principles, for he did believe in enfranchising the working-man, and went on with the Bill. The " Adullamites ", joining with Disraeli, de-

Lowe and the Adullamites

feated the new Reform Bill. Lord John resigned, and the Tories came into power.

Tories in power: Disraeli (1866)

The new Prime Minister was *Lord Derby*, but the true leader was the Chancellor of the Exchequer, *Benjamin Disraeli*, who now stood forward as the great opponent of Gladstone. The rivalry between these two men was to give zest and a personal excitement to all Victorian politics. Not often has England had two such outstandingly able men competing to serve her, and never, perhaps, two contemporaries with such picturesque personalities. In some ways Disraeli seems unbelievably exotic,[1] but actually the mid-Victorians were far more exuberant in their dress and way of life than we always appreciate. He came from a family of Italian Jews. His father was a literary man, and Disraeli himself first won fame as a novelist — a contrast with Gladstone, whose first publication had been a book on the principles regulating the relations between Church and State.

Gladstone had progressed easily from Eton and Oxford to a seat in the House. Disraeli left school at fifteen, went into a solicitor's office at seventeen, and had tried four times for a seat before he was successful in 1837. Where Gladstone had been recognized from the outset as a speaker of extraordinary promise, Disraeli's first efforts were complete failures, and his maiden speech was laughed down.[2]

Now, however, time had shown his great ability and dexterity, and having won his position through his opposition to Peel and the repeal of the Corn Laws, he was now the recognized leader in the opposition to Gladstone and his policy of reform.

Disraeli was abnormally quick in foreseeing the way

[1] A lady who met him at a dinner party when he was a young man describes him as wearing a black velvet coat lined with satin, purple trousers with a gold band running down the outside seam, a scarlet waistcoat, and white gloves with several brilliant rings outside them.

[2] He merely said in conclusion, " I will sit down now, but the time will come when you will hear me."

Disraeli's Reform Bill (1867)

things were developing; he was said to " have his ear to the ground ", and he realized that further extension of the franchise must come. So he decided that his party should have the credit, and though he had brought about Gladstone's defeat on this very measure, he now decided to " dish the Whigs ". With some difficulty he convinced his own party. So the new *Tory* party brought in a Reform Bill. Disraeli was sincere in that he had no great love for the rich middle classes, and he had much sympathy for the workers, of whom he spoke as the second of the " Two Nations " [1] into which he thought Britain was divided. His later life was to show his belief in social reform.

He did not intend at first, however, that this extension of the franchise should be as wide as it turned out to be. His move to win popularity was met by his opponents. Gladstone and Bright began a great campaign which swept the thickly populated manufacturing districts. They brought forward amendments in the House, and Disraeli dared not oppose them. So the second *Reform Act* was passed (1867), with far wider changes either than Gladstone's original Bill or than Disraeli's. It gave the vote in the towns to all householders who paid poor rates, and to all lodgers who paid £10 a year in rent and had been in their lodgings for twelve months; and in the counties to all occupiers paying rates on an assessment of £12 a year. This really enfranchised the working-man. The reception given to the Act perhaps showed Disraeli what he had done. His own leader, Lord Derby, called it a " leap in the dark ", and *Carlyle*, who was neither a coward nor a reactionary, said it was like " shooting Niagara ". The future *Lord Salisbury*, who opposed his leader Disraeli on this point, bluntly called it " a piece of political dishonesty unexampled in our history ". Disraeli might remain unmoved by these remarks, but he had more than harsh words to bear. A general election had to be held

[1] His works, especially *Sybil*, show knowledge of and sympathy with the conditions of the workers.

in the next year (1868), and Disraeli had believed that the new voters would show their gratitude by voting for his party. Gratitude, however, does not exist in politics, or, rather, party principles are stronger.[1] The Liberals were returned to power, and Gladstone became the new Prime Minister till 1874.

CHAPTER 66

GLADSTONE'S FIRST MINISTRY AND REFORMS (1868–1874)

Gladstone had come back as a minister supported by the working-class vote. He was resolved to carry through social reforms, and he began with *education*, for, as Lowe commented, " now we must educate our masters ". **Education**

Sometimes people have urged that votes should depend upon a test of a certain standard of education, but history has shown that the opposite rule prevails — grant people a vote and improvement in their standard of education follows (*Note 143*).

Up to 1870 children were not obliged to go to school, and, indeed, there were not schools for them all to attend. Education for the working-classes, such as it was, had been provided by the churches, which had raised large sums for the purpose. The Church of England had built many schools, especially in the country districts, the non-conformists had built others, and the Government had given grants to both.

W. E. Forster, a Quaker, was given charge of Gladstone's measure for educational reform. By his Act (*Elementary Education Act*, 1870) England and Wales were divided into districts, and in each district there was to be an elected **Education Act (1870)**

[1] Lord Baldwin made the same miscalculation over the " flapper vote " in 1928. He thought the newly enfranchised women, between the ages of 21 and 30, would vote Conservative, but they did not.

School Board. In every district where there was no school, the State would provide one, paid for by special education rates. But in most places where schools were provided by the various churches, they were to continue, and were to receive grants out of public funds. All schools alike were to be inspected. Until the new schools had been built, it was useless to make it compulsory for children to attend, but ten years later (1880) all children were obliged to attend school up to the age of thirteen. Parents had to pay fees, and not till 1890 was education made " free "; that is to say, parents were no longer obliged to pay specifically for their children's schooling. We should note, however, that as all parents are both tax-payers and ratepayers (usually, though not in Scotland, rates are included in rents), they do certainly provide, though more indirectly, for the sums spent on national education.[1]

Universities (1871) Next came an improvement in university education. Hitherto no one could hold a scholarship or fellowship in or be a member of the universities of Oxford and Cambridge, unless he was a member of the Church of England. This " religious test " was now abolished by the Repeal of the Tests Act of 1871.

Ballot Act (1872) One of the Chartist demands was realized, when in 1872 the *Ballot Act* made voting for members of Parliament secret, and voters no longer had to fear intimidation or reprisals as a result of voting publicly. This did away with a great deal of the corruption and disorder of elections (such as Dickens caricatured in the *Pickwick Papers*), for it was useless to bribe a man to vote when you could no longer tell how he actually voted. Though opponents of the reform said that the secret ballot would " sap the manly independence of the voter ", it really had the opposite effect.

Civil Service As the State was extending its activities, it needed more officials, and it was perfectly clear that the old system of nomination must be changed. The entrance to the Civil

[1] In 1872 a similar Education Act was passed for Scotland.

Service was therefore made to depend on examination, open and compulsory to all applicants for admission to its ranks.[1]

The army: Cardwell's reforms

Democracy was gathering strength, and Gladstone's ministry carried its influence even into the stronghold of the army. The reforms brought about by *Edward Cardwell*, the Secretary for War, were then called "revolutionary". He adopted ideas from the Continent, where Prussia had just shown the effectiveness of her system in her "lightning" wars against Austria and France. Great Britain had a professional army, recruited on the basis of a twenty-year service with the colours. This meant that the soldiers of her army were often too old for active service, and there were no reserves. Germany and France had the system of conscription, whereby all young men had a period of military training and then went back to civil life. Great Britain, without the need for a great army, would not have accepted conscription. Cardwell aimed at getting some of the benefits of that system by "short-term" service, under which men enlisted for twelve years, and then went into the reserve. He also tried, by abolishing the purchase of commissions, to prevent the army being officered by such incompetents as had mismanaged the Crimea. He tried, too, to meet the special difficulties which our Empire had to face, by the "linked battalion" method. This meant that in a regiment one battalion would serve abroad, while the other trained at home, and each pair came from one special area where the regiment had its depot for recruiting, thus getting the benefit of local feeling. Finally, there was swept away the hopeless system against which Florence Nightingale had raged, of having separate authorities for different departments — one for stores, another for clothing, and so on. There was to be one Army Council, with the Secretary for War at its head.

[1] Macaulay's Report had long since made this system to be applied to the Indian Civil Service.

During this time the Trade Unions had been going steadily ahead in membership and in organization (*Note 144*). They had given up the wilder policy of the Chartists, and many had struggled to give their members wider interests.[1] As the Unions collected more funds, so they felt stronger, and they now wished to make their legal existence secure. For though the formation of unions was no longer forbidden by law, they were declared by the justices to be " in restraint of trade ", and so could not sue dishonest officials who misused their funds. In 1868 the Unions had a great joint meeting, recognized to-day as the first Trades Union Congress. Gladstone decided to meet their grievances. His *Trades' Union Act* (1871) gave them proper legal existence and their funds were safeguarded against dishonest officials.

Trade Unions

Trades' Union Act (1871)

Apparently in politics it always happens that after a while men tire of any ministry, and what is called the " swing of the pendulum " comes into play. Gladstone had done a great deal, and he wanted to do more. He wished to reform the trade in drink and set to work on a Licensing Bill. He had already vexed many Nonconformists over education, for they disliked paying rates in areas where there was only a Church School. He had upset the Church of England by his Bill disestablishing the Church in Ireland (1869). Now this new Bill, which his opponents said would " rob the poor man of his beer ", lost him the workers' votes.

The country was vaguely discontented, too, with what was thought to be Great Britain's loss of prestige abroad. People were dissatisfied with the mild line taken by Gladstone in 1872 in paying the U.S.A. compensation for the *Alabama* (p. 808). Nor were they happy over European politics. 1870 was the year of the Franco-Prussian war. Napoleon III had most mistakenly given Bismarck the opportunity he needed. France had thought herself strong, but she proved to be lamentably weak. The British Court

[1] Various societies " for the diffusion of useful knowledge " were formed, and one man wrote in 1864, " This year I gave up buying beer and took to buying books."

and many others were in favour of Prussia, for Napoleon III was universally distrusted, and Britain sympathized with the union of Germany which followed the war. But as a result of the preoccupation of the great powers in the west, Russia at this point repudiated the Treaty of Paris and opened the Black Sea to her warships (1871). Britain was always nervous of Russia, and this move seemed to her ominous. So, moved partly by panic, partly by pique, the electorate turned against Gladstone, and in 1874 he went out.

CHAPTER 67

DISRAELI AND "TORY DEMOCRACY" (1874–1880)

Disraeli and the Queen

Thus at length (1874), Disraeli had triumphed (*Note 141*). His party was in power after twenty-eight years in opposition, and he was Prime Minister. He was jubilant, for he had behind him a party which he had won over to his new programme. He was destined, too, to find his path smoothed in another direction through the personal liking felt for him by the Queen. Victoria had suffered very greatly from the death of her dearly-loved husband. For years she had shut herself up, refusing to come to London or to take her share in public life,[1] and discontent at this attitude had been general. In Disraeli she found, at this stage in her life, a man whom she treated as a friend. He knew exactly how to please her, in a way that the stiffer and more sedate Gladstone had never been able to achieve. She was happy in this friendship with her new Premier, and persuaded by him she began once more to emerge from her retirement. Disraeli was sincere in his admiration for the sovereign. He had a conception of Great Britain as an Empire in which he whole-heartedly believed, and at the head of that Empire, acting as a link

[1] One newspaper published a mock statement: "The Queen will come to London and stop one whole week."

with all the parts, was the Crown. He wished to emphasize that link and to make the Crown popular, and he used his influence to induce the Queen to take her place amongst her people. Gladstone was every whit as loyal; indeed, his regard for the sovereign was his undoing, for he always alienated the Queen by his stiff and austere respect. Disraeli had a far more human touch,[1] and he was, of course, perfectly aware of his advantage. He knew, and so did everyone else, that the Queen was one of his warmest friends, and that anything he did was sure of her approval.

Policy of Disraeli

In domestic affairs Disraeli had a policy which he himself called "Tory Democracy". He genuinely wished to improve the conditions of the working classes, and also to strengthen the Empire. He meant, too, to play a more striking part in foreign policy than had Gladstone, and this was the sphere in which he personally most desired to distinguish himself. So he left the details of his social measures largely to *Sir Richard Cross*, the Home Secretary.

Trade Unions

Cross guided through the House a Bill concerning the Trade Unions (called the Conspiracy Act, 1875), which declared that no Union could be prosecuted for anything that would not be illegal if done by an individual. This was of immense importance to the Trade Union movement, but workers might not, by use of a strike, cause loss of life or interrupt the supply of gas and water to the community.

Public Health Act (1875)

In this same year was passed the Public Health Act, which gave to county and borough councils power to take measures for public health. The novelists of that period often deal with the frightful epidemics of "cholera" and typhus which ravaged town and country alike. This measure was the first attempt to get at one of the causes of such outbreaks by the provision of proper water sanitation. Each district was now to have a Medical Officer of Health.

[1] Comparing his attitude towards Queen Victoria with Gladstone's, Disraeli once said, "Gladstone treats the Queen like a public department; I treat her like a woman." The Queen spoke of Disraeli after his death, as her "dear, great friend."

Another feature of town life in those days was the terrible slums,[1] and the Artisans' Dwelling Act of 1875 gave local authorities power to pull down such places and rebuild them. It is a reflection on our civilization that in all the many years since that Act was passed, slums have not yet been obliterated.

Housing

One other bad development of the industrial age was touched upon. Ships, greedy for freight, often went to sea in bad repair and overloaded. In 1876 the Merchant Shipping Act gave the Board of Trade the right to inspect all ships before they went to sea. A mark called the " Plimsoll Line ", after the man who introduced it, was from that time painted on the side of every ship to show the depth to which it could be loaded.

The Merchant Shipping Act (1876)

All these Acts form part of the efforts to improve the conditions of the working-classes which were really shared by Liberal and Conservative alike. In foreign affairs, however, Disraeli showed where he really differed fundamentally from Gladstone. In one sense Disraeli's policy gave a marked and persistent character to his party, for he deliberately emphasized the idea of *Imperialism.* He believed whole-heartedly in the British Empire, and he wanted to glorify it.

Foreign affairs

He was specially attracted by India, and this interest led to one of his successful coups, when in 1875 he bought £4,000,000 of shares in the *Suez Canal* which were being sold by the Khedive. This helped us to control the Canal route to India, and proved in addition a paying investment. Next he arranged for the Prince of Wales to visit India, and finally, in 1876, he put through an Act making the Queen " Empress of India ". The Empress was proclaimed at Delhi on 1st January, 1877. Concern with India had again and again made Britain nervous of Russia, disliking the idea of that great Empire creeping down into the Mediterranean,

Suez Canal shares (1875)

Empress of India (1877)

[1] Dickens gives an unsurpassed picture in *Bleak House*, of " Tom-all-alone's " slum.

RUSSIA AND THE BALKANS. 1876–1878

too near her trade route. Britain dreaded, too, lest Russia should push through Asia and come near the Indian frontier. This nervousness Disraeli carried further, with a policy hostile to Russia in the Near East (*Note 142*).

In 1876 the people of the Balkans, who were miserably oppressed by the Turks, burst into revolt. That revolt, especially in *Bulgaria*, was put down by the Sultan with most appalling ferocity. The stories of the *Bulgarian Atrocities* roused Gladstone to a campaign in which his burning indignation and eloquence evoked the sympathy of the working-classes. The Czar, considering himself the champion of a Slav nation and of his co-religionists, asked Britain, Germany, and Austria to join in a protest to the Turks against the massacres. Disraeli refused, for he said that we must not weaken the Sultan's authority. The Czar threatened to act alone. In vain did Gladstone write one of his best and most effective pamphlets, in vain did he urge that the Turk should be turned out of Europe " bag and baggage ", in vain did vast meetings in the north and midlands support him — the Conservative Party feared Russia and preferred to bolster up the Turks. The Czar finally did take action. In 1877 he sent his troops to invade Turkey, and though the Turks fought well and gained renown by their defence of *Plevna*, they were defeated and forced to make peace in the Treaty of San Stephano. The Balkans were to be free and the two chief States, Serbia and Bulgaria, were to be independent. But the terms imposed by Russia were such that Great Britain could not acquiesce in them, nor could Russia be allowed to settle the Eastern Question without reference to the other Powers concerned.

The Near East: the Bulgarian Atrocities

The Russo-Turkish War (1877–78)

Disraeli, who had just been made *Earl of Beaconsfield*, intervened. He was determined that no settlement should be imposed by Russia alone, and he declared that as the Treaty of Paris at the end of the Crimean War had fixed Turkey's boundaries, so now all the Powers must be consulted if these boundaries were to be altered. Russia hesitated, but Disraeli sent troops to Malta and the British fleet to Constantinople. Sullenly Russia gave way, and agreed that a European Congress should be called. That Congress met at Berlin in 1878. Bismarck presided, and as he did not want his two friends, Austria and Russia, to quarrel, he had already tried to act, in his own words, as an " honest broker " in facilitating a settlement between Great Britain and these

Congress of Berlin (1878)

two Powers. Thus, when the Congress met, the business consisted mainly of carrying into effect decisions already made by means of secret and direct negotiations between the Powers concerned. Disraeli returned from this Congress with the boast that he had brought "Peace with honour", but unfortunately final peace was not to be achieved on the terms of the settlement.

For as the main object of Disraeli's diplomacy was to check Russia and save Turkey, one of the chief measures of Berlin was to put back a large part of the newly freed Bulgaria under Turkish rule. Another measure was that Bosnia, which had also been freed, was placed under Austrian "control". This led ultimately to the fatal intrusion of Austria into the Balkans and her rivalry there with Russia, which in 1914 was one of the causes of war. Disraeli accepted Cyprus for Great Britain, so long as Russia held her conquests in northern Asia Minor, in return for a pledge to support the Sultan's Asiatic Empire by force of arms if necessary, a pledge which she was never asked to fulfil. He had achieved his main object, namely to save the Turks, though he also earned the enmity of Russia. Yet so overwhelming was the dislike of Russia that, on his return from the Congress,[1] he was greeted by his party with the utmost enthusiasm, and the Queen, who openly and ardently agreed with his policy, gave him the Order of the Garter.[2]

Trouble in India (1878–80)

This anti-Russian policy led Beaconsfield into further entanglements. He believed that Russia had "designs" on India, so he sent his friend *Lord Lytton* as Viceroy, and instructed him to get control of Afghanistan and so block Russian advances there. Accordingly a British mission was

[1] Bismarck's opinion of Disraeli at the Congress was "Der alte Jude, das ist der Mann!" (The old Jew, he's the man!) Disraeli in a letter described Bismarck thus: "Bismarck soars above all: he is 6 feet 4 I should think; with a sweet and gentle voice, which singularly and strangely contrasts with the awful things he says: appalling from their frankness and audacity. He is a complete despot here, and all tremble at his frown and most sedulously court his smile."

[2] He had been made Earl of Beaconsfield in 1877. Gladstone, when offered a peerage, refused.

dispatched, but within a few months the British agent was murdered in Kabul. A British general, *Sir Frederick Roberts*, was sent (1879) to march to Kandahar, and gained much prestige. But it was clear that a mistake had been made. To control Afghanistan effectively a garrison would have to be maintained. This was not practicable, so Britain, discomfited, had to reverse her policy and to do her best to win over Afghanistan by peaceful friendliness.

And in Africa

Troubles in Africa with the Zulus and the Boers (see p. 895) completed the gloomy story. The time had come for a general election, and to everyone's astonishment Gladstone burst out of his retirement and undertook a campaign against the Government in the autumn of 1879. He was seventy years old, but he went off to Midlothian, which was in those days a " safe " Conservative seat. There, in his famous " Midlothian Campaign ", he spoke with all and more than all his former vigour and fire, denouncing Beaconsfield's policy towards the Turks, his stirring up of trouble in Afghanistan, and his failures in South Africa. His indignation and his eloquence chimed in with people's uneasiness, and the Liberals were returned triumphantly to power (1880).

Beaconsfield himself did not long outlive his defeat. He died the next year [1] (1881). He must always remain a strange and romantic figure, not at all typical, in his foreign and flamboyant style, of the party he led. His genuine belief that Great Britain's rule was " beneficent ", and that the Pax Britannica brought good to the nations, caused his imperialist ideas to strike deep roots. The other side of his policy, social reform or " Tory Democracy ", ceased to exercise so much influence on his party.

[1] Queen Victoria sent primroses to his funeral bier, with the label " his favourite flower "; she intended to refer to the Prince Consort, but the idea prevailed that Beaconsfield's favourite was meant. Hence the Conservative body formed to carry out his ideals is the " Primrose League ".

CHAPTER 68

GLADSTONE'S LATER MINISTRIES: FOREIGN POLICY (1880–1885)

2ND, 3RD, AND 4TH MINISTRIES

Second Ministry (1880–86)

The " Grand Old Man " found himself responsible for a very troubled country. In one sense he was unfortunate in his successful defeat of Disraeli, for actually he inherited a legacy of troubles, and there was little he could do to put matters right.

Difficulties ahead

In every direction he was to earn unpopularity. First there came Africa. Here Gladstone had utterly disapproved of Disraeli's " imperialism ", and he had objected to the annexation of the Transvaal. He was ready therefore to take the resistance of the Boers as a true reason for going back on that policy and to make peace by recognizing the independence of the Boer Republics (see p. 898).

Next came problems nearer home. Ireland had always been in Gladstone's thoughts, and now he devoted his best energies to an attempt to remove the source of so much trouble, the land question. But his whole Irish policy is so momentous that it must be dealt with elsewhere (see p. 864).

Egypt

Third, the question of *Egypt* came to the front. Here we come to a very interesting development — the gradual arrangement between England and France, which resolved itself eventually into a perfectly amicable withdrawal of the French and the establishment of English influence.

Originally it looked as if France would be the power to control Egypt. She had vast territory in North Africa, she had easy communications, and above all she was responsible for the creation of the Suez Canal. A French engineer, *de Lesseps*, had originated and carried through the scheme, and the money invested in it was held part by the Khedive (the ruler of Egypt), who was only nominally responsible to the Sultan,[1] and part by French bondholders. In 1863 *Ismail Pasha* was Khedive, and by his senseless extravagance, plunged head over ears into debt. In an effort to raise funds, Ismail, as we have seen, sold his shares in the Suez Canal (1875), Disraeli buying them for the British Government for four million pounds. This, however, was but a drop in the bucket, and a few months later Ismail repudiated the State debts which had risen to over 100 million pounds. This money had been lent directly by British and French investors, and France was eager to act in the interests of her own people. Britain was unwilling to let France act alone, and as a result, after negotiations with the Sultan of Turkey, Britain and France jointly took over the control of Egypt. A puppet ruler, Tewfik, son of Ismail, was set up (1879).

Ismail Pasha's debts

The Dual Control

Gladstone thought poorly of this whole policy, and his apprehensions were soon justified. The Egyptians thoroughly disliked the " Dual Control ", and in 1881 the army, led by *Arabi Pasha*, rebelled. The troops had not been punctually paid, though French and British had duly received all interest on the loans amassed under Ismail. The French and British fleets were sent to Alexandria, but Gladstone was very reluctant to order any action. Riots broke out in *Alexandria* and Europeans were killed. Goaded on, Britain determined to act, and though the French drew back, the British fleet bombarded Alexandria. War could not now be avoided. The French were afraid to become entangled, for Bismarck was threatening attack on them, and they decided that it was better to abandon Egypt. So Britain acted alone. In 1882 Arabi's army was defeated by *Sir Garnet Wolseley* at *Tel-el-Kebir*. Furthermore, the army revolt being thus suppressed by British forces, the Khedive

Arabi's revolt (1881)

Tel-el-Kebir (1882)

[1] He was the independent ruler of Egypt, but still owed a nominal allegiance to the Sultan of Turkey, Egypt having been originally part of the Turkish Empire.

was obliged to let Great Britain try to restore order in the finances, and *Sir Evelyn Baring* was sent out to act as adviser.

The Sudan and the Mahdi

To the south of Egypt lay the vast district of the Sudan. There Ismail's misrule had wrought complete havoc, and discontent had long been acute. Now this broke out into rebellion. The Sudanese were stirred up by the appearance of a preacher, the " Mahdi ", whose advent was supposed to mean the conversion of the world to Mohammedanism, and under the influence of whom the Sudan declared itself independent. The Khedive could not himself put down the revolt, and he appealed to Great Britain. Gladstone and his Cabinet decided that it was no part of their duty to reconquer the Sudan for the Khedive. But scattered about in that country were Egyptian garrisons, commanded by British officers who had taken service in Egypt, and it was decided that these garrisons must be rescued and then some course of action decided upon. Most unfortunately the man sent out (1884) to supervise this withdrawal was *General Gordon*.

General Gordon

Gordon was a strange man, full of a personal magnetism which won him ardent friends. He had made a great name for himself in China,[1] and he had been Governor of the Sudan under the Khedive from 1874 to 1879. Himself an intensely religious man, he had set his mind on converting the Sudanese to Christianity, and he could not tolerate the thought of abandoning them to the wild priests of the Mahdi. He either did not understand his instructions, or decided to ignore them. He knew that the Khedive did not wish to evacuate the country, and he knew that the British Government had vaguely talked of the " future welfare " of the Sudan. So he advanced right up the Nile to *Khartoum*, instead of withdrawing the garrisons, and from there he began to send back dispatches to England.

Gordon at Khartoum (1884)

[1] Gordon's most famous exploits were in China. He commanded a force known as the " Ever-victorious Army ", on behalf of the Chinese Government in the formidable Taiping rebellion. His force won thirty-three engagements in under two years (1863–4), and stamped out the rebellion. Gordon led the storming-parties in person, carrying a little cane. His soldiers regarded it as a magic wand, protecting his life and leading them to victory.

He believed that we should " smash the Mahdi ", and he asked for more troops to be sent out for that purpose. The inevitable result of this pause at Khartoum was that the Mahdi's troops closed in round him. He and his small force were cut off. At this critical moment the Cabinet in England quarrelled violently. One party had always opposed the policy of withdrawal, and Gladstone felt with anger that Gordon was working with this section to induce him to send out a large force and re-conquer the Sudan. Nothing would induce him to do this. In the end *General Wolseley* was sent, but delays occurred, and when the relieving force arrived at Khartoum, they were just two days too late — the citadel had been stormed, and Gordon killed. The news created an absolute passion of indignation in Great Britain. Pictures were sold everywhere showing the " lonely man " in the tower, watching and waiting for the relief that never came. The full fury was directed against Gladstone, who was treated as individually responsible. He had the self-restraint to accept the blame, and to a certain extent he was bound to do so. For his Cabinet had made a mistake in appointing Gordon at all — he was not the sort of man to carry out this particular mission. Having done so, the Cabinet delayed too long in sending relief. Gordon's own conduct in not withdrawing had contributed to the disaster, but he had died a hero's death and his mistakes were forgiven, while Gladstone's were not.

Death of Gordon (January, 1885)

Thus in almost every direction, Gladstone met with trouble. He scored only one success. He completed the enfranchisement of the workers by his *Country Franchise Act*, an agreed measure as between the two parties, which gave the vote to the agricultural population, and increased the vote of the town-dwellers. This Act laid down that every occupier and lodger in town or country, paying £10 a year in rent, was given a vote. People no longer had to be in a " borough " to exercise the franchise. Actually, though this Act has received comparatively little attention, it was

Reform of country franchise (1884)

one of the most practically effective of the Reform Acts. More than two million new voters were added to the register — nearly half the total, for in Great Britain in 1884 there were, including the new voters, a total of five millions on the register. Gladstone also "redistributed" members, limiting towns with less than 50,000 inhabitants to one member each, and transferring the extra members to London and the great cities. Finally, he tried to check corruption by the Act which limited the amount of candidates' election expenses.

Split in the Liberal Party

Thus in too many directions Gladstone had achieved little except unpopularity. The "imperialists" resented his lenient policy to the Boers; Gordon's death had been visited on him; and he could point to no definite advantages gained for the people. In June, 1885, he brought his second ministry to a close by resigning office. No election could be held until new voting lists were ready, so for six months (till December, 1885) Lord Salisbury took office.

Gladstone's Third Ministry (1886)

Then the general election (November – December, 1885) gave the Liberals a majority, and Gladstone began his Third Ministry. He meant to solve the problem which most weighed on his mind — Ireland. He was by now convinced that Home Rule must be granted (see p. 868), and Ireland have her separate parliament. In consequence there appeared the fatal split which was to ruin the Liberal Party. Many of his followers did not agree with Home Rule, and they were led by one of the most important men in the Party, *Joseph Chamberlain*. Hitherto Chamberlain had been an advanced Radical (see p. 871), but he thought that "union" with Ireland must be maintained, and would not agree to an Irish parliament. He and eighty other Liberals therefore broke away and voted against their leader (June, 1886). In the election which followed, Gladstone was defeated, for the country as a whole would not grant Home Rule. The "Grand Old Man", now over seventy-eight, was driven from office.

For six years the Conservatives ruled (see p. 869), and then in 1892 Gladstone returned to office once more, this being his fourth ministry. He tried patiently and perseveringly to carry out his Irish policy, but he could not succeed. This time his Bill passed the Commons, but the Lords rejected it (see p. 870). He now accepted defeat, and felt that his day was really done — he was past eighty-three years old. He went back to his home at Hawarden, where he died four years later.

The last phase: Gladstone's Fourth Ministry (1892–94)

We can see how he had clung all his life to what we would now call " self-determination ". His foreign policy had been based on that idea; his colonial policy, especially his handling of the Boer question, had been rooted in it; and so was all his Irish policy. Here he had the great difficulty that Ireland includes two races and two religions. He believed that by granting " Home Rule " to the island as a whole, the two sections might settle down together, but his countrymen did not agree with him and they felt that he did not maintain Great Britain's prestige. They turned instead to what has been called a " forward " policy and " imperialism ". Gladstone had, however, done an immense amount to give political power to the working-classes and to improve their social conditions, and he was the greatest exponent of " Liberal " ideals. The effect he produced on his contemporaries was tremendous, and with his death men felt that a great force had passed away.

Perhaps he had been in advance of his time, for the two chief policies for which his opponents blamed him, Home Rule for part of Ireland and self-government for the Boers, have both been conceded in later times though in both cases a legacy of bitterness has poisoned the situation, and so far no permanently happy solution of the problems has been found.

CHAPTER 69

IRELAND (1848–1893)

The Fenians

The years of famine in Ireland, 1846 and 1847, had left that country fearfully exhausted. Yet in 1848, when all Europe was in revolution, the Irish too rebelled. A party was formed called *Young Ireland*, led by *Smith O'Brien*, which tried to win Irish liberty. The people were, however, too worn out with misery for this to be anything but a feeble flicker, quickly put out by the British. Ten years later a more formidable organization appeared in the *Fenian Society*. These men, knowing Ireland was too weak to rebel, believed in using force and outrages to draw attention to her grievances. For example, they sent members over to England with bombs. Thousands of Irish had emigrated to the United States, and the Fenians there planned a raid into Canada. The British Government, by the use of spies, discovered the various Fenian plots, and hundreds were arrested in Ireland and given long sentences of imprisonment. The Canadian raid was easily crushed. In England Fenian bombs were used in an attempt to blow up Clerkenwell gaol, where some Irishmen were imprisoned, and at Manchester the police were attacked and one policeman killed (1867).

This campaign of terrorism frightened and angered the British nation. Gladstone became Prime Minister when the movement was at its height, and he declared that repression was not enough, and that some attempt must be made to remedy the grievances which perturbed Ireland (*Note 139*).

Gladstone and the Irish Church Act (1869)

His first effort was to deal with religious trouble. The Irish were, of course, a Roman Catholic nation, with the exception of Ulster, which was largely Presbyterian. But the Protestant Episcopal Church was by law the "established" one, and the Irish were compelled to pay tithes for its support. Gladstone's own devotion to the Church of England made him feel specially strongly on the religious question. He believed that a church which represented only a tiny fraction (one-tenth) of the population, ought not to be in this privileged position. In 1869, therefore, he brought in his Bill for the *Disestablishment of the Irish Protestant Church.* This meant that the Episcopal Church in Ireland was put on an equality with other churches there, that tithes were not to be paid it, and that part of its great wealth was given to other objects, chiefly the relief of the poor.

The land question

The *Land Question* next engaged Gladstone's attention. The poverty of Ireland shocked all fair-minded men. The Irish had few manufactures, the people were too poor to be able to develop their land, the Irish system of inheritance meant that a peasant holding was divided and subdivided amongst a family until each part was too small to support anyone. The great landowners were often absentees living in England, and their agents' chief object was to squeeze rent from the peasants. In Ireland the tenant had to be responsible for repairs to buildings and for gates, but he got no compensation for his expenditure on these items. In England the landlord was responsible. Nor had he any security of tenure. He was a "tenant-at-will"; that is to say, the landlord could turn him out at any time, or, if he chose, raise his rent. Thus a decent peasant who improved his farm could, and often did, find the result was that his rent was put up, and if he could not pay he was evicted and the farm, on which he had worked, was let to anybody who could pay more.[1] Gladstone saw clearly that the miserable condition of the agricultural population must be remedied, and his first *Land Act*, 1870, was an effort to rectify this state

[1] Maria Edgeworth's novels *The Absentee*, etc., show the evils of this system at work.

The Irish Land Act (1870)

of affairs. It laid down that compensation must be given to any out-going tenant who had improved his farm. Also, any tenant who was evicted for any other reason than non-payment of rent or the refusal to accept "reasonable" conditions of tenure, must also receive compensation.

The Land League

More than this Gladstone could not do, for he had to contend with the House of Lords, which stood up for all the privileges of landlords. Yet the need for more action was soon made clear. Tenants were often too poor to pay rent if times were bad, and landlords could, even under the 1870 Act, evict them. In 1871 *Michael Davitt*, who had been a Fenian, started the *Land League*. This aimed at preventing evictions by binding all tenants together in an undertaking not to offer higher rents for a vacant holding, and to adopt a "rent strike" in the case of harsh landlords. Anyone who broke this rule was to be "isolated from his kind as if he were a leper of old", no one was to supply him with food, and, in the case of a landlord, no one was to work for him in any way.[1] Then in 1879 came another potato famine, and the landlords evicted thousands of miserable peasants who were utterly unable, starving as they were, to pay their rents. Driven out of their homes, these desperate men took to violence and murder, attacks on the landlords broke out, and many horrible crimes were committed. It was said to "rain outrages", and it was reckoned that there was a policeman or soldier in Ireland for every thirty people.

Irish Land Act (1881) the three F's

When Gladstone came back after his Midlothian campaign in 1880 (p. 857) he resolved to make a further effort to put Ireland on a better footing. With a big majority behind him, he could be firm. So 1881 saw the *Second Land Act*, which has been nicknamed the *Act of the Three F's* (Fair rent, Fixity of tenure, and Free sale). This said that rents were to be the subject of arbitration — that is to say,

[1] This was called "boycotting", as the first person to be treated in this manner was a Captain Boycott who evicted some of his tenants.

a tenant could appeal to an independent tribunal to fix what his rent should be; if he paid that rent he could not be evicted, and if he wished to leave his holding he could sell his " interest ". This was meant to allow tenants to plead bad times, and to give them support against harsh landlords. But the Irish were by now too embittered, and they refused to go to these new " Land Courts ".

The reason for this lay in the rise of a new leader and a new movement, destined to have very great effects on both Irish and British history. Parnell had organized the demand for Home Rule.

Parnell and Home Rule

Charles Stewart Parnell was a Protestant and his father was a landowner. He had been educated in England, and, his mother being an American, he had visited the United States. He had great gifts of eloquence and an even greater gift of organization. Himself hard and cold, he had the very quality of iron resolution which was needed to bind together the fiery Irish. Believing that Ireland would never win reforms or proper attention to her grievances from Great Britain, he held that the true remedy for Irish misery was to give her back her own parliament and let her have " Home Rule ". Gladstone came to share these views, but the Conservative Party clung fast to " union ", and with some Liberals, called themselves " Unionists ". Parnell thought that instead of committing outrages in Ireland, the more effective way was to agitate in Parliament in England. So he organized his block of Irish M.P.s and began a policy of " obstruction ". The Irish members would " block " every debate by arranging for relays of speakers to take it in turn to make interminable speeches. Hours of time were wasted and it became almost impossible to carry on the business of the House of Commons.

The Unionists

Coercion Act (1881)

Parnell worked with the Land League, and English public opinion was so infuriated by the troubles in Ireland, coupled with the tactics in the Commons, that against his own judgment Gladstone was induced to try repressive measures. "Coercion" was probably the only means of restoring order, at that stage, and, of course, had Gladstone felt that he could not introduce it, he could have resigned office. A Coercion Act was passed (1881). This meant that the ordinary rights of the subject were suspended, the police were given special powers, and magistrates could imprison people "on suspicion" without trial. This roused the Irish members to violent anger and opposition, and finally Gladstone allowed Forster, who was Chief Secretary in Ireland, to imprison Parnell himself, who had committed no "crime", though as head of the party he had great responsibility for what occurred.

The mistake of such a policy was soon clear, for outrages at once grew worse and more frequent. Gladstone made a bargain with Parnell, called at the time by the nickname of the "Kilmainham Treaty" after the gaol in which Parnell was imprisoned. Parnell was to induce his followers to stop lawlessness, and Gladstone was to bring in a bill to help peasants who were in arrears with their rent. Any hopes that this pact might have worked, were destroyed by a political murder. Some of the most violent Irish wished to

Phœnix Park murders (1882)

murder one of the political Secretaries, Burke. By mistake they also murdered *Lord Frederick Cavendish*, the Chief Secretary, as he was walking with Burke in the Phœnix Park, Dublin. This roused such a passion of anger in England that, as Parnell (himself horrified at the murder) foretold, all hope of conciliation vanished. A fresh Coercion Bill was the direct result.

Gladstone and Home Rule

Yet Gladstone stuck to his principles. It was clear that repression might punish crimes, but had no effect on the grievances which drove men to commit them. Gladstone saw this, and resolved that the Liberal Party must give Ireland what she wanted. He could not convince all his followers, and his most promising young Liberal, *Joseph Chamberlain*, left the party on this issue (p. 870). Still Gladstone persevered, and in 1886 brought in his Home

Rule Bill. This would have given Ireland her own parliament in Dublin, to deal with Irish affairs, while control of the army, navy, customs duties, and foreign policy, would have remained with Great Britain. It was a return, indeed, to the policy which had existed before Pitt's Act of Union. He could not carry the measure. A block of Liberals voted against it, and the Government was defeated.

Defeat of Home Rule (1886)

The next few years make dreary reading in the history of both countries. The Conservatives came into office, and their remedy was stronger repression. The *Crimes Act* (1888) suspended trial by jury in Ireland (for no Irish jury would convict), and men were tried by special magistrates appointed by the Government. Strict policing of the country and imprisonment of hundreds did something, but, perhaps, more was produced by the collapse of Parnell's party. The leader in 1890 was involved in a divorce action. The Irish, as Roman Catholics, did not recognize divorce, and not only did many of Parnell's followers in the House of Commons break away from him, but the priests in Ireland turned people against him. The party which had been so effective when united, now split hopelessly, and even on Parnell's unexpected death in 1891, it could not be restored. Arthur Balfour became Irish Secretary, and his policy was to repress disorder by coercion on the one hand, but to give relief to economic grievances with the other.

The Unionists and repression

In 1885 a *Land Purchase Act* (Lord Ashbourne's Act) had been passed, under which the British Government lent money at a very low rate of interest to enable small tenants to buy their land, if their landlord would sell. The Conservatives now made a further effort to remedy the eternal land question and in 1891 Balfour was able to pass another Land Purchase Act.[1] He also passed such Acts as the Light Railways Act and the Congested Districts Board Act, hoping thereby to bring greater prosperity to Ireland.

Land Purchase Acts (1885, 1891)

[1] The interest on the loans given under these Acts and the Land Purchase Act of 1903 was paid by the Irish, and formed the "Annuities" withheld by the Irish Free State in 1932 and subsequently repudiated.

Home Rule again rejected (1893)

One last effort was made by the fiery old man who still wished to make one final contribution to peace. In 1892 Gladstone came back to power at the age of eighty-two. He came back with but one object — to carry Home Rule. He passed his Bill triumphantly through the Commons, but the Lords rejected it by an enormous majority. Against that verdict Gladstone himself could not struggle, and he resigned. Southern Ireland was, therefore, by the vote of the Upper House, left to her discontent until twenty years later a Liberal Ministry was prepared to deal with the House of Lords.

CHAPTER 70

SALISBURY AND CHAMBERLAIN (1893–1906)

The Unionist Party

When Gladstone was finally defeated over Home Rule, power passed into the hands of the party which began to style itself "Unionists" to show its determination to maintain the union with Ireland through one parliament. The party really had three sections — first, the Conservatives proper, led by *Lord Salisbury* (*Note 145*); then a section of old-fashioned Whigs, led by *Lord Hartington*, who had originally followed Gladstone but had turned back from his more advanced ideas; finally the Radicals, led by *Joseph Chamberlain* (*Note 146*), who had been ardent reformers but who could not accept Gladstone's Home Rule policy.

Ireland: resolute government

If we first take Ireland, which had originally produced the secession of these last two groups from Liberalism, we shall see how logically things developed. The Unionist Party owed its position to its determination to refuse Home Rule. Yet Ireland was seething with discontent. The course taken by the Unionists was to deal severely with Irish disorders, and twenty years of "resolute government" followed. *Arthur Balfour* (Salisbury's nephew), as has been seen, was sent as Chief Secretary in 1886. He was armed with a more severe Crimes Act, under which trial by jury was totally suspended. With special paid magistrates to enforce this Act, political crime was stamped out. Land purchase was made easier (see p. 869) and for a while peace seemed to prevail. Irish hopes of Home Rule were so dashed that quiescence settled over the country.

Chamberlain as a Radical

This negative policy as regards Ireland was in sharp contrast with the other developments of the Unionist Party. *Joseph Chamberlain* claimed to be the heir to Disraeli's "imperialism", but he breathed new life into the conception. Chamberlain had begun life as a Radical. He was a successful manufacturer in Birmingham, and made his name in local politics. He became Radical Lord Mayor of Birmingham, and as such showed great energy. He advocated public control of essential supplies such as light and water, he was ardent for slum clearance, and under his influence the city acquired an Art Gallery, a Free Library, a Public Park, and a University. Thus, when he first took Government office, it was appropriate that he should be President of the Local Government Board. Yet, after all, the sphere in which he made his mark was not that of home affairs. His interest was drawn to the colonies and especially to Africa. He was a man who radiated energy and enthusiasm, and his personality made an immense impression on the people with whom he came in contact.[1]

In the first phase of his life he was an ardent admirer and supporter of liberty. Thus he always advocated free education on secular lines, with no religious teaching in State schools. He consistently pressed for the extension of the franchise, wishing to see manhood suffrage. He wanted payment of M.P.s (going back to that old demand of the Chartists) in order to give the poorer men a chance to sit in Parliament, and not leave all power in the hands of the

[1] His appearance, his clear incisive face, sharp nose, monocle, and orchid in buttonhole, made him a godsend to caricaturists.

well-to-do, whom he bitterly attacked in his speeches. He had urged land reform, so that peasant proprietors might own their holdings. He had wished for heavier taxation of unearned incomes, so that more money could be spent on social reforms.[1] Yet as a Unionist he split the Liberal Party, and turned against his leader over the question of giving Ireland the freedom she demanded, and the right to manage her own affairs in her own parliament. His defection had completely alienated him from the Liberal Party.

Chamberlain as Imperialist

Probably his attitude over Ireland was connected with the policy which he was now to develop — his belief in imperialism and the supremacy of the British Empire. He threw the whole of his strength into efforts to strengthen the ties of the colonies. The *Imperial Federation League* had been founded in 1884 with the idea of binding the colonies closer to Great Britain, and in 1887 the first Colonial Conference was held in London. But the colonies, now fully aware of their own development, wished to carry out their own policy, and considered nothing further was to be looked for in the way of federation, preferring independence.

Tariff Reform

Chamberlain's interest in the colonies led directly to the economic policy which he now began to advocate. The nineteenth century had seen the movement for Free Trade. Huskisson, Peel, Gladstone, had all removed customs duties from goods coming into England. Chamberlain now took up what he named *Tariff Reform*. He wished to see duties placed on foreign goods, so that home manufactures should gain, by being "protected" from foreign competition. He also wished, by giving a "preference" to goods from the colonies (i.e. letting in colonial goods either free, or with a lower duty than that charged on foreign goods), to draw the ties between the Empire closer. Many Conservatives did not agree with this policy, and the party was so sharply divided that Chamberlain ended by giving up

[1] He put forward all these points in his "Unauthorized Programme" of 1885.

office, so that he might devote all his energies to converting others. Free Traders opposed him bitterly, declaring that while tariffs might help the " protected " industries, it was at the expense of our export trade, and that the colonies did not offer us large enough markets. They held that tariff " arrangements " would lead to " tariff wars ", and embitter both colonial and international relations.

Chamberlain failed to convert the country to his policy, and the General Election of 1906 saw a " landslide " in favour of the Liberals, who returned to power with the largest majority hitherto gained by any party.

Lord Salisbury, who had been Prime Minister during the period of Unionist government (which with very brief intervals had lasted from 1886 to 1906), was a great contrast to Chamberlain. He was a member of the Cecil family, descended from Queen Elizabeth's minister, and was a learned man with a gift for writing. He lacked Chamberlain's remarkable gift for making friends, and was rather a solitary individual, with a sharp biting mode of speech. He had always been of an independent turn of mind (he once said he was an Ishmael, his hand against every man and every man's hand against his), but he showed his great gifts in two directions. He was a great party leader, keeping together the sections which formed his composite party. And he was deeply interested in foreign affairs; the policy he followed was important because of the extraordinary changes now taking place on the Continent.

Salisbury

Salisbury had begun his training in foreign affairs long before, when in 1878 he had gone with Beaconsfield to the Congress of Berlin. There he had been impressed, as all were, by Bismarck, and Salisbury retained an admiration for Germany and a belief in her declaration that she was a satisfied power and needed no further expansion. To Salisbury, France seemed the Power which threatened most trouble, and it began over Egypt. After the crushing of Arabi's rebellion, Great Britain had decided that she must

Foreign policy: Egypt

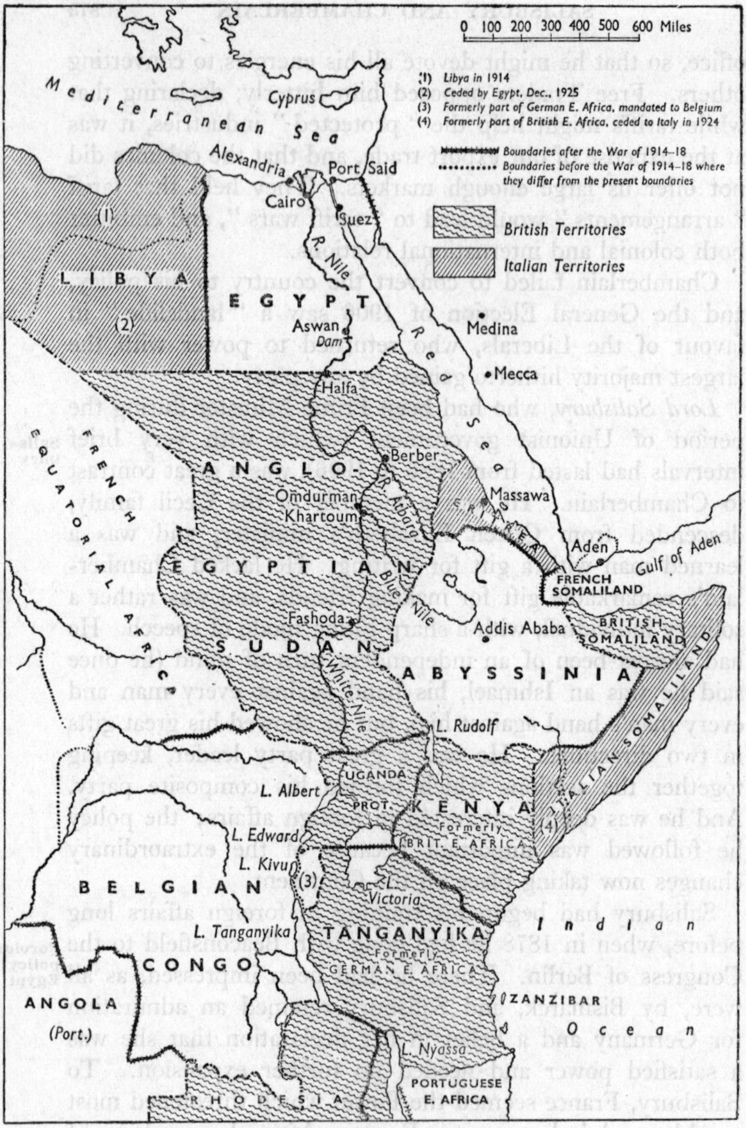

EGYPT AND EAST AFRICA

remain in " provisional occupation " of Egypt. In strict theory the Sultan of Turkey was overlord, and the Khedive his local administrator. The Sultan was paid an annual tribute, and Egyptians were his subjects. In actual fact, neither Sultan nor Khedive ruled, but Great Britain. The British army garrisoned Egypt, and a British Consul-general, *Lord Cromer*, previously Sir Evelyn Baring, managed all her internal affairs. Cromer has been called the " creator of modern Egypt ". In some ways he resembles Dalhousie, for his work was centred in improving the material prosperity of the country, while he did not succeed in winning the support of the people for an alien regime.[1] He first put the finances in order, checking the wholesale bribery and corruption that prevailed, and lessening the burden on the native cultivator. He stopped forced labour, which reduced the fellaheen to what was not far removed from slavery, accompanied by cruel floggings. He set on foot, above all, vast constructive schemes to improve irrigation on which the life of Egypt depended. Land that had been desert was now irrigated and cultivated, and great dams were built to regulate the flow of the Nile. With Egypt itself thus becoming not only solvent, but extremely prosperous, it was possible to deal with the *Sudan*. The lawlessness of the Mahdi's tribal rule made conditions there intolerable. The Egyptian army had now been trained and officered by the British, and in 1896, under the command of *Kitchener*, it undertook the reconquest of the Sudan. The Dervishes were defeated at *Omdurman*, and Khartoum, the capital, was recaptured. What the Mahdi's rule had implied, may be judged from the fact that the population of the Sudan under him had dropped from 8 millions to 4½.

Omdurman (1898)

Trouble with France

The French were both jealous and anxious over our progress, and over the consolidation of Great Britain's position in Egypt. They wished to stop the expansion south-

[1] Lord Cromer, when he finally left Egypt after 25 years of devoted service, had to drive through streets lined by armed British soldiers.

wards, and accordingly made a bid to secure the region of the Upper Nile. Major *Marchand* had gone to raise the

Fashoda (1898)

French flag at *Fashoda.* This would have given France power over the waters of the Nile on which Egypt depended. Kitchener, fresh from victory at Omdurman, sent troops and forced Marchand to withdraw. The French Government felt great bitterness at this, and it almost looked as if war might threaten. Salisbury, however, was determined to be conciliatory as far as possible, and the matter was smoothed over.

South America

He took pains too, to conciliate another Power. A quarrel over boundaries had broken out in South America, between British Guiana and Venezuela (1896). The President of the United States intervened and said that Britain would not be allowed to back her claims, for the *Monroe Doctrine* forbade any European power to interfere in the affairs of the two American continents. Salisbury agreed to arbitration.[1] Great Britain wished for no dispute with the U.S.A. — she was too much occupied elsewhere.

The "Grab for Africa"

The Egyptian question was only a part of the major problems now agitating the European powers — the general development of Africa. This has been called the "grab for Africa", and it is indeed hard to give it any better designation.

Living-stone and Stanley

Africa for centuries had been the "dark continent", and had possessed little to tempt the powers. But the wonderful journeys (1840–73) of *Livingstone* had revolutionized men's ideas. He had shown that Central Africa, far from being "sandy deserts into which rivers ran and were lost", was an area of forests, rivers, and lakes.[2] *Stanley* had continued his work of exploration, and the journeys of these two men caught the general imagination. Their romantic meeting in the centre of the continent won fame, and a new era

[1] A Commission sat which decided in favour of Great Britain.

[2] "His spirit", said Curzon, "hovers over Central Africa just as that of Cecil Rhodes, of many of whose ideals he was the unconscious parent, broods over the South African regions that bear his name."

began. Individual Europeans of every race swarmed out to Africa. No doubt their motives were somewhat mixed. With some it was the love of adventure; with others, as it was with Livingstone, it was missionary zeal. Some hoped to find gold or diamonds or to make openings for trade; others were inspired by a patriotic enthusiasm to secure for their country, before it was too late, the influence they thought it ought to possess in that vast continent (*Note 152*). The enthusiasm for Africa spread from individuals to governments, and the European powers began a general scramble for more territories and " spheres of influence ".[1] It is easy to condemn this invasion of Africa by European people, and its partition by European governments. But the white people were warmly welcomed, at all events at first, by the black people. And it is well to remember what " Africa for the Africans " at that time meant —" the dead, effortless degradation which it represented, broken only by interludes of blood lust, slaughter, slavery, and unspeakable suffering."

Clearly this " partition " of Africa would lead to jealousies amongst the nations, and the ultimate results were strange and momentous, especially in view of Germany's position.

In 1880 Stanley had been sent out to Africa by the King of the Belgians, who thereby secured the vast Congo district, for Great Britain had at that moment no wish whatever for the annexation of territory in Central Africa. She was too much occupied with the first Boer War (p. 896).

After peace had been restored in the south, Salisbury came to office and fully grasped the importance of the partitioning of the north and centre. Accordingly in 1884, the *Conference of Berlin* was held, at which, after much negotiating, each Power received both actual territory and

Partition at Berlin (1884)

[1] " When I returned to the Foreign Office in 1885," said Lord Salisbury, " the nations of Europe were almost quarrelling with each other as to the various portions of Africa which they could obtain. I do not exactly know the cause of this sudden revolution. But there it is. It is a great force — a great civilizing, Christianizing force."

a limitation of its "sphere of influence". Bismarck presided over the Conference, and declared that he personally had no ambition to see Germany a colonial power. He had succeeded in bringing about the union of Germany, he had won for her Alsace-Lorraine and Schleswig-Holstein, and he did not envisage Germany as a colonial or naval power. Hence he made no effort to gain for her any great acquisition of territory. On the contrary, he deliberately encouraged the formation of a French colonial empire, hoping thereby to distract France from her losses in Europe, and so soothe the humiliation left by the Franco-Prussian war. France obtained a vast tract of north-west Africa, reaching from Algiers to the Congo, twenty times larger than France herself. In the remaining years of the nineteenth century there were six international agreements over Africa. As a result, France in 1911 obtained control over Morocco. Belgium was confirmed in the possession of the Congo. Spain got territory in the north, opposite her own coasts. Italy was given part of Somaliland on the Red Sea, Portugal got a part of East Africa. Great Britain already had the Cape Colony, to which she added Rhodesia (p. 899). She controlled Egypt, and at Berlin she gained possession of two other areas. She acquired Nigeria in the west, and the "East Africa Company" gave her a protectorate over Kenya and Uganda. Germany, where public opinion had developed, now wished for colonial possessions, and she obtained German East Africa and German West Africa.[1]

At that time no one could have foreseen the future consequences of these arrangements. France, for example, has so developed her African territories that they have not only shown her success as a colonizer, but have given her a vast reserve of native troops on which she can draw. Germany,

[1] In the course of this division of Africa, figures show the acquisitions:

Great Britain,	5	million	sq.	miles with	90	million	inhabitants.
France,	3½	,,	,,	,,	40	,,	,,
Germany,	1	,,	,,	,,	17	,,	,,
Belgium,	1	,,	,,	,,	30	,,	,,

on the other hand, later became jealous and sore at her comparatively small share, and declared under her later ruler that she had been denied her " place in the sun ". Italy's entry on to the African scene also caused her to embark on the policy which led to her conquest and annexation of Abyssinia in 1936.

The extension of Great Britain's possessions was not confined to Africa. This period, in the last part of the nineteenth century, is sometimes called the time of the creation of her " Third Empire ". Her earlier acquisitions seem to have come about incidentally in the course of her great wars with European Powers. Now, stimulated by Chamberlain's theories, Britain began to talk of her " Imperial destiny ", and her " Empire on which the sun never sets "[1].

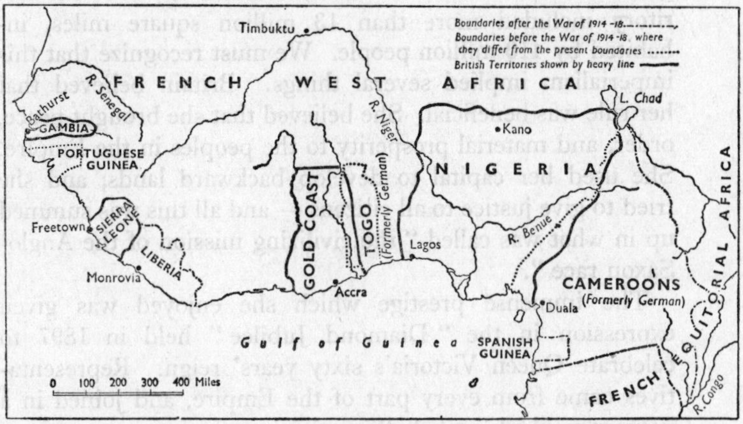

WEST AFRICA

The " Third Empire "

She tightened her hold on the Straits Settlements, and the Federation of Malay States was created in 1896. She obtained a protectorate over North Borneo and Sarawak.[2]

[1] Kipling's writings sum up this phase more completely.

[2] Till 1946 was ruled by descendants of Brooke, the Englishman who made himself Rajah of Sarawak. In 1946 became a colony under the Crown.

She acquired the Fiji Islands and various others in the South Seas. Finally in China, where she already had Hong-Kong, she obtained a lease of the port of Wei-hai-wei.

Extension of British Empire Thus, in the twenty years from 1880 to 1900, Great Britain increased her Empire by 5 million square miles and added 90 millions to her population. Other nations gained too (see p. 934), but when Britain's acquisitions were added to her previous possessions, she became one of the greatest Empires the world had ever seen. By 1914 her territory included more than 13 million square miles, inhabited by 410 million people. We must recognize that this imperialism implied several things. Britain believed that her rule was beneficial. She believed that she brought peace, order, and material prosperity to the peoples in the Empire. She used her capital to develop backward lands, and she tried to give justice to all citizens — and all this was summed up in what was called " the civilizing mission of the Anglo-Saxon race ".

The immense prestige which she enjoyed was given expression in the " Diamond Jubilee " held in 1897 to celebrate Queen Victoria's sixty years' reign. Representatives came from every part of the Empire, and joined in a pageantry which united all in rejoicing.

Working-class discontent Yet, side by side with all this outward expansion and success, there existed a less happy state. The " trade cycle " as we now call it, had resulted in the prosperity of the mid-Victorian period being followed by a depression. The Franco-Prussian war dislocated trade, and from 1870 onwards there was great industrial distress. All this coincided with the spread of education and the extension of the franchise. The working-classes suffered, and their criticism of their condition was now directed into new channels. The unskilled workers, the poorest of all, united to struggle for better conditions. A new form of Trade Unionism was to appear. And, above all, British Socialism, and a Labour Party, were to arise.

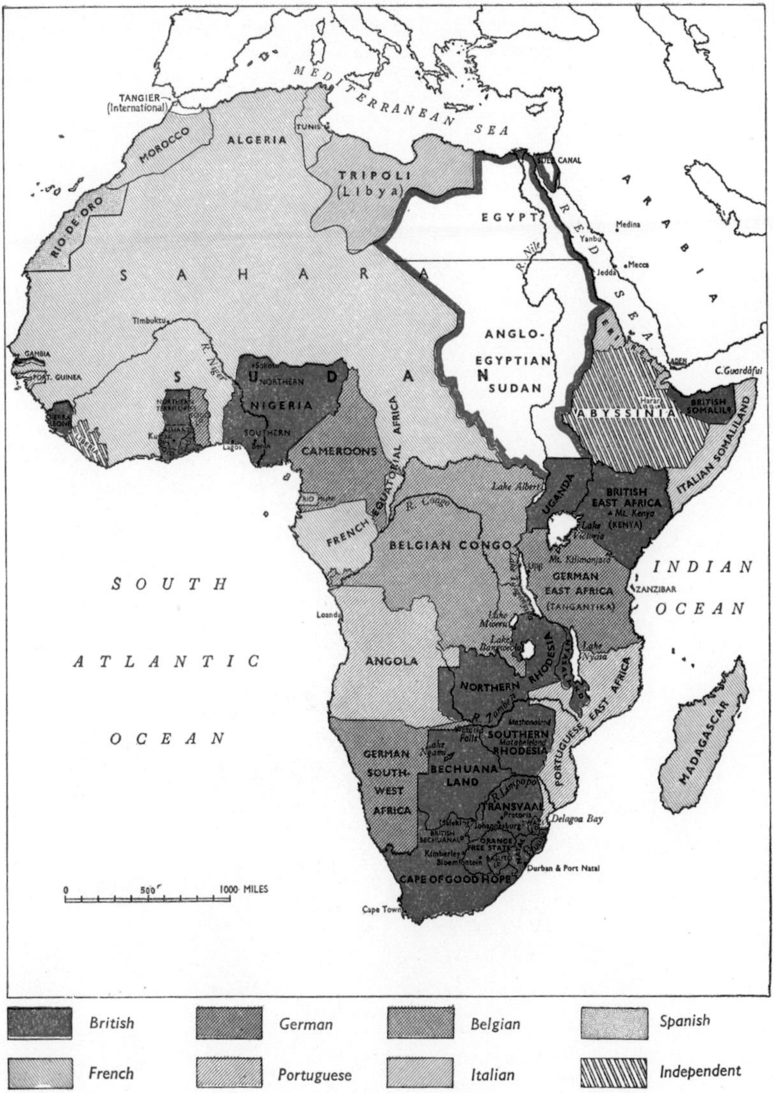

AFRICA IN 1914

F 938

In 1865 *Karl Marx* [1] published *Das Kapital*, the book which has had such immense influence on the history of the modern world. Marx taught that " capitalism " as a system whereby individuals own one of the main factors of production, was wrong. Capital should be collectively owned by the workers. A class war must inevitably be fought and the workers must seize industrial power and create a State controlled by workers. Marx's ideas spread, and when the *Socialist movement* came into being, men took it up all over the world. In Great Britain Socialism as a political force was to develop later, and its first victories were won in industrial life. Trade Unions had been steadily going ahead, but the fact that weekly contributions had to be paid by members, meant that the poorest class of workers and those in casual employment, could not afford to belong.

Karl Marx: "Capital"

Some of the workers' leaders, stirred up by the ideals of Socialism and egged on by the distress which was general in 1889, organized one large section of casual labourers, the *dockers*. *John Burns*, who was to be one of the first Labour men elected to Parliament, led them. Public feeling supported them, for their erratic hours and low rates of pay won them universal sympathy.[2] Their demand was for a wage of 6*d*. an hour, but the employers would not even meet them for discussion. After one of the most celebrated strikes in industrial history, they won the day. From then on a new form of Trade Unionism sprang up. It flourished amongst the poorer-paid workers, and it was immensely influenced by the ideals of Socialism which had not appealed so much to the better paid and highly skilled workers of the older Unions. The leaven had begun to work. The Trade Union movement decided to use part of its funds to send working-men to Parliament. When Chamberlain's

The great dock strike

Trade Unions and Parliament

[1] He was a German Jew who was exiled from Germany under Bismarck's repressive regime, lived in London, and used the British Museum Reading-room when collecting material for his writings.

[2] Cardinal Manning supported them warmly. In their processions they carried poles on which were stuck bad onions and rotten fish heads, to show the food on which they subsisted.

Tariff Reform policy split the Unionist Party in 1906 and a General Election was held, no less than twenty-nine " Labour " members took their seats.[1]

CHAPTER 71

CANADA AND AUSTRALIA

1. CANADA

The grievances felt by the Irish had been made more bitter because they declared that they were refused the right of self-government given to other parts of the Empire. We must turn now to see what had indeed been happening in our colonies and lands overseas. For the developments of the nineteenth century really altered not only our own conception of Empire, but the standard for political developments all over the world.

The idea of self-governing colonies traces its origin to events in *Canada* (*Note 147*). As far back as 1791 that great country had been divided into two provinces, *Upper Canada* and *Lower Canada*. Each had a Governor sent out from Britain and a Council nominated by the Crown, and each had an elected assembly. Discontent grew, because this elected body had no control over finance. In addition, each province had its own grievance. The Upper or English province resented the fact that all the chief posts were invariably given to members of a certain few families. The Lower or French province disliked the British settlers and quarrelled incessantly with them. Grievances were also to be found in the great grants of land which the Government made to British settlers, and in the territory given to the Episcopal Church, which was not the church of the majority. In 1837, when Queen Victoria came to the throne, both provinces

Rebellion of 1837

[1] The first working-men ever to enter Parliament had been elected in 1874. They were both miners and their names were Thomas Burt (Morpeth) and Alexander Macdonald (Stafford).

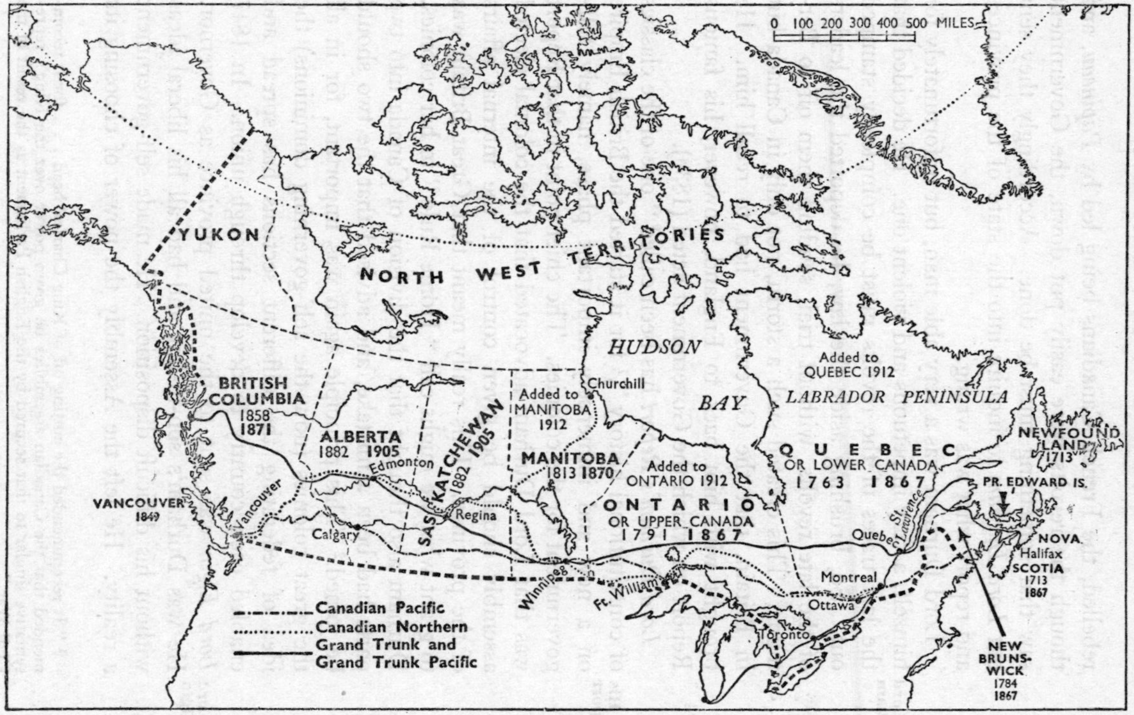

CANADA SINCE 1783

Dates in thinner numerals show foundation of colonies; dates in heavier numerals show entry into Dominion.

rebelled, the French Canadians being led by *Papineau*, and though the revolts were easily put down, the Government saw that something must be done. Accordingly they sent out *Lord Durham* to inquire into the state of the provinces and report what was wrong.

Lord Durham

Lord Durham was a very able man, but unfortunately for himself, a very impetuous and violent one. He decided that the last traces of the revolts must be completely stamped out. So, brushing aside the law, he deported the leaders of the late revolts, without trial, sending them off to Bermuda. This created such a storm, not only in Canada but in Britain, that the Government had to recall him. He brought with him back to England, however, his famous Report on which the Government acted (1839).

His Report

Lord Durham's Report has been called " one of the classics of constitutional history ",[1] for it started the British Empire on a new and immensely important phase, namely self-government for the colonies. The chief point in that Report was that Lord Durham advocated that the colonial elected assembly should be given control of the internal affairs of the province. This really meant that Great Britain was to grant what we might call " Home Rule " to her colonies. Durham also thought that the division of Canada into two parts had been a mistake, and advised that the two should be joined.[2] This principle again was important, for in all the great colonies (now the self-governing dominions) the idea of federating the different sections has spread and enabled each country to develop through union. In 1847

Lord Elgin

Lord Elgin was sent to the united province as Governor. He was Durham's son-in-law and had all his liberal ideas without his difficult disposition. He made self-government a reality. He left the Assembly the power of choosing its

[1] " It recommended the cutting off of King Charles' head . . . for it recommended that the Canadian assemblies be given power over the King's representative similar to that secured by the English Parliament as the result of the Civil War."

[2] This was done in 1840.

own ministry, and to that ministry he left the conduct of affairs. He, as Governor, only gave advice.

So far, Upper and Lower Canada had been joined together, but as the century advanced, so the great outlying regions of the country were developed. In 1867 by the British North America Act, the *Dominion of Canada* was created, and the old Upper Province (now called Ontario) and the old Lower Province (now called Quebec), were federated with Nova Scotia and New Brunswick. Three years later the Hudson's Bay Company sold to the new Dominion its vast lands, part being formed into the province of Manitoba, and in 1871 British Columbia was joined. In 1905 the two last provinces to be created, Alberta and Saskatchewan, became members. This enormous region, therefore, was now united in one federal self-governing dominion. The building of the Canadian Pacific Railway both joined the territories and helped to develop their resources. Canada with her vast wheat areas, her forests, and her orchards, began a career of increasing prosperity.

Dominion of Canada (1860)

Various disputes with the United States over frontier questions were settled by compromise and arbitration, and the peoples of North America can proudly boast that while their common frontier is one of the longest in the world, it is also one which it is unnecessary to fortify.

2. AUSTRALIA

In Australia, also, the idea of self-government developed, though on rather different lines (*Note 148*).

In 1770, *Captain Cook*,[1] after exploring New Zealand, sailed along the east coast of Australia for more than 2000 miles. He saw the fertile areas there and reported on them,

Captain Cook (1770)

[1] Cook, the son of an agricultural labourer, first came into notice through his successful pilotage of the British fleet up the St. Lawrence in 1759. His primary duty in his famous expedition was astronomical — to observe the transit of Venus in the Pacific — and this being accomplished he proceeded on his famous voyage of discovery.

but Britain in those years was not anxious to add to her territories. She had lost the American colonies, and the general belief tended to be that expansion was not needed. Still, in 1788 a small settlement called *Botany Bay* was made in what was to become New South Wales. Then came the French Revolution, and in Britain the Government feared revolution and began a campaign to stamp out possible "sedition". Political prisoners were sentenced to transportation [1] and together with long-term criminals were sent out to Botany Bay. It should be noted that the early Australian settlements were thus in part formed from political offenders, rather than from felons. The ships carrying the first convicts landed at the harbour later called Sydney, after the Home Secretary who had arranged this transportation.

Botany Bay founded (1788)

Political prisoners

In the early nineteenth century *Gibbon Wakefield* began to develop his ideas on colonization, which had great influence. He was a well-educated man but he ran off with an heiress who was a ward in Chancery, and was sent to prison. His career in England being ruined, he decided to emigrate (though in fact he did not leave England for some years), and this led him to study the idea of colonization. He became so enthusiastic that he founded the *Colonization Society* (1834) and set to work to popularize his views. He saw that the empty colonies could give living-room to the growing population of Britain, and he believed that the colonies could grow raw materials and take our manufactures in return. This was no new idea — it had been the basis of our trade with our American colonies — but Gibbon Wakefield had the advantage of dealing with quite undeveloped territory which, above all, needed agricultural settlements. The difficulty was, then as now, that there was no labour available on the spot, and that the poor and unsuccessful, if sent out from Britain, had naturally no capital, and most of them no skill, with which to make a start. Nor

Gibbon Wakefield (1796–1862)

[1] Thomas Muir, one of the "Scottish Martyrs", was sent to Botany Bay for having bought a copy of Tom Paine's *Rights of Man*.

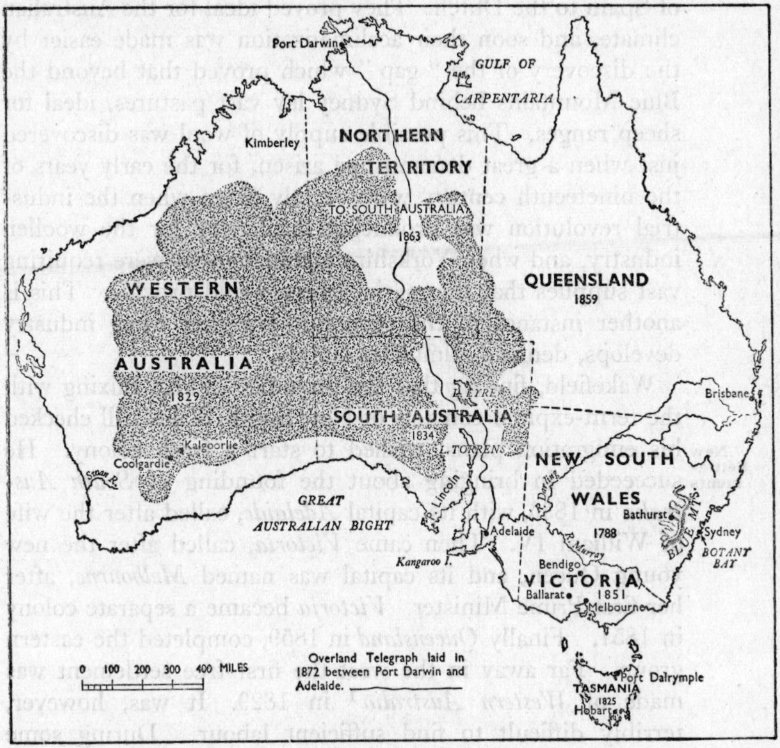

AUSTRALIA SINCE 1788

Dates show foundation of each colony. Desert areas are shaded.

would good-class settlers willingly go to a country which had been given such a disagreeable reputation through the convict settlements.

Also, during the early years of settlement, it was not at all clear for what Australia was best fitted, as the climate and lack of labour made arable cultivation impracticable. In 1797, Captain Macarthur, one of the officers of the British garrison, had imported to Australia some sheep from the Cape. These were merino sheep, originally sent by the King

Sheep farming

of Spain to the Dutch. They proved ideal for the Australian climate, and soon their acclimatization was made easier by the discovery of the " gap " which proved that beyond the Blue Mountains behind Sydney lay vast pastures, ideal for sheep ranges. This possible supply of wool was discovered just when a great demand had arisen, for the early years of the nineteenth century were exactly those when the industrial revolution was producing machinery for the woollen industry, and when Yorkshire manufacturers were requiring vast supplies that the merino sheep could provide. This is another instance of the economic law that when industry develops, demand stimulates supply.

New Settlements

Wakefield, finding that the prejudice against mixing with the term-expired convicts of New South Wales still checked his emigration plans, wished to start a fresh colony. He succeeded in bringing about the founding of *South Australia* in 1836, with its capital *Adelaide*, called after the wife of William IV. Then came *Victoria*, called after the new young Queen, and its capital was named *Melbourne*, after her first Prime Minister. *Victoria* became a separate colony in 1851. Finally *Queensland* in 1859, completed the eastern group. Far away in the west the first free settlement was made of *Western Australia*[1] in 1829. It was, however, terribly difficult to find sufficient labour. During some years convicts were sent out to supply this need, and this cheap labour, added to free Government grants of land, made Western Australia more attractive to settlers than the colonies where Wakefield's policy prevailed. Real expansion came when the British Government abolished transportation of convicts. In 1853 this was done in the eastern colonies though it lingered on in the western areas. The bad times which marked the " hungry forties " in England drove men to try to find work elsewhere, and emigration really set in. By 1850 the population of New South Wales alone had risen to a quarter of a million.

[1] First called the Swan River Settlement.

Then (1851) came the discovery of gold in Victoria. A "gold rush" set in and men poured out to the new fields.[1] **Gold.** Though the gold discovered did not prove as permanent a source of wealth as in South Africa (for the bulk of Australian gold was not in a solid reef, as on the Rand), yet the immense increase in population meant that the colony needed all sorts of supplies, and industries grew up in response.

By 1850 the policy of self-government had been proved successful in Canada. It was decided that the same **Self-government** principle should be applied to Australia. Self-government was granted to the settlements, and Australia began to follow the lines which seemed to be those of healthy growth. Each of the various provinces first developed its own State, and then gradually the wish for federation appeared. The continent clearly formed a whole, and in 1900 the final step was taken. All the provinces, while retaining local **The Commonwealth founded (1900)** assemblies for local affairs, united to form the Commonwealth of Australia, the capital of which was ultimately built at *Canberra.*

3. NEW ZEALAND.

In Australia the chief obstacle to settlement was the difference in climate and conditions from those to which **New Zealand** the early settlers were accustomed. But across the southern sea lay the islands of New Zealand, where climate and soil were both more like those of Great Britain. There a different, and in some senses a more difficult, problem awaited solution. The original inhabitants of Australia were so primitive and so low down in the scale of native culture, that they could not in any way oppose the white man. They simply faded back into the barren regions, and all the efforts of later administrations have been directed towards trying to save the remnants of the race by helping them to survive in changed conditions.

[1] Only two policemen were left in Melbourne — the rest had gone to look for gold.

In New Zealand, however, the *Maoris* were very different. They were a tough, warlike race, and they were prepared to fight to keep their land. Moreover, the Christian missionaries, sent out by the great Societies at home, were anxious to save the native race, and in this they were warmly backed up by the Colonial Secretary in Britain, *Lord Glenelg* (1837), who, like Shaftesbury, was a devoted Evangelical. Glenelg, holding the views which led Wilberforce to champion the cause of the negro slaves, first put forward the view that the white races should act as guardians and helpers of the more backward coloured people. These views did not fit in with Gibbon Wakefield's ideas. Wakefield sent his brother to form a " New Zealand Company " in 1839, and his settlers fell out with the natives over the acquisition of land. Fighting broke out, and the Government at home decided on annexation. They were obliged also to act because France was planning to send an expedition and settle a French company in the islands. The Maori chiefs were asked to come to a conference, and in 1840 they made the *Treaty of Waitangi*, recognizing Queen Victoria.

The Maoris

Treaty of Waitangi (1840)

A Governor was sent out, Sir George Grey, who was an enlightened man, interested in helping to preserve native races. He paid the tribes to cede part of their lands, which he then resold to the white settlers. Here again, the pastures proved magnificent for sheep, though in this case not wool, but mutton, was produced. " Canterbury lamb ", so called from the New Zealand city in the middle of the great sheep-farming area, was to be one of the great sources of New Zealand's wealth, when the invention of refrigeration made its transport to Britain possible.

Grey's reforms

Actually, under Grey's sympathetic and wise rule, the natives flourished and the white people learnt to live peacefully beside them. In astonishingly few years self-government was granted, and in 1855 New Zealand, too, became a country with its local provincial legislations and one central Assembly at *Wellington*. In these assemblies after 1867 the

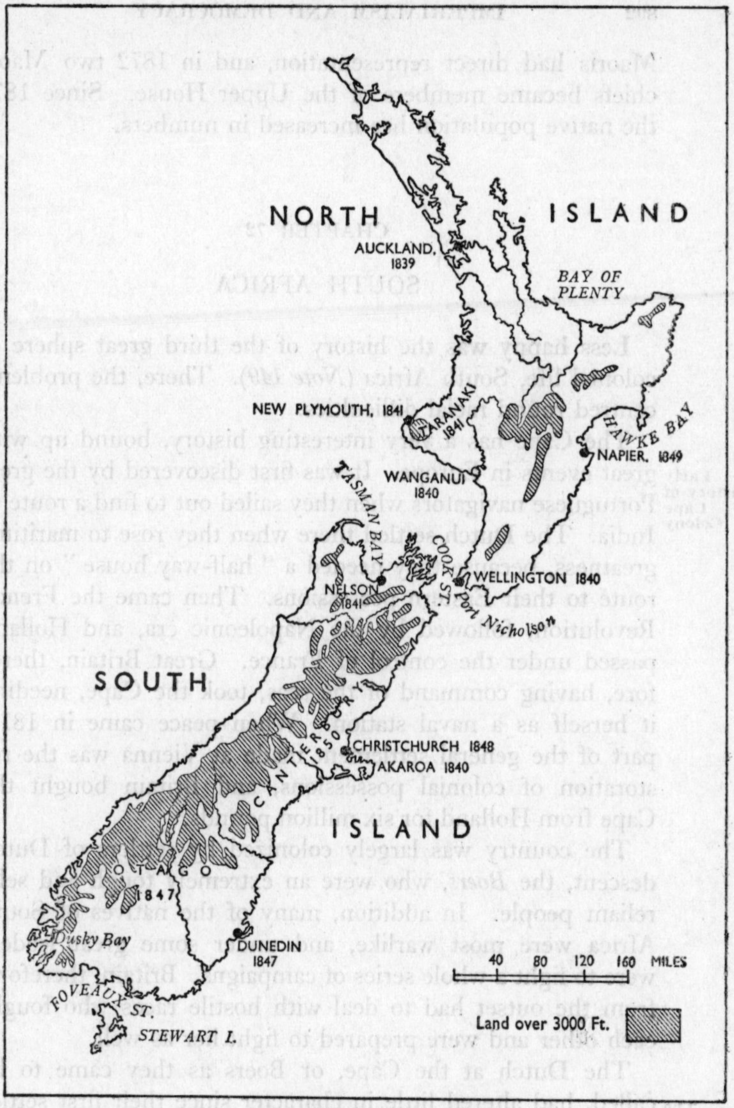

NEW ZEALAND SINCE 1769

Dates show foundation of each settlement.

Maoris had direct representation, and in 1872 two Maori chiefs became members of the Upper House. Since 1874 the native population has increased in numbers.

CHAPTER 72

SOUTH AFRICA

Less happy was the history of the third great sphere of colonial life, South Africa (*Note 149*). There, the problems centred round racial difficulties.

Early history of Cape Colony

The Cape has a very interesting history, bound up with great events in Europe. It was first discovered by the great Portuguese navigators when they sailed out to find a route to India. The Dutch settled there when they rose to maritime greatness, because they needed a " half-way house " on the route to their Eastern possessions. Then came the French Revolution, followed by the Napoleonic era, and Holland passed under the control of France. Great Britain, therefore, having command of the seas, took the Cape, needing it herself as a naval station. When peace came in 1815, part of the general settlement made at Vienna was the restoration of colonial possessions, and Britain bought the Cape from Holland for six million pounds.

The country was largely colonized by settlers of Dutch descent, the *Boers*, who were an extremely tough and self-reliant people. In addition, many of the natives of South Africa were most warlike, and under some great leaders were to fight a whole series of campaigns. Britain, therefore, from the outset had to deal with hostile races who fought each other and were prepared to fight her as well.

The Boers

The Dutch at the Cape, or Boers as they came to be called, had altered little in character since their first settlement in the country. Upon them, as upon the Puritans of the seventeenth century in England, whom indeed they resembled in many respects, it was the teaching in the Old Testament rather than that in the New that had the greater hold. They had the same intense conviction as the Puritans that God was with them in all their decisions, and the supreme self-confidence and self-righteousness that such a conviction engendered. The rugged, obstinate, simple Boer farmer, incurably suspicious of everything new, and ardently tenacious of his rights, had little in common with the eager sympathies, progressive ideas, and, it must be added, the somewhat ignorant sentimentality which characterized a large portion of the British public during the nineteenth century.

The native tribes

There was also an enormous coloured and semi-barbarous population in South Africa; part belonged to the *Hottentot* race, but the great majority of tribes, such as the *Kaffirs*, *Zulus*, and *Basutos*, belonged to the race of the *Bantus*. Even at the present time, in the territories comprising the Union of South Africa, the Kaffirs outnumber the people of European descent by nearly five to one, and, of course, a hundred years previous to the Union the disproportion was much greater, the total number of Europeans in South Africa in 1815 being only some thirty thousand.

Friction over natives

This question of the natives led to friction between the British and the Boers. In the nineteenth century Great Britain definitely took up the cause of the negroes, and in 1833 slavery was abolished throughout her dominions. This affected the Boers of the Cape who had slaves, and though compensation was paid to the owners, they declared that the amount was quite insufficient and really only represented a third of their value.

A greater shock was felt to be the granting of political rights to natives in Cape Colony on the same terms as to white men. The Boers could not tolerate this. The final touch was given when the Kaffirs threatened invasion from the north. *D'Urban*, Governor of the Cape, drove them back and took some of their territory to form a "buffer" province.

The Home Government considered this unjustified, and gave the Kaffirs back the land. The Boers resented this and felt themselves both threatened by the Kaffirs and deprived of protection by the British.

They decided to move out of the territory, and in 1836 thousands of them set out on the *Great Trek*. They moved in their wagons across the veld, in a movement resembling the migration of the Biblical patriarchs, until they came to unoccupied spaces, and there they settled. The first new territory was called *Natal*, but the British followed them, and as the Home Government wished to keep access to the coast from the Boers, Natal was annexed in 1843. The Boers moved on again and formed a State on the other side of the *Orange* river, with a capital, *Bloemfontein*, and others went still farther across the Vaal, and called that territory the *Transvaal*, with a capital at *Pretoria*. These new settlements consisted mainly of scattered farms, and were weak in defence against the Kaffirs and Zulus. Great Britain declared, therefore, that the new territories must be annexed to give safety to the Cape, and this was done in 1847.

The Great Trek (1836)

Natal annexed (1843)

Then, however, came a change of policy. In Europe Britain was becoming concerned with the Near Eastern question, and the Crimean War was not far off. South Africa was felt to be troublesome, and the Government therefore tried to lessen its obligations. In 1852 the Boers were given independence, and their two States recognized as republics, Great Britain saying that she "had no desire for responsibility beyond the Orange River" (*Sand River Convention*).

Independence of Boer States

The Sand River Convention (1852)

Two circumstances led to that policy being abandoned, and again we can see how a mixture of motives led us on. First came endless difficulties over the natives. Bordering the Orange Free State lay *Basutoland*, and there trouble began when the natives of that district attacked the Boers. The Free State was not strong enough to deal adequately with this war-like tribe, and in consequence Britain stepped

Native wars

in, put down the Basutos, and annexed their territory (1868). **Basutoland annexed (1868)**

Meanwhile, a whole series of campaigns against the *Kaffirs* went on, lasting almost continuously till 1878. This meant that the territory from the Cape right up to the Orange River, became, after conquest, consolidated with the Colony. Moreover, the Cape government prospered, and when diamonds were found at Kimberley (1871) thousands flocked out to the diamond fields. The country round Kimberley was annexed by the British Government, wealth increased with numbers, and at last the Colony, in 1877, was given self-government in accordance with what was now recognized as Britain's policy towards her colonies. **The diamond fields**

In contrast with these advances made by the Cape were the misfortunes which had overtaken the Boer republics. They were poor, with a very scattered agricultural population. The district round Kimberley, where the diamond fields lay, had not been incorporated with the Orange Free State, and now danger threatened from the most formidable of all the native races, the *Zulus*.

This race of magnificent warriors was full of vigour and vitality. The men were of wonderfully fine physique, and with their great painted shields and their assegais, were truly formidable as fighters, whilst their impis (bands of trained warriors) were severely disciplined, and thus formed an army in the strict sense of the word. They were now ruled over by a great man, *Cetewayo*, who collected his army of over 40,000 fighting men and threatened to invade the Transvaal. Such an invasion was not likely to be beaten off by the Boers, and fearing general danger to all the white populations of South Africa, Britain once more intervened, and in 1877 annexed the Transvaal. **The Zulus** **Transvaal annexed (1877)**

Actually this step brought about the very war it was intended to avert. The Zulus had up to this point been on good terms with the British, though they disliked and despised the Boers. They took the annexation of the Transvaal as an insult to themselves, and said "the English cow has neglected her own calf, Zululand, and given her milk to a strange calf, the Transvaal." In the war which followed (1879), the Zulus at first won successes, largely through the incompetence of the British generals who underestimated their enemy and made no effort to reckon on the nature of the country. At *Isandhlwana*, a British force was cut off and massacred. In another ambush the Prince Imperial, son of the late Emperor Napoleon III, was amongst the killed. He had insisted on going out to fight for Britain, which had given refuge to him and his mother. His detachment was surprised by the Zulus and he was killed by their assegais.

The Zulu War (1879)

At *Rorke's Drift* a tiny British force won fame by holding out behind barricades of biscuit tins till rescued. Finally, the Zulus were defeated at *Ulundi* (1879). Cetewayo was captured and sent as a prisoner to the Cape. Later he came to England and an agreement was made whereby he was to have a large part of his country returned to him. But he could not win back control over his own fierce people, and a brief civil war ended in his defeat and death. Continual fighting in Zululand and raids into the Transvaal went on, until in 1888 the last chief, Dinizulu, was defeated, and the country annexed.

The first Boer war (1881)

While this struggle with the Zulus was raging, the British found themselves with another war on their hands. The Boers had naturally resented the annexation of the Transvaal, but they had gloomily acquiesced, believing that they, like the rest of South Africa, would be given self-government. When they found that this was not the case (for Disraeli, and Gladstone who came into office in 1880, did nothing in the matter) they decided to rebel. As soon as the victory of Ulundi made the collapse of the Zulus certain, the Boers rose. They first repulsed a British attack at *Laing's Nek* (1881) and then themselves stormed and took *Majuba Hill*, a place with a top shaped like a saucer, the rim of which was held by the British. The Boers stormed

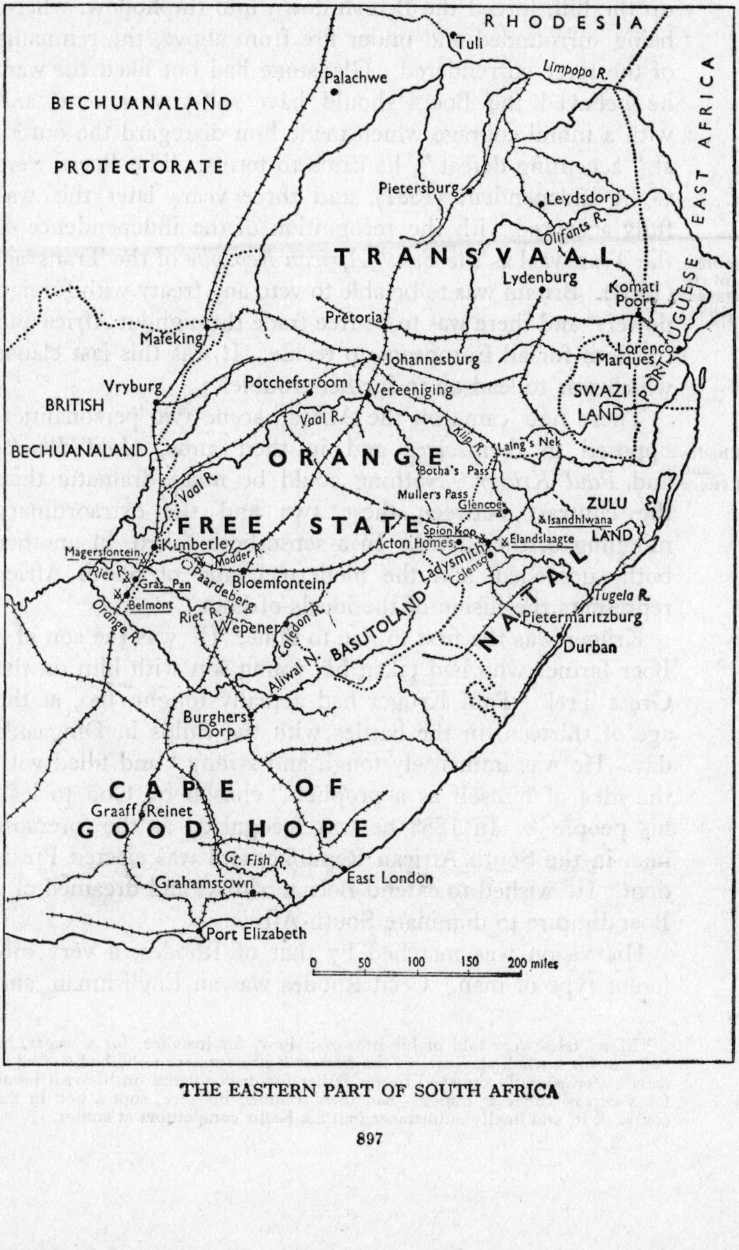

THE EASTERN PART OF SOUTH AFRICA

up the hill, forced the British down into the hollow, where, being surrounded and under fire from above, the remnants of the force surrendered. Gladstone had not liked the war; he believed the Boers should have self-government, and with a moral courage which made him disregard the outcry at " accepting defeat ", he came to terms. The Boers were to be independent (1881), and three years later this was fully accepted with the recognition of the independence of the Transvaal as the *South African Republic* of the Transvaal (1884). Britain was to be able to veto any treaty with foreign powers, and there was to be free trade throughout Africa and freedom for all Europeans to reside. It was this last clause which was to lead on to further trouble.

Republic of the Transvaal (1884)

There now came on the African scene two personalities, opposed in themselves and in their aims, *Cecil Rhodes* and *Paul Krüger*. Nothing could be more dramatic than the contrast between these two and the extraordinary mingling of their lives. In a sense both failed, in another both succeeded, and the modern Union of South Africa represents the fusion of the ideals of both.

Rhodes and Krüger

Krüger was the first to rise to fame. He was the son of a Boer farmer who had taken his young son with him on the Great Trek. Paul Krüger had actually fought, too, at the age of thirteen, in the battles with the Zulus in Dingaan's day. He was immensely tough and strong [1] and filled with the idea of himself as a prophet " chosen by God to lead his people ". In 1883 he was recognized as the foremost man in the South African Republic, and was elected President. He wished to extend Boer territory, and dreamed of a Boer Empire to dominate South Africa.

His vision was matched by that of Rhodes, a very different type of man. Cecil Rhodes was an Englishman, and

[1] Many tales were told of his prowess; how, for instance, for a wager, he had run for a whole day against the fleetest Kaffir runners — he had started at dawn, been soundly thrashed by his father for disobedience on his visit home for a cup of coffee at midday, had then resumed his race, shot a lion in the course of it, and finally outdistanced all his Kaffir competitors at sunset.

the son of a country clergyman. He was sent to South Africa as a boy because of his delicate health, and though he managed to return to Oxford, he always spent his long vacations in Africa.[1] He was that rare combination, a visionary who is also a superb man of business. He believed passionately in the idea of " imperialism ", which was then filling the minds of men in England, and he took as his ideal the extension of British influence from " Cape to Cairo ". Like Krüger, he envisaged a great dominion of South Africa, where Boer and Briton would combine, but he meant it to be part of the British Empire.

Rhodesia (1895)

The hard, practical side of his nature drove him on to seek power through wealth, unlike Krüger who remained a simple farmer. Rhodes went into the diamond market, and so outstanding was his ability that he succeeded in forming a great combine controlling the output of diamonds, and in amassing for himself an income which was said to reach the fabulous sum of a million a year. He used the influence which this gave him to further his political ideals. He urged the Cape Government to annex *Bechuanaland*, knowing that the Boers had their eye on the territory. When his arguments failed, he induced the Home Government to declare it a Protectorate. This went against the grain with him, for he disliked rule through the Colonial Office. Then he went on to a greater achievement. He created the Chartered Company of South Africa, and took up the development of that vast region now called after him, *Rhodesia.* He settled men there, Boers and British, built railways and roads, and made schemes for the development of agriculture and mines (1895).

Gold and the Transvaal

Then fate seemed to play a trick upon him. He had done all he could to thwart the Boer Republic, and now gold was found in the Transvaal in such quantities that clearly here was to be one of the great gold-producing countries of the

[1] His love of Oxford persisted all his life, and when he died he left part of his vast wealth to found the Rhodes scholarships there. These are held by young men from all parts of the Empire and the U.S.A. and from Germany.

world. The reef of the *Rand* was inexhaustible, and yet its control was in the hands of the Boers, a government of "backward" farmers. Moreover, the Boers were determined to keep that power in their own hands. People poured into Johannesburg in thousands upon thousands. The income of the State from taxation rose from £150,000 to over £3,000,000 and almost the whole of that taxation was paid by the foreigners or *Uitlanders*, as they were called. The Boers specially altered their constitution so that it was practically impossible for these newcomers to acquire votes.

The Jameson Raid (1895)

Rhodes thought he saw his chance. If the Boers would not allow taxation and residence to qualify for representation, then he considered it justifiable to overthrow the government. He was then himself Prime Minister of the Cape and he was Chairman of the Chartered Company of Rhodesia. The Uitlanders planned a rising, and Rhodes promised to send a force from Rhodesia under the controller of that district, *Dr. Jameson.* To us the wrongheadedness and folly of such a plan seems obvious, for even had it succeeded, the disgrace of such methods would have been great. Rhodes actually knew himself to be a dying man, and impatience and illness urged him on. Yet at the last moment he drew back, and sent word to Jameson to abandon the whole scheme. But Jameson made an even greater error. He did not wait for the Uitlanders to rise, which would at least have given a semblance of reason to the proceeding, but started his "raid" and crossed the frontier of the Transvaal with 600 men. Of course he was easily defeated and had to surrender with all his men. Rhodes was too clearly implicated and he had to resign the Premiership and retire from all public life.

The second Boer war (1899–1902)

The Jameson Raid roused dreadful bitterness. The Boers naturally resented the plot, and, triumphing in its failure, were more harsh than ever against the Uitlanders, who, finding conditions unbearable, appealed to Great

Britain for help. The British Commissioner in South Africa was *Lord Milner*, and the Colonial Secretary in England was Joseph Chamberlain. Both were strong imperialists, and both thought the position intolerable. Besides utterly refusing to do anything to meet the grievances of the Uitlanders, Krüger had opposed Britain in other ways, and held up the progress of all South Africa. He had refused to join a Postal Union, and he had also refused to join in common railway developments and had favoured the line made to the Portuguese harbour in Delagoa Bay. Moreover, since the Jameson Raid, he had clearly prepared for war, buying munitions and bringing in foreign soldiers, especially Germans, as instructors.

Britain had always retained certain rights, even when she had recognized Boer independence (p. 898), and she now declared herself " paramount ". Krüger sent an ultimatum, and in October 1899, war was declared.

The idea of the British Empire at war with two very small republics, was not a popular one in Europe, and most continental powers sympathized with the Boers. The Kaiser had shown his support of the Transvaal, at the time of the Jameson Raid, by sending a famous congratulatory telegram to Krüger. Now Germany, Holland, and France all condemned Great Britain. Nor did the early course of the war do anything to raise our prestige. The Boers fought heroically and adapted their methods to the country. The British on the other hand, made many mistakes. We were far from our base, and at first too few troops were sent, with insufficient munitions. The Boers surrounded and besieged small British forces in the three towns of *Ladysmith*, *Kimberley*, and *Mafeking*, and they then invaded Cape Colony, where they believed the Dutch population would rise. In this they were deceived. They also made two other mistakes. They hoped that some of the European powers would come to their help, but none would go so far. They also, remembering their victorious peace at the end of the first Boer war, believed that Britain would not persevere. But now Britain felt that more was at stake. After a series of reverses (December, 1899) the Government at home saw that serious measures must be taken, and in consequence fresh troops were poured out, including colonial contingents of volunteers from Canada and Australia and New Zealand. *Lord Roberts* and *Lord Kitchener* were sent to direct operations. As a result, by February, 1900, Kimberley and Ladysmith were relieved, Pretoria was captured in June, and the Orange Free State and the Transvaal declared annexed. For two years the Boers continued to fight, but at length they gave up the hopeless struggle and peace was signed in June, 1902, at *Vereeniging*.

Annexation of Boer Republics

The British Government may be said to have done its best to allay the anger and bitterness left by the war. The Dutch language was to be used in schools and in the law courts. The native question was to be decided by the States, and as it turned out, the two Boer States both refused to enfranchise their native populations. Self-government was promised for the future. Five million pounds were spent on helping the Boer farmers to return to their homesteads, and forty millions lent to develop the countries. Actually, in less than five years, the promise made in the peace treaty was fulfilled, and self-government was given in 1906.

Self-government and the Union of South Africa (1909)

A few more years passed, and then the dreams of Krüger and Rhodes were fulfilled, for South Africa decided on federation. In 1909 the provinces of the Cape, Natal, Orange River, and Transvaal united to form the Union of South Africa, and the first united Parliament met in 1910. The first Prime Minister was *Botha*, one of the Boer generals who had fought hardest against the British. Federation actually gave much power to the Boers, who preponderate in numbers over the British settlers, but the Union itself remains part of the British Empire. The *Statute of Westminster* (p. 961) gave it absolute self-government and " dominion status ".

CHAPTER 73

RELIGION; ART; LITERATURE IN THE VICTORIAN AGE

The great Russian, Tolstoy, once wrote a beautiful story, *What Men Live By*, to illustrate the theme that men's lives depend on living "not by bread alone" but by the things of the spirit. So, when we read of the prosperity of the Victorian age, we must realize that besides the material side of life, men of the day woke to a stronger spiritual life as well (*Note 151*).

Evangelicals

The Church of England has always included men of different shades of belief. The settlement of Queen Elizabeth tried to include both those who clung to the old ritual, and those who wanted Puritan simplicity. So, when the Victorian age saw men stirring and wakening from the apparent deadness of the eighteenth century, these two streams of religious life appeared once more. The *Evangelicals*, as their name implies, revived the simplicity of the Gospel. Great men such as Wilberforce and Shaftesbury believed in, and lived their lives in accordance with, the doctrine of the brotherhood of man. One large section of the Church was inspired to fresh life and activity in this direction. What people called "philanthropy" sprang to life through this movement, and efforts were made along these lines to help the poor. Bible Societies, "ragged schools", orphanages, foreign missions, all sprang up, and besides the practical results achieved, there was something perhaps more useful — an awakening of the public conscience to general ills, and the responsibility of men towards each other. In that period the time was not ripe for the State to undertake many of the activities which private persons performed, but the Evangelicals forced into the limelight the bad conditions which needed attention.

In the other direction, the *High Church* movement, as it was called, appealed to a different side of man. The *Oxford Movement* was led by *Keble* and *Pusey* and *Newman.* It began by the writing of the famous *Tracts for the Times* at Oxford, and aimed at revivifying religion by reviving the ceremonies and some of the doctrines of the early church. More ritual and greater beauty were brought to church services. This roused opposition from those who saw in it a return to Roman Catholic beliefs. Great heat arose in controversy, especially when *Newman* (in 1845) and later *Manning*, went over to Rome, both of these great men eventually becoming cardinals. Newman's fame rested chiefly on his writings, especially his *Apologia* or story of his spiritual life and conversion. Manning showed his great ability as an organizer, and the work he did amongst the poor and his sympathy with working-class movements won him great respect and were emphasized by the vast crowds of working people who attended his funeral. He took a prominent part in settling the great Dock Strike in 1889.

Oxford Movement

Newman and Manning

All sections of religious belief, indeed, shared in this recognition of Christian duty " towards one's neighbour ". A party called the *Christian Socialists* carried on a regular campaign to secure better conditions of life for the poor. Their chief exponent was *Charles Kingsley*, who wrote many of his novels to show the need for such practical reforms as sanitation, and described the miseries suffered by " climbing boys " who used to sweep chimneys.[1] Another clergyman, *F. D. Maurice*, worked for the education of working-men, and went on to be one of the pioneers of education for women.

Christian Socialists

So, when we look back on the mid-Victorians, we can see that besides the growth of England in riches and her advance in all material things, all classes were showing signs of an advance in intellectual and spiritual ways. There were real changes in the attitude of man to man, and this rise in

[1] As in the famous *Water Babies.*

" social consciousness " is one of the main characteristics of Victorian England.

It is always interesting to notice that vitality in a nation in one respect, such as trade and commerce, often seems to coincide with vitality in other, and very different, ways. Thus, while the Victorians traded and made money, and incidentally built streets of Victorian houses which they filled with solid Victorian furniture, they also produced a remarkable outburst of literary and scientific activity. It was really an age when men respected and appreciated letters and art, though we may not at present think their standard of taste good. Standards vary, and we now consider that the Victorians had a totally different idea of beauty from ours. They had a marked style, in houses, clothes, furniture, and ornamentations, and to-day some think it ugly and in-artistic.[1] The Victorians themselves were completely self-confident. They felt themselves to be rich, and strong, and they expressed their wealth and vitality in their surroundings. Thus their houses and their furniture were well and solidly built, Victorian workmanship was excellent, and they aimed at, and obtained, solid comfort. Where some think they failed was in their lack of simplicity, and their fussy ornament.

Victorian solidity

Yet they were keenly interested in art, and the rich Victorian business man patronized painting with enthusiasm. Crowds visited the exhibitions held at the Royal Academy, and celebrated paintings had regular " mobs " seething round them and won renown not equalled to-day. Vast sums were earned by the popular painters of those days, and not only did the original paintings of *Landseer*, *Leighton*, *Millais*, *Alma Tadema*, sell for thousands of pounds, but engravings and reproductions made those same pictures familiar all over the land. Landseer's dogs and stags may seem very meaningless, and we think Leighton's mock classical scenes, with men and women in Grecian draperies, and great stress laid on marble and its bright reflecting

Painting

[1] There is, however, a revival of interest in Victorian taste.

surface, very artificial. Nor do we all admire Millais' narrative picture " The North-West Passage " or his renowned " Bubbles ". Yet these pictures had an immense appeal at the time, such as few modern paintings have. Scarcely a home but had its copy of " Dignity and Impudence " or " Wedded Love " or " A Summer Shower ".

Some may think that enthusiasm misplaced, and fail to see artistic merit in those works, but we ought to recognize and respect the fact that the immense success of Victorian painters was at least a tribute to the importance which that age attached to art. A few men still stand out, whom moderns recognize as great. *Whistler's* influence was profound, and his portraits of his mother, and of Carlyle, are famous.

Rossetti, *Burne-Jones*, *Millais*, and *Watts*, form a separate and distinctive group. In 1848 when political revolution broke out all over Europe, a little band of men tried to produce an artistic revolution in England. Led by *William Morris*, Rossetti, and Millais, they formed a " Brotherhood ", which they called the *Pre-Raphaelites* because they wished to go back to the period before Raphael, considering that since his day art had gone off on to wrong lines. They aimed at simplicity of line and form, and opposed the " fussy " elaboration of mid-Victorian decoration, much of which was meaningless. They tried, too, to restore a love of pure colour, and their pictures glowed brilliantly with vivid tints. Morris was very successful, for he applied his ideas to the home, and his designs for wallpapers and stuffs had great influence and are still used. He inspired one man, *Arthur Liberty*, to search for and discover the secret of clear dyes for silks. Burne-Jones and *Holman Hunt* also won larger favour. Though the paintings of the Brotherhood later lost popularity, yet certainly their destructive attacks did rid the world of a mass of Victorian ugliness. They also represented a genuine and conscious attack on machine-made things; they stood for the hand-

The Pre-Raphaelites

made work of the craftsman, and they succeeded in keeping alive the craftsman's beautiful work in printing, painting, decoration of furniture, weaving, and pottery.

We must admit, then, that the Victorians were interested in art, and believed they were encouraging beauty, but to us they were astray in their standard of taste, and all their vigour and vitality were wasted by false values.

Literature

But when we turn to literature, we have the curious fact to face that whereas the Victorian writers were just as prolific, and just as popular as the artists, we still admire the writers, though we condemn most of the painters. The nineteenth century novelists form a band of whom we are still proud. *Scott*, *Thackeray*, *Dickens*, the *Brontës*, *George Eliot*, remain giants in the land, and their books are read not only in English-speaking countries, but are recognized as classics and studied by people of other races all over the world. They show to perfection not only the vast energy of the Victorian age, but its many-sidedness, for these writers of course differ completely in their contribution to the novel. Scott the romantic, Thackeray the satirist, George Eliot the unsurpassed portrayer of English rural life, the Brontës, claimed as the forerunners of modern realistic and "passionate" novels, all gave the Victorian world a richness and variety which makes it a splendid period.

The novelists

Poets, too, attained very great influence. *Tennyson* became the most popular poet England had ever produced, while another group, the *Rossettis* and the *Brownings*, represented, we may say, the cult of "intellectual" poetry.

The poets

Ruskin had immense influence in trying to improve artistic taste on sound principles. His famous dictum was, "have nothing but what you know to be useful and believe to be beautiful." He fought a tremendous battle for good workmanship and design, though here again some deplore his dislike of "classical" influence and his belief in what he thought to be "Gothic" tradition. Ruskin in one sense is the epitome of the cultured Victorian, for while he was a

Ruskin

skilled art-critic, and gave half his energies to preaching on behalf of beauty, he was also keenly interested in social questions. He advocated the importance of the education of women, and his interest in economics and his desire to improve the conditions of the working-classes was profound.

This intellectual wish to "popularize" culture touched all classes, and *Carlyle's* immense vogue as lecturer and writer showed the wide-spread interest in the philosophical ideas which he himself had derived from Germany.[1]

Science

Science was on the verge of a spectacular advance, and Darwin's *Origin of Species*, published in 1859, is recognized as a book which marks an epoch.

Altogether, when we look at this flowering of intellectual life, and realize how many-sided it was, we may agree that "there were giants in those days", and that the Victorian epoch takes its place among the great periods of English development.

Women

One interesting point to notice is that in the latter part of the nineteenth century, women begin to take a prominent place as writers. In the early part of the century it was still considered "unwomanly" to show the possession of brains, much more so to use them in writing and making money by the pen. "George Eliot" took a man's name to conceal her sex, and the Brontës at first wrote under pen-names taken to represent men. This attitude had entirely altered by the end of the century, and women novelists had become a commonplace. Better education and, more important perhaps, wider opportunities, later enabled women to advance beyond "fiction", and in sociology, travel, religion, and art, modern women can win recognition on their own merits.[2] Indeed, women writers actually outnumber men to-day, but they must still admit, like the men, that they have not yet surpassed their Victorian predecessors.

[1] It is interesting to read *Heroes and Hero Worship* or *Frederick the Great*, and see how German theories of the dominant super-man were put forward then.

[2] A list of a few writers to illustrate this particular aspect might include Mrs. Webb, Freya Stark, Evelyn Underhill, and so on.

CHAPTER 74

EDWARD VII (1901–1910)

REFORMS OF THE LIBERAL PARTY

In 1901 Queen Victoria died. She had reigned for over sixty years, and her reign had been one during which Great Britain had made the most immense strides forward. The Queen was herself a great personality, in a period which was very rich in notable men and women. Perhaps her greatest gift to her people was that she did create a definite link through the Crown between the widespread territories which formed her Empire. She proved that Burke's contention was true: "Kindred blood and common memories are ties which, though light as air, are yet as strong as links of iron."

With the new century a fresh phase began. *King Edward VII* succeeded his mother, and many of the chief personalities of the reign now vanished. Lord Salisbury retired from politics in 1902, Chamberlain in 1906. The Unionist Party was hopelessly divided, and in 1905 the Liberals, revivified by their battle for Free Trade, came into office determined on a great policy of social reform (*Note 153*).

New conditions and parties

This was made inevitable by the advance in the organization of the working-classes, and by the spread of the new ideas. The removal of social injustice was the theme of the new *Socialist Party*, and the immense growth of *Trade Unionism* and the formation of a *Labour Party*, clearly challenged both Conservatives and Liberals.

The ministry which took office in 1905 was composed of men whose abilities fitted them for the accomplishment of what proved to be a minor revolution. *Sir Henry Campbell-Bannerman* (Prime Minister, 1905–8), *Asquith*, *Sir Edward Grey*, *R. B. Haldane*, *David Lloyd George*, were all conspicuous for brains and for energy.

The problem of poverty

They had to deal with the problem of poverty, and they therefore had to consider how best to help people suffering from unemployment, ill-health, or the failure to earn simply because of the onset of old age. Some reforms were carried out during the short period of Campbell-Bannerman's premiership, and when *Asquith* became prime minister in 1908 the ground was prepared for a great advance in what we call "social reform".

Old Age Pensions (1908)

The first reforming measure was the *Old Age Pensions Act* (1908) which gave a weekly pension to men and women over seventy. This enabled many old people to leave the workhouses and live with their families.[1]

National Insurance (1911):

The problems of ill-health and unemployment were next tackled. Germany had tried to suppress her socialist movement by force, and at the same time to conciliate her working-classes by improving their conditions. Great Britain now adopted some of the Germans' best ideas. So far, people who were out of work or in distress had either to seek help given under the Poor Law, or to rely on the Trade Unions and Friendly Societies. The Liberals now introduced the idea of insurance, which was first applied to workmen who lost their employment through illness. In 1911, Lloyd George brought in his National Health Insurance Act. By this Act practically all manual workers and many non-manual workers paid a weekly sum (while in work) which was supplemented by weekly contributions from the employer and by the State.[2] In return for these payments, an insured worker who fell ill was entitled to free medical attention and to sickness benefit. Maternity benefit was also included to help working-class women with the expenses of child-birth.

(a) Health Insurance

The National Health Insurance Act also included a similar contributory scheme enabling workers in certain industries

[1] Age later lowered to 65. For later developments of pensions legislation see p. 980.

[2] The slogan was "9*d*. for 4*d*.", as the worker paid 4*d* and the total weekly amount was made up to 9*d*. A great campaign was launched against the scheme, on the grounds that people would object to "sticking stamps" on a card.

to insure against unemployment. In 1921, this scheme was extended to include practically all industries.

(b) Unemployment Insurance

There remained the Poor Law itself, which had come to be associated in the minds of the working-classes with harshness and the " stigma of the workhouse ". Reformers, such as the Webbs, agitated for the " break-up " of the Poor Law, and a Royal Commission was appointed, which presented its report in 1909. The commissioners did not agree, the majority asking for certain reforms, the minority being much more drastic in its proposals. Both sections, however, agreed in the many evils of the system under which those in distress and needing help, suffered. Thus the Report unanimously recommended the abolition of the Boards of Guardians, and the transference of their duties to the County and Borough Councils.

Poor Law

Yet no action was taken by the Government, beyond the adoption of the Unemployment Scheme contained in the Act of 1911. It was not till twenty years later that the Guardians had their duties regarding workhouses and relief of distress taken from them, by the Local Government Act of 1929. An effort was then made to get rid of the old miserable associations by naming the new committees of the Borough and County Councils which dealt with these matters *Public Assistance Committees.*

Before entering on its programme of social reform, the Liberal Government had dealt with a point of great importance to Trade Unions. In 1901 by a famous legal decision (the Taff Vale Case) it was laid down that the funds of a Trade Union could be made liable for damage done by its members during strikes. The *Trade Disputes Act* of 1906 stated that action could no longer be taken against a Union in " a corporate capacity " — that is to say, only an individual could be sued for illegal actions.[1]

Problems of workers

Trade Disputes Act (1906)

[1] In what is known as the " Osborn " case (1908) the appeal court decided that Trade Unions could not use their funds for political purposes, and this decision was confirmed by the House of Lords in 1911. The Trade Unions overcame the difficulty by having two rates of contribution, one for industrial and one for political purposes — but no member was obliged to pay the political contribution.

Other Reforms

Other reforms carried out by the Liberal Government before the outbreak of the Great War in 1914 included the reorganization of the army by *Haldane*, who embodied his ideas in the constitution of the *Territorial Army* (*Territorial and Reserve Forces Act*, 1907). Another measure of importance was the decision by Parliament in 1911 that members of the House of Commons should be paid; it was thus made much easier for a poor man to enter Parliament.

Territorial Army (1907)

Problems of the Constitution: the House of Lords

All these and other reforms were carried through the House of Commons with the greatest of ease, for the Government had an enormous majority of Liberals and in its social legislation it had also the support of the Labour members.[1] They could also often reckon on the support of the eighty Irish members. When, in 1908, Campbell-Bannerman resigned, Asquith became Prime Minister and Lloyd George Chancellor of the Exchequer. At once he brought in a Budget which became famous. It was called the *People's Budget* because it was openly defended by Lloyd George as being meant to " take money from the rich in order to help the poor "; in other words, it meant that more money was to be raised by direct taxation to finance the Government's social measures.[2]

The " People's Budget " (1909)

The Government's majority could ensure the passage of the Budget through the Commons, and what is called the " custom of the constitution " made it usual for the House of Lords not to touch a money bill, the underlying principle being the famous one that taxation is the concern of representatives elected by the people. But so fierce was the opposition of the wealthier classes to what they called " confiscation of wealth ", that the Lords threw out the Budget. At once the Liberals took up what was a true challenge. They went to the country (January, 1910) on

[1] John Burns was given office as President of the Local Government Board. This he held from 1905 till 1914. He then became President of the Board of Trade, but resigned on the outbreak of war.

[2] Income Tax was to be 1*s*. 2*d*. in the £ for incomes over £3000; incomes over £5000 were to pay an additional super-tax of 6*d*. in the £.

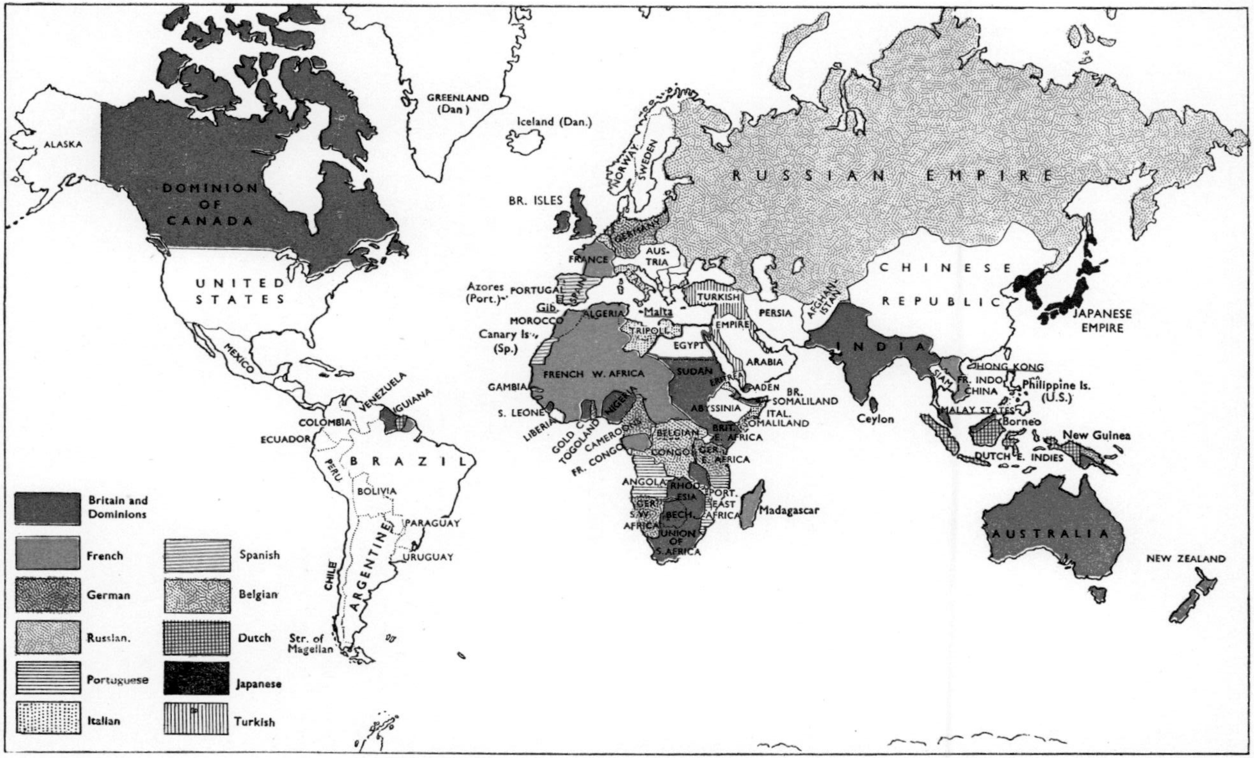

EMPIRES AND COLONIES IN 1914

the question whether the Lords could over-ride the elected Chamber in finance. The country sent them back again to power, though with so reduced a majority that they were dependent on either the Irish or the Labour members. The Lords passed the Budget (April, 1910).

The agitation over the Budget had scarcely begun to die down, before King Edward's sudden death (May, 1910) took the country by surprise. His short reign had seen the great flowering of the Liberal policy of social reform, and it had seen, too, a notable change in our foreign policy, in the friendship with France, of which King Edward had been a warm champion (see p. 919).

King George V became King, and at once the constitutional conflict was intensified.

The Parliament Act. Reform of the Constitution (1911)

Liberals had long suffered from the rejection of their bills by the Upper House, which now was predominantly and permanently Conservative. Such measures as Gladstone's famous Home Rule Bill had been passed by the Commons only to be rejected by the Lords. With the advent of a social policy which might be perpetually fought by the Upper House, it was clear that not only would trouble arise, but that the Conservatives, even if defeated at the polls, could keep power through the Lords.

The rejection of the Budget made the position impossible, so the Liberals now brought in the *Parliament Bill.* This Bill sought to deprive the Lords of their power to destroy the work of the Lower House, and give them the power only to delay. Any measure brought in by the Commons and passed by them in three successive sessions, was to become law, even if the Lords threw it out each time. Moreover, the House of Lords was to be deprived of all power to reject a money bill. A terrific battle took place over this bill, and the Lords would not accept it. Another General Election was fought (the second within the year 1910) and the country showed its feelings by sending the Liberals back with a majority again. Yet, still the Lords threatened to wreck the Bill, and introduced amendments which quite altered its scope. Now recourse was had to one of the odd but useful expedients of our Constitution. Any Bill must receive the consent of the Lords, therefore the Parliament Bill itself must do so. It seemed unlikely that the existing House of Lords would pass it, but it was possible for the Crown to create peers from amongst men who supported the Bill. (This procedure had last been threatened in the case of the Reform Bill of 1832).

King Edward VII had died in May, 1910, just when the Bill was introduced. His successor, King George, now had to act. The Prime Minister announced that he had assurances from the Sovereign that, in accordance with the will of the people, which had been fully shown by the recent election, the King was prepared to create enough Liberal peers to secure the passage of the Bill. The House of Lords now recognized that nothing could be done.[1] The Parliament Bill was therefore accepted by them and became law.[2]

Constitutional reform being thus made prominent, it is not surprising that another movement sprang to life at this time — the demand that women should be given the vote. Hitherto women were classed with "infants, criminals, and lunatics", and, though they might be property-owners and tax-payers and citizens, had no votes. For many years reformers, both men and women, had urged the injustice of this, and now various influences combined to strengthen the campaign. Gradually the various professions had been thrown open to women on the same terms as men; Socialism made no distinction in its demands for equality; and the stress laid on the connection between payment of taxes and political power which the struggle with the Lords had emphasized, now recoiled on the Liberals. For the Govern-

Votes for women

[1] The creation of about 600 new peers would have wrecked the House, for it would clearly be a ridiculous assembly, and as a result, more drastic "reform" might follow.

[2] It also reduced the duration of any parliament from 7 to 5 years.

ment refused to listen to the women, and bills brought in by private members were rejected.

Hitherto all the agitation had been carried on by peaceful methods, such as meetings, processions, petitions. Now a new organization which used "violence" was created, the Women's Social and Political Union, headed by *Mrs. Pankhurst*. This society meant primarily to force the women's claims on public attention. To obtain "publicity" its members broke shop windows, attacked prominent members of the Government with whips, chained themselves to railings in front of the House of Commons and to the Strangers' Gallery in the House. They were imprisoned for their actions, and this led to unforeseen results. In the first place, they went on "hunger-strike", and had to be "forcibly fed". This proving very dangerous to life, the Government fell back on an extraordinary measure. A Bill was passed, nicknamed "Cat-and-Mouse", under which a prisoner in danger of dying from hunger-strike would be temporarily released, and when sufficiently recovered, taken back to prison. The other effect produced was more beneficial. Many of the women who went to jail were influential persons, and all had a most active and intelligent organization behind them. The state of the prisons, and the bad conditions under which women prisoners lived, was so emphasized that prison reform had to be undertaken.

Women use "violence"

Opinions will always vary as to whether this "violent" agitation would have achieved its object. For just as the movement was swelling, everything was interrupted by the advent of war in 1914. The immense part played by women in that war induced the Government to grant them the franchise in 1918. At first the vote was given only to women with a property qualification, and over the age of thirty. Later this was altered, and to-day women are on an equality with men and all alike receive the vote at 21, on the sole qualification of six months' residence in one place.

Besides the political troubles, the Liberals also had to face industrial strife. Great Britain, after the South African War, once more had to endure a period of depression. People now began to realize that trade went in " cycles " of " boom followed by slump " and that war accentuated depression. Unemployment increased, and trade fell off. In consequence the workers suffered, and their discontent led to a series of strikes. The great Trade Unions, being the workers' organizations with funds behind them, largely financed the Labour Party. They provided the funds for election campaigns, and they helped to pay the expenses of members in the House.[1] But the small block of Labour members could not achieve any very great result, and more " direct action " was demanded by the workers. Hardly had the country recovered from the political battle over the Parliament Act, when it found itself faced by great strikes. First came a railway strike (1911). The Railway Companies refused to recognize the right of the men's Unions to negotiate for them. This meant that the workers would lose the advantage of collective action, and they fought for their claims and won. Then came a miners' strike, to obtain a minimum of 5*s.* a day for men and 2*s.* a day for boys. This lasted so long and was so ruinous to our coal export trade, that at last the Government took action, arbitrated between the two parties, and regulated the trade by Act of Parliament, machinery to fix a minimum wage being set up.

Strikes

Finally, a climax was reached in the conflict over Ireland. The Liberals had a majority in the House over the Conservatives only when the Irish block of eighty members voted with them. The Irish, seeing that they controlled the situation, now demanded Home Rule. The Liberals believed in this measure and were prepared to grant it, and a Bill was accordingly introduced; an Irish Parliament was to sit at Dublin, to deal with purely Irish affairs. This

The Irish troubles

[1] The £400 (see p. 935) a year salary did not by any means cover the total expenses of members.

Bill passed the Commons. It was thrown out by the Lords, re-introduced, and passed a second time by the Commons, If passed a third time (as it was in 1914), it must, under the Parliament Act, become law, for the Lords could not stop it. Racial and religious differences and antagonisms were, however, so long-standing and so bitter that Ulster refused to accept the Act which the Protestants there believed would put them under the domination of a Roman Catholic Parliament. They declared that they would rebel rather than agree.[1] The Conservative Party in England warmly supported them. Feelings rose to fever pitch, and a climax was reached when most of the officers at the garrison at the Curragh camp let it be known that they would rather be dismi sed from the army than undertake active operations against the Ulstermen. This " mutiny " caused Asquith, the Prime Minister, to take over the office of Secretary for War. But the Ulster " rebellion " never came to a head, for a great European war was imminent.

Ulster (1914)

CHAPTER 75

GEORGE V (1910–1936)

CAUSES OF THE WAR OF 1914–1918

Prussia, throughout the nineteenth century, had been rising to the position of a great power. Under *Bismarck* the States of Germany had been united into the German Empire. He had (see p. 878) declared her a " satiated " power, with no wish for expansion, but the next generation did not share these views. *Kaiser Wilhelm II* succeeded his father in 1888, and Bismarck fell from power. Bismarck had humiliated France and annexed Alsace-Lorraine, but he did not wish

Rise of Germany

[1] Their supporters said, " Ulster will fight and Ulster will be right ".

to take more from her, and he wished to preserve peace in Europe through alliance between Germany, Russia, and Austria. The Kaiser's policy did not follow these lines. He fell out with Russia and showed hostility to France. These two powers therefore began to draw together. On the face of it, friendship between Czarist Russia and Republican France was extraordinary, but fear drove them to form the *Dual Alliance* in 1893. Each was to help the other, if either were attacked by Germany or Austria. Against this union stood Germany and Austria, who, being joined by Italy, formed the *Triple Alliance*.

The Triple Alliance

Here, it seemed, was that source of uneasiness and insecurity, a " balance of power "; for a balance can easily be upset. Great Britain stood aloof. She had deliberately wished for " splendid isolation ", and actually up to 1900 she seemed more in sympathy with the German bloc. She had always feared and disliked Czarist Russia, and her Egyptian policy had caused her to quarrel with France. Her Royal Family's close connection with the Hohenzollern dynasty of Germany might have been expected to strengthen the ties between England and Germany,[1] and Salisbury had supported a pro-German policy. (For this chapter see *Note 155*).

The German navy

The new century showed that all was changing. The most potent single cause of trouble was the building of a German navy. That navy could not possibly help German efforts directed against France or Russia. Land forces would be decisive there, and Germany was already far the most formidable military power on the Continent. A German navy could be aimed only at Great Britain, and in fact we know now that it was so aimed. At first Great Britain tried to come to terms. She offered to negotiate alliances with Germany in 1891, in 1901, and again in 1912. Her offers were refused.

Moreover, Britain became rather uneasy over the East.

[1] The Kaiser's mother was Queen Victoria's daughter.

Germany obtained the concession to build the great railway to Baghdad. This gave her influence in Near Eastern Europe, and she began to lay the foundations for her alliance with the Turk.

Germany and Turkey

Britain meanwhile felt herself "isolated" in the wrong sense. The Boer War showed her most plainly how unpopular she was on the Continent, and she began to think that she had better seek for friends. Germany was most clearly formidable, and she was also unfriendly.

Great Britain, therefore, made the momentous decision to join the other side. In 1904 she embarked on what was known as the *Entente Cordiale* with France. That is to say, she became friendly with France, though no definite alliance was made. This was perhaps intended to warn Germany what hostility to England might involve.

Policy of Great Britain

Entente Cordiale

Then came the Russo-Japanese War (1904), which again had an unforeseen effect. Britain had been pro-Japanese, but the total defeat of Russia removed fears of Russian aggression. So Britain accepted Russia as a friend, while herself making a treaty with Japan (1905). Thus the beginning of the century saw Europe divided into two "armed camps", and never has there been a greater demonstration of the untruth in the saying, "if you wish for peace, make ready for war". European powers all began to arm, but their efforts for peace were not to succeed.

So angry and threatening was the situation, that when the Liberals came into power in 1906, they began to accentuate the "race for armaments". Germany had voted unheard-of millions for her naval budget, and now Great Britain followed suit. Threats of war began to be bandied about, the Kaiser making his famous speeches as to Germany's "shining armour" and "sword rattling in the scabbard". Looking back, we must think that Germany was deliberately provocative, though we cannot now tell whether she wished for war, or thought she could gain her ends by threats and bluff.

The race for armaments

At first it looked as though France were again to be attacked. She was twice involved in "incidents". In 1906 Germany quarrelled with her over Morocco, and insisted on the French Foreign Secretary, Delcassé, being dismissed.

The Agadir Incident

In 1911 the Kaiser sent a German warship to Agadir, a Moroccan port. France was desperately anxious to avoid war, and in the negotiations which followed, she gave up large stretches of the French Congo in return for German acceptance of French control over Morocco.

German complaints

The Germans, on the other hand, have always put forward two points in justification for their policy. They had moved on from Bismarck's position, and they now wanted a colonial empire, a "place in the sun" as they put it, for they felt that their African colonies were not worthy of the prestige of what was now a very great power. They wanted room to "expand" with their growing population, and spoke of "living-space"[1]. Yet only a tiny proportion of Germans settled in the colonies they already had. Their economic grievances could not be reckoned acute, for the British Empire was then based on free trade, and not only could every country then, as now, buy raw materials freely from any part of her dominions, but they could also at that time send their goods free of duty into Great Britain.

One complaint which the Germans put forward was that owing to the "entente" of Britain, France, and Russia, Germany was now "encircled", for with France on the one side and Russia on the other, she had enemies on two fronts. It should be noticed, however, that with Austria, Italy, and Turkey as friends, her road into the East was clear.

Austria and the Balkans

Finally, and here was where the true occasion for the war was to arise, she wished to "push towards the East".[2]

Austria

Germany's partner, almost her subordinate, was Austria-Hungary, but the Austro-Hungarian Empire had fallen on evil days. It consisted of a number of States, alien to one another in race and religion; Bohemia (part of what later

[1] *Lebensraum.* [2] This policy was called the *Drang nach Osten.*

became Czechoslovakia), Hungary, Austria, and the southern Slav provinces (Styria, Carinthia, Bosnia, and Herzegovina). All were united only by the tie of the Imperial Government. Austria dreaded lest Russia should expand into the Balkans. That storm-ridden peninsula, after centuries under Turkish rule, and many efforts, at last freed itself in the Balkan wars (1911–13). Austria had many Slavs in the southern part of her Empire, and, though she kept them in check, she was afraid lest the Balkan Slavs should call in the help of the greatest Slav power of all, Russia. Afraid of revolt in Bosnia and Herzegovina, afraid lest Russia should acquire undue influence with the Balkan League, she decided that " attack is the best form of defence ".

Serbia

In 1914, the heir to the Austrian throne, while on a tour in Bosnia, was assassinated at Sarajevo. Even now people dispute as to whether this was the genuine action of rebellious subjects of Austria (the actual murderer was a Slav living in Austrian territory) or action influenced by Serbia, or even deliberate action by Austrian intriguers who disliked the heir's policy and wanted a pretext for war. In any case, the effects were the same. Austria accused Serbia of having instigated the deed, demanded outrageous terms of compensation, and, when Serbia refused, declared war.

The murder at Sarajevo

Instantly, Serbia appealed for aid to Russia. Russia was perfectly willing, and, despite all the appeals which flew across Europe, mobilization began.

Russia

Germany was bound by treaty to assist Austria, and she may have urged and wished for moderation. Austria would not draw back. Russia called upon France to fulfil the obligations which bound her too. France and Russia prepared for war with Austria and Germany.

Belgium

What would Great Britain do? She was not bound by any treaty to fight for either France or Russia. The country and the Cabinet were divided. The action of Germany herself brought Britain in, for one treaty did exist by which Britain *was* bound. When Belgium had been declared an independent kingdom in 1839, her neutrality had been "guaranteed" in the Treaty of London, by Germany, France, and Great Britain. That neutrality had been respected in the Franco-Prussian War, but Germany now prepared to break it. German army plans were based on an invasion which should sweep through Belgium and on into France.

Belgian Neutrality

Great Britain had a solid tradition behind her in demanding that Belgian neutrality must be respected. She would not tolerate the armed forces of another great power in the sea-coasts opposite her shores. When the Germans broke the Treaty of London and invaded Belgium, Britain made up her mind. She called upon the Germans to withdraw, but they declared it folly to make war "for a scrap of paper", and refused to give way. War between Great Britain and Germany was then declared on 4th August, 1914.

The Prime Minister (Mr. Asquith) in a speech said: "If I am asked what we are fighting for, I reply in two sentences. First to fulfil a solemn international obligation . . . second to vindicate the principle that small nationalities are not to be crushed in defiance of international good faith by the arbitrary will of a strong and overmastering great Power."

NOTES ON PERIOD ELEVEN (1867–1914)

BRITISH SOVEREIGNS

VICTORIA (1837–1901)
EDWARD VII (1901–1910)
GEORGE V (1910–1936)

IMPORTANT FOREIGN RULERS

FRANCE:	NAPOLEON III, Emperor (1852–1870)
	THIRD FRENCH REPUBLIC (1870–)
AUSTRIA:	EMPEROR FRANCIS JOSEPH (1848–1916)
GERMANY:	WILLIAM OF PRUSSIA proclaimed Emperor of Germany (1870–1888)
	FREDERICK I Emperor (1888)
	WILLIAM II, Emperor (1888–1918)
RUSSIA:	ALEXANDER II (1855–1881)
	ALEXANDER III (1881–1894)
	NICHOLAS II (1894–1917)

BRITISH PRIME MINISTERS

DERBY-DISRAELI:	(1866–1868)
1ST DISRAELI:	(1868)
1ST GLADSTONE:	(1868–1874)
2ND DISRAELI:	(1874–1880)
2ND GLADSTONE:	(1880–1885)
SALISBURY:	(1885–1886)
3RD GLADSTONE:	(1886)
SALISBURY:	(1886–1892)
4TH GLADSTONE:	(1892–1894)
ROSEBERY:	(1894–1895)
SALISBURY:	(1895–1902)
BALFOUR:	(1902–1905)
CAMPBELL-BANNERMAN:	(1905–1908)
ASQUITH:	(1908–1916)

NOTE 139. — GLADSTONE AND IRELAND

1867. Fenian movement created trouble in Ireland and England. Gladstone determined to remedy grievances.

1. Causes of Irish Discontent.

(*a*) *Church.* Irish forced to pay tithes to Church of Ireland. Irish majority were Roman Catholics; Church of Ireland Protestant.

(*b*) *Land.* No security of tenure, landlords rack-rented their tenants, many absentees, as many landlords were English. Irish peasants sub-divided farms, till too small to be efficient; lack of capital made farms poor.

(*c*) Ireland depended on agriculture, and had no alternative industries.

(*d*) Population was very large for poor resources of the country. Holdings could not support families. (Hence dependence on potatoes, and terrible result of famine.)

2. Gladstone's Irish Policy.

(*a*) Disestablished Irish *Church* (1869).

(*b*) *Land* Acts.

(i) 1870. Compensation for improvements to be paid by landlords. Evicted tenants to be compensated if had paid rent. But landlords still might evict tenants by raising rents so that tenants could not pay.

Land League (Davitt's league) to organize rent strike.

(ii) 1881. Second Land Act (Three F's). Fair rent; free sale; fixity of tenure. Act not accepted by Irish, who were now too embittered and wanted political independence.

(*c*) *Political.*

Parnell headed movement for *Home Rule.*

(i) i.e. Irish Parliament to manage Irish affairs. Gladstone converted to Home Rule. **But**

(*a*) Disorders in Ireland led to first *Coercion Act* (1881). Parnell imprisoned. Gladstone came to terms with him (*Kilmainham Treaty*, 1882).

(*b*) Phœnix Park murders (1882) roused hostility of people in England.

(ii) 1886. 1*st Home Rule Bill* introduced by Gladstone. Failed to pass; many Liberals against it. (Chamberlain left Liberals on this issue.)

(iii) Conservatives in power (1886) — more Coercion. In 1890 Parnell's disgrace ruined the "Nationalist Party". Conservatives passed *Land Purchase Act,* to lend money to enable peasants to buy land.

(iv) Gladstone brought in *2nd Home Rule Bill* (1893). Passed by Commons. Rejected by Lords. Gladstone retired from public life (1894).

Note 140. — GLADSTONE

1. **Finance.** A great financier and Chancellor of the Exchequer.
   (*a*) Britain became a Free Trade country. (Abolished taxes on paper, " tax on knowledge ".) Completed Peel's policy of abolishing duties on goods (1852–55).
   (*b*) Trade Treaty with France (1860).
2. **Parliamentary Reform.**
   (*a*) *2nd Reform Act* proposed (1867) to give vote to working-class householders by lowering property qualification. Thrown out — and Disraeli then carried a Bill based on Gladstone's. Gladstone forced wide amendments on Disraeli.
   (*b*) 1884 — gave vote to *all* occupiers and lodgers in town and country paying £10 in rent. Enfranchised *agricultural* labourers.
   (*c*) *Ballot Act* (1872) made voting secret.
   (*d*) *Corrupt Practices Act* (1883) limited amount of money a candidate could spend.
   (*e*) *Redistribution Act* (1885) disfranchised boroughs under 15,000 inhabitants and merged them into counties; gave boroughs of less than 50,000, one member; redistributed these seats to new constituencies.
   This measure made electoral districts more equal.
3. **Social Reforms.**
   (*a*) *Education. Forster's Act*, 1870, provided for schools in every area and for education rate.
      (i) 1880, education made compulsory.
      (ii) Religious test at Universities abolished (1870).
   (*b*) *Civil Service* entrance made to depend not on nomination but on examination.
   (*c*) *Trade Union Act* (1871) gave Unions legal existence and safeguarded funds.
4. **Army Reform** under Cardwell (1871).

   Note: Gladstone's " Reform " ministry lasted from 1868–74. Most of his measures came in this period, and were only rounded off in his later ministry.
5. **Gladstone's Foreign Policy.**
   (*a*) Supported Italian freedom and unity and opposed Austrian rule in Northern Italy (1866).

(*b*) Advocated arbitration with U.S.A. and paid compensation over *Alabama* (1872).

(*c*) Opposed Turkish misrule. Bulgarian "atrocities" agitation (1876). Opposed Disraeli's "backing" of Turkey and maintained Balkans should be freed.

(*d*) In *Egypt* objected to Disraeli's policy of control in Egypt. But responsible for "provisional occupation". Ordered withdrawal from *Sudan*. Thus held responsible for death of *Gordon*.

(*e*) In *South Africa* objected to attacks on Boers, so made peace with Boers and recognized the *independence of Boer Republics* (1881).

Summary. Gladstone's policy was based on belief in right of small nations to self-government and reluctance to interfere. Based also on belief in peace, and objection to war of intervention.

NOTE 141. — DISRAELI

1. **Policy of Imperialism,** or extension of British Empire.
2. **Policy of Popularizing the Crown,** as a personal tie between Empire.
3. **Policy of Converting Tories to "Tory Democracy",** i.e. reforms.

---

1. Foreign Policy of Disraeli.

(*a*) *Russia.* Strongly opposed to Gladstone's ideas of peace and non-intervention. Disraeli was aggressive and therefore opposed Russia and favoured Turkey.

(i) In Near East, 1876, supported Turkey against the Bulgarians.

(ii) Sent British fleet to check Russians at Constantinople (1878).

(iii) At *Congress of Berlin*, 1878, thwarted Russian plans and supported Turkish power.

(iv) Sent Afghan expedition to check Russian designs on India (1878).

(*b*) Obtained share in control of Suez Canal, to give Great Britain control of route to India, and check French in Egypt (1875).

2. Imperial Policy.

(*a*) Queen Victoria, Empress of India (1877).

(*b*) Fought Afghan War to secure safety of India (1878–80).

(*c*) In Africa dealt with:

(i) Annexation of Transvaal (1877).

(ii) Zulu Wars (1879–80).

3. **Home Policy.** "Tory Democracy". Carried through reforms supplementary to those of Gladstone.
   (*a*) *Parliamentary Franchise.* Thus, in 1867, he took over Gladstone's Bill and was obliged to widen its provision. Vote given to "lodgers" who paid £10 a year. (This Act enfranchised the working-man.)
   (*b*) *Combination Act* (*Trade Union Act*) (1875) making strikes legal and legalizing "peaceful picketing".
   (*c*) *Public Health Act* (1875).
   (*d*) *Artisans' Dwelling Act* (1875) — improved houses and started clearance of slums.
   (*e*) *Enclosure of Commons Act* (saved public land from enclosures) (1875).
   (*f*) *Merchant Shipping Act* (1876), causing "Plimsoll Mark" to prevent over-loading of ships

Note 142. — BRITAIN AND RUSSIA (1815–1878)

1. 1827, Canning joined with Russia in helping Greek Independence, for once overcoming British fear of Russia.
   Growing hostility to Russia, due to Russia's tyranny in Poland, her aid in suppression of the revolution of 1848 in Austrian Empire, and fear of her interference in India. All combined to create feeling which led Britain to contemplate war.
2. *Crimean War*, to prevent Russia gaining influence, and to bolster up Turkey (1854–56).
3. In 1870 during the Franco-Prussian War, Russia repudiated peace terms made after Crimea, and restored her warships to Black Sea.
   Britain could not oppose Russia single-handed.
4. 1878. Disraeli opposed Russia's attack on Turkey, and at *Congress of Berlin* thwarted Russia. "Peace with honour" was claimed by Disraeli; as no European war followed. Disraeli considered he had checked Russia.
   (*a*) Bulgaria, though part of it now forced back under Sultan's suzerainty, did in the end get free.
   (*b*) Britain accepted Cyprus.
   (*c*) Bosnia put under protectorate of Austria to check Russia, and this led to Austria's attitude in the Balkans and helped to cause war of 1914.

Summary: Disraeli's policy was based on the idea of extending the power and prestige of the Empire. Also wished to reform social conditions. Strong interest in the Near East, also in India. Helped to restore the popularity of the Crown.

NOTE 143. — EDUCATION (1815–1914)

1. Education at first carried on by voluntary societies, the *National Society* (Church of England) and the *British Society* (Non-conformist). In 1833 State grants given to these societies, and inspectors appointed.

2. 1870. **Forster's Education Act** (Gladstone's ministry).
   (*a*) Schools to be set up in every parish.
   (*b*) Existing schools to have State grants.
   (*c*) Elected boards to manage schools.

3. 1880. **Attendance at Schools Compulsory.** Schools had now been built in areas where formerly had been none.

4. 1890. **Education made Free.** That is, parents no longer charged fees. (But parents pay for education through payments of rates.)

5. 1899. **Board of Education Set Up.** A government department now responsible for education of children.

6. 1902. **Education placed under Control of Town and County Councils.** (Old school boards abolished.)

Secondary education encouraged by provision of " places " for children from elementary schools, in return for State grants.

NOTE 144. — DEVELOPMENT OF TRADE UNIONS

1 After *Combination Acts* repealed (1824), Robert Owen forms Grand Amalgamated Union. *Trade Unions* could be formed, But
   (*a*) Magistrates often punished leaders for " intimidation ".
   (*b*) Trade Union funds could not be protected from dishonest officials.
   (*c*) A strike might still be a " conspiracy ".

2. 1871. Gladstone passed *Criminal Law Amendment Act.* Trade Union officials could be prosecuted for dishonesty, so *funds protected.*

3. 1875. Disraeli passed *Employers' and Workmen's Act. Strikes made " legal "*, and unions could not be prosecuted for doing anything collectively that would be legal if done by individual.

4. 1901. *Taff Vale Judgment* struck at Unions, for judges decided that Unions were liable for all losses to employers caused by illegal acts of members.

   This removed by *Trade Disputes Act* (1906), saying that Unions not liable for losses caused by such acts.

5. Trade Unions, to protect their interests, used their funds to send members to Parliament (before members were paid, no means to send working-man to Parliament). This declared illegal by judge in *Osborne Judgment* (1909). Hence *Trade Union Act* (1913) said Unions could use funds for political purposes if (*a*) such funds kept separate from industrial funds, and (*b*) any members objecting, need not pay.

NOTE 145. — LORD SALISBURY (1830–1903)

Leader of Conservatives (1881–1902). When Gladstone's Home Rule policy split the Liberals, a joint Conservative-Unionist party formed, Conservatives under Salisbury (1885), "Liberals" led by Hartington, and "Radicals" led by Chamberlain.

(Salisbury had been in Disraeli's ministry, 1866, but would not accept his Reform Bill.)

1. **Ireland.** 1886. Salisbury advocated "resolute" government as opposed to Gladstone's Home Rule.
   (a) *Balfour* sent as Chief Secretary.
   (b) *Crimes Act*, suspending trial by jury. Special resident-magistrates to crush disorder (1887).
   (c) *Land Purchase Act* to lend peasants money at very low rate, to purchase land (1887).

2. **Colonial Policy** — dominated by Chamberlain (see Note 146).

3. **Foreign Policy.**
   (a) In 1878 had gone with Disraeli to Congress of Berlin. Had shared Disraeli's hatred of Russia and his support of Turkey.
   (b) Impressed by Bismarck and friendly to *Germany*.
   (c) Feared *France* and her growing African Empire.
   (d) *Egypt*:
      (i) Lord *Cromer* administered Egypt excellently, British influence supreme (1883–1907).
      (ii) *Sudan* reconquered (Kitchener) (1898).
      (iii) French tried to check this. *Fashoda*, triumph for Britain (1898).
   (e) *South America*, quarrel with *Venezuela* — Britain accepted U.S.A.s intervention, and Salisbury conciliatory (1899).

4. **African Policy.** Conference at Berlin (1885) to settle division of Africa. Salisbury worked with Bismarck. Secured for Britain Nigeria, Kenya, Uganda. France given northern areas, to console her after Franco-Prussian war.

5. **" Splendid Isolation ".** Salisbury would not interfere in the continental quarrels raised by Germany, but kept Britain in isolation. He shared opinions generally held then:
   (a) That France was dangerous.
   (b) That rise of Germany was a good development; and
   (c) That the struggle on the continent did not concern Britain.

NOTE 146. — JOSEPH CHAMBERLAIN (1836–1914)

Started life as an extreme Radical and Republican.

1. **Municipal Career.** Began public career in Birmingham. Carried through series of municipal reforms.

2. **Radical M.P.** under Gladstone. Left the party over Home Rule, and split it (1885). Many " Liberals " joining the Conservative party which now called itself " Unionist " as maintaining union with Ireland.

3. **Accepted office as Unionist** under Salisbury (1895). Now developed true interest of his life as Colonial Secretary.

4. **Imperialism.**
   (*a*) Desired extension of British territory. Thus encouraged " Empire on which sun never sets ". Straits Settlements acquired 1896.
   (i) North Borneo and Sarawak Protectorates, Fiji Islands.
   (ii) Encouraged Rhodes in creation of *Rhodesia* (1895).
   (iii) Supported *2nd Boer War* and conquest of two Dutch Republics, 1899–1902.
   (*b*) Desired tightening of colonial ties, hence promoted Colonial Conference (1897). Colonies not very anxious for further federation, preferred greater independence.
   (*c*) Started campaign for " Tariff Reform " (1903), i.e. wished duties put on foreign goods entering Britain with a *preference* for colonial goods. Aim, to make trade relations with colonies closer.

   Note: Colonies and dominions being independent, could and did impose own tariffs, and tariffs against Britain.

   Policy defeated at Election of 1906, and Liberals returned to power. " Tariff Reform " split the Conservative party now, just as Peel's Corn Law Repeal had split it earlier. In both cases, the Opposition returned to power.

NOTE 147. — CANADA (1791–1905)

In 1791 Canada divided into two provinces (Pitt's Canadian Act) — Upper Canada (English), and Lower Canada (French). Each had local elected assembly.

1837. *Rebellion* under Papineau, due to discontent over grant of land to Englishmen, and to grant of land to Episcopal Church. Rebellion crushed.

1. 1838. *Lord Durham* sent out to inquire into revolt.
   (*a*) Deported leaders of revolt without trial.
   Opposition to this caused his recall.

(*b*) Famous *Report* issued. Advocated:

(i) Union of two provinces once more (1840).

(ii) Grant of colonial assembly and full control in internal affairs.

2. 1847. *Lord Elgin* made governor, and under him, *responsible self-government* was fulfilled.

Lord Elgin governed through a *Ministry* which was responsible to the *Assembly*, and depended on a majority there.

3. *Federation* of Canada.

(*a*) 1867. *Dominion* of Canada created, by federation of provinces. Ontario (Upper), Quebec (Lower), Nova Scotia, and New Brunswick.

(*b*) 1870. Part of Hudson Bay territory formed into province of Manitoba.

(*c*) 1871. British Columbia added.

(*d*) 1905. Alberta and Saskatchewan added.

Note 148. — AUSTRALIA AND NEW ZEALAND

1. **Early Developments.**

1. (*a*) 1770. Captain Cook explored Australian coast.

(*b*) 1788. First settlement in New South Wales.

(*c*) 1789. During repression of the French Revolution, political prisoners transported to Australia, as well as convicts, to Botany Bay.

(*d*) In 1797 Macarthur had imported *sheep*, which gave Australia a great industry. Helped by discoveries of *Gap in Blue Mountains* with great pastures beyond.

2. **Development of States.**

(*a*) *New South Wales.*

1788. First convict settlement.
1823. Made Crown Colony.
1840. *Transportation abolished.*
1842. Granted representative government.

(*b*) *Victoria* (originally part of N. S. Wales).

1851. Separated from N. S. Wales.
1851. Gold discovered.
1854. Granted responsible government.

(*c*) *Queensland* (originally part of N. S. Wales).

1859. Separated from N. S. Wales.
1859. Granted responsible government.

(*d*) *South Australia.*

1836. Founded by *Edward Gibbon Wakefield*, through his *Colonization Society*. 16,000 " Free " colonists settled there.

1836. Adelaide founded.

1854. Granted responsible government.

(*e*) *Western Australia.*

1829. " Free " settlement.

1849–68. Convicts sent.

1868. *Transportation abolished.*

1850. Granted representative government

1890. Granted responsible government.

3. Federation.

1855. Federation of N. S. Wales, Victoria, and South Australia.

1897. Convention held at Adelaide to discuss federation of all the States.

1900. *Australian Commonwealth Act.*

(i) Commonwealth Parliament created.

(ii) State Parliaments continued in each State.

(iii) Commonwealth Capital to be created at Canberra.

1926. Australia became a *Dominion.*

NEW ZEALAND

1817. Early settlements founded.

Maoris resisted settlement and fought. *Lord Glenelg* championed Maori cause. Quarrelled with Gibbon Wakefield's settlers.

1839. Annexation proclaimed.

1840. *Treaty of Waitangi* — Maoris accepted Queen Victoria's rule and New Zealand becomes Crown Colony.

Sir George Grey preserved native lands. Sheep introduced — " Canterbury lamb " trade.

1852. New Zealand granted *self-government* with assembly at Wellington.

1867. Maori representatives elected.

1907. New Zealand (which had refused to federate with Australia) given title of Dominion of New Zealand.

Note 149. — SOUTH AFRICA

Cape Colony acquired from the Dutch (1814).

1. Large *Dutch* population. In addition, numerous **native** races. **Friction** between British and Dutch, over the natives. Boers turned them into *slaves*, and resented Britain's abolition of slavery (1833).
   (*a*) This led to *Great Trek*, 1836. Boers migrated to Natal (1838). In 1843 Britain annexed *Natal*, and Boers trekked again to Orange and Vaal districts.
   (*b*) 1852. *Sand River Convention.* British recognized independence of *Orange Free State* and *Transvaal*.
   (*c*) Representative institutions granted to the Cape (in 1853) and to Natal (in 1856).
2. Great Britain by series of wars acquired:
   (*a*) *Basutoland*, and by war against Kaffirs, controlled Cape Colony up to Boer portion (1868).
   (*b*) 1877. *Transvaal annexed* — on grounds that Boers could not protect territory against warlike Zulus.
   (*c*) *Zulus* provoked war and Zululand conquered. Later annexed (1887).
3. **Wars with Boers.**
   (*a*) *First Boer War.*
      (i) 1881, Boers rose against British. Won Laing's Nek and Majuba. Gladstone made peace and recognized *Boer independence* as *South African Republic* (1884).
      (ii) *Cecil Rhodes* acquired Rhodesia for Britain (1895) checked Boer attempt to expand.
      (iii) Quarrel over *Uitlanders* in *gold mines* of *Transvaal*. (1895.) Jameson Raid, provoked Boer hostility.
   (*b*) *Second Boer War*, 1899–1902. *Transvaal* and *Orange Free State* annexed.
4. **Union of South Africa** (1909). All 4 provinces (except Rhodesia) united (Orange Free State, Transvaal, Cape Colony, Natal) and given *self-government.*

Note 150. — DEVELOPMENT OF SELF-GOVERNMENT. SUMMARY

1. **Canada** federated in 1867. **Dominion of Canada.**
2. **Australia** federated in 1855. Completed by joining of new provinces in 1893. **Commonwealth of Australia** in 1900.
3. **New Zealand** given self-government in 1852 and called a Dominion in 1907.
4. **South Africa** federated and **Union of South Africa formed,** with grant of self-government in 1909.

NOTE 151. — RELIGIOUS REVIVAL IN THE NINETEENTH CENTURY AND ITS EFFECTS

1. **Evangelical Movement** ("Low Church").
Started in Church of England partly owing to the influence of *Wesley* (1703–91), whose followers left the Church. Took practical view of "brotherhood of man", based on Bible teaching, so active members were active philanthropists.
Most eminent members, *Shaftesbury* (1801–85) (Factory Acts, etc.), and *Wilberforce* (1759–1833) (Abolition of Slavery).
Also encouraged education (*Hannah More*) (1769–1833).

2. **"Oxford" or Tractarian Movement** ("High Church").
Founded by a group of men at Oxford (1833), published "Tracts for the Times" emphasizing continuity of Church of England with the Catholic Church. Revival of ritual.
(After Tract 90 which tried to prove that the 39 Articles of the Church of England had nothing contradictory to the Roman Catholic Church, many left and joined the Roman Church.
Most prominent men, *Newman* and *Manning*.)
Encouraged work in poor parishes, encouraged founding of nursing and teaching sisterhoods, and encouraged building of Church schools.

3. **Christian Socialists.**
Led by a group of writers, *Charles Kingsley* (1819–75), and *F. D. Maurice* (1805–72). Encouraged working-class education, founded working-men's college. Very active in hygienic reforms — sanitation, and so on. The writers used their novels to forward their views (*circa* 1854).
General revival of religious life, which led on to movement to encourage "philanthropy" and work for, and amongst, the poor.

NOTE 152—THE "GRAB FOR AFRICA"

Exploration of nineteenth century showed Africa vast continent.

1. *Burton* and *Baker* discovered the great Lakes, Tanganyika and Victoria. Speke discovered the source of the Nile. (1857–64.)
2. *Livingstone* explored Zanzibar, discovered Victoria Falls and Lake Nyassa (1849–73).
3. *Stanley* explored the Congo (1874–79).
4. *European powers* decided to divide up Africa.

Begun at Conference of Berlin (1884) and continued in a series of conferences and agreements down to 1906.

(*a*) *France* got north-west Africa, Algeria, French Congo, Tunis, and control of Morocco.
(*b*) *Spain* got Spanish Morocco.

(*c*) *Belgium* got Congo.

(*d*) *Italy* got Somaliland, Libya (and in 1911 Tripoli).

(*e*) *Portugal* got Portuguese West and Mozambique (on West).

(*f*) *Germany* got German East and West.

(*g*) *Britain* got Nigeria, Kenya, Uganda. Already had Cape Colony, and Rhodesia, and protectorate over Egypt and Sudan.

NOTE 153.—SOCIAL REFORMS OF THE LIBERALS (1906–1913)

Rise of Socialist party led all parties to take greater interest in social reform.

Liberals introduced:

1. Social Reforms:

(*a*) *Old Age Pensions* (1908).

(*b*) *Reform of Poor Law.* Workhouses to be classified and efforts made to keep people out of them, by finding them work if able-bodied, and other reforms took many people out of the workhouses, e.g. pensions led old people to live with relations.

(*c*) *National Health Insurance* (1911).

(*d*) *Children.*

(i) Provision of meals for children in need (1906).

(ii) Medical inspection in schools (1907).

(iii) *Children's Charter* set up special Children's Courts for crime (1908).

(*e*) *Labour.*

(i) *Trade Disputes Act* (1906), protected funds of Trade Unions.

(ii) *Sweated Industries Act*, set up minimum wage boards in low-paid trades (1909).

(iii) Labour exchanges set up, to enable men and women to find work (1909).

(iv) *Shop Hours Act* to limit hours (1911).

(v) *Trade Unions Act*, enabled Trade Unions to use funds for political purposes (1913).

2. Army Reform. Haldane reorganized Army, and created Territorial Army (1906–13).

3. Political Reforms.

(*a*) " People's Budget ", to pay for cost of social reforms led to disputes with House of Lords (1909).

Result, *Parliament Act* of 1911, abolished power of Lords to veto bills for more than a limited period..

(*b*) Payment of Members (to enable working-men to sit in Parliament) (1911).

(*c*) *Home Rule Bill* passed 1912. Never put into operation owing to resistance of Ulster and to war of 1914.

NOTE 154. — INDIA — MOVEMENT FOR SELF-GOVERNMENT

1. **Demand for Self-government** on same lines as Dominions.

Obstacles: (*a*) Differences of race and religion in India. Clash between Hindus and Mohammedans.

(*b*) Poverty and illiteracy of Indians, making self-government more difficult. Illiterate population difficult to organize politically, and poverty makes provision of education difficult.

2. **Growing Discontent in India.** Outbreaks of disorder, especially in Bengal, where terrorists used firearms. Objection to partition of Bengal under Curzon (1905).

3. **Liberal Proposals for Reform** (1906).

Morley (secretary of State for India in England), and *Minto* (Viceroy), introduced " Morley-Minto Reforms " (1906–10).

(*a*) Elected representatives to sit in Imperial Legislative Council.

(*b*) Elected representatives to be in majority on the Provincial Legislative Councils.

(*c*) Indians to sit on Viceroy's Council and Council of State in England.

4. **Montague - Chelmsford Reforms** (1918–1919) — " Dominion Status " promised. *Montague* (Secretary of State) and *Chelmsford* (Viceroy).

(*a*) Certain departments in provincial governments placed under Indian ministers, responsible to elected assemblies (responsible government).

But, this not applied to all departments. Some were " reserved " for officials appointed by Britain (hence called *Dyarchy*). " Reserved " departments include *finance* and *maintenance of rule*.

If system worked well, then after 10 years extension to be granted.

Rise of opposition movement, headed by *Gandhi*, has led to dissension and no further grant yet made.

(*a*) Council of State for all India, Legislative Assembly for all India.

(*c*) Provincial Legislatures to have wide powers, but certain powers to be reserved for Governor, and if Legislative Council refuses to act, the Governor can take over.

TIME CHART FOR PERIOD ELEVEN (1867–1914)

Sovereign.	Prime Minister.	Great and Greater Britain	Dates.	Other Powers.	Dates.
Queen Victoria (1837–1901)	RUSSELL.				
	DERBY.	Dominion of Canada formed; Second Reform Bill.	1867		.
	DISRAELI.	Transportation to W. Australia stopped.	1868		.
		Irish Church Disestablished.	1869	Opening of Suez Canal.	1869
		First Irish Land Act; Education Act.	1870	Franco-Prussian War (1870–71); Republic in	1870
	1868–74	Universities opened to Non-conformists; Trade Union Act.	1871	France; Formation of Empire of Germany.	1871
	GLADSTONE.	Ballot Act.	1872		.
			.		.
			.		.
	1874–80	Suez Canal shares purchased.	1876	The Bulgarian Atrocities.	1876
		Queen becomes Empress of India.	1877	Russo-Turkish War.	1877
	DISRAELI.	Second Afghan War.	1878	Treaty of San Stephano; Treaty of Berlin.	1878
		Zulu War; Dual Control in Egypt.	1879		.
			.		.
		First Boer War; Battle of Majuba.	1881	Alexander III becomes Czar.	1881
	1880–5	Bombardment of Alexandria; Battle of Tel-el-Kebir.	1882		.
			.		.
	GLADSTONE.	Third Reform Bill.	1884	The "Grab for Africa" begins.	1884
		Annexation of Upper Burma; Fall of Khartoum.	1885		.

Sovereign.	Prime Minister.	Great and Greater Britain.	Dates.	Other Powers.	Dates.
Queen Victoria (1837–1901)	SALISBURY.	First Home Rule Bill.	1886		.
	GLADSTONE.	Jubilee of Queen Victoria	1887		.
		Local Government Act.	1888	William II German Emperor.	1888
	1886–92 SALISBURY		.		.
			.	Fall of Bismarck.	1890
			.		.
	1892–94 GLADSTONE.	2nd Home Rule Bill	1893		.
			.	Nicholas II becomes Czar.	1894
	1894–95 ROSEBERY.	Jameson Raid.	1895		.
			.		.
	1895–1902	The " Diamond Jubilee " of Queen Victoria.	1897	War between Turkey and Greece.	1897
		Re-conquest of Sudan; Battle of Omdurman.	1898		.
		SOUTH AFRICAN WAR.	1899	Peace Conference at the Hague.	1899
			1900		.
Edward VII (1901–1910)	SALISBURY.	Federation of Australia.	1901		.
		Treaty of Vereeniging.	1902		.
	1902–05		.		.
	BALFOUR.	Anglo-French Agreement	1904	Russo-Japanese War, 1904–05.	1904
		Anglo-Japanese Treaty.	1905		.
	1905–08		.		.
	CAMPBELL-BANNERMAN.	Anglo-Russian Convention.	1907		.
			.		.
		South Africa Act; Indian Councils Act; Union of South Africa.	1909		.
George V (1910–1936)	1908–16		.	Portugal becomes Republic.	1910
		Parliament Act; National Health Insurance Act.	1911	War between Turkey and Italy.	1911
	ASQUITH.	3rd Home Rule Bill.	1912	First Balkan War	1912
			.	Second Balkan War	1913
		Britain declares War on Germany.	1914	Assassination of Archduke Francis Ferdinand. Germany declares War on Russia and France.	1914

EXAMINATION QUESTIONS ON PERIOD ELEVEN

1867–1914

1. Describe Gladstone's attempts to remedy Irish grievances. (NUJB 1935)

2. Give an account of the foreign policy of Gladstone. (LGS 1936)

3. State the services of Disraeli (*a*) to his party, and (*b*) to the improvement of social conditions. (LGS 1937)

4. Describe the principal achievements of Disraeli. (NUJB 1936)

5. Trace the growth of British power in Egypt and the Sudan from the establishment of the Dual Control in 1876 to the end of this period. (NUJB 1938)

6. Describe the main reformers in England of Gladstone's first ministry (1868–74). (NUJB 1937)

7. State the services to the British Empire of *two* of the following Lord Dalhousie, Lord Durham, Joseph Chamberlain, Cecil Rhodes. (LGS 1936)

8. Give an account of the work of *either* Joseph Chamberlain or Cecil Rhodes. (LGS 1937)

9. Give a brief study of the foreign policy of Disraeli. (LGS 1923; NUJB 1930, 1932)

10. What was the attitude of this country towards the Eastern Question? (OC 1932)

11. Discuss the contributions of Disraeli to the development of the Conservative party. (LM 1926)

12. Relate the course of events in Egypt leading up to the death of Gordon. (LGS 1922, 1925; OL 1929; UW 1931)

13. Compare the aims and methods of O'Connell with those of Parnell. (LGS 1923)

14 Compare the Evangelical and the Oxford Movements. (OC 1935)

15. Sketch in outline the history of the English novel between 1815 and 1914. (LGS 1935)

16. Describe society in the Victorian age as it appears in the works of any Victorian novelist. (OC 1932)

17. What were the main contributions made by Englishmen to the advancement of science between 1815 and 1914? (LGS 1935)

18. Give a brief account of the relations between England and France from 1870 to 1914. (NUJB 1935)

19. Write a brief account of two of the following: (*a*) the Introduction of Railways in England; (*b*) the Rochdale Pioneers; (*c*) the Irish Famine of 1845–7; (*d*) the Women's Suffrage Movement. (NUJB 1933)

20. What part did Britain play in "the scramble for Africa"? (Illustrate with a map.) (CWB 1931)

21. What is meant by "Responsible Government"? Show how and when it was gained by either Canada or Australia. (UW 1932)

22. Outline the principal measures affecting education in England during the nineteenth century. (LGS 1922, 1924; OL 1932)

23. Trace the development of Trade Unions during the latter part of the nineteenth century. (LGS 1922, 1924; LM 1924; OL 1930; D 1931)

24. Outline the course of franchise reform during the nineteenth century. (LGS 1924, 1925; UW 1932,; OL 1932)

25. Outline the development in England of factory legislation. (LM 1924; CL 1930)

26. Outline the relations between England and Turkey during the latter half of the nineteenth century. (LM 1924)

27. Describe some of the improvements in communications effected during the nineteenth century. (LGS 1924; LM 1931)

28. Discuss the growth of British power in India during the second half of the nineteenth century. (LGS 1925)

29. In what dangers was Great Britain involved at the end of Victoria's reign by her isolation from continental affairs? (LGS 1925)

30. What efforts were made by legislative means to improve the conditions of the people between 1900 and 1914? (OC 1930)

31. Between 1815 and 1915 the conditions of life of the working classes improved enormously. What were the chief factors that brought about this improvement? (LGS 1937)

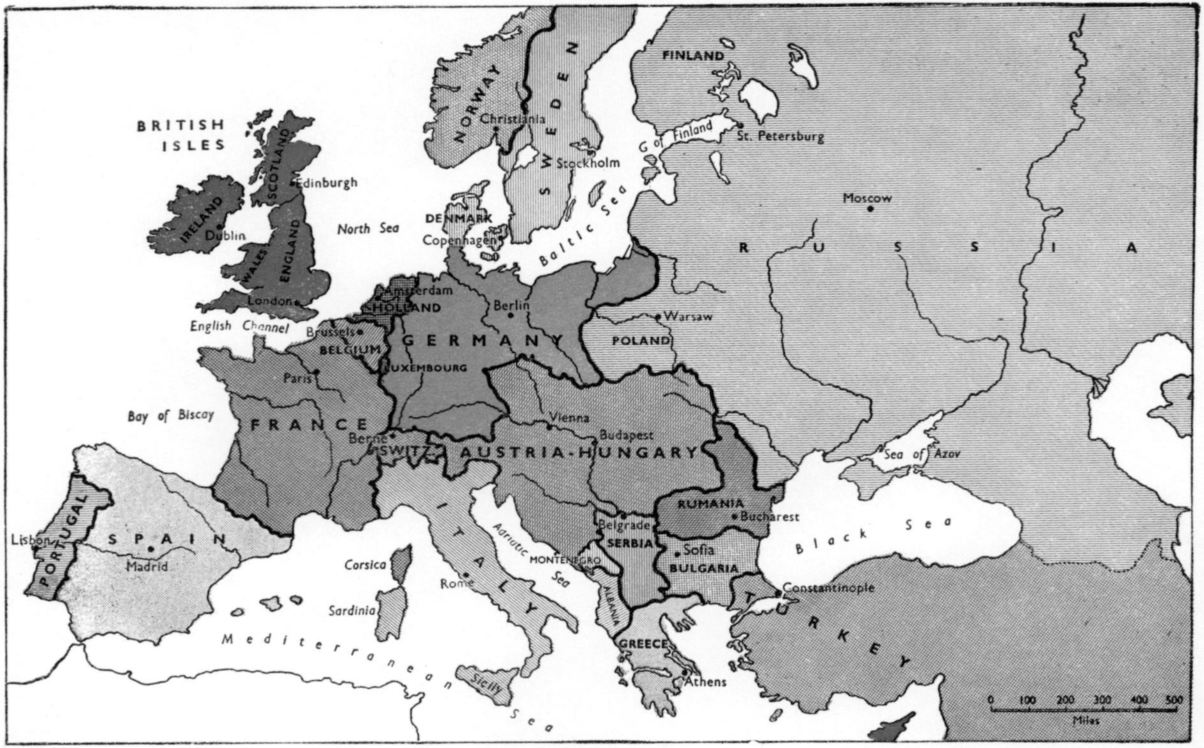

EUROPE IN 1914

F 938

PERIOD TWELVE

WAR AND AFTERMATH (1914–1939)

CHAPTER 76

WORLD WAR (1914–1918)

The World War (*Note 156*) was fought on a scale unapproached in any previous century. For the first time, "Nations in Arms" fought one another, and instead of tens of thousands, millions faced one another — altogether the war saw the employment of no less than 50 millions of armed men. Moreover, not only were old weapons transformed and multiplied beyond measure,[1] but the war was fought in new elements and with new weapons. War in the air and under the water was developed enormously. Air forces — aeroplanes or airships or balloons — were used, for instance, for scouting and for obtaining information, chiefly by means of photography, of the hostile dispositions; for assisting artillery by checking and registering; for bombing hostile forts and railway stations; and for attacking the enemy on the march. The under-water weapons, again, as we shall see, transformed the conditions of naval warfare. As the war progressed, weapons became more and more deadly and diabolical; hand-grenades, gas, artificial fog, liquid fire, and tanks were all gradually brought into operation. The result was that the strain on men's nerves in the later stages

Modern warfare

[1] The British had on the West front at the beginning of the war 486 guns and howitzers, of which 24 were of medium calibre; at the end they had 6437, of which 2211 were of medium and heavy calibre.

of the war was of a kind incomparable with that in any previous warfare.

The Germans had to fight on two fronts; on the west against France and Great Britain, and on the east against Russia. They hoped by a " knock-out blow " to concentrate their army in the west, sweep through Belgium, thus getting round the French line, and reach Paris.

Conquest of Belgium

They nearly succeeded. Though the Belgians fought hard, they could not stand against overwhelming force, and in three weeks the Germans reached the French frontier. They then wished to get between the allied Franco-British armies to Paris. The French sent all the troops they could get,[1] and the Germans were driven back to the River Aisne. They were then aligned facing the French and British armies, and from September, 1914, for the next four years, the lines reaching from Rheims to the Vosges scarcely shifted. Trenches were dug, barbed wire entanglements put up, and " trench warfare " began.

The Western Front

Tannenberg (1914)

The Eastern Front

Meanwhile, in the east the Russians met with disaster. They advanced into Germany, and at *Tannenberg* amongst the lakes, were totally defeated (1914). The next spring the Germans followed this up, drove the Russians far back, and established themselves on Russian territory.[2]

Two possibilities: Gallipoli (1915)

There was now a difference of opinion between military commanders and statesmen. The soldiers wished to confine the war to these two long-drawn frontiers. The statesmen believed that trench warfare meant " stalemate " and that we should seek to pierce the Austro-German defences in other areas. So one attack was planned on *Gallipoli*, held by Germany's ally the Turks, and another on *Mesopotamia*. The object of the landing at Gallipoli was to get in touch with hard-pressed Russia, to defeat Turkey, and thereby to induce Bulgaria to join us. A naval attack was first planned, but the Turkish floating mines sank some of our ships, and

[1] Many were sent from Paris in vehicles hastily commandeered.

[2] The Germans conquered all Russian Poland and Lithuania.

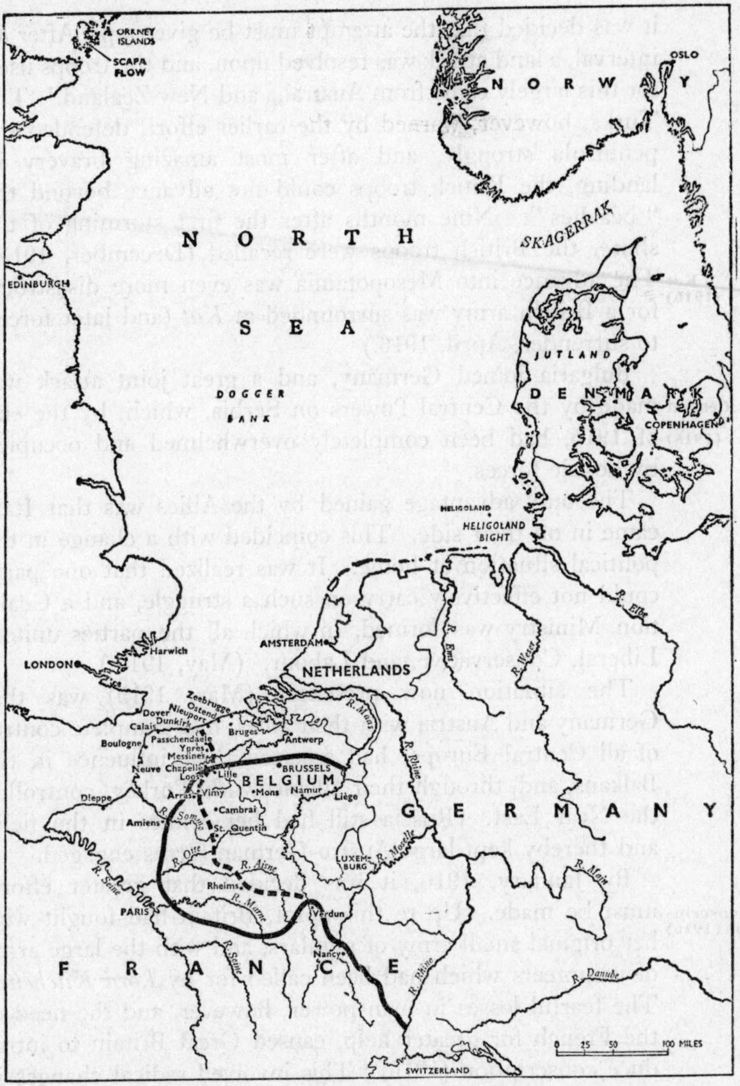

THE NORTH SEA AND THE WESTERN FRONT, 1914–1918

——— Enemy front line at time of Marne. - - - Line before the great attacks of 1918

it was decided that the attempt must be given up. After an interval, a land attack was resolved upon, and the troops used for this largely came from Australia and New Zealand.[1] The Turks, however, warned by the earlier effort, defended the peninsula strongly, and after most amazing bravery in landing, the British troops could not advance beyond the " beaches ". Nine months after the first storming of the shore, the British troops were recalled (December, 1915).

Kut (1916) The advance into Mesopotamia was even more disastrous, for a British army was surrounded at *Kut* (and later forced to surrender, April, 1916.)

Central Europe (1915) Bulgaria joined Germany, and a great joint attack was made by the Central Powers on Serbia, which, by the end of 1915, had been completely overwhelmed and occupied by hostile forces.

The only advantage gained by the Allies was that Italy came in on their side. This coincided with a change in the political situation at home. It was realized that one party could not effectively carry on such a struggle, and a Coalition Ministry was formed, in which all the parties united, Liberal, Conservative, and Labour. (May, 1915.)

The situation now presented (May, 1915) was that Germany and Austria with their allies, had complete control of all Central Europe, had asserted their influence in the Balkans, and, through their alliance with Turkey, controlled the Near East. Russia still had her armies in the field, and thereby kept large Austro-German forces engaged.

Conscription (1916) By January, 1916, it was decided that greater efforts must be made. Up to this point, Britain had fought with her original small army of regulars, and with the large army of volunteers which had been called for by *Lord Kitchener*. The fearful losses in man-power, however, and the need of the French for greater help, caused Great Britain to introduce conscription (1916). This involved radical changes in

[1] Thus the name " Anzac " from the initials of Australia and New Zealand Army Corps.

industry. With man-power drawn off to the armed forces, and with the increased and always increasing demand for munitions, women had to take the place of men. They were admitted to the factories, and the Trade Unions agreed, in the interests of the nation, to "dilution". This meant that unskilled labour was allowed in industries and occupations hitherto reserved for skilled workers. Women also worked on the land, drove trams, acted as postmen, and in every way helped to set men free for work women could not do.

The Western Front throughout this period was the scene of continuous bombardment. As such a form of warfare had not been foreseen, there were no proper "dug-outs" or trenches, and the men suffered greatly from cold and above all from mud in the winter. Yet it was in this area that both sides hoped for decisive victory.

War in France

Verdun

First the Germans made a violent attack on the French at *Verdun* (February to August, 1916), and to the French this was the great struggle of the war. They held out against all the massed attacks of the Germans, despite appalling casualties. Over 400,000 Frenchmen were killed in the defence of Verdun, but they showed that the Germans could not batter their way through.

The Somme

Then the Allies launched their attack along the river *Somme*. Again thousands upon thousands of men were killed, and gigantic quantities of munitions were used up, but small advance was made. Indeed, as became clear later, such terrific bombardment of any ground by high-explosive shells reduced the terrain to such a condition that no army could advance across it. The Germans were, so Ludendorff reported, "absolutely exhausted" by these struggles, but they withdrew their lines and were thus able to continue the war.

Russia

The Russians at this time made one final effort to help their allies; they attacked the Austrians in the east and won some successes, while the Italians harassed them by an attack from the south. Rumania joined the Allies (August, 1916), only to be defeated.

Lloyd George Prime Minister

This period, mid-way through the war as it proved, was one of crisis. It was marked by the replacement of Asquith by Lloyd George as Prime Minister. As the land war became more and more one of great forces camped immovably against each other, the Germans began to fix their hopes on victory through sea power. Great Britain had, at the very outset of the war, driven German shipping off the oceans. A few German warships had remained on distant stations. These had, in the first months of the war, defeated and sunk a weaker British squadron at *Coronel* (1914), only to be themselves, one month later, defeated and sunk at the *Falkland Islands*. But the navy had many duties to perform. First, it had to protect the shores of Great Britain from German raids or invasions. A few raids were made, as for instance on Lowestoft and Scarborough, but the Germans were able to make no attempt at invasion.

The war at sea

Second, the navy had to transport and convoy all the soldiers and munitions and supplies of all sorts to the many fields of war — twenty million men were conveyed to and from France alone during the four years of war, and without the loss of a single soul.

Third, the navy had to sweep the enemies' merchant flags from the sea, and to strangle their foreign trade. The strangulation of their trade and the stoppage of their imports were among the most important of the factors which brought about the final downfall of the enemy Powers.

Fourth, the British navy had to protect and encourage British and allied commerce. Great Britain's very existence depended on her imports — and if the navy had failed, Great Britain would have been starved into surrender in a few weeks.[1] At the beginning of the war the navy had to

[1] Two-thirds of the foodstuffs eaten in the United Kingdom came from abroad, as did all the cotton and three-fourths of the wool; and the available supplies in the United Kingdom, at any one time, would not have lasted more than five or six weeks.

stop hostile cruisers escaping from German ports, and to clear the seven seas of the cruisers already there.[1] Later, the navy, in its protection of commerce, had to meet a more formidable menace in the submarine — but of that we shall say something shortly.

The paramount duty of the navy, however, on which all else depended, was the fifth. This was to look after the German High Seas Fleet, to confine it to port, and to bring it — or any portion of it — to action if it put to sea. That, in the first two years of the war, was the business of our Grand Fleet, under the command of Admiral *Jellicoe*[2] till November, 1916, and later under that of Admiral *Beatty*. But, of course, the conditions of naval warfare since our last great sea fight in Nelson's time had in many ways altered. It was not only that steam or oil-driven ironclads had displaced sailing vessels, or that the vessels themselves were much larger, and the range of their guns enormously extended,[3] but also that entirely new factors had been introduced. One was the underwater torpedo, discharged either from a submarine or a destroyer or a battleship. Another was the mine, laid under the sea, which exploded when brought into contact with a ship. Our battle-fleet had always to beware of being drawn over prepared minefields, and the torpedo, with its extreme range of 15,000 yards, was still more to be feared. Again, in the old days, ships could not slip away unperceived

[1] At the opening of the war there were five German cruisers in the Pacific. These destroyed, off Coronel in Chile, two British ships of an inferior squadron. The Admiralty immediately dispatched two battle-cruisers to the Falkland Islands. The day after their arrival the five German ships, unaware of danger, appeared; and before evening they were all, except one, at the bottom of the sea. Of the other German cruisers, the *Emden* had the greatest fame; one of her exploits was to sail with an additional false funnel, so as to resemble a British cruiser, to Penang, an island off the Malay Peninsula, and there to destroy a Russian cruiser and a French destroyer.

[2] "Jellicoe", it has been said, "was the only man on either side who could lose the war in an afternoon." This gives some measure of his responsibilities.

[3] Nelson's flagship, the *Victory*, was of 3400 tons, and her whole broadside only weighed 1160 lb., with a range of 1760 to 2500 yards. The *Iron Duke*, Jellicoe's flagship, had a displacement of 25,000 tons, and could throw a single projectile of 1200 lb., with a range of 18,000 to 20,000 yards.

except in a fog or at night—but artificial smoke screens enabled a modern fleet to conceal its movements.

The British fleet could no longer, under the new conditions, be kept, as in past ages, outside the enemies' ports. For the greater part of the war it was either in *Scapa Flow* or the Firth of Forth; and when it did come out, it had to be protected and flanked by large numbers of destroyers and by cruisers, and often preceded by mine-sweepers. Although there were minor actions, for nearly two years the British Grand Fleet and the German High Seas Fleet fought no great battle. But on the last day of May, 1916, came the *Battle of Jutland*—the only encounter of the two main fleets. Poor visibility, perhaps, robbed the British fleet of what appeared to be a splendid chance of victory. As it was, both sides expressed themselves satisfied. The German fleet maintained that, though met by a force superior in the ratio of eight to five, it inflicted twice as much damage as it suffered, and destroyed three British battle-cruisers; whilst Great Britain maintained that the German High Seas Fleet was so much battered that never again would it risk another fight.

The Battle of Jutland (1916)

If the Germans had thus failed as regards fighting our battle fleet, they had formidable weapons still to use. They could attack our merchant shipping, and that of neutrals trading with us. From 1915 they used their submarines to destroy commerce, and in 1917 they declared that they would wage *unrestricted* submarine warfare; that is to say, all ships of whatever nation proceeding to or from a British port, would be sunk. This campaign proved terribly effective; in April, of every 100 ships leaving England, 25 were sunk, and over a million tons of shipping lost.

"Unrestricted" submarine war

Various results unexpected to Germany followed. The Admiralty started the *convoy system*, which reduced our losses. It also equipped "Q-boats", that is, ships disguised in various ways, but really armed to destroy submarines—which proved very effective. Rationing was introduced in

Great Britain, to conserve our food supplies. America, first perturbed by the sinking of the British liner, the *Lusitania*, when 1200 lives were lost, including 120 American citizens (May, 1915), then inflamed by the sinking of her own ships and the breach of international law, declared war on Germany (April, 1917).

This actually marked the turn of the tide, though at first it was not apparent. Gradually the British got the better of the submarines, yet before troops began to pour across the sea from the United States, one further dramatic event occurred.

Russian Revolution (1917)

Russia had struggled on in the east, but the incompetence and corruption of her leaders had led to a total breakdown in the supplies of her armies. Men were sent to fight against the Germans and Austrians with no munitions, no guns, no rifles. The casualties became a slaughter. At length the nation could stand no more. Revolution broke out, and the Tsar abdicated (March, 1917). So utterly was Russia at the mercy of Germany that she had to accept the *Treaty of Brest-Litovsk*, giving up to Germany vast areas of her territory, including all her western provinces.[1]

The West, 1917

The collapse of Russia was a great blow to the Allies, and 1917 brought them no corresponding gain. The French made great attacks on the Aisne, which failed totally, and so frightful were the French losses that there were mutinies and great discontent in their armies. This necessitated attacks by the British to draw off the Germans. An attack was made on the Germans at *Messines* which was a great success, and repeated attacks, lasting over a period of five months, for the possession of *Passchendaele* which were most terribly costly in men, gained little. Italy suffered a crushing defeat at *Caporetto*. Finally, the use of the tank, a new weapon invented by Britain, was tried at Cambrai. It proved a marvellous success, and the German line was broken. But this was not followed up, and by the end of the year it was

[1] These included Finland, Estonia, Latvia, Lithuania, and Russian Poland.

known that not only had these offensives gained us relatively little ground, but had resulted in losses far outweighing any we inflicted on the Germans.

Palestine

Even *Allenby's* success in *Palestine* did not appear to offer much hope. He took Jerusalem, and another British force took Baghdad, but the Turks remained full of fight.

So 1918 opened with apparently not much hope of change. Yet really the war was to enter a different and a decisive phase.

Crisis in the west, 1918

Germany had not succeeded in starving Britain, but she was herself starving. Though she controlled the Balkans, and though her ally Turkey had access to the East, she could not get supplies for her people. Her leaders resolved to make one final violent effort, in the hope that they could win a victory in the west before the American troops arrived. Every available man was transferred to the west, and in March she began a massed offensive on the British. So terrific was her onslaught that the British lost 400,000 killed and wounded, and 80,000 taken prisoner; all the hard won gains of the previous year were lost (including Messines and Passchendaele Ridges), and the Germans threatened Amiens, the great centre of our railway communications.[1] Then the attack was halted — the Germans could win no more ground here.

To hearten the British, on St. George's Day there was a brilliant attack on *Zeebrugge*, when a smashing raid was made on the mole, and the canal through which the submarines came was partially blocked.

Hard on this, the Germans struck at the French. All during May, June, July, wave after wave was flung on the French lines, which were pushed back to the Marne, and

[1] The Germans held for part of one day the village of Villers-Bretonneux from which they could command Amiens. Hindenburg writes in his memoirs: "We ought to have shouted in the ear of every single man 'Press on to Amiens! put in your last ounce. Perhaps Amiens means decisive victory. Capture Villers-Bretonneux whatever happens, so that from its height we can command Amiens with masses of our heavy artillery.' It was all in vain; our strength was exhausted."

once there the Germans were within forty miles of Paris. But on 18th July the Allies in their turn attacked. American troops had poured in since April, munitions had been provided in overwhelming quantities, and in March *Foch* had been given unified command of the Allied forces. All along the line, in different places, French and British attacked. The German line was pierced, and in every part all through August, the Allies went steadily forward. By 8th August, Ludendorff decided that Germany must make peace. He tried to hold the field a little longer, but behind his back the German allies were collapsing. First Bulgaria gave in, then Turkey, then Serbia was recovered by the Allies, and in October the Italians smashed the Austrians at the battle of *Vittorio Veneto*. It was hopeless for Germany to struggle on. Her troops had been beaten and driven back everywhere, her allies had all been forced to surrender. Now the civilian population in Germany could bear no more. Revolution threatened, and the Kaiser fled from Berlin. The German army chiefs resigned, and on 11th November, Germany was granted an armistice. The war was over.[1]

Armistice (11th November, 1918)

CHAPTER 77

THE PEACE OF VERSAILLES

The armistice which ended the war was signed on 11th November, 1918; there followed a great Conference, held in Paris during many months, and finally, in June, 1919, peace was signed at *Versailles* (*Note 157*) and later treaties followed. The faults of those Treaties have been so loudly proclaimed, and so many of Europe's subsequent difficulties

[1] The war cost 50,000 million pounds and led to the enlisting of 50 millions of armed men; there were 30 million casualties and not far short of 9 million deaths. In France alone 21,000 factories, 630,000 houses, and 1659 townships were completely destroyed. The National Debt was in 1914 before the war 25 billion francs — in 1921 it was 302 billion francs. The National Debt of Great Britain was in 1914 before the war £708 millions — it was £7435 millions in 1919.

have been attributed to them, that they have to be clearly examined.

Influence of U.S.A.

First, we must notice the great influence which the United States of America exercised through *President Wilson*, who came to Europe himself. The U.S.A. was not exhausted by the war, they were not so tainted by the bitterness left by the struggle, and Wilson's "Fourteen Points" were held to represent the ideals of the Allies. (See note on p. 998.) Wilson was inspired by two great beliefs. He held that democratic forms of government must be established in every country, and he believed in "self-determination"; that is, in the right of each racial group to independence or to decide as to its form of government. Now, this principle led at once to difficulties. Small States were to be set up and given "self-government", but the idea could not be logically carried out, for Europe is filled with "racial groups" too small to live alone.[1]

"Self-determination"

Acting, however, on this principle, Europe was now "reformed".[2] Taking the territorial changes in Europe, Germany lost Alsace-Lorraine which was restored to France (on the basis of being primarily French in race), and she had to hand over her eastern or Polish provinces to the Republic of Poland.[3]

Poland

As the newly-formed Republic of Poland needed an outlet to the sea, they created the "corridor", a strip of land running between East and West Prussia, and ending in the port of Danzig. Danzig was to be "free", that is to say neither Polish nor German. This corridor revived the position in old days long before Poland had been divided up in the eighteenth century, and it was hoped thereby to

[1] Thus the State of "Czechoslovakia" was formed, which actually contained people of opposed nationalities — Czechs, Slovaks, Germans, Ruthenians, who were all grouped together because Czechoslovakia did form a geographical whole, and occupied an important position as a buffer between Russia and Germany, and as a "bastion" or outpost between Germany and Austria.

[2] In Eastern Europe the number of States rose from 7 to 14.

[3] Since the partitions of 1799 the Polish Republic had ceased to exist. It was now revived.

let Polish trade flow down its natural route, the river Vistula, while the Germans were to use trains running across the "corridor" and giving them access to their eastern province.

Austria-Hungary disappeared as an empire. She was broken up into her component parts, and a series of small independent republics were created, of which Austria, Hungary, Czechoslovakia, and Poland were the chief. In addition, the new Kingdom of Yugoslavia was formed by giving to the original Serbia more parts of the Austro-Hungarian Empire on the southern borders which were inhabited by Slavs, and Montenegro. Rumania gained a slice of former Russian territory, which was inhabited by Rumanians (Bessarabia), and also obtained Transylvania from Hungary, thus almost doubling her territory.

The Break-up of Austria-Hungary

Turkey lost nearly all her European territory and some of her outlying provinces, and Syria and Palestine became independent States under the guardianship of France and Britain respectively, who ruled under mandate from the League of Nations. (See p. 1000.)

Turkey

Russia, which by the Treaty of Brest-Litovsk had great fragments of her territory torn off by Germany, now had most of that land restored, but she had to cede her Polish provinces back to Poland, and to recognize the independence of the little Baltic republics of Finland, Lithuania, Estonia, and Latvia.

Russia

Italy gained the provinces to her north, Trentino, Trieste, Istria, and part of Tirol, though here " self-determination " did not prevail, for a large block of the inhabitants of Tirol were Germans.

Italy

So far, the motives actuating the peace-makers are clear. They meant to give liberty to these small States who desired it, and they meant as far as possible to group races together. These measures were intended to be constructive.

" Security against aggression "

The other provisions of the Treaty raised very different problems. The French wished to prevent the possibility of further German aggression. They insisted, therefore, on very severe terms. Germany had to pay a vast indemnity; surrender her fleet; give up all her colonies; and accept her "war guilt" as an aggressor.

The League of Nations

Finally, the *League of Nations* was created, and the "Covenant of the League" drawn up (*Note 158*). This was intended to provide a means for ensuring peace by setting up a body to prevent disputes degenerating into war. Three-quarters of the nations of the whole world joined as members, but the U.S.A. herself refused to join.[1] All these nations were to meet in an annual Assembly held at Geneva, which represented, as it were, a "parliament of nations". The business for that Assembly was to be regulated by a Council, which was to meet three times a year. It was originally intended that this Council should consist of representatives of the U.S.A., British Empire, France, Italy, and Japan who were to have permanent seats, together with representatives of four other member-States to be selected from time to time by the Assembly. The failure of the U.S.A. to join the League reduced the permanent seats to four,[2] and later the number of non-permanent seats was raised to nine.

Economic consequences of the peace

The highest hopes were felt that through the League war would really be prevented, but the decade that followed saw these hopes gradually fade. For that we can now see certain reasons more clearly. The actual territorial arrangements at Versailles were imperfect. Many "minorities" were included in the new States, and thus fresh grievances were created. Germany was embittered by her humiliation, and, most potent of all, the economic consequences of the war and of the peace led eventually to widespread depression and misery, and in the end to the collapse of the German Republic and the rise of the Nazis. When we judge the Treaty of Versailles, therefore, we can see that the men who made it tried to solve different problems in different ways.

[1] Wilson's policy was repudiated by his country when he went back after the Conference.

[2] When Germany joined the League of Nations in 1926, she was given a permanent seat on the Council.

They tried to give liberty to small nations; they tried to secure the world against future wars; but they tried to make Germany pay for the damage she had caused. They did not foresee the economic consequences of their actions, and still less how out of that misery political consequences would ultimately follow.

CHAPTER 78

CONSEQUENCES OF THE PEACE

A General Election held in 1918 returned Lloyd George to power at the head of another Coalition ministry. The whole country hoped now for peace and prosperity, but peace did not bring prosperity. The vast economic waste caused by war always leaves an aftermath. Capital had been destroyed, trade terribly damaged. Those who insisted on vast *reparations* from Germany were warned by the economists what would be the result. "Reparations" mean payments, but payments on a huge scale from one country to another must give rise to a dilemma (*Note 160*).

Economic consequences

Either the reparations would take the form of goods, and then the countries receiving them (in this case Britain, France, and U.S.A.) would be flooded with the manufactures and such goods as coal, of their defeated enemy. Or they must be paid in gold, in which case the countries receiving payment would be filled with gold and the effect would be a disastrous rise in prices. These results did indeed follow. On the other hand, the financial ruin of Germany meant the ruin of a country which had been amongst our best customers; they could not buy from us, so our export trades were bound to suffer.

Reparations

The economic clauses of the peace treaties were therefore in the nature of boomerangs, coming back to injure us. Two other factors were to add to our troubles. Great

Unemployment

Britain had borrowed largely from the U.S.A., and she had used her credit to obtain goods for her allies, whose credit was not as high as hers. She was now bound herself to repay the money borrowed from the U.S.A., while as time passed her debtors ceased to pay her. In addition, the demobilization of the armies and the cessation of work on munitions, dislocated employment. Hundreds of thousands of munition workers lost their jobs, while the returning soldiers could find none. The cost of living had doubled during the war and did not fall to its original level, while employers wished to reduce wages from their very high war levels.

Changes in industry: strikes and tariffs

Modern developments have hit most hardly what were once our most flourishing industries. Coal-mining and railways have obviously suffered from the advance of petrol-using motor-cars, from the substitution of oil for coal in the navy and in industry, and from the growing rise in the use of gas and electricity. So trouble became acute in these industries. The miners first threatened to strike, and a Commission appointed to inquire into their grievances, advocated that the State should take over the mines. This the Coalition Government delayed to do, and then other events swept it from power. In 1922 the " uneasy partnership " between the Lloyd George Liberals and the Conservatives broke down, and the Conservatives won the General Election and took office under Bonar Law. When Bonar Law retired in 1923, Baldwin became Conservative Prime Minister, and he wished to introduce a " full-blown " tariff. During the war, in order to save space in our ships, heavy duties had been put on a few categories of goods which were considered " luxuries " to a country fighting for its life.[1] Now the Conservatives wanted a general

Government changes

[1] These included motor-cars and clocks. The duties were known as McKenna Duties from Mr. Reginald McKenna, the Chancellor of the Exchequer who introduced them. In 1921, by the Safeguarding of Industries Act, certain " key " (i.e. vital) industries were protected by the imposition of import duties. The purpose of this and of similar Acts was to establish in Great Britain industries which were vital to the nation both in peace and in war, and to make the country independent of imports of such things as scientific glassware, fine chemicals, dyestuffs, magnetos, etc.

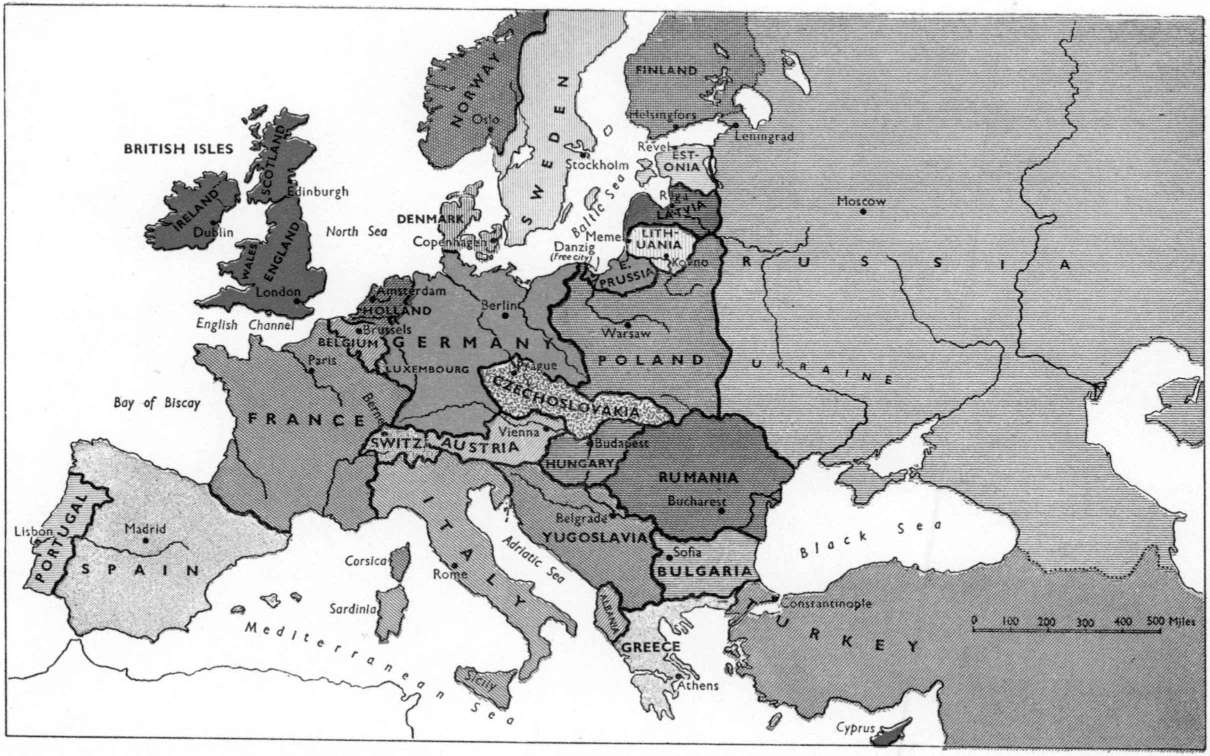

EUROPE AFTER THE PEACE SETTLEMENT, 1919–1923

F 935

tariff, but a general election at the end of 1923 showed that the country did not accept this policy. The Conservatives still formed the largest party in the House of Commons but they had not a majority over the combined Labour and Liberal members, and when Parliament met in January, 1924, the defeat of the Government and the resignation of Baldwin followed almost as matters of course.

The First Labour Government (1924)

The *Labour Party* was then called on to form its first Government, and this it did with *Ramsay MacDonald* as Prime Minister. As it was only the second largest party in Parliament, it had to rely on the support of the Liberal members, and this it did receive at first. This advent of the Socialists to power was regarded with great apprehension by the propertied classes; they feared "confiscatory taxation", and there was much vague talk of the influence of Russian Bolshevism on English Labour. Actually, as the Government depended on the Liberal votes in the House, it undertook nothing startling in the way of legislation. Right from the beginning, however, it was clear that its position was precarious, and in the autumn of 1924 trouble arose over its Russian policy. The Labour ministry was defeated in the House of Commons and the general election which followed (October, 1924) gave the Conservatives an absolute majority over all other parties. Stanley Baldwin then formed his second Conservative Government. The result of this 1924 election was possibly greatly influenced by the publication in the newspapers, five days before the polling date, of a letter which was said to have been written by Zinoviev, one of the Bolshevik leaders, and which contained instructions to persons carrying out subversive activities in Britain.

The Zinoviev Letter

Six years had now passed since the war ended, and it might have been expected that trade would have revived and the world been given what it most wanted — work and food. Actually the position had become steadily worse, as the economists had predicted that it would. The evils of "reparations" had become so clear, and the condition of Germany as a debtor was so hopeless, that now the nations began to try to rectify their mistakes. The *Dawes Plan* (1924) [1] greatly lowered Germany's contributions, though those of Great Britain to America continued. Thus Britain's debtors did not pay her, while she continued to pay her debts.

The Dawes Plan

But more constructive efforts were not attempted. No measures of reform were brought in, and in Great Britain unemployment continued and discontent grew. The miners who were suffering increasingly from the decline in the demand for coal, were faced with reductions of their wages, for the new Conservative Government gave up the control of the mines, which had been in Government hands since 1917. The Government subsidy, which had reached very large proportions, was withdrawn. The mine-owners decided, in view of the depression in the trade and the rise in cost of production, to lower wages or lengthen hours.

Discontent in Britain

Against this the miners struck, and they were soon supported by the two other great Unions, the railwaymen and the engineers. All Labour rallied to their support, and a *General Strike* of all Trade Unionists was declared (May, 1926). It failed, and very quickly. The Government could not allow the existence of the country to be threatened, and took steps to provide transport and food. Motor transport brought supplies to the towns; the workers themselves, with funds depleted by years of unemployment, could not stand the strain; and the general feeling of the public told against this resort to industrial war. After a week, the Unions recognized their defeat — all but the miners, who struggled on all summer and then had to accept the owners' terms.[2]

The "General Strike" (1926)

[1] The Dawes Plan was drawn up by a committee of the Powers, under the chairmanship of the American General Dawes.

[2] The outcry against the General Strike also led to protests that the Unions used their funds for "political" purposes. Hence the Trade Disputes and Trade Union Act of 1927 was passed, which made any "sympathetic" or "general" strike illegal.

The " General Strike " was a symptom of the unrest and discontent due to falling trade, growing unemployment, and all the misery and suffering these involve for the workers. When, after three years, no improvement came, and no legislation, the workers used their votes, and in 1929 the Labour Party was returned the largest party in the House of Commons, but still without a majority over all other parties combined (they had 289 seats representing over 8 million votes). They accepted office, however, and Ramsay MacDonald formed his second Government, again relying on Liberal support. It proved a bad moment for Labour to assume power. Economic conditions were unfavourable and the burden of reparations prevented the revival of prosperity. Efforts were made to deal with this, but these measures did not prove effectual. Germany again had her reparations reduced by the *Young Plan* of 1929 and the *Hoover Plan* of 1931. Great Britain was still paying the U.S.A., her industries had suffered from the strikes, and her unemployment continued to grow.

Second Labour Government (1929)

In 1931 the whole world was struck by a terrible " slump " in trade. Great Britain had her scheme of unemployment insurance, and now the immense demands on the Unemployment Fund meant that its money could not meet the weekly payments, and it had to borrow from the Treasury. At the same time, naturally, as trade was universally bad, our " balance of trade " suffered, and our revenue decreased. The Budget, therefore, would not balance, and a demand was made for drastic economies. A financial crisis created a panic, and gold began to drain out of the country. (In one week, 25th July, 21 millions in gold were withdrawn to France.) The Labour Government could not, by itself, deal with so serious a situation, and the Prime Minister, Ramsay MacDonald, accordingly asked Conservatives and Liberals to join him and form a " National Government ". Some of the Labour Cabinet resigned rather than accept the programme put before them, objecting in par-

The financial crisis (1931)

ticular to the proposed reduction in the rate of unemployment benefit, and thus Labour, like the Liberals, was split into groups. At the election which followed, the new National Government secured 554 seats, the Labour Party only 52.

The National Government had first to restore confidence, and this it did by very drastic measures. Taxation was increased sharply, wages of all government officials (including the judges) and employees were reduced, and unemployment benefit was cut down. In this way, and also owing to the psychological effect of a " National Government ", panic was checked.[1]

Tariffs imposed (1932) A very far-reaching change was now made in our financial and economic policy. Great Britain abandoned Free Trade. Tariffs were put on many goods coming into the country, with the idea of checking purchases from abroad which had tended to upset our balance of trade.

Hopes of recovery Gradually the panic subsided and trade began slowly to revive. A *World Economic Conference* was held in 1933 to try to solve financial problems. One of the most useful of the activities of the League of Nations was its efforts to tackle economic problems. The nations met at Geneva to consider the best ways to check trade depression and to stimulate prosperity. It might have been hoped that common sense would show that all have common interests. If one nation prospers, others who sell to it will also prosper; if one is impoverished, others will suffer from loss of markets. Moreover, it was most clearly recognized that war was the worst enemy of prosperity. Therefore it might have been anticipated that the nations would work together, not only in limited ways, but in the supreme effort to preserve peace. These hopes were all frustrated, and to understand what happened we must turn to the events which had been passing in other nations and in other parts of the Empire.

[1] Britain also " went off the Gold Standard "; that is to say, gold could not be used as currency.

CHAPTER 79

THE "THIRD EMPIRE"

The war had a great influence on the constitution of the British Empire (*Note 159*). In the first place, the great Dominions had entered the war and attended the Peace Conference as equals with the mother country. Then, new territories were attached to Great Britain under conditions different from any that had hitherto existed.

"Independent nationhood"

Thus, at the Treaty of Versailles, each of the self-governing Dominions had its own representatives, each signed that Treaty separately, and each signed the Covenant of the League separately. It was recognized that the Dominions had attained control over their own foreign policy, and could make treaties as independent States.[1] This led to an *Imperial Conference* in 1926, when it was declared: "Great Britain and the Dominions are autonomous communities within the British Empire, equal in status and in no way subordinate to each other in any aspect of their domestic or external affairs, though united by a common allegiance to the Crown, and freely associated as members of the British Commonwealth of Nations". This declaration was embodied in the *Statute of Westminster* (1931), which recognizes the "independent nationhood" of the Dominions.[2] "The Crown is the golden link" that now holds the Empire together.

The Statute of Westminster (1931)

As a result, the Dominions were free to act as they chose in every respect. Thus, when King Edward VIII abdicated

[1] This was emphasized in 1925 when the Dominions refused to sign the Treaty of Locarno. Canada would not sign because in that Treaty Great Britain guaranteed the frontier between France and Germany, and Canada (like the U.S.A.) objected to "guarantees" in Europe being binding on her.

[2] The British Government cannot veto any Dominion legislature, cannot control foreign policy, and the Governor-Generals representing the King are not nominated by the British Government, but by the Sovereign on the advice of the Dominion government concerned.

(in December, 1936), each Dominion accepted the abdication and recognized King George VI through its own Parliament. When war broke out in September, 1939, each Dominion again was free to join in the war or not. The solidarity of an Empire based on such freedom was in point of fact brilliantly demonstrated by the fact that every Dominion, but not Eire, ranged itself voluntarily by the side of Great Britain.

Progress towards self-government

The British Empire, therefore, shows what the world has not seen before, an Empire whose members are in some cases completely self-governing, and in others are progressing towards that stage. We may think that this characteristic is our unique contribution to the art of governing. But all parts of the Empire have not reached that point.

"Trusteeship"

Many of the colonies and dependencies now have all their government departments staffed by local people and responsible to elected assemblies. Others are so backward that they must still be governed by Britain. Yet here, again and again, the British Government stresses the idea that it is a "trustee" for these backward peoples. Modern policy, too, tries definitely to preserve what is good in native civilization, so that each dependency shall contribute what is characteristic to its culture, while at the same time Britain can give them what is most helpful in hers, such as medical services, agricultural knowledge, better communications. In 1923 Parliament laid down the lines on which Britain considered her colonial policy must be based; "The interests of the native must be paramount, and if and when these interests and the interests of the immigrant race (i.e. white settlers) should conflict, the interests of the natives must prevail."

Mandated territories

There remains another group of territories, whose position has caused much heart-burning, namely the "mandated" territories. This is a group of what were formerly German colonies or Turkish provinces, taken from these countries after the Great War. They are mostly in Africa (formerly

German East and German West), and are held under a "mandate" from the League of Nations, which calls for reports on their government and progress. In accepting the mandate for Palestine, taken from the Turks after its conquest by Great Britain, we involved ourselves in much trouble. We promised to give the Jews a "national home" there, and accordingly many Jews emigrated, especially after the Nazi persecution started in Germany and Austria. But Palestine had its Arab inhabitants, who bitterly resented these entrants, and as a result, trouble between Jew and Arab led the Arabs to revolt against the British. The problem of reconciling the two claims has been extremely difficult, and the warfare and bloodshed involved led to much bitterness. It was not found possible to give self-government to a country so divided, and Great Britain incurred a great deal of blame and hostility.[1] **Palestine**

The mandate system led to trouble in another direction. During the war *Lawrence of Arabia* had devoted himself to stirring up the Arab "Revolt in the Desert" against the Turks. He had succeeded marvellously, and he believed that as a result an independent Arab State could be formed to include Syria and Mesopotamia ('Iraq). The French, however, were given a mandate for Syria, and they drove out Lawrence's friend Feisal from Damascus.[2] In compensation, Great Britain made him King of 'Iraq, which was ultimately recognized as an independent State (1932). **Arab States**

One other Eastern State also achieved independence. *Egypt* had been a British Protectorate, but after the war Britain realized that Egyptians would no longer tolerate this control. She withdrew the protectorate, and Egypt was recognized as an independent sovereign State (1922). Yet, as the Suez Canal is vital to British commerce and forms her connecting link with India, Britain retained control of the **Egypt**

[1] The great pipe-line bringing oil from 'Iraq runs out to Palestine, and the question of its control leads to further difficulty.

[2] Lawrence's bitter disappointment led to his withdrawing from public life.

Canal. The long and close connection of Great Britain and Egypt is interesting in many ways, and not least in this close to a chapter. Britain, and not France, had been the power to influence Egypt, and now she acted in recognition of the principle that this State had a right to its independence.

Modern India

The movement towards independence had thus been shown in various directions. The great Dominions achieved theirs without any friction whatever. Now we must turn to that great member of the Empire, India, which by 1939 had not yet attained " Dominion status ", though wishing for it.

India had come to the help of Great Britain in the war of 1914. Her troops had crossed the ocean, had fought in France, and had won the highest military honours. In 1917 the British Government officially promised " the progressive realization of responsible government in India as an integral part of the British Empire ". This was to be made possible through a series of reforms,[1] which were intended to give Indians gradual control of their own affairs. As India progressed, so she wished more for development in two directions. First, she wanted to see Indians employed in larger numbers in the administration, and second, she wished for self-government through elected assemblies.

Here one of the difficulties in Indian affairs showed itself, for the two main religious bodies of the country, Hindus and Mohammedans, often clashed. If complete self-government through assemblies elected on a uniform suffrage were granted, the Mohammedan " minority " would be outvoted. Moreover, India was not considered to be fit for the immediate grant of full self-government. Accordingly, a plan, called *dyarchy*, was adopted; this was to be tried for ten years, and if it was successful, further development was then to follow.

The *Government of India Act* was passed in 1919. This set up a Council of State and an elected Legislative Assembly

[1] These were advocated in the *Montagu-Chelmsford Report* (1917), Lord Chelmsford being then the Viceroy, and Edward Montagu, Secretary of State for India.

representing all India. Each Province was also given its own elected Legislative Council, from which ministers were to be chosen by the Governor. These Councils were to take over the administration of their Provinces, though finance and the maintenance of order were not entrusted to them, but were "reserved" for the Governor and his Executive Council.

The Government of India Act (1919): "Dyarchy"

A large volume of Indian opinion did not think that this measure went far enough, and a most interesting personality, the Mahatma Gandhi, came forward and organized the opposition on "peaceful" lines. He was entirely opposed to violence, and preached that India must win her self-government, but not through force. He and his followers refused to "co-operate" with Great Britain, that is to say they would not work with the British. The strike was to be their weapon and the boycott of British goods. Gandhi himself, when imprisoned, used the hunger-strike as his weapon of defence. National feeling rallied to Gandhi, and his movement swung many in India into line behind him. Himself wishful for reforms, he included in his programme the abolition of caste and full co-operation with Mohammedans. So widespread did the agitation become, that Britain had to recognize the necessity for some effort being made to meet it. As a result of the report made by a Government Commission under the chairmanship of Sir John Simor which went to India in 1928, *Round Table Conferer* representing both India and Great Britain, were h 1930 and 1931, and it was decided that the solutio Indian problem lay in a Federation of All Indi course, self-government for the central and p semblies. When the National Government c in Great Britain in 1931 it was faced with ing what steps should be taken to accor Indians themselves were unable to c the British Government took the m and issued a scheme of constituti

Mahatma Gandhi

Non-Co-operation

The Government of India Act (1935)

scheme was finally embodied in the *Government of India Act, 1935,* which provided for the establishment of an All-India Federation if and when the British Parliament considers that the time is ripe. Certain provisions were also made for the establishment of provincial autonomy, and these came into force in 1937.

The 1935 Act really gave India a new constitution, and in 1937 India started to pass through a transitional period between the old constitution and the establishment of complete Federation. The *Indian National Congress* (the nationalist party led by the Mahatma Gandhi) regarded this transitional period as an unnecessary irritation and never ceased to agitate for immediate independence. There were, too, other and more violent agitators against whom repressive measures had to be used.[1] On the whole, however, reasonably satisfactory progress was being made along the road to self-government,[2] when the outbreak of war in Europe in September, 1939, brought Britain to one of the gravest hours in her history and caused Congress to abandon temporarily its objections to violence and to give Britain and the Empire every help within its power, though unfortunately this co-operation was not to last.

CHAPTER 80

EUROPEAN REVOLUTIONS OF THE TWENTIETH CENTURY

In the nineteenth century, after the close of the Napoleonic wars, Europe first had a period of economic distress,

[1] Thus, in certain provinces, such as Bengal, crimes of violence led to the suspension of trial by jury, and agitators were deported on the order of the Governors.

[2] In 1947 India received complete independence, and divided herself into the two states of India and Pakistan. Both, so far, have voted to remain members of the British Commonwealth.

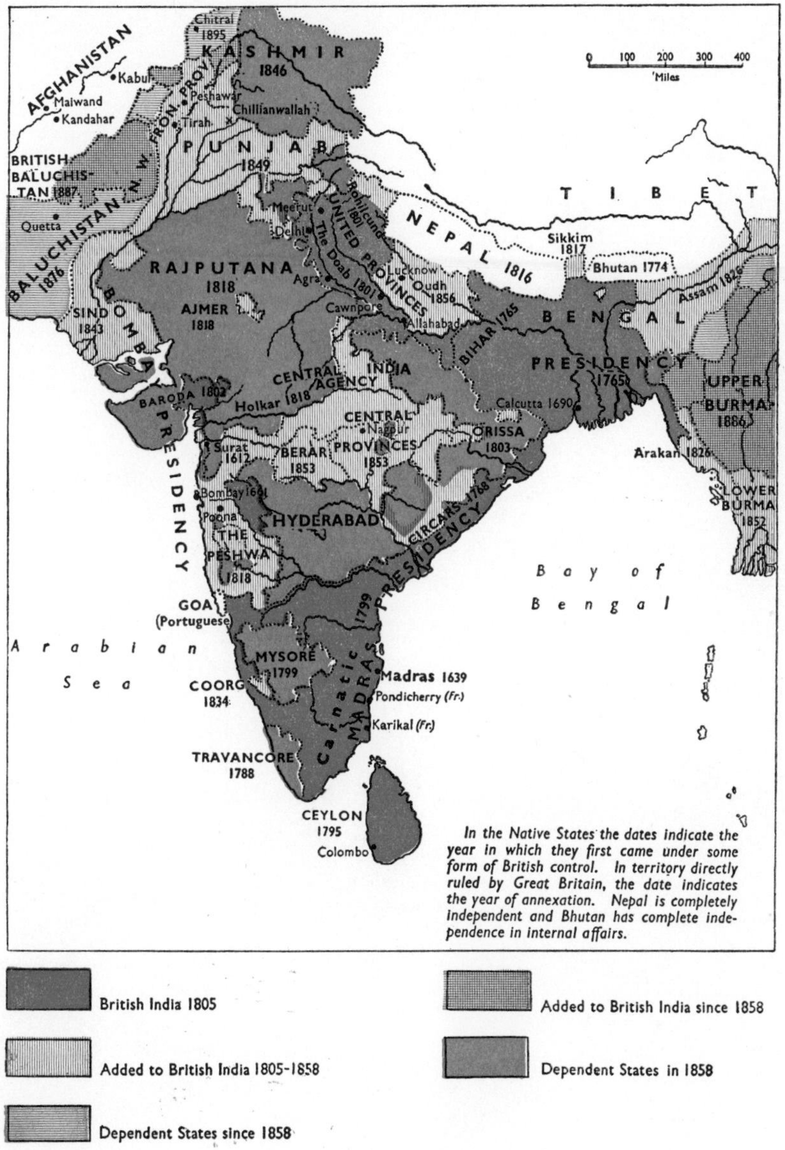

INDIA, 1805–1939

F 938

followed (in 1830 and in 1848) by a series of political revolutions. The close of the war of 1914–8 was followed by similar events. We have already dealt with the post-war economic distress, and we have now to say something about the series of " revolutions " which followed the peace made at Versailles.

Russia and Bolshevism

The first Russian revolution of 1917 had meant the overthrow of the Czar and the establishment of a republic. That republic was moderate in character, but was at once opposed by extremists. These were led by *Lenin*, head of the Communist Party,[1] which wished not only for a political but for a social revolution, and for the setting up of rule by the workers, for the workers. When the Great War ended in 1918, civil war continued in Russia. The struggle of the moderates against the Communists was made more difficult by attacks of the " Whites ", or reactionary parties, who wished to overthrow the Republic. The Allies, France and Britain, gave help to these " Whites ", and invasions were made into Russia at Archangel, and into Siberia. These attacks all failed, but the moderate party in Russia fell, and the Communists formed the Union of Socialist Soviet Republics.[2] This was a major event of the century; one of the world's vastest countries adopted a completely Communist form of government, and organized its whole life and industry on Communist lines. The State took over the ownership of all land and the organization of all production. " Capitalism ", meaning production for private profit, was replaced by production for the uses of the State.

Opponents of the regime were ruthlessly exterminated, and, moreover, the Bolsheviks openly declared (as had the earlier French Revolutionaries) that they wished to extend their doctrine over the whole world. This roused the appre-

[1] The Russian Communists are generally known as Bolshevists, a word derived from *bolshinstvo,* which means " majority " and was originally applied in 1903 to the majority Radical faction (led by Lenin) of the Russian Social-Democrat Party.

[2] A union of the various provinces of Russia, organized into republics of which the political units are Soviets or Councils of Workers.

hension of most of Europe, and in various countries violent reactions took place.

Italy, like the rest of Europe, suffered from the slump which followed peace, and distress gave rise to a good deal of disorder. The government was feeble and Communism was making advances. Against this, a new party now appeared, the *Fascisti*, led by Signor *Mussolini*. He had himself been originally a Socialist, but he now headed the anti-Communist party. Organizing his followers, he marched on Rome (October, 1921) and set up a government, which developed into a dictatorship. Parliamentary government was abolished, and the rule of the Fascist Party made supreme. No opposition was, or is, allowed. At Versailles Italy had acquired territory, and her population had now risen to over 40 millions. Yet, not being a rich or highly industrialized country, she needed an outlet for the growing population which her own land could not support. Here she was hard hit by the effects of the great "slump" in the U.S.A. When that country found herself suffering to an unparalleled extent from unemployment, she began to limit the number of people allowed to immigrate into her territories. Italians had hitherto flocked in thousands to the U.S.A., but they now found themselves deprived of that outlet. Italy's colonial possessions did not afford much help, and she began to feel restless. Moreover, the tariffs imposed by all European countries after the war, acted as a check to international trade, and all nations began to experience a shrinkage in their foreign trade.

Italy and Fascism

The Fascist Government therefore, in 1935, embarked on the conquest of *Abyssinia*, giving as "pretext" outrages said to have been committed by the Abyssinians, and desiring to acquire a land which was believed to be rich in minerals.[1] Great Britain opposed this act of aggression, and the League of Nations being invoked, "sanctions"

Italy and Abyssinia

[1] Italy also believed herself justified because in 1880 she had asserted a "protectorate" over Abyssinia, though later compelled to withdraw.

were put into force. This meant that Italian goods were boycotted, no financial loans were made to Italy, and an embargo was placed on the export of certain goods to Italy. This embargo did not apply to oil needed for aeroplanes and the army, since the U.S.A., not being a member of the League, did not apply sanctions, and the League Powers considered it useless for them to refrain when supplies poured in to Italy from the U.S.A.

The results of the war were, first the speedy conquest of Abyssinia, which was entirely annexed to Italy in 1936; second, bitter animosity between Italy and the two " democratic " powers, Great Britain and France, who had led the opposition. Italy now turned away from her former allies, and began the policy of friendship with Germany, which developed into the close alliance known as the *Rome-Berlin Axis*.

The Rome-Berlin Axis

This same period which saw Italy become a dictatorship,[1] saw the transformation of Germany in 1933 from a democratic Republic to a *totalitarian* State ruled by an absolute dictator, and saw too the new Germany become once more a great military power, with a policy of expansion based on aggression.

Germany

Those who believed in democracy, that is in government by the people through elected representatives, and in freedom of speech, freedom of the press, and the right to hold public meetings, thus had to face a Europe in which more than half the territory was ruled by dictatorships where no democratic institutions and no freedom were allowed to survive.[2]

In the case of Germany the dictatorship led to the renewal of European war. We have to see how this came about.

Germany, after Versailles, was organized as a Republic.

[1] Turkey too, under Mustapha Kemal (Kamal Ataturk) adopted government through a dictator.

[2] Stalin (son of a shoemaker), Hitler (son of an Austrian official), Mussolini (son of a blacksmith), all began their political careers as Socialists, and all ended as dictators.

The government had terrible difficulties to contend with, chiefly connected with economics. The payment of reparations was an intolerable burden, and gradually this was recognized by the Allies. In the years immediately after 1918 she suffered from inflation of her currency and from the results of the war. Her financiers borrowed immense sums, chiefly from the U.S.A., and in the years 1927 and 1928 she borrowed more than five times the amount she had to pay out in reparations. Her debt, therefore, rose to over 1200 million Reichsmarks in 1929. By degrees, and in successive years, the reparations were reduced, until in 1931 they were entirely " suspended " by the plan put forward by President Hoover. But the whole world was then on the verge of a " slump ", which in the next few months developed until every country was suffering. In Great Britain, as we have seen (p. 959), the Government fell and Britain " went off gold ".

The Nazis

In Germany the depression led to the rise of the *Nazis*[1] and the advent of *Adolf Hitler*. This " National-Socialist " party owed its origin firstly to the misery caused by the economic depression, secondly to the humiliation felt by Germans from their defeat. (France had felt the same humiliation after 1870, and it took years before she recovered.) Hitler had appeared as leader of what seemed a totally unimportant party in 1923, when he staged a revolt which was suppressed with great ease.[2] In 1929 he and his party were so obscure that the German " Director of Political Studies ", lecturing in England on " German political parties ", never even mentioned Hitler's name.

The distress due to the world slump gave Hitler and his backers their chance, and they began to gain adherents. They pointed out that Germany could not bear the burdens

[1] " Nazi " is an abridgment for the German equivalent of the title " National Socialists " (National Sozialisten).

[2] The British Ambassador in Berlin wrote: " He was released after six months and bound over for the rest of his sentence, thereafter *fading into oblivion*." Lord d'Abernon's *Ambassador of Peace* (published, 1929).

of the war settlement, and they promised to win her release. Yet Germany for some further time was not converted to National Socialism. Even at the elections held in November, 1932, the Nazi vote dropped. No one then anticipated trouble, but by a political intrigue, the old and failing President Hindenburg was induced to make Hitler Chancellor of the Republic.

The Reichstag Fire

He had only 196 followers in the Reichstag out of a total of 584 members. Fresh elections were due to be held in March, 1933. In February the Reichstag [1] was burnt down, and at once the Nazis declared that this was the work of Communists. This was the signal for a coup d'état. All Communist deputies were promptly arrested, and hundreds of people all through Germany were imprisoned on the Chancellor's orders. But even then at the elections the Nazis held only 288 seats out of 647. They used their power of intimidation, and passed a Bill abolishing parliamentary government and giving dictatorial powers to the Nazi Party and its leader (March, 1933).

Hitler: "Mein Kampf"

From that moment Germany fell under the absolute rule of Hitler. His opponents were utterly suppressed, persecution of the Jews followed, and the doctrine of "racial superiority" was proclaimed.

We may trace the subsequent development of German policy to that doctrine, fully set forth, together with all it means, in Hitler's book, *Mein Kampf* (My fight). Briefly, Hitler there laid down his programme: (1) All people of German race must be united into "Great Germany". (2) Further territory must be acquired for the "support of the people". (3) World-power must be attained. In order to win his nation over to that policy, the bitterness over Versailles must be inflamed, so that the nation would acquiesce in rearmament.[2]

[1] The Parliament House of the Republic.

[2] "What a use could be made of the Treaty of Versailles! . . . How each one of these points could be branded into this people till a cry was wrung from it 'we will re-arm!'."

Hitler was completely successful. Though it was against the terms of the Treaty, Germany rearmed at first secretly, then openly. In March, 1935, Hitler reintroduced conscription and announced the building of an air force, both of which had been forbidden by the Treaty of Versailles. The rest of Europe did not interfere. All were " war-weary ", all were involved in the struggle with their economic difficulties. Germany refortified the Rhineland and began to rebuild a fleet. She found an ally in Italy, bitterly angry with Britain and France over Abyssinia. Yet British — and French — statesmen still did not take action. A naval pact was made between Germany and Britain in 1935, and continuous efforts were made for peaceful settlement of disputes.

Rise of German military power

A whole series of treaties of " non-aggression " were signed, notably between Germany and Poland, France and the U.S.S.R., the U.S.S.R. and Czechoslovakia, the U.S.S.R. and Finland, etc. Germany did not now put forward with any vehemence the demand for the return of her colonies. She could not allege that they were needed to take her surplus population, for previous to 1914 the proportion of Germans emigrating to her colonies was infinitesimal. She did desire the return of these colonies, but chiefly for reasons of " prestige ".

Non-aggression

Then, in February, 1938, action came swiftly. Hitler occupied Austria by force of arms, and declared her union with Germany. He then, as summer wore on, threatened Czechoslovakia. Here he still put forward his theories of the German race. Czechoslovakia included a body of Germans some of whom had been settled within Bohemia by the Emperor Ferdinand in the seventeenth century. Hitler declared that these districts and their inhabitants (the *Sudeten Germans*) must be joined to Germany. By threat of war he obtained his ends. Neville Chamberlain's three famous journeys by air to Berchtesgaden (15th September), Godesburg (22nd September), and Munich (29th September),

Austria annexed (1938)

The Sudeten Problem (1938)

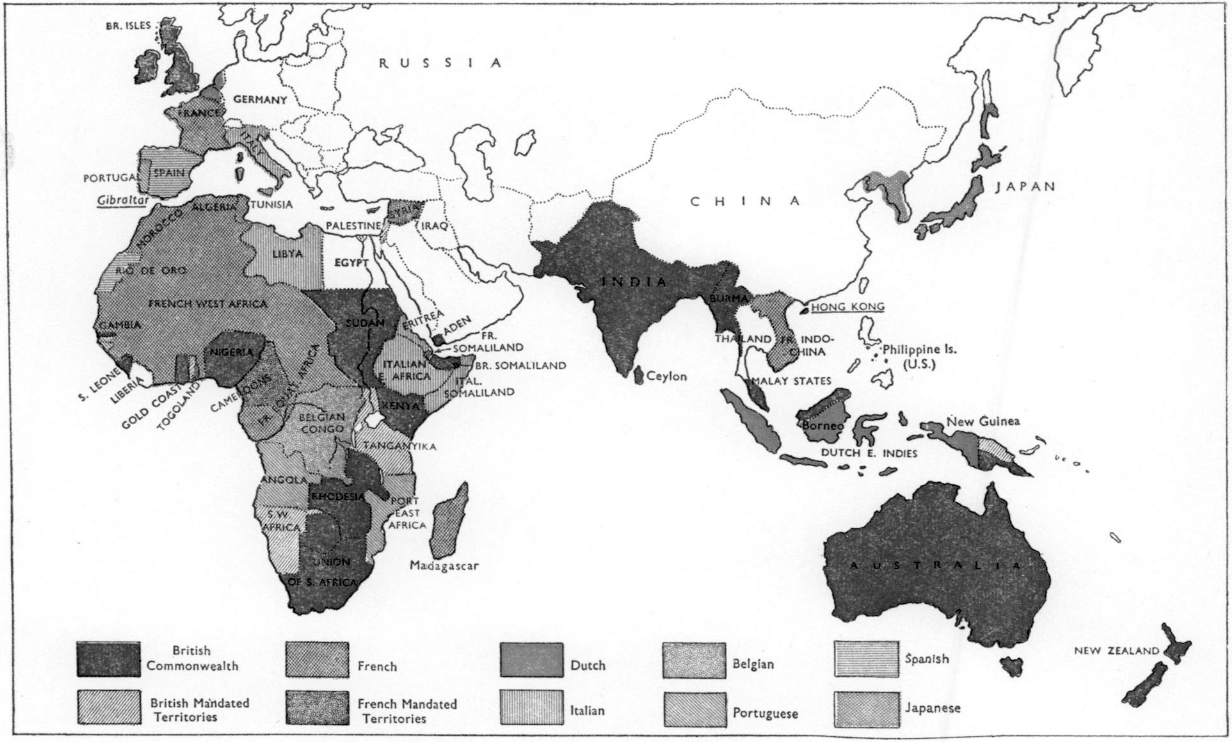

EUROPE, AFRICA, AND ASIA, 1939

F 938

ended in the *Munich Agreement* (30th September), by which Britain and France agreed that the *Sudeten* districts should be taken from Czechoslovakia and given to Germany. Actually it was known that Hitler's policy was based on a planned " advance to the east ". This had been in part Germany's policy before 1914. France and Britain knew that such an advance might involve Germany in war with Russia. They possibly hoped that Hitler would be satisfied with the annexation of districts with German populations, and that henceforward he would be content with economic development of Germany's connection with Eastern Europe. In any case, whether they clung to these theories or not, events soon proved them to be a fallacy. **Munich (1938)**

In March, 1939, Hitler, breaking every pledge, attacked the remnant of the Republic of Czechoslovakia and annexed it. Now Europe saw the real position. Germany had gone beyond all her theories of " race ", and Hitler had proceeded to the second point of his programme, the acquisition of " fresh territory ". His excuse was that Czechoslovakia " threatened " Great Germany, and for the safety of her people Germany must remove this danger. Britain and France prepared feverishly for what they began to be convinced lay before them — war. Hitherto they had acquiesced in all Hitler did, for two reasons; everyone dreaded war, and everyone knew that Britain and France were not prepared. They had hoped, too, that Hitler himself would not go too far. The annexation of the Czechoslovak Republic by Germany showed that not only could no reliance whatever be placed on any pledges made or treaties signed by Hitler, but also that there were no limits to his aggression. **Conquest of Czecho-slovakia (1939)**

Then, in August, 1939, Hitler demanded the cession of *Danzig* by Poland.[1] Poland, knowing that if she gave up Danzig she would henceforth be almost completely cut off **Poland**

[1] By the Treaty of Versailles Danzig with the surrounding territory was established as a Free City, under the protection of the League of Nations. Danzig was, however, a unit in the Polish customs administration.

from the sea, and her commerce and life placed at Germany's mercy, refused. Hitler invaded and conquered Poland, declaring now that she too must be annexed to give Germany "living space". The invasion of Poland meant European war. France and Great Britain had promised Poland that if she were invaded they would come to her assistance. They had made efforts, throughout 1939, to induce the U.S.S.R. to join in resisting Germany, but in August it was announced that Russia and Germany had come to agreement. Hitler may have believed that this agreement would frighten the two democracies into abandoning Poland, or he may always have intended to make war. In any case, whatever he anticipated, Great Britain and France did not abandon their ally, and on 3rd September, 1939, they declared war on Germany.

War breaks out, 3rd September, 1939

CHAPTER 81

POST-WAR POLITICAL DEVELOPMENT IN BRITAIN

EDWARD VIII — JANUARY, 1936 – DECEMBER, 1936
GEORGE VI — DECEMBER, 1936–

We should be mistaken if we thought of the years after 1918 as leading on solely to catastrophe, for in many respects they were years of progress; there were an extension of the franchise, a settlement with Ireland, and development in the relations with the Empire.

Progress after 1918

1. REFORM OF THE FRANCHISE

First, there came various developments in the theory of democracy. The *franchise* was given to women by the Reform Act of 1918, but not on the same terms as men. It was given to all men over twenty-one, but only to women

The franchise

over thirty.[1] Women could also be elected to Parliament.[2] Exactly ten years later, women were enfranchised on the same terms as men, so that Great Britain has now equal and universal suffrage.

This obviously involves the grant of political power to the working-classes, who, being numerically superior, have the control of elections. As men do not think alike, so the workers do not vote alike; they vote as Conservative, Liberal, and Labour.

Different ideals of Labour and Conservatism

Labour opposes Conservatism in its ideal for the organization of society. Labour believes that Capitalism is a wrong basis, that the community should control the land (as the source of wealth), the banks and financial system, industry and transport; that private profit should be eliminated and that, instead, the State should use the profits earned for the benefit of the community. The Labour Party differs from Continental Socialism in preferring to work for this ideal through constitutional and not revolutionary methods. Conservatism believes that under Capitalism, industry gains through the encouragement of private enterprise, and that reforms can be made to adapt it to modern conditions.

Communism

Communism, which aims at achieving social revolution by revolutionary action, has so far very little footing in Great Britain, though Parliament has had a small group of four or five Communist people.[3]

2. IRELAND

Ireland

One great problem with which the British Government had to deal after the war of 1914–18 was Ireland. At the outset of war in 1914, it had been mutually agreed that

[1] 13 million men were enfranchised by this measure, and 9 million women.

[2] The first woman elected was the Irishwoman, Countess Markievicz, but she would not take her seat. The first woman to sit in the House was Lady Astor.

[3] In the coalition of parties made during the war, in the summer of 1940, one solitary Communist formed the official Opposition.

"Home Rule" should wait till the war ended. This had been accepted by the Irish Party in the House of Commons, and many Irishmen enlisted as volunteers in the war. But the decision was not accepted by all Ireland, and in 1916 what is called the *Easter Rising* broke out. A body of Irishmen, wishing for an independent Ireland, rose in revolt. They were prepared to accept German help, and *Sir Roger Casement's* story is a dramatic illustration of the state of affairs. Casement had been a British official and had gained honour through the work he did in exposing the Congo atrocities. But he believed intensely in Irish independence, and turned against Great Britain. He was in Germany when war broke out, and in 1916 came in a German submarine and landed in Ireland. He was caught by the British, taken to London, tried, and hanged. The other leaders were captured in Dublin and executed there. Great bitterness was aroused, and the vast majority of Irishmen became supporters of the new party of *Sinn Fein* ("ourselves alone") which demanded complete independence.

Easter Rising (1916)

Casement

Sinn Fein

In the elections of 1918, this party was completely triumphant, carrying all before it. Its members refused to recognize the British Parliament or to take their seats. Violence broke out, and individuals on both sides were murdered.

Now began a struggle which was really "civil war". The Sinn Feiners attacked British soldiers and officials. The British Government retaliated and sent troops.[1] For two years bloodshed went on, ruthlessness being shown by both sides. The world was horrified and British public opinion was disturbed. A "Home Rule" Bill was passed (1920), dividing Ireland into two. Ulster was to be allowed to remain part of the United Kingdom, but the rest of Ireland was to be united into one "Free" State, with its own Parliament in Dublin. The years of struggle, however,

Ulster declared for union with Britain

[1] This force was composed of men who had fought in the Great War, but it was not part of the British army; it was specially recruited for this Irish war. Its members had no regular uniform at first, and from their motley appearance were nicknamed "Black-and-Tans".

had proved fatal. Irishmen would not accept the measure. Ulster wished to have her own local Parliament and also representatives in the British Parliament. She elected her own Parliament and King George V went to open it, but the rest of Ireland remained absolutely determined. Matters went from bad to worse, with reprisals on both sides. At last the British Government decided to try to come to terms, and in 1921 the Irish leaders negotiated a treaty with Great Britain. **The Treaty of 1921**

The *Irish Free State* was set up, consisting of the three provinces, Munster, Leinster, Connaught, with her own Parliament at Dublin, and the status of a Dominion in the British Empire. Ulster (six counties) was left separate, for she refused to join the Free State, preferring to have her own local Parliament, and to retain her closer connection with Great Britain. She took the name of Northern Ireland. **The Irish Free State (1921)**

Many of the Irish, however, were now far too hostile to accept even "Dominion Status"; they wished for an Irish Republic, completely severed from Britain. The Treaty was not accepted by these extremists, and Ireland was desolated by another civil war, fought this time between these two Irish parties.[1] The contest ended in the defeat of the republicans, and the Irish Free State began to function. **Republicans refuse to accept Treaty**

The whole chapter was a sad one, and Irish feeling could not forget the episodes of "reprisal". Though the first Free State Government carried on for nine years, it was consistently opposed by the Republicans. Gradually these gained more support, and in 1930 *Mr. de Valera* won the election and became the head of a Republican government. Great Britain, however, was resolved that strife should not be renewed. She therefore accepted the Irish position. **Victory of Republicans**

Mr. de Valera at once took action over another cause of friction. The Land Acts of 1891 and 1909 had provided for money being advanced by Great Britain for the purchase **Land Annuities**

[1] Michael Collins, who had fought hard against the English, but who negotiated the Treaty, was killed by the Republicans in this struggle.

of land by tenants (see p. 869), and payments of interest on this loan, called the *Land Annuities*, was now refused by Mr. de Valera. Great Britain, in retaliation, put a customs duty on Irish cattle entering the country, to make up the equivalent of the amount due. This led to unforeseen difficulties, but English farmers lost through no longer importing Irish stock, and trade as a whole between the two countries was checked. Both countries suffered from this, and finally Great Britain gave up her "retaliatory" measures. A policy of conciliation would, it was hoped, at length allow old wounds to heal, and the revival of trade bind the countries by economic ties, though political ones had gone.

Mr. de Valera and his party were, however, resolved to sever as far as possible all political connection with Britain, and accordingly in 1932 the oath of allegiance, formerly demanded (in the Treaty of 1921) to be taken by all members of the Irish Parliament, was abolished. In 1933, appeals to the Privy Council were forbidden. In 1936 the office of Governor-General was abolished, and a High Commissioner now represents the United Kingdom in Dublin, his position being the same as the High Commissioners to the other Dominions. At the same time the Senate was done away with as part of the legislature.

The Oath of Allegiance

Privy Council

Governor-General

Then, at the close of 1936 came the abdication of King Edward VIII, and it became necessary for the Irish to decide what they should do. Mr. de Valera's government decided to bring in a new Act amending the Constitution, and this was passed early in 1937. By this Act a republican government was declared established, "sovereign, independent, and democratic". The new State was to be called "Eire" (or in the English language Ireland). It was to have its own national flag, a tricolour of green, white, and orange. Irish was to be the official language. New stamps and new coins, the latter with beautiful Celtic designs, were issued. A President was to be the head of the State,

Eire (1937)

and he was to appoint the Prime Minister on the nomination of the Dail (Chamber of Deputies). Eire was to have complete control of its internal and external policy.[1] She was, however, to remain in one sense connected with the British Empire. She was, as long as she chose to do so, to be " associated with the following nations, that is to say, Australia, Canada, Great Britain, New Zealand, and South Africa ". So long as these countries allowed the King " to act on their behalf in appointing diplomatic and consular representatives ", Eire would agree that he should do the like for her.

It remains vague as to how far this connection through the Crown has any definite meaning.

Eire was to have her own army, and could, if she chose, build herself a navy,[2] and she gave a solemn assurance that her territory would never be permitted to be used as a base for attack upon Great Britain.

Position of Northern Ireland

The constitution set forth by the Irish themselves stated that it was to apply to " the whole of Ireland ". Northern Ireland, however, refused to be included, and Great Britain, when she recognized the new constitution in June, 1937, while acknowledging the new State did so with the reservation that it did not involve jurisdiction over Northern Ireland, " or in any way affected the position of Northern Ireland as an integral part of the United Kingdom ". In other words, Eire was recognized as that area formerly known as the Irish Free State.[3]

3. OTTAWA CONFERENCE

When the National Government returned to power, after the election of 1931, one of the steps it took was to

[1] Thus when Great Britain went to war against Germany in 1939, Eire remained neutral.

[2] The naval ports and Admiralty property at Cork Harbour, Lough Swilly, and Berehaven were handed over to Eire in April, 1938.

[3] The total population of Ireland is 4,300,000; of this, 2,930,000 are inhabitants of the former Free State, 1,370,000 of Northern Ireland.

Tariffs within the Empire

introduce a *general tariff*, the aim being partly to reduce our purchases of goods from abroad, and so restore the "balance of trade". Great Britain abandoned Free Trade, duties were put on most goods coming into the country, with a lower rate on goods from within the Empire. Gradually these taxes have been extended to practically all articles except bread.

Ottawa conference.

In 1933 an Imperial conference was held at *Ottawa*, in an attempt to settle an economic policy for the Empire. The chief difficulty lay in the fact that the different Dominions all had their own tariffs, protecting their own industries. The conference granted to all the Dominions "equal privileges in the United Kingdom market", and it attempted to pave the way for a policy whereby each Dominion should "specialize" in its best products,[1] though this proved very hard to apply in practice.

King Edward VIII

Abdication

King George V celebrated his jubilee in 1935, having then reigned for twenty-five years. In the following year (January, 1936) he died, and was succeeded by King Edward VIII, who as Prince of Wales had travelled in all parts of the Empire. King Edward VIII, however, abdicated after only a few months, and was created Duke of Windsor. He was succeeded by his brother, who became King George VI and who was crowned in 1937.

George VI

The early years of the reign of George VI saw the change in the status of Ireland, noted above. They also saw some social reforms. In 1936 pensions were granted at the age of 65 to men who had been insured, and their wives could also obtain a pension on reaching the age of 60. Widows and children of insured men were also granted pensions, and spinsters who were themselves insured. Blind persons over 40 who were not insured were given pensions, and, of course, any person over 70 still received a non-contributory pension. A campaign was to be launched for better housing; the

[1] The difficulty here lay in the fact that some Dominions, e.g. India, wished to increase their own "self-sufficiency" and produce goods in which they were inferior to others.

school age was to be raised; and further social advances might have been expected but the outset of his reign was soon clouded by the approach of European war.

CHAPTER 82

THE TWENTIETH CENTURY — SOCIAL CHANGES

The fact that the first half of the twentieth century has seen two great European wars, may at first seem to stamp the period as one of re-action. Yet the failure in the sphere of international politics cannot wipe out the advances made by mankind as a whole. For it is clear that the way of life of the bulk of mankind has changed, and changed in many ways for the better.

1. TRANSPORT

Transport: the motor-car

The most striking change probably is due to the invention of the motor-car, which has brought about a positive revolution in the habits of the people. This was first made possible when Daimler, a German, invented the petrol engine in 1885, but real progress was not made till later. The first cars went very slowly; they could only achieve a speed of four miles an hour, and even then they were considered highly dangerous vehicles to be let loose on the roads, and it was laid down that a man must walk ahead of them carrying a red flag. Fairly soon cars were improved, and people became used to them, King Edward VII helping to popularize them by his instant adoption of a " Daimler ". In 1896 the 4-mile speed limit was abolished, and the " flag-man " was also done away with. At first the new and speedier cars raised vast clouds of dust along the roads, which was inconvenient to motorists, to pedestrians, and also to all those whose houses or cottages bordered the high-ways. This was remedied by the improvement of road surfaces, and soon " Tarmac " transformed the "white roads" which had characterized Britain since the earliest days, into shining black tracks.

Cars were at first expensive, and were therefore the luxury of the few, but new methods led manufacturers to take up "mass production" and standardization, and thus produce small cheap cars. The principle was originally applied by Ford, in the U.S.A., and there the worker now usually has his own car, bought on the instalment plan. In Great Britain the idea was taken up by Austin and Morris (Lord Nuffield), two men who have both built up huge businesses and brought the cheap car (often bought on the "hire-purchase" system) within the range of many.

Standardization

The cheap car

More influential perhaps on the lives of the working-classes has been the development of the motor omnibus and the char-a-banc. As regards the towns, the buses have enabled thousands to move out from the crowded areas and densely packed streets to live in the suburbs or even in the country districts. Where formerly people travelled comparatively little, and holidays away from home were denied to the majority, now they travel frequently, and the town dweller is no longer cooped up, but can get out into the countryside and to the sea.

The motor omnibus

Gains of town dwellers

The villager, too, has gained. Where before he could go only as far as his legs would carry him, now he can go far afield, and the country-woman can go in to shop at her neighbouring town, and buy many things she could not get at home. Country people as a whole have lost what to them was usually a burden, the sense of isolation, and can, if they choose, have something they never had before, namely, the power to leave their villages and see and share in the advantages of the town. To all alike, in both country and town, the motor-car has brought the possibility of recreation, of change of scene, and the pleasure of visiting the too often unknown beauties of their native land.

Gains of country people

We must also note that the revival of road traffic has brought fresh life and prosperity to the country districts, and many towns and places which had lost all vitality with the growth of the industrial cities, have sprung into fresh vigour with the advent of the touring motor-bus. The vast increase in motoring has involved the reorganization of our road system and the expenditure of millions of pounds yearly on the improvement of services and the laying out of new traffic routes, thus creating a vast mass of employment. A *Ministry of Transport* has been set up, with a special department to deal with and administer these problems of roads.

Revival of rural prosperity

Ministry of Transport

The development of the motor-car and consequent increase in road transport had a serious adverse effect on the railways which, after a period of Government control during the War, were grouped into four great systems in 1921 (see map on p. 748).

The next striking development in transport has been aviation. Man has long dreamt of the conquest of the air, and as far back as the late fifteenth century, Leonardo da Vinci made elaborate drawings of a flying machine. In the Victorian period men were interested in " lighter-than-air " balloons, and in 1870 Gambetta escaped from besieged Paris in a balloon filled with gas. No great progress, however, was achieved in this direction, and men therefore concentrated on efforts to produce a " heavier-than-air " machine which would fly. This was made possible by the discovery of the internal-combustion engine, and the use of petrol. Once those principles had been combined, flying became practicable. Two American brothers, *Orville* and *Wilbur Wright*, were the first men to fly in one of these machines, in the year 1903. Six years later, *Blériot*, a Frenchman, flew across the Channel. In 1919 came the first flight across the Atlantic, by *Alcock* and *Brown*, both British. *Lindbergh*, an American, was the first to cross alone. *Amy Johnson*, an Englishwoman, was the first woman to make a solo flight to Australia.[1]

Transport aviation

Earlier balloons

Internal-combustion engine

Petrol

The pioneers of aviation

[1] Graham White and Rolls (of the Rolls-Royce firm) were also amongst the British pioneers of the early days.

Now we have become familiar with the use of the aeroplane in both civil and military life. Air-routes traverse every country and link every continent. Men fly from city to city, crossing seas and deserts, without difficulty. Trans-Atlantic services have become a commonplace. Remote parts of Africa, Australia, South America, and the ice-bound North have all been opened up. Here again, it is the most isolated parts of the world which have received much-needed help. In such places as the jungles of the Amazon basin, or the remote parts of northern Canada, or the great desert areas of Africa and Australia, lie scattered little communities which cannot be reached by rail or road. To them the aeroplane (and the air ambulance) can bring help in emergency, can act as a link in bringing mails or supplies, and may develop trade, as it has already done in the case of the gold-mines buried deep in the bush of the New Guinea mountains. This beneficial side of aviation needs to be stressed, for it will develop further, and there is a tendency to lose sight of it in the more terrible use to which air-power has been put in war.

Air routes

Help for isolated areas

The *auto-gyro*, perfected by a Spaniard, *Cierva*, now makes it possible for an aeroplane to rise and descend vertically. This obviously extends the possible uses of aeroplanes enormously, for it makes landing in a small space practicable.

The auto-gyro

2. ELECTRICITY, GAS, OIL

We turn now to another great development of modern times, the use of electricity, and gas, and oil. These three have come to be used enormously, displacing to a large extent the use of coal. Thus factories are worked by electric power, streets and houses are lit by it, and, except in the remote country, cooking is now done by gas or electricity. Petrol has become largely used in land transport, and fuel oil in shipping. A very large proportion of ships, including most of the navy, are now driven by oil (Diesel engines) or

Electricity, gas, oil

(a) in industry

(b) in domestic life

burn oil in place of coal. This has had a two-fold effect. The mining industry has suffered, and Great Britain has to a certain extent suffered too, in losing one of the factors which gave her such predominance in the first industrial revolution. But on the other hand, new industries have sprung up in the place of the old, and labour has shifted from the decaying mining industry to the newer trades created by the use of electricity and oil.[1] Nor can anyone doubt the immense gain of these new developments.

Their effect on employment

Perhaps one of the most widely appreciated changes is that which has been made in the home. The laying on of electricity and gas has become possible even in country cottages, and houses have become cleaner and lighter as well as easier to run. "Labour saving" has enormously lightened the work of the woman in running her home, and as gas and electricity become cheaper, and are applied to more devices, so the "housewife" gains, and her family too.

"Labour saving"

So vital are these new services that, whereas at first gas was provided by private companies run for profit, by the time electricity came to be developed, it was realized that it should (like the water-supply of a community) be in the hands of public authorities. Thus in very many parts of the country now, electricity is provided by the municipality and profits go back into the revenue of the community.[2]

Control by public authorities

One other point concerned with household life may be noted. The development of refrigeration has made it possible to import meat, butter, and fruit. This has not only cheapened these commodities, but has allowed of greater variety. (The introduction of the banana and the grape fruit are instances of this.) In the same way improvements in canning have led to an increase in the use of canned food, and here again besides saving of labour a more important result is an increased variety of diet.

Refrigeration

[1] e.g. the whole industry connected with the cinema, wireless, motoring.

[2] In this way too, privately owned undertakings, such as gas companies, cannot raise their prices beyond those of the publicly owned works, for the consumers would then simply transfer from the one to the other.

3. HOUSING: SLUMS, FLATS, ARCHITECTURE

As the standard of " amenities " in household life has risen, so the standard of housing itself has improved. The " slums " have for long been a thorn in the national conscience, and efforts have been made under " slum clearance " schemes to remove them. The movement has been reinforced by new ideas in architecture, for with the appearance of " flats ", which have been adopted by all classes in place of " houses ", it has become easier to plan and build blocks of dwellings for the workers.

Housing

Modern " clearance " schemes now often transform an area where formerly squalid rows of miserable little houses were huddled together, into places with well-planned blocks of flats supplied with space for play-grounds, balconies, roof-gardens, and, above all, ample windows, for the twentieth century reckons amongst its discoveries, the use of sunlight. Light, air, space for recreation, and labour-saving devices, these are the characteristics of the new buildings, whether flats or " council " houses, which both private and municipal effort have given as their contribution to modern housing.

Architecture

In this connection, we may note that the twentieth century has seen the adoption of new styles of architecture. The rise in land values has led in the cities, and especially in London, to the pulling down of older buildings to make room for larger erections. Modern use of steel framework and ferro-concrete has produced blocks of flats and of shops which rise to greater heights than were formerly possible.[1] Thus such beautiful streets as Regent Street in London, built in the classical style of the early eighteenth century, have disappeared.

[1] The building regulations of such bodies as the L.C.C. have had to be altered to permit of these higher buildings.

4. HEALTH. PUBLIC HEALTH. MEDICINE

Improvement in housing conditions may be considered as a movement which goes hand in hand with another advance, that is the increased importance attached to the health of the nation. King Edward VII is said to have remarked, when told of the incidence of " preventible " illness amongst the population of Great Britain, " If preventible, why not prevented?" The modern community, whether in town or country, does now make greater efforts than ever before to " prevent " illness, by rearing a healthier race of children. School medical inspection is compulsory; school clinics deal with ailments, and with dental cases; mothers now in most areas can attend " baby welfare " clinics, and also receive treatment themselves; great efforts have been made to improve the milk supply and milk is supplied to school-children, either at cost price, or, in necessitous cases, free. In all these ways efforts are made by the State to give its young citizens a healthy start in life.

Health

Public health

Side by side with this development of preventive treatment has gone a great advance in medicine. Here again, the new force, electricity, has been used to help mankind. X-rays have been brought into universal use both in hospital and in private practice. The *Curies* by their discovery of radium (in December, 1898) gave a new weapon to be used against disease.

Medicine

X-rays

Radium

Sir Ronald Ross by his discovery of the part played by the mosquito in infecting man with the germ of malaria made possible the treatment and cure of what has been one of the greatest scourges of millions of men in tropical countries. Snake-venom, too, has been found to cure the disease known as " bleeding ". *Sir Frederick Hopkins*, by his discovery of Vitamins, added to the health of the world by helping to correct deficiency-diseases, through diet. The discovery of *insulin* has meant life, instead of death,

Treatment of malaria

Vitamins

to thousands. In every direction science has come forward with new remedies to help suffering mankind in its struggle against disease. This is a field where the record is one of unmatched progress.

5. ART AND LITERATURE

If now we turn from material things to those of the mind, we find that here also the twentieth century has shown change. The mental side of man's life has altered, as it alters in every age.

Art

Some of the products of modern art show a great departure from the Victorian concept. The "Victorian" painter often concentrated either on efforts to reproduce faithfully the objects he was studying, or to give "interest" to his picture by its "story". With the opening of the twentieth century a new school of painting made its influence felt. This originally was inspired by the painters of France, and England was slow to accept its ideas. These artists called

The Post-impres-sionists

themselves *Post-Impressionists* and among the characteristics of their work were the painting of light, the use of pure colour, and the aim of producing the impression left on the mind by any subject rather than its outward appearance. The extent or permanency of their influence cannot be judged when we stand so near in time to the artists, nor can names of individual painters be singled out. But, of the older artists of the twentieth century, *Brangwyn*, *Sickert*, *Augustus John*, and *Sargent* are all recognized as pre-eminent.

Sculpture

Sculpture, too, has shown a radical departure from previous standards. *Epstein* has had a profound influence. *Eric Kennington* is another exponent of modern ideas, while *Sir Edward Lutyens* has represented in his "Cenotaph" an aspect of modern sculpture which has won ready acceptance and admiration.

Just as some painters have tried to break away from the old styles, and to use greater freedom in their treatment of their subjects, so too have many writers of both poetry and prose tended to adopt new forms. **Literature**

Modern verse perhaps has shown a greater change in technique. It is obviously more " free " in its structure and rhythm, though here we must differentiate between two streams. *W. B. Yeats*, the Irish poet, wrote his beautiful verse more strictly in the older tradition, and so did *Robert Bridges*, though his *Testament of Beauty* in some respects showed the new ideas which were making themselves felt. *A. E. Housman*, in his *Shropshire Lad*, also retained more of the " classical " tradition, as did the young poet *Rupert Brooke*, who died in the war of 1914 before he had developed his full gifts. *T. S. Eliot* is one of the most notable and influential of modern exponents of the " new " verse. **Poetry** **The Georgian poets: Yeats, Bridges, Housman**

Dramatic writers of the period are outshone by one man, *George Bernard Shaw*. Shaw, an Irishman, is an outstanding example of the man who satirizes English conduct, English standards, and English " romanticism ", but who does so by entertaining and amusing the people he satirizes. His plays do what he, through one of his characters, declares to be highly beneficial — they administer a stimulus by providing a shock. **Drama** **G. B. Shaw**

Shaw's realism and satire had their counterblast in the works of *J. M. Barrie*, whose fantasies (such as *Peter Pan*, and *Mary Rose*) represent the opposite extreme, and deal with a world of escape from reality. **Barrie**

One other point may be noted. The twentieth century saw a great interest in continental drama (in the plays of Ibsen, for example), and many plays translated from foreign languages won widespread recognition, especially in many provincial cities where *Repertory* theatres sprang to life and success. **Interest in foreign drama**

The visit of the Russian Imperial Ballet in 1913 also led to an immense revival of the art of the ballet in England, and to the reopening of the Sadler's Wells Theatre, for the **Ballet** performance of ballets, largely composed and danced by English people, trained in English schools of dancing.

As regards the " general reader ", all other literary competitors have really been outdistanced by the novel, which has become the chief food of the new population of readers. A whole host of writers have won their way. Just as Thackeray was the great satirical writer of the Victorians, so *Thomas Hardy* attained supremacy as the ironical writer of the Edwardians. His " Wessex " novels, with their beautiful pictures of country life and country landscapes, give, however, something Thackeray never gave to his description of life in towns, and at the same time, because they deal with the slow-changing countryside, they seem to go back and reflect an earlier period. More characteristic of the modern scene are the scientific romances of *H. G. Wells*, with his almost prophetic descriptions of new machines. *John Galsworthy* gave in his series known as the *Forsyte Saga* a wonderful reproduction of English upper-middle-class life, which won him recognition not only amongst his fellow countrymen, but abroad, where foreigners read with delight books which gave a portrait of a class, and a way of life, held to be unique to Great Britain.

The Novel

Hardy

Wells

Galsworthy

In a lighter vein, one English writer of the period won world-wide fame, and may be said to have founded a new school of fiction. *Conan Doyle*, when he wrote the Sherlock Holmes stories, which have been translated into almost every living language, including Chinese, began the stream of detective fiction which has developed into such amazing proportions.

Conan Doyle

6. AMUSEMENT – CINEMA, RADIO, SPORT

While the twentieth century has shown its own style of progress in the arts, we have also to realize that if art provides culture, there is another side to life which has received even greater stimulus. All human beings need amusement,

Amusement

but in the past, opportunities have been more closely limited to what were called the leisured classes. Now a most striking change has taken place, due primarily to the invention of the cinema and the wireless. Here again we have the coming together of certain scientific discoveries, each supplementary to the other. Electricity, petrol, and machinery, have combined to revolutionize not only work, but play.

The cinema

The cinema has proved one of the most universal sources of amusement and pleasure yet found by mankind. Beginning with the " silent moving-pictures ", it has, since 1918, moved on into the " talkies " and the coloured film. No one can deny the improvements both in technique and in the artistic presentation of the stories portrayed. The social results of the invention may be noted in the very marked decrease in convictions for drunkenness, for now the public house is no longer the chief place of amusement in most districts.

Wireless

In much the same way the development of wireless has opened a whole new field of possible happiness. To *Marconi*, an Italian who carried out his researches in Great Britain, must be ascribed the immense step forward taken when in 1902 he sent the first wireless message from Cornwall to Newfoundland. Companies were speedily founded to develop this new invention, under Government control, for clearly here was a new and very important means of communication. To-day wireless is of the utmost value for sending messages and for holding telephone conversations over long distances.

Communication

One of its most obvious benefits has been its use at sea, where the famous S.O.S. signal has in countless instances brought help to ships in distress.[1]

From the sending of messages, wireless has gone on to be used as a means of entertainment. " Radio ", or broad-

[1] So marked is this, that marine insurance has been greatly affected, for fewer ships are now lost at sea.

Broad-casting

Radio in the home

cast wireless, has brought music and entertainment into almost every home, and again the greatest benefit is perhaps felt by lonely places and by people isolated from ordinary life by such misfortunes as blindness or illness.

In Education

One other aspect, besides that of amusement, is less marked. Education does now make more use of the wireless for lectures, talks, and concerts. This side of broadcasting is found to be specially useful in dealing with very poor and primitive communities, such as are found in many parts of the Empire.

In poor communities

A link with the Empire

Another aspect of the influence of wireless lies in the link it provides between parts of the Empire. We have grown accustomed to Empire broadcasts where men, women, and children all speak and are heard from the most distant corners of the world, and the fact that the King and the various Prime Ministers speak to the whole Commonwealth at special times, has proved a valuable bond of union.

Outdoor sport

We may turn from indoor occupation to another sphere where we find obvious improvement. Outdoor sport and exercise have become common to all classes. Town councils build swimming baths and provide tennis-courts and playing-fields; youth hostels enable men and girls to go for walking tours; organized games are provided by the State schools. The better health of the nation is a tribute, not only to medical inspection and treatment in the schools, but to the widespread recognition that the young need outdoor recreations.

News-papers

Picture papers

In a different direction, large sections of the people now derive amusement and interest from a new source. The "picture papers" though condemned by some as being too sensational, yet do bring news and interest into houses where the more sedate press would never have entered. They owe their existence partly to the improvement in the art of photography and printed reproduction, partly to the influence of the U.S.A., where the "popular" press showed the way to present news in a brief and perhaps too striking way. The first popular paper in Great Britain was the famous weekly, *Tit-Bits*, and it was in its office that Alfred Harmsworth learnt his trade. Harmsworth really founded the popular press in Britain with his *Daily Mail*, started in 1896, and he and his brother went on to create a whole chain of newspapers, their example being followed by other groups.

7. POSITION OF WOMEN

Another change that has become more marked in the twentieth century is that in the position of women. In the political sphere, as has already been noted, they have been granted full citizenship. In the social life of the nation, however, there has also been advance. Girls and boys all receive equal education from the State. Women can enter many professions formerly closed to them, such as medicine, law, and the civil service. Moreover, science always makes strength of less importance than skill, so women now have not the inferiority which their lesser physical strength formerly imposed. A woman can drive a car, or fly an aeroplane, or work a machine, besides using the typewriter and operating the telephone. Thus, with more openings available, woman's wages have risen and woman's status improved. Even in smaller matters, women may reckon themselves happier. Their dress has altered with their way of living, and where the Victorian wore long, heavy, tight dresses and took little exercise, the modern woman can wear short comfortable clothes and join in any form of sport or exercise she likes.

Position of Women

8. SUMMARY

Thus, if we contrast the life of the people to-day with what it was at the beginning of the century, we can see how changes have made for an increase in human happiness. To those who most needed help, we may hope that most help has been given. The chief evils of poverty are perhaps the insecurity and suffering caused by illness, loss of work, old age. Against these, the State in the twentieth century has afforded some protection. The man or woman out of employment receives unemployment pay; those who are ill receive sick-pay; the old and widowed receive pensions. The young receive education for a longer period, and increased attention is given to technical training. Slum clearance is recognized as a policy to be pursued. Though in many respects we have not advanced very far along these roads, still we have made a beginning, and we can be sure that there will be no turning back. Science and invention have given us new powers. Man has shown once more that he holds in his hands the possibility of making further progress.

NOTES ON PERIOD TWELVE (1914–1939)

BRITISH SOVEREIGNS

George V (1910–1936)
Edward VIII (1936–abdicated)
George VI (1936–1952)

IMPORTANT FOREIGN RULERS

France:	Third Republic
Italy:	King Victor Emmanuel
	Benito Mussolini (1921)
Germany:	The Third Reich
	Adolf Hitler (1933)
Russia:	Czar Nicholas II (1892–1917)
	Union of Socialist Soviet Republics (1917–)
Spain:	Alfonso XIII (1886–1931)
	Republic (1931–)

BRITISH PRIME MINISTERS

Asquith:	(1908–1916)

(Coalition of three Parties, Liberal, Conservative, Labour, from 1915 to 1922.)

Lloyd George:	(1916–1922)
Bonar Law:	(1922–1923)
Baldwin:	(1923–1924)
MacDonald:	(1924)
Baldwin:	(1924–1929)
MacDonald:	(1929–1935)

(National Government from 1931.)

Baldwin:	(1935–1937)
Chamberlain:	(1937–1940)
Churchill:	(1940–1945)

NOTE 155. — CAUSES OF WAR (1914–1918)

1. **Germany** rose to great power, built great navy.
2. **Austria** wished to gain expansion in the Balkans, and hence came into conflict with Russia. After *Balkan wars* (1912–13) saw her opportunity passing. Balkans free from Turkey.
3. **France,** having been humiliated by Germany in various incidents, (1906, Delcassé retired; 1911, " Agadir "), wished for alliance with *Russia.*
4. **Great Britain,** which had kept in " isolation " began to fear Germany's naval power, so sought for allies. *Entente* with France followed (1903–4) and this indirectly meant alliance with Russia (1907).

   Hence gradually two armed camps — Germany and Austria (Italy formed an alliance with them, but when war broke out repudiated it) against France and Russia, which were allies, with Great Britain connected by vague entente.

   Germany declared herself encircled by French policy.
5. **Occasion for War.**
   (*a*) Austrian Archduke assassinated (June, 1914) (in Croatia, a part of Bosnia annexed by Austria) and *Austria* declared Serbia had instigated crime. Ultimatum to Serbia by Austria (July).
   (*b*) *Serbia* appealed for help to *Russia,* who mobilized. This brought in *France,* her ally.
   (*c*) *Germany,* in order to attack *France, invaded Belgium,* whose neutrality had been guaranteed by France, Germany, and Britain. This brought in *Great Britain* (August).

NOTE 156. — COURSE OF THE WAR (1914–1918)

1. **Period of Attacks by Allies; Failure.**
   (*a*) 1914.
   (i) Germany invaded *Belgium.* Great Britain entered the war. Her task then to prevent Germany reaching the sea. Retreat from Mons. Stand by British and French from Rhine to Vosges. This line roughly held throughout war.
   (ii) Russians invaded Germany, but were themselves overwhelmed at *Tannenberg.*

   (*b*) 1915.

   Russians attacked Austria, Germany sent troops. Russians defeated, and Russian Poland occupied by Germans.
   (i) Britain to help Russia, attacked Turkey at *Gallipoli.* Failed.
   (ii) *Bulgaria* joined Germany and *Serbia overwhelmed.*

(*c*) 1916.

(i) French beat off great German attack on *Verdun*, and in July Anglo-British attack on the *Somme*. Small progress made. Italians attacked Austrians. *Rumania* joined Allies and was totally defeated and overwhelmed.

(ii) Expedition to attack Turks in *Mesopotamia* failed. Surrender at *Kut*.

2. Sea Warfare.

(*a*) German ships in Pacific at outset of war defeated British at *Coronel* (1914); were themselves defeated at *Falkland Islands* (1914).

(*b*) Submarine warfare meant that battle fleet did not keep at sea, or blockade ports. In May, 1916, German battle fleet came out. *Battle of Jutland*, German fleet retreated to port and stayed there.

(*c*) In 1917 the Germans fell back on *unrestricted submarine warfare*, and sank ships of every nature. This ended by causing *United States to join allies* (April, 1917).

3. Crisis of the War, 1917.

(*a*) Submarine warfare very deadly, but gradually overcome.

(*b*) *Russian Revolution*, Russia made peace with Germany at Brest-Litovsk.

(*c*) U.S.A. enters War (April).

(*d*) *French offensive* failed and mutiny followed. *British attacks* on German front; battles of Vimy Ridge; Messines Ridge; Flanders. General failure to make ground; offensive with tanks at Cambrai also failed.

(*e*) Italians defeated by Austrians at *Caporetto*.

But, in March, allies took *Baghdad* and in December, *Jerusalem*.

4. German Final Offensive, 1918.

(*a*) Germans saw submarine attack had failed, so general attack in France, at Amiens and Ypres on British who lost much ground; at Soissons against French, who were driven back to the Marne.

(*b*) July, 1918, Allied advance began in France. Aided by

(i) Unity of command under Foch.

(ii) Arrival of Americans.

(iii) Exhaustion of Germany's supplies owing to blockade. General advance through July and August.

(*c*) *Bulgaria* defeated by Allies. Palestine conquered by British; *Turkey* made peace; *Austria* defeated by Italians at *Vittorio Veneto*, made peace.

(*d*) Mutinies in German fleet and revolution in Berlin.

(*e*) *Collapse of Germany*.

Note 157. — PEACE OF VERSAILLES

Germans asked for armistice in November, 1918. Peace Conference met at Versailles three months later, Jan., 1919. (A series of treaties really; Treaty of Versailles with Germany in June; Treaty of St. Germain with Austria; Treaty of Neuilly with Bulgaria; Treaty of Trianon (1920) with Hungary; Treaty of Lausanne (1923) with Turkey).

Wilson's Fourteen Points.

Peace was to be made on basis of *Wilson's Fourteen Points.* The majority of these were accepted by both sides and were:

1. No more secret diplomacy.
2. Freedom of the seas (to check Britain from seizing neutral cargoes useful to the enemy. Britain never accepted this).
3. No tariff barriers (this was never carried out by any one).
4. Armaments to be reduced to a minimum.
5. Colonial claims to be settled according to the interests of the populations (resulted in " mandate " system, but Germany lost all her colonies).
6. Unhampered development for Russian Republic, " under institutions of her own choosing, with cordial assistance from other nations ". Meant to help establishment of Republican rule, as contrasted with Czar's autocracy. (But Allies made war on Russia from fear of extremists after 1918.)
7. Belgium to be evacuated and restored.
8. Alsace-Lorraine to be restored to France. (Germany had annexed it in 1871.)
9. Italian frontier to be " readjusted " (Italy was given Trentino provinces and part of Tirol, which was formerly Austrian).
10. " Subject " races of Austro-Hungarian Empire to be given independence.
11. Balkan frontiers to be " readjusted ".
12. Ottoman Empire to give its non-Turkish subjects home rule.
13. Independent Polish State to be set up " with secure access to the sea ".
14. " A general association of nations " to be formed for " neutral guarantors of political independence "

Terms of Treaty.

1. *Alsace-Lorraine ceded* by Germany to France.
2. *Poland restored* as a Republic, with her former territories which at end of eighteenth century had been divided up by Austria, Germany,

and Russia. She was given " secure access to sea " by a corridor. This cut off East Prussia from rest of Germany. *Danzig* to be a free port.

3. *Austrian Empire broken up.* Separate republics formed: *Czechoslovakia* (Bohemia and Slovakia); *Hungary*; *Austria.*
4. Serbia joined with former Austrian territories and formed Republic of *Yugoslavia.*
5. *Rumania* received Transylvania and Bukovina (parts of Austro-Hungarian Empire) and Bessarabia (from Russia).
6. Republics of *Finland, Latvia, Lithuania,* and *Estonia* created. Formerly Russian conquests.
7. *Italy* gained Trentino and part of Austrian Tirol.

Thus the peace treaties fulfilled some of Wilson's 14 points, but not all. The " general association of nations " was first part of the Treaty, but the United States withdrew and refused to join the League.

Note 158. — THE LEAGUE OF NATIONS

The League of Nations was set up in accordance with Wilson's fourteenth point, " in order to promote international co-operation and to achieve international peace and security by the acceptance of obligations not to resort to war ". To this every party to the Treaties agreed.

1. **Constitution of the League.**
   (*a*) Council and Assembly to be set up. France, Britain, Italy, Japan, and originally the United States, were always to have seats on the Council. (Germany allowed to join in 1925. She withdrew in 1934.)
   (*b*) Four other members of Council to be elected by the Assembly.
   (*c*) Decisions by the League must be unanimous (this proved a source of weakness, as any one or two small nations could hold up entire League).

2. **Measures to Avoid War.**
   (*a*) Members " *undertake to respect and preserve the territorial integrity and existing political independence of all members of the League.*"
   (*b*) Any dispute to be submitted to arbitrators and " in no case is resort to be made to war until three months after award by arbitrators ".
   (This was meant to afford chance of settling a dispute and of giving time for peace efforts to prevail).
   (*c*) Any member resorting to war to " be deemed to have committed an act of war against all the other members of the League ", who were bound " to sever all trade and financial relations ".

(*d*) In event of such war, the Council to settle what forces each member should contribute to "protect the covenant of the League".

Note: It was this obligation for joint action which was seized on by the American opponents of the scheme, as both likely to involve U.S.A. in Europe and (which they feared even more, unlikely as it seemed) interference of Europe in the U.S.A.

The American Senate rejected the Covenant, rejected the Treaty, and U.S.A. made a separate peace with Germany later on.

3. Colonial Settlement.

Colonies which had been taken from Germany and which were "inhabited by peoples not yet able to stand by themselves", were to be considered as a "Trust".

This was interpreted in the *Mandate* system, under which countries receiving mandates had to render account of their rule to the League.

(France had mandate for Syria; Britain for Palestine, 'Iraq (later given up), Tanganyika, South-West Africa (mandate to Union of S. Africa), and part of New Guinea (mandate to Australia).)

4. Disarmament.

Council to draw up plans for general disarmament to be revised every ten years.

Note 159.—THE PERIOD AFTER THE WAR OF 1914–1918

1. Changes in Great Britain.

(*a*) *Franchise.*

(i) 1918. *Reform Act* gave the vote to all men over 21 and all women over 30 (i.e. no property qualification). Women could sit in Parliament; first woman M.P., Lady Astor (by birth an American) who was elected for the constituency represented by her husband before he became a Peer. (An Irish woman had been previously elected, but never took her seat.)

(ii) 1928. *Equal Franchise Act.* Women given the vote on the same terms as men, i.e. all men and women over 21, who have resided for 6 months in one place. Electorate thus became 15 million women and 13 million men. Compare with the Reform Act of 1832, a hundred years before, when the total electorate was 1 million.

(*b*) *Trade Disputes Act* (1927) made "sympathetic" strikes illegal, i.e. one Union cannot strike merely in support of another. (This was passed after the General Strike (1926) and was meant to protect community against joint action in vital industries.)

2. Changes Abroad — The British Empire since the War.

(*a*) *The Dominions.*

(i) The Dominions became members of the League of Nations as separate nations.

(ii) They had always disliked idea of closer federation, and in 1921 the Imperial Conference decided against it.

(iii) Independent foreign policy for Dominions after the war.

(*a*) Canada made her own treaty with U.S.A. over the Fisheries dispute (1923).

(*b*) Canada and South Africa refused to join in attacks on Turkey (1922).

(iv) *Statute of Westminster*, 1931, declared that:

(*a*) Dominions were completely self-governing; equal in status; " in no way subordinate in any respect of their domestic or external affairs ".

(*b*) Bond of Union to be only " common allegiance to the Crown " and " free association as members of the British Commonwealth of Nations ".

The Dominions include Canada, Australia, New Zealand, and South Africa.

(*b*) *The Colonies.*

The Colonial Empire consists of territories which are more closely connected with Great Britain; they have not control of their foreign policy, and the Crown has an element of control in their government. This varies very much from place to place.

Chief colonies include Kenya, Uganda, West Indies, etc., etc.

NOTE 160. — CONSEQUENCES OF THE PEACE

1. Britain.

(*a*) " Reparations " and deflation added to cessation of munition work and return of troops, led to *general dislocation* of *trade* and *great unemployment.*

(*b*) Conservatives wished to introduce general tariff on goods. Defeated at election, and *first Labour Government* (1924). Conservatives returned to power nine months later.

(*c*) *General Strike* failed, 1926. Unionist Government passed Trade Disputes Act (1927).

(*d*) *Financial Slump* (1931). " National " Government formed (1931). Strict economy, and tariffs; Britain abandoned free trade.

(*e*) *Irish Free State* set up (1921).

2. In the Empire.

(*a*) " Dominions " recognized as independent. Statute of Westminster (1931). (See Note 159.)

(*b*) Increased self-government in the colonies.

(*c*) Movement for " Dominion Status " in India (see note, p. 936).

(*d*) " Mandated " territories. 'Iraq given independence (1932).

(*e*) In *Egypt* British Government withdrew, and Egypt became completely independent (1922).

3. In Europe.

(*a*) In *Russia* the moderate revolutionaries replaced by the *Bolsheviks*, who set up a complete Soviet Republic. (State ownership and control of production) (1919).

(*b*) In *Italy*, the *Fascist* party seized power (1921), and Signor *Mussolini*, after his " March on Rome ", became Dictator.

Italy not highly industrialized. Large population, which owing to the " slump " in America found emigration stopped. This in part led to the *Abyssinian War* (1935). Italy and Abyssinia were both members of the League of Nations; Italy therefore broke the Covenant. The League imposed partial break-off of economic relations. But action was weakened as U.S.A. not being a member of the League, sold war materials, notably oil, to Italy. Hence the other powers refused to put an embargo on oil.

Result: Conquest of Abyssinia and shattering of prestige and influence of the League.

(Prestige had previously been weakened when in 1932 League failed to take effective action against *Japan* when she invaded Manchuria.)

(*c*) In *Germany*, the First (Weimar) Republic contended against payment of overwhelming reparations. These gradually abandoned. " Dawes " plan reduced them. " Hoover " plan suspended them. Up to 1932 the Republic was settling down, and payment of reparations had ceased. Germany had been accepted as a member of the League of Nations.

After the world slump of 1931, rise of the *Nazis* to power under *Hitler*.

(i) In March, 1935, Hitler re-introduced conscription.

(ii) In 1935 refortified the Rhineland, and made pact with Italy (embittered over Abyssinian war).

(iii) In 1938 Hitler occupied Austria (February).

(iv) In 1938 (autumn) he at *Munich* obtained cession of part of Czechoslovakia (Sudetenland).

(v) In 1939 (March) he occupied all Czechoslovakia.

(vi) In 1939 (August) he attacked Poland.

(vii) On 3rd September, 1939, war declared by Great Britain and France who had guaranteed Poland.

TIME CHART FOR PERIOD TWELVE (1914–1939)

Sovereign.	Prime Minister.	Great and Greater Britain	Dates.	Other Powers.	Dates.
George V (1910–1936)	1908–16 Asquith.	Britain declares War on Germany.	1914	Assassination of Archduke Francis Ferdinand; Germany declares War on Russia and France; Germany enters Belgium.	1914
		Coalition Government.	1915	Italy declares War on Austria.	1915
		GREAT		WAR United States of America declares War on Germany; Russian Revolution.	1917
	1916–22 Lloyd George.	Armistice.	1918		
		Representation of People and Education Acts			
		Treaty of Versailles; Government of India Act.	1919		
		Peace Treaty ratified; Irish Home Rule Act	1920		
		Great Coal Strike.	1921		
	1922–23 Bonar Law.	Irish Free State constituted; Egypt independent.	1922		
	1923–24 Baldwin.		1923	Treaty of Lausanne.	1923
	1924 MacDonald.	First Labour Government in United Kingdom.	1924		
	1924–29 Baldwin.	Locarno Pact signed.	1925		
		General Strike.	1926	Germany admitted to League of Nations.	1926
		Representation of the People Act.	1928	Kellogg Pact signed.	1928
	1929–31 MacDonald.	Church Union in Scotland.	1929	Rhineland evacuated.	1929
		India Round Table Conference (First Session).	1930		
		India Round Table Conference (Second Session); National Government formed; Statute of Westminster.	1931	Spain becomes a Republic; World Economic Crisis.	1931
	1931–35 MacDonald.	Imperial Economic Conference at Ottawa.	1932		
				World Economic Conference.	1933
				Hitler seizes power.	1933
	1935–37 Baldwin.	Government of India Act.	1935	Italo-Abyssinian War.	1935
Ed. VIII ('36)					
George VI (1936–)	1937–40 Chamberlain.			Hitler seizes Austria; Sudetenland ceded.	1938
		Britain declares war on Germany.	1939	Czechoslovakia seized; Russo-German agreement; Poland invaded	1939

EXAMINATION QUESTIONS ON PERIOD TWELVE

(1914–1939)

1. Describe the reforms achieved or attempted by the Liberal party between 1906 and 1914. (NUJB 1938)

2. Do you think colonial rivalries were the main cause of the Great War (1914–18)? Give your reasons. (NUJB 1937)

3. Why did Britain go to war in 1914? (LGS 1937)

4. State the main facts in British foreign policy between 1902 and 1914. (NUJB 1936)

5. What effect did sea power have on the World War? (OC 1931; LGS 1940)

6. Is (*a*) the country labourer, (*b*) the town artisan, better off now than he was in 1900? (OC 1929)

7. What were the chief changes made in the map of Europe by the Treaty of Versailles? (LGS 1940)

8. What is "Dominion Status"? How has the connotation of the phrase been enlarged since 1914?

9. How far were the Fourteen Points embodied in the Peace Treaties? (LGS 1939)

10. Describe the constitution of the League of Nations. What part did the League play in European politics between 1919 and 1931? (LGS 1940)

11. *Either* (*a*) Give some account of the Russian Revolution of 1917 and its results; *or*

(*b*) What led to the Fascist Revolution in Italy? On what lines did the Fascists reconstruct the government of the country? (LGS 1940)

12. Explain the part played by the Labour Party in politics between 1919–1931. (LGS 1940)

INDEX — BOOK TWO

[*The names of Battles, Wars, Rebellions, Plots, Treaties, Statutes, etc., are grouped under these headings respectively.*]